# Environment

# Environment

## RESOURCES, POLLUTION & SOCIETY

## William W. Murdoch, Editor
University of California, Santa Barbara

SINAUER ASSOCIATES INC. • PUBLISHERS

STAMFORD CONNECTICUT

**For Joan**

ENVIRONMENT
© 1971 by Sinauer Associates, Inc.
20 Second Street
Stamford, Conn. 06905

Printed in the United States of America

Library of Congress Catalog Card No. 70-155367

SBN: 0-87893-500-2

# Editor's Preface

The appearance of yet another book on environment, amidst the present plethora of such books, requires some defense. I believe that much of the current writing lacks sufficient depth; some of it is simply alarmist without providing the rationale for alarm, and much of it is confusing and hardly conducive to rational discussion. There is a certain satisfaction in viewing with alarm; people in general seem to enjoy predictions of cataclysm and catastrophe. But continual postponement of impending Armageddon blunts the sensitivity of the listener. This book tries to distinguish truly alarming situations from those which are simply serious. I have aimed, above all, to produce a book which will provide a solid basis for the study and discussion of environmental problems.

There are also few books which bring together the multiple facets of these problems. Environmental problems and their implications for society and its institutions cover an enormous range of disciplines. Here, authors representing this range of disciplines have presented authoritative analyses of the problems we face now and in the foreseeable future.

The idea for a textbook of this type originated at the end of 1969 and each of the authors began working on an original chapter in the spring of 1970. We have tried to cover most of the major environmental topics, though a few remain undiscussed, notably chemical and biological warfare research, the problems of solid waste, noise pollution, and the general disfigurement of town and landscape. Those interested in expanding upon the book would do well to consult recent issues of the magazine *Environment*.

The organization of the book is straightforward. Although the chapters can be read in any order, they come in a logical sequence. Chapters 1 and 2 provide a useful background; it would also be better to read some of the earlier chapters before reading the final section on environment and society. Among the chapters on resources, Chapter 8 differs from the others in taking a single specific biological resource and showing the complications which flow from its exploitation. The subject of environmental degradation has been divided along systems lines but again one chapter (Chapter 13) deals with a specific kind of pollutant — pesticides — and another (Chapter 14) is devoted to suggesting ways in which we can reduce this pollutant while doing the job of pest control better.

Opinions about environmental problems are almost as numerous and diverse as the problems. The 21 authors represented in this book, like any other such group, hold somewhat different views on some aspects of the problems, especially with respect to their social implications. No attempt has been made to suppress these differences; indeed, I hope they will stimulate discussion.

We intended this book mainly for undergraduates taking courses that deal with the interaction between man and the environment, particularly interdisciplinary courses. Because the issues are fundamental the chapters have been written so that they are mainly understandable by a lay audience, and we hope that members of the general public will also use this as an environmental sourcebook. At the same time, the book seeks to explain the underlying basis of the problems, and in some chapters, such as Chapters 5, 9, and 12, this has meant describing quite complex material. The implications of the material come through clearly without detailed study, but I hope that the reader will find it rewarding to spend the extra time on the material needed to develop a more sophisticated appreciation of the analyses.

I hope that the book will go some way to instilling in its readers an ecological attitude. The most important capacity we can develop in dealing with the environment is not any particular piece of knowledge but the ability to see environmental problems in a proper ecological perspective and in relation to other environmental and social concerns. Man is part of the biosphere and does not exist outside its physical and biological constraints. His future comfort and survival require a widespread understanding of the environment and wise application of this knowledge.

Many people have helped me in preparing this book. Friends and colleagues who have provided stimulating discussions or who have made comments on my manuscripts include, from the University of California at Santa Barbara, William Chambliss (Sociology), Preston Cloud (Geology),

Otis Graham (History), Jack King (Biology), and James Sullivan (Economics); from Animal Ecology Research Group at Oxford, C.S. Elton, H.N. Southern, K. Southern, and J. Lawton; from Imperial College Field Station, England, G.R. Conway, W.D. Hamilton, S. McNeil, T.R.E. Southwood, Miss N. Waloff, and M. Way; and D.B. Mertz (University of Illinois at Chicago, Biology Department), J. Rhodes (Department of Applied Economics, Cambridge University), and my wife Joan.

My special thanks go to two UCSB colleagues with whom I have discussed these problems in recent years: to Joseph Connell (UCSB, Biology) for keeping me on the ecological straight and narrow and to Carroll Pursell (UCSB, History) who helped me to see ecological problems in a broader perspective. Finally, my thanks go to Prof. T.R.E. Southwood, Director of Imperial College Field Station, who provided peace and quiet while the book was being edited.

*William W. Murdoch*

# Contents

# 1 Ecological Systems

William W. Murdoch

One of the best known plots of land in the world is the Evans Old Field: 12 acres on the E.S. George Reserve of the University of Michigan. The subject of many ecological papers, the Old Field was farmed until about 1920 and then, largely because of low productivity, allowed to revert to the wild. It has passed through a succession from mainly grasses to a rich mixture of forbs (herbs) and grasses — a total of 140 species. Left alone, it would eventually become a mixed deciduous woodland like the surrounding community; but the grazing of a herd of wild deer continually prevents the invasion of small trees. During the past 20 years more than 1800 species of insects and about 250 species of birds, mammals, and other animal groups have been found there. And we have very little idea of the number of species of protozoa, bacteria, fungi, and other small organisms. In a rather more complex area, 2 square miles of mixed woodland, grassland, and streams near Oxford, England, Charles Elton has kept records for many years. Just over 4000 species of insects have been re-

WILLIAM W. MURDOCH is Associate Professor of biology at the University of California, Santa Barbara. He received his B.S. in zoology from the University of Glasgow (Scotland) in 1960. From 1960 to 1963 he did graduate research on insect population dynamics with Charles S. Elton at the Bureau of Animal Population, Oxford. In 1963 he obtained his doctorate from the University of Oxford. During 1964 and 1965 he did post-doctoral research on community ecology at the University of Michigan with Francis C. Evans. Since 1965, at Santa Barbara, he has been doing experimental and theoretical work on predator-prey populations and population regulation.

corded and probably over 6000 insect species occur there, which is about a fifth of the total British insect fauna.

These figures would seem insignificant if comparable data were available for the number of species in a tropical rain forest. A typical midwestern deciduous woodland has about 11 species of tree per hectare, but J.H. Connell of the University of California, Santa Barbara, found over 200 species of tree on a hectare of rain forest in New Guinea, and this is not a record for the tropics. In the vastness of Alaska, only 222 breeding species of bird have been found, compared with 667 species in tiny Panama. This pattern of increasing complexity as one moves toward the tropics is quite general, and the richness and diversity of tropical rain forests is almost beyond belief. Much of this diversity has not even been cataloged. Thus although about 1 million insect species have been described, there are probably from 4 to 8 million insect species on earth.

The Old Field, an English woodland, and the tropical rain forest illustrate the striking complexity of biological communities. To study them, we must either find or invent some organizing principles. In fact, ecological communities do appear to be organized on levels which can be studied, although to some extent ecologists have imposed on them slightly artificial classifications and structure. In this chapter we shall examine ecological systems in terms of the flow of energy and materials, food webs, populations, and communities; and we shall try to see what has been discovered by each of these approaches.

Two processes impose a gross pattern and organization on ecological systems. These are the flow of energy and the cycling of materials.

*Energy*

Energy sources on earth include tidal energy, nuclear energy, the heat of the earth's core, and so on. But for living systems the unique energy source is solar radiation. Biological systems depend on the flow of this energy from the sun, through the system, and back into outer space in the form of heat. The earth is in a steady state so that, over any appreciably long period, the amount of energy entering from the source is equal to the amount lost as heat to the "sink" (outer space). The existence of both source and sink is essential since the earth must maintain this energy balance, otherwise it would heat up or cool down and biological systems would not persist (Chapter 5). The earth is thus an "open" system with respect to energy.

Energy flows and in so doing produces material cycles. The water cycle (Chapter 7) is an example. Part of the solar energy eventually absorbed by the atmosphere and oceans produces temperature differences which cause convection currents in the air and produce winds. The heat energy absorbed by water also produces evaporation, and water vapor is then convected high in the atmosphere. If the water vapor precipitates over land (releasing the heat energy absorbed during evaporation) the cycle is completed when the water returns to sea level via runoff, rivers, and lakes, the potential energy of the water being finally dissipated as heat. Man "concentrates" the potential energy by building dams and converting it to hydroelectric power.

Other sources of energy which play a part in cycles include the thermal energy of the earth, which produces volcanoes and mountain uplifting, and the solar energy trapped by plants, which drives biological cycles. This latter energy is transferred as food from one part of biological systems to another, each transfer involving biochemical rearrangements during which heat is produced, so that eventually all of the energy first trapped by photosynthesizing plants leaves the system as heat.

*Materials*

In contrast to the case for energy, the earth is essentially a closed system with respect to matter, the amount being fixed so that it merely passes from one state to another. For some elements, or some portion of them, the natural cycle is fairly simple. For others, for example, those 30 or 40 elements used by biological systems, the cycle is more complex. And, of course, man now uses almost all the elements, complicating and disrupting cycles.

The most perfect or complete cycles tend to be those in which there is a gaseous phase, for example, water, nitrogen, and oxygen. These, in particular, are balanced cycles, in that the amount in any one phase (such as oxygen in the air) tends to be constant. Small disturbances are corrected for naturally and changes are only temporary. However, as Hutchinson[1] has noted, these cycles may not be able to return to the steady state following large disturbances which may cause severe disruption of the cycle.

From man's point of view, small, gradual changes may also have profound environmental effects. The $CO_2$ in the atmosphere forms an important reservoir in the carbon cycle, and the oceans and the world's plants together act to regulate its quantity. However, we produce enough $CO_2$ in burning fossil fuels to exceed the capacity of these regulators and the $CO_2$ content of the atmosphere is increasing (Chapter 15).

A second type of cycle involves movement of materials from land to sea and back again. Elements going through such sedimentary cycles generally take millions of years to cycle and the cycles tend to be less perfect than those with a gaseous phase in that some of the element may get "stuck" in one phase of the cycle. In the sedimentary cycles materials are leached or eroded from rocks on land and carried by rivers to the oceans. Most of the element is deposited on the bottom of the shallow inshore areas of the oceans and is eventually returned to the land when these sediments are raised into mountains by uplifting. However, there is some slight "loss" of calcium and phosphorus (important elements for biological systems), since small amounts are deposited in deep ocean sediments. These losses to the geochemical cycle probably are permanent.

Biological systems, of course, are important parts of the cycles in many elements. To take but two examples: The guano birds off the Peruvian coast eat ocean fish and produce concentrations of phosphates on land (Chapter 8). This process has probably occurred in other times at other places. Of major importance also is the part played by organisms in the movement of carbon dioxide as noted above.

The phosphorus cycle is illustrated in Figure 1. Phosphorus is a necessary constituent of protoplasm. Notice from this figure that phosphorus continually cycles to some extent within biological communities, going through plants and sometimes animals to soil bacteria and back through plants again. There is always a tendency,

BIOGEOCHEMICAL CYCLE OF PHOSPHORUS. A diagrammatic representation of the phosphorus cycle. Notice that there is a net "loss" to deep ocean sediments.

however, to lose phosphorus in the form of soluble phosphates, in runoff, down streams, and eventually to the ocean. However, rocks and other phosphate sources act as a reservoir and the phosphorus leaving biological communities is partly replaced from these sources by leaching.

It has been estimated[1] that about 20 million tons of phosphorus per year is leached from land to the oceans. In addition, man quarries phosphorite and makes superphosphate of it for fertilizer, most of which eventually reaches the sea. So man adds 1 or 2 million tons to the loss of phosphorus from the continents each year. The major pathway for returning phosphorus to land is the uplifting of marine sediments, but this is a geologically intermittent process. The other major and more continuous process is the deposition of

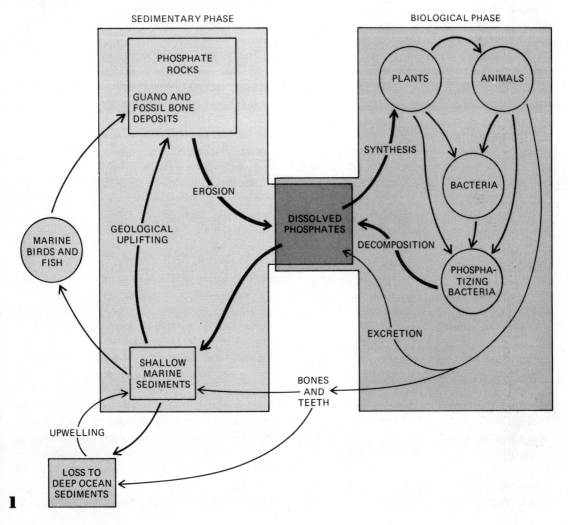

**1**

guano by sea birds, which may return several hundred thousand tons per year. Some thousands of tons are returned by marine fishing, but it is clear that at present the rate of loss to the oceans is much greater than the rate of return.

Man can now use enormous amounts of energy to interfere in a massive way with the cycling of materials, as I have just described for phosphorus. In particular, by mining and drilling operations elements are removed from more or less concentrated forms and dispersed on the earth's surface, a process which clearly cannot persist indefinitely for any element (Chapter 4). This process of dispersion is, for our purposes, a permanent disruption of the cycling process. Thus copper, once mined and dispersed, will not recycle naturally to an extent useful to human populations. Of course, we could recycle it artificially within our industrial system, and do to some extent.

Man disrupts material cycles in exploiting resources. The other side of this coin is that disruption of the cycles leads to pollution. Here it is important to note that we do not "consume" materials, we merely move them around. Pollution frequently involves the breakdown of the natural cyclic processes so that materials accumulate where we don't want them. This results in part simply from the fact that, because we extract materials from the earth at very high rates, the natural cyclic processes cannot cope with the increased rate at which materials are returned to the system. Possibly the most graphic illustration of this is eutrophication (Chapter 10). "Wastes" are spewed into rivers as sewage and as effluent from industries such as pulp mills. Such organic and inorganic materials (for example, phosphates) occur naturally, as described above, but the stream organisms normally responsible for cycling them can only handle a limited rate of input. In eutrophication the rate of input is too high and the cycling is continued mainly by different organisms, often in the absence of oxygen. The results are offensive. It is instructive that this change in QUANTITY of input results in a change in the QUALITY of the biological situation. This illustrates the point that biological systems frequently have thresholds, so that responses to rate changes are not simply linear.

Another example in which part of the problem is simply an increase in the rate of production of materials is the solid waste problem — the junk heaps of metal and other materials littering the landscape. But the solid waste problem illustrates a second aspect of pollution, namely, that technology produces new combinations of materials for which no natural breakdown processes (or poorly developed processes) have been evolved. Plastics are a good example. Various persistent pesticides and phenols from the petroleum industry are also in this category. Some of these new exotic materials are particularly a problem since they are toxic. Of course, some naturally occurring materials are also toxic when they are in high concentrations, and here man's effect of producing them at high rates and in concentrated form provides the toxic effect. Examples are lead from gasoline additives and mercury from pesticides and paper mills.

A peculiar addition to some material cycles is radioactive isotopes from nuclear explosions and nuclear reactors. For example, strontium cycles with calcium in the sedimentary cycle and passes through biological systems. As is well known, radioactive strontium is now involved in this cycle. Ecologists have taken advantage of the fact that radioactive isotopes are easily monitored in organisms to trace the cycling of materials in the system. An example is discussed later in this chapter (See Figure 5).

*The Food Web and Trophic Levels*

We now pursue the subject of energy flow and material cycling in ecological systems in more detail.

In the oceans, energy is trapped and used to synthesize organic tissue, mainly by minute plants — the phytoplankton (algae, diatoms, and so on). The phytoplankton are fed upon by very small invertebrates (the zooplankton) and these in turn are eaten by larger invertebrates and small fish, which are attacked and eaten by large fish, seals, and so on, and these may finally be eaten by killer whales. Each link in this food chain can be viewed as a trophic level — a group of organisms feeding on similar food sources. In this case, and in others, typically the organisms in each trophic level are larger than those in the lower trophic levels. Food chains, or more realistically food webs, are thus the pathways along which energy and nutrients move, and trophic levels are transfer stations along the way at which nutrients are first broken down and used or reassembled into new tissue.

A word of caution about trophic levels is needed. At any one point in time no doubt trophic levels exist in reality; however, many organisms regularly or at different stages in their life history are in different trophic levels. For green plants, of course, this is rarely a problem but in insects, for example, more than half the species may spend time in more than one trophic level[2] and even seed-eating birds feed small animals to their young. To this extent trophic levels are an abstraction which are, however, useful in thinking about ecosystems and in studying energy flow.

For any biological system to persist, there has to be a basic trophic level which traps solar energy and synthesizes food. This function is universally performed by green plants and this first level is called the producer level. Just as necessarily, nutrient cycles must be completed, and organisms must be present which can break down the complex organic materials and molecules in plant tissues. This job is finally done by microorganisms (bacteria and fungi). In general, intermediate activities take place in which the plants are eaten (live or dead) and large chunks of plants and animals are broken down into smaller parts.

There are two more or less clear series of trophic levels, one (the herbivore chain) dealing with live plant materials as a base and containing plants, herbivores (which eat green plants), predators (which eat other animals, mainly herbivores), and parasites; the other using mainly dead materials as a base (the detritus or decomposer food chain). The distinction between the two types of food chains is not complete; for example, snails eat both live and dead plant material. In a perfect, idealized ecosystem the links in these chains form a closed circle so that biological material is being continually synthesized from simple inorganic molecules (for example, phosphates in the soil) by plants and passing

along the circle until bacteria finally complete the decomposition process by breaking down complex organic molecules to inorganic compounds which plants can use again.

Plants, the producers, synthesize organic molecules (carbohydrates, proteins, and so on) from inorganic molecules in the environment ($CO_2$, sulfates, nitrates, and so on) and use solar energy for the purpose. This energy is trapped during photosynthesis, during which carbon dioxide combines with water in the presence of radiant energy and enzymes associated with chlorophyll, to form glucose (oxygen is given off). By far the largest proportion of plant biomass is made up of such carbohydrates.

The amount of solar energy actually available to plants, on the average, is about $5 \times 10^8$ calories per year per square meter of earth's surface and they manage to "fix" about 1 to 5 percent of this energy. All organisms need energy, the ability to do work, for their maintenance, growth and reproduction, and they get it in the form of potential energy, that is, chemical energy stored as food. Thus the total amount of energy fixed by plants sets an absolute upper limit to biological production and activity.

This solar energy is not trapped uniformly over the earth's surface, nor is biomass produced uniformly. The surface of the open oceans is by and large a biological desert — as are the deserts on land — and in these areas, solar heat is almost entirely lost via radiation to outer space, without flowing through a biological community. In contrast, a few places are very high in their annual production. In particular, in the wet tropics intense cultivation can produce 50-80 metric tons per hectare (2.5 acres) in a year, but estuaries, coral reefs, and rich alluvial farmland are also very productive. Some idea of the world distribution of production can be gained from Figure 2.

The most important determinants of production are the climate (rainfall, solar radiation), soil structure and nutrient quality, and the efficiency of the plant community at trapping the incident solar energy throughout the year. Thus the production of the desert can often be increased by irrigating and adding fertilizers. (Production is defined as the amount of organic matter elabo-

GRAMS/SQ. METER/DAY

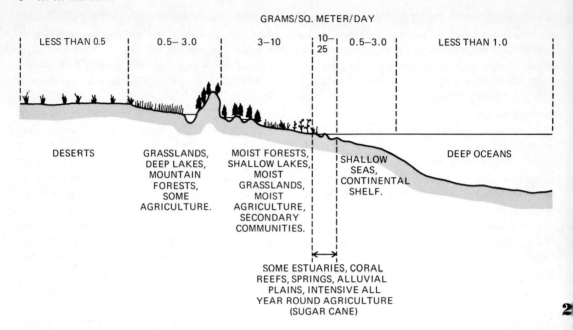

| LESS THAN 0.5 | 0.5– 3.0 | 3–10 | 10– 25 | 0.5–3.0 | LESS THAN 1.0 |

DESERTS

GRASSLANDS, DEEP LAKES, MOUNTAIN FORESTS, SOME AGRICULTURE.

MOIST FORESTS, SHALLOW LAKES, MOIST GRASSLANDS, MOIST AGRICULTURE, SECONDARY COMMUNITIES.

SHALLOW SEAS, CONTINENTAL SHELF.

DEEP OCEANS

SOME ESTUARIES, CORAL REEFS, SPRINGS, ALLUVIAL PLAINS, INTENSIVE ALL YEAR ROUND AGRICULTURE (SUGAR CANE)

WORLD DISTRIBUTION OF PRIMARY PRODUCTION. Source: E.P. Odum, *Fundamentals of Ecology.* W.B. Saunders, Philadelphia, Pennsylvania.

rated over a specified time period, whether or not it all survives to the end of that time.)

The primary plant production is eaten and passes through the various trophic levels. At each transfer, the great proportion of the energy contained in the production of one trophic level is dissipated as heat during the process of forming the production of the next higher trophic level. This follows from thermodynamic and biochemical rules.[3] First, every time energy is transformed naturally from one form to another some portion always goes to heat and is lost. For example, when an animal releases the potential energy in glucose (by oxidation during respiration) about two-thirds of the energy is available for growth and activity (work) and one-third is lost to the environment as heat. Second, not all of the food eaten can be assimilated or used, and a varying proportion is lost as feces which pass to decomposers. Third, organisms need energy to maintain themselves, to move about, and to grow and reproduce. They get this energy by breaking down large food molecules into smaller, simpler molecules which are then further degraded to produce energy plus waste products in the pro-

cess of respiration. An example of maintenance is that every day almost 8 percent of our body protein becomes degraded and is resynthesized. New biomass (growth or reproduction) is synthesized from broken down food molecules.

In addition to these losses, there are more ecological losses. For example, herbivores do not usually eat all of the plant production nor carnivores all the herbivore production. Thus the herbivore food chain is continually "leaking" large quantities of energy to the decomposer food chain in the form of dead organisms and feces.

From this discussion it can be concluded that the amount of energy available to a trophic level and its production of biomass over a period of time must decrease very sharply as we move up trophic levels.

In the herbivore food chain a special constraint applies in converting material from plants to animals. Plants have a chemical composition very different from that of animals. In particular, a gram of plant biomass has a much lower energy (calorific) content than a gram of animal biomass. This is because plants consist mainly of carbohydrates, with very little protein and fat, while animals are very high in protein and fat but low in carbohydrates. The energy in carbohydrates is about 3.7 kcal/gm dry weight, while that of protein is 5.8 and for fats the figure is over 9.0. Therefore a great deal of plant biomass must be degraded to turn the energy into the "concentrated" form found in animals. Clearly, since the food of carnivores is similar to carnivore tissue, they can convert assimilated food into biomass more efficiently than can herbivores.

Some data are available for the efficiency of transfer between trophic levels, though it is not clear how generally applicable they are. This efficiency is the product of (a) the percentage of the production of one trophic level taken by the next higher level and (b) the percentage of this food which is turned into new biomass (production). It is difficult to get such data for major portions of communities, and the data available are approximate. Plants themselves use some of the energy they fix; thus about 10-20 percent is eventually lost as heat during respiration and 80-90 percent of the total energy fixed over a year is available to the herbivore food chain or the detritus food chain as potential energy. This amount is what has been defined as primary production. Herbivores (primary consumers) do not eat all of this plant production (in fact in forests they may eat only 10 percent).[4] Of the plant production actually consumed by herbivores, about 10 percent is turned into new herbivore biomass (that is, herbivore production). Thus for every 100 grams of land plant production in natural systems generally we only get 1 or 2 grams of herbivore production!

Secondary consumers (predators feeding on herbivores) tend to take a large percentage of the production of herbivores (at least 30 percent and possibly sometimes nearly 100 percent). For example, Golley[5] estimated that a weasel population took 31 percent of the production of a meadow mouse (*Microtus*) population and weasels were only one of several predators feeding on the mice. In some areas on the North American seashore snail and starfish predators take almost the entire production of settled barnacles.[6]

The efficiency of predators in converting food to new biomass was previously believed to be about 10 percent as in herbivores, but it may be

as high as 30 percent or more in cold-blooded predators such as invertebrates. An example of such an efficient converter is the larval damsel fly population in a pond shown in Figure 3. The damsel flies feed almost entirely on herbivorous insects. If predators in general were equally efficient, predator production would be about 10 percent (30 x 30 percent) of herbivore production and possibly as high as 30 percent. Estimates for ocean herbivores average 15 percent and for ocean fish predators reach 20 percent.[7] In warm-blooded predators the conversion efficiency is likely to be lower than 10 percent.

It is generally stated that in aquatic systems based on phytoplankton almost all the primary production passes through the herbivores. This is certainly true in some systems, but it is not clear yet if it is generally true. Again, more data are needed. In such aquatic systems where the herbivores consume nearly all the plant production, for every 100 grams of plant production there will be almost 10 grams of herbivore production. As on land, predators may take a high proportion of this herbivore production, so that one might get 20 grams of primary carnivores for each 100 grams of herbivores. Thus a conversion factor of 1-2 percent between the first and third trophic levels may be common in aquatic systems, compared with 0.1 - 0.3 percent for the land.

The kind of information discussed above can be summarized in a "production pyramid." Fig-

ENERGY CONVERSION BY DAMSEL FLY LARVAE. Energy flow in kilocalories per square meter per annum, through a population of damsel fly larvae in a pond. The shaded box represents the standing crop (mean annual diomass). Source: J.H. Lawton, *J. Animal Ecol. 40:* (in press).

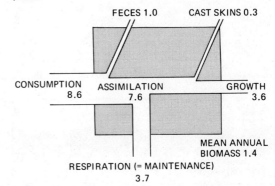

**3**

ure 4 shows the estimated amount of new biomass produced over a year by each trophic level
in all the world's oceans. Herbivores were assumed to convert about 10 percent of the plant
productivity into herbivore productivity, and at
all higher trophic levels the conversion rate between levels was assumed to be 15 percent. Since
interest centered on the potential fish production
of the oceans a small fraction of production was
omitted at carnivore levels to take account of
organisms such as jellyfish, corals, and barnacles
not in the trophic path to fish.

The basic measurements are necessarily rather
rough, but the significance of energy losses between levels is strikingly obvious. Man exploits
the oceans at about trophic level 4 (mollusks and
some fish are at a lower level, some fish even
higher). The 300 million tons of production at
this level is slightly higher than some other recent
estimates, and of this productivity man probably
can harvest rather less than half, that is, not
much more than double the present 57 million
metric tons of harvest. By comparison, on land
man can exploit trophic level 2 for protein. We
have to come in at higher trophic levels in the sea
because the organisms in the first two or three

NEW BIOMASS PRODUCTION PYRAMID. The esti-
mated total annual production at different trophic levels
in the world's oceans, in millions of metric tons. The
areas of the rectangles are proportional to the estimated
production. The estimate of primary production
(mainly by phytoplankton) is 130 billion tons. Source:
*Resources and Man: A Study and Recommendations* by
the Committee on Resources and Man of the Division of
Earth Sciences, National Academy of Sciences-National
Research Council, with the cooperation of the Division
of Biology and Agriculture. W. H. Freeman and Company. Copyright © 1969.

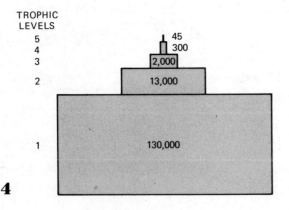

TROPHIC
LEVELS

levels are very small. Tilly[8] has done a recent
study of energy flow in a freshwater community.

Presumably the drastic decreases in production as one moves up trophic levels is a major
reason why ecological food chains rarely have
more than five links from producer to top predator. There probably are other reasons, of course.
For example, predators have to be larger than
their prey generally, so that individual animals
are large and population sizes become very small
in top predators.

By contrast with the herbivore food chain, on
the average and over long periods the decomposer food chain consumes all of the incoming
production and completes the dissipation of biologically fixed energy in the form of heat. If this
were not the case most ecosystems would be
chest-deep in a growing pile of dead and decaying
organisms and detritus. In fact, temporary exceptions (such as bogs and lakes) do occur and some
organic material does accumulate, as we shall see
when the process of succession occurs. Furthermore, important exceptions in the geologic past
permit us now to burn fossil fuels (Chapter 5).

The detritus food chain is crucially important
in nutrient cycling. Here the same thermodynamic and biochemical principles apply as in the
rest of the ecosystem. A system of trophic levels
can be outlined, although perhaps less clearly.
Although many of the species are small and in-
conspicuous by habit, tremendous complexity
exists here also.

There are two rather different parts of the
decomposition process, and both are necessary
for its completion. In the first place, large pieces
of detritus (dead animals, leaves, and so on) are
fragmented and partly decomposed, generally by
invertebrates and by fungi. Second, these coarse
organic particles are decomposed into simple inorganic compounds by simple organisms — bacteria and other fungi. The part played by the
different kinds of organisms varies with soil conditions.

Throughout this discussion emphasis has been
on the quantity of energy transfer and loss between trophic levels. However, it must be
stressed that energy considerations alone may
not explain the limits of production at some or
all trophic levels. Thus primary production by

plants in an area is rarely limited by the solar energy available, since nutrients of some sort usually set a lower limit. This is particularly well illustrated in lakes and in the ocean. In lakes, algal "blooms" of production occur seasonally when the water stratification breaks down and nutrients are brought to the lighted surface waters from the bottom of the lake. In the ocean, regions of upwelling are highly productive; in these regions, nutrients in deep cold water are brought up to the lighted surface and are used by the phytoplankton. (Chapter 8).

At higher trophic levels food quality may be important in determining production. For example, aphids feed on plant sap and it has been shown[9] that the limits to the transformation of this primary production into aphid biomass is set, not by energetics, but by the concentration of nitrogen (an essential ingredient of proteins) in the plant sap. In fact, aphids go into diapause (a sort of suspended animation) and shut off production when nitrogen levels are too low, even though the sap is still an adequate source of energy.

### Biological Concentration

Before leaving the subject of trophic levels and transfer of nutrients, it is important to note that in many cases materials become concentrated as they move up food chains. This is a characteristic of considerable practical importance, as the widespread occurrence of DDT illustrates so dramatically (Chapter 13).

Heavy metals and some radioactive elements also become concentrated as they move up food chains. An example of the latter occurs in Perch Lake in Ontario and is illustrated in Figure 5. Perch Lake is fed by a stream which contains radioactive material which seeps from a nearby liquid "disposal" area of Atomic Energy of Canada Limited. Strontium-90 is one of these radionuclides. Over the 5-year study period the amount of strontium-90 entering the lake each year was fairly constant. Some of the isotope is removed from the water and the substrate by plants and by organisms in the bottom sediment (where most of the strontium-90 occurs) and also directly by animals swimming in the water.

Figure 5 shows concentration factors for radio-strontium in selected organisms in the lake. The concentration in yellow perch, a top fish predator, is 3000 times that in the water.

### Populations

For some purposes we are interested only in particular components of the ecosystem such as the population of a single species. A population is a group of organisms belonging to the same species and living in the same area so that there is a possibility of interactions among its members. Populations thus present us with less of a problem of delineation than do trophic levels. They have birth rates, death rates, age distribution, genetic composition, and so on (Chapter 2). For many purposes the ecosystem can be seen as being organized at the population level and we can examine interactions within and among populations. Frequently we are interested in this level of organization from a very practical point of view. We may wish to maximize the yield from the population of a crop or herbivore and we often wish to reduce the numbers of a pest population. We are also very much interested in the problem of the human population. The general field of study which deals with this level is population biology, and that dealing with population abundance is population dynamics.

A population, of course, cannot be studied to the exclusion of all other parts of the ecosystem. Rather, the population forms the focus and other components are studied as they appear to influence it.

Perhaps most important from a practical point of view (as well as being interesting theoretically) is the question of how the numbers of a population are determined, what causes them to fluctuate, and what helps to stabilize them if they exhibit stability. It is important to get clear that there is more to finding out about populations than merely listing all the things which kill organisms. Animals fall over cliffs, are struck by lightning, die of disease, and perish in many other ways, yet many causes of mortality may not be "important" in the sense that they provide no explanation for the particular question asked of the population. It is sometimes difficult for the

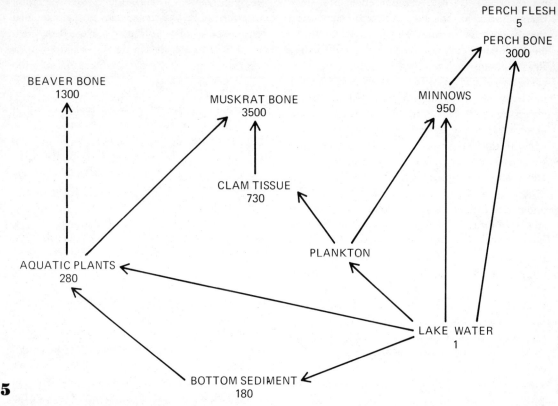

PERCH FLESH
5
PERCH BONE
3000

BEAVER BONE
1300

MUSKRAT BONE
3500

MINNOWS
950

CLAM TISSUE
730

PLANKTON

AQUATIC PLANTS
280

LAKE WATER
1

**5**

BOTTOM SEDIMENT
180

BIOLOGICAL CONCENTRATION OF STRONTIUM-90. The average concentration factors for strontium-90 in the Perch Lake food web. From Ophel, I.L. 1963. The fate of radiostrontium in a freshwater community. Source: *In* Radioecology, V. Schultz and A.W. Klement, Jr., eds.

beginner in population biology to drag his attention away from the specific events which occur to individual organisms and to learn to look at, say, the effect of mortality rates upon populations as they vary through time and with population density. For example, in spite of the fact that there may be many causes of death in a population, it may be possible to explain the fluctuations in the numbers on the basis of changes in the death rate caused by only one or a few factors. This has been shown to be the case in many of the long-term studies of insects, where it has been found (1) that there is one crucial or "key" stage in the life history whose survival is particularly variable from year to year and (2) that much of the annual variation in its survival can be attributed to a single cause or factor. Thus, although dozens of processes affect

the birth rate and death rate of the population, one "key factor" can explain (and serve to predict) most of the annual fluctuations. Some easily measured aspect of the weather often has been the key factor, though in other cases it has been the amount of parasitism (by insects). This recent finding has obvious practical importance in any situation where we want to predict population fluctuations, or where we want to control them.

The numbers of organisms in a population are determined by three processes: birth rate (natality), death rate (mortality), and movements. Movement is sometimes important in determining the numbers of a species as a whole. Thus, the British starling increased its numbers by invading and spreading throughout the United States in this century. Clearly, when it has gone as far as it can go, the net movement West will cease, and its population in the United States will reach some limit. However, emigration from a population which results in lowering the local density must in general be a net loss to the species in the form of eventual mortality, since most species cannot be continually expanding their range in a finite world.

Dispersal is a crucial process in many species, for example, in organisms like plants and barnacles where the adult is sedentary. Migration is important in many bird species, and, for example, in the spectacular case of the California gray whale which migrates between the Arctic and Baja California. Also, organisms which live in temporary habitats (such as some carrion-feeders and crustacea living in temporary ponds) have to have well-developed powers of dispersal.

In managed systems, movements sometimes can be important.[10] Many pest insects, such as aphids and the frit fly, travel large distances as "plankton" in air currents. They descend upon crops, and frequently the factors controlling such invasions determine the size of the pest problem. It has been suggested, for example, that the prevailing wind pattern determines which areas in the Middle East are infected by cereal pests.

For simplicity, we will now ignore population movements and discuss population growth and limitation in terms of birth and death rates. Populations increase in density when births exceed deaths and decrease when the reverse is true. For populations which are approximately constant numerically, the birth rate must equal the death rate. Growing populations, therefore, become limited in numbers either by an increase in the death rate or a decrease in the birth rate or both.

Since populations grow by multiplication, they have the capacity to expand exponentially — that is the numbers present can increase at a constant rate (the numbers can double at a constant interval) even though the numbers get larger at each doubling. This potential for exponential growth, of course, is rarely realized in nature, for a variety of reasons. Populations are usually already at some high density with respect to factors which limit them — although some may frequently decline catastrophically and build up again almost exponentially.

I want to illustrate some features of population dynamics using a well-studied laboratory population. A great deal of work has been done on flour beetles (*Tribolium*) by Thomas Park and

his colleagues at the University of Chicago.[11] Populations of beetles are kept in flour in small glass vials. The beetles lay eggs, the eggs become larvae, the larvae pupate, and new adults appear and then begin to lay eggs. Temperature, humidity, and other conditions are kept constant, so we see "pure" populational events. A typical population growth pattern for one genetic strain of *Tribolium confusum* in Figure 6 shows the numbers of adults in the population over 16 months.

Several interesting features are as follows: (1) There is a very rapid increase in numbers in the first few weeks. (2) The population very quickly becomes limited. The limit is set by the amount of flour given, and the more flour there is, the more beetles there are. (The flour provides space to live in and space is limiting rather than food.) (3) Although space is the limiting factor, this does not explain the mechanism. The beetles are cannibals. As they burrow about in the flour, both the larvae and adults eat eggs and pupae. Most eggs and pupae are eaten, but every month about 20 old adults die and about 20 new ones come through. It can be shown that the frequency of contacts among beetles is the important variable determining cannibalism rate, and this frequency is determined by the amount of living space and the number of beetles present. Thus once they develop a mixed age distribution, these

POPULATION GROWTH OF FLOUR BEETLES. The number of adults of *Tribolium confusum* strain II in 8 grams of flour (average of 10 populations). Notice that abundance is plotted on a logarithmic scale. The data are from an unpublished experiment by D.B. Mertz and the author.

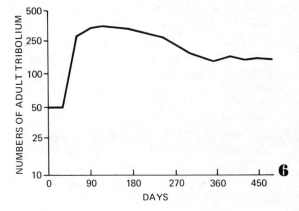

populations are stable and self-regulating and they do this without destroying their food supply. (4) There is an interesting initial overshoot period when numbers exceed the equilibrium density. This overshoot illustrates the existence of lag effects which are universal in ecological systems. The overshoot results from the fact that a large cohort of eggs is produced all at the same time and they develop into adults at a time when there are few other older adults around to be cannibalistic. The long decline occurs as this generation of adults hangs around, cannibalizing all further recruits.

In another very closely related genetic strain of this species, the beetles are very poor cannibals and cannot stabilize their own numbers. These populations become so dense that they ruin their food supply with their secretions, essentially polluting themselves to frequent near-extinction. Thus small differences in the quality of the beetles have very large consequences for the dynamics of the populations.

*Tribolium* populations, then, present a wonderful microcosm, illustrating a variety of important characteristics of natural populations: (1) Self-regulation below the level of food destruction appears to be fairly common in some natural populations, for example, in territorial birds, and various predatory animals. (2) Changes in the quality of animals through time, either via genetics or physiology are being found more commonly to play a role in determining abundance. Examples are being found in cyclic small mammal populations, in various important caterpillar pests in forests, and in locust populations. (3) It is probably true that a species of tree in a forest is less prone to defoliation by pests if it has a more complex or mixed age distribution, just as a beetle population is more stable with a mixed age distribution. This is the case in the Canadian balsam fir forests where outbreaks occur when the spruce budworm attacks even-aged stands of mature trees.[12] (4) The history of a population is to some extent incorporated in its age distribution (the age distribution is a sort of population "memory") and the consequences of this history are prolonged into the future because of the existence of the age distribu-

tion. This sort of demographic time lag is very well illustrated in human populations (Chapter 2).

*Factors Limiting Population*

Populations do not increase indefinitely, in fact, they generally increase for only short periods. This is because all populations are constrained by limiting factors of one sort or another. The following list includes a number of things which can set upper limits to populations or can be important in population dynamics in some other way.

SOURCES OF MORTALITY

Enemies, for example, predators (including insect parasites); disease
Competitors
Food supply (quality and quantity)
"A place to live in," for example, nesting site, shelter
The weather
Factors internal to the population, for example, cannibalism, changes in the quality of organisms, stress from crowding, waste products

FACTORS AFFECTING NATALITY

Food supply (quality and quantity)
Oviposition sites
The weather
Interference among members of the population, for example, territorial behavior, stress, social hierarchy

It is probably the case that many populations in nature are kept at low densities through the action of one or more enemy species. This idea is certainly often implicit in discussions of "natural balance." In fact, there is little direct evidence in the way of detailed population studies that many populations are limited by enemies, but this is probably because there are few thorough studies. (Of course, there is plenty of evidence that predators cause large amounts of prey mortality in many species, but as I have said, this does not necessarily signify that predators actually limit the population.)

Some of the most convincing examples of enemies limiting populations come from studies on the rocky seashore.[13] Examples are also available from the field of biological control (Chapter 14). But we do not have good direct evidence from complex natural ecosystems, such as forests, though such systems strike us as excellent examples of natural balance. A basic problem is that few such studies have been made.

However, it is probably a good assumption that many herbivore species are kept at low densities by their enemies. The indirect evidence which is available comes mainly from comparing managed ecological systems with natural systems. Thus pest populations occur where natural enemies generally are missing. The trouble with such evidence is that in managed ecosystems many factors other than the absence of natural enemies have been altered from the natural system and we are not presented, therefore, with clear controlled experiments.

One example of population control by an "enemy" is particularly illustrative of the difficulties of doing ecological research and of the fact that a historical perspective is necessary in field studies.[14] The St.-John's-wort (*Hypericum*) is an introduced plant in California. Generally it is not very abundant in pastures there. Also, if one searches very diligently, an occasional chrysomelid beetle (*Chrysolina*) can be found, but an analysis of the present scene would rate this insect as unimportant. In actual fact, the plant was once a very important weed in California pastures and it was controlled by introducing the beetle. The beetle has been extremely effective and now the weed is rather rare and patchy and is kept that way by the beetle, which of course is also rare.

The food supply must set the upper limit to the potential population size in most organisms, though it is not clear how often populations reach this limit or if they are usually held below it by other factors. It is again difficult to get clear-cut examples of populations being limited in a simple, direct fashion by the quantity of food available to them. Few instances are known of populations simply eating out their food supply and being limited by mass mortality through starvation, though food limitation need not involve such occurrences. The numbers of animals feeding on plants in the plankton in lakes seem to be limited by food supply in many cases. This can be shown by the increase in their numbers following an increase in the phytoplankton caused by adding nutrients.[15]

There are several good examples of the quality of the food, or the quantity of the right quality of food being limiting. In aphids the quality of the sap can help limit numbers.[9] It seems quite likely that there is a complex interaction between food quality, the behavior of the aphids, and their density. Thus the food quality and the frequency of contact with other aphids may interact to determine when reproduction is shut off.

The aphid example pinpoints two important features of population dynamics. The first is that factors may frequently interact, so that simple explanations of population limitation are not available. Secondly, organisms are not passive nor do their characteristics remain constant under the impact of environmental factors. The effect of such factors must result from an interaction between the factor and the individuals in the population, and both can vary.

There is growing evidence that "self-regulation" occurs in some populations. That is, numbers may be determined largely by the qualities of the organisms in the population and by interactions among them. Perhaps the clearest example is territoriality in birds, where only a portion of the population is allowed to breed, others being excluded by the aggressive behavior of the territory holders. The density in many such cases seems to be geared to the food supply. Self-regulation is also brought about by social hierarchy or aggressiveness in some small mammals. Clearly a *sine qua non* for the functioning of such mechanisms is the existence in the population of animals with different qualities.

Evidence for changes in the quality of organisms playing a part in limiting numbers has been found in several populations. The proportion of "lower quality" animals becomes especially high at times of high population densities (and immediately thereafter in cyclic populations), so

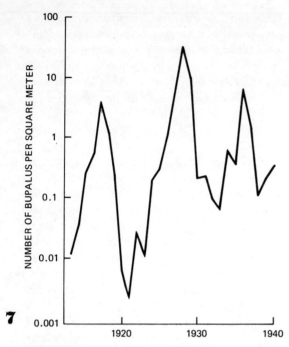

UNSTABLE MOTH POPULATION. The number of hibernating pupae of *Bupalus* per square meter of forest floor at Letzlingen, Germany. *Bupalus* is a moth whose larvae are pests which eat the needles of the pine trees. The population peaks were severe outbreaks causing extensive damage. Note that abundance is plotted on a logarithmic scale and increased more than 10,000-fold between 1920 and 1930. Source: G.C. Varley, *J. Animal Ecol. 18:* 117-122 (1949).

**7**

that the density is then reduced. Such changes in viability have been very nicely shown for the western tent caterpillar,[16] a forest pest, and for locusts. The most controversial case is that of cyclic small mammals such as mice, voles, and lemmings, which have been studied for 40 years and whose numbers show very large oscillations.[17]

To summarize, all populations become limited, and food supply or space usually sets the potential upper limit. Other processes such as predation prevent many populations from reaching this limit. But it is not clear how frequently the various kinds of limiting factors operate, and ecologists are not yet in a position to make generalizations on this subject.

*Population Regulation*

For reasons of clarity I have kept separate the discussion of limiting factors and the mechanisms

acting to keep populations stable. The question of population stability (used here synonomously with regulation) is an interesting and vexing one. It seems likely that some local populations of species are very unstable and frequently become extinct and are reconstituted by immigration. Others are also unstable numerically, though they seem to persist for quite a long time (for example, see Figure 7). Unstable populations are common in simple agricultural systems where pest outbreaks either occur or are continually threatening but are prevented artificially, but some natural populations also erupt when conditions are right. For example in balsam fir forests the Canadian spruce budworm (a moth caterpillar) historically seems to have remained at low densities for 30 or 40 years at a time, and then increased enormously when a combination of climatic and tree "stand" factors were favorable.[18]

On the other hand, there seem to be large numbers of populations which jog along maintaining fairly constant numbers, though different populations fluctuate around different density levels. It may be that most populations in most natural systems are stable, or "regulated," to this extent. Indeed, the fact that populations persist

STABLE BIRD POPULATION. The number of breeding pairs of heron on the Thames drainage area, England. Notice that abundance is plotted on an arithmetic scale and that fluctuations over the entire period were about twofold. Source: D. Lack, *Population Studies of Birds,* The Clarendon Press, Oxford, England. 1966.

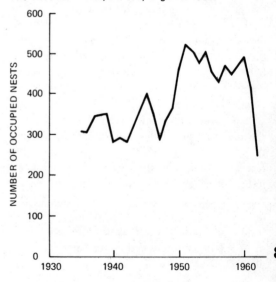

for long periods suggests that there are mechanisms, either in the populations themselves or in the communities they live in, which tend to keep them stable. An example of a stable bird population which has been studied over a long time is shown in Figure 8.

Other evidence is the contrast between the pest problem in our agricultural systems and the continued existence in natural communities of grass, shrubs, trees, and so on, which rarely are destroyed or defoliated, which suggests that herbivores in natural systems rarely become enormously and erratically abundant. Since we would prefer our ecosystems to be dependable and stable, gaining an understanding of natural stability is of great value to us.

Figure 8 shows a stable population, and the fact that territorial birds generally seem to be stable suggests that one important set of stabilizing mechanisms comes under the general heading of self-regulation. These mechanisms help populations to buffer themselves against some vagaries in the environment and probably occur in many kinds of animals.

In fact, populations which ecologists consider as stable do fluctuate, but the fluctuations are relatively small and the average density over several generations in the future will be the same as it was for several generations in the past.

In trying to explain why a given population is stable, we need to discover the mechanisms which tend to make the population decrease when it becomes higher than average and make it increase when it is below average. To illustrate how such mechanisms work, let us take a simplified example. Suppose we are interested in the numbers of adults in an animal population in May of each year, and we observe that every year there are 10 adults per square meter. In this example we·have perfect regulation of the adult numbers. However, each year the birth rate (number of eggs laid) is a density-disturbing process; it tends to be highly variable, so that in some years there may be only 20 eggs per square meter but in other years 500. Clearly, mortality as a whole is regulatory. We assume that adults do not live a second year. Table I shows what happens each year.

| Initial no. of eggs laid in May, year 0 | No. of adults produced in May, year 1 | No. dying | Percent mortality |
|---|---|---|---|
| 20 | 10 | 10 | 50 |
| 40 | 10 | 30 | 75 |
| 60 | 10 | 50 | 83 |
| 100 | 10 | 90 | 90 |
| 200 | 10 | 190 | 95 |
| 300 | 10 | 290 | 97 |
| 400 | 10 | 390 | 98 |
| 500 | 10 | 490 | 98 |

**A MORTALITY-REGULATED POPULATION**

Notice, not only does the number killed increase with increasing initial density, but so does the percentage killed. Thus regulating factors are those which cause an increasing percentage mortality as density increases. Of course, natality can also be regulatory; one hopes it will be so in human populations. Such regulatory factors are said to be DENSITY-DEPENDENT in operation.

Populations which are stable, then, by definition are stabilized by density-dependent processes. To explain such stability we must then search for factors which operate in this way. Since the effect of a factor acting upon a population can result from changes in both the factor and in the individuals in the population, in principle any factor might operate in this way. In general, however, ecologists tend to look to such factors as food, enemies, and nesting sites and to interactions among organisms in the population for density-dependent effects.

The separation of populations into stable and unstable ones here is rather arbitrary. It probably is the case that there is continuous variation from populations which are very stable to those which are extremely unstable.

The importance of the concepts of density dependence, regulation, and stability goes beyond "pure" ecology into the realms of pest control and the management of resource species. Pests are species which are highly unstable and prone to outbreak with great rapidity. The ideal solution is to keep such populations regulated at densities so low that they cause little harm. Thus, ideally, pests should be controlled by density-dependent mechanisms (Chapter 14).

The concept of density dependence is important in resource management.[19] Although the problem of getting the optimum yield from an exploited natural population is complex, at the simplest level, for naturally stable stocks exploitation should be density-dependent over the long run to guarantee the persistence of the population. Disregard of this obvious point has resulted in the past in the near-extinction of the blue whale, sperm whale, and the buffalo, and is now leading to overfishing in some of the world's fishing stocks. Similarly in the management of game-bird stocks the aim is to shoot the "surplus" each year, and this is simply to act as a density-dependent mortality factor.

## The Nature of Population Problems

A great proportion of the problems we face in managing ecosystems are population problems. The enormous and diverse endeavors of growing crops for food and for fibers, of managing forests for timber, of exploiting and managing ocean fisheries, of controlling pests, and maintaining recreational areas in ecosystems, all include population problems. And so, of course, is our own Population Problem. One ought to appreciate, therefore, the nature and difficulty of population studies.

Questions of a populational nature are difficult to answer. Not only are populations affected by a multitude of factors, but they are themselves very complicated. Indeed, natural populations generally strike one as being hopelessly complex at first sight — and often at subsequent sights! The task of explaining the population dynamics of field populations so far has taken very long periods of intensive investigations. The famous cyclic populations of small mammals have been studied for 40 years, and still there are several theories competing to explain the data.

An illustration of the difficulties is the very large scale and intensive work which was carried out on the spruce budworm (caterpillar) which is a pest of balsam fir forests in New Brunswick, and breaks out periodically after several years of good weather.[12] After 15 years' study the major causes of mortality had been found for most of the life stages in the insect, but after this enormous effort, it is still not known what normally limits their numbers or what finally causes the crash after an outbreak. Other 15-20 year studies of animal populations have been made which do not provide a complete answer, and an important lesson is that field studies are difficult and require a long time. This is something which decision-makers have to learn about ecosystems. It also presents a challenge to those dealing with both population ecology and practical population control to develop new ways of getting at least approximate answers with a few years' work.

The reasons for the long times involved in such studies and their inconclusiveness include some unalterable aspects of natural systems. They are complex and it is difficult to disentangle the effects of interacting factors — one may have to wait and see how these change in different circumstances; generally there are great difficulties in making measurements because animals tend to be hidden, and most species most of the time in most places are rare; every situation is to some extent unique, as every species is unique, and it is difficult to cut through the bewildering maze of species' peculiarities to those features which they have in common, so that useful broad generalizations are hard to come by. Finally, ecological systems, unlike physical systems, are often "non-Markovian." That is, the future state of the system cannot be predicted on the basis of the present state alone, but depends upon the population's history. Thus population events not only vary with locality, but are time-dependent.

Of the many approaches and techniques which ecologists have developed to deal with these difficulties it is worth mentioning one in particular which should prove increasingly useful to people involved in managing populations for applied purposes. This is systems analysis. This is a promising approach because it is exactly suited to the peculiar nature of ecological systems. These are composed of very large numbers of different components which interact in a large variety of ways. Each biological component is affected by a large number of physical variables, and all variables change not only in time but from place to place since the environment is heterogeneous. Distant components interact, and one component affects all others in one way or another. Hence "the complexity of the system of interlocking cause-effect pathways confronts us with a superficially baffling problem."[20] Systems analysis is designed precisely to handle such situations. Basically, the system is analyzed in terms of simple components. The variables and processes affecting each component are analyzed and described so that changes through time can be described and predicted. The way the various components fit together is also analyzed, and finally these units are then reassembled in a model of the whole system. Almost invariably this involves the use of a computer to simulate the consequences of changes in the variables controlling the system.

In the case of real ecological systems one does not try to describe every interaction and the relationships among all the variables. No simulation can be complete. Indeed, the art, as in any science, is to draw a caricature of the system, etching in the really crucial lines which describe the major features of the system. This is why systems analysis will be particularly useful to practical ecologists who have to make decisions on an incomplete description of the system. Systems analysis is a method of allowing one to make decisions and to make the best decision on the available data and at different times as the system changes. Examples of the use of systems analysis in managing a very complex biological resource are described in Chapters 8 and 14.

## Succession in Ecosystems

As usual there are various ways of studying ecology at this level. For example, botanists in particular are interested in trying to describe communities in such a way that distinct assemblages of species can be categorized and classified together, while their limits can be delineated and they can be separated from different communities. It is often possible to recognize recurrent groupings of species which make up a large part of a community, so that regularities at this level obviously occur. Thus bog communities are distinct and repeated, as are chaparral, mixed deciduous forests in the midwest, and high alpine valleys.

Another way of looking at changes in communities is to see how they change with time, that is, to study SUCCESSION. Here again, the edges are fuzzy, but patterns emerge and allow one to make predictions about the nature of future communities. The succession of terrestrial communities in various circumstances has been fairly well described and occurs in an orderly way. The initial stages of development may take a long time — for example, filling in a lake or bog, or breaking down a bare rock surface by wind, rain, and the action of small plants — such as lichens — which produce a top soil. Once soil and some plants are present, succession then tends to proceed faster. Each stage or community tends to modify the environment, making it more suitable for some other group of organisms, so that there is an interaction between the biological and physical parts of the system.

Secondary succession on abandoned fields is fairly well studied. In the southeastern United States the order often is grasses → grasses plus forbs → mainly shrubs → pine forest → oak-hickory "climax" forest. This history may take 150 years or more, with each successive stage lasting longer than the preceding one. Various features about the process seem rather general. (1) Low, structurally simple communities which persist for only a short period give way to communities with larger plants, a more complex structure and which persist for longer. (2) The number of species present tends to increase with time (though there may be a slight dip in the number of species in the final "climax" community) and food webs become more complex. (3) The later stages are more stable in the sense that the individuals tend to be longer-lived, that the community tends to stabilize its internal environment (for example, temperature, wind speed), and that later stages last longer and continually replace themselves. Thus diversity and stability seem to go hand in hand.

Other changes occur in succession[21]: The production of plant biomass in early successional stages is high. Typically this is associated with a low standing crop of biomass (production/biomass ratio is high). From one point of view, such early successional stages are highly efficient in that the rate of production of plant material is greater than the rate of "respiratory loss" of energy by the system, so biomass tends to accumulate throughout succession. As this occurs, and we move to a larger, older community with greater biomass, the relative rate of biomass production declines, that is the production/biomass ratio tends to decrease. Climax communities then tend to be balanced, in that the energy fixed by photosynthesis is equal to that respired in maintaining the community, so biomass no longer increases but remains constant. This low production/biomass ratio might be considered inefficient. From another point of view, though, such communities are highly efficient in that the energy fixed is used to maintain a large, diverse, and very stable community which has gained a great deal of "control" over its physical environment. The relative importance of the two basic types of energy pathways also changes during succession. In early successional stages a high proportion of the energy passes through the herbivores, while in later stages most of the energy passes through the decomposers.[21]

Man's typical food-producing ecosystems can be fitted into this scheme as "early succession" types, with a high production (yield)-to-standing crop ratio, short food chains, and great simplicity. We will discuss the simplicity of such systems in greater detail in the next section.

There is a trend during succession from an open to a more closed system with respect to nutrients. Climax communities tend to retain the nutrients they have and continually recycle them (though of course no ecosystem, except the biosphere as a whole, is completely closed with respect to matter). It is estimated, for example, that in a north-temperate watershed covered by climax forest only slightly more than 2 percent of the exchangeable calcium is lost per year — this being replaced by rainfall and rock-weathering.[21] Although no good measurements are available for mineral loss following reduction of forest cover, there is much greater water loss and presumably mineral loss also.

The openness of ecosystems is important since it means that ecosystems are linked by a flow of materials and energy and therefore they are not independent of one another. Freshwater bodies in particular are open systems. Thus streams gain nutrients in the runoff from surrounding terrestrial communities and in the leaves and other debris which fall in from the riparian vegetation. There is a constant downstream drift of nutrients in the form of detritus and organisms, though this is sometimes reversed, for example, when migrating salmon come back as nutrients from the ocean. Lakes receive inputs of potential energy and nutrients from upstream, and while the rate of flow is slowed within lakes, they still pass on nutrients downstream to the estuaries, continental shelf, ocean plankton, and the deep ocean floor. Sometimes the passage of materials occurs on a huge scale: The annual flooding of the Nile, the Tigris and Euphrates, and other great river systems of the world provided rich alluvial farmland with which great civilizations were associated. It is estimated that every year the Mississippi carries 730 million tons of soil — 38 thousand acres 3 feet deep — into the Gulf of Mexico.

In aquatic systems, however, not all of the material is passed downstream. In slow-moving rivers and lakes, particles and dead organisms settle to the bottom, where the organisms are decomposed, and the water body gradually fills up. A pond fills up and becomes a swamp and during the process, as vegetation chokes the pond, the types of fish and other organisms change. The swamp is invaded by vegetation from the surrounding communities and terrestrial succession begins. Thus ecosystems are dynamic, not only in that they are open systems, constantly receiving and losing materials, but because their character changes with time and they develop into different kinds of systems.

*Interactions in Ecosystems*

From our point of view it is of great importance that ecosystems are dynamic, not only in that they change in space and time, but in that enormous numbers of interactions are going on within them all the time. Perhaps feeding interactions are the most significant. On the Old Field mentioned earlier, 31 different categories were needed to classify all the insects simply into general feeding types (predators on insects, parasites, plant feeders, scavengers, and so on).[2] More than half the insect species, mainly parasites, feed on other insects, providing great potential for interactions among species. This point is illustrated by the food web in Figure 9, which is based on only one species of plant (broccoli). This shows interac-

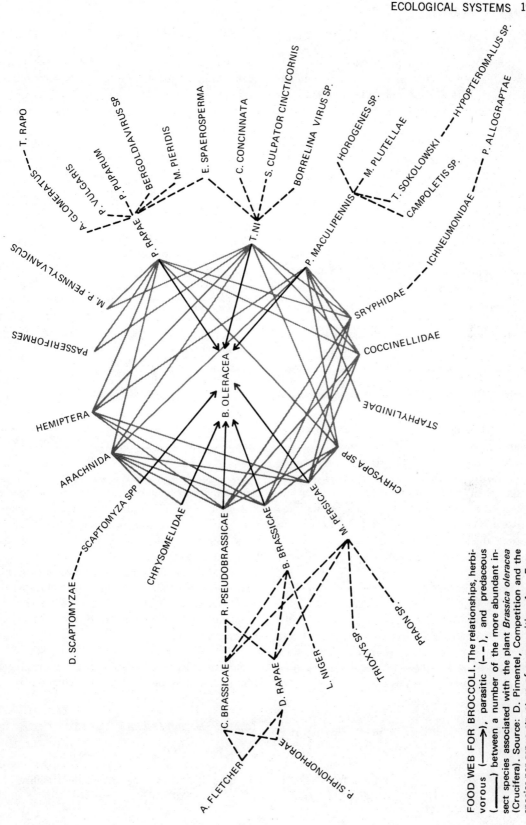

FOOD WEB FOR BROCCOLI. The relationships, herbivorous (———➤), parasitic (– –), and predaceous (———) between a number of the more abundant insect species associated with the plant *Brassica oleracea* (Crucifera). Source: D. Pimentel, Competition and the species-per-genus structure of communities. *Ann. Entomol. Soc. Amer. 54:* 323-333 (1961).

tions among only the 50 most abundant insect species of the 200 in this agricultural community.

Apparently distant components in the ecosystem, as well as adjacent ones, interact and are interdependent. For example, the adult stage of insects which parasitize other insects feed on flowers; thus the time of flowering of plants might indirectly affect the parasitism rate observed in a caterpillar population later in the year. The point can be illustrated and its practical importance emphasized by an example from agriculture.

For 15 years partridges have been declining in England. While these are not a major resource of that nation, they are an important "managed" game resource. The most likely explanation is as follows: For these 15 years cereal crops have been sprayed with herbicides to kill weeds, and this has been fairly successful. However, at a crucial time in their life history, when the young are present, partridges need to feed upon insects, and insects that live on weeds in cereal have been severely reduced. So there has been heavy partridge mortality. A further consequence of spraying for weeds in cereals is that the numbers of aphids are gradually increasing. These insects, of course, are serious pests. It seems that the natural enemy insects of the aphids are disappearing along with the weeds. Furthermore, the herbicides when taken up by the cereal seem to change the cereal's physiology in some way and make them a better host for aphids! For various reasons the aphids do not provide a substitute to the partridges for the lost food supply of weed insects.

The notion that different components of ecosystems interact, and that consequences of perturbing one part of the system are likely to be felt elsewhere in the system, can be extended to interactions between different ecosystems, since all ecosystems are open and are linked together. Migratory species illustrate the classical case of linked ecosystems. Thus the populations of salmon, important oceanic predators, are greatly influenced by conditions in the freshwater river systems in which they spawn.

Perhaps the most dramatic examples can be found in systems managed by man. The well-intentioned but often poorly conceived building

of dams for reservoirs illustrates this. For example, the Aswan High Dam on the Upper Nile was built to provide hydroelectric power. It has had three major bad effects on surrounding systems.[22]

The catch of sardines from the eastern end of the Mediterranean, once 18 thousand tons per year, dropped to 500 tons per year. It is not clear whether this is a consequence of cutting off the nutrients which formerly came into the sea during annual flooding and produced large blooms of phytoplankton, or if it is due to changes in the salinity regime of the area. In either case, the dam is the cause of the reduced catch.

Another ecological effect of the dam has been the replacement of an intermittent flowing stream with a permanent stable lake. This has allowed aquatic snails to maintain large populations, whereas before the dam was built they had been reduced each year during the dry season. Because irrigation supports large human populations, there are now many more people living close to these stable bodies of water. The problem here is that the snails serve as intermediate hosts of the larvae of a blood fluke. The larvae leave the snail and bore into humans, infecting the liver and other organs. This causes the disease called schistosomiasis. The species of snail which lives in stable water harbors a more virulent species of fluke than that found in another species of snail in running water. Thus the lake behind the Aswan Dam has increased both the incidence and virulence of schistosomiasis among the people of the Upper Nile.

Finally, the flooding of the river historically produced rich alluvial farmlands. Below where the dam now sits, these soils are no longer being replenished, and the fertility of the farm soils is decreasing.

The chapters in this book dealing with environmental degradation are replete with examples of interactions between distant components of the environment.

*Complexity and Stability*

Perhaps the most interesting and potentially valuable concept to have come from a study of communities is the notion that the stability of a community is roughly correlated with its complexity. This has become something of a cliche', both in and out of ecology, and one tends to accept it all the more uncritically and easily because it has such obvious parallels in human society: Pluralistic societies tend to be socially stable; economic systems with multiple resources, diverse manufacturing processes and export markets are supposedly less vulnerable to fluctuations in one part of the system, and so on. In fact, as usual, good direct evidence is hard to come by, unequivocal experiments are almost nonexistent, and it is not even clear sometimes what aspects of complexity are important, how they work, or indeed what stability is. The remainder of this section is devoted to an analysis of this relationship.

Stability will be taken to mean that the system is rather constant through time — the species present in the community tend to be similar from time to time, and their abundances do not usually vary wildly. Furthermore, stable systems are those which tend to be resistant to external perturbations, and if such perturbations disrupt the system, it tends to be able to come back to a stable state.

The case for claiming that complexity leads to stability rests essentially on three bases. The first is controlled laboratory experiments, which are few and hard to interpret. The second is general observations; examples are that simple agricultural systems are more prone to pest outbreaks than the native complex systems and that forest pest outbreaks are virtually unknown in the highly diverse tropical rain forest. The third is a priori considerations, for example, that a system with multiple feedback loops is much more likely to be stable than one with few such loops.

There are various kinds of complexity which might produce stability. PHYSICAL COMPLEXITY provides discontinuities, breaking up populations into small units. It also provides refuges, and this may be a crucial reason why predators can persist with their prey species without wiping them out. There is evidence that predator-prey systems in the laboratory persist longer if the physical environment is complex.

The importance of physical complexity in allowing predator-prey systems to persist has been shown very nicely for seashore populations of barnacles. In this study,[6] the barnacle prey had one part of their range which was an inviolable refuge which the predators never invaded. In another study of marine organisms it was found that mussels (prey) and their starfish predators coexisted because there were numerous barriers to dispersal of the predators between populations of prey.[23]

BIOLOGICAL COMPLEXITY comes in many forms, all of which might contribute to stability. At the population level, variability among individuals, either genetic or physiological, may be important in allowing the population to cope with conditions which vary in time and space. We already noted in flour beetles and conifer forests that a mixed age distribution population was more likely to be stable than one with a single age class.

In nature, populations are distributed very patchily and occur in semiisolated clumps. This, combined with physical heterogeneity, introduces a stochastic element into population dynamics. For example, while a disease or predator population may be wiping out one clump of prey, another clump may be increasing and sending out propagules, and the semiisolation may prevent the disease or predator from reaching all clumps simultaneously.

In considering the diversity of whole communities, perhaps simply the high number of species present is itself a stabilizing factor. Elton[24] has suggested that complex communities are stable in part because every niche is filled and so new species are unable to invade empty niches and produce upsets.

It seems certain, however, that more than mere numbers of species are involved and that, as Elton stressed, the myriad interactions are important. Possibly the most significant are predator-prey interactions. When predators eat a variety of prey species, the presence of many prey populations may help ensure that when one prey is temporarily low, the predators can turn to others and so maintain a high potential for attack, rather than becoming rare and allowing prey numbers to "escape." (This is actually a complex theoretical and experimental problem.[25]) The presence of many predator species also means that there is a reservoir of possible control mechanisms for prey species potentially capable of expanding to outbreak proportions.

More generally, we can say that ecologists believe that interactions between trophic levels are a major stabilizing force. They also help to maintain the diversity of communities. Some work on the seashore, referred to earlier, demonstrates this point.[13] Grazing herbivores keep down some species of plant and thereby allow other species to persist. If the grazers are removed, a few plant species increase greatly in density and crowd out other species, thus simplifying the community. The same occurs if the predators of sessile herbivores on the shore are removed. Then barnacles and mussels gradually spread over the area crowding out chitons, limpets, sponges, and other species, thus making the community much less diverse.

Taking these various aspects of species diversity together, they present a multitude of cause-effect pathways which can provide multiple regulatory or negative feedback systems. Natural communities, so to speak, possess a myriad of "fail-safe" systems, so that if one regulating process goes out, there are many others which are still functioning.

In fact, there is disagreement among ecologists as to which kinds of diversity are particularly useful in enhancing stability. For example, to control a pest should we release many species of parasites, or only one species which can attack several prey? Very little work has been done to put this kind of speculation on a solid basis and it presents possibly the most interesting and challenging problem facing the "pure" ecologist today. The very complexity, of course, makes the problem difficult to study.

One final word on the consequences of complexity in ecological systems. Although it may lead to stability and therefore to a gross sort of predictability, it makes predictions on a finer scale much more difficult, and a characteristic of natural communities is that, because of the complex interdependence of components, it is often hard to predict the particular consequences of various perturbations.

It is this ecological principle relating stability to complexity which makes ecologists, in particular, concerned about the stability of human eco-

systems. Let us look now at some of the features of man's ecosystems.

## Man's Ecosystems

Since man's influence is ubiquitous, it might be said that all ecosystems are human ecosystems. However, we can usefully classify as human ecosystems those in which man plays a dominant role. The kind of ecosystem we are interested in includes those which man manages to a large degree, mainly for the production of food and fiber. This capacity to manage and control his environment is surely man's most important ecological characteristic, and, from this capacity to modify, flow the effects elaborated throughout this book. Although we are concerned about the bad effects of management, the power to modify must clearly be recognized at the outset as a highly desirable characteristic. The good sense to use that power well, of course, is an even more important characteristic.

Almost every aspect of ecological complexity discussed above is simplified in agricultural communities. The natural physical and biological patchiness of habitats which produce population discontinuities is removed. Ecosystems are changed from mosaics or patchwork quilts, to monoculture carpets. Two other features accentuate the effect of a carpet of continuous sameness. First, the subpopulations of the same species are frequently genetically very similar; this is especially true of some of the new tropical cereal crops. Second, distances are shortened and physical barriers removed as the speed of movement of organisms increases greatly due to their transport by man. The consequences of these particular simplifications is that large-scale crops are ecologically potentially vulnerable to enemies. They may, of course, be physiologically rather resistant; this is the case with the new wheat and rice strains (Chapter 3). But rusts, viruses, herbivores, and so on, evolve, and presumably they will evolve to attack all of the new strains we produce. In the absence of heterogeneity, the great danger is that any successful pest will sweep throughout the range of the host crop. For example, adaptation by rust to rust-resistant strains of wheat is the rule rather than the exception, generally via the appearance of new strains of existing races of rust. A new strain of the existing wheat stem rust race 15B "emerged" in about 1951 and almost totally destroyed the durum wheat crop in the United States in 1953 and 1954. It is estimated that a new virulent strain of wheat rust evolves every 3-5 years in the United States. This is the average lag time between developing a new wheat strain resistant to rust and the rust itself becoming adapted to the new strain. A problem is that while the geneticists in the advanced countries may be able to keep breeding new crop strains, the underdeveloped countries do not have such technical resources.

The other great simplification is the removal of the complex biological fail-safes of natural communities. When we grow crops, we try to remove herbivores which compete with us, and often also remove their predators and parasites. We are then dependent on our own mechanisms of pest control. This is dangerous, if only potentially, because we are removing our options permanently since genetic material cannot be reconstituted. But we are probably doing more than merely limiting our choices. Complete reliance on chemical pest control may be beginning to fail us and its side-effects are becoming at least tiresome and at worst highly dangerous. These are topics discussed at length in Chapters 13 and 14. I want only to mention them here.

In these managed systems we intentionally simplify communities. However, it seems clear that pollution of all sorts is turning out to be a great accidental and undirected simplifier. It does this by killing off and reducing sensitive species and, in the case of excess nutrients, by greatly increasing the abundance of some species which come to dominate the community. Remarkably, many different kinds of pollution have this effect, including chronic radiation, air pollution, and herbicides.[24] These also tend to cause structural simplification because taller types of vegetation seem to be more sensitive.

Although we do not farm the sea to any extent (except to culture shellfish), we are certainly reducing its biological complexity. In particular, J. H. Connell has pointed out that we tend to remove predators in the ocean, and frequently top predators with wide-ranging food habits. We

have done this for a long time by harvesting whales and fish, though for most fish species we do not yet seem to have had a large effect on their numbers. More recently, we have started to make serious inroads into marine predators by pollution. Pesticides and heavy metals are concentrated in predators, as discussed earlier, and we are now seeing breeding failures in ospreys and pelicans — both at the top of marine food chains. Crude oil spills have most effect on diving birds and, of all marine birds, these are the main predators of fish (Chapter 11).

There is ample evidence that our simple human ecosystems are unstable — otherwise, for example, we wouldn't need pest control. On the other hand, they are efficient, we need them, and it is not altogether practical to suggest giving up farming and allowing nature to go wild — that is, to evolve to climax states. However, the ecologist can make some suggestions towards increasing the inherent stability and viability of human ecosystems.

Even in agricultural systems it is possible to maintain and even increase diversity. Monocultures needn't be all of the same genetic stock, and could be planted in a patchwork of different strains. Where possible agriculture should be diverse, giving a mosaic of species. When integrated control (Chapter 14) comes into wide use, it will be efficient to intersperse cropland with more diverse areas, and in some circumstances with more complex communities. These communities will serve as reservoirs of predator and parasite insects for use in pest control.

A good example of the stabilizing effect of complexity is in forests of balsam fir which are attacked by spruce budworm. Outbreaks of the pest occur where we first have an "outbreak of balsam fir"[12]; that is, where there are extensive areas of dense mature fir trees. It was shown that high pest populations did not develop where the forest was broken up into smaller patches or in forests where other tree species were mixed in with the balsam fir.

In considering the application of ecological principles to agricultural systems, it should be obvious that we cannot simply use the natural ecosystem as a blueprint for managing agricultural systems. Unlike natural systems our managed systems are not self-perpetuating and are always of very limited duration. A useful distinction can be drawn between two types of agricultural system which illustrates that ecological principles have to be applied in a thoughtful and careful fashion.[10] Tree crops such as fruit orchards, timber plantations, and coffee plantations may last half a century, while cereals are planted and harvested in the space of a few months; between times the land is bare and plowed. It follows that in the first kind of system we are more likely to be able to develop stable interactions between pests and enemies, since both can persist over many years. In short-lived crops, however, pests generally can invade the crop early and get a head start on the other enemies. The enemy populations are killed off each year at plowing or burning. It is less likely therefore that any stable interaction will develop in these very temporary communities. Clearly this second type of crop is further from natural stable systems than is the first, and different modifications of ecological principles must be expected in the two cases.

*The Quality of Complexity*

Perhaps, in their considerations of stability, ecologists have somewhat overemphasized the importance of complexity per se. The U.S. prairie or Russian Steppe probably was (or is) a rather stable though relatively simple system, and climax *Sequoia* forests of only one tree species probably have been stable over thousands of years. Perhaps at least as important as complexity is the idea that natural systems are stable and, generally, unnatural ones aren't. This, of course, sounds awfully naive and possibly Pantheistic or Wordsworthian or, worst of all, nonscientific! It may, however, be true. It brings out two important points. First that biological QUALITY is important; if complexity leads to stability it is not because of any old complexity or any old species. For example, if one has a crop of vegetables and increases the complexity by growing a hedge of the spindle bush, one will almost certainly decrease the stability. Spindle is the host plant over winter for pest aphids.

Second, the species in natural communities have had a shared evolutionary history. The re-

sult of this coevolution is exactly that they persist together. Predator populations in natural systems kill prey individuals and have evolved to do this, but the prey also have evolved so that some of them escape predation each generation. There are many examples known of plants which have evolved mechanisms of resisting attack by the local herbivores, and so on. These are dynamic situations, always changing, but they will tend to be stable in the future because of their shared evolutionary past.

This aspect is important in the "green revolution." The new cereal strains developed recently and described in Chapter 3 undoubtedly constitute a magnificent achievement, and one should not try to belittle this. The ecologists' concern, however, is for the future maintenance of high yields and the avoidance of a pest catastrophe. One hopes that no such catastrophe will occur, and it may not, but the inherent ecological risks must be pointed out, and if possible prepared for. With respect to the rice varieties, pest, weed, and disease outbreaks are possible, and difficulties are arising already.

Plant protection officers have said that in India a leafhopper has become a much more serious pest, cutting down yields and requiring spraying with insecticides every 4 or 5 days. Also in India the new rice has developed a severe bacterial blight problem which cuts down yields. In Java the stem borer (larval moth) has become a much worse pest. The new rice stems are larger and the rice requires high nitrogen fertilizer levels, making it nutritious. These two features make it highly suitable for the stem borer which reduces yields by about 25 percent and is now sprayed once a week with insecticide. A gall midge, not previously a serious pest, has become a very bad pest in some areas, again reducing yield by about 25 percent and requiring spraying every week. This pest also appears to be spreading.

While an attempt has been made to breed into the rice resistance to major PRESENT pests and pathogens (such as rice blast disease), they are not broadly resistant. The old local strains of rice may have been resistant to indigenous nonpest organisms, but now these local organisms could expand and turn into pests of the new rice strains.

To deal with croplands only, however, is to take a narrow view. Odum[21] states the case for diversity rather aptly:

> Many essential life-cycle resources, not to mention recreational and esthetic needs, are best provided for man by the less "productive" landscapes. In other words, the landscape is not just a supply depot but is also the oikos — the home — in which we must live. Until recently mankind has more or less taken for granted the gas-exchange, water-purification, nutrient-cycling, and other protective functions of self-maintaining ecosystems, chiefly because neither his numbers nor his environmental manipulations have been great enough to affect regional and global balances. Now, of course, it is painfully evident that such balances are being affected, often detrimentally. The "one problem, one solution approach" is no longer adequate and must be replaced by some form of ecosystem analysis that considers man as part of, not apart from the environment.

> The most pleasant and certainly the safest landscape to live in is one containing a variety of crops, forests, lakes, streams, roadsides, marshes, seashores, and "waste places" — in other words, a mixture of communities of different ecological ages. As individuals we more or less instinctively surround our house with protective, nonedible cover (trees, shrubs, grass) at the same time that we strive to coax extra bushels from our cornfield. We all consider the cornfield a "good thing," of course, but most of us would not want to live there, and it would certainly be suicidal to cover the whole land area of the biosphere with cornfields, since the boom and bust oscillation in such a situation would be severe.

Clearly, most of us do not live in Odum's "pleasant landscape"; we live in cities or suburbs. Furthermore, many city dwellers will not agree that such a landscape is more pleasant than the city. Viewing the environment as a whole, however, Odum is right. Such a mixture, even if we do not live in it but only visit it, would seem to be necessary for our safety. As agriculture becomes even more efficient we may have areas which are purely productive, indeed we have that now, but this is all the more reason to have many areas which are "protective," as Odum used that word.

The most striking example of a "protective" community is a well-developed forest. Forests, of course, protect the area they actually cover by stabilizing temperature and soil, and so on. But they also extend protection beyond their own limits. For example, forests regulate water runoff in watershed areas; they catch and hold water and, when it comes in heavy rain, slow down the water movement across the landscape so that it has time to percolate down into the soil and even deeper. The Chinese cut down their forests 3000 years ago, allowing water to rush quickly to the rivers, thus setting the stage "for the catastrophic floods which in recurrent sequences wrought havoc upon the country for centuries to come."[27] By regulating water runoff forests also help to reduce soil erosion in adjacent areas, and this is further helped by their cutting down on erosion by wind. Borgstrom[27] states that reforestation is a prime requirement throughout much of the world.

The arguments in favor of biological diversity probably are familiar to us all. I have noted above the case for stability of our agricultural crops. I would expect the large-scale and heavy use of pesticides alone to be a very temporary phenomenon in agriculture, to be replaced by a more accurate monitoring of crops for pest species and a finer and more incisive local control of the pest by biological and chemical means. This new kind of control will require a diverse biological pool of species to draw on, just as the continuous development of new strains of crops will require the existence of a diverse genetic pool.

We will need diverse ecosystems, if only to find out how nature manages to keep things under control so well. Natural communities can and do serve as field laboratories. It may even be an important component for man's mental health to live in an ecologically diverse world.

The above reasons, however, are based on considerations of "need" and "efficiency." Efficiency is pressed upon us because we need to maximize yield from and control over our environment. The reason we have this "need' is simply a growing population and a growing standard of living. Yet it is obvious that a maximum population size is not necessarily an optimum population size, and it becomes clearer that maximizing the standard of living probably does not optimize the quality of our lives. We are no longer so under the control of the forces of natural selection that we need maximize the number of offspring that we leave. Clearly, the optimum population will not easily be defined, but it surely will be one which can afford to maintain enormous ecological diversity as an aesthetic pleasure, rather than one which has a minimum of diversity forced upon it as a necessary cost of survival.

*Conclusions*

Certain important features of ecological systems, and of studies of these systems, can be summarized as follows: First, limits are ubiquitous (Chapters 3-8). Not only are there limits to resources, there are limits to the rate at which the environment can receive wastes and return them to the system in usable form, and to its capacity for storing them in innocuous form (Chapters 9-15).

Secondly, ecosystems are made up of interacting and interdependent components, and ecosystems are open and linked to each other. As a result, events at one place in the environment are bound to have repercussions in other places and at other times. Because of the interconnectedness and complexity of the environment, some of the consequences are bound to be unpredictable.

Third, actions which are massive enough, drastic enough, or simply of the right sort, will cause environmental changes which are irreversible. This is partly because the genetic material of extinct species cannot be reconstituted. Furthermore, some changes are ecologically irreversible. If a complex climax community is removed, together with important physical characteristics of its environment, it may not be able to redevelop because the conditions are no longer appropriate for a reenactment of the successional stages. For example, typically when tropical forests are removed and the soil exposed, the mineral nutrients (already poor) are leached by the rain. The soil usually becomes hardened also and thereafter the forest will not grow back again, nor can crops be grown. Such irreversible changes will almost always produce a simplification of the environment.

Fourth, simple communities tend to be unstable and almost without exception man's activities result in simplification. Further, when man's simple ecosystems develop instability, the actions taken (for example, pest control) tend to be inherently destabilizing in the long run. In particular, in artificial simple systems the instability is enhanced because the organisms do not have a shared evolutionary past.

The instability of ecosystems is accentuated by the existence of time lags. As we noted for *Tribolium,* demographic time lags produce population momentum; populations of enemies tend to lag behind their prey populations, producing oscillations in numbers. In simpler systems especially, the existence of time lags can enhance initial perturbations, causing increasingly wild fluctuations in abundance.

In dealing with systems with the above characteristics, the present limitations of methods of study must be remembered. First, the complexity of ecosystems makes them very difficult to study. While systems analysis can help, it has not yet been used for the management or study of whole ecosystems, where we are interested in the behavior of many variables in the output as well as in the input. Secondly, it is not clear that removing portions of the problem to the laboratory for experimentation is an appropriate technique. Possibly the necessary simplification that this involves removes exactly the elements from the system which determine how it functions. Yet field experiments are difficult to do and usually difficult to interpret. Thirdly, ecology is almost the only field of biology which does not boil down to physics and chemistry, and it seems certain that a direct extension of physics and chemistry will not solve ecological problems. Yet exactly such an extension has proved very helpful for the rest of biology. Finally, there is the problem that each ecological situation is different and has a unique history. Therefore, we do not have, and may not have in the future, broad and profound generalizations as a basis for action. Each problem requires particular analysis, and there will generally be a sizable time lag between posing the question and receiving the ecological answer. This does not make all environmental problems hopeless of solution, merely difficult and interesting.

The above observations contain much of what it is important to know in general about ecological systems and the nature of ecology. Together with the material in the other chapters they should help develop in the reader what I have called the ECOLOGICAL ATTITUDE.

## References

1. Hutchinson, G.E. 1948. On living in the biosphere. *Sci. Monthly 67:* 393-397.
2. Evans, F.C., and Murdoch, W.W. 1968. Taxonomic composition, trophic structure and seasonal occurrence in a grassland insect community. *J. Animal Ecol. 37:* 259-273.
3. Morowtiz, H.J. 1968. *Energy Flow in Biology.* Academic Press, New York.
4. Odum, E.P. 1962. *Japan. J. Ecol. 12:* 108-118.
5. Golley, F.B. 1960. Energy dynamics of a food chain of an old field community. *Ecol. Monographs 30:* 187-206.
6. Connell, J.H. 1970. A predatory-prey system in the marine intertidal region. I. *Balanus glandula* and several predatory species of *Thais. Ecol. Monographs 40:* 49-78.
7. Ricker, W.E. 1969. Food from the sea. In *Resources and Man* (Preston Cloud, ed.). W. H. Freeman, San Francisco, California.
8. Tilly, L.J. 1968. The structure and dynamics of Cone Spring. *Ecol. Monographs 38:* 169-197.
9. Dixon, A.F.G. 1970. Quality and availability of food for a sycamore aphid population. In *Animal Populations in Relation to Their Food Resources.* Blackwell, Oxford, England.
10. Southwood, T.R.E., and Way, M.J. 1970. Ecological background to pest management. In *Concepts of Pest Management* (R.L. Rabb and F.E. Guthrie, eds.). North Carolina State University Press, Raleigh, North Carolina.
11. Park, T., Leslie, P.H., and Mertz, D.B. 1964. Genetic strains and competition in populations of *Tribolium. Physiol. Zool. 37:* 97-162.
12. Morris, R.F., et al. 1956. The population dynamics of the spruce budworm in eastern Canada. *Proc. 10th Intern. Cong. Entomol. 4:* 137-149.
13. Paine, R.T., and Vadas, R.L. 1969. The effects of grazing by sea urchins *Strongylocentrotus* spp., on benthic algal populations. *Limnology and Oceanography 14:* 710-719.
14. Harper, J.L. 1969. The role of predation in vegetational diversity. In *Diversity and Stability in Ecological Systems, Brookhaven Symposia in Biology 22.*
15. Hamilton, D.H., Jr. 1969. Nutrient limitation of phytoplankton in Cayuga Lake. *Limnology and Oceanography 14:* 579-590.
16. Wellington, W.G. 1965. Some maternal influences on progeny in the Western Tent Caterpillar, *Malacosoma pluviale* (Dyor). *Can. Entomologist 97:* 1-14.
17. Krebs, C.J., Keller, B.L., and Tamarin, R.H. 1969. *Microtus* population biology: Demographic changes in fluctuating populations of *M. ochorogaster* and *M. pennsylvannicus* in southern Indiana. *Ecology 50:* 587-607.
18. Morris, R.F., ed. 1963. The dynamics of epidemic spruce budworm populations. *Memoirs Entomol. Soc. Canada 31.*
19. Watt, K.E.F. 1968. *Ecology and Resource Management.* McGraw-Hill, New York.
20. Watt, K.E.F. ed. 1966. *Systems Analysis in Ecology.* Academic Press, New York.
21. Odum, E.P. 1969. The strategy of ecosystem development. *Science 164:* 262-270.
22. McCaull, J. 1969. Conference on the ecological aspects of international development. *Nature and Resources (UNESCO) 2:* 5-12.
23. Landenberger, D.E. 1968. Studies on selective feeding in the Pacific starfish *Pisaster* in southern California. *Ecology 49:* 1062-1075.
24. Elton, C.S. 1958. *The Ecology of Invasions by Plants and Animals.* Methuen, Wiley, New York.
25. Murdoch, W.W. 1969. Switching in general predators: experiments on predator specificity and stability of prey populations. *Ecol. Monographs 39:* 335-354.
26. Woodwell, G.M. 1970. Effects of pollution on the structure and physiology of ecosystems. *Science 168:* 429-433.
27. Borgstrom, G. 1969. *Too Many.* MacMillan, London.

## Further Reading

Allee, W.C., Emerson, A.E., Park, O., Park, T., and Schmidt, K.P. 1949. *Principles of Animal Ecology*. Saunders, Philadelphia, Pennsylvania. Pennsylvania.

Andrewartha, H.G. 1961. *Introduction to the Study of Animal Populations*. Methuen, London.

Connell, J.H., Mertz, D.B., and Murdoch, W.W. eds. 1970. *Readings in Ecology and Ecological Genetics*. Harper and Row, New York.

Kormondy, E.J. 1969. *Concepts of Ecology*. Prentice-Hall, Englewood Cliffs, New Jersey.

MacArthur, R.H., and Connell, J.H. 1966. *The Biology of Populations*. Wiley, New York.

Odum, E.P. 1959. *Fundamentals of Ecology*. Saunders, Philadelphia, Pennsylvania.

# POPULATION & RESOURCES

# 2 The Numbers and Distribution of Mankind

## Nathan Keyfitz

*Le temps du monde fini commence.*

Paul Valery

### An Inhabited Satellite and Its Crew

Before this century it did not occur to anyone that the world of human habitation is effectively finite. Discovery of new features on the earth's surface was still in progress, and the maps contained white spaces of unknown topography. Names had indeed been given to the continents and regions within them, and seaports were established around their edges, but men had not seen, let alone possessed, all of their interior space. Today every part of the planet is mapped, and most parts are claimed by some national state; each square mile is under daily photographic and electronic surveillance. World population censuses have been attempted in 1950, 1960, and 1970. We have the outline of precise knowledge about man and his habitat, with enough detail at least to be sure that no new fertile lands will be turned up by a Columbus of the twenty-first century.

But is not our world infinite in the sense that new knowledge will make it ever more produc-

NATHAN KEYFITZ is Professor of Demography at the University of California at Berkeley. In recent years, he has specialized in the mathematics of populations, after an earlier career as a statistician and census taker. He took his doctorate in sociology at the University of Chicago, and has been Professor and Chairman of the Department of Sociology of that University. He has taught demography in Buenos Aires, Santiago, at the Colegio de Mexico, and at the University of Indonesia.

tive? Science and invention have accelerated and their future is open. They seem a modern form of magic, slaves at our elbows to grant all our wishes. Yet just as the wishes in fairy tales are granted, but each with some unexpected rebound that brings calamity on the wisher, so ecologists are finding that the magic of science can bring an assortment of disasters. From the DDT that kills insect pests but ultimately poisons us, to the green revolution that produces mountains of food but encourages an increase of population that defeats economic growth, this book contains many instances of what science can do on the rebound. At least pending the resolution of some major points of ignorance, we have to think of the frontier of science as ultimately closed, just as the land area of the planet Earth is closed. Finiteness in both senses is a theme of this book.

The present chapter can hardly do justice to the discussion of human population growth that has unfolded during the past few years, and it will be confined to the review of a few major themes. These include the inequality of growth in time and in space: the inequality in time includes especially the present acceleration of the rate of increase; inequality in space is both between and within countries, including the concentration in cities.

Is finiteness of the food supply the ultimate limit on growth, as Malthus, living in a simpler age, believed, or is that limit set by poisoning of the atmosphere or exhaustion of fuels? Can we be climbing to a position of instability in the habitat, analogous to the position in which a physical object topples over? If so, the world's capacity for sustaining population could at some future time drop sharply, even below the present level. With separate nations and identifiable races the intergroup competition takes a demographic form, as it has through history; the difference is that now outbreeding one's national, cultural, or racial rivals has planetary implications that it did not have before. Some governments, in both poor and rich countries, are aware that competitive breeding will hardly lead to prosperity for individual countries or for the planet, and they are taking measures to bring their populations under control. More drastic measures are likely to be necessary in many areas before runaway populations are brought to a halt, and some changes in the value system that would permit drastic measures are appearing. These are the principal topics to be discussed in what follows.

## Acceleration of Population Growth

From the beginning of man's appearance to 1825 A.D., a period of 1 or 2 million years, the human race increased from a few savages to a billion people. In only a little over 100 years more, by about 1927, it increased another billion. The third billion took 33 years, until 1960; the fourth is likely to be attained before 1975, or 15 years after the third; the fifth, by 1985. (These future members are the United Nations Medium Variant projection, to which reference will be made again later.)

The time for adding a billion would steadily diminish even if the rate of increase were constant; indeed under constant increase the time would be inversely proportional to the number of billions already here. Thus if the second billion took 100 years, the third would take 50 years, the fourth would take 33 years, and so on. These intervals for attainment of successive billions under a constant rate of increase may be contrasted with the shorter intervals actually observed (Table I).

An alternative way of describing the acceleration is in terms of doubling time.. A doubling took place between 1825 and 1927; a second doubling, from 2 to 4 billion, is in prospect by 1975, or 48 years later; at the rate of increase of 2.1 percent per year already attained doubling would require only about 33 years. On the most optimistic assertions about the number of people that can live on the earth — however uncom-

fortably — only two or three doublings more are possible. Under the best of circumstances we are pushing against a ceiling that will be reached within the lifetimes of children already born.

| | Actual growth | Continuation of growth at the rate of 1825–1927 |
|---|---|---|
| 1st billion by | 1825 | |
| 2nd billion by | 1927 | 1927 |
| 3rd billion by | 1960 | 1978 |
| 4th billion by | 1975 | 2012 |
| 5th billion by | 1985 | 2037 |

POPULATION GROWTH RATES. The much earlier dates in the left-hand column are a measure of the acceleration in world population growth.

The rate of increase is about 20 per thousand per year, and it has been rising. Table II shows changes compiled by the United Nations for the first half of the decade of the 1960s — data for the second half are not yet in. The birth rate of the less developed countries declined marginally, but deaths declined much more, resulting in a rise in natural increase of about 3 per thousand. On the other hand, the more developed countries showed no improvement in their crude death rate, and their births declined, to make a net decline of about 3 per thousand in their rate of natural increase. The decline by the more developed does not offset the rise of the less developed, since the latter have a base 2½ times as great, so that 1960-1965 shows for the planet as a whole a rise in the rate of increase. Just when the peak in the rate of increase will be reached, and what its level will be, are not yet known.

| | Birth | Death | Natural increase |
|---|---|---|---|
| Less developed | | | |
| 1960 | 41–42 | 20–22 | 20–22 |
| 1965 | 40–41 | 16–17 | 24 |
| More developed | | | |
| 1960 | 21 | 9 | 12 |
| 1965 | 18 | 9 | 9 |

NATURAL POPULATION INCREASE. Components of natural increase in less and more developed countries: crude rates per thousand population.

*Population Projections*

Demographers estimate future population from separate calculations of birth and death components. These estimates are often used as predictions of what will actually happen, but their greater value is as projections, for which they have a conditional character; they tell, for example, what will happen if nothing is done to check birth rates.

Table III shows the most recent and realistic estimates the United Nations has made for the years up to 1985 — it is the medium variant. In accord with the figures quoted above, it shows the world total over 4 billion in 1975, and almost 5 billion by 1985, an increase of 100 million per year against present increase of about 75 million. Whether because prospects for population control have worsened or for other reasons, the latest estimate shows 187 million more people in 1985 than the 1985 total as assessed by the United Nations only 6 years earlier in 1963.

| Area | 1965 | 1970 | 1975 | 1980 | 1985 |
|---|---|---|---|---|---|
| World Total | 3289 | 3632 | 4022 | 4457 | 4933 |
| More developed regions | 1037 | 1090 | 1147 | 1210 | 1275 |
| Less developed regions | 2252 | 2541 | 2874 | 3247 | 3658 |
| East Asia | 852 | 930 | 1011 | 1095 | 1182 |
| South Asia | 981 | 1126 | 1296 | 1486 | 1693 |
| Europe | 445 | 462 | 479 | 497 | 515 |
| USSR | 231 | 243 | 256 | 271 | 287 |
| Africa | 303 | 344 | 395 | 457 | 530 |
| Northern America | 214 | 228 | 243 | 261 | 280 |
| Latin America | 246 | 283 | 327 | 377 | 435 |
| Oceania | 18 | 19 | 22 | 24 | 27 |

TOTAL POPULATION ESTIMATES BY MAJOR AREAS. 1965-1985. In millions. Medium variant. Source: United Nations. New findings on population trends, *Population Newsletter No. 7* (December 1969): p. 4.

The difference in the rate of climb between the more and less developed regions — United Nations expressions for rich and poor, respectively — is dramatic. The more developed countries grow by almost 20 percent in 20 years, the less developed by over 60 percent. In fact, the presently less developed countries alone will be more numerous by 1985 than the world as a whole is in 1970; during the 15 years they are expected to increase somewhat more than the total of the developed countries in 1970. Among continents Latin America and Africa increase by the largest fraction, with South Asia only slightly slower.

Even these numbers suppose a fall in fertility. If fertility remains constant at its 1965 level, the less developed regions will contain not 3658 million, but 3925 million, by 1985.

Extrapolation to the future is very dependent on what series one decides to extrapolate. If one assumes that the growth rates of the past continue, the United States will have 300 million or more residents by the end of the century, and about 6 million annual births. If one supposes that the rate of change of the birth rate from 1957 to 1968 continues, the result is very different: the rate fell from about 24 per thousand to 17 per thousand, so its continuance would mean no births at all by the end of the century.

No one can complain of a lack of long-range estimates of future world population. Let us consider the year 2000 and speak only of the estimates produced by one agency, the Population Division of the United Nations Secretariat.

The medium estimate for the year 2000 as made in 1963 was 6130 million. Other estimates ranged around this, from a low variant of 5449 million to a high variant of 6994 million. Even this last was based on the assumption of falling fertility. If fertility of the early 1960s was assumed to persist, the 2000 figure would be 7522 million. By 1969 these numbers were regarded as low, and they are in the process of being raised.

No one knows when the fall in the birth rate, assumed now to have started, will overtake the fall in the death rate. The net increase is given by the United Nations as 22 per thousand in the 1970s, with a fall thereafter to 21 in the 1980s and 19 in the 1990s.

About the sharpest statement that these and other materials permit is that the world population will probably be between 6 and 7 billion by the year 2000 (Figure 1).

We must also remember the importance of time-lag and population momentum in making projections. Suppose, for example, that the United States implemented the policy that the

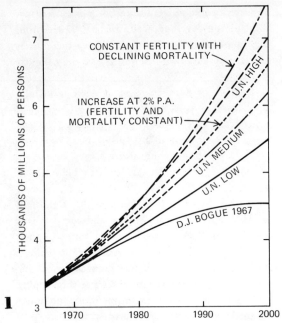

**SIX ESTIMATES OF WORLD POPULATION,**
1965-2000. Sources: *World Population Prospects as Assessed in 1963.* Population Studies No. 41, Department of Social and Economic Affairs, United Nations, New York, 1966. Unpublished estimate by D.J. Bogue, 1967.

average family size is restricted to the number of children needed to replace a nongrowing population. This number is about 2.1 children; it is greater than 2 because some people do not have children. If we started this policy *now* the population would take at least 70 years to stabilize and would grow by 80 million people in the meantime.

### People and Land

The land area of the globe is about 136 million square kilometers. Spread out as a square it would be a little more than 11,000 by 11,000 kilometers, about a 12-hour flight by jet from edge to edge.

If this land were divided equally among its inhabitants, who were estimated to number over 3.6 billion in 1970, then each man, woman, and child would have 3.76 hectares, or about 10 acres to himself or herself (Table IV). Were such a division made in 1920, he or she would have had double this, about 20 acres. Man's estate, as so divided up, seems lavish at the earlier date and

adequate at the present time. In what, then, does the population problem consist?

It consists partly in the varying quality of the estate. Of the 3.76 hectares that each of us would have on this hypothetical division, much would be too hot, too cold, too dry, or too mountainous even to live on, let alone to raise essential food. Desert regions comprise about 17 percent of the world's land area; mountains about 12 percent; ice caps and tundras about 29 percent; thus on nearly 60 percent of the planet human settlement is sparse or impossible. The remaining 40 percent is by no means all ideal for humans: The wet tropical lowlands of the Amazon, for instance, average about one person per square mile, and how much this could be increased is not known. C. Langdon White[1] concludes his survey of such data by estimating that about one quarter of the land surface of the globe is suited to human habitation and food raising. The average of 3.76 hectares per person comes down to about 1 cultivable hectare per person.

This is still more than we need. Several tons of edible cereal can be raised on 1 hectare of agricultural land, and the most that an adult can consume directly in a year is one-third of a ton. Two pounds of bread or rice daily is enough for the adult male and much more than a child needs. A hectare for each man, woman, and child should easily provide meat and vegetables as well as cereals. Such facts have been stressed by Clark.[2] But the population problem is both more subtle and more serious than the threat of starvation because we run out of bread or rice (Chapter 3). The bread standard of living can ultimately satisfy only a few ascetics; most people need pork and beef, as well as clothing, housing, and transport, not only for comfort but to meet minimum standards of dignity. The problem of the minimum is not easy: What is dignity when one claims it for oneself becomes ostentation when claimed by others. The aim is to maximize individual choice.

The question of human need is too wide for this chapter, but population growth in the face of a limited environment sooner or later makes free choice an unattainable luxury. Contrast the

United States of 1870 with Calcutta or Canton of 1970; the degree of planning and regulation in the latter cannot be disassociated from their greater density. To go from a life in which one chooses, to one in which one is allotted what he is presumed to need is an unhappy transition. Population growth is pushing us from a regime of choice to one of need both in rich and in poor countries.

*People and Nations*

That part of the earth's crust not under salt water is mostly divided among national states and humanity is allocated among these. International movement for residence purposes is sharply restricted. Eighteenth and nineteenth century notions of the state and citizenship, after bringing to an end the unity of the European Middle Ages, have now triumphed around the world.

Whatever its other consequences, nationalism has certainly promoted censuses and statistical counting. Present statistical knowledge is an off-shoot of the national state, as the word statistics itself reminds us. Let us briefly review the status of this knowledge for the eight states with the most people.

Mainland China is the largest of the national entities in terms of population, and the one on which information is most conspicuously lacking. Much of what we know pivots around the total of 583 million reported by Peking in 1953. That the total was about 100 million persons more than the regime itself seems to have thought were present up to that time lends a degree of credibility to the result, and this level of evidence is most of what we have to go on. Professionals in the field have accepted the figure, and compilations of world population raised their totals by about 100 million at the time of the announcement.

Even less certain is our knowledge of the rate of increase of the Chinese population. If it is 2 percent per year, which seems a minimum, then it would have long since passed the 700 million mark and this is what we may suppose.

Because of extensive Chinese record keeping in the past, we know a good deal about the population of China over the last two millenia, perhaps more than we know about it today.[3] For other developing countries current information is more reliable than historical.

India's tradition of census-taking was established in British times, and the record up to 1951 has been pulled together and analyzed by Davis.[4] We are reasonably sure that the 1961 population was nearly 440 million; again the census showed the authorities that they had been assuming too

| | Population in millions | | | | | | |
|---|---|---|---|---|---|---|---|
| | 1930 | 1940 | 1950 | 1960 | 1970 | Area in 1000 km$^2$ | Hectares per person 1970 |
| Planet Earth | 2070 | 2295 | 2517 | 3005 | 3609 | 135,767 | 3.76 |
| Poor Countries | 1328 | 1494 | 1683 | 2058 | 2556 | 78,040 | 3.05 |
| Africa | 164 | 191 | 222 | 278 | 352 | 30,313 | 8.61 |
| Asia (except Japan) | 1056 | 1173 | 1298 | 1567 | 1921 | 27,162 | 1.41 |
| Latin America | 108 | 130 | 163 | 213 | 283 | 20,565 | 7.27 |
| Rich Countries | 742 | 801 | 834 | 947 | 1051 | 57,727 | 5.49 |
| Europe | 355 | 380 | 392 | 425 | 461 | 4,929 | 1.06 |
| Japan | 64 | 71 | 83 | 93 | 103 | 370 | 0.36 |
| Northern America | 134 | 144 | 166 | 199 | 226 | 21,515 | 9.52 |
| Oceania | 10 | 11 | 13 | 16 | 19 | 8,511 | 44.79 |
| USSR | 179 | 195 | 180 | 214 | 242 | 22,402 | 9.26 |

**IV**

POPULATION AND LAND AREA OF THE PLANET EARTH. The 1970 figures are extrapolated from 1968 by the author and differ somewhat from those of Table III, which are projected. Source: United Nations *Demographic Yearbook*, 1968, Table 1, p. 83.

few people in their planning and other calculations. If the increase is 2.5 percent per year, as the United Nations *Demographic Yearbook* (1968, Table 2)[5] tells us, then India now stands at over 550 million.

Third is the USSR, which counted 241.7 million people in its census of January 1970.[6] Here the census was only slightly larger than the precensal estimate of 241 million. Like the United States, the Soviet Union has seen a steady fall in its birth rate over the past decade; its increase of 2 million per year is very close to that of the United States.

The United States is the fourth country in respect of population. Its latest census was taken in April 1970, using very modern techniques, and we can expect results in record time. Pending their release we assume the total to be about 205 million.

The fifth country is Indonesia, of which a census was taken in 1961; another is promised for October 1971. The standard authority is Widjojo, N[7], who estimates the 1970 population as around 120 million.

Sixth is Pakistan, with a total very close to that of Indonesia. Seventh is Japan, with just over 100 million at the present time; its drop from fifth in population has coincided with its rise to third industrial power. Eighth is Brazil, with a population now passing 95 million and rising faster than any other country in its size class.

These eight countries account at the present time for over 2 billion people, or nearly 60 percent of humanity. They do not include any of Western Europe, whose statistics are complete enough that we can do what has not been possible for any other continent: compile a grand total of a solid international unit. A recent compilation[8] shows the aggregate of Europe from Ireland to the boundaries of the USSR as 442 million in 1965, and probably about 460 million by 1970, a further 13 percent of the world's total. European data on births and deaths are the best that exist.

Estimates of error are inevitably subjective in those countries whose censuses include no sample check. We probably know China's population within 10 percent; that of Europe and the

United States within 2 or 3 percent; most countries of South America and Asia with accuracy intermediate to these. Adding together such evidence for national units suggests that we know the world total to within about 5 percent and can assert that it is between 3.4 and 3.8 billion in 1970.

We will make some comparisons of growth between the United States and Europe, and then contrast these with two less developed countries: Mexico and West Malaysia for 1966.

*Population Dynamics*

When birth and death rates remain constant in a population a stable age distribution is developed in which the proportion of the population formed by each age group remains constant through time. The crude birth rate for Europe, that is the number born per year per thousand people, was 18.04 in 1965. When projected forward until it comes to a stable age distribution consistent with its age-specific rates of 1965, it shows a birth rate of 17.46 per thousand. The U.S. birth rate was slightly higher than this at the time, but it has continued falling to 1968.

The proportion of children under 15 is necessarily a consequence of birth rates of the preceding 15 years. For Europe in 1965, 25.23 percent of the population was under 15 years. The United States shows 30.67, higher because its earlier (though not its contemporary) birth rates had been higher. The percent of people 65 years old and over was 10.50 for Europe and 9.42 for the United States. The differences here are unimportant: A convergence in demographic as in other parameters is apparent. Similar rates appear for Canada, Australia, and even the USSR.

Close analysis does show slight differences in trends, which barely stand out from the general errors to which the numbers are subject. Male mortality, for example, seems to have improved in Europe more than in the United States in recent years. In 1955 the expectation of life at age zero was 64.88 in Europe and 66.45 in the United States; by 1965, Europe had climbed to 67.69, while the United States stood at only 66.87. But female expectation was about a half a year higher in the United States in 1965. The overall death rate for both sexes, standardized on the United States in 1960, was slightly higher for Europe: 9.45 against 9.30.

We do not have to brood over subtle differences in contrasting developed and underdeveloped countries. Mexico's crude birth rate is 43.96 per thousand, possibly understated, and is more than twice the U. S. figure. However, its death rate is only 9.61, and its rate of natural increase is the difference, $43.96 - 9.61 = 34.35$ per thousand (3.4 percent). Its age distribution is close enough to stable that the ultimate or intrinsic rate of natural increase is 34.65 per thousand, almost the same. West Malaysia's birth rate is 38.06, its death rate 7.20, and its rate of natural increase 30.86 (3.1 percent). The fact that over 44 percent of its population is under 15 years of age makes us ask if births could be understated.

Mexico's rate of increase would double its present 50 millions in about 21 years; quadruple them in 42 years; multiply them by 8 in 63 years. Thus if the pace continues, a child now born will not yet have retired from active life before Mexico contains 400 million people. Anyone who knows the difficulties of employment, schooling, and housing in Mexico now will surmise that it must be making every effort to prevent the exacerbation of these problems that is certain to follow from further population increase.

He would be wrong. The new president, a father of eight, campaigned on the slogan: "To govern is to populate." No birth control is needed; on the contrary, large families are to be encouraged. Empty parts of the country are to be colonized by pioneers engendered by the large families in the older parts. We shall see later that such pioneering has an appeal to national leaders that it lacks for the intended settlers: They prefer to come to the capital city.

Among the difficulties incidental to the high rate of population increase is the large proportion of children to be cared for. Mexico's percentage under 15 in 1966 was 46.26, against that of the United States previously mentioned of 30.67, and Europe's of 25.23.

The objection to children is not personal but economic. A country has only so much available income and savings, and it necessarily, willingly or not, makes a choice on allocation. If it spends more on raising and educating children, then it spends less on the equipment that will give them jobs when they come to working age. If it has fewer children, then it will have more capital for investment (say in factories), so that when these children reach maturity productive jobs will await them. Determination of how much expenditure should go into children and how much into factories, for a combination of the two that will be satisfactory a generation later, is not a simple problem. Its difficulty is further accentuated by the finiteness of the environment, including, for example, the pollution caused by the factories, which is not ordinarily taken into account. To determine for the right population, the right amount of capital to accumulate, the right number of people to employ, the right degree of pollution to be created, is a problem difficult even to formulate, let alone solve. And even its solution would not help much if the real condition for development was inventiveness and organizational skill, and only in a lesser degree capital.

The view (presented in careful detail by Coale and Hoover[9]) that population growth in poor countries obstructs capital accumulation and therefore future prosperity, rather than threatening starvation, is congenial to an age accustomed to technical progress. It would have surprised Malthus, for whom the possibilities of agricultural innovation were limited. We shall review the recent agricultural revolution in developed countries and its spread to less developed ones, information needed for a judgment on the relation of food to population.

*Food and the American Farmer*

In the United States in 1920 over 30 percent of the population lived on farms; by 1967 only 5.4 percent of the population lived on farms. The number of farm population has declined from about 30 million to about 10 million, the number of farms from 6½ million to 3 million.[10]

At the same time the absolute amount of agricultural production has increased. Careful estimates of productivity per man, using two quite independent sources, are available to tell us by how much. The first asked a random sample of individuals, chosen by household, about their activities, as part of the survey of the labor force. This showed that the index of physical output per farmer and farm worker rose from 49.8 in 1947 to 170.4 in 1967. A second source is the survey of producing establishments, and it showed an increase from 49.8 to 171.2 in the same period.[10] We can summarize these independent sources by describing the increase as a multiplication of output per man by nearly 3½ over the 20 years.

To appreciate the magnitude of this, one can compare it with nonfarm activities including manufacturing. Their increase over the same 20 years from 1947 to 1967 was only from 72.9 to 127.0 on the household reports, and 74.1 to 127.6 on the establishment reports. The output per man in manufacturing and other nonfarm activities fell short of doubling over a time when agricultural productivity multiplied by 3½.

Such a change is devastating for the common-sense outlook of a generation ago, according to which factories are naturally more and more productive, while farming, being close to nature, cannot readily be modified. The farmer could move up from the hoe to the tractor in plowing and planting, but harvesting, for example of cotton, had to depend on human fingers. We know now that not only cotton, but grapes, asparagus, lettuce, and many other unlikely crops can be harvested better and more cheaply by machine, and machines are appearing on the market for the purpose.

The main problem has become marketing. The government of the United States, like those of Canada, Australia, and other similarly placed countries, tries to hold down production to what can be sold.

How can anyone seriously talk about shortages and starvation when the surpluses are so conspicuous in all advanced countries with market agriculture? Yet the surplus crops of the advanced countries cannot affect the long-term outcome insofar as the capacity to buy them is lacking, insofar as the poor of Asia and Africa have little to sell on which they can realize the exchange to buy food. For a short period cereals can be shipped to India at the rate of a million tons a month, as in the crisis of 1966, partly as gifts and partly as sales, but such shipments could hardly continue indefinitely. U. S. population increases even if its generosity is unlimited. In the long run the less developed countries are likely to have to live largely on their own food production.

## Agriculture in the Underdeveloped World

During the past 5 years advances in American agriculture have been matched elsewhere. What are now standard research techniques of plant breeding and selection produce similar results in the Philippines and Mexico that they do in the United States; they are almost as effective on wheat and rice as they were on corn. High-yield varieties first developed were subject to "lodging," that is, collapse of the stalks before harvesting; this was avoided by crossing with dwarf varieties. The new agriculture has distinctive features: development of crop varieties responsive to fertilizers, and then the application of fertilizers in 10 or 20 times the ratios previously used; combatting of rust and other diseases and of insect pests; the complementing of research with extension, so that the package of techniques comes quickly into the possession of the average farmer. Such methods, sponsored by the Ford and Rockefeller Foundations and other agencies, have constituted the "green revolution" now proceeding in the underdeveloped world (Chapter 3). It may be thought of as a diffusion outwards from the United States, Britain, Holland, and elsewhere, not so much of specific research, but of the research method, including statistical procedures.

Some of its results have been spectacular, first in the Philippines and Mexico, then in Pakistan, and most recently in extensive parts of India.[11] The 1969-1970 Indian output of food grains was 100 million tons, 11 million more than in 1964-1965, the best earlier year. Wheat yields per acre have risen 52 percent over 5 years. In the Punjab especially, innovation-minded wheat farmers have dug many thousands of tubewells and applied fertilizer in ratios as high as 50 kilograms per acre. Unfortunately rice, which accounts for twice as much acreage as wheat in India, has not fulfilled the promise of early research results in the same degree. Peasants have not responded well to the "miracle" strains from the Philippines and Taiwan, even though these double or treble yields per acre in experimental plots. The lag in rice is partly due to a different kind of peasant, one with a smaller holding, less financial strength to buy the inputs, less disposition or capacity to take risks. Partly also, the new rice is a less attractive product according to local food preferences, and it sells at a discount. The rice farmers of India may or may not eventually follow the wheat farmers.

Even if the green revolution goes forward, as seems on balance likely, through the innovation-mindedness of the better-off farmers, some immediate social problems will arise. The successful farmer becomes a business man; he has to borrow for purchases of fertilizer and other inputs, and repay the loans on time; he ceases to be a peasant and comes to think of his balance sheet first and foremost. He becomes less and less patient with traditional sharecropping, which is no longer an economic way for him to secure labor, and wants to get rid of conventional claims and obligations and simply engage wage-labor. If the labor is inefficient he turns to labor-saving devices, and these in any case accord with requirements for harvesting, threshing, and drying the new varieties.[12] Meanwhile, unless unprecedented economic growth in the cities draws them off, landless rural laborers increase rapidly.

In this situation population increase intensifies social unrest in the countryside. India as a whole can easily be seen as attaining self-sufficiency in food, which will certainly improve its balance of payments. But the internal distribution of the crop is less easily foreseen, and with inequality and unrest the green revolution could turn to red.

During the 20 years to 1966 food hardly kept pace with population increase; in Latin America food produced per capita actually diminished. Now food has jumped ahead, and the prospect is that the population increase will be looked after for the next decade. This rise in one of the ceilings on population provides a breathing space. If it becomes the occasion to relax efforts to bring runaway populations under control — and there are signs that it may in a few countries — then humanity will bump its head on the ceiling again in 1980. And this time the scale of the problem will be larger, the dependence on fertilizer greater, and the social situation more fragile. Most important of all, capital per worker will not be greater if the increment of food has been turned into people. The problem is to turn that food into economic development.

## Automation and the End of Exploitation

The United States, Western Europe, and the USSR are now moving into a new period, with the United States in the lead. The controlled chemical synthesis which enables a modern factory run by a few technicians to produce the same rubber as a tropical plantation with thousands of laborers constitutes a liberation of production from human hands as well as from the natural landscape. A Dutch concern making synthetic fiber now fills much of the demand for Indonesian sisal of colonial times. But synthetics are not the only example of the new industrial power.

A few examples of the direction which industry is taking will serve. Men with pickaxes have not been important in American coal mines for some time; but even men working underground with mechanical diggers and loaders are giving place to strip mining, in which the largest earth-moving equipment ever constructed pushes away the few hundred feet of soil above the coal deposits, and then mechanical shovels take it out several tons at a time. Open strip mining now accounts for over 20 percent of American coal production. The extraction of oil and natural gas is even cheaper, and these are moved effortlessly through pipelines to where they can be converted into electricity in nearly unmanned thermal plants.

The decline of employment in the automobile industry at the same time as more automobiles are being sold is partly due to numerical control of machine tools which is spreading rapidly through this and other industries. Instead of craftsmen working with elaborate jigs, we have a library of control tapes (themselves made by computer from engineering drawings), and an operator who mounts whichever one is required. Make-ready time is reduced from days to minutes; inventories may practically be dispensed with when it is possible to make pieces one at a time as cheaply as several hundred at a time. Engineers can make designs which are more elaborate, being no longer held to what a craftsman can produce by hand. In electronics printed circuits have reduced the man-hour content of electronic equipment in the same way that numerical control has reduced the labor content of automobiles.

Computers are the most spectacular labor-savers. Whether for department store billings, for insurance company records, or for airline reservations, they produce a quality and quantity of work that makes previous methods unacceptable. Operations like searching a file or multiplying two numbers, for which a clerk takes minutes, can be done by the computer in microseconds. It is an understatement to call a large-scale computer the equivalent of 500 people. Even based on this understatement, the 100,000 computers expected to be in existence in the United States by the mid-1970s will be the equivalent of 50 million people in their capacity for nearly all varieties of clerical work. Within 25 years of the first working models − the computer era does not antedate 1950 − computers will be doing as much adding and recording as could have been performed by the entire labor force of the United States in 1950.

*Internal Labor Displacement*

Both economic theory and current experience show that, far from causing unemployment, the worst that automation need do is to move people from one occupation to another. The new one is usually more challenging; the work of a computer programmer is incomparably more exciting than that of a billing clerk. It is true that the shift-over cannot always take place in the same generation; many men in the transition may have to retire somewhat younger than they would like.

The major discovery has been that the level of unemployment can be kept wherever one wants by adjusting demand. If there is not enough work making automobiles we can fill the gap by going to the moon. We could equally have filled the gap by planting flowers in the parks, but this has

less appeal. We do not want the dull public works of the 1930s; our public works must be cosmic. They give employment to engineers, physicists, and technicians of all kinds. They require the expansion of the facilities for the production of such people, chiefly an expansion of the university system. And this has indeed gone forward with all possible rapidity.

*External Labor Displacement*

The same satisfactory observations cannot be made on the external displacements caused by progress. While these have not ordinarily been spoken of in the same breath, yet the Indonesian plantation worker dismissed because synthetic rubber limits the market for natural rubber is automated out as decisively as the Detroit automobile worker displaced by numerical control. The difference is that we offer no way for the Indonesian to get back into the system.

Our synthetics attack the economy of the underdeveloped country at the point where the colonial power had put its principal demand for tropical labor − the production of raw materials. Here the comparative advantage of tropical sunshine and cheap labor is greatest. If these were already being undercut in the colonial period, when Europeans owned the plantations, they will be undercut by western factory operators even less regretfully when the plantations are in the hands of independent and sometimes hostile states. And while the former colonies can sell less, they want to buy more, especially the capital goods needed to industrialize themselves.

But could the ex-colony not turn to what it can now do best, relative to Western capitalized industry? Cannot India make textiles and sell them abroad, using abundant labor and local techniques, and so finance her own industrialization? Japan helped industrialize herself (without the benefit of Western good will) by selling textiles made by cheap labor. I am arguing that it may today be too late for another Asian country to do this.

Suppose Western industry were so mechanized that the competitive wages for unmechanized production would not suffice to enable the worker to buy the food that would keep him. We are actually at this point in some fields of Western production. An Indian worker with a hand loom produces about 3 yards of fabric in a long day's work; the value added in a world market whose prices are set by machine-made cloth is barely sufficient to buy him a pound of rice. India lacks capital to put her redundant population into factories and so make them competitive.

I have calculated that about 50,000 Calcutta clerks could do the work of a modern computer. Could they have been organized and trained by someone to take the contract for the computation of the Apollo project? Even if every other difficulty of coordination could be surmounted, it would turn out that the clerks could only be paid about 4 cents a day each (allowing a computer rental of $250 an hour or $2000 for an 8-hour shift), and this would not feed them, let alone feed and shelter their families.

At each point where the West learns to accomplish an industrial process at below what might be called physiological cost, that is, more cheaply than it could be done by unequipped labor willing to work for food alone, one more means of sustaining the overpopulation of the underdeveloped world is removed.

## Beyond Exploitation

Much concern has been expressed on behalf of the exploited of the world. But now a lower level of the human condition has appeared: the man who is unexploitable. It is not worth anyone's while to use his labor; no one can make a profit by setting him to work, even at starvation wages.

This situation could only come about when to the technological leap of the advanced countries is added population density in the poor ones. If there were sufficient land everywhere, and each peasant could grow his own food, then there would be no urgency. The peasant in the delta of the Irrawaddy can even today produce three times what he and his family need to eat; he can sell the surplus abroad and buy himself consumer goods; his government can preempt the surplus and buy machinery. The peasant could even be exploited in a factory in his spare time — since he feeds himself no floor is set to his wages. This description does not apply to Java nor to India, which are net importers of food. Increasing proportions of their people are functionless in relation to national and world production. They each come with two hands as well as a mouth, in Mill's phrase, but without either land or capital they cannot be productive enough to feed themselves, to say nothing of contributing to progress.

Two factors act to bring about this condition of apparently surplus population: (1) Population growth means that an increasing number of residents of the tropics cannot find enough land to raise their own food. (2) The technological advance of the West means that the unequipped poor cannot produce enough — say working on foreign raw materials — so that they can buy their own food with the proceeds of export. This phase of history is now beginning. In the last third of the twentieth century the world seems to be crossing a kind of height of land that threatens to divide it decisively into two non-intercommunicating parts, between which reciprocal trade is impossible. The weapon of low wages, which historically enabled the poor to compete with those possessing capital, becomes ineffective when capital passes a certain point of productivity.

## The Nature of the Ceiling

In times of rapid technical change statements about the ceiling that the environment sets on population do not have much value. The Asian food ceiling has been decisively pushed up since 1966. The thickening smog over American cities in recent years has shown their ceiling to be lower than was formerly thought. Malthus went out of style in Europe partly because his food ceiling on population was repeatedly raised by discovery of new lands and new techniques. Should population continue to grow at its present pace, he could become relevant again when the limits on agriculture begin to reveal themselves.

If the ceiling were an entirely rigid one, no sudden tragedy could ever occur. By a rigid ceiling I mean a clear and patent division of space, food, and other resources such that a moment comes when the last sustainable person is born, and that moment is easily recognized. From then on mankind would be compelled to stay within its income, that is, its food supply. From the moment the limit was reached we could add no further population, except that as individuals died Nature would permit us to replace them. With such an overt ceiling the population problem would require no foresight of us and would be stripped of all its difficulty. Nature is like a moneylender who allows — even encourages — us to borrow beyond our means and beyond our needs, and then calls the debt when we are most extended. The Malthusian ceiling was not rigid, but flexible; it demanded foresight of men.

But meanwhile even the Malthusian flexible ceiling may be nullified by a certain instability that ecologists have come to fear as a result of man-environment interaction in our technological age. Instead of living with a ceiling over our heads, which is bad enough, we may be on a melting iceberg that can turn over at any moment. This raises the amount of foresight demanded to much higher levels. Let us look into some aspects of the potential instability under which we may now actually be living.

That the analogy of our world to an iceberg that could turn over is not far-fetched is seen in many examples throughout this book. To add one more illustration of the mechanism, at least on a local scale, we can cite the Sumatran or Laotian hill country where slash-and-burn agriculture has been practiced for centuries. Each year a family burns the trees on about an acre of land, plants with digging stick its cassava, tobacco, and corn or other cereal, and after a year or two abandons the site and makes another clearing in the forest. This neolithic agriculture is perfectly stable as long as people are few.

Above a certain population density, however, each family has to return to the same plot before the forest has had time to reestablish itself. When population increase compels such a premature return the landscape changes in the course of a few cycles, and instead of forest a tough grass, called *alang-alang* in Sumatra, comes to prevail. It cannot be cut with primitive implements, and effectively puts the land out of use indefinitely. The land could have sustained 20 people or so per square kilometer under shifting agriculture, but the attempt to make it sustain 40 has reduced its carrying capacity to virtually zero. This story can be repeated in respect of overgrazing, overfishing, and other attempts to exceed the (unknown, but none the less existent) limit imposed by the environment. Fortunately the cases have so far all been local, and people could move somewhere else and have another chance. For violation of the population ceiling on the planet as a whole no second chance would be possible.

That populations can fall tends to be overlooked during a century of rapid and nearly universal increase. And yet many well-documented instances exist — in Europe with the Black Death, in the Americas after the advent of the Spaniards, in some Pacific islands. Schmitt[13] brings together available figures for Hawaii and concludes that at the arrival of James Cook in 1778 some 300,000 persons were living in the islands, after which the number fell gradually to the 56,897 counted at the end of 1872. The 1930 census was the first that showed more people than were present in Cook's time. The decline has been attributed to wars, measles and other diseases, disorganization of economic life, and other causes.[14] We need more study of instances of population decrease as well as of population growth, even though past declines do not have the same causes as possible future ones.

We know little about instability in local situations now and can only speculate on its operation on a larger scale in the future. When the farmer replaces horses with a tractor, he need no longer grow oats and hence increases the output of human food on his land. Based on this larger output, population comes into existence. But on what will the additional people be sustained when the fossil fuels that drive the tractor are exhausted?

More immediately threatening, the farmer eliminates species that are not of use to him, including weeds, rats, and other pests, and so increases effective yields. Again population grows on the increased production. One instrument used by the farmer to produce the increased yields is DDT, and DDT turns out to be an active poison. It concentrates in the fat and bones of animals up food chains throughout the world.

What happens to the population built up on it when its use has to be discontinued?

Aside from any specific effect of this kind, ecologists fear agricultural procedures that drastically reduce the number of species coexisting in an area. In simplifying the ecosystem man can engage mechanisms of instability that are not yet thoroughly understood. He builds one device on another in a complex structure; at each stage production is increased, but always with an unknown risk that the whole structure will collapse.[15]

Because the number of inhabitants is set by such considerations we do not know whether the long-term carrying capacity of the earth is 1 billion or 5 or 10 billion people. Much more research is needed, and it could tell us that the limit is below or above the present total of about 3.6 billion.

The preceding discussion has provided three images or ways of thinking about the problem. One is in terms of a rigid ceiling by which we would know immediately when we had reached the last person the environment could sustain; if Nature provided such a warning, the need for men to exercise responsibility in their affairs would be greatly diminished. The second is a flexible ceiling of the kind Malthus envisioned, that permits some temporary excess population. The third is a potential instability, by which a moment would be reached that would drastically reduce the population sustained, like the crash observed in lemmings and other species.

We turn now from considerations of carrying capacity to distribution in space.

## Urban Agglomeration

Even in developed countries half the population is rural and small town, and in the less developed countries four-fifths is rural and small town (Table V). But the trend everywhere is toward large urban centers. During the period 1960-1980

POPULATION DISTRIBUTION. Total, agglomerated, and rural and small town population in the world and major areas, as projected for the period 1960-1980 (millions). Source: United Nations Department of Economic and Social Affairs. *Growth of the World's Urban and Rural Population, 1920-2000.* Population Studies No. 44. United Nations, New York, 1969.

| | 1960 | 1970 | 1980 | 1980 as percentage of population 1960 |
|---|---|---|---|---|
| *Total population* | | | | |
| World total | 2991 | 3584 | 4318 | 144 |
| More developed | | | | |
| major areas | 854 | 946 | 1042 | 122 |
| Europe | 425 | 454 | 479 | 113 |
| Northern America | 199 | 227 | 262 | 132 |
| Soviet Union | 214 | 246 | 278 | 130 |
| Oceania | 16 | 19 | 23 | 144 |
| Less developed | | | | |
| major areas | 2137 | 2638 | 3276 | 153 |
| East Asia | 794 | 911 | 1041 | 131 |
| South Asia | 858 | 1098 | 1408 | 164 |
| Latin America | 212 | 283 | 378 | 178 |
| Africa | 273 | 346 | 449 | 164 |
| More developed regions | 976 | 1082 | 1194 | 122 |
| Less developed regions | 2015 | 2502 | 3124 | 155 |
| *Agglomerated population (localities of 20,000 inhabitants and over)* | | | | |
| World total | 760 | 1010 | 1354 | 178 |
| More developed | | | | |
| major areas | 389 | 472 | 568 | 146 |
| Europe | 188 | 214 | 237 | 126 |
| Northern America | 115 | 142 | 177 | 154 |
| Soviet Union | 78 | 105 | 141 | 181 |
| Oceania | 8 | 11 | 13 | 158 |
| Less developed | | | | |
| major areas | 371 | 538 | 786 | 212 |
| East Asia | 147 | 198 | 267 | 182 |
| South Asia | 118 | 176 | 266 | 226 |
| Latin America | 69 | 107 | 163 | 234 |
| Africa | 37 | 57 | 90 | 246 |
| More developed regions | 450 | 546 | 661 | 147 |
| Less developed regions | 310 | 464 | 693 | 223 |
| *Rural and small-town population (localities of less than 20,000 inhabitants)* | | | | |
| World total | 2231 | 2574 | 2964 | 133 |
| More developed | | | | |
| major areas | 465 | 474 | 474 | 102 |
| Europe | 237 | 240 | 242 | 102 |
| Northern America | 84 | 85 | 85 | 101 |
| Soviet Union | 136 | 141 | 137 | 100 |
| Oceania | 8 | 8 | 10 | 128 |
| Less developed | | | | |
| major areas | 1766 | 2100 | 2490 | 141 |
| East Asia | 647 | 713 | 774 | 120 |
| South Asia | 740 | 922 | 1142 | 154 |
| Latin America | 143 | 176 | 215 | 151 |
| Africa | 236 | 289 | 359 | 152 |
| More developed regions | 526 | 536 | 533 | 101 |
| Less developed regions | 1705 | 2039 | 2431 | 143 |

V

the increase of rural parts is expected to be 33 percent, of urban 78 percent, the urban population being defined for this purpose as that living in agglomerations of 20,000 persons or more. (The word "agglomeration" rather than "city" shows a fine awareness on the part of our source, the United Nations, of what has happened to urban life in this age of mass society.) This continues earlier trends. Between 1920 and 1960 the world total increased by just over 50 percent, while the urban population on this definition multiplied by more than 2½.

The differential in growth between the more and less developed regions, conspicuous in total population, is even more striking in respect of urban population. Between 1920 and 1960 the total population of the more developed doubled, while the less developed multiplied by 4; in respect of urban population the more developed multiplied by 4½, the less developed by 20.

A striking change in the meaning of urbanization stands out from the United Nations figures. While urbanization was essentially a phenomenon of industrialization in 1920, so that there were 198 million people in urban agglomerates of developed countries and only 69 million in those of less developed regions, we are now approaching the time when the absolute numbers will be the same in more and less developed regions, and by the year 2000, again according to the United Nations projection, the more developed regions will have only 901 millions, the less developed 1436 millions, in places of over 20,000. In Latin America the projection shows a fivefold increase between 1960 and 2000, in Africa even more. Considering what the agglomerations of rich countries have now become — Manhattan is an example — we can only begin to imagine the problems that will confront even larger urban places in Asia and elsewhere, remembering that these latter will have to face most of the same difficulties with only a small fraction of the income.

When analysis reaches the level of individual metropolitan areas we find that the growth is especially concentrated in those that are already the largest. This is true for the United States as for the Soviet Union. The Soviet effort to persuade people not to move to Moscow, but rather to help develop the mineral and other resources of Siberia, has hardly prevented Moscow from growing; one of the surprises of the 1970 Soviet Census was finding 400,000 more people in Moscow than the planners thought were there.[16]

At the other extreme, little Panama's census of May 1970 shows an increase of 32 percent for the country as a whole, 53 percent for the capital city, since 1960. One-third of Argentinians live in greater Buenos Aires. The argument that a country needs people to fill its empty spaces is rendered specious by current migration from relatively empty spaces to the capital city.

That cities everywhere draw people from the countryside is by no means due to their esthetic attractiveness. Large numbers of new residents who lack a tradition of urbanity have more than offset the efforts of planners and builders to create a physical milieu that would encourage civility, and a flight from the older parts of cities is in progress. That pride in community of ancient Athens, indeed of New York only a generation ago, seems to have left the central city and, insofar as it exists at all, moved to the suburbs (Chapter 16). The suburban shopping center has become the Acropolis of the modern community.

The importance of urbanization has attracted good minds to its study in recent years. In addition to the work of Harris on the Soviet Union[16], there are Hodge and Hauser[17] who have studied the United States, and Kingsley Davis, who is preparing a series of monographs on the facts and dynamics of world urbanization.

*The Sun Belt*

Movement to cities may be seen as part of a loosening of the chains that have historically bound productive activities to particular locations. Subsistence farming is the main example of location-determined production, but there are many others. Iron-ore mining goes on in a section of the United States just west of Lake Superior and coal mining in Pennsylvania; the production of steel tends to be located along the land and water routes of the territory between these two areas. Recent discoveries of iron ore in northern

Australia have brought settlement to that part. Oil production is concentrated in Texas and Venezuela, where the crude is located; citrus fruit is produced in Florida and California, which have the soil and climate for it.

Other activities depend much less on locality. The film and later the aircraft industries did not need to locate on the West Coast, and where on the West Coast they settled was even less determined. A university whose student body is national can locate anywhere on the national transportation network, which provides a good deal of choice. With better transport even automobile assembly plants, computer manufacture, and printing become loosed from the location of their raw materials. Those who determine the location of such activities may well do so merely on the basis of how pleasant the climate is, as among other things giving then an edge in attracting staff.

Generally such decisions are not made once and for all, but rather the firms and other activities that have the climatic advantage grow at the expense of those that do not. The free movement of individuals becomes determining. Free movement is even more decisive when no currently productive activities at all are involved — of old people on pension, for example.

This liberation from place applies to increasing fractions of the population as the economy shifts from primary activities — agriculture and mining — to tertiary activities — service — and as the proportion on pension and similar incomes increases, both with earlier retirement and with a greater proportion of old people. The 1970 census of the United States shows the process in full motion. Nevada grew by 69 percent, Arizona by 35 percent, Florida, California, and Colorado by over 25 percent. Very few other states grew by as much as 25 percent, according to census returns up to August 1970. The sun belt, running from Florida west and somewhat north across the continent, has emerged as a population magnet. One can anticipate that the trend will continue with further affluence, with technological advance that makes industries less dependent on bulky raw materials, with air transport that comes to include overnight air-cargo

service through much of the country, with miniaturization in some products that lessens the volume of both raw and finished goods to be shipped.

A major direction of movement is to where people already are, that is, to cities. With increasing fractions of income going into services, agglomerations grow on the opportunities that the very numbers of people create.

Let us contrast the new gravitation to cities and to the sun belt allowed by modern affluence with the older competitive process in agricultural communities.

*Ecological Competition*

Hughes[18] shows with North American examples how people enter into ecological competition, using as weapons high fertility and a simple way of life. German settlers displaced Yankee, and French Canadians displaced English; simple living and industriousness on the one hand enabled them to save the money to buy land from earlier residents, and on the other hand they bore many sons who could be settled on this land. Some groups, like the Japanese fruit growers on the West Coast and the Dutch in Illinois, settled less desirable lands that had been bypassed by native farmers, taking these as their initial ecological niche, but then spreading out from them. Many other instances can be found of quiet, often unwitting, competition among peoples whose locus is fertility and hard work.

The struggle takes a different form when politically conscious groups engage in it. It becomes more articulate, with plentiful invention of slogans and ideologies. The Malays and Chinese in Malaysia watch each other's birth rates to see how they respectively stand in the electorate, or how they would emerge in street fighting if it came to that. Ceylon's ruling Sinhalese have recently abandoned part of the official birth control program for fear that the Tamils will outbreed them. Lebanese Christians and Muslims are so close in numbers and caught in such rivalry that the government has avoided taking a census, which it feared might accentuate the hostility.

*National Rivalries*

Among countries the concentration on numbers has been even more intense. The classic instance is the demographic rivalry between France and Germany; France, for a long time the more advanced technically and militarily, dominated Europe with her 25 million population right into the nineteenth century; then she dropped down to a modern birth rate, while Germany remained feudal. France accumulated a colonial empire, and Germany turned to technology, and it was this rather than population that enabled her to defeat France in three wars. The demographic issue between the two countries, like the economic one, seems to have been bypassed only at the end of World War II. With the technical advance of industry, the competitive struggle among nations is determined not by numbers of people but by their knowledge and the capital they have to work with, a fact that has been understood in France since the 1950s.

Nonetheless, population retains a symbolic meaning for national electorates. Frondizi, in a famous electoral campaign in the Argentine, proposed to be the president of 20 million Argentinians, at a time when the census takers were not sure that there were quite that many in the country. Sukarno's target for Indonesia was 250 million people. Mexico is proud to reach the 50 million mark. Chinese leaders have referred to a billion Chinese, though they have been relatively liberal in permitting birth control.

The worldwide census-taking of the present day, supported by the United Nations and other agencies, and usually most strongly by those statesmen and officials who believe that population should be brought under control, has enabled many new countries to establish their numbers in 1960 and again in 1970. Population control is likely to be undertaken more seriously and hence more effectively if the facts of present population are known.

One is therefore alarmed at the instances in which the census total becomes a symbol of national prestige. Argentina's 20 million; Mexico's 50 million; Brazil's 95 million; these and many other numbers came to be valued and frequently exhibited like the national flag. By a

vague kind of association some Brazilians think that if they can only have as many people as the United States they will be as rich and as powerful as the United States. On present trends in the two countries Brazil would catch up numerically in little more than half a century. Unfortunately this numerical achievement would delay rather than hasten the closing of the gap in skill, capital, and affluence.

Thus, of the competition among families, among language groups, and among nations, the last has become prominent in several recent instances. But responsible efforts to bring fertility under control represent the more widespread official orientation of the 1960s and 1970s.

*Official Birth Control Programs*

The support of birth control varies among countries in the ratio of official to unofficial effort. Active official policies and programs are found in many Asian countries, including both Chinas, Pakistan, India, Ceylon, Indonesia, and Malaysia, as well as Iran and Turkey in Western Asia; a few African ones (only Ghana and Kenya south of the Sahara), and virtually none in Latin America.[19]

Countries lacking formal official policies do have one degree or another of informal or private activity in the field of birth control. Chile allows its maternal and child health clinics to provide family planning services. In Colombia and Costa Rica birth control activities are also relatively overt. Mexico has a private Family Planning Association that is operating effectively, even though the advertising of contraceptives is illegal. In Hong Kong birth control has been successful enough to affect the official birth statistics substantially, the procedure being government subsidy of the private Family Planning Association. Government subsidy to private medical and other family planning activity is to be found also in Korea and Taiwan.

Where contraception is being introduced officially the method varies. In India sterilization is said to be applied by just under 5 million couples out of 6.6 million using one kind of contraception or another.[19] Pakistan has favored other methods, and over a million women have been fitted with intrauterine devices (IUDs). In the United Arab Republic the predominant method is oral contraceptives, now used by 374,000 women, or about 8 percent of those of ages 15-44. Jamaica supports contraception and officially encourages emigration as a major means of population control.

Most of the countries with national family planning programs provide the necessary supplies, free, and a few provide some incentives. India offers 10 rupees (the equivalent of $1.30) to men who undergo sterilization, and 40 rupees to women; South Korea offers 800 won, the equivalent of $3.00, to each.

No country encourages abortion, but the degree to which it is actively opposed varies from Latin America and the Philippines at one extreme to Eastern Europe and Japan at the other. The practice of abortion varies much less than does the sternness of official injunctions against it. The United States has been a leader among those countries whose laws condemn abortion but whose women practice it. Its laws have made medically safe abortion expensive, and in consequence a certain proportion of hospital beds are occupied by poor women suffering the consequences of operations by amateurs and unskilled professionals. In Latin America the disjunction of law and practice has had even more tragic effects.

Until contraception attains complete reliability abortion seems required as a backstop for its failures. Those poor who can afford children least, and whose contraception is least likely to be effective, need it most. A legal system that in effect permits abortion to the rich and withholds it from the poor hardly sets an example of fairness and responsibility.

That our values are changing rapidly in the face of population growth is indicated by attitudes towards abortion revealed both in opinion polls and in institutional action. As recently as 1967 the House of Delegates of the American Medical Association adopted a report opposing induced abortion except for therapeutic reasons and under very restricted other conditions. Only 3 years later it is in process of reversing this policy, and moves are afoot to allow the decision to interrupt pregnancy to be made simply by the woman and her physician. In this the AMA is catching up with the removal of restrictions on abortion in New York and several other states. Altogether 15 states have liberalized their laws in one degree or another since Colorado's action in 1967. That abortion with impunity can follow by only a few years laws which provided jail sentences for the sale of contraceptives shows that the legal system can be influenced by objective conditions.

### Official Reasons for Birth Control

Governments adopting family planning policies advance varied official reasons, among which economic growth of the country is the most frequent. For the United Arab Republic, "This increase (of population) constitutes the most dangerous obstacle that faces the Egyptian people in their drive towards raising the standard of production in their country . . . ." Turkish government statements mention economic development and the income per capital ratio, and how the ratio benefits if its denominator is not allowed to become too high. Kenya emphasizes the problem of providing jobs as the adult male population increases, and the burden of child dependency. Singapore stresses the welfare of the individual family and especially the incapacity of its breadwinners to support many children. Malaysia speaks of its population problem as engendered by lower mortality due to medical and health services and sees it as necessary to complement this health support by family planning if economic progress is not to be inhibited. Indonesia says that "the aim of family planning is in the first place to promote the welfare of the family, especially of mother and child."

Berelson[20] sums up by saying that in the entire developing world today about 65 percent of people live in countries with policies favorable to birth control. "In Asia and Africa the movement is mainly based on the effect of population growth upon social and economic development . . . In Latin America it is based more on medical and humanitarian concern with the prevalence of induced abortion."

The ecological view, that population out of balance with the habitat leads to disaster, is barely hinted at. The closest I see, for instance in the collection of governmental statements on family planning provided by the Population Council[21], is for India, which does refer to pressure on resources as at least a subsidiary reason for family planning in its First Five-Year Plan (1951-1956). Pakistan refers in introducing its population policy for the Third Plan (1965-1970) to the 3.5 acres held by the average cultivator, and hence must be counted as aware of the ecological problem, at least in its gross form.

While little is said officially about the need to limit population to accord with the finiteness of the environment, much is spoken about vast natural resources. These are indeed the stock-in-trade of political discussion of population in Brazil and other countries of Latin America today, and in Indonesia during Sukarno's regime. Dusty notions about resources that had some substance when these two countries each contained 40 or 50 million people become obsolete when they reach the 100 million mark.

If little is said officially about the limits of national resources requiring a limiting of population, the notion of a planetary limit of resources appears not at all. That anyone should curtail his own family because the planetary environment must be protected would seem incomprehensible, if not laughable, to officials of underdeveloped countries, who face pressing day-to-day problems. For the ecologists writing in this book that is ultimately the reason for population restraint.

But we should not complain if countries adopt the right policies, even if for inadequate reasons. The underdeveloped world may be gradually coming to see how its own interest is served by population control. Not content to leave things to take their own course, country after country is officially promoting birth control.

## Voluntary Birth Control

The dominant approach is one of providing the means to voluntary birth control, which is to say, offering cheap and effective contraceptives to those parents that feel they have enough children. Some optimists consider that this would solve the population problem — they implicitly assume that the desires of individuals for children and the carrying capacity of the earth's surface are in natural harmony. That such an assumption is gratuitous appears from many studies.[22]

To cite the most thorough of the investigations now extant, Freedman and Takeshita[23] found that for Taiwanese wives 35-39 years old live births averaged 5.2, living children 4.6, and children wanted 4.2. Availability of birth control to the population under survey would reduce fertility, but would still leave it very high. Some assumptions about proportions unmarried and unfertile, as well as about mortality, are required to translate a figure of 4.2 children wanted into a population rate of increase, but even with maximum adjustments for these, a mean of 4.2 births per woman comes out to an increase of over 50 percent per generation.

The groups classified as more modern want fewer children. Professionals in the Taiwan sample, for instance, stated a mean number children wanted of 3.4, against 4.9 by farmers. Women 30-34, moreover, wanted slightly fewer than did women 35-39: 4.1 against 4.2; among wives of farmers, those 30-34 wanted 4.5 children, against 4.9 wanted by wives 35-39. That younger women, and those in the modern sector, wanted fewer children is encouraging for any country that is moving rapidly towards modernization. But the number of children wanted by even the most advanced groups is far from suggesting that approach to a stationary condition will follow automatically from present economic trends even in Taiwan, let alone in Nepal or Bolivia.

In developed countries as well, the perfecting of contraceptive techniques by which couples will be able to have exactly the number of children they want by no means promises a stationary population. Reconciling the value placed on children with what the economy and ecology can stand is a worldwide problem, surmounted so far only in Japan and in Eastern Europe.

The birth control movement has placed rather exclusive emphasis on voluntary family planning. United Nations Secretary-General U Thant speaks of "the right of parents to determine the numbers of their children," in the context of a statement on overpopulation. Is it possible that in a near future this slogan will be taken over by populationists and used to shout down those who initially devised it?

## Individual and Collective Goals

Any realistic treatment must start with the fact that most people want children. If there is any one constant of human aspiration it is this. Nearly every culture incorporates a desire for progeny, and in most cultures children are more highly valued than wealth. Even among Americans, who would not take the trouble to conceive ten children if no further obligation was attached? The Kennedy model would be universally accepted.

In fact, children are some cost and trouble to their parents everywhere, and hence most couples do not have ten children. In industrial societies where the labor of caring for children is priced high, particularly where women have alternative opportunities of employment, the ideal family size may drop down to three. In preindustrial groups where alternative employment that could give satisfaction equal to that of childbearing is not to be had, the ideal family size is around 5 children, and even higher numbers have been reported. Hundreds of surveys of ideal family size have now been carried out, each question presumably answered by each respondent on the assumption that the costs of having children and the alternatives to having children are what they are in the community of the respondent, and no large group has stated as its ideal an average as small as two children surviving to maturity. Yet this, or slightly more to allow for infertile couples, is what the long-run human average must be.

Whether seen on the national scale or on the world scale, the solution of putting safe, reliable, and easily applied contraception within the reach of every couple is only a first stage; it will enable them to have only the number of children they want. The second stage is somehow causing them to want the number of children that the crust of the earth can support. And in view of the urgency of the problem, it would be unpardonable complacency to put off facing the second stage until the first stage is disposed of.

The influencing of parents is part of the ethics of population, a field developed by John Noonan[24], whose encyclopedic work is a necessary introduction to any contemporary discussion.

## Measures of Population Control

If voluntary parenthood, the slogan under which contraception has made itself acceptable in wide circles, still leaves a disequilibrium, what is the next step? Must parenthood be administratively controlled? Should we require that couples fill out a form and submit it at the wicket of a government agency, wait several months, and then return to find it stamped as approved or disapproved? This is what we require of anyone adding to the national population in later life as an immigrant. Yet an immigrant entering the United States at the age of 25, his education completed and his working life just beginning, is not the burden that a newborn infant is.

While our ethics allow officials to make choices among foreigners, we would be repelled by their making choices among natives — deciding which Americans could be parents cannot be left to administrative decision. Should we, then, allow each couple to have two children and no more? This quantitative regulation is analogous to what we now have in respect of marriage: most countries set at one the number of wives a man may have at any moment. And yet his having two wives places less strain on the community than a couple having four children. The members of the community who support laws against bigamy — presently the majority — would presumably support compulsory family limitation as soon as they realized that unrestrained reproduction does more harm than unrestrained marriage as such could do. They might even favor sterilization after the second child!

Or should limitation be made consistent with market freedom by giving every girl at puberty two coupons, each entitling the holder to a child.[25] Coupons are used to ration consumer goods in wartime, but here the woman could be allowed to sell the coupons, or buy others, and so the rights to children would drift into the hands of those who most wanted to be the parents of the next generation. Specifically, the coupons would drift into the hands of those who both wanted children and had the financial capacity to give them good schooling and expensive upbringing. It makes all the difference that the payment for the excess over two children would have to be IN ADVANCE of their conception, rather than after their birth. Here, as in consumer goods generally, an installment system by which one can make the decision to purchase long before he has to pay encourages improvidence. Of course, the coupon system would only be a test of foresight and saving as a prerequisite for having children if parents were forbidden to borrow to raise the amount needed to buy the coupons. We do have laws restricting purchase of stocks on margin, and such would have to be applied for children.

There are incidental benefits of the scheme. The girl who was poor would sell the two coupons at the high prices that would prevail in the market if children are desired as much as surveys of married couples show them to be. For an upwardly mobile couple cash from the sale of the coupons could be a dowry, sufficing for the groom's education or to set the couple up in a business.

The children would be born to those financially stronger, and therefore better able to care for them. They would be made comparable to yachts or other expensive consumer goods; those who could afford the high initial cost would be those best able to stand the upkeep. But the citizens who find it objectionable that yachts are allocated in this way would be aroused to revolutionary fury if children were so allocated, and very drastic changes in values would have to occur before such a proposal could be taken seriously.

The scheme would, in any case, require a new contraceptive technique not under the control of the couple. Guarding the nation's frontiers against illicit immigration would have its counterpart in policing the nation's wombs against unauthorized reproduction. A device would have to be invented to make women temporarily infertile and would be administered to all through the water or in some other way. Only on obtaining permission to have a child would couples be provided with a suitable antidote.

An alternative is a tax, fixed at the level that will just produce the average of two surviving children per couple needed for stability. Taxes are how we discourage the consumption of cigarettes and liquor. This would be going back to an earlier and fairly successful method of population control. When schools had to be paid for by the parents of the pupils, and free lunches were unknown, many expenditures that today are public costs had to be covered privately by those benefitting. In effect there were heavy charges on children in nineteenth century England and France, in contrast to the present day when children are income tax exemptions. Can we restore the nineteenth century arrangement by a tax in the nature of a user charge on schools, and so on, similar to the gasoline tax that pays for highway construction and maintenance? People being taxed differentially is not in itself abhorrent; the exemptions at the present time, which are passed down in laws inherited from an epoch of underpopulation, in effect tax couples who do NOT have children. The principle of a tax incentive relative to reproduction is well established in our laws, but heed for the environment would reverse its direction and load the tax burden on the prolific rather than the careful.

This approach of charging parents the full cost of their children has a serious disadvantage: That not the parents alone but in whole or in part the children would pay. We do not want to discourage parents from having children by means that result in poorer food and poorer education for the children that are born. Parents might well try to maintain their own level of living and scrimp on their children.

A subsidy for those who do not have children would have more appeal than a tax on those who do. Women would be invited to register for the payment, and to return to the registry office each 4 months, say, to be inspected for nonpregnancy. After a suitable number of such inspections they could collect their subsidy.[26] Since a woman may be fertile for over 30 years, and 10 years are more than enough to contribute to a dangerous overload on the environment, the subsidy per year of nonreproduction would have to be graduated upwards with the length of time. Its administration for effectiveness would offer problems unknown in the U. S. Department of Agriculture, where farmers are paid for leaving their soil uncultivated on a year-by-year basis.

This discussion is intended only to show the dilemma posed by the desire of individual couples to have children in the face of the incapacity of the earth's surface to contain more than a certain number of people. The balance in all previous history was maintained by bacterial diseases; now that bacteria have been substantially conquered we need some moral equivalent to them. Those who find the above suggestions repulsive, as this writer admits he does, have to ask themselves whether they are as painful as the restoration of disease or starvation would be.

## References

1. White, C. L. 1965. Geography and the world's population. In *The Population Crisis: Implications and Plans for Action* (L. K. Y. Ng and S. Mudd, eds.), pp. 11-20. Indiana University Press, Bloomington, Indiana.

2. Clark, C. 1967. *Population Growth and Land Use.* Macmillan, London.

3. Ho, Ping-ti. 1959. *Studies on the Population of China, 1368-1953.* Harvard University Press, Cambridge, Massachusetts.

4. Davis, K. 1968. *The Population of India and Pakistan.* Russell & Russell, New York. First published by Princeton University Press, 1951.

5. United Nations. *Demographic Yearbook 1968.* United Nations, New York.

6. New York Times. 1970. April 18, page 3.

7. Widjojo, N. 1970. *Population Trends in Indonesia.* Cornell University Press, Ithaca, New York.

8. Keyfitz, N., and Flieger, W. 1971. *Population: Facts and Techniques.* W. H. Freeman, San Francisco, California, to be published.

9. Coale, A. J., and Hoover, E. M. 1958. *Population Growth and Economic Development in Low-Income Countries.* Princeton University Press, Princeton, New Jersey.

10. U. S. Bureau of the Census. 1969. *Statistical Abstract of the United States, 1969,* 90th annual ed. U. S. Government Printing Office, Washington, D.C.

11. Ladejinsky, W. 1970. Ironies of India's green revolution. *Foreign Affairs 48:* 758-768.

12. Brown, L.R. 1968. New directions in world agriculture. *Studies in Family Planning No. 32.* (The Population Council).

13. Schmitt, R. C. 1968. *Demographic Statistics of Hawaii: 1778-1965.* University of Hawaii Press, Honolulu.

14. Petersen, W. 1969. *Population,* 2nd ed. Macmillan, London.

15. Ehrlich, P. R., and Ehrlich, A. H. 1970. *Population, Resources, Environment: Issues in Human Ecology.* W. H. Freeman, San Francisco, California.

16. Harris, C. D. 1970. *Cities of the Soviet Union: Studies in Their Functions, Size, Density, and Growth.* Rand McNally, Chicago, Illinois.

17. Hodge, P. L., and Hauser, P. M. 1968. *The Challenge of America's Metropolitan Population Outlook, 1960 to 1985.* Frederick A. Praeger, New York.

18. Hughes, E. C., and Hughes, H. M. 1952. *Where Peoples Meet: Racial and Ethnic Frontiers.* Free Press, Glencoe, Illinois.

19. Nortman, D. 1969. Population and family planning programs: a factbook. *Reports on Population/Family Planning.* The Population Council.

20. Berelson, B. 1969. National family planning programs: Where we stand. In *Fertility and Family Planning: A World View* (S. J. Behrman, L. Corsa, and R. Freedman, eds.), University of Michigan Press, Ann Arbor, Michigan.

21. Population Council. 1970. Governmental policy statements on population: An inventory. *Reports on Population/Family Planning.*

22. Davis, K. 1967. Population policy: Will current programs succeed? *Science* 158:730.

23. **Freedman, R., and Takeshita, J. Y.** 1969. *Family Planning in Taiwan: An Experiment in Social Change.* Princeton University Press, Princeton, New Jersey.

24. **Noonan, J. T., Jr.** 1966. *Contraception: A History of Its Treatment by the Catholic Theologians and Canonists.* Harvard University Press, Cambridge, Massachusetts.

25. **Boulding, K. E.** 1964. *The Meaning of the Twentieth Century.* Harper and Row, New York.

26. **Enke, S.** 1963. *Economics for Development.* Prentice-Hall, Englewood Cliffs, New Jersey.

27. Written at the East-West Population Institute, Hawaii. Acknowledgement is made of NSF Grant GZ995, NIH Research Contract 69-2200, and teaching grants to the Department of Demography at Berkeley from the National Institute of General Medical Sciences (5 TO1 GM01240) and the Ford Foundation.

# 3 Man, Food and Environment

Lester R. Brown and Gail Finsterbusch

Man may have first appeared in the thin film of life that covers the earth as early as 2 million years ago, which is very recent in geologic time. For hundreds of thousands of years he hunted and gathered wild food, living as a predatory animal, a primitive hunter. His life was largely a search for food, and starvation was a constant threat. While he depended entirely on hunting and gathering for his food, his numbers probably never exceeded 10 million — the estimated human population that the earth could support under these conditions.

Then somehow, perhaps as recently in man's existence as 10 to 12 thousand years ago, he learned to domesticate animals and plants and began the great transition from hunter to tiller. Today only a small fraction of 1 percent of the human race live by hunting. The transition from hunter to tiller is virtually complete. Man has substituted the vicissitudes of weather for the un-

LESTER R. BROWN is currently a senior fellow of the Overseas Development Council. He was formerly Administrator of the International Agricultural Development Service, the technical assistance branch of the U.S. Department of Agriculture. He has written numerous articles and three books on the world food problem, the latest of which is *Seeds of Change, the Green Revolution and Development in the 1970's*.

GAIL FINSTERBUSCH has taught sociology at the University of Wisconsin and Fairleigh Dickinson University. She and Brown are the coauthors of a book on food and environment to be published by Harper & Row.

certainty of the hunt.

Man the hunter had an exceedingly limited capacity for intervening in his environment. But man the tiller developed a seemingly endless capacity for altering his environment, shaping it to his ends, and multiplying his numbers in the process. Initially quite simple and limited in scope, his interventions became successively more complex and widespread. Eventually some of the consequences of his interventions were to exceed his understanding of them, creating worrisome problems. Some of these problems are largely local; but others, the more serious ones, are global in scale.

Although still a mystery just currently being unraveled, scholars agree that the beginnings of agriculture occurred in southwestern Asia, in the hills and grassy northern plains surrounding the Fertile Crescent. Climate was hospitable and food resources relatively abundant. Wheat and barley grew wild there, as did sheep, goats, pigs, cattle, horses, and deer. To this day wild barley and two kinds of wild wheat (emmer and einkorn) flourish in the region. Available evidence indicates that the earliest agrarians were herdsmen.

The great Neolithic achievements of agriculture and husbandry gave man a more abundant and secure food supply, allowing him to increase his numbers and establishing the base for civilization. Grain fields fed growing urban populations. But the problem of obtaining enough food remained; it has plagued man since his beginnings. A succession of technological advances have expanded the earth's food-producing capacity. Spurts in food production have permitted man's numbers to increase, and these increases have in turn exerted pressure on the food supply, forcing man to innovate and devise still more effective means of producing food. These two mutually reinforcing factors have brought man to the point where he must attempt to arrest the vicious cycle.

The history of agriculture following the domestication of animals and plants is filled with technological advances of varying importance, each of which has increased the earth's population-sustaining capacity. A few stand out: the discovery of irrigation, the harnessing of animals for draft purposes, the exchange of crops between Old World and New, the development of mechanical power, and the advances in soil chemistry and in plant genetics.

After the invention of agriculture itself, irrigation was the next major effort by man to change his environment in such a way that it would produce more food. The emergence of a distinctly irrigated agriculture in contrast to a predominantly rainfed agriculture occurred around 6000 years ago on the Tigris-Euphrates flood plain and quite possibly also that early along the Nile. It was irrigated agriculture that provided the surplus food and spurred the social organization necessary for the rise of the earliest civilizations.

Man's discovery that animals could be harnessed as a source of power augmenting his own limited energies was another early farming breakthrough. It is not possible to say just where and when man first hitched primitive plows to cattle or horses, but the breakthrough was early, certainly before 3000 B.C. The animal-drawn implements were crude, little more than pointed sticks, and hitches were inefficient. Plows were often hitched directly to the horns of draft animals, as pictured on Sumerian and Egyptian monuments. The technique of harnessing remained crude and inefficient throughout classical times.

But inefficient as early hitches were, man was no longer dependent on his meager energies alone for tillage. With the use of animals for breaking the ground as well as for hauling, threshing, and operating water lifts, man's energy supply expanded greatly since draft animals subsisted largely on roughage indigestible by man.

It is not customary to associate Columbus with a major technological advance in the earth's population-sustaining capacity, but his contribution was profound. For among the strongest supporting evidence for the independent origins of agriculture in the Old and New Worlds is the fact that crops domesticated in the two regions were quite different from each other. Thus, when Columbus crossed the Atlantic in 1492 and established the link between the Old World and the New, he set in motion an exchange of crops between the two worlds, some of which found a much better ecological niche in the world to which they were introduced than in the one from which they originally came. As this exchange of crops progressed, the earth's population-sustaining capacity expanded greatly.

The introduction of the potato into Europe and China augmented the food supply considerably, permitting marked increases in population. Ireland illustrates this most dramatically. The Irish population grew rapidly for several decades on the strength of the expanded food supply which the potato — originally adopted as a means of protecting the food supply against burning by English enemies — made available. Only when the potato crop was devastated by blight was population checked in Ireland.

Corn, the only cereal crop indigenous to the New World and the only one of man's three principal grains — wheat, rice, and corn — to be widely used as both human food and animal feed, is now produced on every continent. It has become a leading feed grain in many countries and a dietary staple in others. Corn is the principal staple in Kenya, where more is consumed per person than in any New World country. Corn exports from Thailand now exceed those of rice.

Wheat, rye, barley, and oats were all carried from the Old World to the New, where an environment highly complementary to these small grains existed. Interestingly enough, without them much of the vast land area of the lower rainfall region in the United States might have remained in grass. For corn required more moisture than is commonly available over much of the Great Plains. Wheat grown in America has fed millions elsewhere in the world in recent years. And wheat in extraordinary modern varieties from Mexico is now revolutionizing agriculture in many parts of the world, including its ancient homeland in southwestern Asia.

In the United States the principal source of vegetable oil and the principal farm export is the soybean, introduced from China several decades ago. Grain sorghum came across the Atlantic from Africa with the early slaves. Today, the United States is the world's leading producer and exporter of grain sorghum. In the Soviet Union the principal source of vegetable oil is the sunflower, a crop domesticated by pre-Colombian Indians that still grows wild on the Great Plains.

The exchange of crops between the New World and the Old has been very much a two-way exchange. But this was not originally the case with livestock. The New World is indebted to the Old for all of its livestock, except the llama and the alpaca, and, with the exception of the turkey and Muscovy duck, for all of its poultry.

The movement of crops between the two worlds, among continents and countries, continues as man alters the nature of the crops themselves through genetic manipulation, as he alters the environment, and as these two factors interact with the changing demands of the marketplace. During the centuries between the linking of the Old World and the New at the end of the fifteenth century, and the modern agricultural revolution in the twentieth century, some of the most dynamic advances in world agriculture and in the population-sustaining capacity of the globe stemmed from the exchange of crops set in motion by Columbus.

Through the past two centuries scientific advances in harnessing mechanical power, in soil chemistry, and in plant genetics have opened new horizons in man's quest for food, permitting him to intervene in his environment more extensively than ever before. Although Watt's development of an efficient steam engine in the latter half of the eighteenth century did not profoundly affect agricultural technique, it set the stage for mechanization and the later development of the internal combustion engine. The farm tractor introduced a new era in world agriculture. Man suddenly had at his command a vast new source of energy, petroleum, to use for producing more food. It was now possible to substitute petroleum for oats and hay that fueled draft animals, to substitute the products of photosynthesis from eons ago for that occurring on farms at present. The substitution of petroleum fuels for oats, hay, corn, and other feedstuffs increases the potential energy supply per person working on the land severalfold. In the United States the displacement of horses by tractors during the first half of the twentieth century released for other purposes some 70 million acres formerly used to feed the nation's horses.

During the nineteenth century the foundations for another major technological advance in agriculture were established by the German chemist von Liebig, known as the father of modern soil chemistry. Von Liebig identified the importance of the major nutrients in plant growth — particularly nitrogen, phosphorus, and potassium. He demonstrated that the soil's natural fertility could be restored or enhanced by adding these nutrients in the proper proportions. On the basis of this demonstration, he recommended the use of mineral (inorganic or chemical) fertilizers by farmers. Eventually farmers were to learn to substitute fertilizer for land as the frontiers disappeared.

At the time of von Liebig's findings, the land resources in much of the world still provided ample opportunity for expanding the area under cultivation to meet man's expanding food needs. It was not until the twentieth century and the disappearance of most of the frontiers that the use of chemical fertilizers became widespread. But widespread it did become and, as we begin the 1970s, the world's farmers are using roughly 60 million metric tons of plant nutrients on 3 billion acres of cropland — about 45 pounds per acre (50 kilograms per hectare).

Although there is much nitrogen in the atmosphere, this gaseous nitrogen is not assimilable by higher plants or animals, both of which require nitrogen. It is changed into an available form in the soil by bacteria, the best known of which are the nitrogen-fixing bacteria associated with nodules on the roots of leguminous plants. Historically, agricultural rotations were often designed to include a leguminous plant such as clover to periodically restore or boost the soil's nitrogen content. During the current century, man has learned to synthesize atmospheric nitrogen into inorganic compounds. The result is low-cost nitrogen which can be applied to soil in the form of nitrogen fertilizer, such as ammonium sulfate or ammonium nitrate, making the application of nitrogen fertilizer more economic than the use of leguminous crops, such as clover, alfalfa, or soybeans, in rotation.

The supply of nitrogen is seemingly without limit. In the case of potassium or potash ($K_2O$), reserves in the rich potash fields in Canada alone are estimated to be sufficient to meet world needs for several centuries. The nutrient which is least plentiful and most likely to become a constraining factor in food production is phosphorus. About 3.5 million tons of phosphorus wash into the ocean each year from the earth's land masses. If there is to be a great demand for a mining of nutrients from the ocean bed, the economic pressures to mine phosphorus might be among the earlier ones to develop.

Usage of chemical fertilizers varies widely among countries and geographic regions (Table I). In densely populated industrial countries located in high-rainfall, temperate regions usage is intensive, while in some poor countries chemical fertilizers are scarcely used at all. In countries practicing intensive agriculture such as Japan, chemical fertilizers are applied at a rate of more than 300 pounds per acre yearly and account for a large share of the food supply. Stated otherwise, if the use of chemical fertilizers were discontinued in these countries, soil fertility would decline rapidly, dropping food production by perhaps half or more. If the use of chemical fertilizers were discontinued on a global basis, man's total food supply would probably be reduced by at least one-fourth.

Along with the development of mechanical power and the understanding of soil chemistry, the third major breakthrough of the past two centuries that has contributed immensely to man's food-producing capacity was the breakthrough in plant genetics made possible by Mendel's experiments with the garden pea. Building on the work of Mendel and others subsequent to him, plant breeders have learned to select, classify, and combine, in order to alter, literally dozens of plant characteristics. Plant breeders can make plants shorter or taller, more responsive to fertilizer, more resistant to drought, more tolerant of cold, more resistant to disease; they can change the quantity and quality of protein

and the cooking characteristics of various crops.

The scientific advances which made possible farm mechanization, widespread use of chemical fertilizers, and the dramatic improvement in plants occurred largely during the nineteenth century. But it was not until well into the twentieth century that the application of this knowledge occurred on a widespread, commercial basis.

## Hunger and Malnutrition

Since the discovery of agriculture, man's capacity to increase food production has grown several hundred fold, enabling him to sustain a human population today of more than 3 billion in contrast to the 10 million limit on his numbers set by the hunting economy. An adequate diet has been assured for most of that third of mankind living in North America, Western Europe, Eastern Europe, and Japan. For most of the remaining two-thirds of mankind, those living in

| | Average 1952/53 – 1956/57 | 1966/67 | Consumption per hectare arable land, kilograms, 1966/67 |
|---|---|---|---|
| Western Europe | 7.5 | 13.9 | 134 |
| Eastern Europe and USSR | 3.5 | 11.2 | 39 |
| North America | 5.9 | 13.5 | 61 |
| Oceania | 0.7 | 1.6 | 41 |
| Japan | 1.1 | 2.1 | 350 |
| Total for developed countries (including Israel and S. Africa) | 18.8 | 42.7 | 64 |
| Latin America | 0.5 | 1.8 | 17 |
| Far East (excluding Japan and Mainland China) | 0.6 | 2.7 | 10 |
| Near East | 0.2 | 0.7 | 16 |
| Africa | 0.1 | 0.4 | 2 |
| Total for developing countries | 1.4 | 5.6 | 9 |
| World Total | 20.2 | 48.3 | 36 |

CONSUMPTION OF COMMERCIAL FERTILIZERS. World use of the commercial fertilizers N, $P_2O_5$, and $K_2O$, in terms of nutrient content. Data are given in million tons. Source: reference 1.

the poor countries of Asia, South America, and Africa, the diet is not adequate but the ancient and ever-present threat of famine has been lifted — at least for the time being.

Man's existence in relation to his food supply has always been precarious. But largely as a result of United States' initiative, the world has been spared from massive famine due to natural causes in recent decades. The last great famine due to the vicissitudes of weather occurred in West Bengal in 1943 when flooding destroyed the rice crop, costing some 2 to 4 million lives. After World War II the United States decided it had the agricultural technology and the food production capacity to assume a global famine relief role on a continuing basis, a role that became institutionalized in 1954 with the passage of Public Law 480. Sending food aid to other countries both relieved food shortages abroad and served to reduce American food surpluses to more acceptable reserve levels. This famine relief policy was followed even in the mid-1960s when massive food needs developed in India after surpluses in the United States had been eliminated. It was necessary to bring idled United States cropland back into production for food aid purposes. One-fifth of the United States' wheat crop was required to stave off famine in India in 1966 and 1967 when the monsoons failed. Sixty million Indians were fed entirely by food shipments from the United States.

Since World War II the global production and distribution system both among and within countries has evolved to the point where large quantities of food can be moved from one country to another on a scale sufficient to avoid any readily envisaged natural catastrophe. The huge quantity of grain transported to India to avert famine required some 600 ships, the largest maritime assemblage since the Allied Forces crossed the English Channel on D-Day.

A major part of the human race is not well nourished, however. The exact numbers of mankind suffering from undernutrition (lack of calories) or malnutrition (lack of essential nutrients, particularly protein) is unknown because data are severely limited. In 1963 the United Nations Third World Food Survey estimated that 20 percent of the residents of poor countries were undernourished and 60 percent malnourished. The survey concluded that at least half the people in the world as a whole were hungry and/or malnourished.[3]

Man's food energy, or calorie, requirements vary with physique, with climate, and with level of physical activity. Calorie standards for an adequate daily diet range from an average of 2300 calories per capita for the Far East to 2700 per capita for Canada and the Soviet Union. People in most of the rich countries of North America, northern and eastern Europe, and parts of South America and Oceania consume between 3000 and 3200 daily calories. The result is that many of their residents suffer from overnutrition, a modern nutrition problem of growing proportions.

Perhaps the most careful global assessment of the incidence of hunger is that in the U. S. Department of Agriculture's World Food Budget (Figure 1). The analysis divides the world into diet-adequate countries and diet-inadequate countries on the basis of recommended minimum caloric intake. In 1960 an estimated 1.9 billion lived in countries where the average intake was below the recommended minimum. The daily food energy deficit averaged 300 calories per person. For some countries and for countless individuals the gap was far wider, of course. The hungriest nations in terms of just not having enough food to eat are those of Central America and Communist Asia. Although there was little change in diets between 1960, when the Food Budget calculations were made, and 1967, preliminary information suggests modest improvements in several poor countries since 1968.

Calorie intake, while a good quantitative indicator of diet adequacy, is not a good indicator of quality. Protein intake is the key indicator of diet quality in today's world. Most people suffering from calorie malnutrition suffer also from protein malnutrition. Protein malnutrition is exacting an enormous toll in both the mental and physical development of a great majority of the youngsters in the world today.

The problem is not just a lack of protein per se — of which 60 grams per day including at least 10 grams of animal protein is the recommended standard — but a lack of protein of

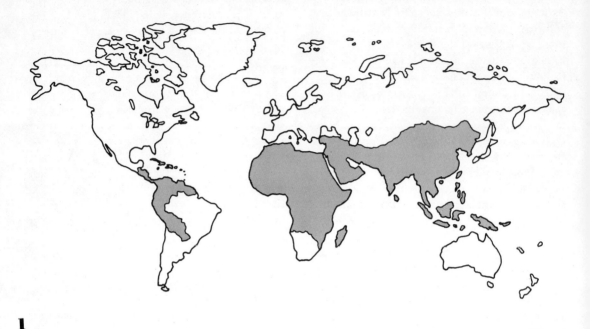

**1**

CALORIE–PROTEIN–DEFICIENT AREAS. Source: reference 2.

high quality like that found in animal products or legumes (peas, beans, soybeans). The serious deficiencies are in Asia and in the corn-, potato-, and cassava-eating populations of sub-Saharan Africa and Latin America.

The problem of malnutrition is inseparable from that of poverty. Traditional food habits, lack of nutritional education, and internal parasites contribute to malnutrition, but these are in many ways simply additional manifestations of poverty. Even in the United States, malnutrition is often found where there is poverty. The connection is impossible to ignore in the poor countries. The World Food Budget shows that the 1.1 billion people living in diet-adequate regions had an average yearly income of $1070 per person; the 1.9 billion in diet-deficient countries had an average income of $97.

In Zambia 260 of every 1000 babies die before their first birthday. In India and Pakistan the number is 140 in every 1000. In Colombia it is 82. Many others die before reaching school age, and more during early school years. Where death certificates are issued for preschool children in the poor countries, death is generally attributed to measles, pneumonia, dysentery, or some other disease. These children are likely to be basically victims of malnutrition whose ability to resist disease has been reduced.

The effects of good nutrition on physical development were dramatically illustrated when India held its Olympic track and field tryouts in New Delhi in the summer of 1968 to select a team to go to Mexico City that fall. Unfortunately, not a single Indian, male or female, met the minimum qualifying standards required to participate in the Olympic competition in any of the 32 track and field events. Outdated training techniques and lack of public support were partly responsible, but undernourishment of most of the population certainly contributed to this poor showing. The effects of nutrition on physical development can also be seen on the streets of Tokyo today. Japanese teenagers, well nourished from infancy as a result of the enormous rise in income and in proper nutrition in Japan, tower inches above their elders. Some speculate that Japanese may surpass Americans in physical measurements in the not so distant future.

Although the relationship between diet and physical performance is well known, the parallel relationship between nutrition and mental performance has only recently been demonstrated. Protein shortages in the early years of life impair development of the brain and central nervous system, permanently reducing learning capacity. Furthermore, this damage is irreversible. Protein shortages today are depreciating the stock of human resources for at least a generation to come. And no amount of investment in education can correct this damage.

*The Ocean as a Source of Food*

Calorie and protein shortages have caused man in recent years to look with quickening interest to the ocean as a source of food. Man's intensified fishing efforts since World War II have tripled fish production, with the world fish catch reaching 64 million tons in 1968, 12 million tons of which (including fish meal) was usable protein.[4] At present fish provide man with only 1 percent of his calorie intake and around 20 percent of his protein supply, including both direct consumption and indirect consumption in the form of products from animals (mainly poultry) which have been fed on fish meal.

The closer man has looked, the more apparent it has become that the ocean is not a limitless storehouse of food forever there for the catching. The ocean, covering around 70 percent of the earth's surface, is not one ecosystem equally fertile and productive throughout. The open sea — an estimated 90 percent of the ocean — is considered a biological desert, contributing almost nothing to current world fishing and offering little potential for the future. Half of the oceanic fish supply is produced in coastal waters and a few offshore regions, together comprising almost 10 percent of the ocean area. About 80 percent of the world fish catch is landed in these regions. The most biologically productive regions of the ocean are the nutrient-rich upwelling areas such as those off the coast of Peru, California, and parts of Africa. Upwelling areas form only about 0.1 percent of the ocean, but produce half of the world's fish supply.

Estimates of fish produced annually in the sea — based on what is known of primary (photosynthetic) production of marine plants as well as conversion efficiencies along oceanic food chains — range from 200 million tons to 300 million tons of the species now utilized by man. Some production estimates reach as high as 2000 million metric tons, but this assumes the future utilization of species further down the oceanic food chain. And this production, of course, far exceeds the economically feasible harvest. Man must be careful to leave a significant part of the annual fish population in order to assure sustained maximum catch.

John Ryther of the Woods Hole Oceanographic Institute judges potential economically sustainable fish harvest to be around 100 million tons annually.[5] Others estimate that sustainable fish catch could reach between 150 and 200 million tons by the year 2000.[6] These latter amounts are doubtful because of the costs of the increased fishing effort, because of the as yet incompletely understood effects of oceanic pollution, and because the pressure of man's current fishing is resulting in overexploitation and decline in several fisheries. Fish per capita based on oceanic hunting may actually decline by the end of the century. Some fisheries that have declined include Antarctic blue whales, East Asian sardine, California sardine, Northwest Pacific salmon, Atlantic herring, Barents Sea cod, and Antarctic fin whales (reference 4, p. 100). Some stocks that are overfished in the sense that increased effort does not bring increased yield include tunas in the Atlantic, Pacific, and Indian Oceans; herring, cod, perch, flounder, and hake in the North Atlantic; anchovy in the southeastern Pacific; plaice and haddock in the North Sea and Barents Sea; and menhaden in the Atlantic, Pacific, and Indian Oceans. This situation contrasts with 1949, when only a few species were considered overfished.

Man dreams of farming the ocean expanses with methods similar to those used on land. Severe technological, economic, and political constraints exist, however, and the transition from fisherman to farmer in the ocean is not imminent. Man's hope for the immediate future lies not with the ocean but with increasing the productivity of the land.

## Expanding the Cultivated Area

The earth's land surface is estimated to be 32.5 billion acres. Man has extended cultivation to about 3 billion acres — around 10 percent of the total. Expressed in these terms, the area cleared by man seems small. But in terms of the earth's land area actually supporting vegetation, it is quite large. In terms of the land area potentially capable of supporting crops useful to many, it is larger still.

Perhaps the largest estimate of the earth's potentially arable land — based on an analysis of soils and climate — is 8 billion acres.[7] This amount is more than double the current cultivated area. However, any such estimate of the area of new land to be brought under cultivation must, to be meaningful, specify at what cost this is to be accomplished.

Little, if any, potential for new farm lands exists in Asia and Europe and relatively little in the Soviet Union. Most countries of North Africa and the Middle East, dependent as they are on irrigation or dryland farming, cannot significantly expand the area under cultivation without developing new sources of irrigation water.

In several countries of the world the area of cultivated land is actually declining. In Japan, the area of cultivated land reached a peak in 1920 and has declined substantially since. Some countries in Western Europe, notably Sweden, Norway, Ireland, and Switzerland, have been losing agricultural land to the construction of highways, airfields, factories, and homes for the past several decades. Land now being farmed in many parts of the developing world should be withdrawn from cultivation because soils are being depleted and destroyed.

Sub-Saharan Africa and the Amazon Basin of Brazil are the only major regions where there are sizable portions of well-watered, potentially arable land. Any substantial expansion in these two areas awaits further improvements in man's ability to manage tropical soils once the lush natural vegetation is removed. Mineral nutrients are easily leached from most tropical soils once the natural cover is gone.

Apart from these possibilities, no further opportunities to expand farm area are likely to arise until the cost of desalinization is reduced to the point where it is profitable to use seawater for large-scale irrigation, or until it is technically possible and economically feasible to alter rainfall patterns to shift some of the rainfall normally occurring on the oceans to arid land masses capable of being farmed. This will probably not occur for another decade or two at best. (Chapter 7).

The United States is the only country in the world that in recent years has had a ready reserve of idled cropland — around 50 million acres compared with a harvested area of 300 million acres. The bold fact is that man is already occupying and farming most of the best and readily cultivable land of the earth.

## Transition to Increasing Yields

Through the centuries as population grew, increases in the world's food supply resulted more from expanding the land area under cultivation than from raising the productivity of land already being farmed. Man moved from valley to valley, country to country, and continent to continent with his crops and farming methods. Only as the frontiers gradually disappeared during the twentieth century was man forced to concentrate his energies on significantly raising yields on the existing cultivated area. In coaxing significantly higher yields from an acre of land the technologies developed in plant breeding, agricultural chemistry, and mechanization, as well as in water supply and control were applied on a commercial basis.

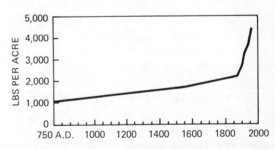

JAPANESE RICE YIELDS. The rice yields in Japan from 750 A.D. to 1960. Historical estimates from the Japanese Ministry of Agriculture. Source: U. S. Department of Agriculture.

The takeoff in yield — a transition from a condition of near static yields to one of rapid, sustained increases — may have occurred first in Japan around the turn of the century. Toward the close of the nineteenth century this densely populated, archipelagic country was forced to turn to the oceans for protein and to use her limited land for producing starchy staples, principally rice, to meet food energy needs. Through intensive farming Japan's rice yields began to rise in the early years of this century and have risen steadily year by year for seven decades, except during war (Figure 2). Some of the countries of western Europe, such as Denmark, the Netherlands, and possibly Sweden, may have achieved yield takeoffs around the same time.

Generating a yield takeoff is difficult and requires an abrupt departure from traditional ways of farming. It was not until 1940 that another group of industrialized countries including the United States (Figure 3), the United Kingdom, and Australia achieved yield takeoffs. But the mid-twentieth century proved to be a global turning point in the man-land-food relationship. For the first time in history, increases in productivity came more from the rising productivity of land than from expanding the land area under cultivation (Figure 4).

It was clear, however, that advanced farm technologies were confined mainly to the rich industrial countries and to plantation or export crops in the poor countries. This was unfortunate because in the decades following World War II Malthusian forces were vigorously at work in the poor countries, which, with the exception of Taiwan and Mexico, had failed to achieve a yield takeoff. Population growth rates soared as new medical and sanitation technologies spread. New land that could easily be brought under the plow

was being used up. And food production lagged behind population growth.

Asia, Africa, and Latin America, which had each been net cereal exporters prior to World War II, shipping largely to Europe, suddenly found that enlarged populations were consuming what had once been their exportable surpluses. By 1950, the poor countries were importing several million tons of grain each year from the rich countries, principally from North America. By 1960, this flow of food grains had increased to 13 million tons. In 1966, it reached a peak of 32 million tons, consisting in large part of food aid shipments from the United States. Cereals supply 53 percent of man's calorie intake and a large portion of the rest in the form of meat, eggs, and milk.

The situation was alarming. The U. S. Department of Agriculture produced a chart in 1966, using a series of conservative assumptions regarding production prospects, which indicated that by 1985 the United States would no longer have the capacity to produce exportable surpluses sufficient to cover the food deficits anticipated in the poor countries. In 1967 the President's Science Advisory Commission report pointed out that during the first half of the 1960s population in the poor countries was increasing at 2.5 percent a year whereas food production was growing at only 1.6 percent. In short, food and population were on a collision course. Some observers were predicting massive famine in Asia by 1975.

At the time these gloomy projections were being made, six of the world's seven most popu-

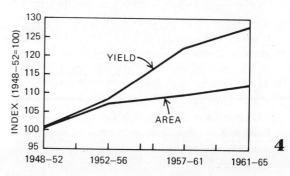

WORLD GRAIN: INDEXES OF AREA AND YIELD. Since about 1950 some 70 percent of worldwide increases in grain production have resulted from rising grain yields. Only about 30 percent of the increases have resulted from expanding the area planted to grain. Source: U. S. Department of Agriculture.

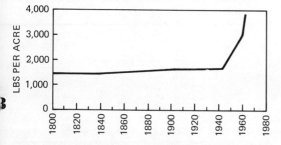

CORN YIELDS IN THE UNITED STATES: 1800-1963. Source: U. S. Department of Agriculture.

lous countries were food-deficient: China, India, the Soviet Union, Indonesia, Pakistan, and Japan. Of the seven, only the United States remained a net exporter of food. As a result of stagnating production in many developing countries and two consecutive monsoon failures in the Indo-Pakistan subcontinent, per capita food production in the less-developed countries had fallen for three consecutive years (Figure 5).

### Agricultural Breakthrough

Just in the past few years — in the late 1960s — a breakthrough in food production has occurred in the poor countries that has measurably improved the prospects for feeding the increasing numbers of people which are predicted for the future. The main impetus for the current agricultural breakthrough, popularly called the Green Revolution, is the successful introduction and rapid diffusion of new high-yielding varieties of wheat and rice in several of the larger poor countries — India, Pakistan, the Philippines, Indonesia, Turkey, and Mexico, for example. Mexico, once importing one-third of its wheat needs, is today exporting wheat, corn, and rice. The Philippines has ended half a century of dependence on rice imports. In Pakistan and India annual increases in wheat yields following the introduction of the new varieties are double the increases in corn yields in the United States following the introduction of hybrid corn a generation ago (Figures 6, 7). In Asia the area planted to high-yielding cereals in the 1964-65 crop year was estimated at 200 acres, and that largely for experimental and industrial purposes. By 1968-69, 34 million acres, or about one-tenth of the region's cropland, were covered.

The new varieties — dwarf wheats developed in Mexico by the Rockefeller Foundation and dwarf rices bred in the Philippines at the International Rice Research Institute — are not just marginally better than traditional or indigenous varieties. They actually double yields, with proper management.

Key to the productivity of the new varieties is a remarkable feat of biological engineering that greatly enhances their responsiveness to fertilizer. Plant breeders redesigned the wheat and rice

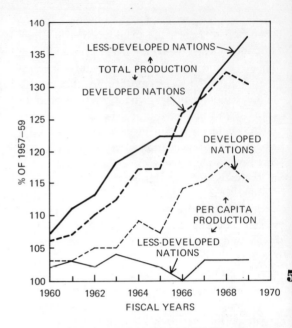

**5**

WORLD AGRICULTURAL PRODUCTION. Indexes of agricultural production in the developed and less-developed nations. Note that per capita food production in less-developed nations fell during three consecutive years, 1963-1966, due to stagnating production and monsoon failures. Source: U. S. Department of Agriculture.

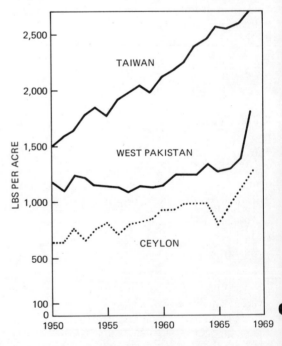

RICE YIELDS IN WEST PAKISTAN, CEYLON, AND TAIWAN. Source: reference 8.

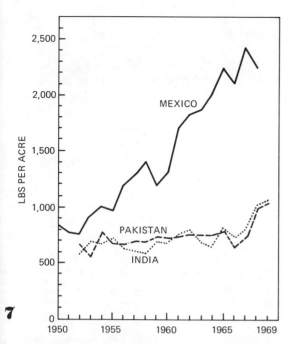

**7**

WHEAT YIELDS IN MEXICO, PAKISTAN, AND INDIA. Source: reference 8.

plants, producing plants with short, stiff straw that stands up under the weight of heavier yields. With the old thin-strawed varieties, yields began to decline when the application of nitrogen reached 40 pounds per acre. The grain would become too heavy and lodge or fall down. Yields from the new varieties increase until nitrogen application reaches 120 pounds per acre. The new varieties not only respond to much larger quantities of fertilizer, they also use fertilizer more efficiently. Thus, a given level of production can be reached using far less fertilizer with the new seeds.

The Green Revolution, still in its early stages, has had a pronounced impact on per capita cereal production in several countries. In Mexico, for example, where the Green Revolution is most advanced, per capita cereal production has risen from 495 to 680 pounds (Table II). Once per capita cereal production rises above 400 pounds in a nation, the additional cereal produced is converted largely into animal protein.

The Green Revolution is not a universal phenomenon in the poor countries. It is limited largely to wheat and rice crops. Geographically it is limited to those areas with an adequate con-

trolled water supply. The new plants, responsive as they are to heavy applications of fertilizer, demand a more intensive and well-managed use of water. Even with these constraints, however, unprecedented gains in cereal production have been realized.

The new varieties not only double the level of production over the levels of local varieties, but in doing so they often triple or quadruple profits. Millions of farmers have suddenly found themselves earning incomes that they had not dreamed were possible. The aspirations of millions of others, especially rural laborers without land, are being aroused in the process. As the new varieties and the new technologies associated with them spread, they introduce rapid and sweeping changes, creating a wave of expectations throughout society and placing great pressure on the existing social order and political systems. Distributing the benefits of the new varieties equitably and in ways that do not excessively exacerbate tensions between social groups, for example, between landowners and tenant farmers, between landless laborers and other farmers, between city dwellers and rural people, and between regional groups — is one of the challenges issuing from the Green Revolution.

The most immediate obstacle to the agricultural revolution is the woefully inadequate state of marketing systems in countries where the new varieties are being planted. With the new technologies, farmers' marketable surpluses of cereals have increased far faster, proportionately, than

| | INDIA Wheat | PAKISTAN Wheat | CEYLON Rice | MEXICO All Cereals |
|---|---|---|---|---|
| 1960 | 53 | 87 | 201 | 495 |
| 1961 | 55 | 83 | 196 | 496 |
| 1962 | 59 | 87 | 213 | 525 |
| 1963 | 51 | 86 | 218 | 546 |
| 1964 | 46 | 83 | 213 | 611 |
| 1965 | 56 | 90 | 150 | 639 |
| 1966 | 46 | 71 | 188 | 649 |
| 1967 | 49 | 80 | 216 | 655 |
| 1968 | 76 | 116 | 247 | 680 |
| 1969 | 80 | 121 | na | na |

**II**

**IMPACT OF PRODUCTION USING NEW SEEDS.** Annual production of selected cereals in countries using new seeds, given in pounds per person of total population. Source: U.S. Department of Agriculture.

production. A farmer who is accustomed to marketing a fifth of his wheat harvest finds his marketable surplus triples when his crop suddenly increases 40 percent. Even after retaining more for home consumption, as many are doing, farmers who have doubled their output with the new seeds are increasing their marketable surpluses severalfold.

The Green Revolution found some countries with marketing systems oriented to a considerable extent toward handling imported grain. Now domestic marketable surpluses are threatening to overwhelm all the components of the marketing system — storage, transport, grading and processing operations, and the local market intelligence system. In West Pakistan, land planted to the new IR-8 rice rose from 10,000 acres to nearly a million in one year (1967-1968). West Pakistan suddenly found itself with an exportable surplus of rice, but without the processing, transport, and pricing facilities needed to handle an export trade efficiently.

There is no agronomic reason why people in any less-developed country should be deprived of the benefits of the Green Revolution. High-yielding varieties exist that are adapted to almost every ecologic zone in the tropics and subtropics. The spread of the Green Revolution depends primarily on the commitment of political leadership, not on technology. How rapidly the Green Revolution progresses will also depend on the extent of financial and technical assistance from the rich countries. Many poor countries, for example, are not able to finance imports of as much fertilizer as they need. The cost of India's fertilizer imports in 1967 totaled almost 20 percent of its foreign exchange.

However exciting and encouraging in the short run, the current wave of yield takeoffs in the poor countries should not reduce concern over the population problem. The Green Revolution is clearly not a solution to the food-population problem, but it is buying time with which to stabilize population growth.

*Redefining the Population Problem*

When Thomas Malthus published his treatise on the principle of population in 1798, he defined the population problem primarily in terms of food supplies and the threat of famine. Ever since, the threat of overpopulation has been perceived largely in these terms. In the 1960s, when national and international leaders were preoccupied with food scarcities in the poor countries, the population problem was regarded as virtually synonymous with the food-population problem.

The Green Revolution forces us to redefine the population problem. By lifting the specter of famine in the immediate future, expanded food supplies make it possible to focus concern on other dimensions of population pressure such as employment, urbanization, and the environment. By 1975 we will in all likelihood be equating the population problem, in its most immediate sense, with the employment-population problem.

With more and more young people entering the job market, the day of reckoning with the explosion in population growth has arrived. In some countries the number of young people coming of employment age will double in less than two decades. If these millions of young people are not able to find jobs, the "labor force explosion" could pose an even greater threat to peace and stability than did the threat of famine in the sixties.

In dealing with the population problem in the years ahead, man must avoid repeating the errors of the past by not focusing exclusively on one dimension of the problem to the exclusion of others. Although employment looms large for the immediate future, it is far from the only one that must be considered. Just as important are the ecological implications of meeting future food requirements.

In considering future food requirements we must keep in mind that there are two sources of additional demand for food: population growth and rising incomes. Projecting food demands on the basis of population growth alone assumes that future populations are no better or worse fed than at present. But every government in the world is aiming at raising incomes. If realized, rising incomes will also increase claims on the world's agricultural resources.

The average North American diet requires some 1650 pounds — nearly a ton — of grain a year. Of this, 150 pounds or so is consumed directly in the form of bread, pastry, and breakfast cereals. The rest is consumed indirectly in the form of meat, milk, and eggs. In contrast, the average person in the poor countries has about 400 pounds of grain available to him each year. Of this, 10 percent is used for seed for next year's crop, leaving 360 pounds, or about a pound a day, for actual consumption. Nearly all of this must be consumed directly simply to meet minimum energy requirements and to keep body and soul together. As incomes rise, the amount of grain required per person climbs steadily, not for direct consumption purposes but for indirect consumption in the form of meat, milk, and eggs (Figures 8, 9, 10).

Historically, diets improved significantly only when grain supplies began to exceed direct consumption needs, leaving large quantities to be converted into high-protein livestock products.

INCOME AND PER CAPITA GRAIN CONSUMPTION.
Source: U. S. Department of Agriculture.

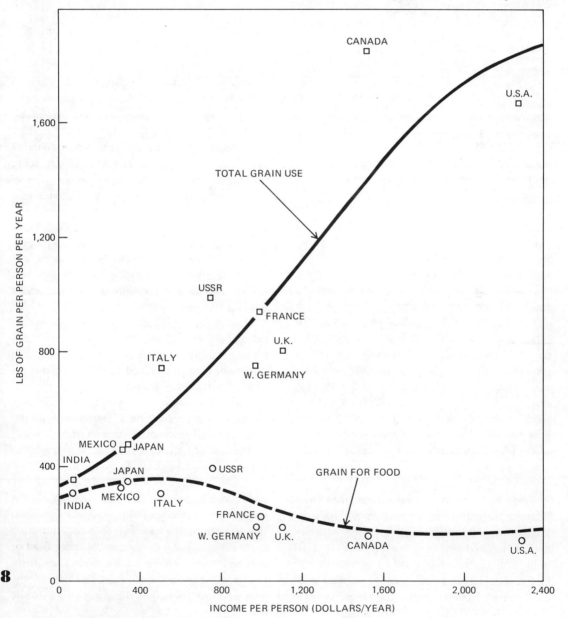

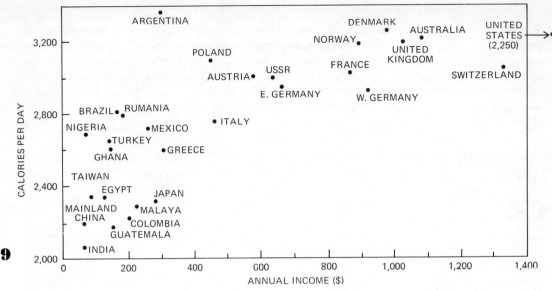

INCOME AND FOOD ENERGY SUPPLY PER PERSON. Source: U.S. Department of Agriculture.

But improving diets via this conventional route is costly because livestock are inherently inefficient in converting plant materials into animal protein and fat. Livestock return to man only about 10 percent of their energy intake in edible food products. They use the other 90 percent to grow, keep warm, and reproduce.

Finding ways to shorten the livestock cycle has caught the imagination of food technologists and other scientists. Advances in food technology in the industrial countries are beginning to offset some of the increases in grain requirements by substituting vegetable products for animal products. Scientists are also developing cereals with improved protein content and fortifying cereals with proteins. But despite these gains in food technology, the overall prospect for the next few decades is for increased claims on the world grain supply as a result of rising incomes.

*Pressures on the Agricultural Ecosystem*

Since the beginnings of agriculture, man's successive interventions in the environment have enlarged the earth's population-sustaining capacity several hundred fold — from the estimated 10 million of the hunting world to greater than 3 billion today. This development took place over more than 10,000 years. Unless population growth is halted, man may have to enlarge food production by two or three times in the next 30 years to accommodate the anticipated doubling of his numbers and the almost universal desire for better diets.

The net effect of the projected doubling in man's numbers and the hoped for future prosperity, particularly among the world's poor, is growing pressure on the earth's agricultural ecosystem. The key question that man must ask and answer is: Will the earth's agricultural ecosystem, already showing signs of stress and strain, hold up under such pressure?

Man places two kinds of pressure on the agricultural ecosystem. One may be called EXTENSIVE PRESSURE, since it results from extending cultivation to marginal land areas. The other is INTENSIVE PRESSURE because it results from intensifying farming on the existing cultivated area through the increased use of water, agricultural chemicals, and more productive seeds.

The cost of more extensive cultivation is often the destruction or loss of that thin mantle of topsoil, measured in inches on most of the earth's surface, on which man depends for his food supply. Increasing human population invariably results in the clearing of more and more land, either for the production of more food or as a result of the demand for fuel. Since fossil fuels are not available to most residents of the poor countries, wood is the desired fuel. In the more densely populated poor countries, fuel demands for warmth and cooking have long exceeded the replacement capacity of local forests. As a result the forested area has declined to the point that in many parts of the world there is little forest land left. In these circumstances, as in the Indo-Pakistan subcontinent, people are reduced to using cow dung as fuel for cooking purposes. The number of people in the world today who rely on cow dung for fuel probably far exceeds those using some of the more modern fuels such as natural gas.

Increase in human population in the poor countries is almost always accompanied by a nearly commensurate increase in livestock population. As cattle populations increase in order to expand draft power, food, and fuel, they denude the countryside of its natural grass cover. Overgrazing by goats and sheep contributes to denudation, also. Overgrazing by animals, combined with the progressive deforestation occurring particularly as a result of the population expansion of the last few decades, is resulting in a total denuding of the countryside, creating conditions for a rapid spread of soil erosion by wind and water. Literally millions of acres of cropland in Asia, the Middle East, North Africa, and

Central America are being abandoned each year because severe soil erosion by both wind and water have rendered them unproductive or at least incapable of sustaining the local inhabitants with existing technologies.

It takes centuries to form an inch of topsoil through natural processes, but man is managing to destroy it in some areas of the world in only a fraction of that time. The problem associated with the loss of topsoil does not end with the abandonment of the severely eroded land. Much of the topsoil finds its way into streams, rivers, and irrigation canals, and eventually into irrigation reservoirs. A dramatic and unfortunate example of this indirect cost of soil erosion is provided by the Mangla Reservoir, recently constructed in the foothills of the Himalayas in West Pakistan. The feasibility studies undertaken in the late 1950s, justifying the investment of $600 million in this irrigation reservoir, were based on a life expectancy of at least 100 years. As the rapid population growth in the watershed feeding the Mangla Reservoir has progressed, so has the rate of denuding and soil erosion. The result is that the Mangla Reservoir is expected to be completely filled with silt within 50 years or less.

History provides us with many examples of man's abuse of the soil which sustains him. North Africa, once fertile, highly productive, and the

INCOME AND TOTAL PROTEIN SUPPLY PER PERSON. Source: U. S. Department of Agriculture.

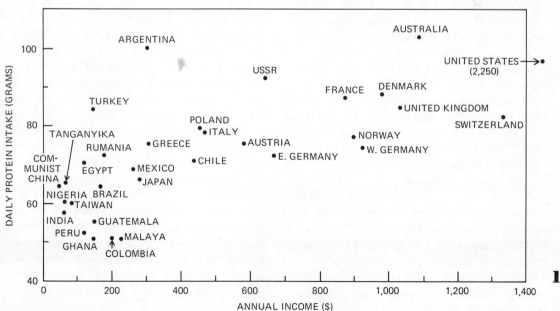

**10**

breadbasket of the Roman Empire, has today lost the natural fertility it had and is heavily dependent on food imports under the United States food aid program.

The United States has also learned of the costs of abusing its rich agricultural inheritance. As a result of overplowing and overgrazing of the southern Great Plains during the early decades of this century, wind erosion gradually worsened, culminating in the dust bowl era of the 1930s. The United States responded to this situation by fallowing 20 million acres and by constructing literally thousands of windbreaks in the form of rows of trees across the Great Plains. The situation eventually stabilized. Today erosion in the Great Plains is negligible and yields are good. Had not the United States responded in this fashion, much of the southern Great Plains, like the once fertile fields of North Africa, would have been abandoned.

Many of the world's densely populated regions, such as those in western India, Pakistan, Java, Central America, and China, facing similar problems of severe wind and water erosion of their soils because of acute pressure of human and livestock population on the land, do not have the slack in their food systems to permit the diversion of large acreages to fallow. Their situation requires a massive effort involving reforestation of hundreds of millions of acres, the controlled grazing of cattle, terracing, contour farming, and systematic management of watersheds, all of which require an enormous array of financial resources and technical know-how not yet in prospect.

The alternative to bringing more land, much of it increasingly marginal, under the plow, is to shift to the more intensive use of existing farmland through the use of agricultural chemicals and other inputs. This brings about another set of ecological problems — those of environmental pollution — which are concentrated thus far in the rich countries. Pesticides and compounds of phosphorus and nitrogen originating in fertilizer and animal wastes are all pollutants. The use of DDT and other chlorinated hydrocarbons as pesticides for agricultural and other purposes such as malaria eradication is beginning to threaten at least some species of animal life. Animal wastes and chemical fertilizers are primarily affecting water, both the quality of the water supply and the complex of plant and animal life inhabiting lakes and inland waterways. (See Chapter 10.)

In his efforts to increase his food supply man has lately been faced not only with a scarcity of land, but of water as well. To acquire the amount of water needed, he has been gradually bringing the rivers under control through large irrigation systems. These irrigation systems, such as the Aswan in the United Arab Republic, the Volta River Project in Ghana, the Colorado River system in the United States, and some of the even more massive irrigation systems in Asia, are altering the environment in immeasurable ways. In addition to reducing the annual deposition of fertile silt on the river flood plains, disturbing the migrational paths and feeding grounds of fish, and displacing population in the vicinity of the reservoirs, they are creating ideal conditions for the spread among humans of schistosomiasis, a debilitating parasitic affliction which is transmitted to man via snails. Also known as snail fever, this disease today afflicts an estimated 250 million people, 1 out of every 14 people now alive and more than any other disease now that the incidence of malaria has been greatly reduced.

As the demand for food multiplies in the future as a result of both population growth and rising incomes, particularly among that two-thirds of mankind now poor and malnourished, man will be forced to intervene more and more in the environment while just beginning to understand the consequences of doing so. The use of chemical fertilizers is projected to increase steadily over the remaining decades of this century. The use of pesticides to protect crops must also increase greatly as crop stands become more specialized and more lush, and as year-round cropping spreads in the tropics. The demand for water for agricultural purposes will most likely far exceed the water available from conventional sources. Man will then be forced to desalt seawater for irrigation purposes or, what may prove more feasible, to alter the world's climatic patterns with the purpose of shifting some of the rainfall now located over the oceans over some of the earth's land masses. But the consequences of extending man's intervention to climate control are not known.

Various estimates have been made of how many people the earth can feed. Some of these estimates are several times the current population size. It is now becoming increasingly clear that those making the estimates have been asking the wrong question. The question is not, How many people can the earth feed? but, What are the environmental and social consequences of attempting to feed so many?

When this latter question is asked, the answer is much more disquieting. Even at the current level of food production, inadequate as it is for our current population, signs of stress on the earth's ecosystem are beginning to appear. Species are being endangered by agricultural chemicals, and deforestation is threatening wild life, as well as soils, particularly in Asia and Africa. Agriculture is a prime contributor to the eutrophication of lakes, ponds, and rivers. In light of what we now know, there is growing doubt that the earth's agricultural ecosystem can support the 6.5 billion people projected for the year 2000. The growing evidence argues strongly for the stabilization of global population growth well before the end of this century.

## References

1. **Food and Agriculture Organization of the United Nations.** 1968. *The State of Food and Agriculture 1968,* Rome.
2. **Economic Research Service, U.S. Department of Agriculture.** 1965. *The World Food Budget 1970.* Foreign Agricultural Economic Report No. 19.
3. **Food and Agriculture Organization of the United Nations.** 1963. *Third World Food Survey,* Freedom from Hunger Campaign, Basic Study No. 11.
4. **Ricker, W. E.** 1969. Food from the sea. In *Resources and Man,* pp. 87-108. National Academy of Sciences — National Research Council; W. H. Freeman, San Francisco, California.
5. **Ryther, J. H.** 1969. Photosynthesis and food production in the sea. *Science 166:* 76.
6. **Holt, J. S.** 1969. The food resources of the ocean. *Scientific American 221:190.*
7. **U. S. President's Science Advisory Committee.** 1967. *The World Food Problem,* Report of the Panel on the World Food Supply, Vol. 2.
8. **Brown, L. R.** 1970. *Seeds of Change: The Green Revolution and Development in the 1970s.* Praeger, New York.

## Further Reading

**Asian Development Bank.** 1969. *Asian Agricultural Survey.* University of Tokyo Press, Tokyo; University of Washington Press, Seattle, Washington.

**Borgstrom, G.** 1965. *The Hungry Planet.* Macmillan, New York.

**Borgstrom, G.** 1969. *Too Many.* Macmillan, New York.

**Brown, L. R.** 1969. Breakthrough against hunger. In *Science Year.* Field Enterprises, Educational Corporation, Chicago, Illinois.

**Brown, L. R.** 1963. *Man, Land, and Food.* Government Printing Office, Washington.

**Brown, L. R.** 1967. The world outlook for conventional agriculture. *Science 158:* 604-611.

**Ehrlich, P. R., and Ehrlich, A. H.** 1970. *Population, Resources and Environment.* W. H. Freeman, San Francisco.

**Hardin, C. E.** 1969. *Overcoming World Hunger.* Prentice-Hall, Englewood Cliffs, New Jersey.

**Wharton, C. R., Jr.** 1969. The green revolution: Cornucopia or Pandora's Box? *Foreign Affairs 47:* 464-476.

# 4  Mineral Resources in Fact and Fancy

Preston Cloud

Optimism and imagination are happy human traits. They often make bad situations appear tolerable or even good. Man's ability to imagine solutions, however, commonly outruns his ability to find them. What does he do when it becomes clear that he is plundering, overpopulating, and despoiling his planet at such a horrendous rate that it is going to take some kind of a big leap, and soon, to avert irreversible degradation?

The inventive genius of man has got him out of trouble in the past. Why not now? Why be a spoil-sport when brilliant, articulate, and well-intentioned men assure us that all we need is more technology? Why? Because the present crisis is exacerbated by four conditions that reinforce each other in a very undesirable manner: (1) the achievements of medical technology which have brought on the run-away imbalance between birth and death rates; (2) the hypnotic

**PRESTON CLOUD** is Professor of Biogeology at the University of California, Santa Barbara. He received his doctorate from Yale University in 1940. Although his thesis was on fossil brachiopods, the war soon involved him in studies of strategic minerals for the U.S. Geological Survey: manganese, bauxite, and petroleum. He taught briefly at Harvard University, then returned to field work with the Geological Survey, where his interest turned toward marine geology, early records of earth history, and the origin of life. In 1961 he returned to teaching. His work has taken him to some of the most remote spots on the globe, but he has concluded that there is really no place to hide: "If we care about man's future, we must do what we can to assure that there will be one, and that it will be something to look forward to."

but unsustainable national dream of an ever-increasing real Gross National Product based on obsolescence and waste; (3) the finite nature of the earth and particularly its accessible mineralized crust; and (4) the increased risk of irreversible spoilation of the environment which accompanies overpopulation, overproduction, waste, and the movement of ever-larger quantities of source rock for ever-smaller proportions of useful minerals.

Granted the advantages of big technological leaps, therefore, provided they are in the right direction, I see real hope for permanent long-range solutions to our problems as beginning with the taking of long-range views of them. Put in another way, we should not tackle vast problems with half-vast concepts. We must build a platform of scientific and social comprehension, while concurrently endeavoring to fill the rut of ignorance, selfishness, and complacency with knowledge, restraint, and demanding awareness on the part of an enlightened electorate. And we must not be satisfied merely with getting the United States or North America through the immediate future, critical though that will be. We must consider what effects current and proposed trends and actions will have on the world as a whole for several generations hence, and how we can best influence those trends favorably the world over. Above all, we must consider how to preserve for the yet unborn the maximum flexibility of choices consistent with meeting current and future crises.

## Nature and Geography of Resources

Man's concept of resources, to be sure, depends on his needs and wants, and thus to a great degree on his locale and place in history, on what others have, and on what he knows about what they have and what might be possible for him to obtain. Food and fiber from the land, and food and drink from the waters of the earth have always been indispensable resources. So have the human beings who have utilized these resources and created demands for others — from birch bark to beryllium, from buffalo hides to steel and plastic. It is these other resources, the ones from which our industrial society has been created, to which my remarks are directed. I refer, in particular, to the nonrenewable or wasting resources — mineral fuels which are converted into energy plus carbon, nuclear fuels, and the metals, chemicals, and industrial materials of geological origin which to some extent can be and even are recycled but which tend to become dispersed and wasted.

All such resources, except those that are common rocks whose availability and value depend almost entirely on economic factors plus fabrication, share certain peculiarities that transcend economics and limit technology and even diplomacy. They occur in local concentrations that may exceed their crustal abundances by thousands of times, and particular resources tend to be clustered within geochemical or metallogenic provinces from which others are excluded. Some parts of the earth are rich in mineral raw materials and others are poor.

No part of the earth, not even on a continent-wide basis, is self-sufficient in all critical metals. North America is relatively rich in molybdenum and poor in tin, tungsten, and manganese, for instance, whereas Asia is comparatively rich in tin, tungsten, and manganese and, apparently, less well supplied with molybdenum. The great bulk of the world's gold appears to be in South Africa, which has relatively little silver but a good supply of platinum. Cuba and New Caledonia have well over half the world's total known reserves of nickel. The main known reserves of cobalt are in the Congo Republic, Cuba, New Caledonia, and parts of Asia. Most of the world's mercury is in Spain, Italy, and parts of the Sino-Soviet bloc. Industrial diamonds are still supplied mainly by the Congo.

Consider tin. Over half the world's currently recoverable reserves are in Indonesia, Malaya, and Thailand, and much of the rest is in Bolivia and the Congo. Known North American reserves are negligible. For the United States loss of access to extracontinental sources of tin is not likely to be offset by economic factors or technological changes that would permit an increase in potential North American production, even if present production could be increased by an order of magnitude. It is equally obvious that other peculiarities in the geographical distribution of the world's geological resources will continue to encourage interest both in trading with some ideologically remote nations and in seeking alternative sources of supply.

*Recoverable Mineral Reserves*

Consider now some aspects of the apparent lifetimes of estimated recoverable reserves of a selection of critical mineral resources and the position of the United States with regard to some of these. The selected resources are those for which suitable data are available.

Figure 1 shows such lifetimes for different groups of metals and mineral fuels at current minable grades and rates of consumption. No allowance is made for increase of populations, or for increased rates of consumption which, in the United States, tend to increase at twice the rate of population growth. Nor is allowance made for additions to reserves that will result from discovery of submarine deposits, use of submarginal grades, or imports — which may reduce but will not eliminate the impact of growth factors. Data are updated from the U.S. Bureau of Mines compendia *Mineral Facts and Problems* and its *Minerals Yearbooks,* as summarized by Flawn.[1] The open bars represent lifetimes of world reserves for a stable population of roughly $3.5 \times 10^9$ at current rates of use. The heavy bars represent similar data for a United States population of about 200 million. Actual availability of some such commodities to the United States will, of course, be extended by imports from abroad, just as that of others will be reduced by population growth, increased per capita demands, and perhaps by political changes. The dashed vertical line represents the year 2042. This is chosen as a reference line because it marks that point in the future which is just as distant from the present as the invention of the airplane and the discovery of radioactivity are in the past.

The prospect is hardly conducive to unrestrained optimism. Of the commodities con-

MINERAL RESERVE LIFETIMES. Apparent lifetimes of known recoverable reserves of 20 mineral commodities at currently minable grades and existing rates of consumption. (Except for helium, whose lifetime is estimated from U.S. Bureau of Mines data on reserves, conservation practices, and expected increases in demand). Such lifetimes tend to increase with new discoveries and technological advances and to decrease with increasing population and per capita consumption rates but resources to left of vertical dashed line are in obvious danger of depletion.

sidered some are in very short supply. Only 11 for the world and 4 for the United States persist beyond the turn of the century; and only 8 for the world and 3 for the United States extend beyond 2042. I do not suggest that we equate these lines with revealed truth. Time will prove some too short and others perhaps too long. New reserves will be found, lower-grade reserves will become minable for economic or technological reasons, substitutes will be discovered or synthesized, and some critical materials can be conserved by waste control and recycling. The crucial questions are: (1) How do we reduce these generalities to specifics? (2) Can we do so fast enough to sustain current rates of consumption? (3) Can we increase and sustain production of industrial materials at a rate sufficient to meet the rising expectations of a world population of

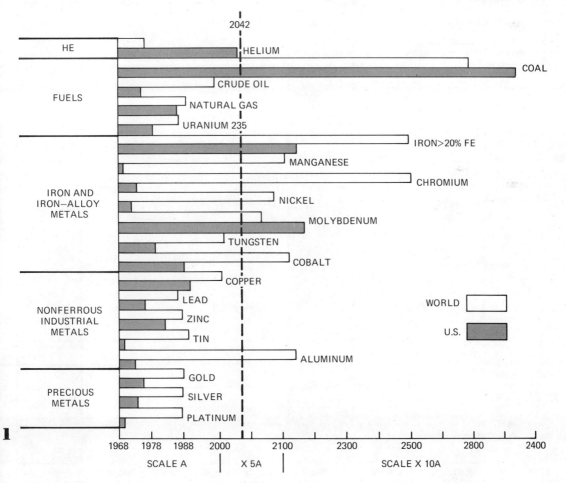

1

74   P. Cloud

3½ billion, growing with a doubling time of about 30 to 35 years, and for how long? (4) If the answer to the last question is no, what then?

A more local way of viewing the situation is

DISTRIBUTION OF RECOVERABLE MINERAL RE-SOURCES. Estimated recoverable reserves of minerals (above sea level) for which U.S. reserve estimates exceed, equal, or fall only slightly below those of the USSR plus Mainland China. Source: Data on lignite, chromium, phosphate from Flawn, reference 1; on petroleum from M.K. Hubbert, in reference 6.

to compare the position of the United States or North America with other parts of the world. Figures 2 to 4 show such a comparison for 16 commodities with our favorite measuring stick, the USSR plus China. Figure 2 shows the more cheerful side of the coin. The United States is a bit ahead in petroleum, lignite, and phosphate, and neither we nor Asia have much chromium — known reserves are practically all in South Africa and Rhodesia. Figure 3, however, shows the USSR plus China to have a big lead

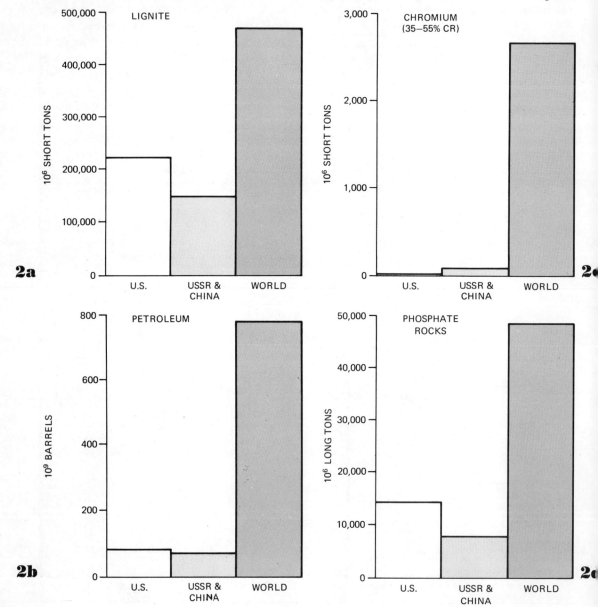

**2a** LIGNITE — $10^6$ SHORT TONS (500,000 to 0): U.S., USSR & CHINA, WORLD

**2b** PETROLEUM — $10^9$ BARRELS (800 to 0): U.S., USSR & CHINA, WORLD

**2c** CHROMIUM (35–55% CR) — $10^6$ SHORT TONS (3,000 to 0): U.S., USSR & CHINA, WORLD

**2d** PHOSPHATE ROCKS — $10^6$ LONG TONS (50,000 to 0): U.S., USSR & CHINA, WORLD in zinc, mercury, potash, and bauxite. And Figure 4 shows similar leads in tungsten, copper, iron, and coal.

Again there are brighter aspects to the generally unfavorable picture. Ample local low-grade sources of alumina other than bauxite are avail-

able with metallurgical advances and at a price. The U.S. coal supply is not in danger of immediate shortage. Potassium can be extracted from sea water. And much of the world's iron is in friendly hands, including those of our good neighbor Canada and our more distant friend Australia.

No completely safe source is visible, however, for mercury, tungsten, and chromium. Lead, tin, zinc, and the precious metals appear to be in short supply throughout the world. And petrol-

DISTRIBUTION OF RECOVERABLE MINERAL RESOURCES. Estimated recoverable reserves of minerals (above sea level) for which U.S. reserve estimates are less than those of the USSR plus Mainland China. Source: Flawn, reference 1.

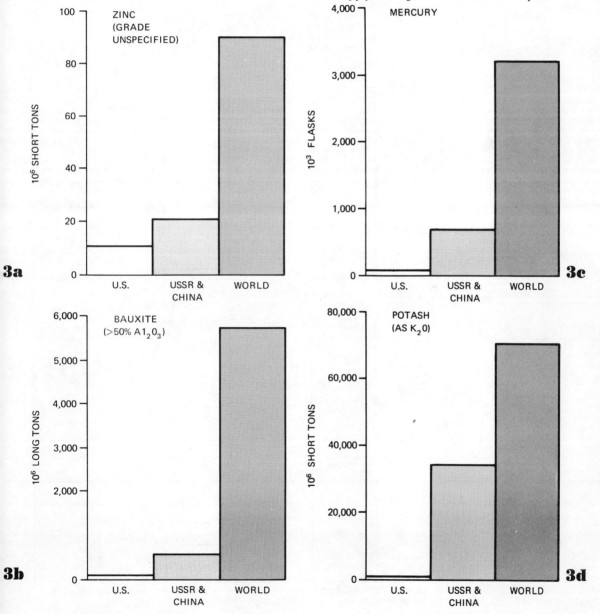

eum and natural gas will be exhausted or nearly so within the lifetimes of many of those alive today unless we decide to conserve them for petrochemicals and plastics (Chapter 5). Even the extraction of liquid fuels from oil shales and "tar

DISTRIBUTION OF RECOVERABLE MINERAL RE-SOURCES. Estimated recoverable reserves of minerals (above sea level) for which U.S. reserve estimates are less than those of the USSR plus Mainland China. Source: Data on iron, tungsten, and copper from reference 1; on coal from Paul Averitt, 1969, *U.S. Geological Survey Bull.* 1275.

sands," or by hydrogenation of coal, will not meet energy requirements over the long term. If they were called upon to supply all the liquid fuels and other products now produced by the fractionation of petroleum, for instance, the suggested lifetime for coal, the reserves of which are probably the most accurately known of all mineral products, would be drastically reduced below that indicated in Figure 1 — and such a shift will be needed to a yet unknown degree before the end of the century.

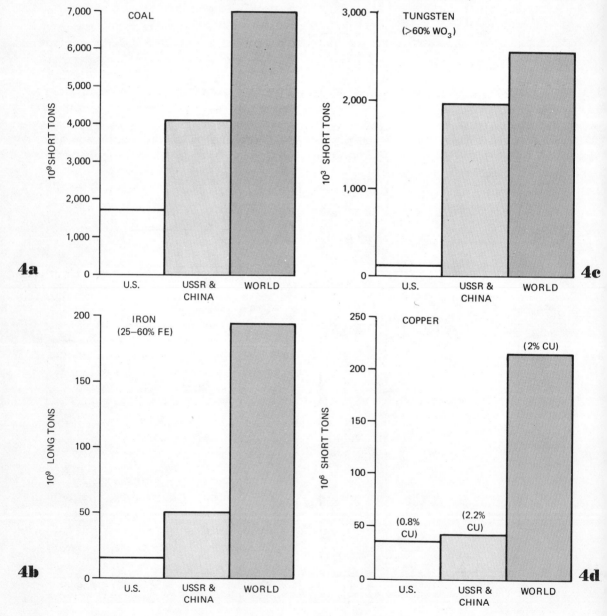

*The Cornucopian Premises*

In view of these alarming prospects, why do intelligent men of good faith seem to assure us that there is nothing to be alarmed about? It can only be because they visualize a completely non-geological solution to the problem, or because they take a very short-range view of it, or because they are compulsive optimists or are misinformed, or some combination of these things.

Let me first consider some of the basic concepts that might give rise to a cornucopian view of the earth's mineral resources and the difficulties that impede their unreserved acceptance. Then I will suggest some steps that might be taken to minimize the risks or slow the rates of mineral-resource depletion.

The central dilemma of all cornucopian premises is, of course, how to sustain an exponential increase of anything — people, mineral products, industrialization, or solid currency — on a finite resource base. This is, as everyone must realize, obviously impossible in the long run and will become increasingly difficult in the short run. For great though the mass of the earth is, well under 0.1 percent of that mass is accessible to us by any imaginable means (the entire crust is only about 0.4 percent of the total mass of the earth) and this relatively minute accessible fraction, as we have seen and shall see, is very unequally mineralized.

But the cornucopians are not naive or mischievous people. On what grounds do they deny the restraints and belittle the difficulties?

The six main premises from which their conclusions follow are:

PREMISE I. The promise of essentially inexhaustible cheap useful energy from nuclear sources.

PREMISE II. The thesis that economics is the sole factor governing availability of useful minerals and metals.

PREMISE III. The fallacy of essentially uninterrupted variation from ore of a metal to its average crustal abundance, which is inherent in Premise II; and from which emanates the strange and misleading notion that quantity of a resource available is essentially an inverse exponential function of its concentration.

PREMISE IV. The crucial assumption of population control, without which there can be no future worth living for most of the world (or, worse, the belief that quantity of people is of itself the ultimate good, which, astounding as it may seem, is still held by a few people who ought to know better[2]).

PREMISE V. The concept of the "technological fix."

PREMISE VI. The naive and unsupported faith that if all else fails the sea will supply our needs.

Now these are appealing premises, several of which contain large elements of both truth and hope. Why do I protest their unreserved acceptance? I protest because, in addition to elements of truth, they also contain assumptions that are gross oversimplifications, outright errors, or are not demonstrated. I warn because their uncritical acceptance contributes to a dangerous complacency toward problems that will not be solved by a few brilliant technological breakthroughs, a wider acceptance of deficit economy, or fallout of genius from unlimited expansion of population. They will be solved only by intensive, wide-ranging, and persistent scientific and engineering investigation, supported by new social patterns and wise legislation.

I will discuss these premises in the order cited.

*Premise I*

The concept of essentially inexhaustible cheap useful energy from nuclear sources offers by all odds the most promising prospect of sweeping changes in the mineral resource picture.[3] We may be on the verge of developing a workable breeder reactor just in time to sustain an energy-hungry world facing the imminent exhaustion of traditional energy sources (Chapter 5). Such a development, it has been persuasively stated, will also banish many problems of environmental pollution and open up unlimited reserves of metals in common crustal rocks. There are, unhappily, some flaws in this delightful picture, of which it is important to be aware.

Uranium-235 is the only naturally occurring spontaneously fissionable source of nuclear power. When a critical mass of uranium is brought together, the interchange of neutrons back and forth generates heat and continues to do so as long as the $^{235}U$ lasts. In the breeder reactor some of the free neutrons kick common $^{235}U$ over to plutonium-239, which is fissionable and produces more neutrons, yielding heat and accelerating the breeder reaction. Even in existing reactors some breeding takes place, and, if a complete breeding system could be produced, the amount of energy available from uranium alone would be increased about 140-fold. If thorium also can be made to breed, energy generated could be increased about 400-fold over that now attainable. This would extend the lifetime of visible energy resources at demands anticipated by 1980 by perhaps 1000 to 3000 years and gain time to work on contained nuclear fusion.

The problem is that it will require about 275,000 short tons of $6.00 to $10.00 per pound uranium oxide ($U_3O_8$) (not ore, not uranium) to fuel reactors now on order to 1980, plus another 400,000 tons to sustain them until the turn of the century, burning only $^{235}U$ with currently available enrichments from slow breeding. Only about 310,000 of the 675,000 tons of uranium needed is known to be available at this price, although known geologic conditions indicate the possibility of another 350,000 tons. Thus we now appear to be somewhat short of the $U_3O_8$ needed to produce the hoped-for 150,000 megawatts of nuclear energy on a sustained basis from 1985 until the end of the century without a functioning breeder reactor. Unless we find more uranium, or pay more money for it, or get a functioning complete breeder reactor or contained nuclear fusion within 10 or 15 years, the energy picture will be far from bright, especially in view of the fact that other nations from whom we might purchase uranium are eager to develop their own nuclear energy plants. There is good reason to hope that the breeder will come, and after it, contained fusion, IF the $^{235}U$ holds out — but there is no room for complacency.

If and when the breeder reactor or contained fusion does become available as a practicable energy source, however, how will this help with mineral resources? It is clear immediately that it will take pressure off the fossil fuels so that it will become feasible, and should become the law,

to reserve them for petrochemicals, plastics, essential liquid propellants, and other special purposes not served by nuclear fuels. It is also clear that cheap massive transportation, or direct transmittal of large quantities of cheap electric power to, or its generation at, distant sources will bring the mineral resources of remote sites to the market place — either as bulk ore for processing or as the refined or partially refined product.

What is not clear is how this very cheap energy will bring about the extraction of thinly dispersed metals in large quantity from common rock. The task is very different from the recovery of liquid fuels or natural gas by nuclear fracturing. The procedure usually suggested is the break-up of rock in place at depth with a nuclear blast, followed by hydrometallurgical or chemical mining. The problems, however, are great. Complexing solutions in large quantity, also from natural resources, must be brought into contact with the particles desired. This means that the enclosing rock must be fractured to that particle size. Then other substances, unsought, may use up and dissipate valuable reagents. Or the solvent reagents may escape to ground waters and become contaminants. Underground electrolysis is no more promising in dealing with very low concentrations. And the bacteria that catalyze reactions of metallurgical interest are all aerobic, so that, in addition to having access to the particles of interest, they must also be provided with a source of oxygen underground if they are to work there.

Indeed the energy used in breaking rock for the removal of metals is not now a large fraction of mining cost in comparison with that of labor and capital. The big expense is in equipping and utilizing manpower, and, although cheap energy will certainly reduce manpower requirements, it will probably never adequately substitute for the intelligent man with the pick at the mining face in dealing with vein and many replacement deposits, where the sought-after materials are irregularly concentrated in limited spaces. There are also limits to the feasible depths of open-pit mining, which would be by all odds the best way to mine common rock. Few open-pit mines now reach much below about 1500 feet. It is unlikely that such depths can be increased by as much as an order of magnitude. Moreover, the quantity of rock removable decreases exponentially with depth because pit circumference must decrease downward to maintain stable walls.

It may also not be widely realized by non-geologists that many types of ore bodies have definite floors or pinch-out downward, so that extending exploitative operations to depth gains no increase in ore produced. Even where mineralization does extend to depth, of course, exploitability is ultimately limited by temperature and rock failure.

Then there is the problem of reducing radioactivity so that ores can be handled and the refined product utilized without harm − not to mention heat dispersal (which in some but not all situations could itself be a resource) and the disposal of waste rock and spent reagents.

Altogether the problems are sufficiently formidable that it would be foolhardy to accept them as resolved in advance of a working efficient breeder reactor plus a demonstration that either cheap electricity or nuclear explosions will significantly facilitate the removal of metals from any common rock.

A pithy comment from Peter Flawn's book on *Mineral Resources*[1] (p. 14) is appropriate here. It is to the effect that "average rock will never be mined." It is the uncommon features of a rock that make it a candidate for mining! Even with a complete nuclear technology, sensible people will seek, by geological criteria, to choose and work first those rocks or ores that show the highest relative recoverable enrichments in the desired minerals.

The reality is that even the achievement of a breeder reactor offers no guarantee of unlimited mineral resources in the face of geologic limitations and expanding populations with increased per capita demands, even over the middle term. To assume such for the long term would be sheer folly.

*Premise II*

The thesis that economics is the sole, or at least the dominant, factor governing availability of useful minerals and metals is one of those vexing part-truths which has led to much seemingly fruitless discussion between economists and geologists. This proposition bears examination.

It seems to have its roots in that interesting economic index known as the Gross National Product (GNP). No one seems to have worked out exactly what proportion of the GNP is in some way attributable to the mineral resource base. It does, however, appear that the dollar value of the raw materials themselves is small compared to the total GNP, and that it has decreased proportionately over time to something like 2 percent of the present GNP. From this it is logically deduced that the GNP could, if necessary, absorb a severalfold increase in cost of raw materials. The gap in logic comes when this is confused with the notion that all that is necessary to obtain inexhaustible quantities of any substance is either to raise the price or to increase the volume of rock mined. In support of such a notion, of course, one can point to diamond, which in the richest deposit ever known occurred in a concentration of only 1 to 25 million, but which, nevertheless, has continued to be available. The flaw is not only that we cannot afford to pay the price of diamond for many substances, but also that no matter how much rock we mine we can't get diamonds out of it if there were none there in the first place.

Daniel Bell[4] comments on the distorted sense of relations that emerges from the cumulative nature of GNP accounting. Thus, when a mine is developed, the costs of the new facilities and payroll become additions to the GNP, whether the ore is sold at a profit or not. Should the mine wastes at the same time pollute a stream, the costs of cleaning up the stream or diverting the wastes also become additions to the GNP. Similarly if you hire someone to wash the dishes this adds to GNP, but if your wife does them it doesn't count.

From this it results that mineral raw materials and housework are not very impressive fractions of the GNP. What seems to get lost sight of is what a mess we would be in without either!

Assuming an indefinite extension of their curves and continuance of access to foreign markets, economists appear to be on reasonably sound grounds in postulating the relatively long-term availability of certain sedimentary, residual, and disseminated ores, such as those of iron, aluminum, and perhaps copper. What many of them do not appreciate is that the type of curve that can with some reason be applied to such deposits and metals is by no means universally applicable. This difficulty is aggravated by the fact that conventional economic indexes minimize the vitamin-like quality for the economy as a whole of the raw materials whose enhancement in value through beneficiation, fabrication, and exchange accounts for such a large part of the material assets of society.

In a world that wants to hear only good news some economists are perhaps working too hard to emancipate their calling from the epithet of "dismal science," but not all of them. One voice from the wilderness of hyperoptimism and over-consumption is that of Kenneth Boulding[5] who observes that, "The essential measure of the success of the economy is not production and consumption at all, but the nature, extent, quality, and complexity of the total capital stock, including in this the state of the human bodies and minds included in the system". Until this concept penetrates widely into the councils of government and the conscience of society, there will continue to be a wide gap between the economic aspects of national and industrial policy and the common good, and the intrinsic significance of raw materials will remain inadequately appreciated.

Economic geology, which in its best sense brings all other fields of geology to bear on resource problems, is concerned particularly with questions of how certain elements locally attain geochemical concentrations that greatly exceed their crustal abundance and with how this knowledge can be applied to the discovery of new deposits and the delineation of reserves. Economics and technology play equally important parts with geology itself in determining what deposits and grades it is practicable to exploit. Neither economics, nor technology, nor geology can make an ore deposit where the desired substance is absent or exists in insufficient quantity.

The reality is that economics per se, powerful though it can be when it has material resources to work with, is not all powerful. Indeed, without material resources to start with, no matter how small a fraction of the GNP they may represent, economics is of no consequence at all. The current orthodoxy of economic well-being through obsolescence, over-consumption, and waste will prove, in the long term, to be a cruel and a preposterous illusion.

*Premise III*

Premise III, the postulate of essentially uninterrupted variation from ore to average crustal abundance, is seldom if ever stated in that way, but it is inherent in Premise II. It could almost as well have been treated under Premise II; but it is such an important and interesting idea, whether true or false, that separate consideration is warranted.

If the postulated continuous variation were true for mineral resources in general, volume of "ore" (not metal) produced would be an exponential inverse function of grade n.ined, the handling of lower grades would be compensated for by the availability of larger quantities of elements sought, and reserve estimates would depend only on the accuracy with which average crustal abundances were known. Problems in extractive metallurgy, of course, are not considered in such an outlook.

This delightfully simple picture would supplant all other theories of ore deposits, invalidate the foundations of geochemistry, divest geology of much of its social relevance, and place the fate of the mineral industry squarely in the hands of economists and nuclear engineers.

Unfortunately this postulate is simply untrue in a practical sense for many critical minerals and is only crudely true, leaving out metallurgical problems, for particular metals, like iron and aluminum, whose patterns approach the predicted form.[6] Sharp discontinuities exist in the abundances of mercury, tin, nickel, molybdenum, tungsten, manganese, cobalt, diamond, the precious metals, and even such staples as lead and zinc, for example. But how many prophets of the future are concerned about where all the lead or cadmium will come from for all those electric automobiles that are supposed to solve the smog problem?

Helium is a good example of a critical substance in short supply. Although a gas which has surely at some places diffused in a continuous spectrum of concentrations, particular concentrations of interest as a source of supply appear from published information to vary in a stepwise manner. Here I draw mainly on data summarized by H. W. Lipper.[7] Although an uncommon substance, helium serves a variety of seemingly indispensable uses. A bit less than half of the helium now consumed in the United States is used in pressurizing liquid fueled missiles and space ships. Shielded-arc welding is the next largest use, followed closely by its use in producing controlled atmospheres for growing crystals for transistors, processing fuels for nuclear energy, and cooling vacuum pumps. Only about 5.5 percent of the helium consumed in the United States is now being used as a lifting gas. It plays an increasingly important role, however, as a coolant for nuclear reactors and a seemingly indispensable one in cryogenics and superconductivity. In the latter role, it could control the feasibility of massive long-distance transport of nuclear-generated electricity. High-helium low-oxygen breathing mixtures may well be critical to man's long-range success in attempting to operate at great depths in the exploration and exploitation of the sea. Other uses are in research, purging, leak detection, chromatography, and so on.

Helium thus appears to be a very critical element, as the Department of the Interior has recognized in establishing its helium-conservation program. What are the prospects that there will be enough helium in 2042?

The only presently utilized source of helium is in natural gas, where it occurs at a range of concentrations from as high as 8.2 percent by volume to zero. The range, however, in particular gas fields of significant volume, is apparently not continuous. Dropping below the one field (Pinta Dome) that shows an 8.2 percent concentration, we find a few small isolated fields (Mesa and Hogback, New Mexico) that contain about 5.5 percent helium, and then several large fields (for example, Hugoton and Texas Panhandle) with a range of 0.3 to 1.0 percent helium. Other large natural gas fields contain either no helium or show it only in quantities of less than 5 parts per 10,000. From the latter there is a long jump down to the atmosphere with a concentration of only 1 part per 200,000.

Present annual demand for helium is about 900 million cubic feet, with a projected increase in demand approaching 2 billion cubic feet annually by about 1990. It will be possible to meet such an accelerated demand for a limited time only as a result of Interior's current purchase and storage program, which will augment recovery from natural gas then being produced. As now foreseen, if increases in use do not outrun estimates, conservation and continued recovery of helium from natural gas reserves will meet needs to somewhat beyond the turn of the century. When known and expected discoveries of reserves of natural gas are exhausted, the only potential sources of new supply will be from the atmosphere, as small quantities of $^3$He from nuclear reactor technology, or by synthesis from hydrogen — a process whose practical feasibility and adequacy remain to be established.

Spending even a lot more money to produce more helium from such sources under existing technology just may not be the best or even a very feasible way to deal with the problem. Interior's conservation program should be enlarged and extended, under compulsory legislation if necessary. New sources must be sought. Research into possible substitutions, recovery and reuse, synthesis, and extraction from the atmosphere must be accelerated — now while there is still time. And we must be prepared to curtail, if necessary, activities which waste the limited helium reserves. Natural resources are the priceless heritage of all the people, including those yet to be born; their waste cannot be tolerated.

Problems of the adequacy of reserves obtain for many other substances, especially under the escalating demands of rising populations and expectations, and it is becoming obvious to many geologists that time is running out. Dispersal of metals which could be recycled should be controlled. Unless industry and the public undertake to do this voluntarily, legislation should be generated to define permissible mixes of material and disposal of "junk" metal. Above all the wastefulness of war and preparation for it must be terminated if reasonable options for posterity are to be preserved.

The reality is that a healthy mineral resource industry, and therefore a healthy industrial economy, can be maintained only on a firm base of geologic knowledge, and geochemical and metallurgical understanding of the distribution and limits of metals, mineral fuels, and chemicals in the earth's crust and hydrosphere.

*Premise IV*

The assumption that world populations will soon attain and remain in a state of balance is central to all other premises. Without this the rising expectations of the poor are doomed to failure, and the affluent can remain affluent only by maintaining existing shameful discrepancies. Taking present age structures and life expectancies of world populations into account, it seems certain that, barring other forms of catastrophe, world population will reach 6 or 7 billion by about the turn of the century, regardless of how rapidly family planning is accepted and practiced (Chapter 2).

On the most optimistic assumptions, this is probably close to the maximum number of people the world can support on a reasonably sustained basis, even under strictly regularized conditions, at a general level of living roughly comparable to that now enjoyed in Western Europe. It would, of course, be far better to stabilize at a much smaller world population. In any case, much greater progress than is as yet visible must take place over much larger parts of the world before optimism on the prospects of voluntary global population control at any level can be justified. And even if world population did level off and remain balanced at about 7 billion, it would probably take close to 100 years of intensive, enlightened, peaceful effort to lift all mankind to anywhere near the current level of Western Europe or even much above the level of chronic malnutrition and deprivation.

This is not to say that we must therefore be discouraged and withdraw to ineffectual diversions. Rather it is a challenge to focus with energy and realism on seeking a truly better life for all men living and yet unborn and on keeping the latter to the minimum. On the other hand, an uncritical optimism, just for the sake of that good feeling it creates, is a luxury the world cannot, at this juncture, afford.

A variation of outlook on the population problem which, surprisingly enough, exists among a few nonbiological scholars is that quantity of people is of itself a good thing. The misconception here seems to be that frequency of effective genius will increase, even exponentially, with increasing numbers of people and that there is some risk of breeding out to a merely high level of mediocrity in a stabilized population. The extremes of genius and idiocy, however, appear in about the same frequency at birth from truly heterogeneous gene pools regardless of size. What is unfortunate, among other things, about overly dense concentrations of people is that this leads not only to reduced likihood of the identification of mature genius, but to drastic reductions in the development of potential genius, owing to malnutrition in the weaning years and early youth, accompanied by retardation of both physical and mental growth. If we are determined to turn our problems over to an elite corps of mental prodigies a more sure-fire method is at hand. Nuclear transplant from various adult tissue cells into fertilized ova whose own nuclei have been removed has already produced identical copies of amphibian nucleus-donors and can probably do the same in man.[8] Thus we appear to be on the verge of being able to make as many "xerox" copies as we want or need of any particular genius as long as we can get a piece of his or her nucleated tissue and find eggs and incubators for the genome aliquots to develop in. Female geniuses would be the best because (with a little help) they could copy themselves!

The reality is that without real population control and limitation of demand all else is drastically curtailed, not to say lost. And the prospect that such limitations may take place voluntarily is not bright. The most fundamental freedom should be the right not to be born into a world of want and smothering restriction. I am convinced that we must give up (or have taken away from us) the right to have as many children as we want, or see all other freedoms lost for them. Nature, to be sure, will restore a dynamic balance between our species and the world ecosystem if we fail to do so ourselves — by famine, pestilence, plague, or war. It seems, but is not, unthinkable that this should happen. If it does, of course, mineral resources may then be or appear to be relatively unlimited in relation to demand for them.

*Premise V*

The notion of the "technological fix" expresses a view that is at once full of hope and full of risk. It is a gripping thought to contemplate a world set free by nuclear energy. Imagine soaring cities of aluminum, plastic, and thermopane where all live in peace and plenty at unvarying temperature and without effort, drink distilled water, feed on produce grown from more distilled water in coastal deserts, and flit from heliport to heliport in capsules of uncontaminated air. Imagine having as many children as you want, who, of course, will grow up seven stories above the ground and under such germ-free conditions that they will need to wear breathing masks if they ever do set foot in a park or a forest. Imagine a world in which there is no balance of payments problem, no banks, or money, and such mundane affairs as acquiring a shirt or a wife are handled for us by central computer systems. Imagine, if you like, a world in which the only problem is boredom, all others being solved by the state-maintained system of genius-technologists produced by transfer of nuclei from the skin cells of certified gene donors to the previously fertilized ova of final contestants in the annual ideal-pelvis contest. Imagine the problem of getting out of this disease-free world gracefully at the age of 110 when you just can't stand it any longer!

Of course this extreme view may not appeal to people not conditioned to think in those terms. But the risk of slipping bit by bit into such a smothering condition as one of the better possible outcomes is inherent in any proposition

that encourages or permits people or industries to believe that they can leave their problems to the invention of technological fixes by someone else.

Although the world ecosystem has been in a constant state of flux throughout geologic time, in the short and middle term it is essentially homeostatic. That is to say, it tends to obey Le Chatelier's general principle — when a stress is applied to a system such as to perturb a state of near equilibrium, the system tends to react in such a way as to restore the equilibrium. But large parts of the world ecosystem have probably already undergone or are in danger of undergoing irreversible changes. We cannot continue to plunder and pollute it without serious or even deadly consequences.

Consider what would be needed in terms of conventional mineral raw materials merely to raise the level of all 3.6 billion people now living in the world to the average of the 200 million now living in the United States. In terms of present staple commodities, it can be estimated[9] that this would require a "standing crop" of about 30 billion tons of iron, 500 million tons of lead, 330 million tons of zinc, and 50 million tons of tin. This is about 100 to 200 times the present annual production of these commodities. Annual power demands would, of course, increase proportionately. To support the doubled populations expected by the year 2000 at the same level would require, of course, a doubling of all the above numbers or substitute measures. The iron needed could probably be produced over a long period of time, perhaps even by the year 2000, given a sufficiently large effort. But, once in circulation, merely to replace losses due to oxidation, friction, and dispersal, not counting production of new iron for larger populations, would take around 200,000 tons of new iron every year, or a drastic curtailment of losses below the present rate of 1 percent every 2 or 3 years. And the molybdenum needed to convert the iron to steel could become a serious limiting factor. The quantities of lead, zinc, and tin also called for far exceed all measured, indicated, and inferred world reserves of these metals.

This exercise gives a crude measure of the

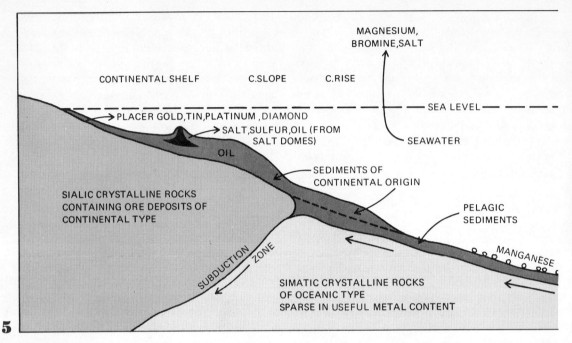

MARINE MINERAL RESOURCES. Sites of possible marine mineral resources. Highly diagrammatic and not to scale.

pressures that mineral resources will be under. It seems likely, to be sure, that substitutions, metallurgical research, and other technological advances will come to our aid, and that not all peoples of the world will find a superfluity of obsolescing gadgets necessary for the good life. But this is balanced by the equal likelihood that world population will not really level off at 6.5 or 7 billion and that there will be growing unrest to share the material resources that might lead at least to an improved standard of living. The situation is also aggravated by the attendant problems of disposal of mine wastes and chemically and thermally polluted waters on a vast scale.

The "technological fix," as its informed proponents well understand, is not a panacea but an anesthetic. It may keep the patient quiet long enough to decide what the best long-range course of treatment may be, or even solve SOME of his problems permanently, but it would be tragic to forget that a broader program of treatment and recuperation is necessary. The flow of science and technology has always been fitful, and population control is a central limiting factor in what

can be achieved. It will require much creative insight, hard work, public enlightenment, and good fortune to bring about the advances in discovery and analysis, recovery and fabrication, wise use and conservation of materials, management and recovery of wastes, and substitution and synthesis that will be needed to keep the affluent comfortable and bring the deprived to tolerable levels. It will probably also take some revision of criteria for self-esteem, achievement, and pleasure if the gap between affluent and deprived is to be narrowed and demand for raw materials kept within bounds that will permit man to enjoy a future as long as his past, and under conditions that would be widely accepted as agreeable.

The reality is that the promise of the "technological fix" is a meretricious premise, full of glittering appeal but devoid of heart and comprehension of the environmental and social problems. Technology and "hard" science we must have, in sustained and increasing quality, and in quantities relevant to the needs of man — material, intellectual, and spiritual. But in dealing with the problems of resources in relation to man, let us not lose sight of the fact that this is the province of the environmental and social sciences. A vigorous and perceptive technology will

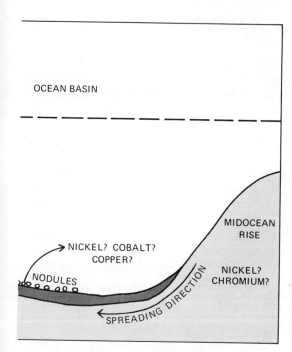

OCEAN BASIN

MIDOCEAN RISE

NICKEL? COBALT? COPPER?

NICKEL? CHROMIUM?

NODULES

SPREADING DIRECTION

3. Sediments other than placers, and sedimentary rocks that overlie crystalline rocks (a) on the continental shelves and slopes (about 15 percent of the total sea floor), and (b) beyond the continental margins (about 85 percent of the total sea floor; the truly oceanic realm).

4. Crystalline rock exposed at the sea floor or lying beneath sediments (a) on the continental margins, and (b) beyond the continental margins.

The sea contains about 1.3 billion cubic kilometers of SEAWATER — an amount so large that quantities of dissolved substances are large even where their concentrations are small. Yet recovery of such substances accounts for little more than 2 percent of current production of marine minerals and chemicals. Only magnesium, bromine, and common salt are now being extracted in substantial quantities, and, for them, the seas do contain reserves that can be considered to be "inexhaustible" under any foreseeable pressures.

At the other extreme of accessibility is the 10 billion metric tons of gold in seawater — about 0.0013 troy ounce of gold in every million liters of water. Although capable people and corporations have worked intensively at the problem, the amount of gold so far reported to have been extracted from seawater is trivial.

Sixty-four of the 90 naturally occurring elements now known on earth have been detected in seawater. Of these only 15 occur in quantities of more than 1.8 kilograms per million liters. Only 9, all of them among the first 15 in abundance, represent 1965 values of more than $2.50 per million liters (chlorine, sodium, magnesium, sulfur, calcium, potassium, bromine, lithium, and rubidium). These 9 (or their salts), plus boron, fluorine, and iodine, offer the best promise for direct recovery from seawater through ion exchange, biological concentration, or more novel processes.

Omitting these 12, and very few others, the metal elements we are likely to have greatest need to extract from seawater offer little promise for direct recovery

PLACER DEPOSITS now offshore were formed by gravitational segregation in and beneath former beach and stream deposits when the sea

be an essential handmaiden in the process, but it is a risky business to put the potential despoilers of the environment in charge of it.

*Premise VI*

What, finally, about marine mineral resources, often proposed as a veritable cornucopia, waiting only to be harvested?[10] This notion is so widely accepted that it is worth considering in some detail what we actually know about prospective mineral resources from the sea.

In 1964, mineral production from the sea represented about 10 percent of the total known value of the specific products recovered and about 5 percent of the entire world mineral output. Sizable quantities of oil and gas, sulfur, magnesium, bromine, salt, oyster shells, tin, and sand and gravel are currently being produced from the sea.[6,11,12] What are the future prospects for these as well as for other substances not now being recovered in quantity?

Mineral and chemical resources from the sea may be found among the following (see also Figure 5):

1. Seawater.

2. Placer deposits within or beneath now-submerged beach or stream deposits.

stood lower or the land higher. The outer limit at which such deposits can be expected is about 100 to 130 meters, the approximate position of the beach when Pleistocene glaciation was at its peak.

Diamonds, gold, and tin are being recovered from submarine placers (the diamonds, up to 1967 at least, at a cost in excess of their value). Approximate 1964 global values, omitting cost of recovery, were as follows: diamonds, $4 million; tin, about $21 million; gold, unknown.

Submarine placers of tough heavy metals such as gold, tin, and platinum offer the best prospects for the practicable recovery of mineral resources from the sea other than magnesium (from seawater) and oil and gas (from continental shelf sediments).

Continental-shelf SEDIMENTS and salt-dome structures that penetrate them, account for nearly 98 percent of the mineral and chemical wealth currently produced from within and beneath the sea — by far the greater part of this being oil and gas. About 17 percent of the world's petroleum and natural gas now comes from offshore, nearly half the fields and about one-fourth the production being adjacent to the United States.

From data available in 1965, it has been estimated that about 700 to 1000 billion barrels of liquid fuels are potentially recoverable from offshore areas worldwide, which is about equal to or somewhat more than that remaining to be discovered and produced on land.

The oil-producing salt domes in the Gulf of Mexico also yield sulfur. More than 5 percent of the world's sulfur now comes from such sources. Current reserves, however, will have been depleted by about 1990, and new discoveries or other sources will have to take up the slack.

Sediments and sedimentary rocks beyond the continental shelves and slopes are strikingly different from those that mantle and comprise the continental margins. Here is where we find the curious and geologically interesting manganese nodules and crusts. Despite the extravagant claims that have been made, however, their prospects for future mineral production remain to be established.

Finding and exploiting mineralized CRYSTALLINE ROCKS on the sea floor — even on the continental shelves — involves the same problems as on land, and many more. Although it is clear from geological data that the substructure of the shelf and slope is of a continental rather than an oceanic type, and that mineral deposits comparable to those found on the adjacent land are to be expected, problems peculiar to the region hamper their discovery and exploitation. Nevertheless, it seems statistically certain that ore deposits exist in crystalline rocks somewhere on or beneath the continental shelves. How many of them will eventually be discovered and worked is another question.

Beyond the continental margins the difficulties increase. The crystalline rocks of the ocean basins appear to be mainly basalts, probably limited both in the variety of included minerals and in the degree of enrichment to be found. Nickel, chromium, copper, and platinum may be present, but the first submarine ore of any is yet to be found. Iron and magnesium are probably the most abundant metal elements in the oceanic rocks, but such ores, if any, could not compete with sources from dry land and from seawater.

Mineral and chemical resources of the sea that will be significant for man over the next half century are those that can be extracted from seawater or recovered from the seabed of the continental shelf (and perhaps the oceanic rises). About 5 percent of the world's known production of geological wealth came from the shelves and seawater in 1964 and the trend is upwards. Oil and gas are by far the most important products, although their duration at expected rates of consumption will be limited. Seawater can supply ample magnesium and bromine, as well as common salt and some other substances. It will, however, supply few important metal elements other than magnesium, sodium, potassium, iodine, and perhaps strontium and boron. Oyster shells (used in the recovery of magnesium and for road metal, and by no means an inexhaustible resource) are being taken from the shallower parts of the shelves in relatively large quantities. The use of nearshore submarine sand and gravel, not yet large, will probably increase as coastal cities expand over and use up other local sources.

The sediments of the continental shelves and the crystalline rocks beneath them can be expected to produce mineral commodities similar to those of the immediately adjacent land. One way of guessing the magnitude of such resources is to reflect the hundred-fathom depthline across the shoreline. It then defines an onshore area equivalent to the continental shelf and having roughly similar geology. For the equivalent onshore area in the United States (in 1966 dollars), the total cumulative value of minerals extracted since the beginning of the U.S. mineral industry, is about $160 billion, exclusive of oil and gas, or $240 billion with oil and gas. Because of geological differences from the land, and other obstacles that complicate discovery and recovery in the subsea environment, however, this figure is doubtless considerably larger than what we can expect from the continental shelves.

The ocean basins beyond the continental margin are not promising places to seek mineral resources.

A "mineral cornucopia" beneath the sea exists only in hyperbole. What is actually won from it will be the result of persistent imaginative research, inspired invention, bold and skillful experiment, and intelligent application and management — and such resources as are found will come mostly from the continental shelves, slopes, and rises. Whether they will be large or small remains to be seen. It is a fair guess that they will be substantial; but if present concepts of earth structure and of seafloor composition and history are correct, minerals from the seabed are not likely to compare with those yet to be recovered from the emerged lands. As for seawater itself, despite its volume and the quantities of dissolved salts it contains, it can supply few of the substances considered essential to modern industry.

## The Nub of the Matter

The realities of mineral distribution, in a nutshell, are that it is neither inconsiderable nor limitless, and that we just don't know yet, in the detail required for considered weighting of comprehensive long-range alternatives, where or how the critical lithophilic elements are concentrated. Stratigraphically controlled substances such as the fossil fuels, and, to a degree, iron and alumina, we can comprehend and estimate within reasonable limits. Reserves, grades, locations, and recoverability of many critical metals, on the other hand, are affected by a much larger number of variables. We in North America began to develop our rich natural endowment of mineral resources at an accelerated pace before the rest of the world. Thus it stands to reason that, to the extent we are unable to meet needs by imports, we will feel the pinch sooner than countries like the USSR with a larger component of virgin mineral lands.

In some instances nuclear energy or other technological fixes may buy time to seek better solutions or will even solve a problem permanently. But sooner or later man must come to terms with his environment and its limitations. The sooner the better. The year 2042, by which time even current rates of consumption will have exhausted presently known recoverable reserves of perhaps half the world's now useful metals, is only as far from the present as the invention of the airplane and the discovery of radioactivity. In the absence of real population control or catastrophe there could be 15 billion people on earth by then! Much that is difficult to anticipate can happen in the meanwhile, to be sure, and to center faith in a profit-motivated technology and refuse to look beyond a brief "foreseeable future" is a choice widely made. Against this we must weigh the consequences of error or thoughtless inaction and the prospects of identifying constructive alternatives for deliberate courses of long-term action, or inaction, that will affect favorably the long-range future. It is well to remember that to do nothing is equally to make a choice.

## References

1. **Flawn, P.** 1966. *Mineral Resources.* Rand McNally, Chicago, Illinois, 406 pp.

2. **Clark, C.** 1967, *Population Growth and Land Use.* Macmillan, New York, 406 pp.

3. **Weinberg, A., and Young, G.** 1966. The nuclear energy revolution. *Proc. Natl. Acad. Sci. (U.S.), 57,* 1-15.

4. **Bell, D.** 1967. Notes on the post-industrialist society II. *The Public Interest,* No. 7, pp. 102-118.

5. **Boulding, K.E.** 1966. The economics of the coming spaceship earth. In *Environmental Quality in a Growing Economy* (H. Jarrett, ed.), Resources for the Future, Johns Hopkins Press, Baltimore, Maryland, 146 pp.

6. **National Academy of Sciences,** Committee on Resources and Man 1969. *Resources and Man.* W.H. Freeman, San Francisco, California, 259 pp.

7. **Lipper, H.W.** 1965. Helium: In *Mineral Facts and Problems,* pp. 429-440. U.S. Bureau of Mines, Bull. 630, 118 pp; **Moore, B.J.** 1969. Helium: Preprint from 1968 *Bureau of Mines Minerals Yearbook,* 4 pp.

8. **Lederberg, J.** 1966. Experimental genetics and human evolution. *Bull. Atomic Scientists, 22:* 1-11.

9. **Brown, H., and others** 1957. *The Next Hundred Years.* Viking Press, New York, 193 pp.; 1967. *The Next Ninety Years.* California Inst. of Technology Press, Pasadena, California, 186 pp.

10. **Mero, J.L.** 1965. *The Mineral Resources of the Sea.* Elsevier, New York, 312 pp.

11. **Emery, K.O.** 1966. Geological methods for locating mineral deposits on the ocean floor. *Marine Technol. Soc., Trans. 2d Marine Technol. Soc. Conf.,* pp. 24-43.

12. **Bascom, W.** 1967. Mining the ocean depths: *Geosci. News, 1:* 10-11, 26-28.

13. This discussion is adapted, with permission of the editors and publishers, from a 1968 paper by the author: Realities of mineral distribution *The Texas Quarterly,* Summer 1968, pp. 103-126.

## Further Reading

**Brown, H.** 1954. *The Challenge of Man's Future.* Viking Press, New York, 290 pp.

**Clawson, M.,** ed. 1964. *Natural Resources and International Development.* Johns Hopkins Press, Baltimore, Maryland, 475 pp.

**Cloud, P.** 1969. Our disappearing earth resources. *Science Year,* pp. 166-181.

**Landsberg, H. H.** 1964. *Natural Resources of U.S. Growth.* Johns Hopkins Press, Baltimore, Maryland, 256 pp.

**Lovering, T. S.** 1943. *Minerals in World Affairs.* Prentice-Hall, Englewood Cliffs, New Jersey, 394 pp.

**Park, C.** 1968. *Affluence in Jeopardy.* Freeman, Cooper & Co., San Francisco, California, 368 pp.

**Skinner, B. J.** 1969. *Earth Resources.* Prentice-Hall, Englewood Cliffs, New Jersey, 150 pp.

**U.S. Bureau of Mines.** 1965. Mineral facts and problems. *Bureau of Mines, Bull. 630,* 1118 pp.

# 5 Energy Resources

M. King Hubbert

## Energy and Power

Inasmuch as this chapter deals with energy and power, both of which are precisely defined physical quantities, it will not be possible to discuss these quantities intelligibly unless their meaning and the units in which they are measured are understood.

In physics, the ENERGY of a system is measured in terms of its capacity to perform WORK. Work, in turn, is measured by the product of an applied force and the distance the object acted upon by the force is moved. Hence,

Work = force x distance

---

M. KING HUBBERT is a research geophysicist with the U.S. Geological Survey in Washington. In 1964, after 20 years of research in petroleum exploration and production for Shell Oil and Shell Development Companies, he accepted dual appointments, one with the Geological Survey, and a second as Professor of Geology and Geophysics at Stanford University, devoting part time to each. Prior to that, he taught geology and geophysics for 10 years at Columbia University, and did geophysical work for the Amerada Petroleum Corporation and for the Illinois State and U.S. Geological Surveys. His scientific education, with a major jointly in geology and physics and a minor in mathematics, was received during 1924 to 1930 from the University of Chicago, where he received both his undergraduate degree and his doctorate. His subsequent researches have been principally in mineral exploration, mechanics of geologic structures, physics of underground fluids, and on the consequences of human exploitation of the earth's mineral and energy resources.

There are as many units of work as there are units of force and of distance, but here, for brevity, we shall limit ourselves to the most nearly universal system of measurement, the metric system. In this system, the unit of length is the meter, the unit of time, the mean solar second (the second or ordinary clock time), and the unit of mass, the kilogram. The unit of force is the newton, which is defined as that force which, when applied to a mass of 1 kilogram free to move without friction, will cause it to accelerate its velocity at a rate of 1 meter per second for each second the force is applied. In free fall, the force of gravity acting upon a 1-kilogram mass causes it to accelerate at a rate of approximately 9.8 (m/sec)/sec. The force must therefore be approximately 9.8 newtons. This is expressed by saying that a 1-kilogram mass weighs 9.8 newtons. A mass that weighs 1 newton would accordingly be

1 kilogram/9.8 = 0.102 kg = 102 grams

The unit of work in the metric system is the joule, defined by

1 joule = 1 newton x 1 meter

Hence, approximately, 1 joule is the amount of work required to lift a mass of 0.102 kilogram a height of 1 meter. The word "approximately" is emphasized because the force of gravity on a 1-kilogram mass is not exactly 9.8 newtons nor is it constant. In fact, this force varies somewhat both with elevation above sea level and with latitude. The magnitude of the joule, however, is defined independently of gravity.

Bodies may possess two kinds of mechanical energy, POTENTIAL and KINETIC. Potential energy is an energy of position, or of configuration.

Thus, if a mass of 1 kilogram rests on a shelf 1 meter above the floor, it is said to possess 9.8 joules of potential energy with respect to floor level, because this is the amount of work that it could perform in being lowered to the floor. A moving body possesses kinetic energy with respect to a state of rest. This is the amount of work required to change the body from a state of rest to that of motion, and it is also the amount of work that could be done by the body in having its motion arrested.

A different manifestation of energy is that of thermal energy, or HEAT. When work is done on a mechanical system having friction, it is a common observation that heat is produced. Careful measurements have shown that when a given amount of work is performed on such a system, the same amount of heat is produced. This makes it possible to measure heat in units of work. The heat produced by the expenditure of 1 joule of mechanical work is defined to be 1 thermal joule.

In a similar manner, the work or heat involved in all kinds of physical processes — mechanical, thermal, electrical, or chemical — is measurable in joules. In fact, it has been found that in all such systems, when energy in a given form disappears, an equivalent amount of energy in some other form appears, and the total amount of energy remains constant. This is known as the principle of conservation of energy, or the First Law of Thermodynamics.

A very important extension of this principle is due to Albert Einstein, who, in a short paper published in 1905, deduced theoretically that there must also be an equivalence between the energy of a body and its mass. Einstein showed that when a body of mass $m$ loses an amount of energy $\Delta E$, the mass is also diminished by an amount $\Delta m$, given by

$$\Delta m = \Delta E/c^2$$

where $c$ (equal to $3 \times 10^8$ meters per second) is the velocity of light.

The validity of this equation has subsequently been amply confirmed experimentally. If both sides are divided by the mass $m$, the equation can also be written in the form

$$\frac{\Delta m}{m} = \frac{1}{c^2} \cdot \frac{\Delta E}{m}$$

For ordinary chemical reactions, such as combustion, the ratio of the energy $\Delta E$ generated per unit of mass $m$ is the order of $10^7$ joules per kilogram. When this is multiplied by $1/c^2$, the value of $\Delta m/m$ is found to be about $10^{-10}$. Hence the mass reduction is only about 1 part in 10 billion, which is negligible for chemical purposes. For nuclear phenomena, on the other hand, the ratio of the energy released per unit of mass, $\Delta E/m$, is very much larger — on the order of $10^{13}$ joules per kilogram, or about a million times larger than the energy per unit mass released by chemical reactions. In this case, the ratio of the mass reduction to the original mass, $\Delta m/m$, is about $10^{-4}$, or 1 part in 10,000. Such a mass reduction accompanying the release of energy is of fundamental importance when dealing with nuclear phenomena.

There are many processes involving work or energy to which no definite quantity of energy can be assigned. A waterfall is such a process. This is capable of doing a given amount of work per unit of time, but the total amount of work that can be done increases without limit as time increases. For such a process, we require a different measure, namely the rate at which work is done, or POWER. Accordingly, we define the power of such a system by

Power = work/time

When the work is measured in joules and the time in seconds, the power is expressed in joules per second, or watts. For larger units of power, we have the kilowatt (1000 watts) and the megawatt (1 million, or $10^6$ watts).

Power and time can also be used to express quantities of energy. Since, by definition, 1 watt is equal to 1 joule/second, then it follows that

1 joule = 1 watt-second

Other similar units of energy are the kilowatt-hour and the megawatt-day. The kilowatt-hour is the familiar unit for which one pays his monthly electric bill. This represents 1000 watts for 3600 seconds, or 3,600,000 joules. A megawatt-day represents 1 million watts for 86,400 seconds, or $8.64 \times 10^{10}$ joules.

*Degradation of Energy.*

While energy can be transformed from one form to another without diminution of its amount, energy changes, in general, have a uni-directional and irreversible character. For example, when an object has a higher temperature than its surroundings, heat spontaneously flows from the warmer body to the cooler surroundings. The reverse, however, never occurs, and the system cannot be restored to its original state except by some external means. In mechanical systems, such as a free-swinging pendulum, the mechanical motion is retarded by friction and the system eventually comes to rest. The potential and kinetic energy possessed initially are completely converted by friction into heat. The reverse process, however, never occurs.

Yet, as the steam engine demonstrates, heat can be converted into work. This is only possible provided a difference of temperature exists. In the case of the steam engine, we have a higher temperature heat reservoir, the furnace, and a lower temperature reservoir, a supply of cooling water. Heat at high temperature is absorbed by the boiler and steam is produced at high pressure. This, upon expansion, drives an engine which does mechanical or electrical work. Finally, the expanded steam is passed through the condenser, from which the heat is discharged to a stream of cooling water, which is increased somewhat in temperature. The steam is condensed to a liquid which is then pumped back into the boiler, and the cycle is repeated.

During this cycle, a quantity of heat $Q_1$ is taken from the furnace; a fraction of this is converted into work $W$, and the remaining heat $Q_2$ is discharged to the cooling water through the condenser. From the principle of the conservation of energy, the sum of the work $W$ plus the heat $Q_2$ discharged by the condenser must equal the amount of high-temperature heat $Q_1$ taken from the furnace. Hence,

$$W + Q_2 = Q_1$$

or

$$W = Q_1 - Q_2$$

The ratio

$$W/Q_1 = (Q_1 - Q_2)/Q_1$$

which expresses the fraction of the thermal energy taken from the furnace that is converted into work, is known as the THERMAL EFFICIENCY of the engine. By a somewhat more elaborate analysis than we can develop here, it can be shown that the maximum possible efficiency of a steam engine is given by

$$(W/Q_1)_{max} = (T_1 - T_2)/T_1$$

where $T_1$ is the temperature of the steam and $T_2$ that of the condenser, both given in degrees on the absolute temperature scale (degrees Celsius plus 273.15°).

From this it is seen that the fraction of the high-temperature heat that can be converted into work is proportional to the difference between the two temperatures. If the difference is zero, no work at all can be obtained. For this reason, in designing steam-electric power plants, an effort is made to obtain as high a steam temperature as possible. For steam-electric power plants in the United States in 1970, the average thermal efficiency is about 0.33 or 33 percent. The largest and most modern plants have somewhat higher efficiencies — up to as high as 38 percent. Present nuclear-electric plants are somewhat less efficient than those deriving their energy from fossil fuels.

In steam-electric power plants, some energy in the case of fuel-fired plants is discharged through the smokestack. Of the thermal energy absorbed by the boiler, about one-third is converted into electrical energy and the remaining two-thirds is discharged through the condenser to the environment at low temperature. The electrical energy, through lighting, direct heating, or frictional dissipation, is also converted into waste heat. Hence, the end product of the entire operation is the conversion of the initial chemical or nuclear energy of the fuel into waste heat at the mean temperature of the environment.

*Flux of Energy*

The flux of energy in the earth's surface environment (Figure 1) involves the maintenance of a near-equilibrium state between the rate at which energy enters this space and the rate at which it leaves. Were this not so, the average temperature over a long period of time would either be steadily increasing or decreasing. It is true that during the past history of the earth there have been climatic changes between tropical and glacial conditions. Even so, these variations, which have occurred very slowly, represent a mean tem-

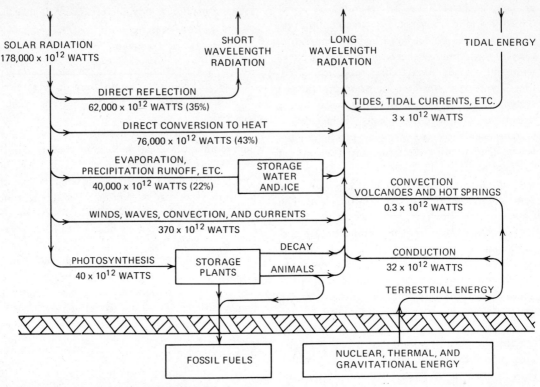

**ENERGY FLOW SHEET FOR THE EARTH.** Source: M. K. Hubbert, 1962, *Energy Resources,*[19] Fig. 1. By permission of National Academy of Sciences.

perature change of only a few degrees Celsius (formerly known as "Centigrade") (Chapter 15).

The sources of the energy entering the earth's surface environment are principally the following:

1. Energy from solar radiation.
2. Tidal energy from the combined potential and kinetic energy of the earth-moon-sun system.
3. Energy from inside the earth, including heat conduction and the convection of energy by the material transport of hot springs, volcanoes, and the uplifting of mountains.

The outflux of energy from the earth is accomplished almost entirely by two processes: (1) the direct reflection, known as the ALBEDO, of incident short-wavelength solar radiation into outer space, and (2) radiation into outer space of long-wavelength thermal radiation characteristic of the surface temperature of the earth.

By a very wide margin, the principal source of energy influx to the earth is the SOLAR RADIA-

TION intercepted by the earth. According to the most recent determinations, the average intensity of solar radiation in space just outside the earth's atmosphere is 2.00 calories per minute per square centimeter of surface area normal to the radiation. This is also equal to 1395 watts/m$^2$, which is about the rate of heat generation in a domestic electric kitchen oven. The total amount of solar radiation intercepted by the earth's diametral plane, having an area of $1.275 \times 10^{14}$ m$^2$, is therefore $1.78 \times 10^{17}$ watts.

In order to compare more readily the magnitude of the solar energy influx with that from other sources, it will be convenient to employ the quantity $10^{12}$ watts as a unit of measurement. Then, in terms of this unit, the rate of solar energy influx amounts to $178,000 \times 10^{12}$ watts. Of this, about 35 percent, or $62,000 \times 10^{12}$ watts, is directly reflected into outer space as short-wavelength radiation. About 43 percent, or $76,000 \times 10^{12}$ watts, is absorbed directly as heat. About 22 percent, or $40,000 \times 10^{12}$ watts, is involved in the evaporation, precipitation, and surface runoff of water in the hydrologic cycle. A small fraction of 1 percent, $370 \times 10^{12}$ watts, is converted into the mechanical energy of winds, waves, and ocean currents, and the convection of water vapor. Finally, an even smaller but very important fraction of the solar energy influx, about $40 \times 10^{12}$ watts, is absorbed and stored as chemical energy in the process of photosynthesis.

The basic reaction of photosynthesis, while more complex in detail, is essentially the following:

$CO_2 + H_2O + 4.69 \times 10^5$ joules of solar energy
$$\rightarrow [CH_2O] + O_2$$

where the expression $[CH_2O]$ represents the unit building block of a series of carbohydrates.

In this equation, the separate chemical terms represent the gram-molecular weights of the respective substances. In particular, during the reaction, 1 atomic weight of carbon (12 grams) from the carbon dioxide of the atmosphere is converted into the FIXED CARBON of a carbohydrate molecule. Accompanying the process, $4.69 \times 10^5$ joules of radiant energy are converted into chemical energy and stored, and 1 gram-molecular weight (32 grams) of free oxygen is released to the atmosphere. This represents a storage of $3.91 \times 10^4$ joules of chemical energy for each gram of carbon.

According to recent estimates, the total rates of carbon fixation by photosynthesis are $20 \times 10^9$ metric tons per year by land plants and $13 \times 10^9$ for the oceans. This gives a total rate of carbon fixation for the whole earth of $33 \times 10^9$ metric tons, or $3.3 \times 10^{16}$ grams, per year. This is at a rate of approximately $10^9$ grams per second. Then, with an energy storage of $3.91 \times 10^4$ joules per gram, the rate of energy storage by photosynthesis for the whole earth amounts to approximately $40 \times 10^{12}$ joules per second, or to $40 \times 10^{12}$ watts.

Although the energy stored by photosynthesis represents only 2 ten-thousandths ($2 \times 10^{-4}$) of the total influx of solar energy upon the earth, through the food chain,

Plants $\rightarrow$ herbivores $\rightarrow$ carnivores, and so on

it constitutes the primary energy source for the biological requirements of the entire plant and animal kingdoms (Chapter 1).

By the reverse oxidation reaction, photosynthesized organic compounds are converted back to their initial inorganic states of $CO_2$ and $H_2O$, and the energy is released as heat. Under undisturbed ecological conditions, these two processes proceed in opposite directions at about the same rates, and the total energy stored in the biomass remains approximately constant. However, during the last 700 million years of geologic time, minute fractions of the remains of the contemporary organisms have been deposited in oxygen-free environments, such as swamps or deep basins of stagnant water, under conditions of incomplete decay. These have subsequently been buried under accumulations of sedimentary muds and sands, and have become the sources of the world's present supply of fossil fuels: peat, lignite, and coal, and the various members of the petroleum family.

The second influx of energy from outside the earth is that of TIDAL ENERGY derived from combined kinetic energies of the earth and moon and from mutual potential energies of the earth-moon-sun system. The gravitational attractions between the earth and the moon, and the sun and the earth, cause a twice-daily distortion of the solid earth, and a rise and fall of oceanic tides involving the filling and emptying of coastal basins, and hence the dissipation of energy into heat by friction. The rate of energy dissipation by the tides is about $3 \times 10^{12}$ watts.[1]

Energy influx into the earth's surface environment from inside the earth — GEOTHERMAL ENERGY[2] — results from two different processes, heat conduction and convection.

When temperature measurements are made in wells, it is found that the temperature increases with depth. Many oil wells have been drilled to depths of 2 to 3 miles (3 to 5 kilometers) or more, and at these depths, temperatures in excess of that of boiling water under surface conditions are frequently encountered. The rate at which the temperature increases with depth varies somewhat widely, but averages about 1 C° per 30 meters of depth. The rate of heat flow to the surface has been found to have an average value of approximately $6.3 \times 10^{-6}$ (6.3

millionths) watts/cm$^2$. Then, since the area of the earth is 510 x 10$^6$ km$^2$, or 5.10 x 10$^{18}$ cm$^2$, the total rate of heat conduction is 32 x 10$^{12}$ watts.

The heat transported to the earth's surface by convection is due principally to volcanoes and hot springs. According to recent estimates, this amounts only to about 1 percent of that by conduction, or to about 0.3 x 10$^{12}$ watts.

The TOTAL ENERGY INFLUX into the earth's surface environment is then approximately as follows:

| | |
|---|---|
| Solar power | 178,000 x 10$^{12}$ watts |
| Geothermal power | 32 x 10$^{12}$ watts |
| Tidal power | 3 x 10$^{12}$ watts |

From this it will be seen that the input of power from solar radiation exceeds that from all other sources by a factor of about 5000. Hence, in terms of the earth's total energy budget, all other sources may be regarded as negligible.

In consequence of the conservation of energy, the energy entering the earth's surface environment must either be captured and retained in some stored form, or else it must leave the earth. Of the 178 x 10$^{15}$ watts of solar power influx, about 35 percent, or 62 x 10$^{15}$ watts, are directly reflected into outer space. Of the remaining 116 x 10$^{15}$ watts, all but a minute fraction is converted directly or indirectly into thermal energy at the temperature of the earth's surface. Were this to remain stored as thermal energy, the mean surface temperature of the earth would steadily increase. In fact, it would require only about 150 years at this rate of storage for the oceans to reach boiling temperature.

However, during the four centuries since the invention of thermometers, there have been insignificant changes in the earth's surface temperature when averaged over periods of a few years. Also, from geological evidence, the earth's mean temperature during the last 600 million years has not fluctuated outside the narrow range required for survival of the biological populations. Therefore, the rate of energy storage must be almost infinitesimal compared with the rate of influx. Consequently, the

average rate of energy flux away from the earth must be almost exactly equal to the rate of influx. This outward flux occurs as long-wavelength radiation whereby the low-temperature heat of the earth's surface is reradiated into outer space. Evidence for this can be seen on winter nights. Because water vapor blocks this radiation, white frosts rarely occur on cloudy nights. On clear nights, however, when the surface heat is radiated away, the temperature drops and white frosts are common.

## Rates of Growth of Energy Consumption

We now direct our attention to the progressive conquest of energy by the human species. With the domestication of animals and plants, the rate of energy conquest by man began an acceleration about 10,000 years ago. This began with the development of agriculture in the Nile, the Tigris and Euphrates, and the Indus valleys and soon led to the city-states of ancient civilizations. The energy conquest was extended to the smelting of metals, and the use of power from wind and water. During all this period, the rates of change were so slow that the growth of the human population was able to keep pace. Consequently, the energy consumption per capita remained only slightly higher than that of the food required.

Freedom from this constraint did not arise until a much larger source of energy became available. This occurred about the twelfth century when the inhabitants of northeast England discovered that certain black rocks found along the seashore, and thereafter known as "sea coals," would burn. Thus began the systematic exploitation of the earth's supply of fossil fuels. In 1857 in Rumania, and 2 years later in the United States, production was begun of the second major fossil fuel, petroleum. The corresponding ecological disturbance accompanying these developments is best illustrated by the resultant increase in the human population (Chapter 2).

Despite the fact that coal had been mined continuously with a steadily increasing rate of production for the preceding six centuries or more, the actual production rates, by present standards, remained small until well into the nineteenth century. By 1860 the annual rate of production of coal and lignite had reached only 140 million metric tons per year, but by 1965 it had increased to 2800. Statistics earlier than 1860 are scanty, but it is known that continuous coal mining began about the twelfth century, and it has been estimated that world production had reached about 2.4 million tons per year by 1660. Hence, during the two centuries between 1660 and 1860 the production rate increased about 58-fold. This corresponds to an average growth rate of 1.225 percent per year, or to an average doubling period of 34 years.

The rate of growth of the world production of coal and lignite since 1860 falls into three distinct episodes: (1) that from 1860 to the beginning of World War I, (2) that from the beginning of World War I to the end of World War II, and (3) that since the end of World War II. The first of these periods was characterized by a steady rate of growth of about 4.4 percent per year, with a doubling period of 16 years. The growth during the second period was oscillatory and very much slower, averaging only about 0.75 percent per year, with a doubling period of about 93 years. Finally, during the third period, a more rapid growth rate of about 3.5 percent per year has resumed, with the doubling period reduced to 20 years.

WORLD PRODUCTION OF ENERGY FROM COAL AND LIGNITE PLUS CRUDE OIL. Source: M. K. Hubbert, 1969, *Resources and Man,*[18] Fig. 8.3. By permission of National Academy of Sciences.

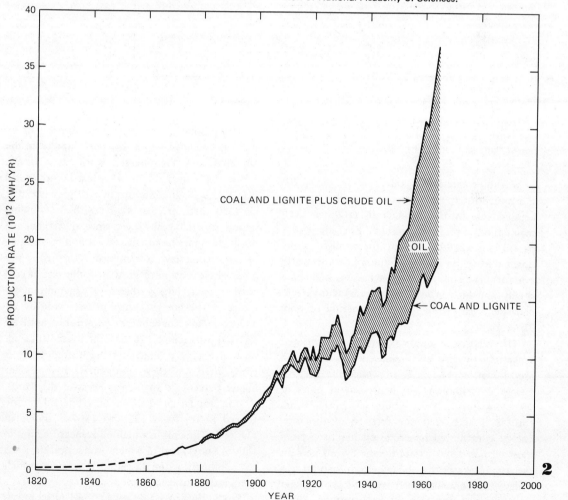

**2**

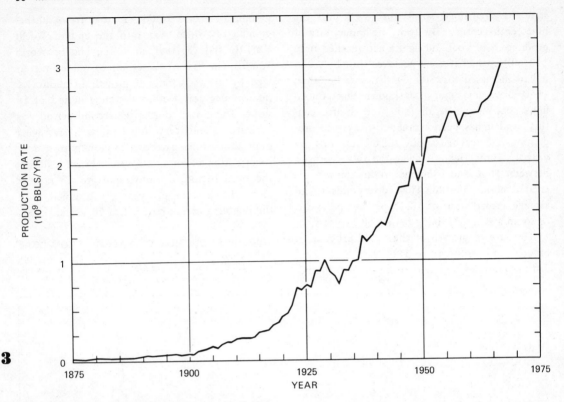

**3**

U. S. CRUDE-OIL PRODUCTION. Source: M. K. Hubbert, 1969, *Resources and Man,*[18] Fig. 8.5. By permission of National Academy of Sciences.

World production of oil began in 1857, but the rate prior to 1880 was very small. A steady acceleration in the production rate has been maintained until the present. For the entire period since 1890, except for a slight slowdown during the decade of the 1930s the world rate ˜of crude-oil production has maintained a steady and high growth rate averaging 6.94 percent per year, with a doubling period of only 10 years.

The relative amounts of energy contributed separately by coal and lignite and by crude oil are shown in Figure 2, in which the thermal energy contributions are expressed in units of $10^{12}$ kwh/yr (kilowatt-hours per year). From this, it is seen that the fraction of the total energy contributed by crude oil has risen from near zero in 1890 to approximately 50 percent by 1965. Were the energy from natural gas added, the contribution of oil and gas together would amount to about 60 percent by 1965, and somewhat more by 1970.

The production rates of major sources of industrial energy have grown more rapidly in the United States than in the world as a whole. From 1840 until about 1910, just before World War I, the production rate of coal grew steadily at 6.58 percent per year, with a doubling period of 10.5 years. Ever since that time, the production rate has oscillated about a mean value of approximately 500 million short tons per year. The cessation of growth in the rate of coal production is largely due to a concomitant increase in the energy contributions made by oil and gas. These have increased steadily until by 1970 approximately 70 percent of the total industrial energy produced in the United States is contributed by these two fuels, a somewhat higher percentage than in the rest of the world.

The annual production of crude oil in the United States from 1875 to 1967 is shown in Figure 3. The unit in which oil is measured in the United States, and in which production statistics are published, is the 42-gallon U.S. barrel, which is equivalent to 0.1590 m³.

Production of crude oil in the United States began in 1859 at Titusville in western Pennsylvania. From 1875 to 1929, the production rate increased steadily at an average growth rate of 8.27 percent per year, with the production rate doubling every 8.4 years. Subsequently, the growth rate has progressively decreased until, by 1970, it has become approximately zero, as the production rate is approaching its climax at about 3.4 billion barrels per year.

The production statistics for natural gas are not quite comparable to those for crude oil since during the first half century of the petroleum industry most of the natural gas was burned because of lack of storage facilities and transportation pipelines. The production statistics until recently have accordingly been limited to "marketed gas." In fact, it has not been until after World War II that pipelines of large diameter appropriate for long-distance transmission of natural gas from the principal areas of production in the Mid-Continent and Gulf Coast areas

to the consumer areas of the north and northeast have become available. Consequently the reserves of natural gas in terms of the rate of production have remained larger than those for crude oil. As a result, the growth in the rate of gas production has not yet slowed down as markedly as that for crude oil. In fact, from 1905 to 1968 the growth rate has remained remarkably steady, averaging 6.57 percent per year, and doubling every 10.5 years. However, during the period 1965 to 1969, this growth rate slowed down to about 6.1 percent per year.

The rate of production of industrial energy from all sources — coal, oil, natural gas, water power, and nuclear power plants — from 1850 to 1965 is shown in Figure 4. These data are plotted on a semilogarithmic scale, that is, the

U. S. PRODUCTION OF INDUSTRIAL ENERGY. Semi-logarithmic scale.

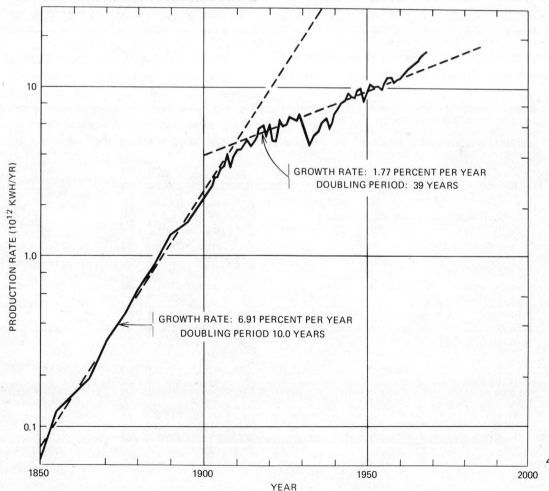

**4**

logarithm of the rate of production is plotted against time on an arithmetic scale. One of the fundamental properties of this representation is that all quantities that are increasing exponentially with time will plot as straight-line segments during the periods of such increase, with the slope of the line, measured from the time axis, proportional to the growth rate. Also, during such periods of growth, the doubling times will remain constant.

In Figure 4 it will be seen that when the total rate of industrial energy production in the United States, versus time, is plotted on semilogarithmic paper, the curve breaks into two distinct sections, each of which may be approximated by a straight-line segment. The first, extending from 1850 to 1910, is characterized by an exponential growth rate of 6.91 percent per year, and a doubling period of 10.0 years. The second, from 1910 to 1965, shows a sharp break in the average growth rate at about 1910, dropping to 1.77 percent per year, with a doubling period increased four-fold from 10 to 39 years.

If the figures for both the United States and the world production of the various fuels dis-

cussed above are plotted semilogarithmically, the pattern exhibited consists of a straight-line increase of the production rate up to a given time and then either an abrupt or a gradual transition to a lower rate of growth. While this may at first glance appear surprising, when one considers the magnitudes involved, it becomes evident that such behavior is inevitable. No physical activity on a finite earth can sustain more than a few tens of doublings without exceeding any possible magnitude of the earth's resources.

## Complete Cycles of Fossil Fuel Production

In order to determine how long a given fossil fuel may be able to serve as a significant source of energy, we need (1) to estimate the producible quantity of the resource initially present, and (2) in addition to our knowledge of past production, to estimate the future rates at which it may be produced and consumed.

In order to estimate the future production of a fossil fuel, we make use of the relation between the annual production and cumulative production. Since fossil fuels exist in finite quantities, the curve of annual production when plotted arithmetically as a function of time, as in Figures 2 and 3, must begin at zero and then increase until it passes one or more maxima, after which it must decline gradually to the limit zero. CUMU-

WORLD MINABLE COAL. Averitt 1969 estimate of initial world minable coal resources. Source: M. K. Hubbert, 1969, *Resources and Man,*[18] Fig. 8.24 By permission of National Academy of Sciences.

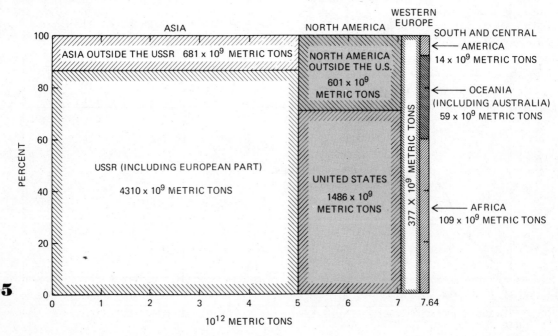

**5**

LATIVE production up to any given time is defined as the sum of all the annual productions up to that time.

On the graph of annual production, consider a small vertical column whose base is on the time axis and whose upper terminus is the graph itself. The base of such a column will be an element of time $\Delta t$, and its mean altitude will be the production rate, $\Delta Q/\Delta t$, where $\Delta Q$ is the quantity of the fuel produced in time $\Delta t$. The area of the column will then be

$$(\Delta Q/\Delta t) \times \Delta t = \Delta Q$$

Hence, the cumulative production from the beginning up to any given time $t$ will be proportional to the area between the curve and the time axis up to that time.

Similarly, the ultimate cumulative production, $Q_\infty$, would be proportional to the total area under the curve from the beginning of production until its end. If we designate the producible quantity of the resource initially present by $Q_i$, then the area $Q_\infty$ subtended by the production curve during its entire cycle must be less than, or at most equal to, that represented by $Q_i$.

*Coal Cycle*

In the case of coal, it is not too difficult to estimate the total amount initially present, because coal occurs in layers, or seams, which extend over extensive areas in sedimentary basins and often crop out on the surface. Hence, from geologic surface mapping and widely spaced drill holes it is possible to estimate the amount of coal in a given basin. Based on such information, inventories of the world's coal resources have been compiled intermittently since 1913. The most recent such study is that of Paul Averitt[3] of the U.S. Geological Survey. These estimates are of coal in beds 0.3 or more meters in thickness and within depths of less than 1800 meters. The estimated amounts of minable coal, assuming 50 percent recovery in mining, for various major areas of the world are shown graphically in Figure 5. In this figure, the scale on the base line represents the quantity of coal and the vertical scale the divisions of each column in percentages. According to these estimates, about 65 percent of the world's initial coal resources were in Asia (in-

cluding the European part of the USSR), 27 percent in North America, and about 5 percent in western Europe, with the three continental areas of Africa, South and Central America, and Oceania (including Australia) combined accounting for less than 3 percent. Of the total, the amount consumed (by 1970) is approximately $135 \times 10^9$ metric tons, or 1.8 percent of the amount initially present.

With this estimate of the world's initial minable coal, and the production history up to the present, we can determine about how long coal can be depended upon as a significant energy resource. In Figure 6, two possible curves for the complete cycle of world coal production are shown. The upper of the two closed curves is based upon Averitt's estimate (Figure 5) of $7.6 \times 10^{12}$ metric tons for $Q_\infty$. The lower curve is based upon a smaller figure of $4.3 \times 10^{12}$ metric tons, which is approximately the quantity of coal resources based on actual mapping. In view of the fact that much of the thin-seamed and deeper beds of coal may never be mined, this smaller figure may be the more realistic of the two.

The scale for measuring the cumulative production by the areas under these two curves is given by the shaded square in the upper right-hand corner of the chart. This has the vertical dimension of $10^{10}$ metric tons per year and the horizontal dimension of 100 years. The area of this square represents, accordingly,

$$10^{10} \text{ met.tons/yr} \times 10^2 \text{ yr} = 10^{12} \text{ met.tons}$$

Therefore, the production curve for $Q_\infty = 7.6 \times 10^{12}$ metric tons can encompass only 7.6 squares; that for $Q_\infty = 4.3 \times 10^{12}$, only 4.3 squares.

Taking the higher figure of $7.6 \times 10^{12}$ metric tons, and assuming only three more doublings in the production rate, we see from the figure that the peak in the production rate would probably occur at about the year 2150. Using the lower figure of $4.3 \times 10^{12}$ metric tons and only a five-fold increase in the present production rate, the peak in the production rate would probably occur about the year 2100.

The dashed curve extending to the top of the chart represents what the production rate would be were it possible for it to continue to increase at the rate of 3.50 percent per year — the rate

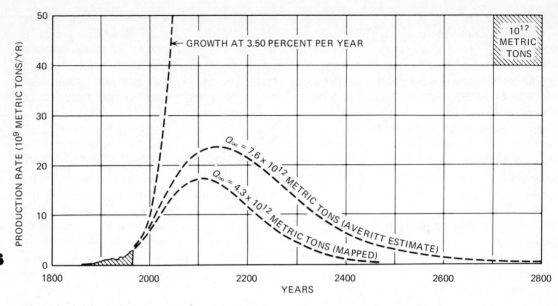

COMPLETE WORLD COAL PRODUCTION CYCLE.
Source: M. K. Hubbert, 1969, *Resources and Man,*[18]
Fig. 8.25. By permission of National Academy of Sciences.

that has prevailed since World II — for the next 70 years. Under this assumption we would run out in 110 years.

These curves can be varied by making the peaks higher and the time scale shorter, or the peaks lower and the time scale longer, but for any likely combination, it is probable that about 80 percent of the world's initial coal resources will be consumed during the next three or four centuries.

Two similar curves for the complete cycle of coal production in the United States can be drawn, using $Q_\infty$ equal to 740 x $10^9$ metric tons, which represents approximately the coal resources established by mapping, or $Q_\infty$ equal to 1486 x $10^9$ metric tons, which includes additional coal not yet mapped but inferred probably to be present. As in the case of world production, if the coal production rate for the United States were to double by but 2 or 3 times, the peak in the production rate would occur about 200 years hence, and the middle 80 percent would be consumed during the interval between approximately the years 2000 and 2400.

*Petroleum Cycle: Oil and Gas*

Unlike coal, which occurs in seams of large areal extent, oil and gas accumulations occur underground in restricted regions of space in the pore spaces of sands and other porous sedimentary rocks. These accumulations have horizontal cross sections ranging from a fraction of a square kilometer up to hundreds of square kilometers, but most are in the range of about 1 to 10 $km^2$. In depth, they occur all the way from 100 meters to as much as 8 km. For these reasons, it is much more difficult to estimate how much oil or natural gas may ultimately be discovered and produced in a given region than it is for coal.

The petroleum group of fuels consists principally of hydrocarbons: crude oil, natural gas, and natural-gas liquids. Crude oil is the liquid petroleum that is produced from oil wells and stored in tanks at atmospheric pressure. Natural gas, consisting principally of methane ($CH_4$), is the petroleum component that is gaseous under conditions of atmospheric pressure and the earth's surface temperature. Natural-gas liquids are the components of natural gas which are liquid under surface conditions of temperature and pressure. Crude oil and natural-gas liquids are referred to collectively as petroleum liquids.

In addition to the above components, all of which are producible from wells, there are heavy tars occurring in tar sands, and also solid hydro-carbons occurring in oil shales. These, in their natural state, cannot be produced from wells, and hence are not to be confused with crude oil.

The difficulty of estimating the ultimate amount of crude oil and natural gas that a given region will produce is well illustrated by the United States (exclusive of Alaska), which is the most intensely explored and best known petro-leum-bearing area in the world. Yet within the last decade, published estimates for the ultimate production of crude oil in the United States (ex-clusive of Alaska) have had a nearly fourfold range, from 165 to at least 590 billion barrels.

CRUDE OIL: EXPLORATION VS. DISCOVERY. Crude oil discoveries per foot of exploratory drilling in the United States, exclusive of Alaska. Source: M. K. Hubbert, 1967, reference 5, Fig. 15, p. 2223. By permis-sion of American Association of Petroleum Geologists.

The highest estimates have mostly been based on the assumption (or a slight modification of it) that the average amount of oil that will be dis-covered in the future per foot of exploratory drilling, up to a density of one well per each 2 square miles, will average approximately the same as that of the past.[4]

This assumption can be simply tested by de-termining whether the discoveries per foot of ex-ploratory drilling have been constant during the past. This has been done and the results are shown in Figure 7, in which the number of bar-rels of crude oil discovered per foot is plotted as a function of cumulative footage of exploratory drilling.[5] This encompasses the experience of the U.S. petroleum industry from 1860 to 1965, dur-ing which $136 \times 10^9$ barrels of crude oil were discovered by $15 \times 10^8$ feet of exploratory drill-ing, averaging 91 barrels per foot. However, the

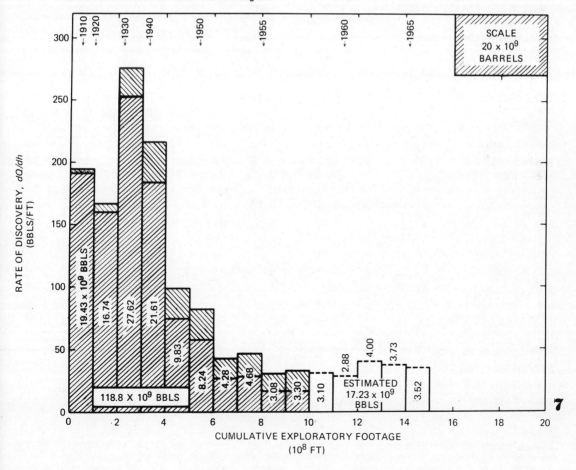

**7**

separate columns in Figure 7 represent the total amount of oil discovered, and the amount per foot, for each successive $10^8$ feet of drilling. It will be seen that for the first $10^8$-foot unit, extending from 1860 to 1920, the rate was 194 barrels per foot; for the second, from 1920 to 1929, it was 167 barrels per foot; for the third, from 1929 to 1936, it reached a peak of 276 barrels per foot. After that, the rate declined precipitously to a present figure of about 35 barrels per foot, notwithstanding the fact that from 1936 to 1966 was the period of the most intensive research and development in petroleum exploration and production techniques in the history of the petroleum industry. As in the case of production rate versus time, the area under the curve of discoveries per foot versus cumulative feet of drilling also represents cumulative discoveries. Extrapolation of this curve gives an estimate for the ultimate discovery of producible crude oil for the conterminous 48 states and their adjacent continental shelves of $Q_\infty = 165 \times$

U. S. CRUDE-OIL PRODUCTION CYCLE. Complete cycle of crude-oil production of United States, exclusive of Alaska. Source: M. K. Hubbert, 1969, *Resources and Man,*[18] Fig. 8.17. By permission of National Academy of Sciences.

$10^9$ barrels. Of this amount, $136 \times 10^9$ barrels, or about 80 percent, have already been discovered.

With this estimate for $Q_\infty$ of $165 \times 10^9$ barrels, it is possible for us to plot a full-cycle curve of crude-oil production for the United States exclusive of Alaska. Such a curve is shown in Figure 8. In this figure, the scale in the upper right-hand corner of the chart shows that one coordinate square represents $20 \times 10^9$ barrels. Therefore, with $Q_\infty = 165 \times 10^9$ barrels, the total area under the curve can only be 8.25 squares. The cumulative production of $81 \times 10^9$ barrels up to 1966 accounts for 4 squares, leaving only 4.25 squares for the future. If this estimate for $Q_\infty$ is even approximately correct, the conclusion is inescapable that the rate of crude-oil production for the conterminous United States must be about at its culmination at the present time (1970).

Other details of Figure 8 worthy of note are the following: The shaded area to the right of 1965, of $55 \times 10^9$ barrels, represents the additional oil that will probably be produced from fields already discovered; the unshaded area of $20 \times 10^9$ barrels represents probable future discoveries. The dashed curve at the top represents what the production rate would be had the aver-

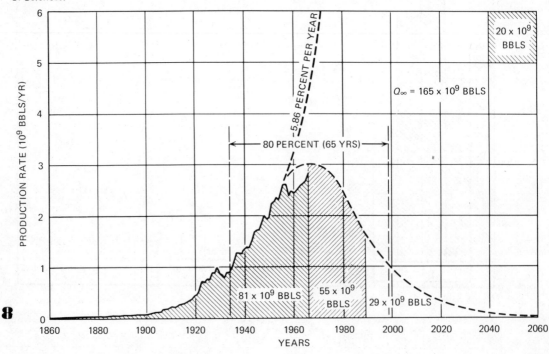

**8**

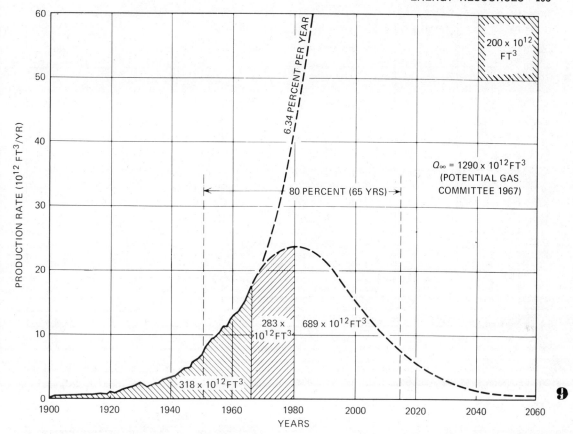

U. S. NATURAL-GAS PRODUCTION CYCLE. Complete cycle of natural-gas production of United States, exclusive of Alaska. Source: M. K. Hubbert, 1969, *Resources and Man,*[18] Fig. 8.20. By permission of National Academy of Sciences.

age growth rate from 1936 to 1955 continued. The two vertical dashed lines represent the times at which cumulative production amounts to 10 percent and to 90 percent of $Q_\infty$. The area to the left of the first line represents the first 10 percent of the ultimate production; that to the right of the second line, the last 10 percent. Between these lines, the middle 80 percent will be produced. It is significant that the time required for this is approximately the 65-year period from 1934 to 1999, less than a human lifetime.

Natural gas is closely related to crude oil in origin, and occurs in the United States at a ratio of about 6500 cubic feet of gas (at atmospheric pressure and 15.56°C) per barrel of oil. This ratio, however, is gradually increasing, with deeper drilling, so, if we assume a higher figure of

7500 cubic feet of gas per barrel of oil for future oil discoveries, we obtain an estimate of the future amount of natural gas to be discovered. When this is added to the present cumulative discoveries, it gives about $1050 \times 10^{12}$ ft³ as the ultimate quantity of natural gas to be produced in the conterminous 48 states of the United States and the adjacent continental shelves. A slightly higher figure of $1290 \times 10^{12}$ ft³ has been obtained independently by the Potential Gas Committee (1968).[6]

The full cycle of natural gas production in the conterminous United States is given in Figure 9. In this case, for $Q_\infty = 1290 \times 10^{12}$ ft³, the area under the curve is 6.5 squares. For $Q_\infty = 1050 \times 10^{12}$ ft³, the area would be only 5.25 squares. The peak in the production rate is estimated at about 1980, or perhaps a few years earlier if the smaller figure for $Q_\infty$ is used. The middle 80 percent of cumulative production will occur during the 65-year period from about 1950 to 2015.

In these estimates, Alaska has not been in-

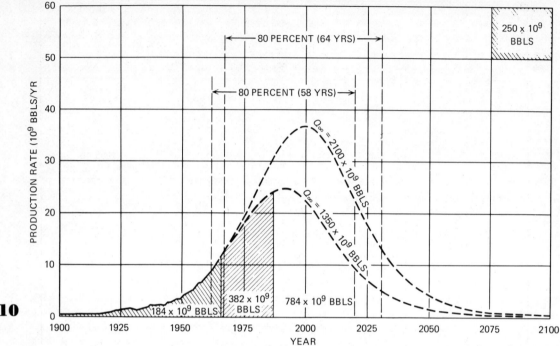

COMPLETE WORLD CRUDE-OIL PRODUCTION CYCLE. Source: M. K. Hubbert, 1969, *Resources and Man,*[18] Fig. 8.23. By permission of National Academy of Sciences.

**10**

cluded because oil and gas production in that state is only now in its initial stage of development and has not yet provided enough data to permit reliable estimates to be made. However, during 1967, the discovery of a large oil field with an estimated ultimate yield of 5 to 10 billion barrels at Prudhoe Bay on Alaska's North Slope, was announced. From present information, a speculative figure of 30 to 50 billion barrels for the ultimate crude-oil production of Alaska may be justified.

Current estimates of the ultimate amount of crude oil that may be produced in the world range from about $1350 \times 10^9$ to $2100 \times 10^9$ barrels. The corresponding figures for natural gas are from $8000 \times 10^{12}$ to $12000 \times 10^{12}$ ft$^3$.

The full-cycle plots of world crude-oil production, for a high value of $2100 \times 10^9$ barrels for $Q_\infty$, and a low value of $1350 \times 10^9$, are given in Figure 10. For the larger figure, the peak of production would occur about the year 2000, with 64 years required to produce the middle 80 per-

cent. For the lower figure, the peak in the production rate would occur about 1990, and the time required to produce the middle 80 percent would be only about 58 years.

Comparison of the full-cycle curves for the world production of coal and petroleum shows that the latter resource is destined to be much shorter-lived than the former. This is the result of two factors: (1) the faster growth rate of petroleum production due to its greater versatility as an energy resource and its greater ease of production and transportation; and (2) the smaller initial energy content of the petroleum group of fuels.

*Petroleum: Tar Sands and Oil Shales*

The best known tar sand deposits in the world are those of Athabaska in northeastern Alberta, Canada, and several smaller deposits in northern Alberta.[7] Together, these are estimated to contain about $300 \times 10^9$ barrels of producible oil, of which about 80 percent is in the Athabaska deposit. A mining operation on this deposit was begun in 1966, and larger-scale operations will doubtless follow when oil from less expensive sources becomes insufficient to meet requirements.

The best known oil-shale deposits are those of the Green River shales in western Colorado, southwestern Wyoming, and eastern Utah.[8] The hydrocarbons in these shales occur in a solid form but distill out as vapor upon heating and condense to a liquid, The oil concentrations range from near zero up to 65 gallons per short ton, and the aggregate oil content of these shales is quite large, about 2000 x $10^9$ barrels, but only about 80 x $10^9$ barrels are considered to be recoverable under present economic conditions.

Oil shales are known in several other parts of the world — notably in South America — and the aggregate recoverable oil is estimated to be about 190 x $10^9$ barrels.

## Summary of the Fossil Fuels

A world summary of the approximate initial amounts of coal and petroleum and of their respective energy contents is given in Table I. From this table, it will be seen that the energy content of the initial supply of minable coal was approximately 10 times that of the initial supply of petroleum liquids and natural gas combined. Also the energies of producible petroleum liquids and of natural gas are approximately equal.

To appreciate the significance of the epoch of fossil fuel exploitation, consider the span of human history extending from 5000 years in the past to a prospective 5000 years into the future. On such a time scale, a graph of the rate of production and consumption of the fossil fuels would rise and fall nearly vertically during a three-century period near the middle of this scale.

It would thus be seen that the epoch of the fossil fuels can be but a transitory and ephemeral event in the longer span of human history — an event, nonetheless, which will have produced the most drastic ecologic disturbance of the world's plant and animal populations, including that of the human species, that has ever been experienced.

Reference to Figure 1 shows the following additional sources of energy or power of such magnitude as to be potentially useful for large-scale industrial purposes: (1) direct solar radiation, (2) water power, (3) tidal power, (4) geothermal energy, and (5) nuclear energy.

## Solar Power

By far the largest source of energy for surface terrestrial processes is solar radiation.[9] After discounting the fraction lost by reflection, this thermal power input amounts to 116 x $10^{15}$ watts, which is about 12,000 times the 1970 rate of heat generation (6.8 x $10^{12}$ watts) from the fossil fuels. The difficulty of using this power for industrial purposes arises from its low areal density and the cost of concentrating it, and from the fact that it is intermittent rather than continuous.

Small-scale uses in areas of abundant sunshine for such purposes as water heating, and household heating and air-conditioning, and the use of photovoltaic cells for charging storage batteries, pose no particular difficulties. The difficulties of large-scale industrial uses, however, are much more formidable. The most promising sites for such purposes would be the desert areas of the near-tropical latitudes, such as the Sahara, southern Arizona, and northern Chile. In such areas the daily solar energy input on 1 square centimeter of horizontal surface has a minimum

| Fuel | Quantity | Energy per unit quantity | Total energy content ($10^{21}$ joules) | Percent |
|---|---|---|---|---|
| Coal and lignite | 7.6 x $10^{12}$ metric tons | 3.05 x $10^{10}$ joules/metric ton | 232 | 89.3 |
| Petroleum liquids | 2,500 x $10^9$ barrels | 5.91 x $10^9$ joules/bbl | 14.8 | 5.7 |
| Natural gas | 12,000 x $10^{12}$ ft$^3$ | 1.09 x $10^6$ joules/ft$^3$ | 13.1 | 5.0 |
| Totals | | | 259.9 | 100.0 |

**WORLD FOSSIL FUEL RESOURCES.** Initial quantities and energy contents of the world resources of fossil fuels.

monthly average of 500 calories, or an average of $2.4 \times 10^{-2}$ thermal watts/cm$^2$. By photovoltaic cells it is possible to convert about 10 percent of the solar energy into electrical energy. Then, for a 1000-electrical-megawatt power plant (which is the size of fossil fuel and nuclear plants now being built), 10,000 megawatts of solar power would be required. This would necessitate a horizontal collection area of $40 \times 10^{10}$ cm$^2$, or 40 km$^2$.

While there is no question that it would be physically possible to build such a plant, the amount and cost of electrical equipment involved, the cost of maintenance, and the cost of the additional storage facilities necessary for continuous operation, renders such an undertaking prohibitive in comparison with other available methods of power generation. Slightly more promising would be the use of solar-electric power for chemical purposes, such as the production of hydrogen by the electrolysis of water, which could be done with low voltages and with intermittent operation.

In summary, aside from the natural processes such as photosynthesis and air and water circulation, the principal uses of solar energy appear to be limited to small-scale, special-purpose applications.

*Water Power*

The largest concentration of solar power is that represented by the potential energy of water precipitated on land at various elevations above sea level. Since the power of running water is proportional both to the rate of discharge of the stream and to the height of fall, the favorable water-power sites are those on large streams either where natural waterfalls occur, or where artificial falls can be achieved by the construction of high dams and the storage of water at the higher elevation.

The potential water-power capacities, and their degrees of development, for various geographical regions of the world are given in Table II. The total water-power capacity of the world is estimated to be $2.86 \times 10^{12}$ watts. Of this, $243 \times 10^9$ watts, or 8.5 percent, had been developed by 1967. The most highly developed areas, Europe, North America, and the Far East, with developed capacities of 90, 76, and $20 \times 10^9$ watts, respectively, together account for 77 percent of the world's developed water-power capacity.

Among the areas having the largest but least developed water-power capacities are Africa, South America, and southeast Asia, with potential capacities of 780, 577, and $455 \times 10^9$ watts, respectively. These combined capacities amount to $1.81 \times 10^{12}$ watts, or 63 percent of the world total. The developed capacity of these three areas amounted by 1967 to only $21 \times 10^9$ watts, or to 1.2 percent of their potential capacity.

Water power also lends itself to installations of large magnitude. In the United States alone, five hydroelectric installations have capacities in excess of 1000 megawatts each and are compar-

| Region | Potential power[a] ($10^3$ Mw) | Percent of total | Developed[b] capacity, 1967 ($10^3$ Mw) | Percent developed |
|---|---|---|---|---|
| North America | 313 | 11 | 76 | 23 |
| South America | 577 | 20 | 10 | 1.7 |
| Western Europe | 158 | 6 | 90 | 57 |
| Africa | 780 | 27 | 5 | 0.6 |
| Middle East | 21 | 1 | 1 | 4.8 |
| Southeast Asia | 455 | 16 | 6 | 1.3 |
| Far East | 42 | 1 | 20 | 48 |
| Australia | 45 | 2 | 5 | 11 |
| USSR, China, and Satellites | 466 | 16 | 30 | 6.4 |
| World | 2,857 | 100 | 243 | 8.5 |

**II**

WORLD POTENTIAL AND DEVELOPED WATER–POWER CAPACITY. Source: M. K. Hubbert, 1970, Table VII.[20]

[a] Francis L. Adams. 1962, *in* M. K. Hubbert, 1962, *Energy Resources,*[19] Table 8, p. 99.

[b] U.S. Federal Power Commission, 1969, *World Power Data, 1967*

able in magnitude to the largest steam-electric plants.

The world's total hydroelectric power capacity of 2.9 x $10^{12}$ watts, were it to be fully developed, would be comparable in magnitude to the 1970 rate of energy consumption from the fossil fuels. The thermal power equivalent of the fossil fuels consumed at the 1970 rate amounts to about 6.8 x $10^{12}$ watts. Converted to mechanical or electrical power at an efficiency of 0.3, this would amount to 2 x $10^{12}$ watts, which is somewhat less than the potential capacity of hydroelectric power.

Since water power depends jointly on solar radiation and the topographic relief of the land surface, it might be supposed that this would be a source of power that would change only about as rapidly as the elevation of the land is changed by geologic processes. Actually, it may be much more rapid than this. Most large water-power installations involve dams and reservoirs. The reservoirs, however, are gradually filled by sediments brought in by the streams, and the time required to completely fill such a reservoir is only about one to three centuries. Unless some effective way of dealing with this problem in the future is devised, the world's major water-power capacity may have a period of usefulness of only about the same length of time as the fossil fuels.

*Tidal Power*

Power from the semidiurnal rise and fall of the oceanic tides[10] is closely related to water power, except that the flow of streams is unidirectional and comparatively steady, whereas tidal flow is oscillatory. Tidal power is obtainable by means of hydroelectric installations in dams across the mouths of bays or tidal estuaries. The amount of power obtainable from a given installation is proportional jointly to the area of the enclosed tidal basin and to the square of the range between low and high tide. Tidal power sites of large potential magnitude are accordingly limited to those coastal areas having naturally high tidal ranges and configurations permitting the large basins.

The total potential tidal power of the world amounts to about 64,000 megawatts, which is only about 2 percent of the world's potential water power. Nonetheless, in favorable sites, such as the Bay of Fundy area on the eastern United States–Canadian boundary, tidal power is possible with large installations and a minimum disturbance of the scenery, the environment, and the ecology.

Small tidal mills for the grinding of grain have been in use since Medieval times, and abortive plans for a tidal project on Passamaquoddy Bay have been under consideration since the 1920s. However, it was not until 1966 that the world's first large tidal electric power project, that on the La Rance estuary in France, began operation. This plant consisted initially of 24 units with capacities of 10 megawatts each and it has a planned ultimate capacity of 320 megawatts. More recently, a 400-kilowatt tidal plant has been installed at Kislaya Inlet near Murmansk in the USSR, and plans for much larger plants in the Kola Peninsula region have been announced.

*Geothermal Power*

In favorable geological localities, it is possible by means of comparatively shallow wells to tap underground reservoirs of steam generated by volcanic heat and to use this steam as a source of power. Such use was begun in the Larderello area of Tuscany in Italy as early as 1904. Subsequently, geothermal power in Italy has been progressively increased to a present capacity of just under 400 megawatts.

Recently, interest in the development of geothermal power has spread to other countries. At Wairakei in New Zealand a geothermal plant began operation in 1958. It has subsequently been expanded to a present capacity of 290 megawatts. In the United States, at The Geysers in northern California, a 12.5-megawatt geothermal plant began operation in 1960. The capacity has subsequently been increased to 82 megawatts, and an additional capacity of 100 megawatts is planned for the near future. Other small installations have recently been made in Japan, in the USSR (Kamchatka), in Mexico, and in Iceland.

Unlike tidal power, geothermal power depends essentially upon stored, and therefore exhaustible, thermal energy. In a recent world review, Donald E. White[11] of the U.S. Geological Survey has estimated the world potential capacity for geothermal power to be about 60,000 megawatts (approximately the same as tidal power), but with a life expectancy of only about 50 years. Potential geothermal power is therefore both of small magnitude as compared with world needs, and short-lived.

## The Atomic Nucleus and Nuclear Reactions

For a final source of energy appropriate for large-scale industrial uses, we now direct our attention to nuclear energy.[12] It has been found possible to release nuclear energy both catastrophically, as in the case of nuclear bombs, and at controlled rates appropriate for the generation of electric power. Concerning the catastrophic release of nuclear energy, either for warfare or for the so-called peaceful purposes, such as digging canals or for mining, few favorable things can be said. In either case, dangerous radioactive products are discharged to the biologic environment with genetic and other harmful effects of as yet undetermined magnitudes (Chapter 12). Therefore, our present discussion will be limited to those uses of nuclear energy in which both the rates and the products of the nuclear reactions are susceptible to human control.

The two contrasting types of nuclear reactions from which large amounts of energy are released are fission and fusion. FISSION involves the splitting of certain atoms on the heavy end of the scale of atomic masses into two roughly equal parts, which represent atoms of chemical elements in the midrange of this scale. FUSION consists in combining light atoms, such as hydrogen, into heavier atoms, such as helium. In both cases, the nuclear potential energy of the initial atoms is much larger than that of the products. The difference is released initially as the kinetic energy of the resulting products, and eventually in the form of heat. This heat, like that from the combustion of coal, can be used to generate steam for an otherwise conventional steam-electric power plant.

An atom is regarded as consisting essentially of a massive core, or NUCLEUS, about which from 1 to more than 100 ELECTRONS revolve in planetary orbits. The nucleus consists of densely packed nuclear particles, or NUCLEONS of two principal kinds, PROTONS and NEUTRONS. Protons and neutrons have approximately equal masses. A proton, however, has a positive electric charge of the same magnitude as the negative electric charge of an electron. Neutrons have zero electric charges. Since a stable atom is electrically neutral, the sum of the positive charges of the protons must be equal to the sum of the negative charges of the electrons. Therefore, a stable atom must have the same number of electrons as protons.

The chemical element to which an atom belongs is determined solely by its nucleus, specifically by the number of protons in the nucleus. By means of the Periodic Table, originated by the Russian chemist Mendeleev about a century ago, chemists have found it possible to arrange the naturally occurring chemical elements into a numbered sequence ranging from 1 for the lightest element, hydrogen, to 92 for the heaviest, uranium. It has subsequently been determined that this atomic number sequence also corresponds exactly to the number $Z$ of protons in the atoms of the respective elements. In addition to $Z$ protons, a nucleus may also contain $N$ neutrons, or a total number $A = N + Z$ of nucleons. Any two of the three numbers $A$, $Z$, and $N$ permit the complete identification of an atom. Ordinarily, only the numbers $A$ and $Z$ are given, $N$ being determined from $N = A - Z$.

To express the identity of an atom by its nuclear composition the following symbolism has now been adopted internationally:

$$^A_Z(\text{chemical symbol})_N$$

but with the $N$ commonly omitted. For example, the nucleus of the common hydrogen atom contains 1 proton, 0 neutrons, or a total of 1 nucleon. Its symbol, therefore, is

$$^1_1H_0 \quad \text{or} \quad ^1_1H$$

The nucleus of the common atom of helium contains 2 protons, 2 neutrons, and, therefore, 4 nucleons. It is symbolized by

$$^4_2He_2 \quad \text{or} \quad ^4_2He$$

Because nucleons are 1836 times as massive as electrons, almost the total mass of an atom resides in its nucleus. Since a hydrogen atom contains but one nucleon, it follows that the mass of a proton, or of a neutron, is approximately equal to that of a hydrogen atom. An atom having $A$ nucleons therefore has a mass approximately $A$ times that of a hydrogen atom. Taking the latter as approximately 1, as in the scale of atomic masses, then the masses of all other atoms, to the nearest whole number, are numerically equal to the number of nucleons, $A$. Accordingly, $A$ is known as the ATOMIC MASS NUMBER.

Since the chemical element to which an atom belongs depends only upon its number of protons $Z$, but not upon its neutrons $N$, it is possible to have several different species of atoms with different numbers of neutrons, and hence different masses, but all belonging to the same chemical element. Such atoms, having the same number of protons but different numbers of neutrons and masses, are said to be ISOTOPES of the same chemical element. This leads to another commonly used notation which is convenient both in speaking and in writing. That is, an isotope is identified by the name of its chemical element and its mass number. For example, the element lead (Pb) has isotopes of masses 204, 206, 207, and 208. The atomic number $Z$ of lead is 82. In the symbolism discussed above these four isotopes may be designated as

$$^{204}_{82}\text{Pb}, \quad ^{206}_{82}\text{Pb}, \quad ^{207}_{82}\text{Pb}, \quad \text{and} \quad ^{208}_{82}\text{Pb}$$

or simply as lead-204, lead-206, lead-207, and lead-208 (or Pb-204, and so on).

*Fission Reaction*

The heaviest of the natural chemical elements is uranium, with atomic number 92. This element, as it occurs naturally, consists of a mixture of three isotopes, uranium-234, uranium-235, and uranium-238, with atomic abundances of 0.006, 0.711, and 99.283 percent, respectively. Hence, each 100,000 atoms of natural uranium contains 6 atoms of uranium-234, 711 atoms of uranium-235, and 99,283 atoms of uranium-238. The amount of uranium-234 is so small that it may be neglected. Essentially then, natural uranium may be regarded as consisting of atoms of uranium-235 and uranium-238 in the ratio of 1 atom of uranium-235 to each 140 atoms of uranium-238.

Stray neutrons exist in nature, and others can be produced by various experimental procedures. It was discovered experimentally by O. Hahn and F. Strassmann in Germany in 1939 that when uranium was bombarded by neutrons, one of the products produced was barium. Shortly afterward, in the same year, this was correctly explained by Lise Meitner and O. R. Fritz as being due to the fissioning of uranium. This result was rapidly confirmed in other laboratories, and it was found further that it was the isotope uranium-235 that was involved. This led to the establishment of the wartime Manhattan Project of the U.S. government. A controlled chain reaction in the fissioning of uranium-235 was achieved at the University of Chicago on December 2, 1942, and the first nuclear-bomb explosion was detonated in New Mexico on July 16, 1945.

Although uranium-235 can fission in many ways, a typical reaction is the following:

$$^{235}_{92}\text{U} + ^{1}_{0}\text{n} \rightarrow ^{95}_{42}\text{Mo} + ^{139}_{57}\text{La} + 7^{0}_{-1}\text{e} + 2^{1}_{0}\text{n} + 204 \text{ MeV}$$

According to this, an atom of uranium-235 is struck by a neutron and splits into one atom of molybdenum-95, one atom of lanthanum-139, seven electrons, and two neutrons. These are all known as FISSION PRODUCTS. Accompanying the process, 204 million electronvolts (MeV), or $3.27 \times 10^{-11}$ joules, of energy are released. If these two neutrons encounter two additional atoms of uranium-235, further fissions occur and a chain reaction ensues. Such a chain reaction may be represented schematically as shown in Figure 11.

Many different kinds of fissioning actually occur and the quantity of energy released by each varies somewhat, depending upon the fission products produced, but the average value per fission has been found to be 200 MeV, or $3.20 \times 10^{-11}$ joules.

FISSION POWER REACTION

U-235 → [FISSION PRODUCTS] + [NEUTRONS] + HEAT

**11**

FISSION POWER REACTION.

Of all naturally occurring species of atoms (or NUCLIDES), only that of uranium-235 is fissionable under ordinary conditions. Hence, initially, all nuclear reactors are dependent upon uranium-235 as their primary fuel. However, if either uranium-238 or thorium-232 (the whole of natural thorium) is placed inside a reactor operating with uranium-235, some of the neutrons are captured by the uranium-238, or the thorium, and the following respective reactions occur:

$$^{238}_{92}U + ^{1}_{0}n \rightarrow ^{239}_{92}U \rightarrow ^{239}_{93}Np \rightarrow ^{239}_{94}Pu$$

$$^{232}_{90}Th + ^{1}_{0}n \rightarrow ^{233}_{90}Th \rightarrow ^{233}_{91}Pa \rightarrow ^{233}_{92}U$$

Thus, uranium-238 absorbs a neutron and is converted into uranium-239. This, by two short-lived radioactive transformations, changes spontaneously into neptunium-239 and thence into plutonium-239. Similarly, thorium-232 absorbs a neutron and is converted into thorium-233. This, in turn, changes radioactively into protactinium-233, and thence into uranium-233. Both of the terminal isotopes, plutonium-239 and uranium-233, are fissile and can be used in reactors as a source of fuel instead of uranium-235.

The process of converting the nonfissile isotopes, uranium-238 and thorium-232, into fissile materials is known as BREEDING and the initial nonfissile materials are known as FERTILE MATERIALS. The breeding reaction is illustrated schematically in Figure 12.

BREEDER REACTION (Schematic).

*Fusion Reaction*

The theory of fusion reactions was first derived by H. A. Bethe[13] of Cornell University in 1939, in two short papers showing the sequence of nuclear reactions whereby hydrogen in the sun and stars is continuously converted into helium-4, with the attendant continuous release of enormous fluxes of energy. Subsequently, the uncontrolled release of energy by fusion has been accomplished by man in the form of the so-called hydrogen or thermonuclear bomb. For about 20 years, intensive research has been under way in various countries in efforts to achieve fusion under controlled conditions. While this has not yet been accomplished, progress is steadily being made, and there is some promise that it may be achieved within another decade or two.

From basic nuclear theory, a variety of physically possible fusion reactions are known, and the amount of energy released by each can be computed. Two of the more promising of these reactions involve, respectively, the fusion of deuterium (a heavy isotope of hydrogen), and of deuterium and lithium, into helium.[14]

The deuterium-deuterium reaction involves the following steps:

$$^{2}_{1}D + ^{2}_{1}D \rightarrow ^{3}_{2}He + ^{1}_{0}n + 3.2 \text{ MeV}$$

$$^{2}_{1}D + ^{2}_{1}D \rightarrow ^{3}_{1}T + ^{1}_{1}H + 4.0 \text{ MeV}$$

Here, the symbol $^{2}_{1}D$ represents deuterium, which is the name given to the hydrogen isotope of mass 2, $^{3}_{1}T$ represents tritium, the hydrogen isotope of mass 3. These two reactions occur

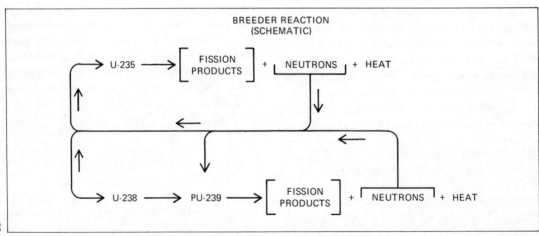

BREEDER REACTION
(SCHEMATIC)

with approximately equal frequencies. The tritium atom produced by the second reaction may then fuse with another deuterium atom in the following reaction:

$$_1^3 T + _1^2 D \rightarrow _2^4 He + _0^1 n + 17.6 \text{ MeV}$$

When these three reactions are combined, they give the net result,

$$5_1^2 D \rightarrow _2^3 He + _2^4 He + _1^1 H + 2_0^1 n + 24.8 \text{ MeV}$$

This gives an energy release of 5.0 MeV, or 8.0 x $10^{-13}$ joules, for each deuterium atom consumed.

An objectionable feature of this reaction is the fact that two potentially troublesome, free neutrons are released for each five deuterium atoms consumed. The following lithium-deuterium reaction, therefore, would be preferable:

$$_3^6 Li + _0^1 n \rightarrow _1^3 T + _2^4 He + 4.8 \text{ MeV}$$

$$_1^2 D + _1^3 T \rightarrow _2^4 He + _0^1 n + 17.6 \text{ MeV}$$

In the first of these two reactions, tritium is obtained from lithium-6 by a neutron absorption. This tritium is then consumed in the second reaction which also provides the neutron required by the first. The net result of the two reactions is

$$_3^6 Li + _1^2 D \rightarrow 2_2^4 He + 22.4 \text{ MeV}$$

In this case 22.4 MeV, or 3.59 x $10^{-12}$ joules, of energy are released, and the only material product is nonradioactive helium-4.

## Burner, Converter, and Breeder Reactions

From what has been said already concerning the fission and breeding reactions, it is clear that energy resources for fission power will be very much greater if breeding is employed than if it is not. The degree to which breeding occurs in a reactor can be specified by the conversion ratio $K$ defined by

$$K = Q/Q_0$$

where $Q_0$ represents the initial inventory of fissile material in a reactor and its auxiliary equipment, and $Q$ the amount remaining after the initial quantity $Q_0$ has been consumed. If no breeding occurs, then $K = 0$, and the reactor is said to be a BURNER. If some breeding occurs,

but $Q$ is still less than $Q_0$, then $K$ is greater than 0, but less than 1, and the reactor is said to be a CONVERTER. Finally, if $Q$ is greater than $Q_0$, then $K$ is greater than 1, and the reactor is a true BREEDER.

The significance of these three degrees of breeding is the following: If only burner reactors are used, then fission power can be generated only so long as the supply of uranium-235 — the rare isotope of uranium — lasts. If only converter reactors are used, then some of the fertile materials can also be consumed, and the total amount of fissile materials will represent some finite amplification of the original stock of uranium-235. Finally, if only breeder reactors are used, the entire supply of the fertile materials, uranium-238 and thorium-232, can be converted into fissile materials, and fission power production can be continued as long as the total supply of uranium and thorium lasts.

## Development of Fission-Electric Power

The speed of development of nuclear power since the initial achievement of a fission chain reaction represents the most spectacular advance in the conquest of energy during the entire history of technology. Within 15 years, the first nuclear electric power station — a 90-megawatt station at Shippingport, Pennsylvania — began operation, in 1957. By the end of 1969, according to the U.S. Atomic Energy Commission report for that year[15], 15 nuclear power stations with a total capacity of 3482 electrical megawatts were already in operation in the United States. Eighty-two additional stations with a combined capacity of about 70,000 electrical megawatts were under construction or contract, making the year-end total about 73,500 megawatts for plants already operable, under construction, or under contract. The AEC's estimate of the U.S. nuclear power capacity by 1980 is about 150,000 megawatts. This is about half of the U.S. fossil fuel, electric power capacity at the end of 1970.

A growth from 3482 megawatts of nuclear central power at the beginning of 1970 to 150,000 megawatts by the beginning of 1980 represents a 43-fold increase in 10 years — an average growth rate of 37.6 percent per year with a doubling period of only 1.8 years. The corresponding forecast for the total U.S. electrical power capacity is for an increase from 233,000 megawatts at the end of 1966 to 600,000 megawatts by 1980 — a mean growth rate of 7.28 percent per year with a doubling period of 9.5 years.

In addition to the nuclear-electric power stations, the United States also has a number of both small and large special-purpose reactors. The U.S. Navy had, by the end of 1969, 86 nuclear-powered submarines, one deep-submergence research vessel, and four nuclear-powered surface ships.

The development of nuclear power in other industrial areas of the world, particularly Great Britain and the USSR, has proceeded in parallel with that of the United States. Statistics for the USSR and its affiliated countries are not available. However, according to a joint report of January 1969 by the European Nuclear Energy Agency and the International Atomic Energy Agency[16], the total nuclear power capacity of the world, excluding the USSR and affiliates, was estimated to reach 25,600 megawatts by 1970, and within the range of 234,000 to 328,000 megawatts by 1980. This would be at growth rates of from 22.2 to 25.5 percent per year, with corresponding doubling periods of 3.1 and 2.7 years, respectively.

*Nuclear Raw Materials*

The raw materials required for nuclear power production depend upon the type of nuclear reaction employed. If the reactors are of the burner, or low-converter, types, the principal raw material required is uranium-235. If breeder reactors are employed, then after uranium-235 is used for the initial fueling, further operation will require only the fertile materials, uranium-238 or thorium-232. Finally, if fusion reactors should be developed, then deuterium obtained from the oceans or other large bodies of water, and lithium, would be the required raw materials.

In the United States, the reactors in operation and under construction by 1970 are overwhelmingly of the light-water-moderated type which

are essentially burners requiring uranium-235 for fuel. A few small experimental breeder reactors have been built, but the research and development for large power reactors based on breeding has only recently been seriously begun; and, according to present time schedules, these reactors are not expected to be in operation before about 1985.

In the meantime, the rapid growth of burner reactors has placed a severe strain on the potential supplies of uranium-235. In 1968, Rafford L. Faulkner[17], Director of the Division of Raw Materials of the U.S. Atomic Energy Commission, pointed out that the U.S. uranium requirements by the year 1980 would have to include not only the amount actually consumed by that time, but also a supply equivalent to the requirements for the next 8 years. This he estimated to be about 650,000 short tons of $U_3O_8$. This estimate, however, was based on an assumed nuclear power capacity by 1980 of only 95,000 megawatts. Since that figure has now been increased to 150,000 megawatts, the uranium requirements by 1980 would have to be increased by a comparable amount, or to about 1 million tons of $U_3O_8$. Against these requirements, the AEC in its 1969 Annual Report, estimates the known U.S. reserves of $U_3O_8$ to be 204,000 tons. To this is then added a speculative figure of 350,000 to 600,000 tons for the "potential resources" of $U_3O_8$ in the western United States. The reliability of this figure is unknown.

Comparable estimates for the entire non-Communist world as of January 1969, have recently been made jointly by the European Nuclear Energy Agency and the International Atomic Energy Agency. The known world reserves were estimated to be about 700,000 short tons of $U_3O_8$, and the cumulative world requirements by 1980 were estimated to be between 563,000 and 739,000 tons of $U_3O_8$, not counting the additional requirements for 8 years of lead time.

From these data, it is evident that with the present type of burner, or low-conversion, reactor a serious worldwide uranium shortage is impending within 25 years. In fact, if nuclear power should continue to be dependent upon such reactors, the entire episode of nuclear energy would probably be over in less than a century.

However, with breeder reactors capable of consuming the entirety of natural uranium and thorium, the situation would be drastically altered. In this case, instead of being dependent upon relatively scarce high-grade ores averaging about 3.5 kilograms of uranium per metric ton, it would be possible to utilize the very much more abundant low-grade ores. For example, the Chattanooga shale which crops out in the Appalachian mountains of eastern Tennessee and underlies most of several states at minable depths, contains a layer 5 meters thick with a uranium content of 60 grams per metric ton. With breeder reactors, the energy potentially obtainable from 1 gram of natural uranium or thorium amounts to $8.20 \times 10^{10}$ thermal joules, which is equivalent to the heat of combustion of 2.7 metric tons of coal or of 13.7 barrels of crude oil. The energy content of 1 metric ton of this rock would accordingly be equivalent to that of about 160 metric tons of coal, or to about 820 barrels of crude oil. The energy content of this stratum underlying an area of 800 square kilometers, or a square of 28 kilometers to each side, would be equivalent to that of all the fossil fuels in the United States.

A comparable amount of thorium is contained in the Conway granite in New Hampshire. This rock, which crops out over an area of 750 square kilometers (300 square miles) and extends to some kilometers in depth, contains 56 grams of thorium per metric ton. A cubic meter of this rock is equivalent in energy content to about 400 metric tons of coal, or 2000 barrels of crude oil.

From such data, it is evident that with breeder reactors the energy obtainable from the fissioning of uranium and thorium is tens or hundreds of times larger than that of all the fossil fuels combined.

Of the fusion reactions cited previously, the preferred reaction is that involving lithium-6 and deuterium. Lithium consists of two isotopes, lithium-6 and lithium-7, with atomic abundances of 7.42 and 92.58 percent, respectively. Other reactions are theoretically possible that involve the fusion of lithium-7 as well as lithium-6. The critical question in lithium-deuterium fusion per-

tains to the relative abundance of lithium and deuterium.

The abundance of deuterium in water, as compared with hydrogen, is one atom of deuterium to each 6700 atoms of hydrogen. From this it can be computed that 1 cubic meter of water contains $1.00 \times 10^{25}$ atoms of deuterium, and the entire volume of the oceans, $1.4 \times 10^{43}$.

Lithium deposits, on the other hand, occur on land. Lithium is produced from the geologically rare igneous rocks known as pegmatites and from the salts of saline lakes. According to J. J. Norton (personal communication), the specialist of the U.S. Geological Survey on lithium resources, an approximate estimate of the world resources of minable lithium, based upon an extrapolation of presently known deposits in North America and Africa, would be about $10^7$ metric tons of elemental lithium. Of this, the lithium-6 content would be 6.43 percent, or 643,000 metric tons.

One metric ton of lithium-6 contains $1.00 \times 10^{29}$ atoms. Therefore, the number of atoms in the estimated world supply would be about $6.4 \times 10^{34}$. Hence, lithium-6 is only about $10^{-8}$ as abundant as deuterium. For this reason, the amount of energy obtainable from the lithium-deuterium fusion reaction would be limited by the supply of lithium. The energy of fusion per atom of lithium-6 is 22.4 MeV, or $3.59 \times 10^{-12}$ joules. Then, for the fusion of $6.4 \times 10^{34}$ lithium-6 atoms, the energy released would be $2.3 \times 10^{23}$ joules. This is approximately the same as the $2.6 \times 10^{23}$ joules for all the fossil fuels, given in Table I.

*Human Affairs in Time Perspective*

From this review of the conquest of energy by the human species, and its physical and biological consequences, two realizations of outstanding significance emerge. One is the brevity of the time, as compared with the totality of past human history, during which the large-scale use of energy for industrial purposes has arisen; the other is that with the advent of nuclear energy, resources of energy sufficient to sustain industrial operations of the present magnitude for an additional millenium or more have become available.

The limiting factors in the future growth in the rate of energy consumption are no longer the scarcity of energy resources, but rather the principles of ecology. The production of power and its associated industrial activities are quite as much components of the world's ecological complex as are the populations of plant and animal species.

TIME PERSPECTIVE. Current human affairs in a time perspective of ten millenia before and after the present. Source: M. K. Hubbert, 1962, *Energy Resources,*[19] Fig. 61. By permission of National Academy of Sciences.

As we have observed, our industrial activities based on energy consumption have been characterized by large exponential rates of growth only during the last two centuries, and the present rate of growth of nuclear power capacity, with a doubling period of but 2 years, represents the most spectacular industrial growth phenomenon in the entire history of technology. However, it is no less true of power plants and automobiles than of biological populations that the earth itself cannot sustain or tolerate any physical growth for more than a few tens of doublings. The resources of the entire earth would

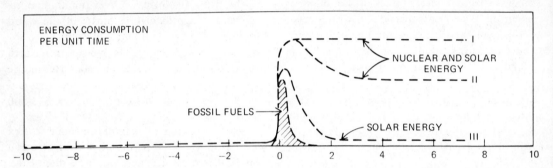

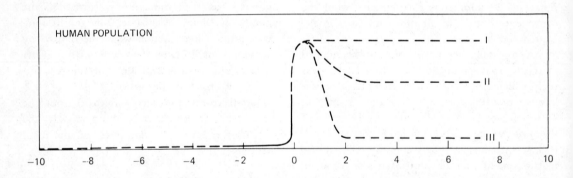

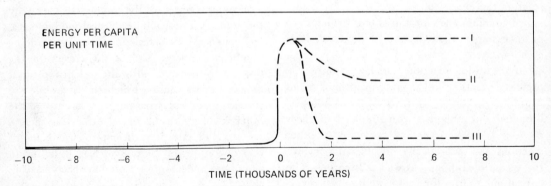

TIME (THOUSANDS OF YEARS)

**13**

not be adequate to support even a bacterial population were it, beginning with one bacterium, to be doubled as many as 100 times. Therefore, any particular physical activity must either cease its growth and, as in the case of water power, level off and stabilize at some maximum or intermediate level that can be sustained, or else it must reach some culmination and then decline eventually to extinction.

Because of the impossibility of sustaining such rates of industrial growth as those which have prevailed during the last century and half, it is inevitable that before very much longer such growth must cease and some kind of stability be achieved. As is indicated in Figure 13, the future period of stability could be characterized either by a continuation of a technological culture with a high level of energy consumption, or by a cultural decline to a primitive low-energy level of existence.

Regardless of which of these courses may actually be followed, it is clear that the episode of exponential industrial growth can only be a transitory epoch of about three centuries duration in the totality of human history. It represents but a brief transitional phase between two very much longer periods, each with rates of change so slow that it may be regarded as essentially a period of nongrowth. Although the forthcoming period poses no insuperable physical or biological difficulties, it can hardly fail to force a profound revision of those aspects of our current social and economic thinking which stem from the assumption that the growth rates which have characterized this temporary period can somehow be sustained indefinitely.

## References

1. Munk, W. H., and MacDonald, G. J. F. 1960. *The Rotation of the Earth, A Geophysical Discussion*. Cambridge University Press, Cambridge, England.

2. Lee, W. H. K., ed. 1965. *Terrestrial Heat Flow*. American Geophysical Union, Washington.

3. Averitt, P. 1969. Coal resources of the United States, Jan. 1, 1967. *U. S. Geol. Survey Bull. 1275.*

4. Zapp, A. D. 1962. Future petroleum producing capacity in the United States. *U. S. Geol. Survey Bull. 1142-H.*

5. Hubbert, M. K. 1967. Degree of advancement of petroleum exploration in the United States. *Amer. Assoc. Petrol. Geologists Bull. 51: 2207-2227.*

6. Potential Gas Committee. 1968. *Potential Supply of Natural Gas in the United States as of December 31, 1966.* Potential Gas Agency, Mineral Resources Institute, Colorado School of Mines, Golden, Colorado.

7. Clark, K. A., ed. 1963. *Athabaska Oil Sands.* Research Council of Alberta, Edmonton, Information Series No. 45.

8. Duncan, D. C., and Swanson, V. E. 1965. Organic-rich shales of the United States and world land areas. *U. S. Geol. Survey Circ. 523.*

9. Daniels, F. 1964. *Direct Use of the Sun's Energy*. Yale University Press, New Haven, Connecticut.

10. Bernshtein, L. B. 1965. *Tidal energy for Electric Power Plants* [English translation of 1961 Russian edition]. Israel Program for Scientific Translations, Jerusalem.

11. White, D. E. 1965. Geothermal energy. *U. S. Geol. Survey Circ. 519.*

12. Glasstone, S. 1967. *Sourcebook on Atomic Energy,* 3rd ed. Van Nostrand, Princeton, New Jersey.

13. Bethe, H. A. 1939. Energy production in stars. *Phys. Rev. 55:* 103; 434-456.

14. Glasstone, S. 1964. *Controlled Nuclear Fusion.* Understanding the Atom Series. U.S. Atomic Energy Commission, Oak Ridge, Tennessee.

15. U. S. Atomic Energy Commission. 1970. Annual report to Congress of the Atomic Energy Commission for 1969. Government Printing Office, Washington.

16. European Nuclear Energy Agency and International Atomic Energy Agency. 1969. *Uranium Production and Short Term Demand January 1969.* Paris and Vienna.

17. **Faulkner, R. L.** 1968. Remarks on uranium reserves before Conference on Nuclear Fuel, *Exploration to Reactors,* Oklahoma City, May 23, 1968. U. S. Atomic Energy Commission, Washington.

18. **Hubbert, M. K.** 1969. Energy resources, Chap. 8, pp. 157-242. In *Resources and Man* (Preston Cloud, ed.). Committee on Resources and Man, National Academy of Science — National Research Council. W.H. Freeman, San Francisco, California.

19. **Hubbert, M. K.** 1962. *Energy Resources.* National Academy of Sciences — National Research Council Publication 1000-D.

20. **Hubbert, M. K.** 1970. Energy resources for power production. In *Symposium on Environmental Aspects of Nuclear Power Stations,* International Atomic Energy Agency, Vienna. In press.

## Further Reading

**Halliday, D. and Resnick, R.** 1960. *Physics for Students of Science and Engineering.* Wiley, New York.

**Rabinowitz, E. I.** 1945. *Photosynthesis and Related Processes,* Vol. I. Interscience, New York.

**U. S. Bureau of Mines.** 1965. *Minerals Yearbook, Vol. II, Mineral Fuels.* Superintendent of Documents, Washington.

**U. S. Bureau of the Census.** 1969. *Statistical Abstract of the United States: 1969.* Superintendent of Documents, Washington.

# 6 Land Resources

Marion Clawson

In the United States we have always used land lavishly. In part, this is because we are relatively generously endowed with land. We now have about 11 acres of land per person. Some of our land is tundra, barren mountaintops, deserts, swamps, or other interesting places which do not produce much in the way of consumable goods for man; but some is rich farm land, some is highly productive forest, some is busy city area, and some is popular park land. Eleven acres is equal to about 3 average size city blocks or to 22 generous size suburban lots. Our land area per person is almost exactly the world's average; but our land supply is relatively generous because of the high quality of our land. Many of the largest nations of the world have a lot of relatively unproductive land — Canada with its immense north, Australia with its great "dead heart," Brazil with its Amazon jungle, and Russia and China with their large relatively unproductive northern areas.

We also use land lavishly because of our history. To the early colonists along the Atlantic Coast, the land area and the forests of the new country seemed limitless. Given their means of transportation and of converting land from its original state into farms and towns, the land area

MARION CLAWSON is director of the Land Use and Management Program at Resources for the Future, Inc., in Washington, D.C. He received his doctorate in economics from Harvard University in 1943, and has served for many years in the Federal departments of Agriculture and Interior. He has published scores of articles and several books, including *Policy Directions for U.S. Agriculture, Man and Land in the U.S., Land for the Future,* and *Land and Water for Recreation.*

was, in fact, limitless for them. But the idea of unlimited resources became ingrained and persisted long after land area and land resources were known to have definite limits. In this connection, we often forget that our colonial history was nearly as long as our national history; for 200 years after the first colonies were established, settlement was confined to a rather narrow belt along the Atlantic Coast, with a vast and unexplored hinterland stretching to unknown distances and shores.

We have not only used land lavishly; we have also used it wastefully and carelessly. It has often been easier to abandon unproductive fields and clear new ones than it has been to protect and restore the ones in production. Land abandonment took place long before the Revolution; many millions of acres have been farmed at one time and abandoned — and some, more than once. We have cut the natural forests, without worrying about regrowth and timber supply for another generation. Millions of acres have been farmed or grazed with consequent soil erosion, in part because farmers often did not know how to prevent it, but often also because they did not care or because it did not pay.

Population growth and economic development, especially during the last generation or two, have made us realize that good land, conveniently located to our needs, is scarce. Such land is valuable and always will be; it should not be wasted, either in the physical sense of deterioration or in the economic sense of use that does not make the most of its value. The people of the United States still are generously endowed with land; there is not an overall land scarcity now, nor is there likely to be one for some generations. We do not face a crisis, a threat of imminent danger. But there are many reasons for careful and wise use of land, and there are many difficult problems in land use to be overcome. Each individual cannot do exactly as he wants, everywhere and on any scale he wants; through one mechanism or another, the wants and actions of different persons and groups must be adjusted, one to another.

The time is ripe for a new look at land use and for some new attitudes about land. Complacency and unconcern can no longer be tolerated, but panic and ill-considered action might be equally dangerous.

*A Brief Look at Land History*

When Europeans first began establishing permanent colonies in what is now the United States, it was the home of 1 million American Indians, more or less. The Indians had immigrated here, perhaps 13 to 15 thousand years earlier, from the opposite direction. They did not possess any of the major domestic farm animals — no cattle, horses, sheep, goats, or pigs; these they got later from Europeans, especially the Spanish. They had never invented the wheel. But they did have fire, and they used it, not merely for their warmth and to cook food, but annually to burn off many land areas to affect grass production and game movements. Given their culture, there were probably as many of them as the land would support. The first successful European colony doomed their way of life.

For more than a century, various European powers contended for areas of the New World, the Pope sometimes acting as referee — and all without concern that they were dividing up the land that belonged to the Indians. Our later record was no better; we continuously pushed the Indians farther west or confined them to reservations. At one time or another, areas now within the United States were colonies of the British, French, Spanish, Swedes, Dutch, and others; but well before the Revolution, the British were dominant within what is now the United States, at least as far as the number of settlers is concerned.

The Revolution gave the new nation most land as far west as the Mississippi River, although

Florida was then a Spanish colony. In a series of bold moves — the Louisiana Purchase, the annexation of Texas (an independent country which had revolted from Mexico), a war with Mexico, a major treaty with Great Britain over the Pacific Northwest, the purchase of Alaska from Russia, and other smaller actions — the territorial expansion of the new country moved swiftly in the next 100 years. The land so acquired became the property of the federal government (except for small areas already in private ownership) in the proprietary as well as the jurisdictional sense. An enormous public domain was created — more than two-thirds of the land in the United States was once the property of the federal government.

Disposal of the federal land and a westward tide of migration dominated the nineteenth century, culturally, economically, and policitally. By 1890, the Bureau of the Census was no longer able to define a "frontier," inspiring Turner to write his famous essay on the influence of the frontier in American history. Land disposal on a large scale continued until about 1930. In total, more than half of the total land area of the United States which was once federal land is now privately owned; if Alaska, with its enormous area of relatively unproductive land, is omitted, the figure is 70 percent.

Well before this process had run its course, thoughtful persons were much disturbed at the reckless exploitation of the land — forests cut, cut-over areas burned until tree reproduction was impossible, streams filled with silt, the rise of tenant operation in farms, and so on. A system of permanent reservation of land in federal ownership began in 1891 with the establishment of what are now called the national forests. National parks, federal wildlife refuges, grazing districts, and other forms of federal land management units have been added, and today include about a third of all the total land area in the country. These lands are managed on conservation principles, with sustained-yield management of forests and grazing areas, and — except for some specialized park and wildlife areas — for multiple uses. They do not include farm lands, nor urban areas; they do include today about half of the timber volume (but far less of the forested area) of the nation and many millions of acres valuable for other purposes.

In the early colonial period, land was plentiful and various legal doctrines and philosophies of land ownership developed and became entrenched, which have continued, with some modification, until today. Law and custom in Britain and in the European countries sought to preserve estates without subdivision; primogeniture, or inheritance by the oldest son and no inheritance by other children, was one such device. There were numerous restrictions on land use and land inheritance. These were gradually abolished in the colonies and in the new nation. We embraced a philosophy of "fee simple" ownership: the land belonged to the individual, to do what he wished with it (even to waste or destroy it) and to will it as he chose to his heirs. In our revolt against restrictions on land use and inheritance, we swung to the opposite extreme.

We also developed various attitudes toward land, including two that were inconsistent and contradictory: Land was valuable, constituted economic security, and was a prime means of saving for one's old age; but land was also a commodity to be speculated in. The first of these attitudes underlay much immigration to the United States; peasants in many European countries who had no hope of landownership in their native country were willing to endure considerable hardship and some risk of life to secure land in the new country. Millions of immigrants came to the United States, at least some motivated by the desire to obtain land. And at least some of the frontiersmen had similar motivation.

The land speculation began early and was in full sway by the time of the Revolution. Most prominent citizens of the day were land speculators; George Washington, for instance, was active in buying and selling land, his work as a surveyor on the frontier often providing him with early knowledge of good land. Land speculation was rife along the frontier throughout its history. Many means were found of thwarting federal laws which were designed to favor the settler or to bring revenue to the federal government. Land was bought and sold, as a trading commodity, long before there were organized exchanges for financial stocks and bonds or for agricultural

commodities. The land speculation philosophy has continued, more or less unabated, until today; now, the center of activity is likely to be in the suburban fringe, not upon the frontier — the latter, in the original sense, has disappeared.

During the past 50 years or so, a gradual expansion of public controls over private land use has been instituted. Public controls are especially marked in the case of land use zoning, but subdivision control, building codes, health codes, and others also exert some control. These controls are not wholly effective nor perhaps always wise, but they do have considerable effect. To take an extreme case, I would not be permitted to erect a smelly glue factory in my backyard. Not only would the neighbors object, but there are laws and courts to enforce their objections. Controls on land use have been more effective in preventing the introduction of nonconforming uses into established residential and other areas than they have been in implementing land use plans for new or developing areas. This is more for political than legal reasons: If someone seeks to introduce a nonconforming use into an established area, the damaged persons protest immediately and vociferously, and are likely to be effective; if one seeks to upset a planned use of a growing suburban area, the damaged persons are really the whole public, and no individuals feel strongly enough to put up a fight. The greatest single policy issue for land use in the future is to find ways for public control over private land use which are fair to the individual but effective in realizing the general public good.

## Land Use Today

The total land area of the United States is 2266 million acres. Because Alaska is such a large part of this (362 million acres) and because Alaska land is so different in its physical characteristics, as well as so located that it is not really a substitute for land in the conterminous 48 states, it is desirable to show land use for the whole 50 states and for the 48 states separately (Figure 1). Land use can be divided simply into (1) the big three — cropland, forests, and grazing land; (2) the important two — urban land and recreation land; and (3) the many miscellaneous uses. Land use depends in part upon physical characteristics of land, but also upon many economic factors.

For instance, Figure 1 (all 50 states) includes about 435 million acres of cropland. For the most part, these are lands with soils of at least moderate adaptability to farming, with enough natural precipitation or with irrigation so that crops have enough water, but with enough protection from flooding that crop production is not seriously impaired, well enough located with respect to markets that their output can be marketed effectively, and so on.

However, the Soil Conservation Service, on the basis of careful land inventories, has estimated that 775 million acres of land in the United States could be farmed permanently, if reasonable care were taken for its conservation and wise management, and if the demand for its output so justified. Much of the land that could be farmed but is not now being farmed would require clearing of forests, or removal of stumps, or protection from flooding, or removal of rocks from the plow zone, or irrigation, or other measures or combinations of measures to bring it into production and to keep it there. By and large, making these changes would not pay under

today's conditions, yet this potential cropland is a great national asset. In some parts of the world — Japan, or Indonesia, or Holland, for example, where good land is scarce — this land would almost surely be brought into use. On some of it, crop production costs would be relatively high and returns relatively low, so that it would take relatively much higher prices of agricultural commodities to make its use profitable.

Over 700 million acres is classed as forest and woodland (Figure 1). Some of this is pasture land or is grazed by livestock, and some naturally supports rather meager stands of trees. Forest growth is very much influenced by soil, climatic, and other natural conditions. A forest is an ecosystem, with competition among various tree species for sunlight, moisture, and soil fertility, but also with various symbiotic relationships, not only among the tree species but between them and various shrubs or smaller plants, and with wildlife of many kinds, to say nothing of an extensive soil microbiology. A forest may have evolved in the presence of fire, either fire caused by lightning or other natural causes or set by man.

When a natural forest, as it has evolved over the decades or centuries, is cut, the ecosystem experiences a major shock, which may be intensified if the slash is burned in a hot fire. Temperature, moisture, sunlight, and other relationships are changed. In time, the natural forest will probably replace itself — but "in time" may mean hundreds of years in some cases. In many areas of the United States, the first-succession trees after cutting were quite different species than were dominant before cutting — species took over which had always been present in the general region, so that seed existed, but had been subordinate to the dominant forest type. The succession forests in turn have been cut, and their succession has sometimes been still different. There is relatively little old growth ("virgin") timber left in the United States, and most of that is in public ownership — national forests, national parks, or other areas. It often supports quite remarkable stands of timber — someone who has known only the badly degraded mixed hardwood forests of the northeastern United States is likely to be flabbergasted

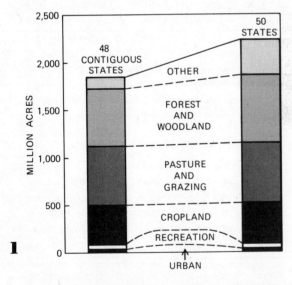

**1**

MAJOR U. S. LAND USES. The data are for 1964. "Other" includes transportation, military, and water management uses; also marshes, bare rock areas, sand dunes, deserts, and other such areas; also all unaccounted for areas, including idle land.

with his first sight of a virgin Douglas fir or red-wood forest.

The vast area of grazing land (640 million acres, Figure 1) is mostly not useful for anything else — grazing gets it by default. Its soils are too rocky or too steep or too shallow for cultivation or its moisture is too limited, or for other reasons it does not grow many or any trees. Native grasses, shrubs, or annual weeds do, however, provide feed for domestic livestock. Output per acre is very low, but use of large areas permits output per man to compare favorably with other types of agriculture.

The urban (29 million acres) and recreation (47 million acres) areas are set aside for their special usefulness for man. By and large, they have been modified greatly, as in the case of urban areas and some parks. Some have been retained in their original condition, as in the case of some national parks, but in either event by special management. Their area is relatively small, their value relatively great.

In addition, some land is given over to miscellaneous uses, such as reservoirs, highways, military reservations, and others. Included in the miscellaneous category is some land whose use is so near zero that it is more accurate to call it unused. or idle. Some of this is highly valuable land; there is a belt of idle land around nearly every city — land no longer used for farming, held in hopes of urban development.

*Who Decides on Land Use?*

Decision-making about land use in the United States is widely dispersed among literally millions of individuals and private organizations, and thousands of public agencies. As a result, no one or no organization is responsible for the result; many have had a hand in it, but none has been decisive.

Some land use decisions are largely in the market place. That is, one person owns some land, another bargains with him to buy or rent it; or the same owner decides to shift the use to something different. The private market is motivated primarily by the hope or expectation of profits — including gains in satisfaction which do not necessarily have a monetary price tag. There

is much to be said for a private market, whether in land or in something else. Different individuals in competition among themselves often put land to its most valuable use. The virtues of the competitive market have been described by many economists in the past, and there is no need to repeat them here.

But the land market, even when largely private, operates within a framework of public decisions and public influence, if not public regulation. Mention has been made of zoning. A unit of government, such as a city or a county, which has the necessary legal powers, establishes land use zones; these may say what uses are permissible, or what uses are forbidden, or both. Within the limits of the zoning ordinance, the private landowner may do as he wishes with the land. If zoned for single family dwellings, he may design his own house, or have an architect do it for him. If the land is not zoned for the use he wishes to make of it, he may usually apply for a rezoning; and, if denied, he can often appeal to some higher authority.

But zoning may not be the only obstacle to use of land as the individual wishes. There may be subdivision regulations affecting the size or shape of lots, or the layout of streets (including grades and curvatures) and other matters. Beyond this, there may be a building code specifying the kind of construction methods which can and cannot be used. This is done primarily on the basis of public safety, to avoid fire and other hazards about which the buyer or occupant would otherwise be uninformed. There may be a health code, backed up by building inspection, especially applicable to rented properties, to see that they do not become a health hazard.

There may be a wide range of public actions which also greatly affect private land use. Construction of main water supply and sewage disposal lines to which the builder or home owner can connect may open up the possibility of using the land for residential purposes. Or the building of a major highway may make an area accessible to employment centers downtown or in the suburbs, and hence make the land more valuable and more attractive for home sites. Or good schools, or good parks, or other high-quality public services, conveniently located, can add much to the value of private land. Needless to say, the lack of any or all of these tends to restrict private land use.

There are still other ways in which public action may affect private land use. Under what terms is credit available, to buy or improve homes? Federal programs for insuring savings deposits have surely encouraged saving, thus making more capital available for home building and buying; federally insured mortgage loans have also increased available credit, to the same end. The federal income tax law stimulates home ownership; interest paid on loans and real estate taxes is deductible from income on which a tax must be paid, thus providing the home purchaser with a definite financial incentive. The fact that increases in land or other property value are taxed as capital gains, usually at a lower rate than the tax on ordinary income, is another incentive to property ownership.

The examples used thus far have applied particularly to urban residential use of land, but similar situations apply to other land. There is a major federal program of assistance to owners of agricultural land: Annual payments are made for adjustments in crop acreage, loans are available on some agricultural commodities in order to support their prices, technical assistance is available free or nearly so to help with soil conservation, and numerous other public programs help the private landowner. In forestry, there are also some public programs, such as help in fire control, and taxing of income from sale of forest products at the capital gains rate. There is also a system of agricultural credit which was initiated with major federal help for a long time but is now largely privately owned and managed by farmers.

In the case of a piece of unimproved suburban land which is converted to residential use, there is or may be a large number of decision-makers. First of all, there is an "original" landowner – perhaps a farmer – who used the land for another purpose. He is likely to sell the land to a dealer, or speculator, or investor, or whatever we wish to call him; the land may pass through the hands of more than one such dealer; ultimately, it is bought by a developer or builder, who erects houses or apartments on it. First,

however, he must get the needed zoning, get approval of the subdivision plan, arrange for the necessary public services such as water and sewerage; and, above all, obtain credit to finance his building of the structures. All of this requires decision-making by public officials and private lending agencies. The builder buys materials and hires labor; this assumes the availability of both and involves local trade unions in many cases. Once a house is built, it must be sold, and this requires some form of marketing organization, either that of the builder or a specialized real estate agent. And, finally, the sale requires a buyer, who may choose only among homes offered, even if none exactly suits him. But he is often the king pin in the process – without his willingness to buy, the whole operation would fall flat. The potential buyer's attitude is conditioned by the availability and cost of credit, and also by the alternative housing, if any, available to him.

The process may actually be far more complicated and circuitous than described so far. All may not go smoothly – in fact, rarely does everything work smoothly. There will be need for consultations, bargaining, and perhaps appeals at many stages. The whole process can be stopped at any point. At least some minimally satisfactory level of agreement must be reached if the whole enterprise is to result in a new home occupied by a new owner. In this long process, any actor may be in the critical role, at least at some stage. It is hard to put one's finger on just who is responsible; there are many decision-makers, no single one with full power.

About a third of all land is publicly owned. This is true in towns and cities, where streets and other transportation areas are mostly public. Parks and recreation areas are mostly public also. In addition, there are very extensive areas of publicly owned forests and grazing lands. The decision-making process for public lands is somewhat different, but not free of pressures and conflicting interests. Although the decision about use of such land is nominally in the hands of the public agency, political pressures, demand for the land or its products, and the general social climate of the times exert many influences upon the public decision-maker.

*Urban Land Use*

The area of land used for urban purposes is not large — on the order of 1 to 2 percent of the total land area; but more than 70 percent of the United States population lives in cities and the value of urban land (without buildings) is 50 percent greater than the value of all rural land. This is why we refer to urban land use as one of the "important two."

We lack good data on urban land use; more seriously, we lack sharply defined concepts and terms to describe the situation. The origin of the difficulty is historical. At one time, a city was clearly bounded — many had walls around them. The city was an economic unit with defined legal and political powers. The physical, economic, legal, and political cities were identical and were clearly set out from their surrounding rural countryside. Today, partly because of the changes the automobile has brought in our daily lives, the physical-economic and the legal-political cities are no longer the same. The physical city may have long outlyers of scattered suburbs, which might be inside or outside of the city's legal boundaries; the economic activity may have dispersed into the suburbs and even into the countryside. But these are nothing, compared with the growth outside of the legal boundaries of the city, which do not begin to include all of the citylike settlement. Thus, when one speaks of the "city," does he mean the legal city, with its defined governmental powers, or does he mean the economic city, or the physical city with all its suburbs?

From a land use viewpoint, there is still another complication. The city (however one defines it) "uses" some land — for the present purpose parks and other permanently reserved open areas are considered used. This is the city planner's approach to urban land use. But, from the viewpoint of rural land planners and users, the city has withdrawn a great deal of land from other uses. Much of the withdrawn area — about half, nationally, as nearly as we can determine — is not actually used, but lies idle, waiting hopefully for development. Farming often becomes difficult in a suburban area, and farmers sell out to land speculators; the latter, by and large, prefer to hold the land idle so as to be able to take immediate advantage of a sales opportunity. Some of the idle land lies within the city's legal boundaries; for instance, Los Angeles has 10 percent and Chicago has 6 percent of its area undeveloped or idle (this excludes parks and other dedicated open areas). But much more of the idle land lies outside of the central city, often outside of even a suburban city; for instance, in the developing suburban fringe area of Fairfax County, Virginia (just west of Washington, D.C.) about 40 percent of the local planning areas have two-thirds or more of their total area vacant and more than five-sixths are more than one-third vacant.

Land passes from this idle suburban state into active use in an uneven manner. Some tracts are bought and become residential subdivisions, while others are passed over. In many cases, the landowner and the potential developer cannot agree on a price, or the owner is not ready to sell just yet, or he hopes to get a different zoning and to make a different use in the future; or the size of the ownership parcel may be either smaller or larger than the developer wants. Whatever the reason, the tide of suburban growth does not flow smoothly; rather, it is a skip and jump matter, with large tracts left undeveloped for years or even decades. The unit of growth is the builder's subdivision. This form of scattered settlement may be called "subdivision discontiguity" — a cumbersome but descriptive name.

The dominant form of suburban growth for many years after World War II, and still the most important one, was single-family homes, each on its own lot. In the past decade, suburban apartments have provided about as many new dwelling units as have single-family houses. Many builders have constructed considerable numbers of houses, up to a few hundred in some cases, on a single subdivision. The combination of irregular development on the subdivision scale, and individual lots which consume a considerable amount of land and yet provide little usable open space, has been termed "sprawl" — and sometimes less complimentary terms.

These suburbs have been widely criticized on social grounds. They have effectively excluded Negroes and poor people of all races; they have frequently been relatively homogeneous groups, as to age, stage in the family life cycle, income, and other respects. They may be called a social "monoculture"; children growing up in them may have no realization that different social, income, and racial classes exist. Sprawled suburbs have also been criticized as being needlessly expensive for what they produce. Eliminating subdivision discontiguity would result in substantial savings — something on the order of $150 per family per year, as a minimum; closer settlement, including clustering of houses to leave larger open areas, would result in further substantial savings. Such savings are realizable only through a greater degree of public control over the private suburban development process.

While the suburbs have been growing, the older city areas have been deteriorating, in the physical sense (Chapter 16). In the United States we have never devised a process whereby land in cities can be rebuilt for the same general land use. An old residential block may be converted to an office building, or even to a high rise apartment, but only rarely to another residential area similar to the present. There are several reasons why this is true. Federal income tax policy positively discourages replacement of old buildings; slum property is often highly profitable. One reason is that each purchaser is allowed to depreciate its cost to him on his income tax return, thus creating a tax-free cash flow for several years; then he sells it, and someone else repeats the process, over and over. If depreciation were limited to once only, a great deal of decadent housing would be unprofitable and would be replaced.

Urban land use is a prime example in modern society of the dependence of each individual on others. The use and value of each piece of land is more affected by what is done on other land than it is by anything that can be done on the tract itself. For instance, if I live in a neighborhood which is drifting downhill, physically and socially, there is little I can do to continue my home as a satisfactory place to live or to retain its value. Likewise, I may neglect my home, yet if the neighborhood stays good, the value of my home does not decline much. These are the externalities and interdependencies of the economist.

Many external effects are negative; someone does something on his property which injures someone else — the factory with its smokestack, for instance. There have been many law cases over such damages. Zoning has as one of its main purposes the avoidance of such secondary negative effects. But sometimes the external effects are positive; my neighbor creates a beautiful garden, and I enjoy its view. Although there are many instances of negative external effects, and a few of positive ones, yet we lack any good social mechanism for reducing the negative ones and increasing the positive ones.

In urban land use, more than in any other land use, social controls in the future must be stronger, while at the same time preserving the maximum of individual rights. If hundreds of thousands or millions of people are going to live in one big urban complex, then clearly each individual cannot be allowed to do just as he pleases. Indeed, he is not so allowed today, but, future controls must surely be tighter. Zoning, subdivision, and other controls will have to be far more stringent than now.

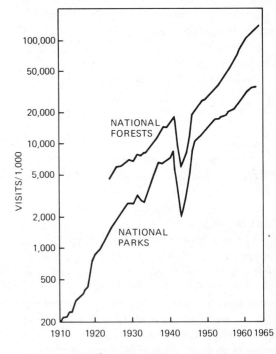

NATIONAL PARK AND FOREST VISITS. The number of annual individual visits to national parks and national forests since 1910.

*Land for Recreation*

Some land is used primarily for recreation — about twice as much as is used for urban purposes, but still a relatively small part of the total land area. Much additional land used primarily for other purposes also provides outdoor recreation. Recreation is a land use which affects many people and is one whose importance is growing rapidly. As with urban land use, we lack good data and clear-cut concepts and terms to describe recreational use of land.

Total attendance at our national parks has increased since 1910 or earlier at a rate closely approximating 10 percent annually (Figure 2). From a total visitation of about 200,000 visits annually, attendance in national parks has risen to over 34 million annual visits, or by more than a hundredfold. Visits to national forests have shown a generally similar trend, but on a higher level each year. These are visits, not persons; they are data like admissions to movies — each entrance is counted, with some people going more than once to a park or to more than one park, while other persons do not go at all. Anyone with a slight acquaintance with the compound interest curve knows that a constant rate of increase, even if small, in time leads to astronomical numbers. Thus far, from the earliest dates at which attendance records were kept, almost every park system shows attendance rising at a relatively constant percent; this cannot continue forever, but there is no sign of a slackening off yet. The day would come when every citizen would have to spend every day at a park; indeed, if the visitation trend to reservoirs built by the Corps of Engineers continued unabated until 2000, every man, woman and child would spend 2500 days annually at such reservoirs — rather difficult to do!

The main kinds of public outdoor recreation areas are city and county parks, state parks, federal reservoir areas, national forests, national parks, and federal wildlife refuges. There are also many private areas used for outdoor recreation but we have very little information about them. In recent years, the mythical average American made two recreation visits to a state park, one to a national forest, one to a unit of the national park system, one to a federal reservoir, and perhaps half a dozen to a city park during the course of a year. Some people went far more than this, others went very little or not at all.

Several major factors have underlain this continued and rapid rise in recreation activity. For one thing, total population has been rising; so have average incomes, so that people can afford to travel and to spend money for recreation to a degree which was impossible in an earlier day. There has been some rise in leisure, not only in the sense of reducing the average hours of work per week, but in longer and more general paid vacations, more years in youth before entering on a job, and more years in retirement — and generally, in better health during retirement. In addition, transportation has improved; car ownership is more widespread, and highways are better. These factors have operated in combination to stimulate outdoor recreation activity; any one of them alone would have had a modest effect. During World War II when gasoline and tire rationing greatly curtailed travel, attendance at national parks and national forests fell by two-thirds, for instance.

The various kinds of outdoor recreation areas form a system. Some parks are located close to where people live, so that they may be used after school or after work. Such parks are usually small — most are city parks — and provide opportunities for activities which can be carried on in a short period of daily leisure. Other parks are located farther away and are used primarily on weekends. Many such areas are state parks; they often include a body of water where swimming, or fishing, or water skiing is possible, and they are likely to have extensive picnic grounds. Sports areas vary from local playgrounds to golf courses with locations and areas appropriate to each activity. Vacation areas are often still further away and are likely to be much larger and often more outstanding in their natural features. Many national parks are visited primarily during vacations. Mountain, seashore, and lake areas are especially likely to be summer vacation areas. Many people use several different kinds of outdoor recreation areas during the course of a year, others use primarily only one kind, and some have poor access to any or do not care to partake of outdoor recreation.

The great and continued rise in outdoor recreation activity has created many important policy issues and problems. Experience has made it clear that an outdoor recreation area has a limited capacity to serve people. One cannot crowd unlimited numbers of people into any defined or restricted area without serious physical effects — human feet, if there are enough of them, can be as destructive as the bulldozer. Many people go to a recreation area for solitude, or privacy, or for a view of nature. Hundreds or thousands of people, each seeking the same thing, may destroy the experience for everyone. Land managers long ago learned that a forest has a limited sustained yield that may be harvested if the productivity of the forest is to be maintained; likewise, a grazing area has a defined carrying capacity which cannot be exceeded if productivity is to be maintained. Similar reasoning applies to recreation areas; there is some limit beyond which use cannot increase without damage to the area. In each case, investments and good management can increase productive capacity above a "natural" or unmanaged level but only within limits.

A first policy issue in outdoor recreation areas, then, is how to limit use to capacity. The best way is to provide alternative areas for people to go to, so that crowding at one site is unnecessary. But more positive controls may be necessary. Entrance fees or other charges might serve as one way of discouraging use; advance reservations might be another; waiting in line until there is a vacancy might be still another; and others can be devised. But it is clear in many areas that unlimited numbers cannot be crowded in. The National Park Service, for instance, finds that the floor of Yosemite Valley in the summer is so crowded that it develops its own smog. This is certainly undesirable, to say nothing of the effect of crowding on one's psychological perception of the wonders of the area. Measures are being taken to reduce total attendance in this extremely popular area.

Another policy question for outdoor recreation use of land and water resources is: Who is going to pay for them, and how? A tradition of free access to parks grew up in this country. Most city parks were, and are, open for use without charge, although charges are increasingly being imposed. Given the easy physical accessibility of many city parks and the absence of park employees during much of the time, it would be administratively impossible to collect charges even if it were desired to do so. In the national forests and national parks, recreation use was once very low and their managers were more concerned to encourage use than to collect revenue from it.

But no area of land and water for outdoor recreation can really be free; it costs money to provide such areas, to construct even the minimum sanitary and other improvements, to clean up the trash, and to provide other services. Someone must pay. Shall it be those who use the parks, or the general taxpayer, or someone else? Sentiment and practice are gradually coming to the conclusion that users should pay a substantial part of the costs. This is not merely equity — those who can afford to travel to an area can afford to pay a modest fee for use — but this may be the only way sufficient funds can be obtained to maintain and manage the areas properly, and people may treat their parks better if they must help pay for them directly. Moreover, when camping at a public campground requires a reasonable payment, then private provision of camping areas becomes more nearly feasible.

But what about the poor people who cannot afford to pay to get into parks? First of all, really poor people rarely are able to get to state parks, federal reservoirs, national forests, and national parks; the travel and other costs are beyond their means. A good case can be made for free city parks, but here the usual situation is for the city parks to be most common in the higher income parts of a city and most deficient in the lower income areas. If we are really serious about providing outdoor recreation opportunities for low-income people, then we should concentrate our subsidies in such parts of our cities.

A special situation exists for wilderness areas. There has been an enormous tide of popular interest in wilderness areas in recent years, much by people who never visit them but want to know that they exist and are preserved. Popular conceptions of a wilderness differ greatly; in one survey, it was apparent that the motorist towing a power boat behind his car thought that the wilderness began the instant he left the paved highway. The original definition was an area large enough to require 2 days or more with a pack train to reach its heart. Many people think of a wilderness as an area exactly as nature made it, untouched and undefiled by man; that kind of an area no longer exists in North America, if indeed anywhere in the world. Man's ecological dominance has spread to wilderness areas as well as elsewhere. All wilderness areas must be managed — the policy issues are, managed for what ends, with what tools, and with what skill? Shall we let forest fires burn uncontrolled — after all, fire is a natural force? But many forest fires today are man-caused, and burned-over areas would leave a fire hazard for years or decades which might lead to ultimate destruction of the whole area. What kinds of approach roads shall we build up to the wilderness boundary? What kinds of trails in the wilderness? What kinds of sanitary facilities shall we construct at popular camping spots? How shall we dispose of our garbage? These and many other such questions could be answered one way when use was at a very low level, but must be answered differently when use rises. With only a very few campers at a spot, each could dig his own latrine or hole, but when one begins digging up the toilet paper of preceding parties it is time to consider a different approach. Wilderness areas are particularly susceptible to overcrowding, and limits on their use must somehow be imposed — or the wilderness will disappear as certainly as if it had been logged or mined.

*Crop and Grazing Land*

Although we showed crop and grazing land separately in figure 1, we shall discuss them together in this section; both are used to produce food and fiber for human use. As we have noted, the concept of cropland is partly a physical one, partly an economic one. This is well illustrated in Table I, which shows changes in cropland use during the past 20 years or so. The area actually used for crops declined about 50 million acres over this period; the former crop land no longer used for crops shows up partly as idle (much of which is under contract to the federal govern-

ment) or is no longer considered as cropland. Some was taken over by the expanding cities; the same physical qualities which make land suitable for cropping also make it attractive for suburban development. But some suburban expansion has taken place on land never used for crops. In spite of the decline in crop acreage, crop production rose substantially during these years; increased yields per acre far more than offset the reduced area.

The data in Table I show that feed crops (for livestock) and hay and forage crops use about 60 percent of all the land in crops; if the cropland used only for pasture is included, the proportion used to support livestock increases even further. Most of this land could produce cereals or other crops for direct human consumption, and could provide food for many hundreds of millions more people in this way. This is another measure of the lavish uses of land in the United States: We are able to produce those foods we most want, even when it requires a lot of land to do so.

Agriculture in the United States has undergone a revolution in the past generation. Total labor used in agricultural production has declined

| Kind of use | 1950 | 1964 |
|---|---|---|
| Cropland used only for pasture | 69 | 57 |
| Cropland idle or in cover crops | 22 | 52 |
| Cropland used for crops, including cultivated fallow | 387 | 335 |
| Total | 478 | 444 |
| Cropland harvested | 345 | 296 |
| Planted crop acreage[a] | | |
|     Feed grains | 147 | 114 |
|     Food grains | 82 | 62 |
|     Hay and forage | 79 | 69 |
|     Oil crops | 19 | 41 |
|     Cotton | 24 | 10 |
|     Vegetables and potatoes | 5 | 5 |
|     Fruits and nuts | 3 | 3 |
|     Tobacco | 2 | 1 |
|     Sugar crops | 1 | 2 |

**I**

U.S. MAJOR CROPLAND USES. The data are given in million acres. The first four lines of figures are for the dates shown; for the rest of the Table, "1950" is the average of 1949-1951 and "1964" is the average of 1966-1968.

[a]Where data permitted, planted acreage; otherwise, harvested acreage.

by two-thirds, and less land is used than formerly. Somewhat more capital (in greatly different forms) and new technologies all have combined to about double agricultural output. This production revolution has largely resulted from public and private research; it has not yet run its course but, on the contrary, future changes may well be greater than past changes. Accompanying it has been a social revolution. The total number of farms has declined more than one-half, primarily because young men have not been attracted into agriculture; average farms are twice as large as they were; small towns in rural areas are often decadent, because farmers increasingly go to larger but more distant towns where better services are available.

The demand for most farm commodities is relatively inelastic; that is, small increases in supply are likely to force very large reductions in price, and increases in income of consumers are likely to bring only small increases in prices at the farm. Agriculture as a whole is vulnerable to fluctuations in output; with small increases in output, prices may fall two, three, or five times as much. The individual farmer, however, produces such a small portion of total output of most commodities that he properly ignores the effect of his output on price. If a new production method is devised which enables him to produce cheaper or to produce more with his labor or both, then he is under strong pressure to adopt it. If other farmers do the same, the resulting increased output may force prices down to unprofitable levels.

It was this situation which led the federal government, at the insistence of farmers, to undertake large-scale programs for control of agricultural output a generation ago. Farmers have been paid to hold land out of production; they have been given loans to store surplus commodities; and, if the price declined, the government took over the commodities without requiring the farmers to repay the loans. Acreage control, price support, and surplus storage have been the trinity of federal agricultural programs. In recent years, direct income payments to farmers have partly replaced price supports, so that prices are now more nearly on a competitive market level. The cost of these programs has risen considerably in recent years. Total appropriations to the U.S. Department of Agriculture (which include other programs but are dominated by production control and income support programs) have reached over $6 billion in recent years, or about $2000 per average farmer. However, the government programs have reached farmers most unequally; low-income farmers have had very little help, while large farmers have received payments of many thousands of dollars. These programs have come under increasing attack, but it is not easy to get out of them — they have become embedded in agriculture, including being capitalized into land values, and their termination will undoubtedly create losses to many farmers. However, the equity or social justice of government aid to large but not small farmers, and at a cost greater than is incurred for many urgent urban problems such as housing for the poor, is increasingly challenged. While prediction of the future is often hazardous, I doubt if the present scale of federal aid to agriculture will be long continued.

Some of the grazing land is privately owned by farmers and ranchers, but much is publicly owned. It is all grazed by privately owned livestock. As we have noted, yield per acre is low, but the livestock efficiently harvest the scanty forage and often produce a high output per man engaged in this kind of operation. There are many interesting technical aspects of good grazing land management which we cannot explore here. In general, a grazing area is an ecosystem; most grazing land has limited moisture, hence competition among plants for available moisture is keen. When domestic animals graze some plants but not others, the ecological balance is disturbed. If they graze too much, the plant vigor is weakened; this is overgrazing, which usually has detrimental effects on the land. Good grazing land management consists of grazing within proper limits and at suitable seasons — and in making a profit in so doing!

Both crop and grazing land have benefited in recent years from improved management, and both are in better physical health today than they were 30 or 40 years ago. The trend in range condition is upward on many areas, or not downward on others, though it is still downward in distressingly large areas. Likewise, about 40 percent of all cropland has been adequately treated against erosion, in the judgment of the Soil Conservation Service, and additional areas have had some, but not full, treatment. Some of the worst erosion areas of 40 years ago, such as in the Piedmont areas of the Southeast, have been abandoned as no longer economic to farm; and trees and shrubs have mostly healed the erosion scars. All is far from ideal, where the physical health of crop and grazing land is concerned, yet some progress has been made. The revolution in agricultural output has been accompanied by some improvement in the basic production plant as well.

*Forests*

When the Europeans first colonized North America, the whole eastern half of the continent (with some exceptions) and large parts of the west were forested. These were forests that had evolved over centuries, each a complex ecosystem, usually but not always with more than one important tree species, other less important species, and other plants and animals. These were by and large "storage" forests; decay equalled growth, and there was no net gain in wood volume, for the land had as much timber as its sunlight, moisture, and fertility would support (Chapter 1). The variety, the size, and the quality of the trees were amazing to the Europeans. The forests were important sources of building material and of fuel to the early settlers; they were also the hiding place from which Indians swooped down upon the settlements.

Forests were long cut without thought of renewal; the doctrine of inexhaustibility or of limitless supply was more firmly held, and longer, for forests than for any other resource. In extensive areas — Ohio, for instance — forests of magnificent trees were cut down and burned, to clear the land for farming. Logs are heavy and even today cannot be transported far. The frontiersmen used what lumber they needed, but much of the forest growth was useless to them, while the land was valuable for farming. Elsewhere, and later, forests were cut to produce lumber for the expanding cities and rural population. Lumbering moved from Maine to the northern Lake states, to the South, and finally to the West. Throughout well over a hundred years of national history, trees were cut faster than they were grown; we were liquidating a large part of our inherited timber supply. This was the age when the "timber barons" were roundly denounced by conservationists, and when the national forests were established to protect our future timber supply.

Today, there is comparatively little old growth or virgin timber left. The national forests and some other federal lands have old growth stands of Douglas fir in the Pacific Northwest, of redwoods in northern California, and of various pines in the Rocky Mountain states. These are rapidly being cut, on a cyclical, or rotation, basis with schedules which are planned to provide mature stands on some land when the old growth is finally all cut. Much of the present cut is quite old; trees of 100, 200, and even 400 years are being cut; but in the future the rotation will be much shorter, generally under 100 years.

By far the greater part of the forests of the nation, however, have been cut over, most several times. Here, too, trees are cut at much younger ages and smaller sizes today than when the original stands were being cut. But the great process of forest liquidation has largely run its course; the low point in timber inventory seems to have been about the end of World War II, or about 25 years ago. Today, annual growth is about 1.6 times annual cut; timber inventory is increasing. This sounds much better than it really is; the excess growth is still in small sizes, less desirable species, and poorer quality stock than the cut, by all odds. Nevertheless, the low point in timber supply seems to have passed, at least for the present.

When inherited natural forests provided such magnificent timber for the cutting, wood products were so cheap — mostly reflecting harvesting costs only — that there was no profit in growing timber. Timber is expensive to grow, in large part because it takes so long; interest on any investment mounts greatly over the years. Moreover, there are risks from fire, disease, and insects. Prices of standing timber — "stumpage" — have risen dramatically since World War II, until today they are 10 times or more higher, for comparable grades of logs.

Today, forests in the United States can be grouped into four broad categories: (1) publicly owned, mostly federal, most of which are in national forests, still largely virgin timber; well managed and well stocked with timber, on the whole; (2) large private holdings, most by timber processors; also well managed and well stocked, on the whole; (3) farm forests or woods, individually small tracts but quite large in the aggregate; mostly poorly stocked and even more poorly managed; and (4) "other," a mixed bag, but more than a million forest landowners, most of whom own very small forest tracts, poorly stocked and poorly managed but quite extensive in total area. There has been considerable selectivity in building up these ownerships. That is, the large timber processors and other large forest owners have sought the more productive forest lands and have had the expertise to manage them well. Moreover, their investments in timber processing plants have given them an incentive to manage their forests for sustained production. Many of the large timber processors are able to practice better forestry than the public agencies, because they have found it easier to set aside funds for capital improvements such as roads.

Many farm forests are badly neglected. They often occupy land that is not suitable for cropping, hence they have never been cleared. But the farmer generally does not have the skill or the interest to manage them well as forests. Often he can make a greater return from his labor and capital by more intensive farm operations than by managing his woodlot better. Many hundreds of thousands of the small "other" forest owners apparently value their forests as recreation areas, or as possible sources of future gains in land value, or for sentimental reasons, more than they do for current income from timber production. Most of them are even less capable of managing their holdings well than are farmers.

The nature of the product from forests has changed. The pioneer often used logs to build his house; later, logs were sawed into lumber for construction purposes. In more recent times, plywood has come to be a major output; logs are literally peeled, and the peelings glued together in layers to form sheets of any desired thickness and size. Plywood sheets 3/4 inch thick and 4 feet by 8 feet in size can be used in much construction work with vastly less labor input than could the old-fashioned boards. Also in recent times, paper has become a major output of many forests, and paper has been substituted for many packaging, building, and other uses. Total lumber production has not risen above the level it attained more than 60 years ago, but plywood and paper consumption have mounted steadily. In the future, wood may be increasingly used as a source of chemical raw material — a building block for all manner of industrial output.

Forests are coming to be valued increasingly for products or services other than wood fiber production. We have discussed outdoor recreation; many forests are prime places for outdoor recreation, and often this need not compete seriously with timber harvest. Forests have important watershed values, which are increasingly recognized. A major difficulty is that the forest owner often does not gain from these other uses; he incurs the costs of good forest land management, but the downstream user of water gets the benefit. The publicly owned forests are mostly under multiple purpose management, but the contentions of various groups for relative emphasis in management create difficult problems for the public forest land manager.

*Miscellaneous Land Uses*

Figure 1 shows 150 million acres, approximately, in miscellaneous land uses when Alaska is omitted and about 350 million when it is included. This is a highly heterogeneous lot of land and of uses; we briefly consider only a few.

Some land is used for reservoirs. There are about 2 million farm ponds in the United States today, with perhaps 4 to 6 million acres in total. These have nearly all been constructed in the past 40 years; they have many uses, including recreation. There are many difficult problems in managing them; they suffer buildups of fertilizer and other chemicals, with consequent algae growth and, in extreme cases, eutrophication (Chapter 10). At best, they are often good local sources of fishing — not to be compared with distant trout water or deep sea fishing, but still pretty good, and convenient. Then there are larger reservoirs, some including many thousands of acres. In addition to their prime water supply and water regulation functions, many of these larger reservoirs are good recreation areas.

Some land is used for defense purposes — military bases, missile sites, and the like. Many people believe that the areas reserved for these purposes are excessive for the need; it is very hard for an outsider to judge. But governmental processes are likely to work faster to set up new areas when needed than to declare surplus an area no longer needed.

Some land is used for transportation. Streets are included in urban uses, as sometimes is other land used for transportation. But there are railroads and highways reaching throughout the countryside which utilize significant amounts of land. There are also airports. All of these are more important in their effect on other land than they are in terms of acreage actually used for transportation. An airport, for instance, may occupy only a few thousand acres, but the sight and sound of airplanes may be evident over several times as large a surrounding area. The highway occupies some land, but it gives value and influences use of other land to several times its extent.

Some land is used for mining; the extent of the surface use varies greatly for different kinds of mineral extraction. Oil can be withdrawn by wells, without major interference with agriculture or other surface uses. At the other extreme, open-pit mining (whether for coal, copper, iron, or other minerals) totally excludes other surface uses; even if the land is restored afterward — and it is not invariably so restored — the subsequent uses are greatly affected. If open-pit operations are carried on in steep hilly land, then the inevitable washing of soil materials affects streams and land for many miles. Shaft and tunnel operations are intermediate in their use of surface; sometimes, mined-out areas subside, with great effect upon the surface uses.

By far the greater part of the "other" in figure 1 represents land whose use is so small, or so difficult to classify, that it can most accurately be classified as idle. Some of this is sand dunes, or deserts, or bare rock mountaintops, or tundra. There is likely to be some animal and insect life,

even if sparse, on all of this, but such areas cannot generally accurately be called wildlife areas. Since some precipitation — even if very little — falls on all of it, it is watershed in a sense, but not really significant watershed. It may have some recreation value, to some groups. Yet, on the whole, it is more accurately designated idle than by any other name.

A special category of "idle" is the land in and around cities, not yet built on but withdrawn from other land uses. We mentioned this in connection with urban land use. Nationally, there is apparently 10 million acres or more in this category. A small idle land area is desirable, in the same sense that a few unemployed persons in the process of changing jobs, are desirable. But there is reason to believe that the extent of the idle land is too great and that it is as undesirable as a very large unemployed labor force would be.

*What of the Future?*

The total population of the United States will increase for the next several decades, at least; even if, by some miracle, Americans could be persuaded to discipline their reproductive processes to a level which would ultimately lead to a stationary population, the present age distribution, with its relatively large component of young people, would lead to population increases for some decades (Chapter 2). If total population increases while total land area stays constant, the inescapable arithmetic is that the land area per person declines.

Does this mean that we are facing a land shortage, or a shortage of the products of the land? Not necessarily; it depends on how well we manage. Land products, such as wheat, require inputs of management, capital, labor, various productive materials, as well as land. As we saw, agricultural output has risen dramatically in the past several decades from a SMALLER area of crop land; the best projections are that the present area of cropland will produce all the agricultural commodities we will need for another generation or longer (Table II). Likewise, forest output could be stepped up considerably from more intensive management of present forest lands. These increases will require thought and work, and will not come painlessly, but there is no reason why the real costs of many products from the land should be higher.

The situation for urban and recreation land use is different, but not necessarily any more serious. These two uses require such modest percentages of total land area that very large percentage increases in them could take place without serious impact upon other land uses — in total, although in some areas the impact would be greater. But there are great possibilities for more efficiency in the use of the land already

| Use of land for | 1900 | 1910 | 1920 | 1930 | 1940 | 1950 | 1980 | 2000 |
|---|---|---|---|---|---|---|---|---|
| Cities of 2,500 or more population[a] | 6 | 7 | 10 | 12 | 13 | 17 | 30 | 41 |
| Public recreation areas[b] | 5 | 9 | 12 | 15 | 41 | 46 | 72 | 95 |
| Agriculture: | | | | | | | | |
| Crops[c] | 319 | 347 | 402 | 413 | 399 | 409 | 388 | 388 |
| Pasture[d] | 77 | 84 | 78 | 73 | 68 | 69 | 70 | 70 |
| Other[e] | 53 | 57 | 58 | 45 | 44 | 45 | 45 | 45 |
| Subtotal | 449 | 488 | 538 | 531 | 511 | 523 | 503 | 503 |
| Commercial forestry: | | | | | | | | |
| Continuous management[f] | 0 | 30 | 60 | 200 | 300 | 359 | 385 | 405 |
| Little or no management | 525 | 482 | 440 | 295 | 188 | 125 | 90 | 50 |
| Subtotal | 525 | 512 | 500 | 495 | 488 | 484 | 475 | 455 |
| Grazing[g] | 808 | 775 | 730 | 735 | 740 | 700 | 700 | 680 |
| Transportation | 17 | 19 | 23 | 24 | 24 | 25 | 28 | 30 |
| Reservoirs and water management[h] | * | 1 | 2 | 3 | 7 | 10 | 15 | 20 |
| Primarily for wildlife | * | * | 1 | 1 | 12 | 14 | 18 | 20 |
| Mineral production<br>Deserts, swamps, mountain tops,<br>    some noncommercial forest, etc.<br>Miscellaneous and unaccounted for | 94 | 93 | 88 | 88 | 68 | 85 | 63 | 60 |
| Total | 1,904 | 1,904 | 1,904 | 1,904 | 1,904 | 1,904 | 1,904 | 1,904 |

PAST AND FUTURE U.S. LAND USE. Land use[a] is given in million acres for selected year, 1900-1950, and projections are given for 1980 and 2000. The data in this table are necessarily estimates in several instances, sometimes on a relatively scanty basis of fact. This table emphasizes land use, as separate from land ownership or control or from vegetative cover. An asterisk indicates negligible use. Source: Marion Clawson, R. Burnell Held, and C.H. Stoddard, *Land for the Future,* Table 5.1 pp. 442-443, Johns Hopkins Press, Baltimore, Maryland, 1960.

[a]Includes municipal parks.

[b]Excludes municipal parks. Includes national park system, areas within national forests reserved for recreation, state parks and acreages around TVA and Corps reservoirs reserved for recreation. Excludes all areas used primarily for other purposes even though they provide much recreation. Excludes actual water area of reservoirs, which is shown later under its own heading. Excludes also wildlife areas, which are shown below. We have assumed that only part of the increased potential demand will be met.

[c]Cropland harvested, crop failure, cultivated summer fallow, and cropland idle or in cover crops. See Tables 11 and 12, *Agriculture Information Bulletin No. 168,* U.S. Department of Agriculture, 1957.

[d]Only pasture on land which is considered cropland is included. This corresponds to the 1949 and 1954 Census of Agriculture definition. The 1900 figure is an estimate. The acreages for 1910 through 1940 are the difference between crops, as shown above, and estimates of cropland potential which included cropland pastured, given in Table 1 of *Agriculture Information Bulletin No. 140,* 1955.

[e]Farmsteads, farm roads, feed lots, lanes, ditches, and wasteland. See Tables 11 and 23, *Agriculture Information Bulletin No. 168.*

[f]This is a roughly estimated figure. For 1950, it excludes commercial forest land with no fire protection or poorly stocked as shown in *Timber Resources for America's Future,* U.S. Forest Service, 1958. For earlier years, it is our estimate of comparable definition area.

[g]Includes some noncommercial forest land used primarily for grazing.

[h]Excluding land around reservoirs and conservation pools of reservoirs, which are included in the recreation areas.

taken over for these uses. This is especially true for urban land; as we noted, the area withdrawn from other uses is now about double the area the cities actually use. If we could invent means of requiring cities to use this withdrawn land (which would not be terribly difficult) and if we had the political strength and courage to carry out the necessary steps (which is enormously more doubtful), then total urban expansion for another generation or so could be accommodated on land already withdrawn by the cities from other uses. There are also great possibilities of more intensive use of urban used land. Recreation areas could be expanded without too great difficulty; if an area equal to the idle crop land were used for recreation, this would add 50 to 100 percent to recreation land. Some of the idle cropland could be used for this purpose, some is too distantly located; but the area relationships remain accurate. A substantial increase in recreation land is desirable, although it is doubtful that we can maintain past liberal land allocation to this use.

Although land supply seems ample for our needs, some adjustments in land uses will be needed — large in some areas, small in others. And they will almost always come hard. Although some land is used today far less intensively than it might be, there is almost always some person or some group which has an interest in having it remain in its present use — they may not own it, but they will protest its rezoning if it is private land or protest its changed use if it is public land. There is an enormous volume and an almost incredible range of vested interests in present land use. One has only to read the daily newspaper in almost any city, to learn of a controversy over a highway location, or an urban renewal project, or a land rezoning proposal, or the filling of a marsh area, or any one of many other land use changes. It is no comfort whatsoever to the persons who think they would lose from this land use change, to point out that the national supply of land is ample for the national need.

All of this may be described in terms of the externalities and interdependencies which we mentioned earlier. What happens on any piece of land is of concern to many people who do not own it, live on it, or otherwise use it directly. I do have a real interest in what you do with your land, as you have in what I do with mine; and the closer we live, the greater is likely to be that interest. Changes in any land use are likely to upset or injure some persons, however great may be their net benefit to the whole public. One can rather confidently predict that controversy over land use will increase in the future.

Likewise, it seems highly probable that public control over private land use, and over changes in land use, will increase. This may be only another way of saying that the extent and the intensity of the interrelationships will increase. Society as a whole will increasingly take a hand in land use decisions; as we pointed out, it already does influence them, but somewhat haphazardly and often without the conviction that sees an issue through. As population increases, as the whole society and economy get more interdependent, it is hard to see how land use can avoid being subjected to more social controls.

In the past few years public interest in decreasing pollution, preserving beauty, and improving the quality of the environment has been on the rise, and it seems likely to continue strongly in the future. This interest will cause the passage of legislation that will affect land use. Land-use decisions formerly based solely on the concerns of the marketplace will be increasingly supplemented by basically political decisions. There will also be increasing public pressure on blatant roadside advertising and waste disposal on the land. Concern for landscape integrity and beauty will become more and more important. Many land-use decisions will still be strongly influenced by economics, but increasingly economics will also be supplemented by aesthetics.

## Further Reading

Clawson, M. 1968. *Policy Directions for U.S. Agriculture,* Johns Hopkins Press, Baltimore, Maryland.

Clawson, M., Held, B., and Stoddard, C.H.

1960. *Land for the Future,* Johns Hopkins Press, Baltimore, Maryland.

Clawson, M., and Knetsch, J.L. 1966. *Economics of Outdoor Recreation,* Johns Hopkins Press, Baltimore, Maryland.

Halcrow, H.G., ed. 1960. *Modern Land Policy,* University of Illinois Press, Urbana, Illinois.

Higbee, E. 1958. *American Agriculture:* *Geography, Resources, Conservation,* Wiley, New York.

Jarrett, H., ed. 1966. *Environmental Quality in a Growing Economy,* Johns Hopkins Press, Baltimore, Maryland.

Thorne, W., ed. 1963. *Land and Water Use,* Publication No. 73 of the American Association for the Advancement of Science, Washington, D.C.

# 7 Water Resources

Tinco E. A. van Hylckama

*For after the rain, when with never a stain*
*The pavilion of heaven is bare*
*And the winds and sunbeams with their convex gleams*
*Build up the blue dome of air*
*I silently laugh at my own cenotaph*
*And out of the caverns of rain*
*Like a child from the womb, like a ghost from the tomb*
*I arise and unbuild it again.*

*Percy B. Shelley, "The Cloud"*

## What Is Water?

The old Greeks, such as Aristotle (350 B.C.), and in a similar manner the old Chinese, held that the universe consisted of four elements: earth, fire, air, and water. (The Chinese, after Lao-tze, 580 B.C., actually recognized five: wood, metal, fire, earth, and water.) If there was a proper balance, all was good, but if the balance was wrong, there were diseases, earthquakes, and other calamities. Although there may have been

---

TINCO E. A. VAN HYLCKAMA is Professor of Hydrology at Texas Tech University. Born in the Netherlands, he studied forestry at the Agricultural University there. He spent nine years in Sumatra, Indonesia, doing research for a private company and later as a prisoner of war during World War II. Forced to leave Indonesia during the Sukarno regime, he came to the U.S. and briefly taught botany and bacteriology at a small midwestern college. After a few years as a research specialist for a frozen-food company, van Hylckama was invited to join the Johns Hopkins Laboratory of Climatology under the late C. W. Thornthwaite. Later he joined the Water Resources Division of the U.S. Geological Survey, where he worked on hydrological topics. He is the author of *The Water Balance of the World*.

times and places when and where no preference was given to any of these "elements," there is no doubt, and ancient literature proves it, that water was considered the base of all living things, especially in such cradles of civilization as Mesopotamia, China, Egypt, and Middle America.

Without water, life as we know it on the earth would be impossible. Not only would all living things dry up, the earth itself would be subject to such extreme termperature fluctuations as to make it uninhabitable. Let us, therefore, examine a few of the important characteristics of water.

In the first place, water is abundant. If we take the crust of the earth to be about 5 km deep, then we have a shell of 2540 million km$^3$ of which 1360 million km$^3$, or more than half, is water.

Secondly, water has an unusual molecular structure. A water molecule consists of one atom of oxygen and two atoms of hydrogen. Atoms consist of a nucleus with electrons rotating around it in one or more orbits. Oxygen has a nucleus and two orbits. The inner one has two electrons, the outer one has room for eight electrons, but there are actually only six. The hydrogen atom consists of a nucleus and one orbit with only one electron, but there is room for two. The result is that there is a strong bondage between the three atoms resulting in a molecule that, unlike most other molecules, is asymmetric with an uneven electrical charge.

Because in most minerals occurring in nature the atoms are held together by electrical attraction, the water molecule with its positive and negative charge can easily squeeze in between atoms in other molecules and this is the cause of the enormous dissolving power of water. There is no other fluid known that can match it. It also explains, in part, the action of water upon the earth's surface, known as erosion. Mountains are continuously dissolved and, over the aeons, washed into the sea.

The irregular shape of the water molecule has other consequences of great importance to our lives. When water becomes a solid (freezes) the molecules become arranged in open crystallike structures. Consequently ice is less dense than water. If ice melts, that is, goes from the solid to the liquid phase, the molecules move around more freely, filling up the holes, and water gets denser. The densest point is reached at 4°C. With rising temperatures, the molecules begin to move faster and faster, occupying more and more space until at 100°C the water boils, that is, it goes from the liquid to the gaseous phase. However, because of the strong molecular attraction, it takes enormous energy to bring water into the gaseous stage.

The opposite is also true. When water condenses enormous quantities of energy are released. This happens in summer time in our cumulus clouds, which on an afternoon in only an hour or so may build up into a thunderstorm. One average thunderstorm has the same energy as is created by the burning of 6000 metric tons of coal.

Summing up then, you may say that (1) water is more abundant than any other substance on the surface of the earth, (2) it is almost the only inorganic liquid that can be found in nature which occurs as gas, liquid, and solid often at the same time, (3) water has a higher solvent power than any other fluid. And these are only a few of the very exceptional properties of water.

*Biological Importance of Water*

Notwithstanding the unusualness of water from a chemical and physical point of view, or rather because of it, water is the source of all life on earth, and the first living things were undoubtedly formed in the primordial ooze. Water is the largest constituent of animal and vegetable tissue; it is the largest part of anything we drink even if we don't call it water; it is the source of enormous energy not only in natural occurrences

such as thunderstorms, but also in man-made devices such as turbines and steam engines. Without water, agriculture would be impossible and a large part of our industries would be rendered impotent.

The inheritance of the origin of life in watery surroundings is still with us. There are only a few living things that contain less than 10 percent of their weight in water, for example, plant seeds and spores of bacteria and fungi. Most of the vegetable matter that we use for food, such as tomatoes, potatoes, lettuce, and carrots contains at the time of harvest 85 to 90 percent water by weight. Even such derived foods as bread contain more than 30 percent water.

Man himself is extremely watery. This author weighs 65 kg; about 70 percent of this, or more than 45 kg, is water and he must continuously strive to keep this ratio as is, otherwise he will die of dehydration long before the water is completely evaporated out of his body. The amount of water man needs varies with the circumstances in which he lives and works. The very minimum probably lies between 2 and 4 liters per day, including the water that is used for cooking his food.

Man and all other animals depend on plant material directly or indirectly, for food. The basic plant-building process is photosynthesis. The total amounts of carbon dioxide and water used for this process are difficult to estimate. As a safe guess we may say that all plants in the world use $600 \times 10^{12}$ kg (600 billion metric tons) of water per year to build their plant material. This amounts to about 600 km$^3$ liquid water or 1 percent of the total water that is evaporated off lakes, streams, and moist soils, and transpires from leaf surfaces of living plants.

But it is not only the sweet water that is of biological importance. The oceans contain more than 95 percent of all the water on the earth and it is not drinkable. Nonetheless, without this salt water, life on this planet would be next to impossible, as we shall discuss later on. First we need to look at what is called the hydrologic cycle.

*The Hydrologic Cycle*

We all know that water does not have to boil to produce vapor. We can see vapor rising from warm water long before it boils, and even out-doors this is observable, for instance, when on a cool morning, warm irrigation water produces a layer of vapor in the air above it. The energy for such processes comes almost entirely from the sun. The total energy intercepted by the earth is $3.67 \times 10^{21}$ calories per day; that is, the same energy as would be produced by 10,000 hurricanes. It is enough energy to evaporate more than 6000 $km^3$ of water. Actually only about one-sixth or 1100 $km^3$ goes into the air every day because not all the energy received from the sun is used for evaporation (Chapter 5).

The total amount of water present in the atmosphere at any one time is estimated to be 13,000 $km^3$. If we divide this number by the 1100 $km^3$ that goes into the air each day, we see that about once every 12 days all the water in the air falls and is replaced.

Most of the water evaporated through the sun's energy is derived from the oceans, but about 16 percent comes from the land surfaces, lakes, streams, moist soils, and the leaves of transpiring vegetation. A large part of the water that is evaporated eventually falls back on the ocean, but about 24 percent falls on the land surfaces. Notice that this is a larger percentage than what evaporates from the land. However, 9 percent does not remain long on the land surfaces. It soon reaches streams and rivers and in a comparatively short time, varying between a few hours and a few weeks, it again arrives in oceans. That leaves 15 percent which remains on the land in forms of ice, snow, and moisture in the soil. It is this water that becomes available to the plants; a small part of it is used to build up their tissue, and a very large part for transpiration. Of course, water perspired and exhaled by animals and that consumed by them, either directly by drinking, or by eating, also is a part of the cycle; but these amounts are so small that we can neglect them.

All this can be briefly summed up by an illustration. Figure 1 is one of the many ways in which the hydrologic cycle can be shown.[1] Due to the sun's energy, water rises from oceans, lakes, and other surfaces, condenses in the air to form clouds, and the water returns to the earth in the form of rain, snow, or hail. The part that falls back on oceans, lakes, and streams has made, so to speak, a short cycle.

What happens to the part that falls on land is another matter. Some penetrates into the soil and becomes available to the plants, but soil, like a sponge, can hold just so much water. When the water holding capacity is reached, water can enter only at the rate that water percolates down under the influence of gravity and capillary attraction. When rain falls faster than the percolating rate, water begins to collect in puddles and ditches, starts to run off, following the slopes of the land, and eventually reaches streams and rivers. The part that has entered the soil and is not picked up by plant roots can continue to travel down and reach what is called the WATER TABLE. If you take a glass bowl, fill it with some sand and then pour water in it, you can see a distinct line marking the position between the wet and dry sand. This line is the water table. Below the line, the sand is saturated, above it, unsaturated or dry. In moist climates such a table can be found at depths of only a few meters or even less; in dry climates there may not be a water table at all. In both places, however, water may have collected in prehistoric times and, due to processes of erosion, sedimentation, and other geological activities, be buried. This is the deep groundwater which plays such an important role in large areas of the western United States, of North Africa, and many other places. Sometimes this water is under enormous pressures, due to the overlying rock and soil formations, and when wells are dug, water may spout several meters into the air, forming a fountain that will last until the pressure in the underlying layers is released. Such water-carrying layers under pressure are called ARTESIAN AQUIFERS. ''Artesian'' comes from the town Artois in France, where the first such well is said to have been dug, and "aquifer" is derived from the Latin words "aqua" for water and "ferre" meaning to carry.

The main thing that the hydrologic cycle illustrates is that water is constantly refreshed and there is plenty of it provided man takes good care of it and manages it wisely. We will discuss this further when we talk about sweet water.

*Salt Water*

More than 7/10 of the earth's surface is covered by water, and nearly all of this water is

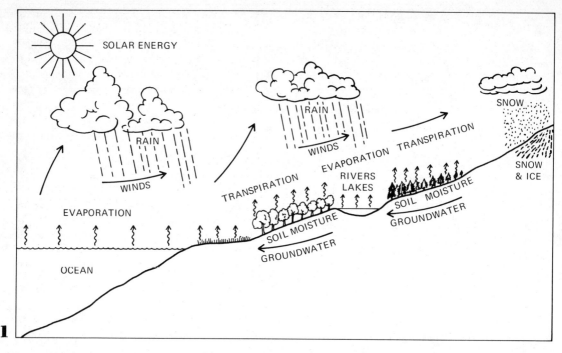

THE HYDROLOGIC CYCLE. *Source:* reference 1.

salty. The total volume has been variously estimated between 1100 and 1300 million km$^3$, slightly more than 0.1 percent of the total volume of the earth.

Ocean water contains on the average 35 grams of dissolved solids for each liter. By far the largest part of these solids, more than 70 percent, is sodium chloride, which we know as kitchen salt. Because of this salt, the properties of oceanic water differ from those of sweet water. Oceanic water does not have its greatest density at 4°C and it does not freeze at 0°C. It freezes at about −2°C and has at that temperature also its greatest density. In consequence oceanic water, when it cools, sinks. The resulting mixing is very important and necessary for plant and animal life. Considered as a direct resource of water the oceans are of little value because the water is unsuitable for agricultural, domestic, and most industrial use. Indirectly, however, the oceans are of enormous importance.

In the first place, there is the fact that in addition to the salts that are dissolved in the oceans, gases also dissolve in water, for example, the two most important ones for aquatic and terrestrial

life: oxygen and carbon dioxide. If the surface of water is cut off from the atmosphere, for instance, by oil slicks, the oxygen content of the water will diminish and life underneath the surface will perish.

Whereas there is little oxygen in water compared to that contained in a same volume of air, the opposite is true for carbon dioxide. The $CO_2$ concentration of the atmosphere has increased markedly since industrial development started to burn increasing quantities of coal, oil, and gas. Now, the oceans absorb huge quantities of this carbon dioxide and thus act as a buffer for changes in atmospheric $CO_2$. The result is that, although a slight increase in the average carbon dioxide content of the air has been observed, the amount is as yet far too small to affect the breathability of the atmosphere. However, even small increases in $CO_2$ content may result in a significant increase of the temperature of the air and thereby affect the climate in the future (Chapter 15).

So we see that the oceans in part are helping to keep the chemical conditions of the atmosphere in equilibrium. They also affect the temperature and the climate of the world. One can get a faint idea of what would happen without the equalizing effect of the oceans by looking at extreme temperature records. In some places remote from the ocean, such as the Sahara, the temperature can rise to over 50°C in the afternoon and fall 12 hours later to below freezing. Without the oceans, these extremes would be even larger, somewhat like those one finds on the moon.

*Sweet Water*

Table I summarizes some important facts about the distribution of all the water on the earth. We see that only 3 percent can be considered sweet water and more than two-thirds of this or more than 2 percent of all the water, is inaccessible for present practical purposes because it is locked up in forms of ice and snow mostly on the Antarctic continents and on Greenland and also as glaciers on the mountains of the world. The total amount thus locked up is variously estimated between 28 and 35 million km$^3$. The table has 29 million km$^3$ of which 200 thousand km$^3$ is glacier ice. If it all suddenly became melted and evenly distributed over the earth, it would form a sea of sweet water about 60 meters deep.

The rest of the water, or only 1 percent of the total, is found in three places: the atmosphere, where it occurs as clouds, fog, rain, and vapor; in lakes and streams, where rainwater or melted snow has been collected; or in the soil and underneath, where rain and melted snow have infiltrated.

The average amount of water present in the atmosphere is comparatively small, as we have seen earlier. If the 13,000 km$^3$ could be extracted and evenly divided over the earth's surface they would form a sheet of water only 2.5 cm thick. In contrast with this, the average rainfall over the earth is about 80 cm. This is made possible through the tremendous turnover which we have discussed earlier. One could say the same water falls 30 times per year.

The total amount of water present in sweet water lakes is about 125,000 km$^3$. That in rivers and streams has been estimated at about 1200 to 1300 km$^3$ at any one time. Because this water is in "perpetual" motion, we might say that it is continuously renewed. It is the "living water" that was, and still is, the main source of supply for our agricultural, industrial, and domestic needs, and that inspired Heraclitus (600 B.C.) to his famous dictum: *panta rei*, "all things flow".

A little arithmetic will show that, on the face of it, the flowing amount of water is an enormous quantity. Suppose the world carries 6 billion people, a number that has been estimated to be the world population by the year 2000. This number divided into 1300 km$^3$ would give 216,000 liters per person. A city dweller in the United States uses about 500 liters per day for his personal use. Thus it seems that there is plenty of sweet water on hand at any time. For several reasons this is not so. Some of the biggest rivers flow in areas that are practically uninhabit-

|  | World | Percent | U.S.A. |
|---|---|---|---|
| **Water on land** | | | |
| Freshwater lakes | 125,000 | 0.009 | 20,000 |
| Rivers (at any one time) | 1,300 | – | 70 |
| Glaciers | 200,000 | 0.015 | 40,000 |
| Ice caps | 28,800,000 | 2.1 | – |
| Saline lakes | 100,000 | 0.007 | 10,000 |
| **Water in the land** | | | |
| Soil moisture | 65,000 | 0.005 | 4,500 |
| Groundwater | | | |
| Within 1000 meters | 4,000,000 | 0.29 | 300,000 |
| In the next 1000 meters | 4,000,000 | 0.29 | 300,000 |
| Atmosphere | 13,000 | 0.001 | 300 |
| World oceans | 1,320,000,000 | 97. | – |
| **Total (in round figures)** | 1,360,000,000 | 100. | 700,000 |
| **Annual evaporation** | | | |
| From land | 56,000 | 0.004 | 4,000 |
| From oceans | 344,000 | 0.025 | – |
| **Total** | 400,000 | 0.029 | |
| **Annual precipitation** | | | |
| On land | 96,000 | 0.007 | 6,000 |
| On oceans | 304,000 | 0.022 | – |
| **Total** | 400,000 | 0.029 | |
| **Runoff of all rivers** | | | |
| Per year (water yield) | 40,000 | 0.003 | 2,000 |

**WATER SUPPLY DATA.** The numbers are given in cubic kilometers (km$^3$).

able such as the Amazon, the three big Siberian rivers, Ob, Yenesey, and Lena, and the mighty MacKenzie in northern Canada. Moreover, a large part of the world population, especially in the United States, lives or wants to live in areas where there are no rivers or only small rivers. In other places the rivers have been so intensely used as sewage canals that the water is unfit for human consumption unless it would be thoroughly and expensively treated. Such is the case with the Mississippi in the United States, the Rhine in Europe, the Ganges in India, and the Volga in the USSR.[2] Since all the water that is out of reach or unusable is part of the 1300 $km^3$, the actual available amount is much less than 216,000 liters per person, maybe only 50,000 liters per person.

Furthermore, we considered only the use of water by city dwellers, but this is just the water for personal use. Far more water is used in industry and agriculture. It has been estimated that in the United States 6000 liters of water per day per person are used to provide each citizen with food, clothing, and the amenities of life he is used to. A large part of this water is being used over and over again, such as water used for cooling in the steel industry. On the other hand, water used in the strip mining and in the paper and pulp industries is unfit for further consumption unless it is purified.

In the past, great civilizations developed along rivers: the Indus in India, the Yangtze and Huang Ho in China, the Euphrates and Tigris in what is now Iraq, and the Nile in Egypt, but it was not always easy. Rivers are fed by rainfall and snow melt. Since quantity and distribution of rain and snow are often erratic, stream flow may be scant at times; at other times disastrous floods may occur. Rivers fed by glacier melt, such as the Rhine, are often more stable, but large floods can occur there too. Especially the Chinese rivers are notorious for such flooding.

This brings us to the greatest difficulty man has in managing his water resources: to regulate stream flow in such a fashion that there will be a predictable supply available at all times. In the dry areas of the southwest United States, the difference between annual maximum and minimum flow in rivers may vary by a factor of 200; in the humid east, the extremes are much smaller, the maximum flow may be only five times the minimum. It is no wonder that the most elaborate examples of stream flow regulation are found in arid lands. By building dams, artificial lakes can be created from which, during times of scanty rainfall, water supplies can be drawn. There are problems connected with reservoir building which will be discussed later. Let it suffice here to say that in heavily urbanized areas, such as New York and Philadelphia which now compete for the same waters of the Delaware basin, the situation could become critical.[3]

Another large source of sweet water occurs as groundwater, present below the water table in aquifers (under pressure or not). There are probably 4 million $km^3$ of water stored in the upper 1000 meters of the earth's crust and possibly another 4 million $km^3$ deeper down. Much of the water that occurs in deep layers is under heavy pressure of the earth above it and has in consequence a high temperature and a high dissolving power. Hence water that is pumped from great depths is often too hot and too briny for use on an economic scale.

Up till recent times only shallow groundwater could be used. Modern pumping technique has made it possible to open up huge sources of groundwater such as found on the high plains of Texas, Kansas, and Nebraska, in the San Joaquin Valley in California, in the deserts around Lake Chad in north Africa, and those in west Pakistan. As a look at the hydrologic cycle (Figure 1) shows, it is possible that the water withdrawn from underground can be replaced by rainfall seeping in through the layers above the aquifer or laterally from hills or mountains in the neighborhood. Such was expected to be the case in California, but it should be realized that water moves through the ground only very, very slowly, a few meters a day at the most, except for the rare places where the water actually runs as underground rivers in limestone areas such as the Karst in Yugoslavia, the Luray caverns in Virginia, and elsewhere. So, unless the withdrawal is equal to the recharge, groundwater is being mined and becomes a nonrenewable resource. This happened north of Phoenix, Arizona where the desert was converted into cotton fields which had to be abandoned when the water levels dropped so far that pumping became uneconomical. A similar situation may soon exist to the south of Phoenix in the fertile valleys around Casa Grande.

Table I further shows that the total amount in fresh water lakes is only a minuscule part of all the sweet water on the surface of the earth and that contained in rivers at any one time is even less. Comparing the columns for the world and the U.S.A., it may come as a surprise that the estimate for the lakes in the U.S.A. is so small, as we are apt to think that the Great Lakes would account for a much larger percentage. But these lakes are shallow, with a maximum depth of 400 meters for Lake Superior, and only 60 for Lake Erie, whereas Lake Baikal in southern Siberia is over 1600 meters deep and contains 26,000 km$^3$ of water, which is more than all the Great Lakes combined. The largest single saline lake is the Caspian Sea, which contains more than three-fourths of all the saline water on the land areas.

Soil moisture, that is the water in the ground above the water table, accounts for only 0.005 percent of all the water, but it is very important because this is the water that is available to the plant roots whereas groundwater is usually too deep. However, because the soil, by a spongelike action, can take up water from below, groundwater can rise into the zone where roots are developed.

Groundwater can also supply water to the lakes and rivers. If the water table is high enough, aquifers act as reservoirs supplying surface streams with water during rainless periods or when the melting snow does not feed the streams. It has been calculated that at the present rate of water seeping to the aquifer, a process which is called natural recharge, it would take 150 years to build up the estimated U.S. supply of 300,000 km$^3$. So groundwater, unlike the water in rivers, does not renew itself annually, and where it is depleted, it may take years to recover even if pumping were stopped altogether.

*Water Use*

When we begin to evaluate how man utilizes the water resources it becomes soon apparent that there are three types of use. In the first place, there is the WITHDRAWAL: the amount of water that is taken out of a stream or pumped out of an underground or surface reservoir. If this water is used in industry, say for the purpose of cooling, it can, after use, be stored in the reservoir and be used again as soon as it has cooled off sufficiently, or it can be released into the stream from which it was taken. If the quality and the temperature have not changed drastically, the released water can be reused and the only loss is that due to evaporation. The same may be said for urban use of water. After it has been used for food and drink supply, for other uses in the household including that in the garden and bathroom, it enters a sewage system (if such is available), undergoes a biological and chemical treatment, and is again usable or could be released into streams as clean water. The Ohio River's water, for instance, is used on an average of four times before it gets to the Mississippi. It is the sad truth that returning the water to the river clean, cool, and drinkable, is far from the general practice (Chapter 10).

The second type of use also starts with withdrawal, but only a small part of the water withdrawn is returned because most of it is used by the plants for transpiration and evaporates from the soils and ditches during the irrigation of crops. The part that is so lost is called CONSUMPTIVE USE. It is not necessary, though, that man is the instigator of this type of use. Plants growing along rivers withdraw water from the streams and some are even capable of withdrawing it from groundwater. Since many of these plants have no economic value, the loss is often considered total, whereas, under agricultural and forest conditions the water contained in the harvested parts is, of course, economically used. A considerable amount of water that has passed through an irrigated field is, at least theoretically, reusable. However, too often, during the irrigation process water has taken up such quantities of salt and silt that it is no longer fit for further use. The Colorado River provides a most revealing example and will be discussed in some detail later on. Another disturbing example is found in west Pakistan. Thirty million people live on the Indus plain, where an enormous irrigation network delivers water to 90,000 km$^2$ of land, but 2000 of these are already lost because of salinity and this number increases every year.[4] If this holds true elsewhere such fertile areas as the Imperial Valley in California may be in danger.

The third use of water is called NONWITH-DRAWAL use. This is the use that is made of water for navigation on rivers, for swimming, boating, and fishing in lakes and reservoirs, and for other recreational purposes. If these were only nonwithdrawal uses they would affect the quality of the water only slightly, but the greatest nonwithdrawal use of water is made by industry, cities, and agriculture when they dump sewage, waste, and everything they want to get rid of into the rivers, lakes, and streams. Lake Erie has been referred to as a garbage dump and the Mississippi has been called the sewage pipe of middle America.

Water use is also classified by type of supply. By MUNICIPAL supply we mean a publicly or privately owned water system that mainly serves a city or suburb and may supply some water to local commerce or industry. SELF-SUPPLIED IN-DUSTRIAL water is derived from a system established by an industry for its own use, such as wells on its own or leased property or a diversion dam in a river. Water withdrawn for hydroelectric power is usually not included in this category. Water supplied to a crop by a system of sprinklers or ditches is called IRRIGATION supply or use, while water on the farm (stock and poultry watering, lawn sprinkling, and so on) not obtained from a municipal system is called RURAL supply. The last two are often combined.

We shall now discuss in some detail the quantities of water used and needed (which is not the same thing) by agricultural, by industrial, and by urban development. Notice that no mention is made of precipitation because: (1) the part that is used directly by plants is no longer available for other use, and (2) the part that reaches rivers, streams, and lakes is later withdrawn for the various uses mentioned above.

*Agricultural Use of Water*

The water withdrawal and the consumptive use by a hectare of any particular crop varies enormously with the climatic conditions. In moist climates, with more or less sufficient rainfall, the withdrawal, either from streams or groundwater, is small and consumptive use is also very small. On the other hand, a hectare of the same crop grown in arid conditions not only requires a large withdrawal, often from groundwater supplies, but also the consumptive use is very large because the plants transpire roughly in proportion to the temperatures of the air and large amounts of water are lost directly by evaporation from the fields and ditches and by seepage from unlined ditches into the ground before the water reaches the irrigated field.

Especially when there is a shortage of water it is very important to know exactly what is the minimum amount of water necessary for maximum production of a crop. The knowledge of these quantities for different crops under different circumstances is very scant and often contradictory. The result is that many farmers, just to be on the safe side, use more water than is actually needed. This tail water, as it is called, runs off at the low side of an irrigated field, sometimes flooding roads and eventually running to waste, although a small part may eventually reach the groundwater again. There is another incentive to such a wasteful practice which is the result of some peculiarities in our water laws. We will discuss these later on.

A very important problem is the overdraft on groundwater caused by tapping aquifers for irrigation water. We have already seen that most groundwater is replenished only very slowly and often from great distances, if at all. The high plains of Texas owe their prosperity to waters accumulated there hundreds of thousands of years ago in an aquifer called the Ogallala formation. This water is pumped out faster than it is renewed by infiltration of snow or rainwater. The water table is dropping at an overall average rate of 3 meters per year. Sooner or later all the water will be used up and unless surface water is imported one way or another, the country will have to abandon its present type of agriculture. The eastern part of New Mexico overlies the same formation but here the water policy is different. Land owners have no unlimited right to pump the water below their properties, and state and federal geological survey hydrologists determine the amount of withdrawal that will ensure a

40-year lifetime for the aquifer. Although this, to a certain extent, is a matter of postponement of execution, it did result in a different land use. There is a significantly higher percentage of ranch land which is even visible from outer space. When in 1960, Apollo 9 flew over the area, the astronauts took photos on which the New Mexico-Texas border showed up as a remarkably clear straight line.

## Industrial Use of Water

In what we call well-developed countries, that is countries with a significant amount of industry, industrial enterprises withdraw about an equal amount of water as is withdrawn by agriculture, but consumptive use is only a fraction of the water withdrawn. Moreover, in many cases the water can be used many times before it becomes unfit for the particular purpose. It takes roughly 100,000 liters of water to make one automobile, but a good part of this water is used again for the next automobile and so on. Some industries can use water that is too acid, alkaline, or saline for agricultural use. This is especially so when water is used for cooling. More than 90 percent of all the water used by industry in the United States is for cooling, and 25 percent of it is saline. There is one industry which deserves particular mention because it neither withdraws nor consumes water, and that is the hydroelectric industry. Whether it uses a natural waterfall, or the artificially created power of water falling through a dam, or the velocity of a flowing stream, the quality of the water is practically unimpaired and only a negligible part is lost consumptively. At most some increase in temperature after use can be noticed. Nuclear power plants cause a much larger increase in temperature of the cooling water, often as much as 10°C. Such heating is sometimes referred to as thermal pollution.

## Domestic Use of Water

Water for domestic use is only a fraction of that used by agriculture or industry. The withdrawal is on the order of 7 percent of the total, but this is an exceedingly important 7 percent because of the requirements of purity, or better drinkability, of this water. The standard requirements vary from country to country, and the deviations from standard probably even more. One notorious example is the drinking water in Philadelphia which, although biologically pure, is heavily contaminated with industrial effluents such as oil, iron, and manganese. Another is found in Buckeye, Arizona, a town of 5000 inhabitants, which used until a few years ago groundwater with a 5000 to 6000 parts per million of dissolved solids, mostly as sodium chloride. The average health standard is on the order of 500 parts per million of dissolved solids. Buckeye got rid of its brackish tasting water by taking out the excess salts, using a process which will be discussed later. In Paris, France, the drinkability problem is partially solved by having two plumbing systems. One used for irrigation, street cleaning, and industrial processes, the other for human consumption and related use.

Urbanites seem to be extremely wasteful with their precious water. Quantities used for bathing and shaving, for instance, are excessive to say the least. On a summer day, a person may easily let five glasses go down the drain in order to obtain one which is cool enough That some improvement is possible was interestingly shown in New York where in 1949 the average water use was more than 1000 liters per person per day. Because of that year's drought, the storage levels in the reservoirs providing the city with water were precariously low, and a campaign began urging people to save water, even to such an extent as to urge the men to grow beards rather than shave. The result was that the water use dropped to 600 liters per person per day and even after the immediate danger of water shortage was over the water remained 200 to 300 liters per person per day below the previous use. Still the per capita use is excessive compared to that in rural areas. Water in cities is indeed so much taken for granted and so cheap that the only time a thought is given to water shortage is when a person opens a faucet and no water appears.

## Water Use in the United States

Water use over the world is difficult to estimate but data for the United States are regularly pub-

**II**

| Supply | For public supplies | | | Rural use | | | Irrigation | |
|---|---|---|---|---|---|---|---|---|
| | Withdrawn | C.U.[a] | Per person | Withdrawn | C.U.[a] | Total | Lost[b] | C.U.[a] |
| Surface water | 60.2 | – | 620 | 3.2 | – | 280 | – | – |
| Groundwater | 30.9 | – | 550 | 12.1 | – | 160 | – | – |
| Total | 91.1 | 19.7 | 600 | 15.3 | 12.1 | 440 | 91 | 249 |

U.S. WATER USE. Water use in the United States in 1965. All figures are given in $10^9$ liters/day, except use per person, which is given in liters/day. Source: reference 5.
[a]Consumptive use (evaporation and transpiration).
[b]Lost in transit (evaporation and seepage).

lished. Tables II and III present some data on water use for various purposes according to the latest available source.[5] The first table shows that about two-thirds of water used for public supplies (that is, mostly municipal water) comes from surface water sources. Of 91.1 billion liters total use per day, 19.7 billion, or slightly over 21 percent, are consumptively used. Of the 15.3 billion liters withdrawn for rural use (that is, both domestic and livestock) about 80 percent is derived from groundwater and an equal amount is consumed. It is an interesting and disturbing fact that 91 billion liters per day, or more than 20 percent of all water used for irrigation, is lost while the water is in transit from the source to the fields, that is, by evaporation from open ditches and by seepage from unlined canals. An additional 56.5 percent is used for evaporation and transpiration in the field itself. Electric utilities can and do use a considerable amount of saline water and Table III shows that nearly two-thirds of all the water is used in the production of thermoelectric power. The consumptive use is just 2 percent and very small compared to the consumptive uses mentioned in Table II.

**III**

| Supply | Electric utilities | Other | Total | C.U.[a] |
|---|---|---|---|---|
| Surface water (sweet) | 348.0 | 113.4 | 461.4 | – |
| Surface water (saline) | 136.0 | 31.8 | 167.8 | – |
| Groundwater (sweet) | 4.2 | 25.7 | 29.9 | – |
| Groundwater (saline) | 0.4 | 1.3 | 1.7 | – |
| Total | 488.6 | 172.2 | 660.8 | 14.4 |

SELF-SUPPORTED INDUSTRIAL WATER USE. Data for water use in the United States in 1965 by self-supported industry, given in $10^9$ liters/day. Source: reference 5.
[a]Consumptive use.

In Figure 2, the total withdrawals from surface and groundwater are presented by water-use regions. Notice that the southwestern part of the country uses far more groundwater in relation to surface water than the east. Figure 3 shows data comparing withdrawal for industry with that for irrigation by water-use regions. Use for irrigation is small compared to that for industry in the northeast, but very large in the dry west. The total average water yield in the United States is 2000 km³ per year (Table I) or 5400 billion liters per day. The withdrawal is 1200 billion liters per day, of which 25 percent is lost by evapotranspiration.[4] Since this loss is only 6.5 percent of the total water yield ($5400 \times 10^9$ liters per day), we could conclude that there is plenty of water. The problem is not in the quantity but in the quality and the distribution.

Table IV is an attempt to look into the future.[6] Noteworthy is the more than fourfold increase in water use by industry expected by the year 2000. Apparently no more efficient water use for rural and irrigation purposes is foreseen. The percentage of water consumed is expected to rise from 56 percent in 1960 to 68 percent in 2000. On the other hand, the increase in water withdrawn for agriculture *per person* would slightly diminish. Piper's figures[6] are based on a per decade increase in population of 17 percent but assume a 14 percent increase in use for irrigation.

He further projects a 19 percent increase in public use, hence a small increase per head. By contrast, industry's use is to jump 47 percent per decade, which means that the per capita use by 2000 will be more than doubled.

It is now useful to compare the data of Table IV with some from Table I. The total withdrawal for the year 2000 is estimated to be $3359 \times 10^9$ liters per day or about 1260 km³ per year. Table

U.S. WATER WITHDRAWAL. Total water withdrawals by water-use regions (excluding hydroelectric power) from surface water (upper number) and groundwater (lower number) in billion ($10^9$) liters per day, in 1965. Source: reference 5.

I shows that the water yield for the United States is 2000 km$^3$ per year, a great deal more than the estimated demands. Moreover the 1260 km$^3$ is withdrawal, therefore a good part of this water can be used one or more times if it is handled wisely. The water consumed, that is, the water that is lost for further use until it returns as precipitation, is only 20 percent of the water withdrawn.

All these are generalized figures summarizing data valid for a large part of a whole continent. On a smaller scale the situation can be much more complicated and, at times, less reassuring as far as the future is concerned. As an illustration two examples follow, one dealing with a pre-

| | Withdrawn | | | | | Consumed | | | | | |
|---|---|---|---|---|---|---|---|---|---|---|---|
| | 1960 | 1980 | %[a] | 2000 | %[a] | 1960 | %[b] | 1980 | %[b] | 2000 | %[b] |
| Public Supplies | 80 | 110 | 137 | 159 | 199 | 11 | 14 | 13 | 12 | 21 | 13 |
| Industry | 530 | 1374 | 259 | 2505 | 473 | 12 | 2.3 | 42 | 3.1 | 91 | 3,6 |
| Rural and Irrigation | 415 | 631 | 152 | 695 | 167 | 232 | 56 | 393 | 62 | 475 | 68 |
| Total | 1025 | 2115 | 203 | 3359 | 328 | 255 | 25 | 448 | 21 | 587 | 18 |

FUTURE U.S. WATER USE. Estimated future water use in the United States, given in $10^9$ liters/day. Source: references 5 and 6.
[a] Increase over 1960; 1960 = 100%
[b] Percentage of withdrawal in same year.

2

IV

dominantly rural area in a dry climate and the other with a very densely populated district, but in a moist climate.

### The Lower Colorado

The head waters of the Colorado River and its tributaries are in the high mountains of Wyoming, Colorado, and Utah. The river enters Arizona just north of Lees Ferry, runs through the spectacular Grand Canyon, and from there winds its way south toward the Gulf of California, a distance of more than 2200 kilometers. Before 1935 the Colorado was an unpredictable stream because the quantities of snow and rain, and the rates of snow melt varied so much that the river was a roaring current at some times and a mere trickle at others. From 1905 to 1923 the average yearly runoff at Lees Ferry was 20 km$^3$ per year, and when in 1922 the seven states that claimed a right to Colorado River water got together and drew up the Colorado River Compact, it was decided that the basin area below Lees Ferry (mostly parts of Nevada, Arizona and California) would be entitled to about half that amount and the area above (mostly parts of Wyoming, Utah, Colorado, and New Mexico) would get the other half. But after 1923 and up until 1963 the river never again reached this average. In only 6 years was the runoff larger than 20 km$^3$ per year, while 22 years yielded less than 15 km$^3$. In other words, the states claimed water that simply was not there.

In 1935 the Hoover Dam was built with the idea of creating a reservoir from which during dry times water could be withdrawn so that the area below the dam could be ensured of a dependable supply. Because the water from upstream carries a heavy load of silt (partly as a

**U.S. INDUSTRIAL AND IRRIGATION WATER WITHDRAWAL.** Self-supplied industrial water withdrawals (upper number) and irrigation water withdrawals (lower number) by water-use regions in billion (10$^9$) liters per day, in 1965. Source: reference 5.

result of poor land management in the hills and mountains), Lake Mead, as the reservoir was called, began to collect mud at a rate faster than was expected. In 1963 Glen Canyon Dam was built, not only to provide power and water for irrigation to areas above Lees Ferry, but also to diminish the rate of sedimentation in Lake Mead. Lake Powell, as the reservoir above Glen Canyon Dam is called, began to fill up in 1963 and it was hoped that there would be enough water to start generating electricity by June, 1964. But 1961 and 1962 had been dry years and, with Glen Canyon Dam withholding water from Lake Mead, the level there got so low that, unless something was done, it would be impossible to keep the generators at Hoover Dam operating. So the Bureau of Reclamation, which is in charge of these works, opened the gates at Lake Powell in order to fill Lake Mead. This made people in the upper states unhappy because they had to wait so much longer before they got their electricity and irrigation water. In the mean time Davis and Parker Dams down the stream from Hoover Dam had been built, again with the idea of providing dependable water supplies not only to farm land but in particular to Los Angeles from behind Parker Dam. Thus two more lakes had been created: Lake Mohave and Lake Havasu. All these reservoirs are in hot country and evaporate great quantities of water, estimated at slightly more than 2 km$^3$ per year or nearly 10 percent of the high average flow from before 1923. (This is enough water to make about 4 million people happy.) As a result of the evaporation, salt concentrations in the river water are high. Below Hoover Dam it is 700, at Lake Havasu it is 800, and at the Imperial diversion Dam just north of Yuma, it is 900 parts per million. From behind Imperial Dam this water is diverted via the All-American canal to Imperial Valley in California. On the Arizona side of the river is the Wellton Mohawk irrigation district which also uses Colorado River water, but because of the poor drainage conditions, the fields there were in danger of becoming saturated with saline water. The water was therefore pumped out and back into the Colorado River behind the Morelos diversion Dam from where the water can be delivered to Mexico. The Mexican farmers protested that a salt level of well over 1000 mg/liter ruined their fields and now the water from the Wellton Mohawk district is often carried around Morelos Dam into the Colorado River and hence directly to the Gulf of California.

We might say that the Colorado River is "overworked." The demand for water is simply greater than the river can deliver even with multiple reuse. There are plans (at least temporarily canceled) to build two more dams, Bridge Canyon Dam above Lake Mead and Marble Canyon Dam a few miles north of the up-river boundary of Grand Canyon National Park below Glen Canyon Dam. They might be useful for generating power but would not create more water. It has been suggested that water be diverted from the Columbia River to the Colorado area, but this belongs in the realm of the "grandiose water plans" and is a different story.

*New York City*

New York City, located on the Hudson River, should have plenty of water both for municipal and industrial use, yet this is not the case. The story, splendidly told by Schneider and Spieker,[3] is quoted here in full.

> In its early years, New York's water was supplied by shallow wells and small reservoirs, all privately owned. None of these sources was satisfactory, and epidemics were frequent. By the 1820's it was clear that a public supply was needed, but there were no adequate reservoir sites nearby. New York's population was then approaching 300,000. A proposal to build a 37-mile aqueduct to a reservoir site near Croton was first considered preposterous but gradually became accepted as a necessity. A cholera outbreak in 1832 killed 3500 people and dramatized the necessity of a new supply, which was authorized in 1834. A disastrous fire in 1835 further demonstrated the desperate need and construction was accelerated. The system was completed in 1842.
>
> At that time the Croton Reservoir was no doubt regarded as the ultimate answer to New York's water needs. Within 20 years, however, it had to be enlarged. Several new reservoirs and a larger aqueduct were needed before the turn of the century. By then all satisfactory sites in the Croton watershed had been exhausted, and the demand was fast catching up with the available supply. Clearly, new sources of supply would have to be sought.

The Catskill Mountains, about 120 miles from New York, were chosen for the new reservoir sites. Construction began in 1907, and the system was completed in two stages: the Ashokan Reservoir was completed in 1917 and the Schoharie Reservoir, in 1928. Although addition of the Catskill system more than doubled the previous supply, the new supply was barely able to keep up with the rapidly increasing demand. By the late 1920's another water crisis was in sight.

This time alternatives were considered. The Hudson River was ruled out because of its allegedly inferior quality. New Yorkers insist on drinking pure mountain water. The Adirondacks were eliminated because of the excessive distance. In 1928, then, it was decided to expand the Catskill system and to develop new reservoirs in the headwaters of the Delaware River basin. The Delaware River is an interstate stream, so the consent of New Jersey and Pennsylvania was needed to divert water from this basin. The issue was resolved after considerable litigation in 1931 by a decree of the U.S. Supreme Court that allowed New York to divert no more than 1665.4 million liters per day from the Delaware River Basin. First the depression, then World War II delayed construction. The first operational phase of the expansion consisted of an emergency diversion from Rondout Creek to the new Delaware aqueduct from 1944 to 1951.

In the meantime, yet another crisis occurred. The postwar urbanization explosion strained the Croton and Catskill systems almost to their limit. Average pumpage exceeded 4 billion liters/day. Abundant rainfall deferred the day of reckoning until 1949, when reservoir level dropped to the danger point. Stringent water conservation measures were enforced, and for the first time the Hudson River was tapped at Chelsea as an emergency source of supply.

Rondout Reservoir, an expansion of the Catskill system, became operational late in 1950 and the diversion from the Hudson was discontinued. Neversink and Pepacton Reservoirs, with their diversion appurtenances, began being used in 1953, but full use of the Delaware system was not achieved until 1955.

History repeats itself. The crisis of 1949 and the forecasts of the even greater population explosion to come made the water planners all too painfully aware that even the Delaware River basin supply system under construction would only temporarily satisfy the city's needs. An additional source would be needed. Thus, planning began for a new reservoir in the Delaware River basin. In 1954 the Supreme Court authorized New York to increase its diversion and in 1955 construction started on the Cannonsville Reservoir. Planners estimated that, with this new addi-

tion, the system would have total capacity of 6.8 billion liters/day, sufficient to meet demands through 1980.

The record breaking drought of 1961-66 occurred, however, before the Cannonsville Reservoir was completed. At one time the existing reservoirs were drawn down to 26 percent of capacity (near the minimum safe drawdown for which the system was designed). The most stringent water-use controls in the city's history were put into effect, and the Chelsea pumping station of the Hudson River was rebuilt. By 1967 abundant rainfall eased the crisis, and the situation returned to "normal." But if history can be taken as any guide, it will not be long before New York is again faced with a water crisis. Indeed, planning has already started on alternative means of meeting expanded needs.

The history of the New York water system has been one of continuing crisis in order to satisfy the demands of the population explosion. Yet part of the water demand might be regarded as unnecessary or artificial. Wasteful and inefficient use of water is encouraged by the absence of metering and unrealistic pricing. While the elaborate network of reservoirs and aqueducts has been built at great cost, the Hudson River, which might supply New York's needs many times over, has, like many other rivers, been allowed to degenerate in quality. The state's Pure Water Program improvements show promise of effecting some regeneration. Planning decisions must be sensitive to economics, politics, and public attitudes. The citizens of New York have become conditioned to drinking "mountain water," and any change in established practices of water supply would require a massive campaign of public information and education.

*The Search for Water*

The old civilizations that developed along the rivers were not in search of water. They saw it, and there was usually plenty of it. By ingenious systems of ditches and dams, they could divert this river water to their land and grow crops on irrigated fields, although climatic changes have forced people for longer or shorter time, to leave such fertile valleys. An interesting case in point is the irrigation system near Phoenix, Arizona where at least from 100 A.D., but possibly earlier, and up to about 1400, a tribe of Indians flourished who diverted river water from the Salt and Gila Rivers and used it to irrigate their fields. Traces of the canals are still visible and many modern ditches of the Roosevelt irrigation district follow the same courses used by the Indians. Later Indians who saw the remnants of irrigation canals and dwellings called the tribe the Hohokam, meaning the vanished one.

Even more ingenious than these surface diversion ditches were the underground canals dug by the Persians some 3000 years ago. Increase in population at the height of their civilization forced them to search for water. Knowing that there was more rainfall in the mountains, they reasoned that water seeped through the rocky soils and was stored underground in the foothills. From the cities they then dug underground aqueducts toward the aquifer. Ventilation shafts were needed at regular intervals, not only for air but also to hoist the debris out of the way and to lower reinforcement rings. The diggers kept track of direction horizontally as well as vertically by rows of oil lamps. The systems are called qanats. Up to this day most of the water in Iran is transported in qanat units, with a total length of more than 250,000 km delivering over 55,000 liters per second or 2½ times the average flow of the Arkansas River in Pueblo, Colorado, which is one of the largest irrigation districts in the United States.

Digging for water vertically has been an old occupation. The Old Testament is replete with well-digging stories and the fights between warring tribes over their possession. Isaac, according to Genesis 26, dug three wells in rapid succession and lost the first two to his enemies. Jacob's well, mentioned in Genesis 29, is still in use. To this day, in many countries such as Greece, Italy, and Mexico, water is taken from wells that existed 2000 years ago. Most of those wells are comparatively shallow; hand-dug deeper wells, however, also still exist.

When man began to understand where groundwater came from and how it was formed (which comprises the science of hydrogeology or geohydrology) scientific exploration for water could begin, but large-scale exploration still had to await the invention of engines capable of drilling fast enough and deep enough. An early drilling occurred between 1829 and 1841 near Paris, France. The drill was driven by man or horses walking on a tread mill. It took 12 years to reach a depth of slightly over 500 meters, but the re-

sults were spectacular because this was an artesian well and water spouted 33 meters high in the air. We know now that such wells do not continue to produce their initial rate of water unless they are continuously fed and this well was no exception. By 1910, it was no longer artesian and water had to be pumped because by that time numerous wells were tapping the same aquifer.

In arid lands, of course, the situation might well be much worse and in many cases is. We have cited cases where groundwater is being mined and when it is used up, the population will have to move or different means of water importation have to be sought.

There are other possible sources of augmenting a water supply. Some of them at the present time seem fanciful, but lots of things that have happened now seemed fanciful only 15 years ago.

There is, for instance, the possible use of the frozen resources, which constitute two-thirds of all the sweet water in the world. It has been proposed to tow icebergs from Greenland or Antarctica to thirsty cities. An average-size Greenland iceberg has a diameter of 150 meters and an initial volume of 15 million cubic meters. This would supply enough water for a town of 60,000 people for a period of a year. Unfortunately, the Greenland icebergs appear in the Atlantic Ocean, whose coastal areas have enough water. Moreover, Greenland icebergs are irregularly shaped and have a habit of going topsy-turvy at times, which makes towing rather risky.

The Antarctic icebergs are flat-topped and are very much more stable and also larger. The small ones may measure 3 x 3 kilometers and be 250 meters thick. It has been figured that one good size tugboat making 1 knot could bring such a berg from Antarctica to Australia in 6 to 7 months at the cost of 1½ million dollars. If we assume that about half of the ice would melt during the trip, there still would be 1 billion $m^3$ of sweet water, or enough water for 4 million people for a year at an average cost per family of about a dollar and a half. Even if one would add the cost of constructing piping, pumps, and other paraphernalia, necessary to deliver the water from the iceberg to the city, such water still would be very much cheaper than that of even the most efficient desalinization plant now available.

The size of the Antarctic icebergs can really be impressive. The biggest one ever seen measured some 20,000 km$^2$ or nearly the size of the whole state of Massachusetts. Tugging such a monster probably would be too costly, if not impossible. One could try to tug the little ones faster to prevent the loss of melting, but the resistance against tugging increases four times as the speed doubles. Hence, it would be desirable to tow with the existing ocean currents and preferably with prevailing winds. This works well for the dry west coast of South America where the Peru currents and trade winds would make towing feasible. The west coast of the southern part of Africa is also favorably located but to go to the east coast of either of these continents would require a roundabout way which would endanger the effectiveness of the towing and much ice would be lost by melting. The California currents would make it possible to tow icebergs to San Francisco or Los Angeles, but such bergs would have to come from the Arctic Ocean through the Bering Sea and icebergs in that area are comparatively rare.

Fantastic as these plans may be, they have the attractiveness of being "natural." Icebergs float around anyway while melting and to have them melt where we want them, would not affect climate or ecology to a noticeable degree.

Another source of solid water is the glaciers. It has been proposed to induce melting which can be accomplished comparatively easily by darkening the surface of the ice. Such coating of surfaces is regularly practiced on a small scale in northern Russia over snow fields. More heat is absorbed, resulting in an increase in snow and ice melt. It must be realized that a systematic treatment of all glaciers in this manner would be equivalent to mining the ice. It would be necessary to go up higher and higher into the mountains until finally the glaciers are used up and the yearly snow fall would be the only renewable resource. Because the glacier supply is very small to begin with (see Table I) the effect of depleting it would not greatly influence macroclimate but would greatly alter the ecology of mountainous terrain and dry up streams that depend on a regular supply of melting ice.

We have seen that in many places water is available but the quality is such that it cannot be used as is. It is at times economically possible to take the undesirable chemicals out of the water by one of the several processes of desalinization. This is especially so when there is a large demand for domestic and industrial use. A small example was already mentioned earlier in connection with the little town of Buckeye, Arizona. Large desalting plants can be found in Aruba and Curaçao in the Netherlands Antilles, and in Kuwait on the Persian Gulf. In these three cases it is mainly the oil industry which makes this expensive process feasible. Another example is the installation on the Guantanamo Bay in Cuba maintained by the U.S. Navy.

All in all, there are at the moment at least 50 desalting plants in operation around the world, mostly close to the seashore because piping water and especially lifting it would make the cost really prohibitive. The cost of lifting water is generally estimated to be 1 cent per 100 meters of lift per 1000 liters. At this rate a city of 150,000 inhabitants at an elevation of 1000 meters, such as Lubbock, Texas, using 1000 liters per person per day would have to pay 10 cents per person per day or more than 5 million dollars per year for LIFTING ALONE, and at least another 5 million for horizontal delivery if ever desalting costs go down as low as 10 cents per 1000 liters (see below).

A very interesting experiment financed by the Rockefeller Foundation is in progress at Puerto Peñasco, Sonora, Mexico. Here the University of Sonora and the University of Arizona have set up a desalting plant powered by a diesel engine which drives an electric generator. The exhaust heat of the diesel engine is used to heat seawater which partially evaporates then condenses to sweet water and is stored for future use. By this process the original 35,000 parts per million of salt are reduced to 200 at the rate of 20,000 liters per day. Next to the desalting plant inflatable plastic greenhouses have been erected in which a constant relative humidity of close to 100 percent is maintained by the use of seawater. The exhaust gases of the diesel engine contain a high percentage of carbon dioxide but also noxious gases. These, by a scrubbing process, are eliminated and the carbon dioxide is fed into the greenhouses, raising the "normal" content of 300 parts per million to 1000 parts per million or over. Many crops respond favorably to this high carbon dioxide content and very high yields are obtained. Because the humidity is so high, the plants use very little water and some of this water comes from condensing transpired water on the walls of the tents. Most of the sweet water is used in the nearby town and hospital.

Desalting seawater costs at the moment between 15 and 80 cents per 1000 liters, which is far too high for agricultural use, for which a price of 2 cents per 1000 liters is considered extravagant and in many cases uneconomical. It has been estimated that desalting will be cheaper as better methods are found, but it is unlikely that distillation of seawater will produce sweet water for less than 2.5 cents per 1000 liters. A nuclear-energy-powered plant under study for use in Israel is supposed to cost between $187 million and $210 million depending on interest rates. The water would cost between 7.5 and 17.5 cents per 1000 liters.[7]

There are several methods of treating water. The oldest one is mentioned again in the Old Testament where in Exodus 15 we read that the water at Marah was too bitter to drink. Moses was ordered to throw a log into the water whereupon it suddenly became drinkable. Present-day systems are much more elaborate and will only be briefly discussed.

The most commonly used method is known as flash distillation. Cold seawater is forced through coils in an evaporating chamber. It is then superheated and introduced into the chamber itself where it rapidly evaporates. The steam condenses on the coils and drips into drains. Usually such a system is set up in batteries. One of the earlier plants was built in Freeport, Texas.

Electrical separation or electrodialysis is not efficient for seawater but works well for brackish water. Water is introduced into a container through which a DC current is passed. The salt molecules are split into negative and positive parts (ions) which go to the positive and negative poles, leaving sweet water in the middle. Buckeye, Arizona has this system.

The cheapest way is to use solar heat to evaporate the salt water, capture the steam, and collect it after condensation. The disadvantage of the system is that it takes a lot of space: about 1 m$^2$ for each 5 liters of water produced.

On the little Greek island of Simi near the Turkish coast with a population of slightly over 4000, such a unit, producing 15,000 liters per day, occupies 3000 m$^2$. The whole island is about the size of Bermuda (54 km$^2$). Notice that the amount of drinkable water the population gets is less than 4 liters per person per day compared to an average use in the United States of 600 liters per person per day. To satisfy such a demand would require a plant or set of plants sprawling over 450,000 m$^2$.

In another type of search, man looks to the heavens for more water. When the knowledge of cloud formations and cloud physics developed and the necessity for the presence of condensation nuclei became known, many scientists, among them Vincent Schaefer and Irving Langmuir, introduced the idea of providing clouds with extra condensation nuclei. Silver iodide was chosen because it matches the molecular structure of ice. Some apparently spectacular successes between 1947 and 1950 resulted in the formation of a large number of private enterprises which claimed, rightfully or not, that they could make it rain on demand. The enthusiasm has cooled considerably and the latest report by the National Science Foundation and the American Meteorological Society concedes that at times a small increase in local rainfall may have been credited to seeding, but very often less rain fell than was expected even without seeding.[8] If ever cloud seeding becomes effective, we are faced with enormous sociological problems, not to mention the possible toxic effect of silver on aquatic life.[9]

Finally, there is the possibility of "importing" water. When groundwater reservoirs become exhausted and when more withdrawal from nearby surface water, because of increase in population, industry, and agriculture, becomes impossible, the populace of such an area fixes its eyes on the big rivers that apparently run uselessly into the sea in other areas. Attempts to transfer water from one basin to another may be costly, but may be economically feasible if authorities or owners of the losing basin do not object to the transfer to the gaining basin. From the snowy mountains south of Canberra, Australia, a river runs south directly into the ocean. By a system of gigantic tunnels this water is diverted to the north side of the mountains to help irrigate the fertile valleys of the Murrumbidgee and the Murray. On their way the waters drive gigantic underground turbines to provide electricity. In California waters from the north are successfully diverted to the fertile valleys and dense population of the south.

We mentioned the plan to divert water from the Columbia River to the south, but the adjacent states seem to object to such a drastic change. No such objection would occur if the plans to divert the Pechora and Vychegda would become a reality. These two rivers, west of the Ural in northern Russia, at present meander northward on their way to the Arctic Ocean. The plans are to lead the waters into the Volga which flows south into the Caspian Sea. This not only would provide more irrigation water for the warmer valleys in the south, it would also stop the level of the Caspian Sea from declining further. Probably neither of these two plans would affect climate, but this is not necessarily so with larger endeavors.

Among such gigantic plans worth mentioning are the North Atlantic Water and Power Alliance (NAWAPA), which hopes to divert huge amounts of water from northern Canada and Alaska to the United States and Mexico; and the South America Lakes Plan, in which dams in the Amazon would create huge lakes connecting numerous points in South America. The execution of such plans may create ecological problems of unprecedented scale.

A different approach to adding to the water supply is to increase the reservoir system. Storing water in reservoirs is attractive because such artificial lakes quite often can be stocked with fish and provide popular recreation areas for boating, water skiing, and diving, but reservoirs eventually silt up, and large quantities of the water are lost due to evaporation. Attempts have been made to cover lakes and reservoirs with thin films (one molecule thick) which would not prevent oxygen and carbon dioxide from entering or leaving the water but would prevent water molecules from leaving the surface. Hexadecanol (which, incidentally, is the base for lipstick) and other fatty alcohols have been tried but wind and wave action make the method far from effective.

If it were possible to store water underground either in artificially created caverns or in the existing aquifer formations which are being mined, at least part of water that is now consumptively lost could be saved, and less land would be drowned by reservoirs. This method of storing is called artificial recharge. It is practiced successfully in many places in and outside the United States, for example, in Israel; Dortmund, Germany; and Los Angeles, California. However, there are at times technical and legal problems here too.

*Problems*

We must now consider the present and future problems related to water resources. As we have seen, there is on the average enough sweet water available even if the world population doubled and even if the water use per person doubled, but this is *on the average*. Arid and semiarid lands, such as the western part of the United States, have not enough water; elsewhere there may be too much water. In many humid tropical lands drainage is the main problem. In general we want water when we want it, where we want it, and of an agreeable quality.

There are only a few places in the world where rainfall is dependable enough and falls at the time when needed. Water is therefore captured directly (stock tanks) or indirectly (a dam in a river forms a reservoir). Building dams creates three kinds of problems. More water is lost by evaporation than would have occurred without the reservoir; the storage capacity will gradually diminish because of silting; and people downstream, especially when they are of different states or nations, may feel deprived of water which they claim is rightfully theirs. If river and dam are big enough there may also be serious ecological and sociological problems.

The evaporation problem is minor compared to all the water that is lost from natural surfaces and vegetation, including agriculture. All man-made reservoirs over the whole world are a mere puddle compared to reservoirs in natural lakes, streams, and groundwater reservoirs. At the moment the knowledge and technique of evaporation suppression is inadequate, but significant progress can be expected in the next 10 to 20 years.

Silting is sometimes combated by dredging, but this is just a matter of a stay of execution. Sooner or later, a reservoir will silt up just as natural lakes will. Man only hastens the process. The real problem may be in the future, even if only four generations from now, but it is a serious one. Dam-building organizations in this and other countries are beginning to run out of dam sites.

The complaints filed by the downstream people are often met by promising them return water, but the difficulty is to provide them with water of the desired quality. We mentioned already the problem on the Colorado River; another example is the Pecos where New Mexico assures Texas a dependable supply. This river gets some of its water from groundwater seeping into the river bed. Pumping groundwater near the river deprived the Pecos of part of its supply and created difficulties in regulating the river flow to restore the agreed water supply to Texas.

Ecological problems have rarely been investigated, but we are more and more aware of the fact that if we manipulate nature, we may cause irreversible damage, for instance, the Texas Water Plan, so far only in the discussion stage,[10] foresees that 15 billion ($15 \times 10^9$) m³ of water per year may need to be imported into the state after 2020. The water would be diverted from the lower Mississippi River and delivered to dry parts of Texas, at an estimated cost of about $6.3 billion. Such a diversion may seriously affect the bayou areas of Louisiana and the estuaries along the Mississippi coast. No one knows whether the resulting changes in mud load and salinity will be detrimental or not. For an example of what might happen though, we can look to the Nile after the Aswan Dam was built. Sediments and nutrients, which fed the coastal sardines, used to be carried to the delta and the Mediterranean Sea. This flow is now stopped and the coastal fishing industry has been destroyed. The delta itself is dwindling due to erosion, and land reclamation projects farther inland are endangered.[11]

The second means of obtaining water when we want it is by developing groundwater resources, but we must remember that groundwater is a reservoir and the only part that is replenishable is what comes from natural or artificial recharge. If the draft on the reservoir is larger, the area will eventually run out of water. If a reservoir supplies water to a river, as it often does, then overpumping will affect the stream flow. This has happened many times, the just-mentioned Pecos River being one example. Here again we have some problems of law and tradition.

In the western parts of the United States, the owner of the land is usually considered also to be owner of the water underneath the land. Under the appropriation doctrine, water is presumed to be a replenishable resource, and the appropriative right has been defined as the right to use a specified rate of flow annually and forever. The quantity of water taken from a stream cannot exceed the quantity that is in it, except for multiple reuse, but for groundwater it is possible to overdraw and the term "annually and forever" becomes meaningless, even if, as we have seen, the use is "stretched" to 40 years.[12] What makes things worse in certain states is that the land owner has the right to the amount of water he "always" used to use. So the farmer is advised by his lawyer to pump much more than he actually needs in order that he maintain the right to more water when he expands his operation. Another interesting problem occurs when artificial recharge is successfully practiced. Whose water is this? It is impossible to solve such a problem except by changing the existing laws and traditions. Water sources and reservoirs on and under the land surface will have to be managed by natural units to the benefit of all involved.

Examples, classic and modern, of such cooperation show that it can be done. For centuries the Dutch have managed their polders (tracts of land below sea level, reclaimed from seas or lakes) by appointing a managing body with complete authority to open and close gates, to decide when and how much to pump, and so on. Old civilizations, such as the Hohokam, undoubtedly worked together for the benefit of all in their withdrawal and use of water. Industries and cities along the river Ruhr in Germany got together and made it compulsory for everyone that used water to clean it before he put it back into the river. As a result the Ruhr is no longer a sewage drain.

A different kind of problem, encountered in practicing artificial recharge, is clogging. If recharge is attempted by surface spreading, for example, spreading water on flat porous terrain and letting it seep down, growth of algae may cause clogging; if it is done by injecting it into deep wells, silt in the recharge water may clog the aquifer around the injection pipe. Chemical and mechanical treatment of water may be necessary, but may also be expensive. However, it seems now that in a great many cases artificial recharge will be economically practical.

Problems connected with the desire to have water where we want it are sometimes different in nature, but in many instances are the same. Along rivers and streams the "where" can often be met by multiple use. The problem here is one of degradation of the quality of the water as happened along the Colorado River. There is also an increase in consumptive use, as can be expected. Communities in many arid areas in the United States and elsewhere, want a transfer of water to their dry lands. This may become extremely expensive and create enormous ecological problems on even a larger scale than the one connected with the Texas Water Plan.

If the USSR ever succeeds in reversing all the big Siberian rivers, and Canada and the United States work together to turn around the Canadian rivers now flowing into the Arctic Ocean, we may expect changes in oceanic currents. This, in turn, may change climates drastically, affect the flora and fauna in the oceans, and even the food chain, including the one from fish to man.

Desalting plants, also a matter of "where we want the water," create a different kind of problem. It is proposed that nuclear power plants be used for desalting the water at the rate of 400 million liters per day.[7] This means that per day 14,000 tons of salt will have to be disposed of. Even if this is done far off shore, a large area of the oceans will be made uninhabitable for plant or fish.

The last problem to be mentioned is in connection with rain making. Present experiments have mostly been made in remote areas and on a comparatively small scale. Suppose an effective method (there is none yet) can be applied to a large area, resulting in disastrous flooding in one place and/or serious drought in another. The legal complications alone are staggering; to say nothing of ecological changes that might occur.

Finally, it should be noted that in the United States we could endure in equilibrium with our water supply by using the available "water yield" (amount of runoff) wisely. By the year 2000 we may be approaching an equilibrium condition when daily withdrawals reach $5300 \times 10^9$ liters not counting reuse. All of the additional means of obtaining water described in this section involve greater or smaller environmental disturbances including possible climatic changes and, without proper costly precautions, perhaps dangerous increases in radiation (Chapter 12).

Summing up then, we might conclude that there are water problems, but they are not those of quantity and not even necessarily of quality. It is the attitude of people and their concern for each other which become the problem. Man will have to learn to live with man, not on a competitive but on a cooperative basis, and this is probably the biggest problem for man and his environment.

References

1. van Hylckama, T. E. A. 1956. The water balance of the earth. *Publ. Climatology 9:* 58-177.

2. Abelson, P. H. 1970. Shortage of caviar. *Science 168:* 199.

3. Schneider, W. J., and Spieker, A. M. 1969. Water for the cities — the outlook. *Geol. Survey Circ. 601-A,* 6 pp.

4. Nace, R. L. 1969. *Water and Man: A World View.* UNESCO, 46 pp.

5. Murray, C. R. 1968. Estimated use of water in the United States; 1965. *Geol Survey Circ. 556,* 53 pp.

6. Piper, A. M. 1965. Has the United States enough water? *Geol. Survey Water-Supply Paper 1797,* 22 pp.

7. Clawson, M., Landsberg, H. H., and Alexander, L. T. 1969. Desalted sea water for

agriculture: Is it economic? *Science 165:* 1141-1148.

 8. **National Science Foundation.** 1968. *Weather Modification, 10th Annual Report.* U.S. Government Printing Office, 141 pp.

 9. **Cooper, C. F., and Jolly, W. C.** 1970. Ecological effects of silver iodide and other weather modification agents: A review. *Water Resources Res. 6:* 88-98

10. **Texas Water Development Board.** 1968. *The Texas Water Plan,* 227 pp. Austin, Texas.

11. **McCaull, J.** 1969. Conference on the ecological aspects of international development. *Nature and Resources (UNESCO) 2:* 5-12.

12. **Thomas, H. E.** 1961. Groundwater and the law. *Geol. Survey Circ. 446,* 6 pp.

Further Reading

**Battan, L. J.** 1962. *Cloud Physics and Cloud Seeding.* Doubleday, New York, 144 pp.

**Davis, K. S., and Day, J. A.** 1961. *Water, The Mirror of Science.* Doubleday, New York, 195 pp.

**Furon, R.** 1963. *Le probleme de l'eau dans le monde,* Payot, Paris, 251 pp. Translated in 1967 by P. Barnes as *The Problem of Water,* American Elsevier, New York, 208 pp.

**King, T.** 1963. *Water, Miracle of Nature.* Macmillan, New York, 238 pp.

**Kneese, A. V.** 1964. *The Economics of Regional Water Quality Management.* Johns Hopkins University Press, Baltimore, Maryland, 215 pp.

**Kuenen, P. H.** 1955. *De kringloop van het water,* Leopold, N. V., The Hague, 350 pp., Revised translation of 1963 by M. Hollander as *Realms of Water,* Wiley, 327 pp.

**McGinnies, W. G., and Goldman, B.,** eds. 1969. *Arid Lands in Perspective.* University of Arizona Press, Tucson, Arizona, 421 pp.

**Nace, R. L.** 1967. Are we running out of water? *Geol. Survey Circ. 536.*

**Piper, A. M.** 1960. Interpretation and current status of ground-water rights. *Geol. Survey Circ. 432.*

**Savini, J., and Kammerer, J. C.** 1961. Urban growth and the water regimen. *Geol. Survey Water-Supply Paper 1591-A,* 44 pp.

*More advanced study texts*

**Ward, R. C.** 1967. *Principles of Hydrology.* McGraw-Hill, 403 pp.

**White, G.** 1969. *Strategies of American Water Management.* University of Michigan Press, Ann Arbor, Michigan, 155 pp.

# 8  Anchovies, Birds and Fishermen in the Peru Current

Gerald J. Paulik

## Introduction

The human mind has difficulty in grasping the true enormity of extremely large numbers. Peru's anchoveta (*Engraulis ringens*) catch of 11 million metric tons (mmt) is such a number. This catch was taken in the 1969-70 fishing season of a little over 7 months. More than 10 trillion anchovetas are needed to make 11 mmt.

One way of comprehending the meaning of large numbers is to compare them to more familiar quantities or to numbers for which we have some intuitive feeling. The total catch by U.S. fishermen of all species of fish and shellfish was approximately 2½ mmt for 1969; thus Peru's catch is about 4½ times larger than that of the United States.

For all practical purposes Peru's catch is composed of only one species. Comparing the Peruvian catch to the U.S. catch of a single species, the yellowfin (*Thunnus albacares*), which is the most common canned tuna sold in the United States, shows the quantity of anchoveta to be a hundredfold greater than the quantity of tuna. The

GERALD J. PAULIK is a Professor of Population Dynamics in the College of Fisheries at the University of Washington. After earning his doctorate at the University of Washington in 1959, he spent a year as a postdoctoral fellow in the Department of Mathematics at the University of Chicago. His current interests include quantitative ecology and the development of computerized simulation games to teach resource management.

total weight of the annual U.S. catch of five species of Pacific salmon — chinook, chum, coho, pink, and sockeye — is about 250 thousand metric tons or 1/44 of the Peruvian catch.

Fortunately for the United States and unfortunately for Peru, sheer biomass does not measure economic worth. Salmon and anchoveta may be equally nutritious, but the ex-vessel or wholesale price of anchoveta is about $11/ton and that of salmon about $770/ton, making salmon 70 times as valuable per unit weight.

One-tenth is a commonly accepted ecological efficiency factor for stepping up one trophic level in a linear food chain (Chapter 1). If it were possible to feed the anchoveta to a predator species as valuable as the salmon and to salvage 1/10 of their annual productivity, the income to Peruvian fishermen could be 7 times greater.

Another way of viewing the 11 mmt taken in the 1969-70 season is to compare it to the sustainable natural productivity of the anchoveta stock in the Peru Current. The secret of successful and continued harvesting of a renewable natural resource is to use the surplus produced by the resource without reducing the size of the stock enough to damage its productive capability.

During January of 1970 the Food and Agriculture Organization (FAO) of the United Nations, the United Nations Development Fund Program (UNDP), and the Instituto del Mar del Peru (IMARPE) sponsored a meeting of a group of distinguished international experts on population dynamics to determine the maximum sustainable yield (MSY) for the anchoveta stocks in the Peru Current. This panel concluded the best estimate of MSY to be about 9½ mmt.[1] It is ironic that the ink had hardly dried on the panel's recommendation before it was substantially exceeded by the catch of 11 mmt in the 1969-70 season.

The true capacity of the Peruvian fleet is staggering. On April 28, 1970 the total catch reached 9½ mmt. The fishery continued for 10 more days, taking 100,000 metric tons per day. This fantastic catching power could have taken the whole U.S. yellowfin tuna catch in one day, or the entire U.S. catch of all Pacific salmon in 2½ days. Obviously, this type of destructive power must be handled most carefully, and precise management and regulation are essential.

As if to illustrate that extremely large numbers may still be too small, part of the Peruvian industry expressed dissatisfaction with the catch of 10½ mmt taken by May 13. Smaller and less efficient producers petitioned the government for a special season to take advantage of availability of the fish and the high price of meal. They were granted an additional 300,000 tons, demonstrating most vividly the political power of a large number of marginal operators. The remaining 200,000 tons in the total catch of 11 mmt were taken near the southern boundary of Peru, where the anchoveta stocks are fished by both Peru and Chile and neither can be assured that its fishermen and factories would be able to realize the fruits of unilateral conservation efforts.

We have compared 11 mmt to other numbers and we have seen that it can be either too much or too little. In actuality it is a statistical fiction. In the process of unloading the purse seiners, or "bolicheras" as they are known in Peru, water pumped into the hold is mixed with fish and the entire slurry transported to the factory through a pipeline which may extend a quarter of a mile or so from the offshore unloading platform. Considerable losses of fish are sustained in this process, especially when the young fish or "peladilla" form the bulk of the catch in January, February, and March. Further losses are sustained in the pursing operation and occasionally because of intentional dumping of excess catches. Under-reporting of the actual quantities

landed is another source of bias during the peladilla season, when the yield of meal per unit of fish is low. Although some observers believe these losses may be as high as 40 percent, a conservative estimate of the actual quantity of fish removed from the sea during the 1969-70 season is between 13 and 14 mmt.

Mathematicians sometimes think about a large number of things by assigning each thing to an entity in a known set. Enough anchoveta were taken from the sea to provide each of the 13 million or so citizens of Peru with 1 ton of high-quality protein food. This capability rests in a fishery which generates about 11 dollars per person per year in terms of current ex-vessel prices. In terms of fish meal exports (assuming $165/ton for meal), foreign capital of about 33 dollars per person per year is generated for the country. However, under current regulatory policies as the fleet and meal factories accumulate excess capacity, the length of the "veda" or closed season must increase, and as idle equipment deteriorates, scarce capital is oxidized into rust. Although much of the factory equipment and nearly all of the bolicheras are manufactured in Peru, purchase of electronic gear and engines is a serious drain on foreign capital reserves.

The remarkable development of the fish reduction industry has completely bypassed the food fish industry, which continues to operate at an extremely low level of production largely for local consumption and struggles along with obsolete equipment and methods. The Peruvian government recently declared development of a major food fish industry to be a national goal and has inaugurated an ambitious program to accomplish this objective. However, the greatest potential for a food fish industry may not lie in the direction of starting new fisheries for those species traditionally used for food, but rather in transforming the immense and already proven production of anchoveta from the Peru Current into a high-quality product suitable for human consumption. Substantial social and economic benefits would result from using Peru's surplus labor in such an enterprise.

From the catch of 11 mmt in 1969-70, Peru will produce around 2.1 mmt of fish meal. This

## 158   Gerald J. Paulik

quantity of meal fed in the poultry, swine, and cattle industries of the industrialized nations of Western Europe and North America represents a significant transfer of nutrients from the southern to the northern hemisphere.

### Historical Developments

The Peruvian fish industry began life as a war baby. During World War II the United States relied upon Peru for canned and salted fish products as well as fish liver and oil. This food fish industry, with bonito, skipjack tuna, swordfish, and shrimp as its prime products, fell victim to the United States' transfer from a war to peace economy and the post-war replacement of some fishery products by synthetics. However, the fertility of the Peru Current could not be denied, and in 1950 a fish meal factory was set up surreptitiously in a remote Peruvian bay. Secrecy was essential for this prototype operation to conceal it from the guano industry, which then represented a powerful vested interest firmly opposed to any use of anchoveta that might reduce the amount of fish available to the guano birds. Before the guano industry could react to this threat to their source of new material, the fish meal boom was out of control. The industry grew at an astonishing rate; from 1956 to 1963 Peru leaped from obscurity to the largest fish meal producer in the world. Fish meal production statistics from 1951 to 1968 are shown in Table I.

Fish meal became the number one producer of foreign exchange for Peru. Fishery products and copper together account for 54.1 percent of the value of Peruvian export products; fish meal leads copper by 0.1 percent. This fantastic industrial expansion brought employment to approximately 25,000 people; a fleet of 1,700 bolicheras and 150 fish meal and oil reduction factories suddenly materialized; the only ingredient missing was John Steinbeck to record the lusty excitement as fishing towns sprouted from nothing along the barren coast of Peru.

Figure 1 shows yearly catches, in live weight, of the world's leading fishing nations for the decade from 1958 to 1968, the latest year for which total world fish production statistics are available. Clupeoids made up about a third (20½ mmt) of the total 1968 catch. Besides the Peruvian anchoveta, this figure includes sardinella, pilchard, herring, and sardine. Cod-like species accounted for about 9½ mmt; mackerels, 2.3 mmt; flatfish, 1.2 mmt; and various tuna species, 1.4 mmt. While total world landings rose from 33 mmt in 1958 to 64 mmt in 1968, Peru's total catch increased from 0.96 mmt in 1958 to 10.5 in 1968.

| Year | Thousand metric tons |
|------|---------------------|
| 1951 | 7.2 |
| 1952 | 9.2 |
| 1953 | 12.1 |
| 1954 | 16.5 |
| 1955 | 20.0 |
| 1956 | 30.9 |
| 1957 | 64.5 |
| 1958 | 126.9 |
| 1959 | 332.4 |
| 1960 | 558.3 |
| 1961 | 863.8 |
| 1962 | 1,120.8 |
| 1963 | 1,159.2 |
| 1964 | 1,552.2 |
| 1965 | 1,282.0 |
| 1966 | 1,470.5 |
| 1967 | 1,816.0 |
| 1968 | 1,922.0 |

**PERUVIAN FISH MEAL PRODUCTION**

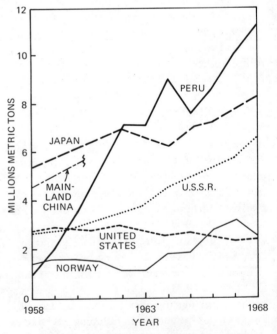

ANNUAL CATCHES OF LEADING FISHING NATIONS. Annual catches in live weight by leading fishing nations of the world for 1958-68.

Today guano birds and large predatory fish must compete with human fishermen for their share of the anchoveta stocks. The guano industry, however, existed long before man began to manufacture fish meal. Over a thousand years ago, the Incas used guano to fertilize the barren coastal soil of Peru. Intense mining of the guano deposits occurred during the latter half of the nineteenth century, when 150-foot high mountains of guano that had taken over 25 centuries to accumulate were removed in a few years. In 1909 the need to regulate the rate of removal and to protect the guano birds was officially recognized when Peru set up the Guano Administration. This administration attempted to restrict the amount removed per year to no more than the amount deposited. Given the magnitude of the annual fluctuations in the size of the bird populations, such a balance could be achieved only with the aid of the sort of highly sophisticated management information system which even today exists only for a very few natural resources. The Peruvian government also concentrated on protecting the birds and their eggs from human and animal predators. The bird sanctuary policy worked well and the numbers of birds began to increase after having been perilously low in the early 1900s.

*An Overview*

The existing and rapidly increasing overcapacity of both the fish meal factories and the fishing fleets, and the inefficient use of labor and capital resulting from the use of extensive closed fishing periods to limit the size of the physical harvest pose grave problems for Peru. She must devise and introduce an equitable means of reducing capacity that will neither encourage economic inefficiency nor foster corruption.

However, the first and most important objective of any regulatory scheme is to preserve the productivity of the resource. Other and almost equally important objectives include the following:

1. To harvest the correct amounts of the right parts of the population to maximize the physical yield of fishery products. At present these products are fish meal, oil, and guano but could include in the near future a product such as FPC (fish protein concentrate) for human consumption.

2. To minimize harvesting and processing costs in order to maximize economic return. This implies regulations that will force evolution of an efficient industry — technologically innovative in its harvesting methods and product utilization.

3. To set up a politically and socially acceptable scheme to distribute profits among fishermen, factory and fleet owners, and the people of Peru.

4. To achieve stability of employment and income from the fishery.

Traditionally fisheries management has taken a very narrow view of its mission and has not properly described to decision-makers the total consequences of alternative courses of action. The calamitous economic performance of such fisheries as those for halibut and salmon on the Pacific coast of the United States can be attributed to an attitude which recognized only the biological aspects of conservation regulations. The anchoveta-based industries are so important to the total national economy of Peru that she cannot afford to run the risk of the disastrous economic and perhaps political consequences that could result from ignoring any significant aspects of the total problem of controlling exploitation of the anchoveta stocks. This chapter presents a broad view of the many background settings in which the regulatory problem is imbedded. Figure 2 is a diagrammatic overview of the current state of affairs and serves as an introduction to the rest of the paper.

In the sections that follow, we will examine many of the factors — physical, biological, economic, and political — acting to shape the destinies of the Peru anchoveta stocks and the many industries and people dependent in one way or another upon maintaining the biological productivity of these stocks.

*The Physical Setting*

Peru's coastal strip is ideally suited for industrialization since the flat desert land provides spacious building sites, and huge inventories can be held with little or no protection from the weather in the stable arid climate. The 1400-mile-long coast of Peru is about 100 miles longer

160    Gerald J. Paulik

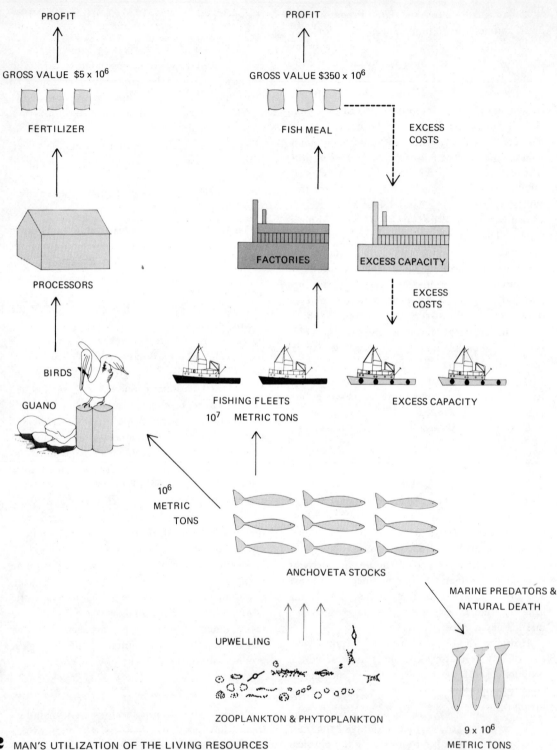

PROFIT

GROSS VALUE  $5 x 10^6

FERTILIZER

PROCESSORS

BIRDS

GUANO

10^6
METRIC
TONS

PROFIT

GROSS VALUE $350 x 10^6

FISH MEAL

EXCESS
COSTS

FACTORIES

EXCESS CAPACITY

EXCESS
COSTS

FISHING FLEETS
10^7    METRIC TONS

EXCESS CAPACITY

ANCHOVETA STOCKS

MARINE PREDATORS &
NATURAL DEATH

UPWELLING

ZOOPLANKTON & PHYTOPLANKTON

9 x 10^6
METRIC TONS

2  MAN'S UTILIZATION OF THE LIVING RESOURCES
OF THE PERU CURRENT. A pictorial systems diagram
showing biological, economic, and social components involved in man's exploitation of the natural fertility of
the Peru Current.

than the Pacific coast of the United States. The narrow strip of coastal desert is usually less than 40 miles wide.

Peru's primary harbor is at Callao, 7 miles west of Lima and about halfway between the northern and southern boundaries. The extent to

which Lima dominates the nation is expressed in an old saying, "Peru is Lima and Lima is Peru". Lima and other cities of the Peruvian coastal plain are being invaded by poverty-stricken migrants from the high mountain areas. Lima itself is surrounded by an incredible array of makeshift housing. Most of the amenities of modern society, such as electricity, water, and sewers, will not be found in these barriadas — or slum areas. Many of Peru's fishermen and fish meal factory workers came from the barriadas.

MAP OF PERU. A map showing major fishing ports, biological production areas, and the epicenter of the May 31, 1970 earthquake. Areas I and II as defined by Cushing[2] for estimation of primary and secondary productivity.

**3**

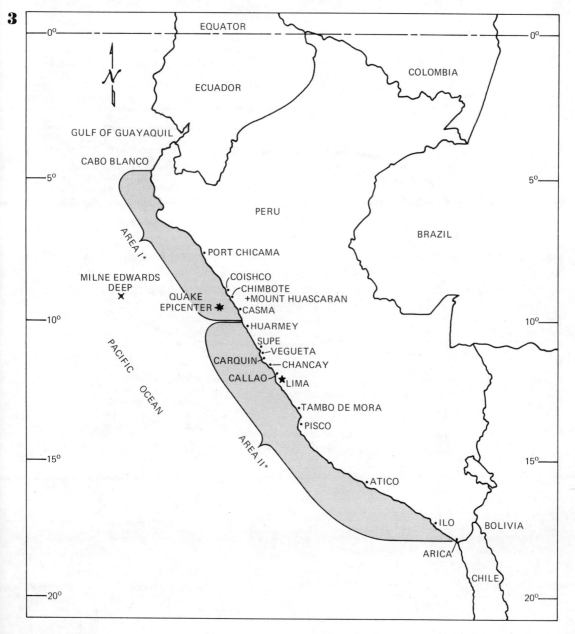

162  Gerald J. Paulik

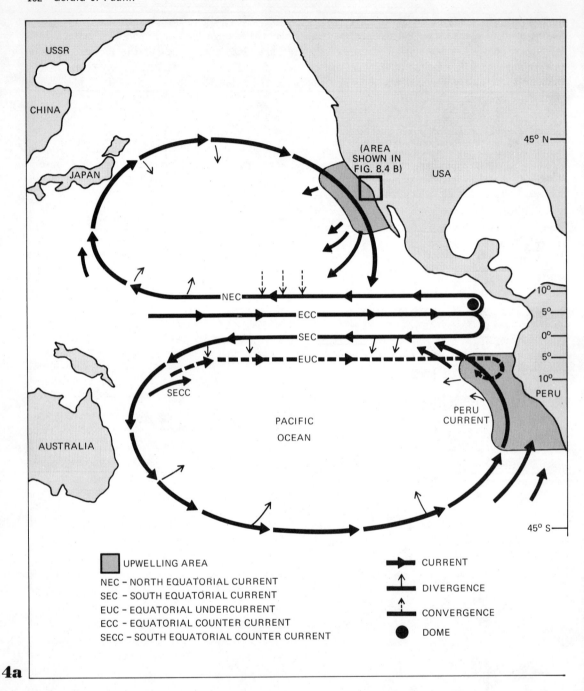

**4a**

PACIFIC OCEAN CIRCULATION. Eastern boundary upwellings and circulation patterns in Pacific Ocean. The solid line represents the upwelling and offshore drift. A secondary upwelling 100 kilometers from shore is shown. Source: Cushing, reference 2.

Peru does not have the broad continental shelves that border many other countries. The western edge of the South American continent begins at the top of the Andes, falls precipitously to the flat and narrow coastal strip, and then plunges into the depths of the Peru-Chile Trench. Just off the coast from 22,205-foot Mount Huascaran, which lost part of its peak in the May 31 earthquake, is the Milne-Edwards Deep, 20,394 feet below sea level (see Figure 3).

Beyond the 100-fathom or 200-meter depth contour — a traditional measure of the outer edge of the continental shelf — the slope of the bottom increases abruptly. It is on the shallower shelf areas that exploitable minerals and petroleum resources are found (Chapter 4). Not only is the narrowness of the shelf an obvious disadvantage, but the marine terrain of a narrow shelf makes economic exploitation extremely difficult. Thus Peru can expect little in the way of nonrenewable resources from her shelf, in comparison with countries with shelves which extend seaward as far as 200 miles below their adjacent waters. Lacking a broad continental shelf, Peru claimed as her own 200 miles of ocean adjacent to her shores. In one sense it is as if Peru regarded the Peru Current as being a substitute for the broad continental shelves claimed by other nations. The Peru Current is about 200 meters deep and approximately 200 miles wide, although these dimensions vary greatly along the coast. More by accident than by design, Peru's claim is a tidy extension of sovereignty in that it encompasses a single and unique marine regime.

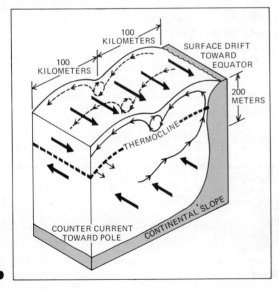

*Ocean Currents and Upwelling*

From Valparaiso, Chile to the Gulf of Guayaquil in Ecuador, the coastal desert of South America is bathed by the cold northward flowing Peru Current. This Current, sometimes called the Humboldt Current, swings to the west just south of the equator and joins the westward flowing South Equatorial Current. Its counterpart in the Northern Hemisphere, the California Current, flows south towards the equator where it swings to the west to join the Northern Equatorial Current.

A rough diagrammatic sketch of the basic dynamics of the swift western boundary currents, the slower and broader eastern boundary currents, and the huge slowly moving equatorial flows in the Pacific Ocean is given in Figure 4.

The interactive response of the winds and the ocean to differential heating between equatorial and polar regions combines with the earth's rotation to produce the northern and southern hemisphere gyres illustrated. Excess equatorial heat is carried toward the poles along the western boundaries of the ocean and eastern shores of the continents. As this flow attempts to restore the heat balance of the earth, it is pushed by the spin of the earth to the right in the Northern Hemisphere and to the left in the Southern Hemisphere (Coriolis force).

The southeast trade winds are channeled by the Andes to blow parallel to the coast. Mountain ranges in California act in a similar manner to direct prevailing winds in a southerly direction. As the Peru Current is pushed northward by the south wind, it is continually deflected to the left by Coriolis force. As the deflected surface water moves off shore, it is replaced by water from below and the resulting upwelling forms huge eddies and spirals flowing in the general direction of the equator. A smaller secondary upwelling associated primarily with wind stress is often generated at about 100 kilometers from the shore, where some of the original upwelling water sinks (see inset in Figure 4).

The intensity of the upwelling varies seasonally with location along the coast of Peru. Over most of the fishing grounds a strong upwelling in the southern winter (May, June, July, and August) disperses the current and the anchoveta populations. When it became necessary to impose conservation regulations on the fishing fleet, the first seasonal closures were imposed during the months of June, July, and August when the dispersed anchoveta were hard to catch anyway.

Upwelling areas constitute only a small fraction of the total surface area of the world's oceans, yet they are exceedingly important in terms of total potential food production. Approximately 50 mmt of the total world catch of 64 mmt in 1968 consisted of marine fishes. Over 15 mmt came from upwelling areas.

Cushing[2] has developed crude but nevertheless useful rankings with respect to potential fish production of the main upwelling systems. The Peru and Benguela Current systems are about the same size, and each produces 20-30 mmt of fish per year. The California and Canary Current systems are somewhat lower, with potential productivities of around 10 mmt. The productivity of the Arabian Sea, where the upwellings are generated by the seasonally shifting winds, is close to that of the California and Canary Currents. Along the eastern boundary of the Indian Ocean in the general vicinity of Indonesia, upwellings are greatly influenced by seasonal monsoons, and estimates of upwelling productivities for this region and for the Western Australia Current involve far more guesswork than for the other five more intensely studied areas. Total productivity for this entire region, including the Gulf of Thailand and Vietnam, appears to be in the 20-40 mmt-per-year class.

One-half or slightly less of total potential production of fish can be harvested by man on a sustainable basis; thus, upwelling areas can produce 50-65 mmt of catchable fish per year. Neither fisheries scientists nor marine biologists have been able to agree upon a single "best" estimate of the potential harvestable production of fish from the sea. A figure of about 125 mmt per year of the types of fish taken today seems to be a reasonable compromise among the available scientific conjectures. We may expect from 2/5 to 1/2 of this total to come from upwelling areas.

*The Biological Setting*

Upwelling systems may be compared to vertical chemostats. At the depths where the upwelling water originates, sparse populations of inoculating phytoplankton are present. Theoretically at least, as the water rises this seed population begins to grow as the plants and nutrients are slowly lifted along an increasing light gradient. The phytoplankton can multiply more rapidly than the herbivorous zooplankton that feed on them. According to this theory, the temporal sequence of events in a volume of upwelling water is similar to the temporal sequence of events during the spring bloom in temperate waters where the phytoplankton build up high densities before they are either overtaken by their predators or have their population growth limited by scarcity of critical nutrients.

Zooplankton, with generation lengths several times those of the phytoplankton, respond after an initial lag to increasing phytoplankton densities and build their own populations at the expense of the phytoplankton. High concentrations of zooplankton often are found far downstream of primary upwelling surface points.

Planktonic animals have difficulty in maintaining spawning populations in a moving habitat as dynamic as the Peru Current. To sustain populations in desirable locations, they must be able to withstand continuous washout from favorable zones or rely upon some mechanism such as a

| | Seasonal average grams C/m$^2$/day | Area km$^2$(x 10$^3$) | Season days | Tons carbon per yr(x 10$^6$) |
|---|---|---|---|---|
| **Area I** Cape Blanco to 10° S | 0.471 | 288 | 270 | 36.64 |
| **Area II** 10° S to Arica | 1.479 | 191 | 270 | 76.27 |
| Total | | | | 112.91 |

**CARBON PRODUCTION IN THE PERU CURRENT. Source: reference 2.**

current/countercurrent system or a gyral to reseed the area with their sex products. How phytoplankton and zooplankton manage to continually inoculate the upwelling water with seed stock remains a nagging but most intriguing scientific problem.

A basic measure of biological productivity is the amount of carbon fixed per unit of surface area per unit time. Some of the highest values ever observed have been found in the Peru Current, where many investigators have observed values greater than 10 grams of carbon per square meter per day. Estimated annual production figures in grams of carbon per square meter per day for two geographical divisions (Figure 3) of the Peru Current upwelling are given in Table II. Production figures for the Peru Current may be contrasted with those for the California Current which, in the most productive of three primary upwelling areas, produces an average of 0.362 grams of carbon per square meter and in the lowest, 0.234 grams.

By extending this productivity to the next trophic level which includes zooplankton and anchoveta, we can estimate total anchoveta production available from the Peru Current. Production in the upwelling farther to the south off the Coast of Chile should not be included in this calculation because of the considerable evidence that the Chilean component of the coastal circulation is separated from the Peruvian component by a belt of warm water at about 20° S.[3]

Zooplankton are usually represented in aquatic food-chain diagrams as a link between the plants or primary producers and the third stage carnivores. Most zooplankton in the Peru Current system consume phytoplankton as they should to fit into a neatly arranged food chain; the anchoveta are not so obliging. Adult anchoveta are far more herbivorous than the very young, which feed upon the larvae and adults of small copepods found in the Peru Current. By feeding directly on phytoplankton, the adults gain access to additional energy; 5-15 grams of phytoplankton are needed to produce every gram of zooplankton the anchoveta consume. By eliminating the zooplankton link, the anchoveta bypass a middleman who otherwise would remove a large portion of the available energy. Some zooplankton, especially the large shrimp-like euphausids which consume other zooplankton and organic debris as well as phytoplankton, occupy about the same position in the food web as the anchoveta.

A standard ecological accounting procedure is to equate some fraction of primary production with production at an artificial second level. While the figure of 10 percent has been widely used as the efficiency of energy transfer from one trophic level to another, in actuality such efficiencies are notoriously variable.

Cushing[2] computed secondary production in the Peru Current by two methods: (1) indirectly, using 10 percent of observed phytoplankton production; and (2) directly, converting average standing crop as measured by net catches of zooplankton by the number of generations produced per season. He assumed the bottom of the layer sampled by nets to be 300 meters and arbitrarily extended generation times by one-fourth from observations made under ideal conditions to account for the intermittent character of upwellings. His figures (using unadjusted generation lengths) for secondary production of the Peru Current are given in Table III.

The last column, trophic efficiency, compares the direct calculations of second-stage produc-

| Area | Net catch ml displaced/ m$^2$ surface area | Grams of C/m$^2$ | Generation time days | Number of generations per season | Carbon tons/yr (x 10$^6$) | Trophic efficiency % |
|---|---|---|---|---|---|---|
| **Area I** | | | | | | |
| Cape Blanco to 10° S | 68 | 3.78 | 52 | 5.18 | 7.50 | 20.47 |
| **Area II** | | | | | | |
| 10° S to Arica | 60 | 3.36 | 52 | 5.18 | 4.43 | 5.81 |
| Total | | | | | 11.98 | |

**PERU CURRENT SECONDARY PRODUCTION. Source: reference 2.**

**III**

tion to the measurements of primary productivity. The low trophic efficiency of 5.81 percent for central Peru may be partly the result of competitive grazing of phytoplankton by anchoveta not included in the zooplankton standing crop measurements.

Recent proclamations on the potential production of fish in the Peru Current system by three eminent scientists provide a rare opportunity to examine the state of the art in estimating potential production of food from the sea. Gulland[4], working primarily from an extrapolation of past fish catch statistics and assuming that about half the total mortality is caused by the fishery, estimates the total productivity of fish in the main Peruvian upwelling area to be on the order of 20 mmt. The accuracy of Gulland's estimate depends upon the implicit assumption that the fishery is currently exploiting all of the anchoveta stocks in the current system and there are no geographically isolated stocks either between major fishing ports or farther out to sea to be discovered in the future. Both possibilities seem unlikely, although the fish resources of the offshore regions of the Peru Current have not been adequately explored.

Two other scientists, Ryther[5] and Cushing[2], used entirely different methods to calculate the productivity of the Peruvian upwelling system and it is most revealing to compare their calculations. Both Ryther and Cushing estimate total production at about 20 mmt and both call attention to the agreement between their calculations and Gulland's. Ryther also cites Cushing's results as supporting the validity of his estimate. While total production estimates turn out to be the same, the components used to construct these two totals differ shockingly. Below, the four factors multiplied by Cushing and Ryther to compute production in the Peru Current system are laid out. (T—C = metric tons of carbon).

ACCORDING TO CUSHING[2]
$(T-C/km^2/yr) \times (km^2)$
$\quad \times$ (2-step ecological efficiency factor of 0.01)
$\quad \times$ (Carbon wet weight conversion factor)
$\quad$ = Metric tons fish

$(235.7) \times (479 \times 10^3) \times (0.01) \times (17.85)$
$\quad = 20.15 \times 10^6$

ACCORDING TO RYTHER[5]
$(T-C/km^2/yr) \times (km^2)$
$\quad \times$ (1½-step ecological efficiency factor of 0.12)
$\quad \times$ (Carbon wet weight conversion factor)
$\quad$ = Metric tons fish

$(300) \times (60 \times 10^3) \times (0.12) \times (10)$
$\quad = 21.6 \times 10^6$

The agreement between the final products is not too reassuring when we compare the individual elements in the equations. If certain elements were interchanged, for example if Cushing had used Ryther's 1½-step ecological efficiency factor of 0.12, he would have obtained about 240 mmt rather than 20 mmt. On the other hand, if Ryther had used Cushing's estimate of the area of biological productivity, he would have obtained 172 mmt rather than 21.6 mmt. The discrepancies between the calculations of these two scientists illustrate existing inadequacies in our understanding of oceanic production. There is a great deal of important work waiting to be done.

*Dynamics of the Anchoveta Stocks*

There are two vitally important reasons for understanding the population dynamics of the Peruvian anchoveta. The most obvious is that unless the population processes are understood and the rate of harvest adjusted to conform with the natural productivity of the stocks, the rapidly expanding industry could destroy the stocks by overfishing. A less obvious reason is that the growing importance to world fisheries of species similar to the anchoveta make it an extremely valuable prototype for an entire group of fisheries of the future. As man's ability to harvest the wild stocks of fish in the farthest reaches of the ocean grows, the larger, more valuable, easier to capture animals are placed in dire jeopardy. The political and practical difficulties of developing suitable international machinery for controlling the total take of high-level carnivores, such as cods, mackerels, tunas, salmons, flatfishes, and sharks, and of dividing the take between nations, may well prove insurmountable. Any future species succession in catches taken from a given region of the ocean will probably involve the replacement of higher trophic level animals with those from lower levels. It is also likely that any such change in species composition will increase the physical yield while reducing its economic worth.

There are indications that such replacements are beginning to occur. For example, the severe overharvesting and near extinction of several of the Antarctic baleen whales has led the Russians[6] to attempt to replace the whales as a harvester of krill. While the sustainable yield from whales was in the vicinity of 1 to 1½ mmt per year, these whales comsumed about 50 mmt of krill per year. So far krill harvesting has not proven economically feasible on a large scale.

The surge of interest by the world's fishermen in anchovies and related species suitable for reduction to fish meal has been examined by W.M. Chapman:[7]

> The overwhelmingly largest change in trend of usage over the years has been as raw material for fish meal and other undifferentiated protein production. In 1938, 8.1 percent of world production was used in this form and by 1968 this had reached 35.6 percent . . . . The reason for this is the rapid spread of modern animal husbandry practices (and particularly poultry production) into the rest of the world. This is really just beginning . . . by the year 2000 a larger proportion of this undifferentiated protein will be used for direct human consumption than at present.

Thus anyone interested in food production from the sea must be concerned about the population dynamics of small, short-lived, anchovy-type species. The prospects for bypassing these animals and harvesting primary producers directly appear to be nil using any foreseeable technology. Until man can separate from the water the microscopic plants that form the basis of the food chain, he will continue to depend upon the herbivores to convert the plants into more available and palatable forms of food.

We shall examine the population biology of the Peru anchoveta as a representative type specimen in a taxonomy based upon the productivity characteristics of animals rather than upon their morphological characteristics. All members of the genus *Engraulis* are pelagic and typically are found in oceanic areas within 200 to 300 miles of a coast line or, in a few cases, in shallow inshore bays and estuaries. They spawn in huge schools or spawning aggregations and spawning is usually spread out over an extended period.

Fisheries scientists have developed a special brand of demographics in which a number of vital population parameters are first measured and then combined in a mathematical model to estimate the maximum sustainable yield of a fish stock. The critical factors include the relation between the stock and the production of young animals subsequently recruited to the population, the rate of natural mortality, and the rate of growth of individual animals. These factors may change with population density, and measurements taken on a virgin stock may be quite different from those for fully exploited stocks. These key processes for the Peru anchoveta will be examined in some detail.

Anchoveta spawn during the entire year in the Peru Current; however, the main spawning activity takes place around September. A secondary spawning peak, smaller and less distinct than the main peak, occurs in the southern fall, that is, sometime in April or May. The anchoveta are recruited to the fishery at about 5 months of age. Thus, the progeny of the first spawning peak enter the fishery in January or February and those of the second in July or August. A large percentage of anchoveta mature at an age of 1 year and fecundity is high; a 2-year-old female may spawn over 20,000 eggs.

These pelagic eggs have an almost negligible store of nutrient material. Consequently, newly hatched anchoveta larvae require a high density of food in their immediate environment if they are to survive. They have only a few wiggles to locate and consume a food particle before their entire energy supply is exhausted and they die. In addition to the ever constant threat of starvation, the pelagic eggs and larvae are subjected to severe predation from a variety of plankton feeders ranging from carnivorous zooplankters to their own parents. The spawning aggregations intermix large numbers of filter-feeding adults with the drifting eggs and larvae, and field observations confirm that the numbers of eggs and larvae consumed by the spawners are sufficiently large that cannibalism during the period of larval drift could serve as a basic mechanism controlling population density and stabilizing the numbers of recruits produced.

By considering the population consequences of the reproductive behavior of the anchoveta, we can obtain insight into the manner in which the population evolved and how it is likely to respond to exploitation. Because of its short life span, the anchoveta is forced to adopt an entirely different reproductive strategy than that of a long-lived species such as cod, which may have upwards of 20 year classes extant in a population at any one time. These long-lived species can survive in highly variable environments where conditions adverse to survival of eggs and larvae during the spawning season may occur for a series of years. Typically, spawning takes place in a very short period of time and, if not properly sequenced in a chain of events controlled by climatic conditions in a given year, will produce almost no recruitment to the population. The anchoveta, with 2 or 3 year classes in its population, cannot afford the luxury of gambling on the weather. Lack of spawning success in a single year could be disastrous. So the anchoveta hedges its bet by spawning over the entire year and increasing its chances of encountering favorable conditions during some part of the extended spawning season. We would expect the combination of this type of spawning behavior, a fairly stable environment, and cannibalism on the eggs and larvae to dampen annual variations in recruitment. Observations support this hypothesis. Recruitment has not varied by more than a factor of 3 for many years and in the last 4 to 5 years, by less than a factor of 2. This consistency is remarkable when compared to longer-lived species of fish.

Peruvian anchoveta suffer high mortalities. Estimates of the fraction of adult fish surviving per year at the level of fishing before the 1969-70 season are in the vicinity of 8 to 15 percent. During the mid-1960s, mortality appeared to be fairly evenly split between the fishery and all other causes of death, including natural deaths from diseases or parasites and from predators such as birds, squid, bonita, mackerel, and hake. In the 1969-70 season increased fishing probably increased man's share from 50 percent to 60 percent, largely at the expense of new re-

cruits that otherwise would have survived until the beginning in June of the 3-month closure.

The decrease in numbers of a hypothetical cohort entering the fishery at an age of 5 months is illustrated in Figure 5. Available data do not justify extension of the numbers-at-age diagram beyond 25 months. For all practical purposes, the maximum possible life span is 42 months.

Growth of anchoveta in length and in weight is also illustrated in Figure 5. Growth is rapid indeed, especially during the first year of life. From ages 5 through 8 months the weight added to a cohort by growth is much higher than the weight subtracted by natural mortality. It is apparent that the Peruvian stocks are now being exploited at a size and an age considerably before first maturity. This means that, in addition to the waste of potential growth and the waste involved with catching and reducing to meal and oil the low-yield peladilla, the present intensity of fishing on the young flirts with the danger of reducing the number of spawners below some unknown but nevertheless real level of abundance needed to sustain the population.

One of the most important problems confronting fisheries biologists is recognizing and regulating self-sustaining population subunits within a population exploited by a common fishery. Such individual stocks may have unique recruitment, growth, natural mortality, and migratory characteristics and may be of quite different numerical abundances. Regulating a mixture of individual stock units on the basis of total allowable catch can be ruinous if the catch is not properly distributed over the stocks. This is precisely the type of management mistake which caused the destruction of several of the Antarctic baleen whale stocks. If the total quota of 16,000 blue whale units had been properly divided among the four main species, it is likely the whale stocks could have sustained this catch indefinitely. Instead the most valuable species was overfished until nearly destroyed and then the fishery concentrated on the next most valuable species. This pattern was repeated until desperate measures were required to save the whales from extinction.

Little is known about the genetic composition of the anchoveta populations in the Peru Current. Some indirect evidence on feeding behavior, intestine length, and number of gill rakers indicates the population off Chile and southern Peru may be genetically distinct from the fish off central and northern Peru. Characters such as vertebral number, size composition, and growth rate have been examined but do not provide definitive evidence for any further separation of the population and cast some doubt on the separateness of the southern from the central-northern stocks. Tagging studies which are just now beginning may be the only means of obtaining indisputable information on stock structure.

From the above description of the Peruvian anchoveta and from published studies[8,9,10] of other members of the genus *Engraulis*, an anchovy type of life history pattern begins to emerge. Anchovy are short-lived animals with extremely high natural mortality even as adults and with maximum ages ranging from less than 3 to at most 6 or 7 years, depending on the species. Spawning activities are generally spread out over long periods and individual females produce large numbers of eggs. Anchovies are filter feeders and their population densities are closely related to the productivity of phytoplankton and zooplankton in particular marine habitats. They browse down their own eggs and by so doing help stabilize their numbers. Most of their growth has been completed by first maturity and ratios of length at first maturity to ultimate attainable length range from 0.6 to 0.8.

Growth during early life is extremely rapid. This type of life history is most productive at extremely high fishing intensities if recruitment

ANCHOVETA GROWTH AND SURVIVAL. Growth in length and weight of Peruvian anchoveta; numbers surviving by age from a hypothetical cohort of 100 fish starting at 5 months.

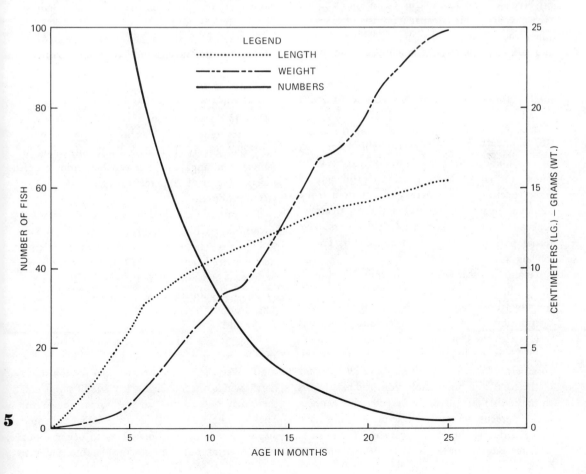

LEGEND
·············· LENGTH
— · — · — WEIGHT
———— NUMBERS

to the fishery occurs at about the time of first maturity and if there is no direct relation between the number of spawning adults and subsequent recruitment. However, this is true only in terms of physical yield, not in terms of net economic yield. The marginal increase per unit of gear added at higher intensities decreases rapidly even though total physical yield may go up. If the natural order does not regulate the age at first entry into the fishery, man must assume the role or else face the prospect of trading a slight increase in production over a very few years for the continued existence of the population as an economically viable fishery resource.

*Guano Bird Stocks*

Manufacture of the finest natural fertilizer known is the specialty of the colonies of guano birds found on the headlands and on the islands off Peru's coastal desert strip. Guano birds crowd every available bit of space on islands located where the ocean provides an especially abundant and available supply of anchoveta and other food. Interspersed with these island "fertilizer factories" along the coast are the shore-based fish meal factories with which they compete for raw material.

The guano birds, all members of the order Pelecaniformes, have an unmistakable pattern of foot webbing joining the hind toe to the front three. Virtually all the guano is produced by three species — the "Guanay" (cormorant), the "Piquero" (gannet or booby), and the "Alcatraz" (pelican). All three of these fish eaters have throat pouches, the most spectacular by far belonging to the pelican.

Guano birds are fairly uniformly distributed along the coast from about 8°S to 14°S, roughly from Chicama to Pisco (Figure 3). The distribution of prime fishing grounds coincides nicely with the distribution of birds. The purest and highest quality guano is produced by the cormorants, which comprised about 80 percent of the total bird population from the mid-1940s to the mid-1960s; about 18 percent were gannets and 2 percent, pelicans. These proportions have changed during the last 5 years and the present relative composition is closer to 60 percent cor-

morants, 35 percent gannets, and 5 percent pelicans.

According to Jordan[11] the cormorants abstain almost religiously from eating anything but anchoveta, which compose 95 percent of their diet. The gannets and pelicans, with 80 percent anchoveta diets, are only slightly less dependent upon a single prey species. The flocks of birds feed most actively at the break of dawn when the plankton and the feeding fish are near the surface. The cormorant, an accomplished diver and powerful underwater swimmer, pursues the anchoveta to depths exceeding 15 meters. The gannet and pelican, on the other hand, dive at at their prey from the air, hitting the water like dive bombers which failed to pull out. While the gannet's effective feeding depth appears to approach the cormorant's, the pelican feeds effectively only near the surface. The fish-catching birds, like their human colleagues, prefer to fish close to home and rarely venture more than 40 or 50 miles offshore.

The rates at which the birds consume anchoveta and produce guano have been the subject of many scientific studies.[11] The most reliable estimate of average per-day consumption of a cormorant weighing 2 kilograms appears to be about 430 grams. From this meal of anchoveta the cormorant produces about 45 grams of recoverable guano. The reader will note that the familiar and apparently inescapable ecological efficiency factor of 10 percent is applicable even to guano production.

The numerical abundances of guano birds and anchoveta catches during recent years are shown in Figure 6. The precipitous drops in abundance that occurred between 1957 and 1958 and also between 1965 and 1966 are associated with the El Niño phenomenon, so named because it occurs around Christmas time, the season of the small child.

When an El Niño occurs, a tongue of warm and low-salinity surface water extends to the south over the Peru Current.[12] Heavy rains and north winds often accompany an El Niño and there may be an active surface flow to the south. The periodicity of El Niño is the subject of some dispute; a severe El Niño seems to occur about every 7 years, but there is considerable evidence than an El Niño is not an all or none phenomenon, but rather a condition whose degree and severity differ from year to year. The biological damage caused by the El Niño is dependent on its duration, magnitude, and the speed with which it invades the southern water.

In spite of the often-repeated statements that an El Niño destroys anchoveta, I believe it does just the opposite. The warm surface water of the El Niño serves as a protective blanket, forcing the anchoveta to sound and avoid the severe bird predation in the top 10 meters. This behavior exerts a selective stress on the birds, discriminating against weak swimmers and divers unable to capture anchoveta or to switch to another type of prey. Census data[13] confirm that weak, immature birds are almost totally decimated by the El Niño.

Why the 1965-66 El Niño should have such a prolonged effect is a mystery; the bird population have completely failed to regain their previous abundance (Figure 6). This failure is in direct contrast to what occurred after severe reductions in the past. After being reduced to 6 million by the severe El Niño in 1957 and then to 5.5 million by a milder El Niño in 1958, the bird population climbed to about 11 million in 1959 and 1960 and by 1963 had reached over 16 million. When the population fell from 17 million in 1964-65 to 4.3 million in 1965-66, it did not recover and according to the most recent census in 1968-69 was only 5.4 million.

We do not know what factors are acting to keep the population at such a low level. Two lines of speculation seem most plausible. One holds that the standing crop of anchoveta has been so reduced by intense fishing that the increased expenditure of energy needed to feed on a more diffuse prey does not leave the birds any excess for population growth. The other conjecture is that the Peru Current upwelling system may trap persistent pesticides just as the oceanographically similar California Current system does, and that these pollutants are concentrated as they move up the food chain to the birds, where they interfere with reproduction (Chapters 11 and 13). In many other parts of the world, DDT has been shown to cause fish-eating birds to produce eggs so thin-shelled that the parents were unable to incubate them. The well-documented demise of the brown pelican in the California Current system is a disturbingly similar example.

Schaefer[14] has articulated the need to maintain some minimum population level of guano birds in order to preserve the species ". . . since this genetic material may be of great future value." The minimum abundance for survival of the species is unknown but it is well established that social birds, such as the guano birds do require some minimum density for successful breeding.

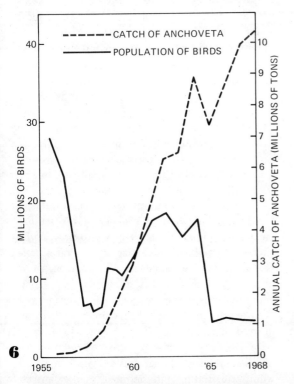

**6**

GUANO BIRD POPULATION AND ANCHOVETA CATCH. Guano bird population census figures and anchoveta catch by year for 1955-1968. Source: Redrawn from figure in Appendix 3 of reference 1.

*The Industrial and Economic Setting*

The same lusty excitement that must have swirled about the boom towns during the Gold Rush in the United States runs through the fishing towns along the Peruvian coast. The fish meal industry grew in a manner reminiscent of the building up during the nineteenth century in the United States of industrial empires based on natural resources such as timber, oil, and minerals. As large and as important as the industry is by absolute measures — total meal production during the 1969-70 season was 1,920,000 tons worth over 350 million dollars; about 20,000 full-time fishermen and 3000 factory workers were employed; capital equipment consisted of 1300 purse seiners and about 125 fish meal plants — such statistics do not even begin to convey the psychological impact of the industrial boom that has culminated in the largest fish meal industry the world has ever known.

To understand why the impressive economic and physical statistics are dwarfed by psychological factors, recall the circumstances under which this industry developed. During the past 15 years, the average population of Peru was about 10 million people. These 10 million people lived in a rigid and stratified society greatly influenced by semifeudal Spanish traditions. Although democratic political traditions have been much stronger in Peru than in some other South American countries, the social hierarchy, which correlates very closely with the economic hierarchy, was dominated by a small elite class of land owners and wealthy urbanites. The industrial explosion that made Peru the world's leading producer of fish meal should be pictured against a background in which social and economic rigidity were maintained by the sorts of institutions allied with the landed aristocracy, the church, and the military.

Opportunities to acquire wealth were heavily weighted in favor of members of a few large and socially prominent families who controlled much of the property in Peru. Because the fish meal industry had no precedent and developed so explosively, it spawned a small but important class of "nouveau riche." It also provided either directly or indirectly many new jobs for middle-class professionals such as lawyers, engineers, boat skippers, factory managers, and white collar workers. During the chaotic growth of the fish meal industry, men of action with brains and good luck became millionaires overnight.

One could hardly blame these industrial empire builders if they were skeptical of the idea

of a fixed limit to the amount of fish that could be removed each year from the giant ocean upwellings so obviously teeming with life. Both the government and the industry are to be complimented on their recognition of the sobering possibility that such a finite limit might exist and that exceeding the limit could destroy the renewable resource upon which the industry depends. The fact that the government has been willing to impose limitations on the industry and that the industry has been willing to accept these limitations is reason for optimism. However, the tremendous excess capacity building in both the factories and in the fleets is severely straining any regulatory agency's ability to impose rational controls on harvesting.

It is interesting to compare Peru's performance to date with the exploitation of natural resources that occurred during the opening of the West in the United States. One great difference is the presence of teams of United Nations scientists and economists and the education of local counterparts. The primary mission of these consultants is to advise the government on the type of exploitation policy that will allow maximum production from the resource without destroying it. To men caught up in the grand enthusiasm of industrial empire building, these consultants must have sounded like prophets of doom. Yet it is abundantly clear that their presence and advice has served to cool down the industrial growth which easily could have raced completely out of control.

In spite of the extreme scarcity of capital in Peru, the fishing industry has managed to acquire far more equipment than it needs to harvest the anchoveta available. Such scarcity generates pressure to employ available capital equipment to its maximum capacity. Many of the fish meal companies which sprang up overnight during the chaotic growth of the industry are models of industrial inefficiency, and their precarious financial state is becoming chronic. When a large number of marginal operators are combined with wildly fluctuating international market prices, the threat of overharvesting the resource becomes very great. The scientists and economists of Peru and from abroad who are responsible for monitoring the industry and for establishing harvesting policies are now engaged in one of the most delicate tightwire acts playing in the international resource circus.

## The Fishing Fleet

In the late 1950s, when it was becoming apparent that the fish meal industry was going to be substantial, tiny shipyards sprouted around Callao. These shipyards turned out wooden fishing vessels with hold capacities from 40 to 100 tons. As the fishery grew, so did the size of the boats, and the large numbers of small vessels were replaced by smaller numbers of much larger vessels. The increases in vessel size were accompanied by increases in the size of the purse seine nets used to surround the schools of anchoveta.

Most of the boats now under construction in Peru have hold capacities in excess of 300 tons and are made of steel; one venturous operator is beginning to build 350 tonners out of fiberglass. The vessels are around 100 feet long and powered by 500-600 horsepower engines. Basic equipment includes the hydraulic power block invented by Mario Puretic which has revolutionized purse seining for salmon and herring as well as for anchoveta. The heavy manual labor formerly necessary to brail the catch from the net to the hold and to stack the net on the deck has been eliminated by power equipment; a pump sucks the anchoveta from the net into the hold and the Puretic power block hauls the net from the ocean. All Peruvian bolicheras are equipped with echo sounders and some have horizontally sweeping sonar or asdic fish detectors.

A 350-ton vessel requires a crew of only 12 to 14 men as compared to the 10-man crews often needed to run a 100-ton vessel. Obviously this labor reduction per ton of capacity is a major source of efficiency associated with the larger vessels.

The net result of the decrease in numbers of vessels and the increases in average hold capacity and power and electronic equipment has been to increase total fishing power of the fleet far beyond that needed to harvest the anchoveta. More frightening, however, than the size of existing fleet capacity is the rapid rate at which capacity is growing.

The fleet existing at the end of the 1969-70 season could be reduced by 25 percent and still easily harvest the quota of 9.5 mmt in 8 months of fishing 5-day weeks. If the boats were allowed to fish as many days as they would like per week, the size of the fleet could be reduced by half or perhaps even 75 percent. If present construction trends continue in spite of the 5-day week and 4-month closure, capacity will be 50 percent greater than needed by 1971-72. The irrationality of the present method of coping with excess capacity is worth examining in more detail.

When free entry is allowed but total removal must be restricted, the management agency finds itself on the horns of a dilemma. As more gear enters and the gear becomes more technologically efficient, the agency, in order to restrict the catch to some preset target quota, limits fishing time. While this regulation negates the effect on the stock of the new technology and the larger fleet, it wastes the economic potential of the resource. Fixed costs of vessel operation (normal depreciation, annual maintenance costs, insurance, and so on) are independent of the total number of days fished. They must be paid whether the vessel fishes 1 day a year or 365 days a year. For the Peruvian fishery fixed costs are about 47 percent of total costs. When the vessels are only allowed to fish 6½ months as in the 1969-70 season, fixed costs become increasingly important and greatly increase the price per ton of removing the fish from the ocean. Consider as an extreme case the difference in costs between catching some fixed quota with one vessel fishing 365 days a year and 365 vessels each fishing one day a year.

There is a limit to such artificial cost raising. The computers of the feed mixers of the world constantly compare the price of fish meal to the prices of competitive protein sources such as soybean, sunflower, bone, blood, ground nut, palm kernel, cotton seed, coconut, and poultry by-product meal. If harvesting inefficiencies become excessive and the resultant price increases, it will cause fish meal to be replaced by other products in the world protein market.

Ownership and fleet size also affect efficiency. In the Peruvian anchoveta fishery and in other industries, private ownership of a piece of capital equipment promotes efficiency in its use. Other efficiencies result from the geographical mobility of the vessels. One of the most successful operators can move his fleet along Peru's 1400-mile-long coast to help supply factories near concentrations of fish. Such mobility requires a certain scale of operation and wide deployment of processing equipment.

Economic considerations alone cannot be used to dictate a scheme for reducing capacity. Social and political factors are sure to play an important, if not dominant, role. For example, as vessels become larger, they require fewer fisher-

men per unit of harvesting capacity. Unemployed fishermen are notoriously difficult to retrain and relocate. Regardless of the scheme adopted, it is quite likely that some element of compulsion will be necessary to make it work and, if so, it will be extremely difficult to be just and equitable while maintaining efficiency and technological innovativity.

### The Meal Factories

The basic anatomy of a modern Peruvian fish meal plant is depicted in Figure 7a. A meal factory is a link in transferring energy from solar

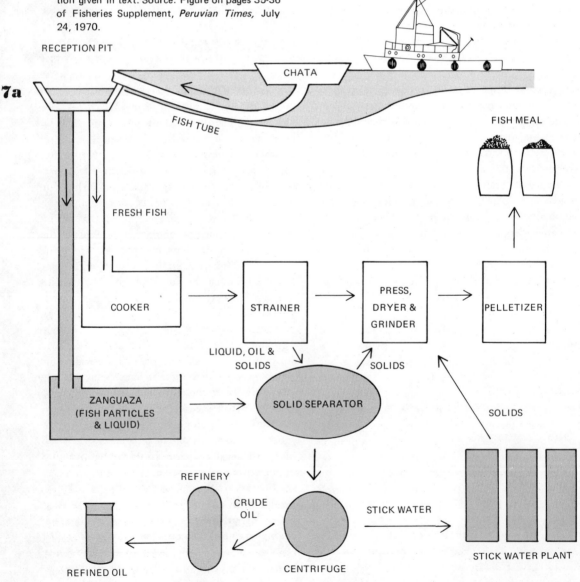

**FISH MEAL FACTORY.** Components of a fish meal factory and flow of material during processing of anchoveta into meal. Detailed explanation given in text. Source: Figure on pages 35-36 of Fisheries Supplement, *Peruvian Times,* July 24, 1970.

7a

RECEPTION PIT

CHATA

FISH TUBE

FISH MEAL

FRESH FISH

COOKER

STRAINER

PRESS, DRYER & GRINDER

PELLETIZER

LIQUID, OIL & SOLIDS

SOLIDS

ZANGUAZA (FISH PARTICLES & LIQUID)

SOLID SEPARATOR

SOLIDS

REFINERY

CRUDE OIL

STICK WATER

REFINED OIL

CENTRIFUGE

STICK WATER PLANT

radiation in the southern hemisphere to the plate of a citizen eating poultry, beef, or pork in an industrialized country in the northern hemisphere. The specific function of the factory is to dewater, crush, cook, and compact the anchoveta so that it can be easily shipped to the animal feed mixers. When the fish arrive at the factory, they have already concentrated the nearly microscopic plants and tiny zooplankton from the Peru Current and transformed unpalatable materials such as cellulose and chitin into high-quality protein. By comparison the factory's job is simple; it must separate the solids and oils from the water in the fish flesh.

The bar-graph diagram shown in Figure 7b shows the amount of fat, solids, and water recovered from the raw fish in the oil and meal output of an efficient plant. The highly publicized fish protein concentrate (FPC) that some persons think will be a major source of animal protein for human consumption in underdeveloped countries is simply a refined version of fish meal with more of the the oils and fats removed. Fishy odor and fishy flavor disappear with the oils and fats.

Figure 7 shows the "chata," or unloading barge, which may be anchored as far as a half mile offshore from the factory. From the chata the fish are pumped into the reception pit dewatered, and weighed. These weights are the official catch statistics. The drain material containing blood and flesh particles is known as "zanguaza" and is processed to separate the oil

from solids recycled into the fish pulp. The raw fish are cooked and then pressed to squeeze out the oil and water. The press liquor is centrifuged to obtain crude oil for refinement and the residual liquid then pumped through a "stick-water" plant to extract soluble proteins and fine solids by a distillation process. As one might guess, the stick water contains the raw materials for glue manufacture. A stick-water evaporator is a sophisticated innovation and a fairly recent development in the Peruvian meal industry; it is found primarily in the large newer plants. Such equipment is one means of increasing output from a limited resource without increasing input. The dried fish pulp is then ground, cooled, and treated with antioxidants to make it less volatile and safer to ship and store.

Most complications shown in Figure 7 were developed to squeeze every last bit of energy from the anchoveta. Any small increase in efficiency of utilization is important for an industry handling 10 mmt of raw material. A 1 percent increase in efficiency salvages an extra 100,000 tons of meal. Removing soluble proteins from the stick water also avoids eutrophication caused by overfertilization of bays and harbors in the immediate localities of the fish plants. In the existing factories, efficiency of utilization varies from 15 to 21 percent. About 20 percent of the plants representing about 60 percent of the total production are equipped with stick-water evaporators. Although capital investment for stick-water evaporators is high, perhaps $250,000 for a fairly large plant, the costs may be recovered in less than 2 years.

According to reliable sources, the Peruvian government will soon make stick-water recovery equipment mandatory for all fish meal plants. Utilization of stick-water by-products is not only economically and ecologically reasonable, but is also consonant with man's innate desire to avoid waste of food.

The processing capacity of the fish factories in Peru has grown far above that needed to reduce a catch of 9.5 mmt to meal. The most reliable estimate of processing capacity operating in the first half of 1970 was 8000 tons per hour. By running 350 days a year, 20 hours a day, these plants could process 56 mmt (or the total world catch of marine fish). Because of geographical and sea-

SOLIDS 19.5

OIL 8.5

PROCESSING →

WATER 72.0

19.5

6.6

1.4

sonal variations in the flow of the raw material and because of operational breakdowns, it is unfair to conclude that factory capacity is 5.6 times greater than needed to process 10 mmt. On the other hand, the immense overcapacity can be neither denied nor minimized. The same sorts of tradeoffs discussed for the fleet exist for the factories. A small number of factories can operate continuously during the year or a large number of factories can operate for a short time. Given a limited supply of fish, adding a new factory means all factories must reduce their operating time. Obviously an infinite number of combinations of capacity and operating time exist. With a 4-month veda and a 5-day week, and providing a comfortable allowance for variability in supply and breakdowns, about 2700 tons per hour of capacity could be retired and the remaining factories could easily process the available catch.

Just why is excess capacity in fleet size and in the number of factories so bad? One answer is purely economic. Surplus specialized equipment ties up capital which could otherwise be employed to generate income for Peru. The country's development is retarded because of misallocation of capital. Even more serious, however, are the less tangible consequences of overcapacity in an industry based on a renewable natural resource. When the industry's harvesting and processing equipment outgrows its resource base, the industry will be in chronic economic difficulty and will be almost impossible to regulate on a rational scientific basis. An FAO—sponsored panel on economic effects of alternative regulatory measures in the Peruvian anchoveta fishery concluded:

> One of the greatest gains of limiting capacity to that capable of dealing economically with a catch of 9.5 million tons is the removal of the temptation to court disaster by significantly surpassing that catch. But, as no value can be put on keeping disaster safely at bay, this is not brought into the reckoning .... [15]

Capacity reduction can be done in such a manner as to reduce costs and at the same time increase the physical and economic yields from a fixed input of raw material. To see how one can have his cake and eat it too, consider the consequences of eliminating 25 percent of the factories at the lower end of the efficiency scale.

First, the amount of meal produced would increase by about 225,000 tons since raw material wasted by the inefficient plants would now be turned into meal by efficient plants. On the cost side of the coin, marginal costs of the more efficient plants are considerably less than the average costs of the less efficient, so transferring fish to them would significantly reduce the cost per ton of meal. Under the reduction proposed, about 6 million dollars worth of additional meal would be produced and 9 million dollars in costs saved. Peru would gain an annual income of about 15 million dollars in direct profit from its fish meal industry. In the short run, part of this money would be used to compensate owners of factories closed and to relocate their employees. Just and equitable compensations could be financed comfortably from the additional 15 million dollars of income generated.

*Marketing*

While Peru's new industrialists were mastering the secrets of harvesting anchoveta from the giant swirls and eddies of the Peru Current, they were also learning the hard way about a different sort of wilderness — the international commodities market. It is said that much of the industry was financed with money and bank credits obtained from the future sales of fish not yet born that would be caught and processed by fleets and factories not yet constructed. In the early years of the fishery, Peruvian producers, unorganized and inexperienced in selling in a world market as complex and sensitive as that for commodities, saw much of the wealth generated by the fishery end up in the pockets of speculators and traders who served as middlemen, buying the meal from Peru and selling it to the animal feed manufacturers in Europe and the United States.

Market prices for meal are determined by the interaction of delicately sensitive market demand and market supply curves. Prices have fluctuated violently during the entire history of the fishery. For example, the average price of meal in 1964 was $108.50 per ton. An intrusion of warm water on the fishing grounds caused catches to drop in early 1965 and sent prices jumping to $207.50 per ton; prices then fell as catches increased. Prices during 1965 averaged $127 per ton. In 1968 meal sold for an average price of $100 per ton. The average price in 1969 climbed to $121 and during the first 4 months of 1970, prices were $180-$205 per ton.

Although Peru's fish oil is much less important on the world scene than her fish meal, oil prices also have exhibited great instability. Fish oil is used for industrial purposes and also for human consumption, primarily as an ingredient of margarine; its market price is controlled by soybean oil and sunflower oil prices. In March of 1969 fish oil was selling for $119 per ton and in March of 1970, $228 per ton.

International traders who not only could follow and interpret events anywhere in the world affecting competitive protein sources, such as soybean meal, but also could monitor the catches and fish meal production of other nations and even knew what was happening in Peru before many of the Peruvian producers, enjoyed a considerable advantage in the market place. Accurate and timely information is exceedingly valuable in a touchy and enormously complicated market. Useful information includes knowledge of all physical and biological factors influencing the quantity, quality, and cost of the catch; industrial problems, such as strike rumors, port congestion, and the flow of sea traffic; and even national and international politics. When many sales are for future delivery, ability to forecast the demand by the poultry, swine, and cattle raising industries of several countries and the fish meal output from Norway, Canada, South America, the United States, Angola, Denmark, Iceland, and Chile becomes most important.

In the first part of 1970 the government in Peru set up a state company, Empresa Publica de Comercializacion de Harina y Aceite de Pescado, EPCHAP, to exercise monopoly control over all fish meal and fish oil buying and marketing activities for Peruvian producers. The government took over the largest of the four industry marketing groups that had conducted most international sales. The other three were disbanded. This government takeover is an attempt to stabilize prices paid to the Peruvian producers primarily by selling directly to the feed mixers, by-passing the international brokers. The government also

has assumed responsibility for providing the short-term financial assistance sometimes required by the industry. It is far too early to know if this government marketing monopoly will be successful.

### The Guano Industry

The magnitude, value, and effect on the anchoveta stocks of the guano industry can be calculated indirectly from bird census, guano production per bird, market price per ton, and anchoveta consumption per day per bird figures. The total bird population is $5.4 \times 10^6$; each bird produces 45 grams of guano per day; guano sells for $56 per ton; and each bird eats 430 grams of anchoveta per day. Thus the birds consume 0.85 mmt of anchoveta to produce 90,000 tons of guano per year. Annual gross value of the guano is 5.05 million dollars.

Comparative gross values of a ton of anchoveta (live weight) are $5.94 in terms of guano and $30.20 in terms of fish meal (assuming 5.3 tons of anchoveta and a price of $160 per ton of fish meal). In the words of the FAO-sponsored special economic mission to Peru:[15]

> If 50% of any fish denied to the birds were caught by Peruvian fishermen, then the loss of $5.94 of guano would result in the addition of $15.10 to the value of meal output. Assuming similar rates of return from the trade in guano and that in fish meal, if the industry's marginal costs of catching and processing one ton of fish into meal are less than the fish meal price to an extent which at least is as great as the cost of exterminating the bird population to the extent required to save two tons of fish (including an appropriate rate of return on the cost of extermination) then it is worthwhile to incur such costs regardless of the price of guano.
>
> . . . . This approach to the matter ignores the threat it presents to the very existence of a bird population that has already reached perilously low levels. Furthermore, the ecological consequences of eliminating the bird populations are not understood. . . . Until more is known about the interactions between the bird and anchovy populations any type of predator control programme to reduce the birds is extremely hazardous.

### The International Setting

In September of 1945, the Truman Proclamation was issued. This document stated that the exploitable resources of the seabed adjacent to the continental United States belonged to the United States and that under certain conditions the United States could establish fish conservation zones on the high seas. Although the Proclamation was originally intended to satisfy certain needs of the petroleum and salmon power politics of the era, it opened a Pandora's box of diverse governmental and industrial activities inimical to traditional concepts of freedom of the seas. When the president of Peru, Jose Luis Bustamante, issued his Supreme Decree of August 1, 1947, declaring that Peru's jurisdiction over its "territorial" waters extended 200 miles off its coast, he cited as a precedent the Truman Proclamation. At present ex-President Bustamante is president of the International Court of Justice at The Hague. However, his interpretation of the Truman Proclamation has been challenged by experts in the field of international law.[16]

In 1952, Peru, Chile, and Ecuador issued a tripartite declaration claiming unilateral jurisdiction by the coastal state over territorial seas of 200 miles. The CEP nations, as these three countries have become known, asserted that this extension of their territorial seas was purely for protection of natural resources and did not in any way involve questions of free navigation. Nations with high-seas distant-water fishing fleets and far-roaming navies such as the United States, Japan, and Russia became skeptical. Irrespective of the logic or legality of their territorial claims, the inescapable fact seems to be that the CEP countries are in a position to enforce their claims. Peru, for example, has a small fleet of modern British-built 110-foot gun boats capable of 30 knots and armed with Swiss Oerlikon anti-aircraft cannon. U.S. tuna clippers are easy prey for such vessels and every tuna season brings with it the drama of high-seas seizures followed by payment of fines and purchase of licenses by adventuresome clippers. The Peruvian navy's greatest victory over a foreign fishing fleet occurred in 1954 when Aristotle Onassis' whaling fleet was caught in Peruvian waters with 3000 whales and fined 3 million dollars by a Peruvian court before the vessels were released.

Peruvian motives are not entirely obvious. One faction in Peru apparently favors using the 200-mile limit as a bargaining point to gain special exemption from the United States' 35 percent *ad valorem* tax on imported canned tuna, while another views extended jurisdiction as providing protection of fishery resources for future use by the coastal state. Another, perhaps more pragmatic faction, welcomes the income generated by selling fishing licenses and imposing various fines and fees on foreign vessels without licenses; there also seems to be some pressure to encourage foreign vessels to set up Peruvian-based operations. United States' response has been to reimburse fishermen the amount of fines levied by CEP nations while at the same time attempting to negotiate with representatives of the CEP nations some sort of settlement that does not recognize 200-mile territorial sea claims. While U.S. diplomats argue against foreign claims to extended jurisdictional zones, spokesmen for certain sectors of the U.S. domestic industry and sports fishing groups are asking that the United States unilaterally declare a 200-mile exclusive fishery zone around the continent and Alaska.

Other interests are maneuvering to set up a new international conference on the law of the sea. Although other powerful nations such as Russia have similar interests in restricting territorial seas to 12 miles, a new Geneva-type conference might very well provide the large number of developing nations with an opportunity to impose wider territorial limits on the more developed nations. Ironically, the U.S. flag fleet (excluding tuna and shrimp fishermen) would be a prime beneficiary of an internationally accepted 200-mile limit. The United States enjoys a broad continental shelf, a huge biomass of lightly or underexploited species, and the world's most important market for seafood. The real losers would be developing nations without seacoasts.

President Nixon, to the amazement and consternation of the petroleum industry, has proposed that the United States renounce any claims to resources of the seabed beyond the 200-meter depth contour and that an agency of the United Nations should manage exploitation of these resources for the benefit of mankind. Informed experts feel the likelihood that such a proposal will be adopted by the United Nations is near zero. With few exceptions, developing nations bordering on the sea have shown no inclination to share potential resources from the seabed.

Peru's extended jurisdictional claims have been one of its most stable policies. In spite of drastic changes in governments, the 200-mile claim has remained invariant. The current military regime in Peru has inaugurated many social reforms and there has been widespread concern since nationalization of the International Petroleum Corporation that similar actions might be taken against foreign-owned or foreign-controlled segments of the fishing industry. So far this has not happened, but more stringent requirements on the percentage of Peruvian interest in fishing enterprises were issued during the first part of 1970. It is perhaps notable that several foreign corporations have been quietly disposing of their holdings in the Peruvian industry.

*Ghosts of Fisheries Past*

Not too many years ago scientists and laymen alike believed there were no practical limits on the amount of fish that could be removed from the sea. In the early 1900s it was clear to any reasonable man that the puny catches taken from huge shoals of herring which sometimes stretched for miles in the North Sea could not possibly damage the populations. Indeed, even in recent years, the steady rise in tonnage of the total world catch supports this view. In 1950 the world's commercial fisheries took about 20 mmt of fish and other aquatic creatures and plants; in 1970 the total will approach 70 mmt.

Given this increase, why are many scientists expressing alarm over the future of the world's fisheries? Are there ominous signs portending trouble? Summary statistics can be misleading and pessimists point at the declining catch records of certain heavily exploited stocks and worry about how long total world tonnage can continue to increase. Fishermen of the world have adopted the motto "move on" as catches from one stock after another reached or exceeded maximum sustainable yields. Without question, some stocks have been so decimated they are no longer worth fishing. Giant distant-water fishing fleets continue to explore new grounds and to exploit previously unfished stocks. The consequences of a "move on" policy actively

pursued in a finite area and coupled with changing environmental conditions can be seen in the Great Lakes. U.S. and Canadian fishermen overexploited local stock after local stock and watched long-lived economically valuable species disappear and be replaced by short-lived species for which no markets exist.

The major catch increases during the past 20 years have come largely from new areas in the southeast, southwest, and northeast Pacific and from the west coast of Africa and the Indian Ocean. It is most significant that no new major resources have been discovered in either the north Atlantic or the northwest Pacific. Fishermen are beginning to run out of unexplored parts of the ocean; within 20 years it appears all possibilities for discovering new major stocks exploitable with conventional gear will have been exhausted.

In 1949 a United Nations Scientific Conference on the Conservation and Utilization of Resources held at Lake Success in New York drew up a map which showed around 30 stocks of fish then believed to be underfished. When reexamined in 1968, at least half of these stocks were either being exploited to their maximum capacities or had already been overexploited.

Fisheries are most profitable in their early years as the expanding fishery harvests a standing stock that may have taken several years, or even decades, to accumulate. When the stock can no longer sustain any further increase in catch or is destroyed, the surplus of harvesting gear built during the expansion phase is available to fish other stocks. As the world's shipyards pour out more fishing vessels, the time between first exploitation and overexploitation is becoming shorter.

For many of the Peruvians who personally witnessed the growth of the anchovy fishery, the idea of a finite maximum sustainable yield is more than just an abstract theory developed by population dynamicists. The first meal factories in Peru were equipped with machinery from idle sardine-processing plants in California.

The California sardine story is well known. In the late 1930s and early 1940s, catches of over 600,000 tons were common. Catches then began to oscillate violently until the early 1950s, when in 3 years they dropped from over 350,000 tons to less than 15,000 tons. Exactly what caused the collapse of the California sardines still generates arguments among fishery scientists, who have not yet completed their autopsies. Recruitment failed as the fishery teetered before its final collapse. At the same time, the anchovy population in the California Current system increased tremendously. What caused the anchovy to replace the sardines is a matter of conjecture. However, we do know most of the older sardines had been caught and the entire fishery depended upon very few year classes, and that water temperatures fell in the California Current system about the time the sardines began to disappear. What would have happened if there had been no fishery? Would the sardines still have disappeared? No one knows and the question seems beyond the capability of even the most sophisticated computerized crystal balls available.

Peruvian vessel and factory builders must have shuddered when they looked to the south and watched Chile dismantle fish meal plants and convert to other uses fishing vessels built to harvest an anchoveta resource much larger than actually exists there. The Chilean fishery has not collapsed; it simply never existed at a level matching up to the expectations of expansion-minded industrialists.

In spite of the half century it has taken for man to realize he is capable of fishing to economic extinction pelagic stocks, at the turn of the century it was clear marine mammals are highly susceptible to overexploitation. Stocks of seals, whales, and sea otters not protected by a national or international conservation agency have been overharvested into oblivion.

Fish with life patterns similar to mammals also have fared poorly. The spiny dogfish (*Squalus acanthias*) is such a species; it does not become mature until 11 to 13 years old and only then produces three pups. Litter sizes increase almost linearly and may reach 14-15 pups for sharks between 30 and 35 years old. Off the northwest corner of the United States, the vulnerability of this life pattern to fishing pressure was exposed with startling clarity. Within a few years, after a good market developed for shark livers during World War II, the waters of Puget Sound, the Strait of Juan de Fuca, and the Georgia Strait were swept almost clean of dogfish. The stocks began to rebuild only after the liver market and the fishery collapsed in 1946 because of synthetic vitamin A production.

The list of individual fish stocks in trouble at this writing is too long to tabulate here but includes representatives of the Gadiformes (cods), Pleuronectoidei (flounders), Salmonoidei (salmon and trout), and Clupeoidei (herrings).

Marine mammals and fish have no monopoly on susceptibility to exploitation. King crab catches by United States, Russian, and Japanese fishermen in the Bering Sea and Gulf of Alaska dropped from 80 "Thousand metric tons" in 1966 to 62 in 1967, 42 in 1968, and 27 in 1969. Stocks of early-maturing penaeid shrimps with short life spans, usually less than 2 years, and high fecundities have been able to withstand severe exploitation, while several stocks of pandalid shrimps, which have much longer life spans and delayed maturity caused by their habit of switching from males to females in their third or fourth year of life, have vanished when fished.

Since the characteristics of an animal's life pattern are so critical in determining ability to sustain a fishery, it is fair to ask if any of the ghosts of former fisheries have relevance for an "anchoveta-type" of life history.

Our collection of fishery ghosts does not include any defunct anchovy fisheries. Either the anchovies are an extremely hardy clan able to withstand tremendous fishing pressure, or anchovy fisheries are such a recent phenomenon they simply have not been in business long enough. It would be tragic if this gap in the taxonomy of dead fisheries were to be occupied by the world's greatest fishery.

The herrings, sardines, and pilchards are a group of species closely related to the anchovies and with a long history of exploitation. Many of these stocks are fished by Peru's competitors on the world fish meal market.

One reason for the sharp rise in fish meal prices in late 1969 and early 1970 was the collapse under intensive fishing of many traditional sources of raw material. The recent experience of the Norwegians who fish the Atlanto-Scandian herring stocks is alarming.

Between 1964 and 1968 Norwegians invested almost a hundred million dollars building up their herring purse seine fleet. Unfortunately the herring stocks were unable to increase their productivity to match the increase in harvesting capacity. In 1967 Norway took 1.2 mmt of herring; in 1968, 0.70; and in 1969, in spite of the massive harvesting power of the expanded fleet, the catch dropped to 0.19 mmt. Norway now owns a huge surplus of herring purse seiners with nothing to catch. The herring stocks appear to have dropped to less than 1/15 of their abundance in 1950. As might be guessed, Iceland's herring fishery, which harvests the same stocks, has experienced a similar disaster — catches from 1966 through 1969 were 0.77, 0.46, 0.14, and 0.05 mmt, respectively. Herring catches off the west coast of Canada, although much smaller than those in the western Atlantic, declined even more severely because of the necessity to impose emergency conservation regulations.

The catch of pilchards in the Benguela Current system off South Africa and southwest Africa appears to be holding up fairly well. However, recent increases in catches of anchovy from this system have caused some scientists to speculate we may be witnessing the type of replacement of a sardinelike species by an anchovy that occurred in the California Current system.

*The Peruvian Anchoveta Future*

Thinking about unthinkable catastrophes is one way of preventing them. Destruction of the world's greatest single species fishery is unthinkable. Could it really occur?

Consider the following scenario: Heavy fishing pressure has so reduced the abundance of 1- and 2-year-old anchoveta that the bulk of the catch is taken from recruits before their first birthday. Most of the catch is made during January through May. A moratorium on vessel construction has held the size of the fleet to 300,000 tons of hold capacity. In the year 197(?) adverse oceanographic conditions cause a near failure of the entering year class and low catches in the southern spring and early summer (September through December) cause fish meal prices to climb to $300 per ton. Weak upwelling currents in January, February, and March concentrate the

residual population in a narrow band extending about 10 kilometers from the coast. The total catch during the first 4 months of the season is 1 mmt and the total biomass of the entire residual population plus the entering recruits is about 5 mmt. Although many danger signals are flashing and scientists warn the industry that fishing effort must be curtailed immediately, the industry's creditors are clamoring for payment of short-term loans, and many factories and fleets are unable to meet payrolls and pay operating expenses while fish meal prices are at an all time high.

The January catches total 0.5 mmt instead of the 2.0 mmt expected. The industry rationalizes that recruitment is later than usual and will occur during the February closure. When the season reopens in March, the entire fleet is poised and the residual population is vulnerable. Within 2 months the entire population of 4.5 mmt is caught and sold at record prices. The government imposes an emergency closure when the catch-per-unit drops to zero at the end of April. The fishery is closed during May but it is too late. The Peruvian anchoveta stocks have been fished into oblivion. Only small scattered schools of anchoveta remain; dead birds, rusting bolicheros, and idle fish meal factories will soon litter the beaches from Chicama to Arica. Just how unlikely is this apocalyptic vision?

During the 1968-69 and 1969-70 seasons, the fishery depended heavily on the entering year class for the bulk of the catch. The hold capacity of the fleet at the beginning of the 1970-71 season is going to be near 225,000 tons. Fish meal prices are flirting with the $200 a ton level and the disappearance of other sources of meal fish may push them even higher. At the time of this writing, no definitive plan for restricting fleet growth and reducing present fleet capacity has been put forth. During the 1969-70 season, the fishermen were allowed to exceed substantially the recommended quota of 9.5 mmt to harvest 11.0 mmt. About 9.0 mmt of this total was caught during January through May when recruitment is high. Is the stage being set for a major ecological disaster?

The close fit of a logistic model with a maximum sustainable yield of 9.5 mmt to the catch history of the anchoveta fishery and the bird populations' failure to increase after the 1965 decline both indicate the stocks may be in some difficulty at present levels of exploitation.

In opposition to this line of reasoning, optimists point to the relative constancy of annual recruitments during the past decade, the short life span of the anchoveta, its high fecundity, early maturity, and extended spawning season.

Beyond the unthinkable lies the unknown. If the Peruvian anchoveta were to disappear, what, if anything, might replace it? Prophets of doom can assemble a long list of noxious or uncatchable marine creatures. If the successor species were a shrimplike euphasid, costs of catching and processing might be too high for the animal feed market; even a small component of poisonous animals in the replacement community could mean detoxification costs that would spell economic disaster. The importance of the huge schools of anchoveta in trapping and recirculating nutrients in the lighted surface layers of the Peru Current is not known. Conceivably if the stocks were removed, the basic productivity of the whole system could be a casualty.

Another possibility is that the anchoveta populations are composed of several functionally independent stocks and that the destruction of one stock (for example, the southern stock that Peru shares with Chile) might lead to major regulatory reforms in time to save the remaining stocks. The racial structure of the population is being investigated at the time of this writing by tagging experiments that should have been conducted long ago.

*Computer Modelling*

Qualitative descriptions of the important variables controlling the performance of the industries dependent upon the anchoveta stocks have occupied most of this chapter. Many of these variables have been incorporated in a computer simulation model by a team of biologists, economists, and computer scientists at the University of Washington. The logical structure of this model of the anchoveta stocks and the meal, oil, and guano industries is shown in Figure 8. This model is being used to explore the sensitivity of

the performance of the total system to modifications in parameter values and to changes in the functions used to describe various processes. Although the model is far too complicated to describe here and has not been tested sufficiently to determine if it will be accepted by, and can provide significant help to, the decision-makers in Peru, it represents a radical departure from earlier fisheries models. It has been specifically designed to incorporate the wealth of data collected by the Instituto del Mar del Peru on the biology of the anchoveta, the catch and effort data accumulated as the fishery developed, and the extensive information on guano birds. A detailed economic sector of the program incorporates available information on harvesters, processors, and markets. The staff using this model plans to explore systematically the strengths and weaknesses of various regulatory strategies. The model can be run in one of two basic operational modes. It can be run as a conventional computer simulation model with built-in management decision-making algorithms specifying the behavior of factory owners, fleets, and regulators, or it can be run with human intervention at frequent intervals to allow intuitive and heuristic decision-making. Mixed modes are also possible For example, a human decision-maker may play the role of factory owner while the computer makes all decisions for the regulatory agency and fishermen.

The primary objective of the simulation exercise is to quantify biological and economic effects of alternative REGULATORY MEASURES that might be imposed in the Peruvian anchoveta fishery. The output is also designed to help social scientists evaluate generalized welfare functions extremely difficult to quantify at the present time. Use of human participants is expected to be especially valuable in detecting regulatory and fiscal policies which encourage administrative corruption.

Ongoing research is investigating the effects upon regulators, harvesters, processors, marketers, and the natural population of the following types of regulations:

1. Input quotas for factories.

2. Output quotas for factories.

3. Quotas assigned to groups of vessels as

COMPUTED MODEL OF THE ANCHOVETA FISHERY. Logical structure of a generalized computer simulation model of the industrial exploitation of the anchoveta stocks off the coast of Peru.

either fixed absolute amounts or fixed percentages of a total national quota.

4. Catch taxes.

5. Harvester licensing schemes.

6. Auctioning of catch quotas for harvesters and for processors.

7. Limitations on number of units of gear.

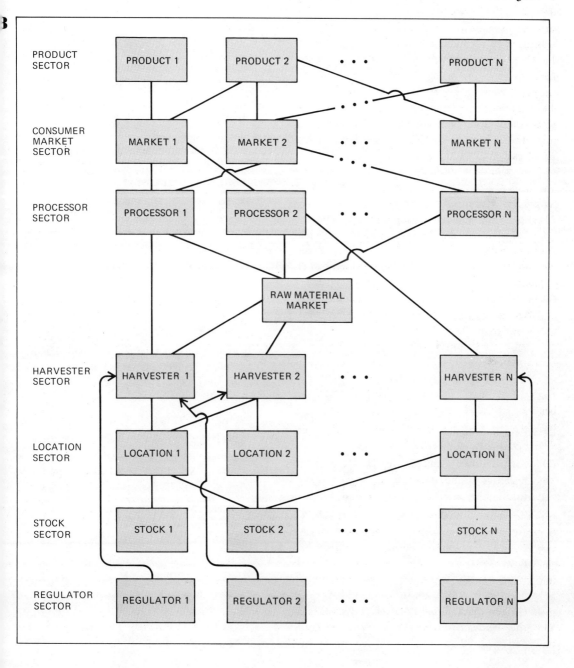

8. Limitations on gear technology and size of individual units.

9. Limitations on lengths and seasonal placements of fishing periods.

10. Catch quotas by area and time.

11. Control of harvesting locations.

12. Combinations of two or more of the above types of regulations.

The number of combinations which could be run is truly formidable and present exploratory work is aimed at narrowing areas of ignorance. For the most promising methods it will be necessary to investigate further their performance in both deterministic and stochastic versions of the model and under a variety of plausible biological hypotheses. The interaction between regulatory policies and a variety of exogenous factors affecting markets and costs of the industry also must be investigated, as well as the value of various types of information to human participants.

One of the most surprising findings to date is the almost total inadequacy of present biological understanding of recruitment mechanisms in fish. Although the computer can help pinpoint such important gaps in current understanding, more field studies are indispensable in order to produce the additional input needed to fuel a realistic simulator.

## References

1. **Ricker, W. E.**, ed. and panel chairman 1970. Report of the panel of experts on the population dynamics of Peruvian anchoveta (unpublished mineo.). FAO Department Fisheries, Rome, Italy, 20 pp.

2. **Cushing, D. H.** 1969. Upwelling and fish production. *FAO Fish. Tech. Paper 84:* 38 pp.

3. **Wooster, W. S.**, 1970. Eastern boundary currents in the South Pacific. In *Scientific Exploration of the South Pacific* (W. S. Wooster, ed.), pp. 60-68. National Academy of Sciences, Washington, D.C.

4. **Gulland, J. A.** 1968. Population dynamics of the Peruvian anchoveta. *FAO Fish Tech. Paper 72:* 29 pp.

5. **Ryther, J. H.** 1969. Photosynthesis and fish production from the sea. *Science 166:* 72-80.

6. **Burukovskii, R. N.**, ed. 1965. Antarkticheskii Krill, Biologiiai Promysel. Kaliningrad, *Antarjucheskii Naukno-issledovatel 'skii, Institut Rybnogo Khoziaistua i Okeanografii.*

7. **Chapman, W. M.** 1969. Seafood supply and world famine — positive approach (unpublished mimeo.). Prepared for delivery at the AAS Symposium "Food from the Sea," September 29, 1969, 26 pp.

8. **Beverton, R. J. H.** 1962. Maturation, growth and mortality of clupeoid and engraulid stocks in relation to fishing. *Rapp. P. — v. Reun. Cons. Perm. Int. Explor. Mer 154:* 44-67.

9. **Beverton, R. J. H., and Holt, S. J.** 1959. A review of the lifespans and mortality rates of fish in nature, and their relation to growth and other physiological characteristics. In *The Lifespan of Animals,* pp. 142-177. CIBA Foundation Colloquia on Ageing, No. 5.

10. **Baxter, J. L.**, ed. 1967. Symposium on anchovies, Genus *Engraulis. Calif. Coop. Oceanic Fish. Invest., Rep. 11:* 28-139.

11. **Jordan, R., and Fuentes, H.** 1966. Las poblaciones de aves guaneras y su situacion actual. *Inst. Mar del Peru. Informe* (10): 31 pp.

12. **Posner, G. S.** 1957. The Peru Current. *Bull. Bingham Oceanogr. Coll. 16:* 106-155.

13. **Fuentes, H.** 1969. Las poblaciones de aves guaneras. *Ser. Informes Especiales IM-54. Instituto de Mar — Callao* (mimeo), 15 pp.

14. **Schaefer, M. B.** 1970. Men, birds, and anchovies in the Peru Current — dynamic interactions. *Trans Amer. Fish. Soc. 99:* 461-467.

15. **Gulland, J. A., Holmsen, A., Laing, A., Paulik, G. J., Popper, F. E., and Watzinger, H.** (members of the panel). 1970. Report of the panel on economic effects of alternative regulatory measures in the Peruvian anchoveta industry (unpublished mimeo.). FAO

Department of Fisheries, Rome, Italy, 34 pp.

16. **McKernan, D. L., and Van Campen, W.** 1970. An approach to solving international fishery disputes. *Trans. Amer. Fish. Soc. 99:* 621-628.


Further Reading


**Gulland, J. A., and Carroz, J. E.** 1968. Management of fishery resources. *Adv. Mar. Biol. 6:* 1-71.

**Murphy, G. I.** 1966. Population biology of the Pacific sardine *(Sardinops caerulea). Proc. Calif. Acad. Sci. 34:* 1-84.

**Schaefer, M. B.** 1967. Dynamics of the fishery for the anchoveta, *Engraulis ringens,* off Peru. *Inst. Mar del Peru, Boletin, 1:* 189-304.

**Scientific American.** 1969. *The Oceans* (special issue devoted to the oceans), Vol. 221(3).

**Wooster, W. S.,** ed. 1970. Scientific exploration of the South Pacific. *Symposium Proceedings, 9th Meeting, Scientific Committee on Oceanographic Research (SCOR).* National Academy of Sciences, Washington, D.C., 257 pp.

# ENVIRONMENTAL DEGRADATION

# 9 Air Pollution

Richard J. Hickey

It seems to be rather generally known, or at least presumed, that atmospheric pollution is "bad for you." Ambient-air quality standards have been established for various specific measures of pollution, with the standards somewhat different in different localities in the United States and in other parts of the world. Emission limitations are sometimes applied locally to industrial or electric power plants and to other facilities, but sometimes there may be concurrent embarrassment because of the presence of government facilities among the more important sources of pollution. Solid proof of what is unhealthy about pollution is not always entirely clear. Acute effects, such as irritation of the ocular and respiratory systems, foul aromas, reduced visibility, and also diminished mental and visual acuity associated particularly with carbon monoxide, are among the characteristics

---

RICHARD J. HICKEY is on the staff of the Institute for Environmental Studies of the Graduate School of Fine Arts of the University of Pennsylvania. He received a B.S. degree in chemistry from the University of Illinois in 1935, and his doctorate in biophysical chemistry from Iowa State College (now University) in 1941. After a number of years working in industrial research and development on microbial processes for manufacturing antibiotics and other biologicals, he became increasingly interested in computer-oriented methods for the analysis of highly complex biological systems, an activity which led to studies in human ecology. In addition to the types of studies noted in this chapter, he has developed considerable interest in ethology and the genetics of behavior, particularly the analysis and theory of behavior in human populations.

which have been primarily used in formulating air quality standards.

Moses Maimonides of Cordova described his observations on the relation of air pollution to human health in the twelfth century, with particular reference to asthma.[1] Atmospheric pollution was found objectionable in England in the fourteenth century when efforts were made to limit the burning of coal because of the resulting smoke and odors. The smoke and smogs of London in the past and at intervals over the last 20 years have been notorious. Such acute pollution episodes have evidently been responsible for significant surges in mortality during these usually relatively short periods of pollution.[2,3] For example, a 5-day London episode in 1952 was associated with about 4000 deaths in excess of the numbers considered normal for the period. In addition to London, other acute pollution episodes have occurred in Donora, Pennsylvania, in 1948, in the Meuse Valley in Belgium in 1930, and in Poza Rica, Mexico, in 1950. The Poza Rica episode resulted from emission of hydrogen sulfide from an industrial source. There have been reports from Japan concerning "Tokyo-Yokohama asthma," and an asthmatic outbreak also occurred in New Orleans in 1958[2]; both were evidently related to air pollution.

Such major episodes, and the acute effects of air pollution with which we are all familiar, are clearly of great importance. However, recent work suggests that various components of air pollution may cause additional, serious long-term health problems. These additional effects are chronic and may result from long-term exposure to rather low concentrations of atmospheric pollutants. Briefly, the hypothesis is that some pollutants cause changes (mutations) in the chromosomes of cells (the DNA); such mutagenic effects increase the occurrence of "degenerative" diseases normally associated with old age (senescence). The evidence for such mutagenic chronic effects is largely circumstantial thus far, and it is rather complex. However, the implications are so serious that I will present the available evidence in some detail later in the chapter.

A cautionary word is needed on pollutants. Over evolutionary time periods man and other life forms evolved in the presence of environmental levels of arsenic, lead, tin, nickel, polycyclic hydrocarbons and other complex compounds (some of which would be classed today as carcinogenic), and numerous other materials found in the earth's crust or which resulted from ancient life processes. Obviously man must have become safely adapted to the presence of all of these materials AT LEVELS WHICH OCCURRED NATURALLY DURING THE EVOLUTIONARY PROCESSES.[4,5] Therefore, there are levels of these materials to which man and other life forms must be safely adapted. Some metals, such as copper and iron are, of course, essential to life. Experimental evidence that tin, lead, cadmium, and other materials are toxic at high levels does not establish that they are toxic and threats to survival at all levels. Simplistic inferences of this nature which ignore evolutionary and ecological facts of life cannot be accepted. Such "logic" would render sodium chloride "toxic."

*Nature of the Pollutants. Data Sources*

Atmospheric chemicals consist mainly of gases and solid or liquid particles. The basic atmospheric gases such as oxygen, nitrogen, and carbon dioxide have been present for millions of years during the evolutionary development of innumerable forms of life, along with the extinction of many of them. Traces of oxides of nitrogen and sulfur, ozone, ammonia, and other gases have no doubt long been present in the atmosphere as a result of lightning, volcanic action, solar effects, and microbial and other life functions. Temporarily high concentrations of some gases may have occurred following volcanic eruptions and fires. But it is only recently that man has mined coal, drilled for oil, and converted minerals to metals; moreover, through industrial

development associated with advancing civilization, he has burned fossil fuels and their derivatives in relatively great and ever-increasing quantities. Among the effluent pollutant gases, prevalent particularly in the air of cities at relatively high concentrations (compared with concentrations during the prehistoric evolution of man), are sulfur dioxide ($SO_2$), nitrogen dioxide ($NO_2$), nitric oxide (NO), carbon monoxide (CO), and ozone ($O_3$). Also present are many other gaseous products, such as traces of hydrocarbons, aldehydes, and other organic compounds.

In addition there are particulates present which are filterable from the air. These particulates are composed of dusts, which may be mineral types such as clay dusts or organic dusts of plant and animal origin, and assorted effluents of industry. They contain organic compounds, nonmetallic chemical entities such as sulfate, nitrate, fluoride, and ammonium functional groups, and also many or most metals. Some metals are usually present in quantities measurable by the currently available analytical methods, while the concentrations of others may be so low as to be undetectable on a practical basis.

To be meaningful, an environmental variable must be defined so that measurements in various places and at different times will be measures of the same chemical material or environmental characteristic. Conglomerates of many variables which cannot be defined rigorously, such as "particulates" and the "benzene solubles" fraction of particulates, are not very useful. In contrast to measurement of copper and sulfur dioxide, "particulates" have great variations in composition, influenced by regional industrial, seasonal, and other characteristics.

Obviously, if atmospheric chemicals affect vital processes, whether deleteriously or beneficially, we need fairly accurate quantitative estimates of their environmental concentrations.

One measurement problem which can lead to complications concerns the valence state of the metal. For example, Schroeder and Balassa[6] point out that naturally occurring pentavalent arsenic, as in arsenate, is less toxic than the trivalent form. Atmospheric data on "arsenic" do not make this distinction. One may also compare the relative toxicities of the sodium salts of sulfide, sulfite, and sulfate, or of nitrite and nitrate.

For anayltic purposes, in the United States particulates have been sampled from the atmosphere by filtering about 2200 cubic meters of air through preweighed, glass fiber filters under relatively standardized conditions in a 24-hour period.[7] Twenty-six days are selected randomly during a year for sampling. From such samples measurements are obtained for (a) total suspended particulates, (b) benzene-soluble organics (extractable from the particulates), (c) $\beta$ radioactivity, (d) nonmetallic inorganic particulates, mainly ammonium, nitrate, and sulfate, and (e) metals. The concentrations of 16 metals are usually reported, along with the other data, by U.S. government agencies. These metals are antimony, beryllium, bismuth, cadmium, chromium, cobalt, copper, iron, lead, manganese, molybdenum, nickel, tin, titanium, vanadium, and zinc. Antimony, beryllium, bismuth, cadmium, cobalt, and molybdenum may sometimes be present in such low concentrations that they are undetectable by the methods used. Soiling indices are also reported.[7] Sometimes data not available from government agencies can be obtained from local sources. A limited number of atmospheric arsenic measurements have been made,[7] but few have been reported recently.

Atmospheric data for a classic cancer-inducing agent, or carcinogen, benzo(a)pyrene (or 3,4-benzopyrene) were given along with air pollution data for 1966. Other information concerning this polycyclic hydrocarbon in air of cities was given by Sawicki et al.[8] To a considerable extent, concentration data for one polycyclic hydrocarbon is indicative of relative concentration data for a number of others.

*Sources of Pollutants*

There are practically endless sources of atmospheric pollution. In geological history there have been volcanic eruptions which polluted the air. Some stupendous eruptions have also occurred during recorded history, such as the eruption of Krakatoa in 1883, which was reported to have placed such large quantities of very fine particulates in the air at high levels that appearances of sunsets were altered for a considerable time in many parts of the world. Such an event may have cooled the weather for a period. There have also been huge forest fires which have caused considerable temporary atmospheric pollution.

Man-made atmospheric pollution arises principally from electric power generation, smelting and other industries, transportation, and home heating, though there are other sources such as private trash burning and municipal incinerators or other municipal trash disposal methods.[3] Table I provides some information on sources, types, and amounts of atmospheric pollutants emitted in 1965. A detailed report on motor vehicles, air pollution, and health appeared in 1962.[9] Information on sources of sulfur dioxide[1,10] and carbon monoxide[11] has been compiled. It was estimated that over 23 million TONS of sulfur dioxide were released to the atmosphere in 1963.[10] Most of this, over 14 million tons, came from coal burning, and over 9.5 million tons arose from electric power generation. Nearly 5 million tons resulted from the combustion of petroleum products. Comparatively little sulfur dioxide originates from the operation of gasoline-burning internal combustion engines. However, major portions of atmospheric carbon monoxide, nitric oxide, and, indirectly, nitrogen dioxide result from petroleum-derivative-powered engines used for trans-

| Source | Carbon monoxide | Sulfur oxides | Hydro-carbons | Oxides of nitrogen | Particulates | Total | % of Total |
|--------|-----------------|---------------|---------------|--------------------|--------------|-------|------------|
| Automotive | 66 | 1 | 12 | 6 | 1 | 86 | 60 |
| Industrial | 2 | 9 | 4 | 2 | 6 | 23 | 17 |
| Electric power | 1 | 12 | 1 | 3 | 3 | 20 | 14 |
| Space heating | 2 | 3 | 1 | 1 | 1 | 8 | 6 |
| Trash disposal | 1 | 1 | 1 | 1 | 1 | 5 | 3 |
| Total | 72 | 26 | 19 | 13 | 12 | 142 | 100 |

**I**

U.S. AIR POLLUTANTS. Some estimates of air pollutants emitted in the United States in 1965, in millions of tons. Source: *The Sources of Air Pollution and Their Control,* Public Health Service Publication No. 1548, U.S. Department of Health and Welfare, Washington D.C., 1966.

portation. About 66 million tons of carbon monoxide of automotive origin were emitted in 1965 (Table I). Ozone and organic peroxides, which are formed by atmospheric chemical reactions involving energy from sunlight, arise largely from the automotive hydrocarbon emissions, and oxygen, oxides of nitrogen, and perhaps catalysts, are among the other important components of photochemical smog, well known in the Los Angeles region[2] as well as in other parts of the world.

While it is obviously important to know the sources and amounts of various atmospheric pollutants, such cataloging can be like stamp-collecting unless it is coordinated with good, critical information on the types of damage caused by pollutants, particularly damage to health. It is this type of information which can lead to regulatory and control action on emissions.

*Photochemical Smog*

Photochemical smog and its irritant and other acute effects were first examined in some depth in the Los Angeles area, but the general problem is now fairly common throughout the world wherever the appropriate air pollutants, weather, and geography occur. Around the end of July, 1970, a unique, seemingly worldwide severe air pollution episode occurred. Reports arose in such cities as New York, Tokyo, Rome, and Sydney, Australia. The problem was especially severe in Tokyo, where photochemical smog is known as "kokagaku smoggu." The air of Sydney was reported to have smelled of "bad eggs," suggestive, of course, of hydrogen sulfide.

The complex chemical reactions involved in photochemical smog formation are not completely understood. However, it is known that hydrocarbons and other organic products along with oxides of nitrogen are intimately involved. Many of the hydrocarbons and the nitric oxide (NO) arise from automotive emissions. A very brief group of chemical reactions are given below which are in no sense definitive, but are involved in the complex smog reaction system. Reaction equilibria are, of course, involved.

All compounds with a "dot" designation, for example, $RO_2^{\cdot}$, are free radicals, quite reactive chemicals. Ozone may also add to unsaturated hydrocarbons, leading to ozonides which, in the presence of water vapor, may lead to peroxides and further to an assortment of aldehydes, ketones, peroxy acids, and other compounds. Sulfur dioxide can also be oxidized to sulfur trioxide, an irritant, which, in the presence of water forms sulfuric acid. The presence or absence of certain metals and other chemicals may influence the course of reactions catalytically. Nitrogen dioxide is a brownish gas. The brownish atmosphere is sometimes apparent when arriving by air at some destinations such as Los Angeles. This is particularly evident in warmer weather.

Some local regions, due to industrial or other characteristics, may have unique pollutants, such as dust from castor bean processing, which may lead to allergic reactions in some people.

Unfortunately, there is a tendency for public officials to be "concerned" only when a pollution episode occurs which has major or minor acute effects. Chronic effects, such as mutagenic effects, do not necessarily irritate, nor are mutagens at low levels necessarily detected by odors. But some mutagens evidently can cause or contribute to the cause of cancer and germinal genetic diseases.

$$NO + O_3 \rightarrow NO_2 + O_2$$
(nitric oxide) (ozone) (nitrogen dioxide) (oxygen)

$$NO_2 + \text{Sunlight} \rightarrow NO + O^{\cdot}$$
(atomic oxygen)

$$O^{\cdot} + O_2 \rightarrow O_3$$

$$O^{\cdot} + R \rightarrow RO^{\cdot}$$
(hydrocarbon) (free radical)

$$RO^{\cdot} + O_2 \rightarrow RO_3^{\cdot}$$

$$RO_3^{\cdot} + NO \rightarrow RO_2^{\cdot} + NO_2$$

$$RO_3^{\cdot} + NO_2 \rightarrow \text{Organic peroxyacyl nitrates}$$

*Acute Health Effects*

When considering the biological effects of chemicals on organisms such as man, there are, broadly speaking, two kinds of effects — acute and chronic. These categories are not mutually exclusive.

Acute effects are those which occur rather rapidly, in minutes, hours, or perhaps over several days, and are usually clearly discernible by the individuals affected. Chronic effects, in contrast, are not necessarily detectable by the affected individuals, but they can develop, perhaps cumulatively, over long time periods, even entire lifetimes.

A specific example to consider is carbon monoxide.[9] The acute effects of carbon monoxide poisoning range from slowed perception and reaction responses to unconsciousness and death. The chronic effects, not so obviously apparent, would be the result of living in a metropolitan environment with low but "acceptable" levels of carbon monoxide present in the atmosphere essentially perpetually, arising from automotive exhaust and other sources. Carbon monoxide has been reported, for example, to be associated with heart disease.[11] Carbon monoxide also forms carboxyhemoglobin in the blood which interferes with the efficiency of the normal oxygen transport mechanisms of the blood. This can lead to fatigue and other symptoms. Inasmuch as chemical equilibrium exists, however, individuals who have heavy occupational exposure, such as traffic officers in a tunnel, would exhale some of their accumulated carbon monoxide on going home, where its concentration should be much lower than on the job.

Chemicals other than carbon monoxide can also react with hemoglobin in somewhat the manner of carbon monoxide. One of these is nitric oxide (NO).[9] Another is nitrite.

The Los Angeles smog problem is well known and the effects became well recognized in 1944 when recurring episodes caused ocular irritation, inflamation of the nose and throat, limited visibility, and damage to plants in the region.[2] Solid fuels were little used for light, power, and heat in the area. In the period near 1960 about 3 million automotive vehicles used about 5 million gallons of gasoline per day. It was estimated that about 1600 tons of hydrocarbons from automotive exhaust were emitted per day into the atmosphere of the Los Angeles basin. A combination of all other sources of pollution was estimated to have supplied less than 25 percent of this quantity. Nitric oxide was emitted from the automobiles, and this plus the hydrocarbons plus sunlight, along with other chemicals, can lead to smog.

In 1955 there was a rather severe problem in Los Angeles which involved both intense air pollution and a heat wave. An increase in mortality occurred during this period and the smog was suspected as a cause. However, evidence eventually indicated that the severe heat was probably more damaging than the pollution in this instance.[2]

Early reports concerning the July, 1970, "smoggu" in Tokyo described the smog as white and misty, and containing sulfuric acid, along with aldehydes, oxides of nitrogen, and, evidently, peroxides, the products of photochemical reactions. Leaves were stripped from trees. Considerable illness was reported, with increases in hospitalizations, along with considerable activity by public officials and resolutions to "do something." Many of those who could afford it left the city. For a period, vehicular traffic was reported to be eliminated from shopping areas of the Ginza and other localities, where shops and gay parasols were set up and refreshments served in the streets. Informal reports stated that the carbon monoxide concentration was reduced from 10.5 to 2.3 ppm within an hour after street closing. During such pollution episodes elsewhere there have been observable increases in mortality rates, particularly among the aged and among those with existing heart and lung disorders.

In New York City during the July, 1970, pollution episode the weather was very hot. It was necessary for the electric power supplier to reduce voltage by 5 percent because of the demands, particularly for air conditioners. In some facilities, air conditioners were turned off. Fears of an electric power blackout led to heavy purchases of batteries for flashlights. Electric powered transportation was reduced. Refuse burning and incineration were reduced or banned. Automotive bans or reductions were considered. With the heat added to the problems of pollution, short tempers were reported as not uncommon.

Clearly, Tokyo and New York have important air pollution problems to be solved. It is most unfortunate that pollution control is particularly important politically only during and for a time after a severe pollution episode. Will it be necessary that catastrophically severe episodes with many thousands of deaths over the "normal" rate occur before meaningful and effective control actions are taken by responsible public officials? If such a reactionary situation exists with regard to ACUTE effects of pollution, which the public cannot miss, how can one expect effective action to be taken regarding SUB ACUTE OR CHRONIC effects, which are not easily detected by the public, but which may increase the risk of cancer, heart disease, and birth defects and may reduce the life span?

*Chronic Health Effects: A Theory*

Chronic effects arise from prolonged exposure to low levels of atmospheric pollutants which demonstrate little or no odor or irritation. There is as yet no conclusive proof of such effects from air pollution, but the evidence is strong enough to warrant a thorough analysis of the problem. I propose here a quite specific mechanism to explain how air pollution can cause chronic health effects; there is some evidence to support the theory. Those wishing to pursue the analysis in many of its complexities should consult reference 4.

It has been observed that there is a correlation between the concentration of some air pollutants and the death rates from certain diseases. These diseases are especially those associated with aging and include various forms of cancer, heart disease, and some other chronic diseases. One hypothesis is that these diseases, and aging in general, are consequences of the deterioration of the genetic material (DNA) in cells of the body. We know that essentially any change in the DNA (a MUTATION) is deleterious. A further hypothesis is that some environmental pollutants cause mutations, that is, they are MUTAGENIC. This action is believed to be one mechanism contributing to the increased incidence of such degenerative diseases.

To test the hypotheses, the following kinds of evidence are applicable:

(1) that some atmospheric pollutants are mutagenic hazards (cause mutations);

(2) that increased mutation rates in somatic cells can cause an increase in the incidence of some chronic diseases;

(3) that increased mutation rates in germinal cells can cause increases in the incidence of birth defects;

(4) that there is indeed a significant statistical relationship between the rate of mortality from these diseases in human populations and the concentration of some atmospheric pollutants. While we cannot experiment with people, urban man in his city is a "test animal"; however, experiments with animals, if properly done, can shed light on the problem.

*Are There Atmospheric Mutagens?*

We know that ionizing radiation causes mutations (Chapter 12) The question is, are there NON-RADIOACTIVE substances among our air pollutants which are also mutagenic?

The genetic information in each cell is carried in the DNA of the chromosomes. The primary building blocks of DNA are four complex compounds called "bases" (adenine, cytosine, guanine, and thymine). Each DNA molecule consists of many such bases in long and varying sequences. The actual sequence largely determines the cells' characteristics (phenotype). The molecule is huge, in biochemical terms, and its spatial structure is also important. Ionizing radiation can cause mutations by causing chemical changes in individual bases (point mutations) and by causing changes in the physical configuration of the DNA molecule. The DNA configuration, and thus any possible changes in it, is especially important when chromosomes replicate (double their number) and then split during cell division, and is even more important when the homologous chromosomes of the sex cells from different parents combine during fertilization.

It has been known for some time that some chemicals such as mustard gas can cause mutations. Nitrous acid, $HNO_2$, a very simple chemical easily derived from the air pollutant, nitrogen dioxide ($NO_2$), is known to be a powerful mutagen. It can alter the structure of amine groups on three of the bases — guanine, adenine, and cytosine. Furthermore, nitrous acid, under certain circumstances, yields nitroso and other nitrogenous compounds some of which can cause cancer[12] (are carcinogenic). Ionizing radiation is both mutagenic and carcinogenic. There is evidence that certain organic compounds, for example, nitroso compounds, are also both mutagens and carcinogens.

While relatively "simple" agents such as ionizing radiation and nitrous acid may change a single base, or "point," in DNA, there does not appear to be any reason why, under proper conditions, groups of bases in DNA may not be changed simultaneously, that is, there may be "multipoint" mutagens. Bisulfite adds to cytosine which is in DNA (and to uracil, which is in RNA).[13],[14] The bisulfite-cytosine product might be considered technically as a base analog.[4] It is known to deaminate in vitro to yield the bisulfite-uracil adduct, which is a direct alteration in structure of a base, cytosine. In DNA, this would be a mutation. But a number of base analogs, such as 5-bromouracil (a thymine analog), are quite notable mutagens.[15],[16] The base analogs function as mutagens indirectly, that is, they act upon DNA replication and cause one or more errors in the newly formed DNA depending upon the number of base analogs present in the original DNA. Base analog mutagenesis is rather complicated chemically,[16] and in the case of 5-bromouracil it involves keto-enol isomerism. It is believed, but not yet proven, that the enol form leads to incorrect base pairing and therefore to genetic errors UPON REPLICATION of DNA. It is hypothesized that the cytosine-bisulfite adduct in DNA may lead to replicative error.[4] Perhaps certain complex chemicals such as thalidomide and benzo(a)pyrene may add to groups or multiple points on DNA in such a way that, upon DNA replication, multiple errors are introduced in the newly replicated DNA. There are various hypotheses and theories regarding the mechanisms of mutagenesis and carcinogenesis, and it might not be entirely surprising if more than one is in part correct.

Related to the preceding, Freese[15] observed that among chemical mutagens are those "which alter resting DNA in such a way that mutations result in subsequent replications." This general description might be interpreted as capable of including certain metals as well as bisulfite adducts and more complicated addition products. Replicative errors in DNA could, under appropriate circumstances, contribute to the general accumulation of mutagenic errors. Somatic genetic degeneration may be a part of senescence.[4],[17]

Known or potential mutagens are probably among the atmospheric pollutants or are easily derivable from them. For example, nitrogen dioxide is a common indirect product of car exhausts and produces nitrous acid when combined with water. Similarly, sulfur compounds, including sulfur oxides, are abundant air pollutants.

If benzo(a)pyrene (and certain other polycyclic compounds) is a mutagen as well as a carcinogen, then it is an atmospheric mutagen, since it is a common ingredient in polluted urban air. It is a product of combustion and is found in automobile exhaust, tobacco smoke, burned toast, charcoal-grilled steaks, some industrial effluents, and effluents from electric power plants and home heating combustion of oil and coal fuels especially.

It should be recognized, however, that mammalian enzyme systems exist which attack benzo(a)pyrene and other polycyclic compounds, so detoxification mechanisms do exist. Furthermore, not all mutations are permanent.[18],[19] There are genetic repair mechanisms, or repair enzymes.[18],[19],[20] But repair is not 100 percent effective, so mutations can accumulate.

In summary, there is evidence that some air pollutants are mutagenic and there are theoretical and other reasons for suspecting that others (for example, bisulfites) are also mutagenic. Not nearly enough has been done to examine these possibilities. For example, it was only as recently as 1964 that Meselson[21] warned that "the possibility that some relatively nontoxic substance might be mutagenic to man deserves careful attention. The prevalence of nontoxic mutagens could go unnoticed until serious genetic damage had already been done."

## Mutagens, Chronic Disease, and Senescence

The second part of the hypothesis to be examined is that accumulated mutations can lead to chronic diseases. Biological senescence may be considered as being to a considerable extent a retrogression from somatic genetic order of youth to increasing somatic genetic disorder as aging progresses, though genetic repair enzymes would tend to reverse the trend toward disorder.

Experiments in radiobiology have demonstrated that in experimental animals individuals of a population exposed to subacute levels of ionizing radiation die sooner, appear to undergo senescence more rapidly, and develop "normal" chronic diseases sooner than control animals.[17,22] The genetic effects, aside from germinal mutagenesis, probably involve to a large extent cumulative somatic genetic degeneration. The senescence process is, however, quite complicated, with no single explanation having described all aspects of it. Somatic genetic degeneration of the pituitary and other glands would be expected to result in endocrinological effects, probably gradually accumulating endocrine deficiences in quantity, quality, or both, which, in turn, affect health of cells and individuals.

Cancer, heart disease, stroke, emphysema, chronic nephritis, diabetes mellitus, general arteriosclerosis, and certain other chronic diseases are known to occur more frequently as age increases, a phenomenon which is consistent with the cumulative somatic genetic degeneration theory of senescence.

*The Use of Statistics*

Next we must examine the link between concentration of pollutants and the mortality rates from chronic diseases associated with aging. Some idea of the difficulties involved with other aspects of this kind of study can be gained from the fact that such correlations are often the best evidence available that certain chemicals might be mutagens. Thus, Crow noted that mutagenic damage "might conceivably be detected by an increased incidence of certain genetic diseases. The hope would be to detect the effect early enough that the cause might be identified before the damage became extensive".[23] This sort of evidence must substitute for direct experimental investigation on human subjects.

Some cautionary words about the use of statistics are necessary. It has sometimes been said that you can prove anything with statistics. There is even a book entitled *How to Lie with Statistics,*[24] in which Artemus Ward is quoted: "It ain't so much the things we don't know that get us into trouble. It's the things we know that ain't so." There are many pitfalls in the use of correlations or associations.

When a high correlation is observed between two or more variables, one proceeds to set forth and test statistical hypotheses to explain the association(s). But such hypothesis testing cannot establish that one variable causes the other. Causality must be established by rigorous scientific method, usually deductive and frequently experimental. It is a commonplace of science, particularly of biomedical and social sciences, to observe correlations between two or more variables, and to attempt to explain the associations by various hypotheses. In 1935, Fisher[25] commented that "the logical fallacy of believing that a hypothesis has been proved to be true, merely because it is not contradicted by the available facts, has no more right to insinuate itself in statistical than in other kinds of reasoning. Yet it does so only too frequently." He observed further that it should be "generally understood that tests of significance, when used accurately, are capable of rejecting or invalidating hypotheses, in so far as these are contradicted by the data; but that they are never capable of establishing them as certainly true."

We cannot infer causality from correlation. Take an example. The correlation coefficient ($r$) is a measure of the covariance between two variables: It is 0 when there is no correlation, +1 or -1 when there is exact correspondence and it takes positive or negative values between -1 and +1 according to the degree of correlation. For example, the summer urban atmospheric concentrations of three different polycyclic hydrocarbons were measured.[8] The correlations between the pairs were very high: benzo(a)pyrene vs. benzo(k)fluoranthene, $r = 0.99$; benzo(a)pyrene vs. perylene, $r = 0.98$; and benzo(k)fluoranthene vs. perylene, $r = 0.96$, where $r$ is the bivariate correlation coefficient. If the atmospheric concentrations of, for example, benzo(a)pyrene in different cities should be found to be correlated significantly with some measure of human pathology in these cities, one cannot conclude that benzo(a)pyrene "causes" the pathology because (1) correlation does not and cannot establish causality, (2) concentrations of both perylene and benzo(k)fluoranthene are strongly covariate with (that is, vary strongly with) atmospheric concentrations of benzo(a)pyrene, (3) one or more testable functional mechanisms must be established in biology or biochemistry which provide the foundation to support and explain the observed statistical relationships.

If a significant statistical relationship is observed between two variables, A and B, then perhaps A causes B, and then again perhaps B causes A, or perhaps a third variable, C, which is a significant covariate of both A and B causes both A and B. Then again, perhaps the association between A and B is the result of a random event with no functional relationship existing.

If a clear, reproducible association exists between A and B, and A is CLAIMED to cause B, perhaps on the basis of "judgment," but if no viable mechanism can be formulated following considerable effort, then the causality claim might be considered as questionable, with causality yet to be proven. Perhaps B causes A, or C causes A and B. Experimental support from a relevant discipline, such as biochemistry, is needed for a casual interpretation of the association to have strength. If the relationship between A and B is ecological, such as the relationship of the concentration of an atmospheric chemical to the mortality rate attributable to a disease, the experimental tests must be ecologically relevant. Experimental design must use the chemical in controlled atmospheres to which experimental animals are exposed. Rubbing the chemical into abraded (wounded) skin or injecting it is not acceptable here.

The statistical approach used here is to examine the variability both within certain human "populations" (cities) and among such populations; the aim is to "explain" mortality rates in the sense of correlating variations in these rates with variations in concentrations of chemical pollutants. It is, therefore, important to understand the nature of variation at the population level. Individuals vary for many reasons. They are genetically different and therefore their physiology and behavior (their phenotypes) also vary. Environmental variables — their diet for example — also affect their phenotype. We certainly expect, and find, differences among individuals in their susceptibility to disease, their age at death, and so on. We therefore find a great deal of variability WITHIN populations. However,

we also find generally that there are differences between or AMONG populations. Thus, the mean value for some characteristic will differ in different populations. Putting it another way, 100 individuals taken at random from the same population will, in general, be more similar than 100 individuals drawn from different populations. The total variation due to that within populations plus that among populations is measured statistically by the VARIANCE. Thus, if we measure individuals from many populations, some of the variance will be that due to differences within the population and some of it due to differences between populations.

Different populations will differ for a variety of reasons. For example, the population of New York is made up of different proportions of various ethnic types than are found in the population of Los Angeles. These populations differ genetically. They also are exposed to different weather, have rather different "average" diets, and so on. So we will never "explain" all the differences between populations, and certainly with respect to death rates, we would not expect to explain all the "between population variance" with one or a few environmental variables. What we are looking for is evidence of strong correlations between death rates and concentration of certain pollutants, especially those which may be mutagenic, and an explanation of as much as possible of the observed variability in death rates.

An additional complication in such analyses is that there are errors of measurement. These arise in estimating chemical concentrations and in determining causes of death. Such errors may tend to obscure correlations.

*Test of the Hypothesis*

The test of the hypothesis that some atmospheric pollutants are mutagenic and increase the death rate from some chronic diseases is now examined using statistical relationships.

The mutagenic effects of ionizing radiation are cumulative.[17,22] Thus, over the course of a year, the total, uncorrected mutagenic damage to all somatic cells of an individual is an additive total of daily uncorrected accumulations. Radiomimetic chemicals should act similarly. In relation to correction of genetic errors, one should consider that there should be and probably are genetic polymorphic variations among individuals with regard to repair enzymes, and their efficiency.[19,20]

The pollutant concentration characteristics of a particular city tend to be similar for that city from year to year for a few years. These pollution patterns are influenced by characteristics of topography, industry, electric power generation, traffic, home heating, climate, and other variables. If one attempts to examine pollution-health relationships for one city, and if the health measures are mortality rates from major chronic diseases such as cancer and heart disease, he finds that the mortality rates for these diseases are relatively constant from year to year over a short period, such as 5 years, for a particular city, but the mortality rates in some cases are markedly different for different cities.[4] The relative constancy of annual mortality rates for chronic disease within Standard Metropolitan Statistical Areas (SMSA), as contrasted with difference in the rates between SMSAs are evident in Table II for the broad cancer category, and in Tables III, IV, and V for cancer of the respiratory system, cancer of the digestive organs, and arteriosclerotic heart disease. The total cancer and heart disease categories may be class-

ed as major causes of death. Similar consistency in mortality rates from year to year within SMSAs are also observed for numerous other categories of chronic disease[4] such as cancer of the liver, breast cancer, and hypertensive heart disease, while marked differences are observed in the rates between SMSAs.

Since there are fairly notable differences in these mortality rates for various SMSAs, one might consider, based on the radiomimetic or mutagenic hypothesis, that environmental variables might contribute to the development or initiation of these diseases, and perhaps might influence the rate of senescence.

If certain environmental chemicals affect the rate of senescence in some proportion to their concentrations, then they should also affect the rate of development and appearance of chronic diseases, and mortality from them in populations. If this is so, then it follows that in metropolitan areas in which the mortality rates for total cancer are high, heart disease rates should be high, and where the mortality rates for one category of cancer are high, the rates for other cancer categories should also be high, and where the rates for one category are low, the rates for the others should also be low.

If pollution and chronic disease data are collected for many SMSAs (for which suitable pollution data are available), then statistical analyses

| Standard Metropolitan Statistical Area | Deaths per year | | | | | Death rate per $10^5$ population |
|---|---|---|---|---|---|---|
| | 1961 | 1962 | 1963 | 1964 | mean 1961-64 | |
| El Paso, Texas | 272 | 274 | 271 | 285 | 275.5 | 87.7 |
| Charlotte, N.C. | 266 | 280 | 318 | 304 | 292.0 | 107.3 |
| Las Vegas, Nev. | 143 | 146 | 171 | 172 | 158.0 | 124.4 |
| Denver, Colo. | 1,165 | 1,163 | 1,192 | 1,266 | 1,196.5 | 128.7 |
| Atlanta, Ga. | 1,252 | 1,287 | 1,419 | 1,382 | 1,335.0 | 131.2 |
| Birmingham, Ala. | 858 | 881 | 900 | 943 | 895.5 | 141.1 |
| Los Angeles, Cal. | 10,005 | 10,093 | 10,658 | 10,834 | 10,397.5 | 154.2 |
| Detroit, Mich. | 5,621 | 5,806 | 5,974 | 5,903 | 5,826.0 | 154.9 |
| Seattle, Wash. | 1,772 | 1,756 | 1,734 | 1,813 | 1,768.8 | 159.8 |
| San Francisco, Cal. | 4,503 | 4,568 | 4,735 | 4,854 | 4,665.0 | 167.6 |
| Chicago, Ill. | 10,696 | 10,548 | 11,074 | 10,907 | 10,806.3 | 173.4 |
| Cleveland, O. | 3,125 | 3,301 | 3,309 | 3,304 | 3,259.8 | 181.4 |
| Philadelphia, Pa. | 7,711 | 7,826 | 7,851 | 8,121 | 7,877.3 | 181.4 |
| New York, N.Y. | 21,284 | 21.404 | 21,591 | 22,087 | 21,591.5 | 201.9 |
| Boston, Mass. | 5,936 | 5,893 | 5,665 | 5,360 | 5,713.5 | 220.7 |

**II**

MORTALITY DATA FOR TOTAL CANCER. Examples of 1961-1964 mortality data for total cancer (ISC No 140-205; see Table VII) showing relative constancy within metropolitan areas and differences in mortality rates between these areas. Source: Adapted from R.J. Hickey, D.E. Boyce, E.B. Harner, and R.C. Clelland. 1970. Ecological statistical studies concerning environmental pollution and chronic disease. *IEEE Trans. Geosci. Electronics (GE 8, No 4, pp. 186-202. Used by permission.*

| Standard Metropolitan Statistical Area | Deaths per year | | | | mean 1961-64 | Death rate per $10^5$ population |
|---|---|---|---|---|---|---|
| | 1961 | 1962 | 1963 | 1964 | | |
| El Paso, Texas | 34 | 44 | 43 | 42 | 40.8 | 13.0 |
| Denver, Colo. | 152 | 177 | 188 | 195 | 178.0 | 19.2 |
| Charlotte, N.C. | 36 | 56 | 69 | 54 | 53.8 | 19.8 |
| Atlanta, Ga. | 208 | 198 | 237 | 254 | 224.3 | 22.1 |
| Seattle, Wash. | 265 | 269 | 281 | 276 | 272.8 | 24.6 |
| Birmingham, Ala. | 147 | 146 | 161 | 176 | 157.5 | 24.8 |
| Las Vegas, Nev. | 22 | 29 | 37 | 43 | 32.8 | 25.8 |
| Los Angeles, Cal. | 1,704 | 1,709 | 1,919 | 1,933 | 1,816.3 | 26.9 |
| Detroit, Mich. | 928 | 1,037 | 1,082 | 1,103 | 1,037.5 | 27.6 |
| San Francisco, Cal. | 744 | 817 | 802 | 892 | 813.8 | 29.2 |
| Chicago, Ill. | 1,757 | 1,759 | 1,904 | 1,922 | 1,835.5 | 29.5 |
| Cleveland, O. | 503 | 582 | 566 | 610 | 565.3 | 31.5 |
| Philadelphia, Pa. | 1,247 | 1,411 | 1,357 | 1,503 | 1,379.5 | 31.8 |
| New York, N.Y. | 3,415 | 3,557 | 3,624 | 3,719 | 3,578.8 | 33.5 |
| Boston, Mass. | 877 | 930 | 875 | 864 | 886.5 | 34.2 |

**III**

MORTALITY DATA FOR RESPIRATORY SYSTEM CANCER. Examples of 1961-1964 mortality data for cancer of the respiratory system (ISC Nos. 160-164, see Table VII) showing relative constancy within metropolitan areas and differences in mortality rates between these areas. Source: Adapted from R.J. Hickey, D.E. Boyce, E.B. Harner, and R.C. Clelland. 1970. Ecological statistical studies concerning environmental pollution and chronic disease. *IEEE Trans. Geosci. Electronics GE-8,* No. 4, pp. 186-202. Used by permission.

may be made for relationships between atmospheric concentrations of chemicals and mortality rates for these chronic diseases.

It is necessary to distinguish genetic damage to somatic DNA from damage to germinal DNA. The former can relate to processes of senescence, while mutations at the germinal level should lead to alterations in developmental biology including, of course, differentiation, and to the

possibility of heritable defects. Among the products of development are the germ cells of the fully developed adult. Since mutations are generally deleterious or degenerative, if there are environmental mutagens which effect somatic DNA and hasten the rate of senescence, it appears necessary that such mutagens could hardly affect somatic DNA without also affecting germinal DNA.

| Standard Metropolitan Statistical Area | Deaths per year | | | | mean 1961-64 | Death rate per $10^5$ population |
|---|---|---|---|---|---|---|
| | 1961 | 1962 | 1963 | 1964 | | |
| El Paso, Texas | ,80 | 82 | 90 | 85 | 84.3 | 26.8 |
| Charlotte, N.C. | 90 | 62 | 70 | 82 | 76.0 | 27.9 |
| Las Vegas, Nev. | 32 | 46 | 58 | 44 | 45.0 | 35.4 |
| Atlanta, Ga. | 319 | 351 | 394 | 379 | 360.8 | 35.5 |
| Birmingham, Ala. | 256 | 247 | 244 | 258 | 251.3 | 39.6 |
| Denver, Colo. | 380 | 364 | 372 | 371 | 371.8 | 40.0 |
| Los Angeles, Cal. | 3,171 | 3,105 | 3,257 | 3,316 | 3,212.3 | 47.6 |
| Seattle, Wash. | 559 | 567 | 569 | 584 | 569.8 | 51.5 |
| Detroit, Mich. | 1,910 | 1,950 | 1,967 | 2,016 | 1,960.8 | 52.1 |
| San Francisco, Cal. | 1,520 | 1,499 | 1,582 | 1,538 | 1,534.8 | 55.1 |
| Chicago, Ill. | 3,890 | 3,768 | 3,910 | 3,811 | 3,844.8 | 61.2 |
| Cleveland, O. | 1,066 | 1,157 | 1,116 | 1,107 | 1,111.5 | 61.9 |
| Philadelphia, Pa. | 2,790 | 2,690 | 2,670 | 2,791 | 2,735.3 | 63.0 |
| New York, N.Y. | 7,870 | 7,777 | 7,757 | 7,802 | 7,801.5 | 73.0 |
| Boston, Mass. | 2,109 | 2,133 | 1,988 | 1,871 | 2,025.3 | 78.2 |

**IV**

MORTALITY DATA FOR DIGESTIVE ORGAN CANCER. Examples of 1961-1964 mortality data for cancer of the digestive organs (ISC Nos. 150-156, 157-159; see Table VII) showing relative constancy within metropolitan areas and differences in mortality rates between these areas. Source: R.J. Hickey and L.A. Tomasello, University of Pennsylvania, Philadelphia, Pennsylvania, 1969, unpublished information.

200   Richard J. Hickey

**V**

| Standard Metropolitan Statistical Area | Deaths per year | | | | mean 1961-64 | Death rate per $10^5$ population |
|---|---|---|---|---|---|---|
| | 1961 | 1962 | 1963 | 1964 | | |
| El Paso, Texas | 295 | 311 | 348 | 302 | 314 | 100.0 |
| Birmingham, Ala. | 1,209 | 1,265 | 1,337 | 1,326 | 1,284 | 202.3 |
| Las Vegas, Nev. | 246 | 263 | 326 | 303 | 285 | 224.0 |
| Charlotte, N.C. | 576 | 652 | 663 | 698 | 647 | 237.9 |
| Denver, Colo. | 2,061 | 2,319 | 2,349 | 2,384 | 2,278 | 245.1 |
| Los Angeles, Cal. | 16,569 | 16,876 | 17,936 | 17,718 | 17,275 | 256.2 |
| Atlanta, Ga. | 1,952 | 2,084 | 2,184 | 2,109 | 2,077 | 264.2 |
| Detroit, Mich. | 9,243 | 10,062 | 10,248 | 10,441 | 9,999 | 265.8 |
| Seattle, Wash. | 3,008 | 3,169 | 3,251 | 3,328 | 3,189 | 288.0 |
| San Francisco, Cal. | 7,748 | 8,040 | 8,497 | 8,194 | 8,120 | 291.7 |
| New York, N.Y. | 41,375 | 41,947 | 42,472 | 42,526 | 42,080 | 293.5 |
| Cleveland, O. | 5,304 | 5,606 | 5,758 | 5,808 | 5,619 | 312.8 |
| Philadelphia, Pa. | 13,779 | 13,893 | 13,784 | 13,408 | 13,716 | 315.8 |
| Chicago, Ill. | 21,226 | 22,517 | 23,542 | 23,386 | 22,668 | 364.4 |
| Boston, Mass. | 11,384 | 11,415 | 11,609 | 10,280 | 11,172 | 431.5 |

MORTALITY DATA FOR ARTERIOSCLEROTIC HEART DISEASE. Examples of 1961-1964 mortality data for arteriosclerotic heart disease (ISC No. 420; see Table VII) showing relative constancy within metropolitan areas and differences in mortality rates between these areas. Source: Adapted from R.J. Hickey, D.E. Boyce, E.B. Harner, and R.C. Clelland. 1970. Ecological statistical studies concerning environmental pollution and chronic disease. *IEEE Trans. Geosci. Electronics GE-8, No. 4, pp. 186-202.* Used by permission.

**VI**

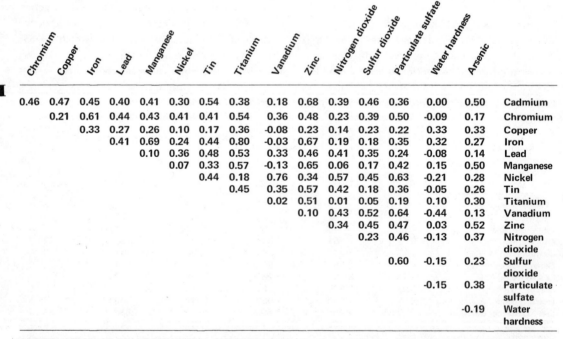

| Chromium | Copper | Iron | Lead | Manganese | Nickel | Tin | Titanium | Vanadium | Zinc | Nitrogen dioxide | Sulfur dioxide | Particulate sulfate | Water hardness | Arsenic | |
|---|---|---|---|---|---|---|---|---|---|---|---|---|---|---|---|
| 0.46 | 0.47 | 0.45 | 0.40 | 0.41 | 0.30 | 0.54 | 0.38 | 0.18 | 0.68 | 0.39 | 0.46 | 0.36 | 0.00 | 0.50 | Cadmium |
| | 0.21 | 0.61 | 0.44 | 0.43 | 0.41 | 0.41 | 0.54 | 0.36 | 0.48 | 0.23 | 0.39 | 0.50 | -0.09 | 0.17 | Chromium |
| | | 0.33 | 0.27 | 0.26 | 0.10 | 0.17 | 0.36 | -0.08 | 0.23 | 0.14 | 0.23 | 0.22 | 0.33 | 0.33 | Copper |
| | | | 0.41 | 0.69 | 0.24 | 0.44 | 0.80 | -0.03 | 0.67 | 0.19 | 0.18 | 0.35 | 0.32 | 0.27 | Iron |
| | | | | 0.10 | 0.36 | 0.48 | 0.53 | 0.33 | 0.46 | 0.41 | 0.35 | 0.24 | -0.08 | 0.14 | Lead |
| | | | | | 0.07 | 0.33 | 0.57 | -0.13 | 0.65 | 0.06 | 0.17 | 0.42 | 0.15 | 0.50 | Manganese |
| | | | | | | 0.44 | 0.18 | 0.76 | 0.34 | 0.57 | 0.45 | 0.63 | -0.21 | 0.28 | Nickel |
| | | | | | | | 0.45 | 0.35 | 0.57 | 0.42 | 0.18 | 0.36 | -0.05 | 0.26 | Tin |
| | | | | | | | | 0.02 | 0.51 | 0.01 | 0.05 | 0.19 | 0.10 | 0.30 | Titanium |
| | | | | | | | | | 0.10 | 0.43 | 0.52 | 0.64 | -0.44 | 0.13 | Vanadium |
| | | | | | | | | | | 0.34 | 0.45 | 0.47 | 0.03 | 0.52 | Zinc |
| | | | | | | | | | | | 0.23 | 0.46 | -0.13 | 0.37 | Nitrogen dioxide |
| | | | | | | | | | | | | 0.60 | -0.15 | 0.23 | Sulfur dioxide |
| | | | | | | | | | | | | | -0.15 | 0.38 | Particulate sulfate |
| | | | | | | | | | | | | | | -0.19 | Water hardness |

CORRELATION OF ENVIRONMENTAL CHEMICALS. Matrix of correlation coefficients for means of mean annual concentrations of environmental chemicals for 38 cities, 1957 through 1964. See text for explanation. Source: Reprinted from R.J. Hickey, D.E. Boyce, E.B. Harner, and R.C. Clelland. 1970. Ecological statistical studies concerning environmental pollution and chronic disease. *IEEE Trans. Geosci. Electronics GE-8,* No. 4, pp. 186-202. Used by permission.

In the first kind of test we examine correlations between two variables at a time (bivariate analysis), remembering that a value of $r = 0$ means no correlation and $r = \pm 1$ is perfect correlation, where $r$ is the correlation coefficient. Using data from many metropolitan areas we can correlate (a) chemicals vs. chemicals (b) chemicals vs. diseases, and (c) diseases vs. diseases, as shown in Tables VI, VII, and VIII, respectively. The data used for analysis are means of mean annual pollution data for several years as available from 1957 to 1964,[7] and the mortality rates are means of annual rates for 1961-1964 for 38 Standard Metropolitan Statistical Areas.[26,27]

Each entry in Tables VI-VIII is a correlation coefficient. For example, the concentrations of iron and titanium tend to vary together ($r = 0.8$ in Table VI); by contrast titanium and nitrogen dioxide vary essentially independently of each other ($r = 0.01$), while there is a tendency for the concentration of vanadium to be high whenever the value for water hardness is low ($r = -0.44$).

The value for, say, titanium versus titanium would of course be $r = 1.0$. While there are several combinations of metals for which $r$ exceeds $+0.50$, the coefficients are rather generally less than plus or minus 0.5, indicating a moderate to small degree of covariance among the concentrations of the different chemical pairs in the 38 SMSAs. High covariance among these predictors is undesirable for multiple regression analysis, which will be described.

The first hypothesis to be tested is that, for various communities, an observable degree of correlation should be evident between atmospheric concentrations of chemicals which are mutagenic hazards, and health effects such as might be detected in cumulative somatic genetic and germinal genetic diseases.

Table VII shows the relevant correlation coefficients. The important point to notice is that high positive $r$ values tend to occur at the top of the table where our suspected mutagens occur ($NO_2$, $SO_2$). Some fairly consistent negative cor-

**VII**

| Gastrointestinal System Cancer (150-156A, 157-159) | Cancer of Respiratory System (160-164) | Cancer of Upper Respiratory System (140-148) | Urinary System Cancer (180-181) | Leukemia - Aleukemia (204) | Genital System Cancer (171-179) | Breast Cancer (170) | Total Malignant Neoplasms (140-205) | Vascular Lesions of the CNS (330-334) | Diseases of Heart (400-402, 410-443) | Arteriosclerotic Heart Disease (420) | Hypertensive Heart Disease (440-443) | Other Bronchopulmonic Diseases (525-527) | Diabetes Mellitus (260) | |
|---|---|---|---|---|---|---|---|---|---|---|---|---|---|---|
| 0.47 | 0.37 | 0.23 | 0.44 | 0.36 | 0.37 | 0.50 | 0.48 | 0.25 | 0.39 | 0.31 | 0.27 | -0.26 | 0.29 | Nitrogen dioxide |
| 0.63 | 0.44 | 0.31 | 0.49 | 0.21 | 0.29 | 0.50 | 0.56 | -0.15 | 0.53 | 0.48 | 0.24 | -0.37 | 0.52 | Sulfur dioxide |
| 0.58 | 0.60 | 0.29 | 0.47 | 0.09 | 0.32 | 0.48 | 0.56 | 0.00 | 0.56 | 0.48 | 0.52 | -0.48 | 0.52 | Particulate sulfate |
| 0.12 | -0.20 | -0.20 | 0.00 | 0.02 | -0.05 | -0.01 | 0.04 | -0.29 | -0.01 | -0.06 | 0.10 | -0.18 | 0.15 | Cadmium |
| 0.28 | 0.37 | 0.03 | 0.15 | 0.06 | 0.26 | 0.11 | 0.28 | -0.01 | 0.29 | 0.11 | 0.40 | -0.11 | 0.34 | Chromium |
| -0.09 | -0.21 | -0.31 | -0.22 | -0.22 | -0.26 | -0.14 | -0.18 | -0.37 | -0.20 | -0.23 | -0.12 | 0.09 | -0.02 | Copper |
| 0.06 | 0.09 | -0.34 | -0.05 | -0.05 | 0.14 | -0.11 | 0.02 | 0.08 | -0.02 | -0.07 | 0.10 | 0.11 | 0.09 | Iron |
| 0.18 | 0.07 | -0.08 | 0.05 | 0.09 | 0.07 | 0.16 | 0.16 | -0.18 | 0.10 | 0.00 | 0.13 | 0.13 | 0.03 | Lead |
| 0.01 | 0.05 | -0.25 | -0.07 | -0.14 | 0.07 | -0.17 | -0.03 | 0.05 | -0.06 | -0.08 | 0.15 | -0.14 | 0.16 | Manganese |
| 0.50 | 0.42 | 0.14 | 0.41 | 0.40 | 0.26 | 0.46 | 0.49 | -0.04 | 0.37 | 0.34 | 0.23 | -0.20 | 0.35 | Nickel |
| 0.10 | 0.10 | 0.02 | -0.06 | -0.13 | 0.22 | 0.06 | 0.09 | 0.08 | 0.01 | -0.10 | 0.37 | -0.23 | 0.11 | Tin |
| -0.19 | -0.23 | -0.54 | -0.28 | -0.10 | -0.16 | -0.33 | -0.23 | -0.18 | -0.20 | -0.27 | 0.00 | 0.21 | -0.23 | Titanium |
| 0.50 | 0.48 | 0.31 | 0.46 | 0.23 | 0.25 | 0.50 | 0.51 | -0.12 | 0.56 | 0.45 | 0.52 | -0.36 | 0.32 | Vanadium |
| 0.25 | 0.12 | -0.11 | 0.17 | 0.05 | 0.20 | 0.15 | 0.21 | 0.04 | 0.08 | 0.03 | 0.11 | -0.17 | 0.22 | Zinc |
| -0.28 | -0.03 | -0.08 | -0.35 | -0.34 | -0.12 | -0.23 | -0.28 | -0.14 | -0.46 | -0.39 | -0.25 | 0.34 | -0.14 | Water hardness |
| 0.17 | -0.22 | -0.22 | 0.15 | 0.16 | -0.03 | 0.04 | 0.07 | 0.01 | 0.05 | 0.03 | -0.04 | -0.25 | 0.01 | Arsenic |

**CORRELATION BETWEEN MORTALITY RATES AND ENVIRONMENTAL CHEMICALS.** Matrix of correlation coefficients between mean mortality rates for chronic diseases and annual mean concentrations of environmental chemicals for 38 SMSAs, 1957-1964. The parenthetical figures are the International Statistical Classification designations of disease, Seventh revision of the International Lists, 1955. Source: Adapted from R.J. Hickey, D.E. Boyce, E.B. Harner, and R.C. Clelland. 1970. Ecological statistical studies concerning environmental pollution and chronic disease. *IEEE Trans. Geosci. Electronics GE-8, No. 4, pp. 186-202.* Used by permission.

relations are observed between mortality rates for a number of the diseases and atmospheric concentrations of copper, manganese, and titanium. This also was found for hardness of drinking water. The negative relationship between water hardness and mortality rates for certain circulatory diseases in different metropolitan areas has been reported before. The findings for titanium may be somewhat novel for this rather ubiquitous element. However, titanium has been reported to suppress oxidation of cysteine, a thiol (a compound which contains the -SH group), which is evidently involved in protection of alveolar macrophages. Cysteine has been reported as being protective against mutagenesis.[4]

Given this support for the first hypothesis, a second hypothesis to be tested is that there should be strong correlations between the mortality rates from different pairs of diseases measured over these various metropolitan areas, since air pollutants are expected to affect the populations through the same mechanisms. Where the cancer rate is high, the heart disease rate should be high and where one is low, the other should be low. The disease data of Table VIII tend to confirm this prediction.

The data show considerable covariance among different metropolitan populations between mortality rates for cancer of the respiratory system (ISC Nos. 160-164), which includes lung cancer (ISC Nos. 162-163), and mortality rates for many other cancer categories including total cancer, arteriosclerotic heart disease, the broader diseases of the heart category, and some other diseases of aging. Figure 1 shows the close correspondence between mortality rate for cancer and that for heart disease in the 38 different metropolitan areas. One could hardly hypothesize that heart disease mortality causes cancer mortality. But both diseases might have largely a common cause, perhaps progressive senescence, the rate of which could possibly be accelerated by effects of environmental mutagens.

Leukemia is rather exceptional. However, viruses or viruslike agents have been reported as being significantly involved in the initiation of

**VIII**

| Gastrointestinal Cancer (150-156A, 157-159) | Cancer of Upper Respiratory System (140-148) | Urinary System Cancer (180-181) | Leukemia - Aleukemia (204) | Genital System Cancer (171-179) | Breast Cancer (170) | Total Malignant Neoplasms (140-205) | Vascular Lesions of the CNS (330-334) | Diseases of Heart (400-402, 410-443) | Arteriosclerotic Heart Disease (420) | Hypertensive Heart Disease (440-443) | Other Bronchopulmonic Diseases (525-527) | Diabetes Mellitus (260) | |
|---|---|---|---|---|---|---|---|---|---|---|---|---|---|
| 0.74 | 0.73 | 0.68 | 0.39 | 0.71 | 0.71 | 0.83 | 0.30 | 0.74 | 0.71 | 0.50 | -0.18 | 0.62 | Respiratory System Cancer (160-164) |
| | 0.63 | 0.91 | 0.67 | 0.72 | 0.90 | 0.97 | 0.32 | 0.90 | 0.88 | 0.35 | -0.26 | 0.70 | Gastrointestinal Cancer |
| | | 0.55 | 0.27 | 0.58 | 0.69 | 0.69 | 0.31 | 0.60 | 0.59 | 0.38 | -0.32 | 0.45 | Cancer of Upper Respiratory System |
| | | | 0.72 | 0.71 | 0.89 | 0.92 | 0.41 | 0.87 | 0.88 | 0.26 | -0.18 | 0.59 | Urinary System Cancer |
| | | | | 0.52 | 0.63 | 0.68 | 0.32 | 0.58 | 0.69 | -0.11 | 0.14 | 0.25 | Leukemia - Aleukemia |
| | | | | | 0.74 | 0.81 | 0.68 | 0.69 | 0.64 | 0.40 | -0.09 | 0.51 | Genital System Cancer |
| | | | | | | 0.94 | 0.40 | 0.82 | 0.80 | 0.36 | -0.24 | 0.52 | Breast Cancer |
| | | | | | | | 0.42 | 0.91 | 0.88 | 0.40 | -0.22 | 0.65 | Total Malignant Neoplasms |
| | | | | | | | | 0.37 | 0.36 | 0.21 | -0.08 | 0.12 | Vascular Lesions of CNS |
| | | | | | | | | | 0.93 | 0.46 | -0.31 | 0.58 | Diseases of Heart |
| | | | | | | | | | | 0.21 | -0.27 | 0.51 | Arteriosclerotic Heart Disease |
| | | | | | | | | | | | -0.37 | 0.49 | Hypertensive Heart Disease |
| | | | | | | | | | | | | -0.30 | Other Bronchopulmonic Diseases |

CORRELATION OF ANNUAL MORTALITY RATES: Matrix of correlation coefficients for annual mortality rates for 38 SMSAs, 1961 through 1964. See text for explanation. The parenthetical figures are the International Statistical Classification designations of disease, Seventh revision of the International Lists, 1955. Source: Adapted from R.J. Hickey, D.E. Boyce, E.B. Harner, and R.C. Clelland. 1970. Ecological statistical studies concerning environmental pollution and chronic disease. *IEEE Trans. Geosci. Electronics GE-8*, No. 4, pp. 186-202. Used by permission.

leukemia.[28] The considerable degree of covariance between mortality rates for respiratory system cancer and other cancer and heart disease categories would suggest that they may have a rather common etiology, and that perhaps the etiology of respiratory system cancer including lung cancer is not uniquely different from the etiologies of these other diseases. This would be in conformity with the principle of Occam's razor, but appears to differ from the general presumption that tobacco smoking, particularly cigarette smoking, is the primary cause of lung cancer.[29] It should be noted here that information on the relationship between smoking and lung cancer is basically statistical; experiments designed to demonstrate a comparable result in animals have been almost entirely negative.

Some of the negative correlation coefficients between diseases in Table VIII may appear rather curious. For example, for the "other bronchopulmonic diseases" category, the coefficients are mostly negative. Since a major component of this category is emphysema, the inverse relationship with respiratory system cancer might seem unexpected. Both lung cancer and emphysema are

chronic diseases whose frequency of occurrence increases with chronological age. However, if emphysema is to a considerable extent a disease of biochemical senescence, and if lung cancer is also a disease of senescence, then perhaps a person with emphysema may be more likely to contract lung cancer than a person of comparable age without emphysema.[4] But if a person with emphysema also contracts lung cancer, he will probably die of cancer rather than of emphysema. If this is the situation, it can explain the inverse relationships based on competition for mortality. The inverse relationship should then also be evident between the "other bronchopulmonic disease" category and other diseases of senescence whose mortality rates are rather highly correlated with the rates for respiratory system cancer, such as other cancer categories and

HEART DISEASE VS. CANCER DEATHS. Mortality rates for diseases of the heart versus total malignant neoplasms for 38 SMSAs in the United States. Source: Redrawn from R.J. Hickey, D.E. Boyce, E.B. Harner, and R.C. Clelland. 1970. Ecological statistical studies concerning environmental pollution and chronic disease. *IEE Trans. Geosci. Electronics GE-8, No. 4, pp 186-202. Used by permission.*

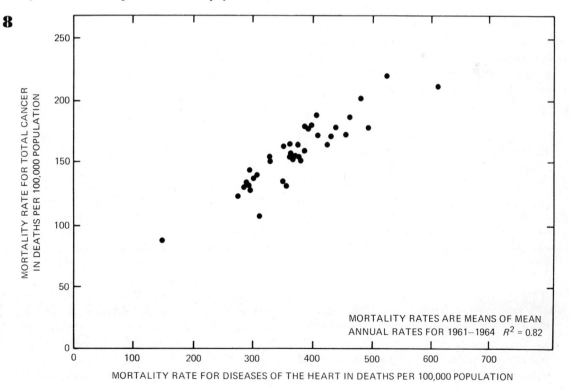

**8**

MORTALITY RATES ARE MEANS OF MEAN ANNUAL RATES FOR 1961–1964   $R^2 = 0.82$

heart disease. This is observed to a noticeable extent except for leukemia.

In the second kind of test of the mutagenic hypothesis we relate a disease rate to several environmental (or other) variables simultaneously. Hence this is multivariate[30] rather than bivariate analysis. There are many dependent variables or criteria involved, such as mortality rates for specified categories of causes of death. The rates differ in different metropolitan areas, as indicated in Tables II through V. Median age, a measure of age structure of populations, can also be investigated as a dependent variable since age structure may be influenced by environmental chemical characteristics and other variables.[4] Independent variables or predictors include atmospheric concentrations of chemicals, drinking water characteristics, demographic, climatic, and other variables.

The particular kind of statistical method used here is OPTIMAL MULTIPLE REGRESSION ANALYSIS. Again, those wishing to pursue details of the analysis and discussions of other methods are referred to Hickey *et al.*[4] In this method, we are searching for an "explanation" of variation in deaths from chronic diseases (statistical variance) among cities by looking for those variables which best serve to "predict" the observed data. As before, good "prediction" or correlation, does not necessarily imply causality. Here we will look for our predictors among the atmospheric pollutants and, in particular, our suspected mutagens. The method allows us to select first the best single predictor, by comparing all the data available, then the best two predictors (which may not include the first, but frequently does), then the best three predictors, and so on. We measure how "good" the predictor is by a statistic, $R^2$, the square of the multiple correlation coefficient. This measures the proportion of the total variance of the dependent variable "explained" by the variable or variables selected as predictors.

A simple regression equation may be expressed by the form, $y = a + bx$, in which $y$ is mortality rate, $a$ is a constant, $x$ is the concentration of a chemical in the atmosphere in micrograms per cubic meter, and $b$ is the regression coefficient. A general form of a comparable multiple regression equation may be expressed as

$$y = a + b_1 x_1 + b_2 x_2 + b_3 x_3 + \cdots + b_n x_n$$

In the present studies, natural logarithmic transformations of $x$ were made, expressed as $\ln c(x)$, such as $\ln c(SO_2)$, where $c$ indicates concentration.

As an example of a simple regression equation is given the equation for mortality rate, $M$, for cancer of the digestive organs and peritoneum. Of the environmental chemicals considered, based on data for 38 SMSAs, $SO_2$ is the best single predictor.

$$M = + 16.470 + 8.734 \ln c(SO_2)$$

The $R^2$ (corrected for sample size) for this equation is 0.385, indicating that about 38 percent of the variance in $M$ is "explained" statistically by atmospheric concentrations of sulfur dioxide. Thus, where the concentration of $SO_2$ is high, $M$ is high, and where $c(SO_2)$ is low, $M$ is low. The multiple regression equations are extensions of this method, and examples are given in Table IX, condensed from Hickey et al.[4]

Statistical findings are, however, worthless without appropriate information on reliability, or levels of statistical significance. For the above simple regression equation, the regression coefficient (+8.734) is significant at the 99.9 percent level of significance. (This is based on a $t$ statistic of 4.92 for the significance of the regression coefficient.)

Table IX shows the ability of the concentration of various atmospheric pollutants (natural logarithm) in predicting the mortality rates for six categories of disease, in 38 SMSAs. As shown in the original table, these results are all statistically significant; in many cases the probability is less than 1 in 100 that such close relationships could arise by chance.

The numbers in the body of the table include the regression coefficients for those atmospheric pollutants which are good predictors of various diseases. The first thing to notice is that increases in the concentration of $NO_2$ and $SO_2$ rather consistently serve to predict increases in the cancer and heart disease categories, while cadmium is a good negative predictor. It can be seen that the relative values of the regression coefficients in the different equations tend to be similar, with $NO_2$ having greater "weight" as a predictor than $SO_2$.

The right-hand column shows that a consistently rather high percentage of the variance be-

AIR POLLUTION   205

tween cities in death rates from these diseases is "explained" by concomitant variation in the concentration of a few pollutants.

The positive coefficients for the $NO_2$ and $SO_2$ variables are consistent with the radiomimetic hypothesis that there are environmental chemicals which are mutagenic hazards to health, and with the hypothesis that senescence is a cumulative somatic genetic disease among whose effects are increased risks of mortality due to cancer and heart disease. As the atmospheric concentration of either one or both rises, the increase is associated with a rise in the mortality rates for several categories of cancer and heart disease. Concentrations of sulfate, nickel, manganese, and vanadium were also found positively associated with certain mortality rate categories, but concentrations of cadmium, copper, titanium, arsenic, zinc, and water hardness were found to be significantly associated negatively. The negative associations suggest possibly beneficial effects of these chemical categories, but such inferences must be considered cautiously, in association with other evidence from, for example, biochemistry.

While a negative association of copper concentration with mortality rate may not be particularly surprising, inasmuch as copper in trace amounts is essential to life, a similar negative association involving cadmium is not in accordance with the general understanding regarding cadmium, which is that it is a toxic, undesirable metal as far as metabolic processes are concerned. A particular caution must be recognized regarding cadmium beyond the usual caution that the result is statistical, and correlation does not prove causality. Some input air pollution data for individual SMSAs were based on single annual mean values. It would be preferable if at least three annual mean measures were available so that annual consistency could be examined. The possibility must be considered, of course, that the cadmium statistical results may be spurious through random influences relating to problems of measurement. Whether the negative association involving cadmium is biologically authentic must await additional and perhaps more accurate data and further developments in biology. The arsenic data were also rather scarce, so the same cautions must be noted.

Death rates from congenital malformations and other chronic diseases have also been analysed, as have other kinds of relationships involving the age structure of different SMSAs. These analyses can be found in Hickey et al.,[4] and in further publications by these authors which had not appeared at the time of writing[31] (1970). It should be noted that significant results were obtained with environmental chemicals as

IX

| Annual mortality rate per $10^5$ population | ISC Nos.[c] | Regression coefficients for ln c(Chemical) predictors | | | | | | | | | % of variance "explained" ($R^2$ x 100) |
|---|---|---|---|---|---|---|---|---|---|---|---|
| | | Constant | $NO_2$ | $SO_2$ | Cd | Cu | $SO_4^{2-}$ | Ti | As | Water hardness | |
| Total cancer[a] | 140-205 | -151.33 | +40.180 | +18.843 | -10.120 | — | — | — | — | — | 55.4 |
| Breast cancer, based on total populations[b] | 170 | -28.00 | +5.523 | +2.018 | -0.992 | -1.510 | — | — | — | — | 58.0 |
| Stomach cancer[b] | 151 | -25.36 | +4.117 | +2.506 | -1.433 | — | — | — | — | — | 49.5 |
| Lung cancer[b] | 162-163 | -28.09 | +4.986 | — | — | -2.197 | +5.462 | -2.103 | -0.6255 | — | 73.2 |
| Diseases of the heart[a] | 400-402, 410-443 | -258.4 | +89.001 | +51.616 | -28.368 | — | — | — | — | -29.964 | 56.1 |
| Arteriosclerotic heart disease[b] | 420 | -254.9 | +71.912 | +41.336 | -24.225 | — | — | — | — | -23.140 | 47.4 |

OPTIMAL REGRESSION ANALYSES. Results of some optimal regression analyses on relationships between concentrations of environmental chemicals and chronic disease mortality rates. Source: Adapted from R.J. Hickey, D.E. Boyce, E.B. Harner, and R.C. Clelland. 1970. Ecological statistical studies concerning environmental pollution and chronic disease. IEEE Trans. Geosci. Electronics GE-8. No. 4, pp. 186-202. Used by permission.

[a]Mortality rate data were means of annual data for 1961-1964.
[b]Mortality rate data were means of annual data for 1959-1961.
[c]See Tables VII and VIII.

predictors for mortality rate for congenital malformations, in accordance with the requirement that environmental mutagens, if they are present, must affect germinal as well as somatic cell DNA.

The important points about the effects of atmospheric pollutants on some chronic diseases can be summarized as follows:

1. There is consistent statistical evidence from 38 metropolitan areas of the United States that increasing concentrations of air pollution and, in particular, of nitrogen dioxide and sulfur dioxide, are associated with increasing death rates from chronic diseases associated with senescence, such as various forms of cancer, total cancer, and diseases of the heart. Concentrations of several metals are negatively associated with such death rates.

2. It is hypothesized that such diseases are caused or their incidence is increased by cumulative somatic genetic degeneration; this is mutations of the cellular DNA which are deleterious and accumulate through life.

3. There is evidence that some atmospheric pollutants, including $NO_2$, $SO_2$, and possibly some metals, may be mutagenic hazards to life.

We must be cautious in interpreting these results; the hypothesis is not PROVEN. There are also other environmental variables, including some demographic variables, associated with variations in mortality from chronic diseases; the situation is complex and enlightenment is emerging slowly.

*Tobacco Smoking and Disease*

A great volume of information has been published concerning the relationship between smoking, particularly cigarette smoking, and chronic disease.[32] Considering that great numbers of people over many years in different parts of the world have derived pleasure and satisfaction from tobacco smoking, it might seem surprising that such a large amount of time, money, and effort have been expended concerning this particular human indulgence largely for the purpose of proving that smoking is a health hazard, and especially that there is a risk of contracting lung cancer. If the mechanism of such a cause-effect relationship were so clear, such a great

quantity of effort might seem unnecessary. Has effort and expenditure gone into studies on causes of chronic diseases generally in proportion to their prevalence?

The evidence implicating smoking, particularly cigarette smoking, as a cause of lung cancer is based primarily on statistical evidence, that is, lung cancer occurs more frequently in smokers than in nonsmokers, and the risk of contracting lung cancer is greater in heavy smokers than in light smokers. It should be noted, however, that nonsmokers do develop lung cancer. There are no major disagreements over whether or not correlations exist between smoking and lung cancer mortality. The associations do in fact exist; but uniformity of opinion does not exist regarding the interpretation of the statistical findings.[33,34] Since statistics are heavily involved, one might inquire whether the statistics have been interpreted with the rigorous objectivity demanded by science. Too often, unfortunately, when statistics are used in a problem which has some "moral" overtones (some religions proscribe tobacco use; puritanism is skeptical of pleasure), biased, subjective interpretations may not be far behind.

It is not possible to discuss the complex smoking-health problem extensively in this limited presentation, but some comment is demanded by the facts that, as reported above, (1) about 73 percent of the variance in the lung cancer mortality rate criterion has been "explained" statistically by a group of several atmospheric chemicals for 38 SMSAs, (2) as shown in the correlation matrix involving diseases (Table VIII), the mortality rate for cancer of the respiratory system is rather highly intercorrelated with mortality rates for total cancer, some specific categories of cancer, and arteriosclerotic heart disease, a finding suggestive of a considerable degree of common etiology, and (3) the mortality rate for cancer of the respiratory system is fairly constant from year to year over several years within metropolitan areas, but is rather markedly different between metropolitan areas.

R.A. Fisher advanced an hypothesis over 10 years ago that an underlying contributing biological variable explaining both the tendencies to smoke and to develop lung cancer might be based on the variability in individual genotypes.[34] Variations on this view have been presented by others.[35,36] Further, as Brownlee has noted, a good, supportable hypothesis for a biochemical mechanism of initiation of lung cancer by tobacco smoking seems to be lacking. It is curious that Brownlee's review[37] of the Surgeon General's 1964 Report on *Smoking and Health*[38] seems to have escaped citation in subsequent Reports. Experimental animal tests intended to induce lung cancer in animals by exposing them to cigarette smoke have been rather uniformly negative. (The use of surgical procedures on animals and "painting" tars on tracheal or other surfaces is hardly ecologically comparable to human experience.) It is also noteworthy that the popular news media, printed and electronic, present nearly exclusively the established view and largely ignore the other side as it has been presented by a number of scientists. The public should be expected to function intelligently on issues affecting it only if it is fully and fairly informed without biased, institutionalized one-sided information.

Great caution is again urged in interpretation of statistics. Two incidental items relating to the smoking problem may be noted: (a) The claim that considerable $NO_2$ is present in cigarette smoke[38] has been challenged by Norman and Keith[39], who found that nitric oxide (NO) was present in fresh smoke, but little or no $NO_2$. (b) The Surgeon General's Report of 1964[38] states (on page 182): "The causal significance of an association is a matter of judgment which goes beyond any statement of statistical probability."

## Implications of Air Pollution Effects

Cooper[11] commented quite astutely in 1966 that "despite our ultrahygienic environment, sterile hospitals, white rooms, air conditioned houses and cars, and all those sanitary and protective modern conveniences that we are blessed with, we have not the slightest qualms about pouring daily approximately 250,000 tons of carbon monoxide, in addition to other pollutants, from motor vehicles alone, into the atmosphere. We regard it as a vast, boundless dumping space for our aerial garbage." Beyond adding that 23 million tons of sulfur dioxide were poured into

the atmosphere during 1963[10], along with other pollution, further comment seems somewhat superfluous. While air pollutants encompass a great variety of chemicals in different proportions, major emission offenders include sulfur dioxide, carbon monoxide, nitric oxide, hydrocarbons, and other organic materials. There are, of course, many types of industrial emissions which may include nitrogen dioxide, chlorinated products, hydrogen sulfide, amines and other products but the preceding chemicals are most important because they lead to other undesirable chemicals (including nitrogen dioxide, peroxides, and sulfuric acid or sulfates) by the reactions which cause photochemical smog.

California standards are among the most stringent, but standards differ in different regulatory agencies. Standards are at times exceeded. Thus far, they are often based largely on acute effects rather than on less readily observed chronic effects. However, in 1967, California standards recognized a number of possible effects of air pollution on "sensitive groups" of people, including (a) acute illness or death, (b) "insidious or chronic" effects, (c) physiological alterations (such as of hemoglobin), (d) "untoward" or unclear symptoms, and (e) discomfort. There tend to be many qualifications regarding standards. For example, less $SO_2$ may be permitted with high particulate concentration than with low. In 1969, recommended California standards included 0.1 ppm of "oxidant, including ozone," 20 ppm of carbon monoxide, 0.1 to 0.5 ppm of sulfur dioxide, 0.25 ppm of nitrogen dioxide, and 100 micrograms/m$^3$ of particulates. Averaging and other measurement conditions vary. For details, source material should be examined. California has also reported data for local regions in hours and days when the standard was equalled or exceeded. During August, 1968, in the Los Angeles area, the oxidant standard was exceeded for 129 hours during 26 days, and the nitrogen dioxide standard was exceeded in Burbank for 12 hours during 5 days.

Construction of more highways rather than mass transportation systems can tend to aggravate the pollution problem. Modification of engine and exhaust systems design can no doubt reduce emissions per transportation unit, but increases in population can lead to increases in numbers of automobiles which will then tend to increase total emissions. A 90 percent reduction of automotive pollution is supposed to be accomplished by 1975 or 1976.

Based on the 1970 midsummer, worldwide pollution episode, one may have serious doubts that pollution control procedures have been or are sufficiently effective. Reductions are being made in sulfur content of fossil fuels burned in electric power plants and other stationary facilities. Electric power from nuclear-powered generators is not developing as rapidly as had been hoped because of technical problems including those of handling heat emission. In addition, partisan pressures have been interfering at times with objective determination of the facts. If certain emissions from fossil-fuel-burning power plants, such as sulfur dioxide, are in fact mutagenic hazards, then those objecting to nuclear electric power plants must weigh the available alternatives. Utopia does not seem close at hand.

Evidence has been presented supporting the hypothesis that among the environmental chemicals to which human populations are exposed are some which are radiomimetic, or mutagenic. Two primary pollutants which appear to be probable mutagenic hazards to life are atmospheric sulfur dioxide and nitrogen dioxide. Peroxides have also been reported to be mutagenic[16]; they are also important components of air pollution.

If such ubiquitous chemicals are in fact mutagenic hazards which can mimic the biological effect of ionizing radiation, then we need safeguards to health comparable to those applied to radioactive materials and ionizing radiation.

The primary danger to life from subacute or chronic exposure to ionizing radiation is mutagenesis. In the event that rigorous scientific evidence develops which establishes beyond doubt that among the urban, nonradioactive atmospheric pollutant chemicals are those which are radiomimetic, and that among their health consequences are increased risk of contracting cancer and heart disease, more rapid aging, reduced life expectancy, and increased prevalence of germinal genetic damage, responsible and rational public and governmental concern could be

expected to develop, followed by remedial action. Warnings have already been issued. (It should be noted that bisulfites, and nitrites are permitted as food additives in the United States. The relevant regulatory agency does not comment on the question of mutagenicity.)

Clearly, if, because of potential chronic effects, we set air quality standards as stringent as those now in existence for radioactive materials, then acute effects would largely or entirely disappear. Air quality standards based primarily on acute effects would then be irrelevant. It should be noted in particular that this would affect automobile exhaust emission. Automobile exhaust devices do not necessarily reduce NO emissions, which can lead to $NO_2$. Yet $NO_2$ is a major suspected mutagenic hazard. This is not to say, of course, that devices cannot be devised to reduce nitrogen oxide emissions. However, unless a chemical is recognized as a health threat, it may not be effectively regulated.

As noted above, if ambient-air quality standards permit 0.25 ppm of $NO_2$ and 0.1 to 0.5 ppm of $SO_2$, based largely on acute effects, in the event that these chemicals are proven to be mutagenic hazards, then governmental regulatory agencies must determine what concentration of mutagenic hazards are "acceptable." If "standards" of 0.01 ppm were set for both $NO_2$ and $SO_2$, severe technical and economic problems would ensue, and "standards" would no doubt be exceeded much of the time in some regions. Levels of mutagenic risk from chemicals comparable to the mutagenic risk of ionizing radiation might be estimated. If levels of equivalence can be estimated, it will be interesting to learn whether standards comparable to the standards for ionizing radiation and for radioactive materials will be applied.

A major problem exists regarding individual and public awareness and the observability of mutagenic effects. The acute effects of pollution, such as those which occurred in Donora, Pennsylvania and in London smogs of the past, cannot be missed. When an event occurs rapidly, causes people to die suddenly, and leads to overcrowded hospitals, it is noticed. But if a large population is exposed continuously or chronically to one or more environmental mutagens at levels which are below the levels of detection by normal, unaided physiological senses, the members of that population will most likely be unaware that anything deleterious is happening. Reduced life expectancy is not obvious. The general public, with some exceptions, might not fully understand this type of genetic problem. It should be a duty of responsible government to protect the public from such hazards even though they may be somewhat arcane and are odorless and non-irritating in the conventional sense. If environmental mutagens lead to a gradual increase in genetic defects in the gene pool, the consequences could be severe. One indicator of increased levels of environmental mutagens could be a gradual increase in the frequency of spontaneous abortions, or a significant statistical relationship between spontaneous abortion rates for populations in different metropolitan areas and concentration of environmental mutagens in these areas.

A serious problem may arise as we respond to ACUTE pollution effects. Acute episodes are, of course, ecological disasters. They are well covered by the news media and tend to result in much public apprehension, study by governmental agencies, and sometimes in governmental action against polluters. London is less polluted today than it was in the past.

However, if such occurrences are minimized by progress in pollution control technology, including reduction in smoke, soot, and other particulates, and if obvious increased mortality episodes occur rarely, a false sense of security may ensue. Atmospheric gases such as sulfur dioxide, nitrogen dioxide, carbon monoxide, and nitric oxide can be present but invisible, along with ozone and other peroxides. Some of these can be detected by individuals through odor and through irritation of the eyes and of the respiratory organs, if the atmospheric concentrations are high enough. There are, however, "thresholds" of biological ability to detect some of these chemicals by odor and irritation which will vary from person to person. Carbon monoxide is odorless and is therefore insidious. In automobile exhaust the other associated chemicals, other

than NO, perhaps, are usually detectable, however. Sulfur dioxide, nitrogen dioxide and peroxides are odorous and are detectable if present in sufficient concentration.

In relation to the findings on chronic diseases reported here, it is interesting to note official attitudes as recently as 1965. An Environmental Pollution Panel of the President's Science Advisory Committee commented as follows: "While we all fear, and many believe, that long-continued exposure to low levels of pollution is having unfavorable effects on human health, it is heartening to know that careful study has so far failed to produce evidence that this is so, and that such effects if present must be markedly less noticeable than those associated with cigarette smoking."

Clearly, capital investment is necessary for the construction of equipment to reduce air pollutant emissions. This is true whether chemical manufacturing, electrical power generation, or automobile exhaust is considered. Added costs for pollution control in already marginal manufacturing operations could render continued operation unprofitable.

It is customary to consider the possibility that certain pollutants may be recovered in some saleable form which may compensate for pollutant removal. This can be quite difficult. Removal of sulfur dioxide from stack gases is an example of the problem. It is known that sulfur dioxide will react with hydrogen sulfide to yield elemental sulfur and water. Where it is feasible to employ this reaction, marketable sulfur becomes available, and water is a reaction by-product. Some types of natural gas contain appreciable hydrogen sulfide. There are also other means of converting sulfur dioxide to sulfur.

Unfortunately, since pollution externalities can be internalized often only at considerable cost, thus reducing profit, the broad goal of maximizing monetary profits can be assisted if pollution is discharged to the atmosphere, to water, and to other environmental resources.

Since atmosphere of proper quality is essential to life, and since polluted air can be a threat to survival, and may possibly lead to shortening of the life span, a serious question presents itself regarding the conflict between (a) maximizing profitability by minimizing costs and (b) the extent to which the public will endure the resultant degradation of its environment along with prospective increased risks of reduced life span, mortality from chronic diseases of senescence, and germinal genetic effects. It should be of some interest to those concerned exclusively with profits that a Presidential Commission concluded in 1964[40] that the annual cost of cancer, heart disease, and stroke in the United States amounted to about $30 billion.

Public officials sometimes express "concern" for such problems, but take no remedial action. R. A. Fisher observed[41] in 1950: "We must face the difficult and responsible task of getting good results actually accomplished. Good intentions and pious observances are no sufficient substitute, and are noxious if accepted as a substitute."

## References

1. **Cooper, A. G.** 1965. *Sulfur Oxides and Other Sulfur Compounds. A Bibliography with Abstracts,* Division of Air Pollution, Public Health Service, U.S. Department of Health, Education and Welfare, Washington, D.C.

2. **Kotin, P., and Falk, H. L.** 1964. Atmosphere pollutants. *Ann. Rev. Med. 15:* 233-254.

3. **American Industrial Hygiene Association.** 1960. *Air Pollution Manual, Part 1, Evaluation,* American Industrial Hygiene Association, Detroit, Michigan.

4. **Hickey, R. J., Boyce, D. E., Harner, E. B., and Clelland, R. C.** 1970. Ecological statistical studies concerning environmental pollution and chronic disease. *IEEE Trans. Geosci. Electronics 8:* 186-202.

5. **Schroeder, H. A.** 1965. The biological trace elements, or peripatetics through the periodic table. *J. Chron. Dis. 18:* 217-228.

6. **Schroeder, H. A., and Balassa, J. J.** 1966. Abnormal trace metals in man: arsenic. *J. Chron. Dis. 19:* 85-106.

7. **National Air Pollution and Control Administration, U.S. Public Health Service.** 1968. *Air Quality Data from the National Air Surveillance Networks,* 1966 edition and corresponding editions for 1957 through 1965. U.S. Department of Health, Education and Welfare, Durham, North Carolina.

8. **Sawicki, E., Hauser, T. R., Elbert, W. C., Fox, F. T., and Meeker, J. E.** 1962. Polynuclear aromatic hydrocarbon composition of the atmosphere in some large American cities. *Amer. Indust. Hyg. Assoc. J. 23:* 137-144.

9. **Public Health Service, Division of Air Pollution.** 1962. *Motor Vehicles, Air Pollution, and Health,* Report of the Surgeon General to the U.S. Congress, House Document No. 489, 87th Congress, 2d Session. U.S. Department of Health, Education and Welfare, Washington, D.C.

10. **National Center for Air Pollution Control.** 1967. *Air Quality Criteria for Sulfur Oxides.* Public Health Service, U.S. Department of Health, Education and Welfare, Washington, D.C.

11. **Cooper, A. G.** 1966. *Carbon Monoxide, A Bibliography with Abstracts,* Publ. No. 1503, Division of Air Pollution, Public Health Service, U.S. Department of Health, Education and Welfare, Washington, D.C.

12. **Clapp, N. K., Craig, A. W., and Toya, R. E., Jr.** 1970. Diethylnitrosamine oncogenesis in RF mice as influenced by variations in cumulative dose. *Int. J. Cancer 5:* 119-123.

13. **Shapiro, R., Servis, R. E., and Welcher, M.** 1970. Reactions of uracil and cytosine derivatives with sodium bisulfite. *J. Amer. Chem. Soc. 92:* 422-424.

14. **Hayatsu, H., Wataya, Y., and Kai, K.** 1970. The addition of sodium bisulfite to uracil and to cytosine. *J. Amer. Chem. Soc. 92:* 724-726.

15. **Freese, E.** 1959. On the molecular explanations of spontaneous and induced mutations. In *Structure and Function of Genetic Elements,* Brookhaven Symposia in Biology, No. 12, pp. 63-75.

16. **Orgel, L. E.** 1965 The chemical basis of mutation. In *Advances in Enzymology* (F. F. Nord, ed.), Vol. 27 pp. 289-346. Interscience-Wiley, New York.

17. **Curtis, H. J.** 1967. Radiation and ageing. In *Aspects of the Biology of Ageing* (H. H. Woolhouse, ed.). Symposia of the Society for Experimental Biology, No. 21, Academic Press, New York.

18. **Watson, J. D.** 1970 *The Molecular Biology of the Gene,* 2nd Ed., W. A. Benjamin, New York.

19. **Cleaver, J. E.** 1969. Xeroderma pigmentosum: A human disease in which an initial stage of DNA repair is defective. *Proc. Nat. Acad. Sci. U.S. 63:* 428-435.

20. **Bootsma, E., Mulder, M. P., Pot, F., and Cohen, J. A.** 1970. Different inherited levels of DNA repair replication in Xeroderma pigmentosum cell strains after exposure to ultraviolet irradiation. *Mutation Res. 9:* 507-516.

21. **Meselson, M.** 1964. Letter to Dr. Donald Hornig, Special Assistant to the President for Science and Technology, December 8, 1964. Noted by Sanders, H. F., Chemical Mutagens. The road to disaster? *Chem. Eng. News,* May 19, 1969.

22. **Casarett, A. P.** 1968. *Radiation Biology.* Prentice-Hall, Englewood Cliffs, New Jersey.

23. **Crow, J. F.** 1968. Chemical risk to future generations. *Scientist and Citizen 10:* 113-116 (June-July).

24. **Huff, D.** 1954. *How to Lie with Statistics.* W. W. Norton, New York.

25. **Fisher. R. A.** 1935. Statistical tests, *Nature 136:* 474.

26. **Public Health Service, National Vital Statistics Division.** 1962. *Vital Statistics of the United States, 1962,* Vol. II, Mortality, Part B. National Vital Statistics Division, U.S. Department of Health, Education and Welfare, Washington, D.C. (and corresponding volumes for other years).

27. **U.S. Bureau of the Census.** 1961. *Census of Population, 1960,* Vol. 1, Characteristics of the Population, Part A, Number of Inhabitants, Table 31, Population of Standard Metropolitan Statistical Areas in the United States and Commonwealth of Puerto Rico: 1940-1960. U.S. Department of Commerce, Washington, D.C.

28. **Graffi, A., Schramm, T., Bender, E., Graffi, I., Horn, K. H., and Bierwolf, D.** 1968. Transmissible leucoses in Syrian hamsters probably of viral etiology. *Brit. J. Cancer 22:* 577-581.

29. **Public Health Service.** 1968. *The Facts About Smoking and Health,* Public Health Service Publication No. 1712. National Clearinghouse for Smoking and Health, U.S. Department of Health, Education and Welfare, Arlington, Virginia.

30. **Morrison, D. F.** 1967. *Multivariate Statistical Methods.* McGraw-Hill, New York.

31. **Hickey, R. J., Boyce, D. E., Harner, E. B., Slater, P. B., and Clelland, R. C.** 1970-1971. Ecological statistical studies concerning the relationships between environmental variables and chronic diseases. Papers in preparation. University of Pennsylvania, Philadelphia, Pennsylvania.

32. **Larson, P. S., Haag, H. B., and Silvette, H.** 1961. *Tobacco. Experimental and Clinical Studies,* and Larson, P. S., and Silvette, H., 1968, Supplement I, Williams and Wilkins, Baltimore, Maryland.

33. **Smith, G. M.** 1967. Personality correlates of cigarette smoking in students of college age. *Ann. N. Y. Acad. Sci. 142:* 308-321.

34. **Fisher, R. A.** 1959. *Smoking: The Cancer Controversy.* Oliver and Boyd, London.

35. **Thomas, C. B.** 1968. On cigarette smoking, coronary heart disease and the genetic hypothesis. *Johns Hopkins Med. J. 122:* 69-76.

36. **Berkson, J.** 1963. Smoking and lung cancer. *Amer. Statistician 17:* 15-22.

37. **Brownlee, K. A.** 1965. A review of "Smoking and Health." *J. Amer. Stat. Assoc. 60:* 722-739.

38. **Public Health Service.** 1964. *Smoking and Health.* Report of the Advisory Committee to the Surgeon General of the Public Health Service, Public Health Service Publ. No. 1103, U.S. Department of Health, Education and Welfare, Washington, D.C.

39. **Norman, V., and Keith, C. H.** 1965. Nitrogen oxides in tobacco smoke. *Nature 205:* 915-916.

40. **DeBakey, M. E., Chairman,** 1964. *A National Program to Conquer Heart Disease, Cancer and Stroke.* Superintendent of Documents, Washington, D.C.

41. **Fisher, R. A.** 1950. *Creative Aspects of Natural Law.* The University Press, Cambridge, England.

42. Some material presented in this chapter is based on recent studies supported in part by grants from Resources for the Future, Inc., and from the U.S. Public Health Service, and by a Special Project grant from The Council for Tobacco Research-U.S.A. as previously noted.[4] This essential aid is gratefully acknowledged. I wish further to thank Dr. David E. Boyce and Mrs. Evelyn B. Harner for reviewing the manuscript and for their suggestions. Any errors, however, are my own.

# 10  Fresh Water Pollution

W. T. Edmondson

Pollution of freshwaters results largely from the ease of disposal of waste there. Lakes occupy low places in the landscape and their inflowing streams are natural collecting systems from the watershed. It is easy to pour wastes into the water and let them be carried away to "somewhere else." But lakes and rivers are used for a variety of other purposes: as sources of drinking water or food (fish), for fun (boating, swimming, water skiing), for camping sites, or simply as parts of beautiful landscapes enjoyed for their existence. Each use depends upon the maintenance of a particular quality, but each of the uses has the possibility of decreasing that quality.

Rivers and lakes may be "enriched" by surface runoff carrying everything that people put into their house drains, put onto their land, or dispose of on the streets: sewage, fertilizers, herbicides, insecticides, and general junk. Up to a point we have been able to get away with this because water and its biota have the capacity to absorb and break down by biological action many kinds of wastes. But some kinds of waste

W. T. EDMONDSON is Professor of Zoology at the University of Washington, Seattle. He did his undergraduate work at Yale University, and earned his doctorate there in 1942, working under G. E. Hutchinson. During World War II he carried out research for the Navy at the American Museum of Natural History and the Woods Hole Oceanographic Institution. He was a member of the biology faculty at Harvard from 1946 to 1949. In 1949 he moved to the University of Washington, where his research has centered on the mechanisms that control the productivity and the populations of lakes, particularly Lake Washington.

cannot be degraded, and any system can be overloaded. And the "somewhere else" turns out to be where somebody else is trying to live and use the water.

As will be shown, several different kinds of unpleasant consequences can be generated in a river or lake by waste disposal. Disposal of sewage into waterways is obviously bad because of the possibility of spreading waterborne diseases, but this is only part of the problem. Much damage is based on the fact that sewage increases the biological productivity in such a way as to interfere with many uses of the waterway. Not all pollution has this effect. Some kinds of waste contain toxic substances that damage biological activity and kill off desirable forms of life. Others impart taste or odor to the receiving water, making it unsuitable for drinking without expensive treatment.

A third kind of damage results from the disposal of large, resistant objects such as cans, worn out tires, and even cars. It is more than simply that the beauty of a place is destroyed. Although one can argue that concepts of natural beauty are cultural and subject to change, for people who have been brought up to value natural beauty, experiencing the sight of a lot of junk dumped into a stream can be psychologically damaging. Surely our mental health is affected by the character of the surroundings we live in and the nature of the visual experiences we have. This effect is entirely out of my field, and I will say nothing about it in this chapter, but it is a point that looms large in the minds of some limnologists as they go about their work.

As a result of decades of overloading the capacity of our natural waste disposal systems, we have built up a pollution debt that now must be paid off if our society is to be able to continue to function. One can make an analogy with a person running a hundred-yard dash. The idea is to run as fast as possible. Under these conditions, it is physiologically impossible for a person to absorb oxygen through the lungs fast enough to keep up with the rate of consumption of oxygen in the muscles. Thus, the muscles are living anaerobically, and lactic acid accumulates from the breakdown of carbohydrate, rather than being completely oxidized to carbon dioxide. This accumulation is called an oxygen debt. The degree of accumulation is limited and one cannot run at top speed very long. After the race, the athlete lies panting on the ground, absorbing oxygen at a rate faster than he is using it, and the extra amount largely goes to resynthesizing carbohydrate from the lactic acid; the oxygen debt is being repaid.

We have been producing wastes much faster than the natural systems can deal with them, producing an accumulation of bad conditions. So, we must learn how to decrease the rate at which we damage the environment. The time has come to pay off the pollution debt.

In order to do this, we have to understand exactly what the different kinds of pollution do and what the possibilities are for modification.

Large volumes of water are involved (Fig. 1 and Chapter 7). In 1965 the rate of water withdrawal for public water supplies was 23.6 billion gallons per day; that is 155 gallons per person. Total use for all purposes including irrigation, farm, and industrial uses was 310 billion gallons per day, or 1600 gallons per person. Different industries have vastly different requirements for water (Table I). The availability of adequate supplies of suitable water is often the key factor in determining the location of factories. Further, the character of the effluents from different industries is enormously varied; consequently the complexity of the effects of industrial waste and the efforts needed to control them also vary greatly. The large numbers in Table I are meaningless in themselves. They must be judged in relation to our total water supply and our requirements. The average stream flow is 1200 billion gallons per day. In some basins, water is used repeatedly.[1]

Many of the uses to which water is put require water of high quality, that is, with a small content of dissolved and suspended material, and lack of bacterial contamination. But some of the uses degrade the quality of the water so that it cannot be used again without treatment. A good example is the domestic use of water in houses with the consequent production of sewage.

*Sewage*

Commonly, sewage has been disposed of simply by letting it run into a river without any treatment.[2] Household drains taking waste from sinks and toilets run into pipes under streets that lead to big collector sewers that in turn lead to the river. Such material is very rich in organic substances that provide nutrition for bacteria and fungi, organisms known collectively as decom-

| Industry | Waste water volume, billion gallons | Process water intake, billion gallons | Suspended solids, million pounds |
|---|---|---|---|
| Food & kindred products | 690 | 260 | 6,600 |
| Meat products | 99 | 52 | 640 |
| Dairy products | 58 | 13 | 230 |
| Canned & frozen food | 87 | 51 | 600 |
| Sugar refining | 220 | 110 | 5,000 |
| All other | 220 | 43 | 110 |
| Textile mill products | 140 | 110 | — |
| Paper & allied products | 1,900 | 1,300 | 3,000 |
| Chemical & allied products | 3,700 | 560 | 1,900 |
| Petroleum & coal | 1,300 | 88 | 460 |
| Rubber & plastics | 160 | 19 | 50 |
| Primary metals | 4,300 | 1,000 | 4,700 |
| Blast furnaces & steel mills | 3,600 | 870 | 4,300 |
| All other | 740 | 130 | 430 |
| Machinery | 150 | 23 | 50 |
| Electrical machinery | 91 | 28 | 20 |
| Transportation equipment | 240 | 58 | — |
| All other manufacturing | 450 | 190 | 930 |
| All manufacturing | 13,100 | 3,700 | 18,000 |
| For comparison: Sewered Population of U.S. | 5,300 | | 8,800 |

**INDUSTRIAL WASTE.** Volume of industrial wastes before treatment, in 1964. Source: reference 8.

posers. As the population of decomposers builds up in the river, the original material is trans-

formed partly into the organic material of the microorganisms, but much of it is liberated to the water in a dissolved, inorganic form. For example, while some of the nitrogen in urea will be absorbed and made into bacterial protein, much will be liberated as ammonia, which may become

ESTIMATED WATER SUPPLY AND USE IN THE UNITED STATES, 1958. Quantities are in billions of gallons per day. Note that the numbers for more recent years, given in the text, are bigger. Source: White, 1969 (see Further Reading).

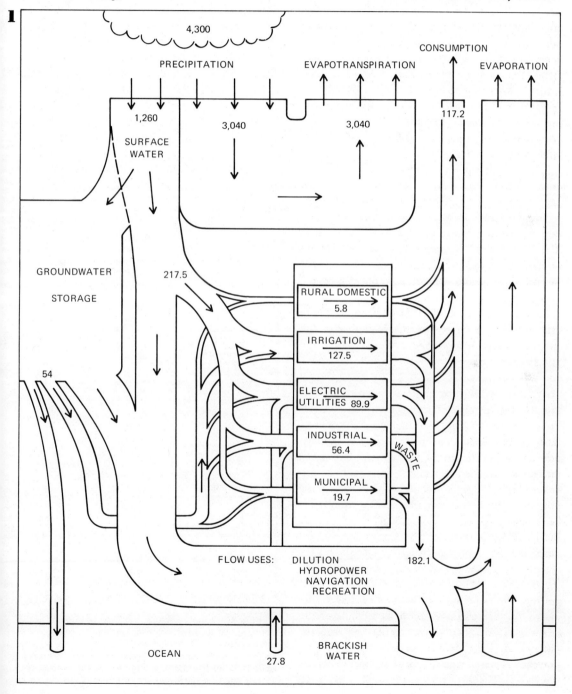

oxidized to nitrate. Phosphorus that was originally part of organic molecules will be liberated as dissolved inorganic phosphate. The respiratory activity of the microorganisms will liberate carbon dioxide containing carbon that was originally part of carbohydrates and other carbon-containing compounds in the sewage.

These processes are a perfectly normal part of the functioning of the ecosystem. Decomposers are very important in nature because of their activities of reducing natural wastes, corpses, fallen leaves, and other by-products of life to their elemental constituents. The recycling of elements permitted by this process is essential for the continued growth of plants, the primary producers (Chapter 1).

All of these processes take time as the water moves downstream, which establishes a series of zones below the input of raw sewage depending upon the stage reached in the series of processes by the time the water passes a given point. As in most biological matters, these zones are not clear-cut regions with sharp boundaries, but blend into each other in a gradual manner[3] (Figure 2).

Immediately below the outfall is the ZONE OF DEGRADATION where stream water mixes with sewage. With the development of increasing numbers of decomposers, the water enters the ZONE OF ACTIVE DECOMPOSITION where the concentrations of organic materials decrease with a corresponding increase of inorganic by-products. If the load of sewage is great enough, the organisms use oxygen faster than it can diffuse in through the surface of the stream, and the water becomes devoid of dissolved oxygen. This SEPTIC ZONE is characterized by the absence of animals and the presence of $H_2S$, which smells like rotten eggs. Eventually, enough of the organic substrates are consumed that the bacterial activity slows down and oxygen reappears, being stirred in from the air as the water moves along. In the following ZONE OF RECOVERY processes take place that change the water back toward its original condition. The dense population of bacteria forms an excellent food supply for a variety of protozoa and small invertebrates. Some of the bottom-dwelling invertebrates are able to live with little oxygen, and sludge worms appear in great num-

bers early in the recovery zone. Further downstream, after more aeration, invertebrates with higher requirements for oxygen increase in numbers.

With the relatively high concentrations of carbon dioxide, phosphate, and other nutrients now present, algae can grow, and luxuriant streamers of filamentous algae attached to stones may develop. By their photosynthetic activity they contribute dissolved oxygen to the water. These algae provide cover and food for invertebrates, so the variety and abundance of animals increases downstream in this zone. Free-floating microscopic algae may develop in large numbers also, providing food for those animals adapted to them.

Eventually, all the decomposable material that entered the stream has been degraded by biolog-

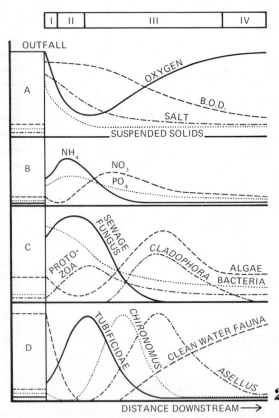

STREAM BELOW SEWAGE OUTFALL. Changes in the condition of a stream below an outfall of raw sewage. A and B show mostly chemical changes; C shows changes in the abundance of microorganisms, and D, changes in abundance of invertebrate animals. The zones described in the text are shown at the top. Source: reference 2.

ical action, and the water is restored to something close to its original condition, the CLEAN WATER ZONE. This series of processes has been described as "self-purification of streams."

Obviously, the discussion just presented concerns the effects only of materials that are degradable by biological action. Some industrial wastes contain highly toxic materials that kill everything and prevent proper action of the natural self-purification processes. Such wastes can damage streams as far downstream as it takes for the material to be diluted below biologically effective concentrations. These wastes will be discussed later in the chapter.

It is clear that the length of river occupied by the affected zone (zones of degradation and active decomposition, septic zone, and recovery zone) will depend largely upon the rate of addition of sewage and the rate of flow of the river. The establishment of a village on a stream early in this century may have produced an affected zone that was relatively short, and this amount of degradation might have been acceptable. But as that village grew to a city, the rate of sewage input would have increased in proportion to the population size and activity, and the length of the affected zone must have increased downstream accordingly. This would present a problem for the next city downstream, which originally stood in a zone of clean water. As the city upstream grew, an increasingly long stretch of river would have been affected, and the downstream city would find its water deteriorating. If the water was used for drinking, the degree of filtration and treatment would have had to be increased. In the meantime, the lower city would be adding its own sewage, so the entire stretch between the two cities and some distance below would be affected. Entire streams have been turned into essentially open sewers by this kind of overloading.

Many cities have been built on lakes and have used the lakes as recipients of their raw sewage. The biological consequences are similar to those in the river, but they are not laid out in such linear order. The surface water of lakes is likely to be blown around and mixed so actively by wind that definite zones are not likely to be seen except in special circumstances. The production of a large quantity of bacteria feeds the animals, and the liberation of nutrients increases algal production throughout the lake.

When it became clear in the early part of this century that streams and lakes were becoming overloaded and that very unsatisfactory conditions would develop, various processes for treating sewage to reduce its unpleasant effects were invented. For example, a typical modern two-stage biological treatment plant operates as follows: Large pieces of solid material are screened out, and preliminary settling in large tanks permits settling of finer material as a sludge that can be removed. The remaining material is led into large tanks where air is bubbled through it. Under these conditions, bacteria and fungi multiply, decomposing the organic materials. Another settling stage permits removal of much of the organisms as sludge. The clear supernatant is then chlorinated to kill bacteria and is discharged into whatever water is convenient.[4]

Obviously, what this kind of treatment does is to carry through the normal ecosystem decomposer funtion in a confined place under controlled conditions. This permits removal of much of the material and prevents it from getting into the stream or lake in the first place.

The disposal of the sludge that settles in the sewage plant presents problems. Normally it is not rich enough to use as a fertilizer without adding phosphorus to it. In some places it is put through an anaerobic digestion process. Methane gas, produced by bacteria, is used as a fuel to generate electricity to operate pumps and heaters. It can be used in composting to develop soil, and experiments are being made to develop its usefulness for land fill. Obviously the capacity of many regions for these uses is distinctly limited.

While it might be thought that treatment would solve the sewage pollution problem, it has solved only part. Disposal of effluent from normal secondary treatment plants can generate bad problems because settled sludge contains a relatively small part of the nutrient elements contained in the original organic sewage. Most are released in dissolved inorganic form. While much of the carbon dioxide is lost during the aeration process, the effluent contains much more phosphorus, nitrogen, and some other elements than do most natural waters. Of these, phosphorus is especially enriched, relative to other elements. Effluent from secondary treatment typically contains about 8 milligrams per liter of phosphate-phosphorus and 20 of inorganic nitrogen including ammonia.[4] While natural values vary greatly with place and time, typical values for an unproductive lake would be, respectively, 0.01 and 0.10 milligrams per liter. The annual human release to sewage is about 1.4 pounds of phosphorus and 11 pounds of nitrogen per person per year. Added to this is phosphate from detergents, which accounts for roughly half the phosphate content of sewage. This means that the effluent is a rich fertilizer and can carry out the last stage of the normal process, stimulating the growth of algae and other photosynthetic organisms. It might be thought to be favorable to increase the biological productivity of a lake by fertilization and up to a point it can be. But this system, like any other, can be overloaded, and there can be very unpleasant consequences of enrichment with treated sewage effluent.[5, 6]

The great increase in the supply of dissolved nutrients increases the production of photosynthetic organisms, and the abundance of the microscopic algae in the open water (phytoplankton) increases. This makes the water cloudy so that one cannot see very far into it, interfering with its use for drinking and recreation. Three other interesting effects magnify the unpleasantness of overproduction of algae. One is that the kinds of algae that grow most abundantly under these conditions (certain species of the so-called blue-green algae) tend to float when the weather is calm, and they concentrate into scums at the surface. Under the sun, they die, and large quantities of decaying algae float around or blow downwind and pile up on beaches. The odor is unpleasant, and if the water is to be used for drinking it requires elaborate treatment. Such conditions have been described as "masses of decaying algae..." which "look like human excrement and smell exactly like odors from a foul and neglected pigsty."

Another effect is that the particular kinds of blue-green algae that form the bulk of the population appear not to be used effectively as food by the small invertebrates in the open water

(zooplankton). Thus, predatory control, which is important in some communities, is at a minimum.

Planktonic algae are not the only ones that respond to fertilization. The filamentous ones that grow attached to stones and docks and boats also thrive and may form dense growths which break away, float around, and wash up on the beach. They contribute to the odor problem, and their presence in masses is unpleasant for swimmers. The alga *Cladophora* has been a nuisance in some of the Great Lakes.

Finally, some of the blue-green algae produce substances toxic to animals. Cattle frequently have died after drinking from a pond with a decaying bloom of such algae. This is unlikely to be a frequent problem for people, but some are sensitive and develop skin rashes or vomiting after swimming in lakes with abundant blue-green algae.

### Life History of Lakes

Before proceeding with an account of how this kind of problem has been handled, it may be useful to consider the normal changes a lake goes through in its life.[6]

Lakes originate from various geological processes, but many of the most familiar lakes in inhabited regions of the temperate zone owe their origin or present form largely to the action of glaciers. Many of the small lakes in the temperate zone originated as blocks of ice left as the glacier melted back at the end of the ice age. Typically, such a lake becomes populated by organisms of various kinds that can be transported by wind, by migrating birds, or by their own movements. Thus algae start growing in the open water, and seeds of water plants germinate on the bottom in shallow water and form stands of underwater vegetation. Animals become established. Eventually a complete aquatic community is developed. In the meantime, similar events are taking place on land in the drainage area around the lake. A cover of vegetation develops which to some extent stabilizes the developing soil against erosion. Before this time, erosion of the land may have delivered large quantities of nutritive elements to the lake. While development of a cover of vegetation may reduce erosion, it does not stop the inflow of nutrients. The plants tap the chemical resources of the soil and make available nutritive elements that are released when dead leaves decompose.

As long as the lake is relatively deep, it enters a long period of equilibrium during which the biological productivity and the abundance of plants and animals match the input of nutritive material from the drainage area. During this time, the lake gradually becomes shallower as the bottom sediment builds up, but as long as there is a rather large volume of water that is deeper than plants can grow, the lake remains in something like a steady state. The steady state may become disturbed by landslides, changes of climate, fires, or other major events that affect the input of material or sunshine into the lake. During this time the lake is stratified in summer, with a distinct layer of warm water floating on top of the lake. The warm layer is stirred by the wind, but it seals off the rest of the lake from contact with air.

Eventually, the lake becomes so shallow that the relation between the shore region and the deep water region are changed in an important way. The area of bottom that can be inhabited by plants increases greatly, so that a larger proportion of the area of the lake is inhabited by massive, long-lived plants that provide cover for animals and surface for attachment of algae and animals. When the lake becomes shallow enough, it is stirred to the bottom by wind all summer instead of being stratified. This changes some of the chemical processes that affect the productivity of plants. The net result is that, toward the end of its life, a lake develops much larger quantities of organisms per unit area than it did earlier. Eventually it becomes filled entirely and covered by land vegetation. When a lake is very shallow at the time of origin, it very quickly goes into the last, weedy stage.

Before the lake becomes too shallow to stratify, important changes take place in the deep water during summer. Because of the increased consumption of oxygen in the deep water by decomposing organisms, the dissolved oxygen may become depleted, rendering that part of the lake uninhabitable by fish. Even a deep lake may lose the oxygen from the deep water if the productivity is increased by sewage enrichment. Typically, enriched lakes have lost their deep water populations of salmonid fish, even though coarse fish may thrive in the upper, shallow layers.

The process of enrichment with nutrients has been called EUTROPHICATION, and lakes with large supplies of nutrients are called eutrophic. Such lakes are usually also very productive biologically. The contrast at the other end of the scale is oligotrophic lakes, which have small nutrient supplies and therefore tend to be relatively unproductive. It has often been thought that the trend in normal succession is from less to more productivity, and it is assumed that this is based on a natural increase in nutrient supply. However, as shown above, the increase in abundance of plants toward the end of a lake's life can take place without a major increase in the input of nutrients.

Such changes have been observed in many lakes. Some of the best-studied cases are in central Europe, where limnology was well advanced in the late part of the last century. The lake at Zürich in Switzerland is a very well-known and well-studied example. In 1898 the algal population abruptly changed, and by 1910 the deep water coreground fish were in trouble. A more recent example of eutrophication by treated sewage in the United States is especially interesting because it has been brought under control by enlightened citizens' action.

### The Lake Washington Story

The city of Seattle lies between Puget Sound and the west side of Lake Washington.[6] Early in this century, the lake was used for disposal of raw sewage and unsatisfactory conditions developed. In the early 1930s, the sewage was diverted to Puget Sound, and for a few years the pollution of the lake was reduced. However, Seattle was expanding and smaller towns around the lake were growing. In 1941, a two-stage, biological sewage treatment plant was established on the lake, and by 1954, 10 such plants had been built. An additional one was built on one of the inlets to the lake in 1959. At the maximum, the inflow of treated sewage effluent was 20 million gallons per day. In addition, some of the smaller streams were heavily contaminated with drainage from septic tanks. Studies of the lake in 1933, 1950, and 1952 showed increases in algae and nutrient content. In 1955, a conspicuous growth of the alga *Oscillatoria rubescens* developed (Figure 3). This event attracted attention because this species occurred early in the process of deterioration of a number of European lakes, including the lake at Zürich. Thus it seemed to be a vanguard of pollutional deterioration, and Lake Washington appeared to be responding to enrichment with sewage effluent. It was exhibiting perfectly normal behavior when it began its increase in the abundance of algae, and it was possible to predict with considerable confidence what would be the consequences of continued or increasing enrichment.

Public concern had been growing about the sewage situation in the entire Seattle Metropolitan area. In 1955, the mayor of Seattle appointed a Metropolitan Problem Advisory Committee to study, among other things, these sewage conditions. The obvious deterioration of Lake Washington and the rather clear-cut predictions that could be made about its future conditions gave focus to the public concern. At the same time, it was recognized that unsatisfactory conditions existed in Puget Sound, and that a broadly based, coordinated program was necessary.

As a result of the Committee's action, a campaign was organized by public-minded citizens' groups to develop a governmental organization to handle the problem (Municipality to Metropolitan Seattle or "Metro"). An active informational campaign was carried out, using to a large extent information about the actual deterioration of the lake and predictions about its future.

After a certain amount of difficulty, the public voted for the authorization of Metro in 1958. A sewage diversion project was started in 1963 and completed in 1968. Much of the sewage that formerly entered Lake Washington is taken to a large primary treatment plant that has its outfall very deep in Puget Sound and far from shore, where strong tidal action dilutes and disperses the effluent. The rest is given secondary treatment and discharged into a river that leads to Puget Sound. These changes are not expected to cause trouble in the Sound.

With the first diversion of about a quarter of the sewage, deterioration of Lake Washington slowed, and further diversions were promptly followed by more improvement, as measured by increased transparency of the water and decreased amounts of phosphorus and algae (Figure 3). During late summer of 1969, some of the deep water had more oxygen than in 1933, phosphate was nearly down to 1950 concentrations, and the summer transparency, as judged by the depth to which a white disk can be seen, was 2½ times as great as in 1963.[7] When the lake was at its worst in 1969, it was still clearer than the best of 1967. It is important to realize that action was taken before the lake had deteriorated very far, relative to the well-known lakes in Europe and the midwest of this country.

The condition of the lake had changed conspicuously enough that there was no doubt about it, but action was taken early in the process. It is clear that Lake Washington responded promptly and sensitively to the increase and decrease in nutrient income. Lake Washington should not be regarded as an unusual lake; many lakes would respond just as sensitively. Many of the results of the Lake Washington study can be generalized and used for evaluating other enrichment situations.

A point of particular interest has to do with the relative importance of phosphorus, nitrogen, and carbon, a matter about which there has been some uncertainty. In Lake Washington, phosphorus has decreased much more than nitrogen or carbon dioxide. The abundance of algae has decreased in very close relation to phosphate, not in relation to nitrate or carbon dioxide.[7] This suggests that, in similar lakes, any limitation on the amount of concentrated sources of phosphorus reaching the lake will be beneficial. Large improvements could be made by reducing the phosphorus content of detergents in regions where phosphorus from sewage is an important part of the concentrated sources. In some places, it may be worthwhile to install treatment processes to remove phosphorus from effluent.

For various reasons, disposal of sewage effluent in Puget Sound is not expected to make nui-

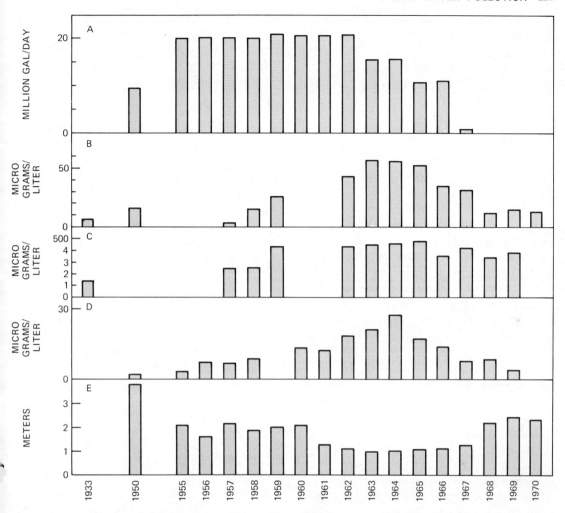

sance problems by overproduction of algae. The water of Puget Sound is replenished about four times per year by tidal action. The water is already rich in nutrients, and the extra load is not expected to make trouble. Part of the Metro operation is to collect 70 million gallons of raw sewage per day that has been entering at the surface and put it through the big treatment plant with its outfall in deep water. This should make a big improvement.

Of course, any body of water can be affected by enough contamination. Care and caution should continuously be used. Particular attention should be given to new developments of potentially toxic household or industrial products which are disposed of through sewers. Puget Sound receives large volumes of industrial and

CHANGES IN LAKE WASHINGTON. Changes in the condition of Lake Washington during the increase of sewage and the subsequent diversion. (A) The amount of sewage as indicated by the total capacity of the sewage treatment plants contributing effluent to the lake; millions of gallons per day. (B) Concentration of phosphate-phosphorus in the surface water, means for January – April, micrograms per liter. [During the winter, dissolved inorganic phosphorus is at a maximum, and it decreases during the spring as it is absorbed by the growing population of the algae (phytoplankton).] The amount of phosphorus in the form of phosphate during winter is about 75 percent of the total phosphorus. (C) Concentration of nitrate – nitrogen in the surface water, means for January – April, micrograms per liter. (D) Abundance of algae in surface water during summer as indicated by the chlorophyll content; means for July and August, micrograms per liter. (E) Transparency as measured by the depth to which a white disk (Secchi disk) can be seen, meters, mean for July and August. Note that the prompt response to even the initial partial diversion of sewage. Phosphate has decreased much more than nitrate.

municipal wastes, and the possibility of damage is present.

*Other Ways of Avoiding Eutrophication*

The solution of the Lake Washington problem was complete diversion of sewage effluent to Puget Sound, where it could not create the problems that it was creating in the lake. Such a solution is not available to most communities. Usually such a move would just send the algae problem somewhere else. For example, in 1936 effluent was moved downstream from Lake Monona, Wisconsin to Lake Waubesa, which promptly started to make nuisance conditions.[6] Therefore, the question arises of what else can be done to avoid eutrophical damage to lakes.

In recent years improved methods have been developed for advanced treatment of sewage, to remove phosphate on a mass scale. The question is whether removal or reduction of phosphate content of sewage will be adequate. This is a field in which considerable controversy exists, and different problems have been mixed up.

On one hand, if we discuss the ecological requirements for production of dense populations of algae, we have to mention that they are affected by the amounts of carbon dioxide, nitrogen, phosphorus, and light, the temperature, and a number of other conditions too. To explain why a given population exists requires a lengthy study. If, on the other hand, we are concerned with what actions we need take to improve a lake that is enriched with sewage the problem becomes simpler. In theory, if we limit any essential element enough, production will be checked, but only a few elements are available for control. For chemical reasons, nitrogen is difficult to eliminate from sewage. Much carbon dioxide is eliminated in secondary treatment, but there are vast reservoirs in the atmosphere, and hard waters especially have bicarbonate that can support plant growth. The element that is most easily eliminated from sewage is phosphorus. Not only can phosphorus be removed chemically in a third stage of treatment, but the initial concentration could be greatly reduced by eliminating the use of the kinds of detergents that are rich in phosphorus. Problems of eutrophication by sew-

age existed before detergents were invented, but detergents have magnified the effect of sewage. It has been calculated that about half the phosphorus entering Lake Erie originates in detergents in the sewage. Thus an important difference in the phosphorus income could be made by this action, but it is not a simple action to take. People want to clean their dishes and clothes effectively, so an effective substitute must be found that will not produce its own problems.

In some places other kinds of beneficial action are possible. A small park lake in Seattle (Green Lake) was greatly improved by dredging soft sediments from the swimming areas and increasing the flow of nutrient-poor water through the lake.[6]

*Agricultural Drainage*

Human sewage is not the only kind that makes problems. Animals in feed lots produce wastes, and some of the material drains into waterways. That which does not offers large difficulties of disposal. Domestic animals excrete from 17 to 45 pounds of phosphorus per thousand pounds of animal per year. The production of animal wastes in the Potomac basin is almost 6 times that of the human population there.[8]

Nor is sewage the only source of concentrated nutrients. In some regions much agricultural fertilizer gets into lakes and can make a great increase in algae. Such conditions seem especially common in the midwest of the United States.[6]

Fortunately, phosphorus is generally more tightly bound in soil than is nitrogen, and water draining agricultural land does not carry a load of phosphorus proportional to its application, relative to nitrogen. Nevertheless, wasteful techniques of application should be avoided, especially on lawns and gardens around small lakes.

A remarkable difficulty has occurred in some regions where excess nitrate originating from septic tank or agricultural drainage has gotten into well water. Nitrate in drinking water becomes reduced to nitrite in the stomach and combines with hemoglobin, reducing the oxygen capacity of the blood. When the concentration of nitrate exceeds about 38 milligrams per liter, the condition can be fatal to infants and cattle, although the Public Health Service standard for drinking water is 45 milligrams per liter.[4]

This problem has become serious in Southern California, which has a long history of pumping water for irrigation, and where drinking water comes from wells replenished by groundwater. Agriculture in Southern California at first depended on pumped groundwater for irrigation. As pumping continued over the years the level of the water table dropped lower and lower, being lowered by as much as 170 feet over a wide area. At the same time, fertilizers were applied and the irrigation water leached nitrate into the soil. In recent years, Southern California has been using water imported from further north, causing a change in the water balance so that the water table is rising again. When water comes in contact with the layers that have been enriched with nitrate, the nitrate is moved into wells used for drinking water. Children of farm laborers have suffered from nitrite poisoning.

*Erosion*

When forests are cut or land is kept in a disturbed state, for example, by repeated plowing without precautions, large quantities of silt are washed into rivers and lakes. The effect is multifold; part of the damaging effect results from smothering the bottom community and from making the water so turbid that light cannot penetrate to support plants. In addition, the increased rate of inwash of eroded materials hastens the extinction of small lakes very greatly. This is particularly serious in small lakes that are near extinction through natural aging. But even large lakes can be affected. Two and a half million tons of silt enter Lake Erie annually. Further, when erosion is from heavily fertilized agricultural land, much of the fertilizer that was intended to increase the production of useful land plants goes to eutrophication instead.

*Radioactive Isotopes*

The problem of environmental contamination with radioactivity from fallout, nuclear accidents, or normal loss from industrial use of atomic energy is widely known. Freshwater organisms concentrate some of the isotopes, such

as strontium, vastly in excess of natural amounts. A special feature of freshwaters is their susceptibility to contamination by leaking underground storage tanks of radioactive wastes. The technology of storage appears not to be advanced enough for us to dismiss the possibility of difficult future problems (Chapter 12).

*Toxic Wastes*

Many industrial wastes contain material that is toxic to organisms and not only interferes with the self-purification processes in streams, but kills the native fauna as well. Some metal treatment processes produce an effluent containing cyanide. A spill of this material, accidental or otherwise, can kill the fish for many miles downstream. While most pollution laws specify disposal of this kind of waste in some other way, trouble continues to be had with it in various places.

A number of materials have the property of being concentrated from the environment by organisms and becoming additionally concentrated from food by the higher members of the food chain (Chapter 1). That is, a substance is absorbed from food and built into the tissues of the feeding animal. As time goes on, the concentration of the substance in the tissues increases and may reach a level at which it interferes with some physiological functions. The most famous case of this sort of problem is with DDT, which has given great trouble both in terrestrial and aquatic communities. Carnivorous fish can develop such high concentrations in their tissues that they are affected and become unsuitable for human food. The successful introduction of the coho salmon into the Great Lakes was met with enormous enthusiasm, but disappointment ensued when the sale and consumption of the fish was banned because of their large DDT content. On land, DDT interferes with formation of egg shells by predatory birds, and several species have been affected. The peregrine falcon has been eliminated from some areas (See Chapter 13).

Some metals have the same property of becoming concentrated in organisms. Rather suddenly, mercury has become recognized as a major health problem in Japan, Sweden, and all parts of the United States. Many inorganic and organic compounds of mercury arc soluble and can be widely dispersed in natural waters. Mercury is toxic. During prolonged exposure to mercury compounds, even at low concentration, mercury accumulates progressively in the nervous system, impairs nervous function, and eventually causes death. The phrase "mad as a hatter" was derived in the nineteenth century from the behavior of hat makers who were in the habit of holding felt in their mouths while fashioning it, and were thus poisoned by mercury compounds used to treat the felt. Even low mercury levels in mothers can lead to abnormalities in their babies.

Mercury enters the environment from many sources. In the past 20 years its use has increased greatly in industry, where it is used, for example, as a catalyst in the production of plastics, and as a fungicide in pulp mills. Untreated effluents from these industries can raise the concentration of dissolved mercury compounds in the water manyfold. Metallic mercury is used for electrodes in production of chlorine and sodium hydroxide, and much of this metal has been discarded into the Great Lakes. In Lake Erie and associated waters, the fish contain so much mercury (1.3 ppm; the legal limit is 0.5) that sale of fish has been banned, and fishing is prohibited in Lake St. Clair.

In agriculture, organic compounds of mercury are used on seeds as fungicides. Eating such seeds has led to the death of many seed-eating birds and the accidental death of children. Some of the mercury is absorbed by the plants that grow from the seed, increasing the mercury content of food. Some of the remainder is leached from the soil into rivers and lakes. This has been a major problem in Sweden, where mercury is still increasing in freshwaters by leaching from the soil, even though agricultural use of mercury was restricted in 1966.

In lakes, various processes result in the accumulation of mercury in animals. One is the usual food chain effect. Some is lost to the sediments in the form of dead organisms, but part of the sedimented material is taken up by invertebrate scavengers and part is released by bacterial action. Bacteria can produce methylmercury, even from metallic mercury; it is soluble and is absorbed directly by fish.

Lead is another metal that is being spread around the landscape, including lakes and streams.[9] Lead is liberated not only by industries, but in the exhaust of automobiles and boats that use leaded gasoline. The vegetation close to major highways has significantly more lead than that a few hundred feet away. Lead deposited on roadways can easily be washed into the nearest water courses by rain. Symptoms of lead poisoning include depression and impaired mental function. While the levels of lead in food animals have not been as high as that of some other metals, lead seems to be contributing one more thing to the burden of toxic substances that we are carrying around in us, each contributing proportionately to the damage of our mental and physical functions.

A very prevalent product of industry is waste oil. Oil spilled over a lake or stream can damage plants and animals and interfere with swimming and drinking. Major oil spill accidents are not the only source of oil problems on lakes. Most of the oil added to the fuel of outboard motors is not burned and contributes to the oil slicks that are becoming prominent on some recreational lakes. Disposal of waste oil is difficult, but putting it down the sewer is a very poor solution. The oil can be broken down by microorganisms, but it takes time, and in the meantime, considerable damage can result.

Oil spills from wells and tankers are mainly a marine problem, but the large lakes are being increasingly affected. Undesirable amounts of oil are liberated even in routine shipping and transfer operations, not just as a result of major accidents. One ordinarily does not think of rivers as being fire hazards, but the Cuyahoga River in Ohio is now famous for an occasion on which a spill of flammable material caught fire and damaged bridges.

*Thermal Pollution*

Thermal pollution simply means the addition of hot water to a stream or lake.[10-13] Stream and nuclear power plants need water for cooling, especially the latter, which produce 60 percent more heat per unit of electricity than coal plants. The water is usually taken from a stream or lake, passed through the cooling system, and returned at a temperature higher by 5° or 10° C. Manufacturing industry used over 9000 billion gallons of cooling water in 1964, and electrical generating plants used almost 42,000 billion gallons. With the projected increase in nuclear power, the requirements for cooling water are growing greatly, and in heavily industrial regions, all the available water could be used for cooling. The cost of cooling increases with the degree of cooling. The difference in construction cost between permitting a $10°F$ increase in the temperature of cooling water or $20°F$ increase in 514 steam plants operating in 1965 would be 132 million dollars.[8]

There is much controversy about the extent of damage caused by thermal pollution. Some animals are killed outright by the hottest water, but with mixing, relatively little water is above lethal temperature. That does not mean it is harmless. It has been suggested, for instance, that spread of a bacterial disease of salmon in the Columbia River (columnaris disease) is facilitated by a slight elevation in temperature. Thus there is the possibility of an interaction of factors, so that a degree of heating, not in itself damaging, may facilitate a damaging condition caused by something else.

On the other hand, fish may congregate near a warm water outfall, and in doing so may be able to grow better during cold weather. This matter is still under study and the situation is not clear. Some people are optimistic that the hot water can be used beneficially, either industrially or to increase productivity of useful fish. However, the temperature adaptations of animals are results of a long evolutionary history. It is unlikely that a major change in environmental conditions can be met without affecting the population. Tropical rivers and hot springs have existed for a long time and populations have adapted to their thermal regime. Doubtless life can continue in heated rivers. The question is whether the resulting changes will be acceptable. The possibility exists that different genotypes will be selected in the newly warmed places, and we may soon be seeing interesting experiments in natural selection.

## Is Lake Erie Dead?

Lake Erie has become the focus of a great deal of attention. Without question it is a very badly polluted lake, receiving all of the kinds of wastes discussed above, and probably more beside.[4] It has been heavily eutrophied, and the productivity increased despite the inflow of toxic wastes. It appears that toxic damage is somewhat localized, and for hydrological reasons, the greatest deterioration is limited to shallow inshore waters. The open part of the lake continues to be inhabited by plankton, bottom fauna, and several species of fish. The species that were most desirable a few decades ago, such as the lake trout and sauger, are no longer present, but Lake Erie produces about 50 million pounds of fish per year, which is about half the entire production of the Great Lakes.[6] The fishery in the mid-1960s was dominated by yellow perch, smelt, and sheepshead. That pollution has been an important influence in Lake Erie is suggested by the fact that some species of fish disappeared from the more polluted western end earlier than from the eastern end.

We should ask what is the condition of a lake that can properly be described as "dead." Surely, a dead lake would be one sterile, devoid of life. It seems anomalous to call a lake "dead" when it is swarming with living things. This does not mean that the lake is in good condition, but it is anything but dead. To call Lake Erie "dead" carries certain implications that confuse one's thinking about how to improve it. After all, death is irreversible, but eutrophication is not. The sight of dead fish washed up on the shore of a lake should not mislead anybody. One can't have dead fish without having live ones first. Of course, this is not to say that a massive die-off is all right.

Lake Erie has been a naturally productive lake during all of recorded history. It was famous in the early part of this century for producing great swarms of mayflies that flew all over, became crushed on street car tracks and made a nuisance by their abundance in the wrong place. These animals spend most of their life as immature aquatic stages in the lake and the vast yield to the air of adults was a sign of the great productivity of the lake. The mayflies no longer swarm because they cannot tolerate the low-oxygen conditions that now exist, but the bottom of the lake supports many sludge worms (*Tubifex*) and other invertebrates.

Lake Erie is but one of the Great Lakes, all of which are generating some concern. Lake Erie is the smallest in volume and the most heavily polluted, so it has deteriorated the most, but all show some signs of effect. There has been a massive decrease in the abundance of desirable species of fish, but not all of the decreases can be attributed to pollution. Some have resulted from the introduction of predatory, nongame fish when the Erie and Welland Canals opened and some have been the result of overfishing. For example, the decline of the lake trout in Lake Michigan by 1953 was importantly influenced by predation by the sea lamprey.[15,16]

Some accounts of eutrophication have mentioned "the point of no return," suggesting that a lake could be damaged so much that it could not recover, no matter what remedial efforts were made. In particular, some people have expressed fear that Lake Erie is beyond repair. I am convinced that it is not. I think that limitation of the input of sewage phosphorus could make a large and noticeable improvement in its condition. The question has been raised whether considerable improvement in lakes can be made by eliminating the use of detergents with phosphate. Whether this, rather than removal of phosphate from effluent, would have enough effect on Lake Erie is difficult to judge. It would seem reasonable to do a certain amount of experimentation on a large scale. In any case, to reduce the loading of concentrated phosphorus on lakes makes sense. Phosphate limitation would not be enough by itself to restore Lake Erie to a fully satisfactory condition. Two other operations would be required to get the lake back to something like its original condition: reduction of the input of concentrated toxic industrial wastes and cleaning up of the junk that has been permitted to accumulate in bays, inlets, and shallows.

While recovery might be slow in coming after a lake is relieved of its burden of pollution, very few situations exist in which improvement could not be expected. Even Lake Erie could be restored to its original mayfly-rich condition. For a lake really to be "killed" would require either that it receive so much toxic waste that nothing could live or that it be filled in to the point where it no longer existed as a lake.

The real question is not whether or not a lake is "dead," but what is the fate of dissolved nutrients and toxic materials. Many factors, such as the rate of replenishment of the lake's water and the amount of nutrients retained in the sediments must be taken into account. To calculate the magnitude of the effect of dissolved materials very exactly in many cases is beyond our present abilities. To make the attempt on some well-selected cases would increase our understanding.

## Air Pollution and Water Pollution

Rain is not simply distilled water. It brings down with it particles and dissolved materials that have been entrapped or absorbed from the air. One of the outstanding problems generated by air pollutants dissolved in rain is caused by sulfur dioxide produced by burning of fuel oil that is rich in sulfur. Sulfur dioxide dissolved in water becomes oxidized to form sulfuric acid; over 5 milligrams per liter of sulfur can be found in rain in industrial regions.[4] In regions of heavy use of sulfurous fuels, the rain can be distinctly acid, with a pH value less than 4.0. This has been especially well studied in Europe where, since 1955, the rain has shown a distinct tendency to become more acid, with values higher than pH 6.0 becoming rare, and values less than 5 becoming prevalent. While the rain is relatively dilute sulfuric acid, it can have pronounced

| Regions | Millions of 1968 Dollars | | |
|---|---|---|---|
| | Total plant required | value of plant in place | Additional investment required |
| North Atlantic | 814.0 | 575.5 | 238.5 |
| Southeast | 276.1 | 208.0 | 68.1 |
| Great Lakes | 973.4 | 784.2 | 189.2 |
| Ohio | 658.5 | 526.7 | 131.8 |
| Tennessee | 80.4 | 47.8 | 32.6 |
| Upper Mississippi | 205.1 | 149.9 | 55.2 |
| Lower Mississippi | 230.1 | 144.8 | 85.3 |
| Missouri | 88.2 | 64.2 | 24.0 |
| Arkansas-White-Red | 49.2 | 33.0 | 16.2 |
| Western Gulf | 286.8 | 168.9 | 117.9 |
| Colorado/Great | 25.9 | 17.0 | 8.9 |
| Pacific Northwest[a] | 167.6 | 121.1 | 46.5 |
| California[b] | 143.3 | 105.6 | 37.7 |
| Total | 3998.6 | 2946.7 | 1051.9 |

WASTE TREATMENT REQUIREMENTS. Regional distribution of waste treatment requirements, 1968. Source: reference 8.

[a]Includes Alaska.

[b]Includes Hawaii.

effects, especially when it forms the water of streams and lakes in regions where, for geological reasons, there is little calcium bicarbonate to neutralize the acid; that is, where the natural waters have little buffering capacity.

The pH of the lakes of southeastern Sweden has been decreasing over the past two decades, and in recent years pH values as low as 3.8 have been observed. The average change has been 0.4 pH unit in the past 20 years. It is no mere coincidence that unusual numbers of dead salmonid fish are now seen in these lakes, and some lakes have become unsuitable for fishing.

Further damage may arise from leaching of calcium from the soil by acid rain, leading to poor growth of trees and crops.

This problem crosses national boundaries; much of the sulfuric acid falling in Sweden originated in the industrial midlands of England.

While the acidified rain does much damage by corroding metals, not the least damage being done is the dissolution of marble and limestone buildings and works of art. The effect has been especially serious in Venice. This city, an art museum in itself, has been irrevocably damaged by the erosion of statues and buildings. Some of the most important ties with our artistic past no longer exist in recognizable form.[17]

*Magnitude of the Clean-Up*

It is obvious that we have many problems, but we understand enough to be able to deal with them very effectively. Before starting, it is necessary to find out how big the problems are, for much of the difficulty is financial: How much are people willing to spend, once they clearly see the consequences of failing to clean up?

It has been estimated that of the total population of the United States, as much as 40 percent has less than adequate municipal treatment of domestic sewage or none at all. To develop adequate facilities would require roughly 8 billion dollars for capital costs alone, and this would provide no more than secondary treatment, thus not really solving the eutrophication problem in much of the country.

Industrial wastes in 1964 amounted to 13,100 billion gallons containing 18,000 million pounds of suspended solids, as compared to 5300 billion gallons of domestic sewage containing 8,800 million pounds of solids.[8] Studies of the problem show that all parts of the country need attention (Table II) and that a wide variety of industries is involved (Table III).

One estimate of the total cost of clean water over the next 5 years, made by a Senate Committee, is $100 billion. But in 1969 only $214 MIL-

| Industry | Annual investment to reduce existing requirement | Total investment to reduce waste treatment requirements and meet growth needs | | | | |
|---|---|---|---|---|---|---|
| | | 1969 | 1970 | 1971 | 1972 | 1973 |
| Food and kindred products | 43.9 | 63.2 | 65.4 | 69.9 | 70.0 | 69.9 |
| Meat products | 7.0 | 10.1 | 11.2 | 11.2 | 11.7 | 11.6 |
| Dairy products | 4.6 | 5.1 | 5.7 | 5.5 | 5.5 | 5.5 |
| Canned and frozen foods | 6.7 | 11.4 | 12.4 | 12.6 | 12.9 | 13.0 |
| Sugar refining | 13.5 | 19.3 | 18.4 | 22.6 | 21.4 | 21.5 |
| All other | 12.1 | 17.3 | 17.7 | 18.0 | 18.5 | 18.3 |
| Textile mill products | 5.3 | 9.8 | 10.9 | 11.1 | 11.0 | 11.6 |
| Paper and allied products | 15.1 | 19.1 | 25.5 | 26.0 | 26.4 | 27.0 |
| Chemical and allied products | 56.0 | 75.7 | 76.9 | 77.7 | 79.4 | 77.9 |
| Petroleum and coal | 15.4 | 15.4 | 18.1 | 30.5 | 31.7 | 32.1 |
| Rubber and plastics, n.e.c. | 6.2 | 7.0 | 7.9 | 7.1 | 7.2 | 7.1 |
| Primary metals | 29.9 | 83.6 | 91.3 | 93.3 | 96.2 | 97.8 |
| Blast furnaces and steel mills | 19.6 | 52.4 | 59.1 | 60.1 | 63.0 | 63.0 |
| All other | 10.3 | 31.2 | 32.2 | 33.2 | 34.2 | 34.8 |
| Machinery | 5.0 | 6.9 | 6.9 | 7.1 | 7.1 | 7.3 |
| Electrical machinery | 1.7 | 3.6 | 3.8 | 3.8 | 4.0 | 4.1 |
| Transportation equipment | 8.3 | 11.7 | 11.9 | 12.2 | 12.1 | 12.3 |
| All other manufacturing | 23.5 | 32.3 | 32.6 | 33.0 | 33.5 | 33.8 |
| All manufactures | 210.3 | 328.3 | 351.6 | 371.7 | 378.6 | 380.9 |

COST OF INDUSTRIAL WASTE TREATMENT IMPROVEMENT. Annual investment required to reduce the existing industrial waste treatment deficiency in 5 years, in millions of 1968 dollars. Source: reference 8.

LION was actually appropriated for this purpose, and for 1970 the figure was $800 million. Thus, to put our waters in a clean condition would cost about as much as the Vietnam war.

The rate of cleaning up is far below the rate of increase of pollution. For an effective clean-up, it will be necessary to make some major readjustments in national priorities. Since production of pollutional effects is linked to population, it is hard to see how in the long run environmental problems can be controlled without population control. Some improvements can be made by reducing per capita quantities of pollutants, but the possibilities are limited, both by limitations of the physical principles involved and by the expectations people have for the requirements of a satisfactory life.

## References

1. **Murray, C. R.** 1968. Estimated use of water in the United States, 1965. *U. S. Geol. Survey, Circular 556.*

2. **Hynes, H. B. N.** 1963. *The Biology of Polluted Waters.* Liverpool University Press, Liverpool, England, 202 pp.

3. **Mackenthun, K. M.** 1969. *The Practice of Water Pollution Biology.* Federal Water Pollution Control Administration, U. S. Govt. Printing Office, 281 pp.

4. **American Chemical Society.** 1969. *Cleaning Our Environment. The Chemical Basis for Action,* American Chemical Society, Washington, D. C., 249 pp.

5. **Edmondson, W. T.** 1968. Water quality management and lake eutrophication: The Lake Washington case. In *Water Resources Management and Public Policy.* University of Washington Press, Seattle, Washington.

6. **National Academy of Sciences.** 1969. *Eutrophication: Causes, Consequences, Correctives.* National Academy of Science — National Research Council, Washington, D. C.

7. **Edmondson, W. T.** 1970. Phosphorus, nitrogen and algae in Lake Washington after diversion of sewage. *Science 169:* 690-691.

8. **Federal Water Pollution Control Administration.** 1968. *The Cost of Clean Water,* 4 vols.

9. **Patterson, C. C.** 1965. Contaminated and natural lead environments of man. *Arch. Environ. Health. 11:* 344-360.

10. **Merriman, D.** 1970. The calefaction of a river. *Sci. Amer. 222 (5):* 42-52.

11. **Clark, J. R.** 1969. Thermal pollution and aquatic life. *Sci. Amer. 220 (3):* 18-27.

12. **Krenkel, P. F., and Parker, F. L.** 1969. *Biological Aspects of Thermal Pollution.* Vanderbilt University Press, Nashville, Tennessee, 407 pp.

13. **Cairns, J.** 1968. We're in hot water. *Scientist and Citizen 10:* 187-198.

14. **League of Women Voters.** 1966. *Lake Erie. Requiem or reprieve?* Lake Erie Basin Committee, Cleveland, Ohio, 50 pp.

15. **Smith, S. H.** 1968. Species succession and fishery exploitation in the Great Lakes. *J. Fish. Res. Bd. Canada 25:* 667-693.

16. **Commoner, B.** 1968. Lake Erie, aging or ill? *Scientist and Citizen 10:* 254-265.

17. **Sargeant, W.** 1968. The crumbling stones of Venice. *The New Yorker Magazine, Nov. 18.*

18. For more details, see references 5, 6 and 7. The work on Lake Washington reported here from 1959 to present has been supported by the National Science Foundation; that in 1957-58 by the National Institute of Health.

## Further Reading

**League of Women Voters.** 1966. Education Fund. *The Big Water Fight.* Stephen Greene Press, Brattleboro, Vermont, 246 pp.

**National Academy of Sciences.** 1966. *Waste Management and Control.* National Academy of Sciences — National Research Council Publication 1400, Washington, D. C., 257 pp.

**President's Science Advisory Committee. Environmental Pollution Panel.** 1965. Restoring the quality of our environment. U. S. Govt. Printing Office, Washington, D. C. 316 pp.

Stewart, R. K., Ingram, W. M., and Mackenthun, K. M. 1966. *Water Pollution Control. Waste Treatment and Water Treatment.* Selected biological references on fresh and marine waters. Federal Water Pollution Control Administration, Washington, D. C., 126 pp.

White, G. F. 1969. *Strategies of American Water Management.* University of Michigan Press, Ann Arbor, Michigan, 155 pp.

Environment. Formerly known as *Scientist and Citizen,* this journal has carried informative articles on many of the topics covered in this chapter.

Environmental Quality. 1970. The first annual report of the Council on Environmental Quality, together with the President's message to Congress. U. S. Government Printing Office.

# 11　Ocean Pollution

Ferren MacIntyre and R. W. Holmes

The ocean impresses both poet and philosopher with the same qualities: bottomless, unutterably vast, and timeless. And so it has been for some 3.5 billion years.

Evocative as this view of the ocean may be, it is largely irrelevant today. We will speak below of oceanic circulation processes that require 1000 years — but if the rate of man's population growth stops increasing and remains at its present yearly 2.1 percent (Chapter 2), in 1000 years there will be only 1 cubic meter of water per person, including the 60 kg in his body. On ther-

FERREN MACINTYRE is a research associate at the Marine Science Institute of the University of California, Santa Barbara. Born in 1930, he took his undergraduate degree at the University of California, Riverside, and his doctorate (in physical chemistry) at the Massachusetts Institute of Technology in 1965. The following year he joined Scripps Institute of Oceanography as an Assistant Professor, a position he held until his present appointment in 1969. Before turning chemist, he worked for eight years as a lumberman, machinist, machine designer and loftsman. His research speciality is the upper layers of the ocean, particularly the interchange of chemicals between sea and air.

R. W. HOLMES is Director of the Marine Science Institute at the University of California, Santa Barbara. Holmes did his undergraduate work at Haverford College and graduate work at Yale University, the Scripps Institute of Oceanography, and received his doctorate from the University of Oslo, Norway. His main interests are the ecology of phytoplankton and the interactions of plants with their physical and chemical environment.

modynamic grounds this represents about the maximum population that the earth can support, but it should be clear that the ocean as we know it will long since have vanished into the plumbing of the world's single city. Any discussion of ocean pollution in which oceanic mixing processes are important must of necessity consider what use man hopes to make of the ocean in the future: Do we want waves and beaches and pelicans, or do we want plumbing?

The conception of the ocean as bottomless is pure romance. The ratio of depth to area, 4 km/361 x $10^6$ km, or better, depth to "width," 4/19,000, is almost exactly that of a sheet of onionskin paper. The ocean is limited with respect to both its capacity to act as a sink for wastes and as a producer of food and other resources. These two aspects, pollution and production, are related. Because different parts of, and processes in, the system interact, we must learn to think in terms of whole systems. This is no easy task.

For instance, to discuss the mere DISTRIBUTION of a marine pollutant requires a knowledge of meteorology, soil chemistry, physicochemical processes, physical oceanography, marine biology, ecology, and so on. Figure 1 shows in a schematic way some of these interactions.

The effects of pollution are equally complex and subtle. Only the blatant effects make headlines: rivers foaming with suds or bursting into flames, killer smogs, extermination of species, oil spills and sewage on tourist beaches, fish catches condemned because of biocides or radioactivity. Actually we may not even be aware of the more important effects. Even though we have begun to understand some of the "20-year problems" related to biocides, we have not the slightest clue to the "100-year problems" or the long-range effects that will accrue from some of our present practices.

From our meager understanding of terrestrial systems we have gathered that diversity is a hall-mark of a "good" ecosystem, that is, diverse ecosystems tend to be stable (Chapter 1). On the other hand, systems with small diversity (like commercial oyster beds) are subject to catastrophic collapse if environmental conditions move outside of the tolerance range of the existing monopolists, or if an overly successful predator or parasite appears. Also, it sometimes happens that the higher members of a food chain are not dependent upon the mere productivity of the low members in terms of the amount of biomass produced, but depend upon having cer-

**1** DISTRIBUTION OF A MARINE POLLUTANT. Some of the routes and processes which determine the fate and distribution of a pollutant after man is through with it. Source: B.H. Ketchum, Man's resources in the marine environment, *Pollution and Marine Ecology* (T.A. Olsen and F.J. Burgess, eds.), pp. 1-11. Interscience, New York, 1967.

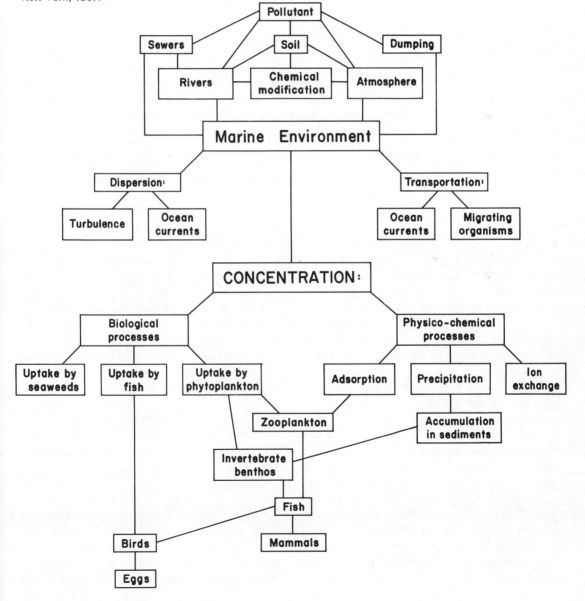

tain prey species available at certain times in their development. Replacing a diverse algal system with a faster growing monoculture will have repercussions throughout the food chain and will not necessarily increase the number of top predators.

Figure 2 shows how diversity drops when pollution hits: to use an analogy, it is as though the ecosystem turned off much of its biochemistry and put all of its energy into those defensive enzymes (organisms) which can consume the infecting agent and return the system to normal. The simplification of the ecosystem is an adaptive way of reacting to stress. The "outbreak" of the worm *Capitella capitata* after an oil spill at Falmouth is a typical example.[2] The worm can live where almost nothing else grows.

Part of the trouble is that when an ecologist says "stable," he means constancy over periods of decades or centuries, and NONE of man's alterations meet this requirement. A power plant may discharge waste heat for a decade, allowing a warm-water ecosystem to begin to establish itself as viable migrants drift into the area and settle. Then comes a week of maintenance during which the boilers are shut down. No heat output: no warm-water species survive. The developing ecosystem has been set back to zero time.

So too with nutrient enrichment: Even if an effluent happens to be poison-free, the fluctuations in man's sewage systems are so very much faster (in terms of outfall extensions, sewage treatment changes, and so on) than the characteristic time of ecosystem establishment, that the systems never progress beyond the first stages. The disturbances we create — frequently in estuaries — are like wounds in an organism. In time they MIGHT heal themselves and the ecosystem might be richer, more diverse, more productive, and more interesting than before. But the first colonizing organisms into such a disturbed environment are an emergency system, like a scab over a wound. Functional, not beautiful, and above all, not permanent, on Nature's time scale. But because the scab doesn't get pretty in a month, we get impatient and pick at it with a bulldozer — when we should call the doctor and design a system that will work with Nature and speed the healing.[3]

In order to put pollution in the ocean into perspective, the next few sections will examine the relevant characteristics of the oceans.

*Food Resources of the Sea*

Until recently there was a tendency to believe that the fishery resources of the sea were vastly underexploited; that foodstuffs from the sea could be expected to become a very important source of protein and energy for the world's expanding population. There is now evidence that our former optimism must be tempered and, furthermore, that food production of the sea can be reduced by man-made alterations of the marine environment. The subject of food production is dealt with in Chapters 3 and 8, which contain appropriate references. Here we will simply summarize the salient points.

Several recent estimates of the potential sustainable world fishery yield are rather similar and range between 100 and 200 million metric tons of fish that could be harvested on a maximum sustainable yield a few decades from now. This is roughly 2-4 times our present world harvest of about 55 million metric tons. The lower part of the range seems to be the most likely — much depends on imponderables such as costs, international cooperation, and the development of competitive protein products. If catches of the order of 100-150 million metric tons per year are realized during the next three decades, the contribution of this added protein source to world protein needs will not be great and will be negated entirely if there is a rise in the rate of world population growth during this period. Mariculture offers an opportunity to increase protein yields from the sea, but as we will see below, this potential is subject to the manner in which coastal zone use is allocated.

Although the coastal zone (depths less than 200 meters) makes up only about 10 percent of the surface area of the sea, by far the great majority of our ocean fish harvest comes from this area. Even when more fish are taken from upwelling zones (still near the coast, Chapter 8) in the future, more than half of the harvest probably will still come from inshore waters, and most of the FOOD fish will come from there. The open sea, which covers nearly 3/4 of the earth's

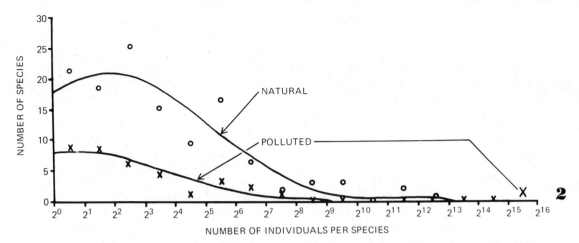

DIATOM COMMUNITIES IN NATURAL AND POL-LUTED WATERS. Pollution may increase "productivity" as measured by total biomass, but it greatly reduces diversity, which is the hallmark of a healthy ecosystem. (Source: R. Patrick, M.H. Hohn, and J.H. Wallace, A new method for determining the pattern of diatom flora, *Notulae Naturae 359* Acad. Nat. Sci. Phila., 1954).

surface and represents about 90 percent of the area of the sea surface, is virtually a desert. It contributes a negligible fraction of the world's fish catch and has little potential for producing more in the future.

The exploitation of our marine fisheries is essentially a hunting endeavor. Since the productivity of the land has been increased enormously by shifting from a hunting to a managed husbandry type of usage, can the effective productivity of the sea be increased by aquaculture? The answer to this, based on present-day and anticipated advancements, is yes, providing the potential marine aquaculture "fields" can be protected from pollution and other deleterious influences, and providing the necessary legal, political, economic, and sociological changes in man's attitudes can be effected. However, to be realistic, the quantitative significance of this added protein to the total world production will not be great in the immediate future unless some form of world population control can be established.

Pasture lands producing cattle yield between 6 and 305 kilograms/hectare/year (kg/ha/yr) (5-250 pounds per acre per year), groundfish on the continental shelf produce 25-60 kg/ha/yr, while the exceedingly productive anchoveta

fishery in the upwelling waters off Peru yields about 375 kg/ha/yr (Chapter 8). Inshore mariculture can yield more than groundfish and cattle, especially if animals are used that feed directly on the phytoplankton. Some yields of mollusks, shrimps, and herbivorous fish are shown in Table I. Some very much higher yields, up to several hundred thousand kilograms per hectare per year, have been obtained in small areas by a variety of methods such as raft-culture of oysters, stocking and feeding fish, keeping fish in running water and adding food or nutrients. However, these figures cannot be applied to an

| Location | Species | Kg/ha/yr | Tons/acre/yr |
|---|---|---|---|
| U.S. | Oysters (national avg.) | 9 | 0.004 |
| U.S. | Oysters (best yields) | 5,000 | 2.00 |
| France | Flat oyster (national avg.) | 400 | 0.16 |
| France | Portugese oyster (natl. avg.) | 935 | 0.37 |
| Australia | Oysters (national avg.) | 150 | 0.06 |
| Australia | Oysters (best yields) | 540 | 2.20 |
| Malaya | Cockles | 12,500 | 5.00 |
| France | Mussels | 2,500 | 1.00 |
| Singapore | Shrimp | 1,250 | 0.50 |

AQUACULTURAL YIELDS. Summary of aquacultural yields. Units in fresh weight, shells of mollusks excluded. Source: J.E. Bardach and J.H. Ryther, *The Status and Potential of Aquaculture, Particularly Fish Culture,* Vol. 2, Parts I and III, Clearinghouse for Federal Scientific and Technical Information, U.S. Department of Commerce, Springfield, Virginia, 1968, pp. 1-225.

I

extensive area because such yields depend upon the animals' getting nutrients from a "catchment area" much larger than the space they occupy. An analogous situation would be the enormous yields derived from chicken ranches, where the maximum is set by how closely the animals can be packed. Over any extensive area, without fertilization and so on, the maximum yield would be not more than 10 or 20 percent of the primary production and is likely to be some hundreds of kilograms per hectare per year.

We noted above how important the coastal waters were for fishing, and this is even more the case for mariculture, which requires inshore and rather sheltered waters. Although mariculture has been employed at least since Roman times, the practice as compared with agriculture is still primitive. Modern genetic practices have not been utilized to improve yields, sophisticated predator and disease control techniques are not presently employed, and many available materials and engineering practices remain to be utilized. In spite of the potential of mariculture there are many constraints which prevent or hinder its expansion in both highly industrialized nations as well as in the developing nations. Except in Japan, the interest in developing maricultural industries in technologically advanced countries is not great. This is due in part to a lack of sufficient demand for seafoods other than luxury items such as lobster, shrimp, mussels, and oysters, because abundant and cheaper sources of protein are presently available from land. There are additional problems associated with the use of the coastal zone by industry. Traditionally fishery resources have been regarded as common property and coastal waters as belonging in the public domain. Thus obtaining rights to coastal waters for mariculture is hampered by both legal precedent and public resistance, and at the same time this use is in competition with other use interests such as recreation, power generation, oil production, and waste disposal. To date, in most developed nations the potential value of coastal waters for food production has been traded off by government and society for more immediate economic gain. In the developing nations, where the need for a sustainable yield of protein is greatest, legal, social, and economic barriers are

in part replaced by other formidable barriers — lack of equipment and technological sophistication, capital, trained personnel, and so on. Even with all of these barriers removed the problems of culturing are by no means solved and a great amount of study will be required to improve techniques and to increase the diversity of organisms available for culture.

At present only about 3-5 percent of the world's food production is derived from the sea. If, as seems unlikely, this production could be doubled by mariculture in the next decade the impact of this added supply would not be great. Famine might be alleviated in certain regions by mariculture using present techniques, but world hunger could not be erased by such limited gains.

Although the potential of mariculture is considerable, in the face of expanding world population and the attendant demands of society upon the coastal zone for purposes other than food production, it is difficult to see how mariculture can contribute significantly to world food production unless there is a marked fundamental change in human attitudes and values.

*Estuaries as Nurseries*

The importance of estuaries to some marine fisheries can be indirectly gathered from the fact that 85 percent of the total U.S. fisheries catch in 1962 was of estuary-dependent species.[4] This is a very high percentage compared with worldwide figures. Some 200 species of fish have been found in Chesapeake Bay and 300 from Indian Ocean estuaries. Similarly, the 1961 fish catch in the Gulf of Mexico showed the following distribution[4]:

| | |
|---|---|
| Freshwater fish | 9.3 million pounds |
| Saltwater fish | 24.4 million pounds |
| Estuarine fish | 1332.2 million pounds |

One reason for this remarkable dependence upon estuaries seems to be that bony fish evolved in fresh water, and their young have neither salt-secreting cells nor mechanisms to protect themselves against the high osmotic pressure of seawater. In other cases, such as some shrimp, prawns, and crabs, the young are spawned at sea but the adolescent stages require, and migrate to, fresh water.

Estuaries, enriched by the runoff of nutrients from land, are at least as productive on an area basis as those rare offshore areas where upwelling deep waters bring nutrients to the surface. Other reasons for the utility of estuaries as nurseries may be the greater diversity of habitats because of salinity and temperature gradients, because the bottom is in the photic zone and can support plant growth, and because nutrients cycle quickly. Freedom from large predators is also important, as is the optimization of the estuarine ecosystem by a form of time-sharing, in which the larvae of different species use the food resources at different times and so do not compete.[4] In addition to estuarine-dependent fish, there are species that come into shallow coastal waters to spawn. So the entire inshore and estuarine zone is very important in the ocean harvest. It is also within easy reach of land-based pollution.

*Atmospheric Circulation*

As any oceanographer will tell you, the ocean is a two-phase system whose vapor phase is greatly diluted with air. The water vapor of the gaseous ocean extends to at least 30 km (nacreous clouds appear at this height[5]), indicating that most, if not all, of the atmosphere is in active exchange with the sea, for if water vapor exchanges, so will all other constituents, including pollutants. In some cases the main effect of this exchange is to clean the atmosphere (dust, $CO_2$, $SO_4$), in others, to dirty the ocean (lead, mercury, DDT).

Both atmosphere and ocean can be divided into a surface (troposphere) and bulk (stratosphere) circulation. In the atmospheric stratosphere zonal, or east-west circulation, is fast, requiring a week or 10 days to circle the earth.[6] The meridional, or north-south, circulation is much slower because it depends upon large-scale eddy diffusion, or mixing by the turbulence associated with weather fronts. Exchange between stratosphere and troposphere occurs intermittently rather than continuously, chiefly in high latitudes in winter. Data from volcanic dust and radioactive bomb debris[5] agree in suggesting that 2 to 3 years are required for certain materials injected into the stratosphere to reach the ocean.

Meridional circulation is driven by the need to move heat from the equator to the poles, and understandably there is little reason for motion ACROSS the equator. Thus, both in stratosphere and troposphere, as well as in the wind-driven ocean surface currents, there is a minimum of mixing across the equator. Pollutants injected into the atmosphere of one hemisphere tend to remain in it: If they are found to have crossed the equator one must postulate more exotic transport mechanisms.

Both vertical and horizontal mixing are rapid within the troposphere (the atmosphere up to about 20 km). For short-range problems the pollutant concentration $C$ (measured in grams/m$^3$) at a distance $d$ (km) downwind of a city of $m$ million inhabitants is given by[7]

$$C = K \times 10^4 \ m/d^2$$

where $K$ is a number which varies somewhat with the pollutant, but may be taken as 5 for a first guess. This equation indicates that one must be 100 km away from a city of 2 million people before the concentration of such things as particulates or sulfate drops to twice the normal unpolluted value. Oceanographic vessels at sea have been able to detect New York by its carbon dioxide some 200 km offshore, and Los Angeles by its carbon monoxide at a distance of 300 km.

*Ocean Circulation*

The "troposphere" of the ocean consists of the sun-warmed, wind-stirred, surface-mixed layer, no more than 200 meters deep, and the thermocline, or region of sharp temperature change, which may extend to 600-1000 meters. Slight differences in temperature or salinity produce density differences which result in stable stratification in the sea, and most motions in the sea occur along such density layers. As one example, radioactive debris from an underwater bomb test rapidly spread out to form a disk 1 meter thick but 100 km in diameter.[8]

The earth's rotation causes the topmost surface water to move 30° to the right of the wind in the Northern Hemisphere and 30° to the left in the Southern Hemisphere. However, because

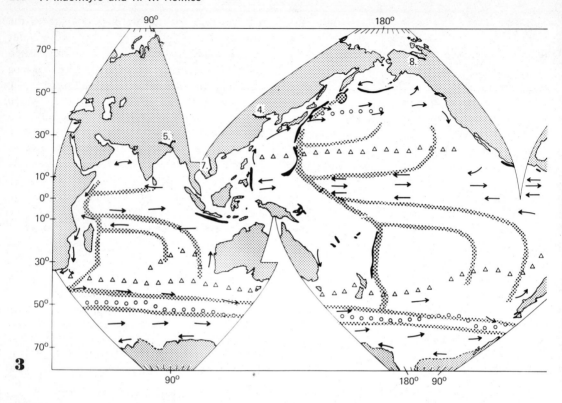

**3**

WORLD OCEAN MAP. World ocean showing surface currents, deep currents, locales of water mass formation, trenches, and major river mouths. For both surface currents and deep currents the world ocean can be thought of as the Antarctic circumpolar system plus three large enclosed bays. The deep currents along the western edges of the oceans are narrow as shown, but the "hooks" extending into the center of the ocean basins represent the sense of motion of an oceanwide slow flow. The rivers are numbered in order of decreasing water volume, since relative pollution input is not readily available. If it were, the ordering would be quite different, with the small rivers (not shown) of Europe and North America dominating.

of frictional coupling between the wind-driven surface and the deeper water, the underlying water moves in a direction even further from the wind, and the NET transport above the thermocline is nearly at right angles to the wind direction. Thus, maps of surface currents (Figure 3) are misleading: the detailed motion of the South Equatorial Current in the Pacific (which, confusingly, lies exactly on the geographic equator, but south of the "climatic equator") is by no means the linear motion suggested. Instead, surface water north of the equator moves southwest. Along the equator itself is a zone of upwelling, where subsurface water from 1-200 meter depth is pulled to the surface. At the edges of the current, this water sinks again and returns toward the equator, moving southwest in the Northern Hemisphere and northwest in the Southern Hemisphere. The overall picture is a pair of corkscrew like motions, back to back.

With this warning, Figure 3 shows the general pattern of surface currents. Note the well-known westward intensification of oceanic circulation — again a phenomenon of the rotating earth — which produces the familiar Gulf Stream and its homologs at the western boundaries of each ocean.

Typical velocities for surface currents are 1 cm/sec over the bulk of the ocean, 100 cm/sec in the cores of the boundary currents.

A WATER MASS is a volume of water with a common origin at which it acquired the particular physical and chemical properties which set it apart from other water masses. Classical oceanographers had only the two probes, temperature

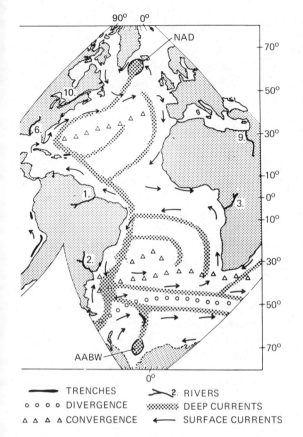

90°  0°

NAD

70°

50°

10

30°

6.

9.

10°

1.

0°

3.

10°

2.

30°

50°

AABW

70°

0°

━━━ TRENCHES     ⌒⌒ RIVERS
o o o o DIVERGENCE     ▒▒▒▒ DEEP CURRENTS
△ △ △ △ CONVERGENCE     ⟵ SURFACE CURRENTS

Antarctica in the wildest windiest part of the world and is pretty well stirred down to about 200 meters, but the deeper portions have been out of touch with the atmosphere for a long time. Weddell Shelf water is formed by excluding salt during the freezing of sea ice, and drips in cold salty fingers from the bottom of the ice to the shallow floor of the Weddell Sea. Thus, neither of the "parents" of Antarctic Bottom water is readily accessible to the atmosphere.

The other water mass formed at depth is the largest body of water in the ocean: the Indian and Pacific Common water, which is made by mixing 10 parts of old Antarctic Bottom water, 3 parts of Antarctic Intermediate, and 4 parts of old North Atlantic Deep water that has travelled from Greenland around the tip of Africa, across to Australia, and up into the Pacific. The only quick way for the atmosphere to equilibrate with the bulk of the deep water is through the small Antarctic Intermediate component of the Common water. Complete equilibration is a thousand-year process.

The "age" of seawater usually refers to the time since the water was last at the surface. This is difficult to measure directly, and must be estimated indirectly. The easiest way is to use the RESIDENCE TIME , defined as

$$t_r = \text{(volume of water mass)/(annual production)}$$

Heat, salt, carbon-14, and isotopes provide tracers for computing the annual production of a given water mass, and the volumes are approximately known, as shown in Table II. However, as Figure 4 shows, the residence time computed in this way is merely the average value of a probability distribution. That is, some parcels of water will leave the water mass long before they have stayed the full residence time, others will remain much longer. Clearly this is an important consideration for the circulation of pollutants. Any calculation must take these probabilities into account. The average age of North Atlantic Deep water is 250 years, but if we wanted something to stay out of sight that long, we might reasonably assume that it could find its way out, perhaps into surface water, in as little as 50 years. Thus, $0.2 \, t_r$ seems a reasonably safe time for calculations like this. If, on the other hand,

and salinity, with which to study the sea, but these turned out to be adequate for identifying and tracking water masses as they spread out from their area of formation, gradually changing their properties by mixing and by biological interactions as they drifted. Nearly all water masses are formed at the surface, because only here can temperature and salinity be changed by exchanging heat and water with the atmosphere. In addition to having a common origin and uniform temperature and salinity, a water mass can be expected to be more or less homogeneous with respect to other chemical constituents. If this is not found to be the case, some specific mechanism must be operating to produce the variability.

There are two major exceptions to surface formation of water masses. The Antarctic Bottom water is formed on the Antarctic continental shelf north of the Weddell Sea by mixing Antarctic Circumpolar water with Weddell Shelf water. The Antarctic Circumpolar water surrounds one desires rapid mixing and dilution, a short residence time is needed, but caution demands a computation time on the order of $2t_r$, because of the possibility of material remaining in its original water mass for that length of time.

But this is not all. The 160-year residence time mentioned in Table II for surface water applies to the water itself, but does NOT a p p l y to carbon dioxide in surface water. The residence time for $CO_2$, obtained from carbon-14 studies, is probably only 4 years and certainly less than 20 years.[9] This difference means that B I O L O G I-CALLY ACTIVE MATERIALS CIRCULATE AT MUCH GREATER RATES THAN BULK WATER: 40 times as fast in the upper, biologically rich, layer, and still 3 times as fast in deep water where there is less biological exchange.

The DEEP CURRENTS are not driven by wind but by heat, or perhaps by cold. We saw that Antarctic Bottom water was made each winter when shelf ice spread over the Weddell Sea; similarly, North Atlantic Deep water is made by cooling surface waters until they are dense enough to sink. But the Bottom water is saltier than the Deep, and so is denser at the same temperature, and when they meet the Bottom water hugs the sea floor and the Deep rides over it.

The deep currents complete a slow circulation which begins with these winter sinkings and ends nearly everywhere in the ocean as subsurface waters are warmed at the bottom of the thermocline and slowly rise through it to become surface water once again. Just as with surface currents, the principal meridional motion occurs in western boundary currents. Along the eastern coast of the Americas there are four layers of boundary currents. Below the southward-flowing Brazil current lies the northward-moving Antarctic Intermediate, then the North Atlantic Deep flowing south, and finally the Antarctic Bottom water moving north. The deep circulation is completed by water moving away at right angles from these boundary currents, and curving gently poleward as it rises through the water column on its way to the surface. The overall pattern is indicated by the shaded bands of Figure 3, but it

| Depth (approx) | Water mass | Where formed (at surface unless otherwise stated) | Volume $10^6$ km$^3$ | Production rate, sverdrups[a] |
|---|---|---|---|---|
| Surface 0–500 m | Surface waters including entire Arctic Ocean | Generally at subtropical convergences: 30° N and 40° S. Also at 5° N & S | 200 | 40 |
| Intermediate 500–1200 m | Antarctic Intermediate[b] (AAI) | Polar Front, c 50° S | 180 | 14 |
| | North Atlantic Deep[b] (NAD) | Southeast of Greenland | 150 | 20 |
| Deep 1200–1400 m | Antarctic Circumpolar | 60° S | 50 | 26 |
| | Indian-Pacific Common (IPC) | Mixing at depth: 16% AAI, 24% NAD, 60% AAB | 410 600 | — 16 |
| Bottom | Antarctic Bottom[b] (AAB) | Weddell Sea | 150 | 12 |

**II**

PRINCIPAL WATER MASSES. Simplified chart of the world ocean showing approximate residence times for the principal water masses. For an insight into the uncertainties attending such apparently simple oceanographic computations, see references. The figures in this table are probably good to within a factor of 2. Depending upon which volume for IPC is used, this table accounts for 83 to 97 percent of the world ocean. Since IPC is itself made

a1 sverdrup = $10^6$ m$^3$/sec.

bThe North Pacific produces small amounts of corresponding water masses.

must be understood that the rightward and pole-ward drift takes place over the entire ocean, and not in discrete streams.

Deep circulation in the Pacific and Indian Oceans is much less well known, but presumably much simpler because of the absence of a North Pacific Deep water. The deep central North Pacific basin is the cemetery of seawater.

Velocities in the deep circulation range from $10^{-5}$ cm/sec in the bulk of the ocean to 10 cm/sec in the boundary currents. But once again, these average values are deceptive. Ripple marks, scour patterns, and denuded rock bottoms at 4-km depth bespeak much faster but little under-stood motions with velocities above 20 cm/sec and sporadic changes in direction every few hours. Turbulence and mixing rate of the deep water is much higher than can be accounted for by looking only at the deep currents.

Redistribution of sedimentary material de-posited by rivers onto the continental shelf oc-curs by occasional TURBIDITY CURRENTS, anal-ogous to turbulent snow avalanches but com-posed of dilute mud (or dirty, heavy, water) flowing down to the abyssal plains at velocities up to 50 cm/sec and with energy enough to break transoceanic telegraph cables.

*Natural Inputs*

Three natural mechanisms carry terrestrially produced or eroded substances to the sea. These are (1) atmospheric transport (including rain), (2) transport by rivers, and (3) transport by ice. This last, although significant on a geological time scale, is in the present context the least im-portant of the three. Man has added a fourth mechanism, direct transport of wastes to the sea, conventionally by pipeline (for example, sewer outfalls) or by dumping from vessels and barges.

It is difficult to estimate an average aeolian (wind-carried) transport to the ocean, but for the tropical Atlantic a layer of 6 x $10^{-5}$ cm/yr of continental dust reaches the sea floor, 50 percent of it larger than 1 $\mu$m ($10^{-6}$ meter) but nearly all less than 20 $\mu$m.[12] This does not sound like much material, but in the North Pacific, where biological deposition is slow, up to 50 percent of the sediment is dust from the Gobi desert and other arid regions.

The natural process of erosion and the subse-quent transport of terrestrial materials to the sea has occurred since the oceans first came into existence. The rate of transport as well as the

| Residence time $t_r$, years | Comments |
|---|---|
| 160 | Residence time for Arctic Ocean, 160 yr, for Mediter-ranean Sea, 75 yr |
| 350 | A small amount of Mediterranean Water (MW) from Gibraltar appears at this depth. $V = 0.3$, $t_r = 6$ years |
| 250 | A small amount of bottom water is made here also |
| 60 | This active water mass provides most of the interocean stirring |
| — | Reference 10 |
| 1200 | Reference 8 |
| 400 | This water occupies all accessible low spots in the sea floor and ventilates the trenches |

from "old" water, the overall residence time for IPC water is perhaps 1500 years. Notice the overwhelming impor-tance of the Antarctic region for oceanic circulation.

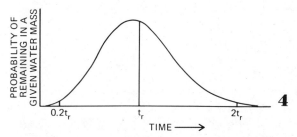

**4**

RESIDENCE TIME. Schematic probability curve show-ing likelihood of a given parcel of water (perhaps con-taining a pollutant) remaining in its original water mass as a function of time. The curve is a Poisson distribution and subjective because we have no real knowledge upon which to build a better model. It serves to show that the residence time $t_r$ is not particularly meaningful in some cases. For instance, if it is essential that a substance remain out of contact with man, it is prudent to use a short "design time" of 0.02 $t_r$ in making estimates; con-versely, if the need is for rapid dilution and mixing, a long design time of 2$t_r$ is safer.

concentrations of suspended and dissolved material being transported has almost certainly varied with climatological conditions and evolutionary development of land plants in the past, and it is being varied now by man's agricultural and engineering changes in watersheds. Despite these variations, the introduction of terrestrial material is essentially a slow process. Coupled with the hydrologic cycle and with slow equilibrium reactions in the sea, it has maintained a complex solution in the sea in which the ratios of major constituents not involved in biological processes remain essentially constant. Except for the alkali metals and halogens, the ocean waters have retained only about 0.01 percent of the substances which have cycled through them.[13]

When river water mixes with seawater dissolved material such as aluminum and iron is precipitated immediately, turning into the fine sediment characteristic of estuaries and river mouths.

However, the ocean ecosystem is prepared to process only certain specific terrestrial products. It can cope very well with particulate minerals and with common soluble chemicals: The ocean doesn't mind mud and salt. But seawater and marine sediments are nearly sterile by comparison to terrestrial environments and contain few bacteria and fungi, which are the commonest decomposers on land. As a rule, things do not rot in the sea, they are eaten and digested and excreted, or they enter into very simple chemical reactions. These factors raise problems when we come to consider man's inputs to the sea.

*Waste Disposal*

The biological and aesthetic consequences of disposing of domestic and industrial wastes into aquatic systems were probably first recognized and documented in fresh water. During the first two decades of this century limnologists characterized bodies of fresh water as being either eutrophic (highly productive, supporting dense communities of phytoplankton resulting from a large input of plant nutrients) or oligotrophic (characterized by low production and sparse plankton communities and a low nutrient input). Oceanographers quickly adopted this terminolo-

gy and it is now widely employed by all aquatic biologists. Limnologists likewise realized that under natural conditions some aquatic systems progressed from an oligotrophic stage to a eutrophic stage, this process being designated as eutrophication. When this natural sequence is accelerated by man it is designated "cultural eutrophication." We feel that this process should be called DYSTROPHICATION, or "bad nourishment." Calling sewage pollution of water bodies cultural good nourishment is like praising cancer for its rapid growth! Both natural and cultural eutrophication are and have been observed in the marine environment as well as in fresh water, although they are best documented in fresh water (see Chapter 10 and reference 14), where the dilution capacities are less than in the sea.

It is well known that streams and rivers in their natural state transport a variety of dissolved inorganic and organic substances, as well as suspended materials, into the sea. While pollution is not likely to affect the gross composition of seawater, for some time our ever-increasing demand for new materials has led us thoughtlessly to dump increasingly greater loads of "useless" by-products of society into natural bodies of water and the atmosphere under the assumption that these materials will become diluted sufficiently to become unobjectionable, either visually, biologically, chemically, or physically. As we will see, this is a mistaken notion and very serious subsequences may follow indiscriminate and uncontrolled waste disposal in aquatic systems, because the systems are not prepared to cope with man's novel materials and have no microorganisms which can break them down.

Since 1965 the cyclic seasonal changes in salinity off the Nile Delta and along the Levant coast have been markedly reduced by the storage of water and manipulation of river flow by the Aswan Dam. It is believed that this modification of the marine environment has resulted in reduced marine productivity, which in turn has reduced the catch of the commercial sardine fishery of this area. Similar control of the Mississippi River flow and alteration of drainage patterns in the Mississippi Delta marsh lands have already led to significant ecological changes.

Former oyster-spawning areas are now barren, but to date the commercial fishery yields do not seem to have been affected.[15]

Figure 3 shows the mouths of the world's major rivers. Note that a disproportionate share of the world's pollution goes into the North Atlantic, partly because of the number of rivers that empty into it (the most polluted are too small to show at this scale, but include the Hudson, the Delaware, the Thames, the Rhine, the Seine, the Rhone, the Tiber — in short, all of the convenient sewers of Western Civilization), and partly because of the large industrial population that surrounds it. Just as the Tiber was once the Cloaca Maxima of Rome, the North Atlantic is the Cloaca Maxissima of the Western world.

*Sewage and Runoff*

Certain dissolved inorganic substances such as nitrogen and phosphorus compounds from sewage and runoff have recently received very considerable attention because they are believed to be important in increasing the productivity of aquatic systems. As in fresh water, the introduction of these nutrients into the sea may accelerate plant growth and increase the general biotic level in the marine area influenced by rivers. Although attention by scientists is largely focused on these particular nutrients, other materials of biological origin such as vitamins and phenols may be of biological importance, as well as the concentrations and ratios of anions such as sodium, potassium, calcium, and of trace elements (for example, arsenic, copper, lead, mercury, and strontium).

Recent studies in British Columbia have shown that a large fraction of the organic materials of terrestrial origin carried into the Strait of Georgia and deposited onto the bottom are readily converted into bacterial biomass which can serve as food for benthic organisms.[16] Some of these same organic materials may also enhance the survival of freshwater bacteria in the sea by acting as chelators or heavy metal binders, which tie up heavy metals and effectively render them nontoxic. Other organic materials such as vitamin $B_{12}$ are also common in land drainage; since this vitamin is required by many marine planktonic plants, this substance may also lead to increased rates of marine primary production. The amount of particulate and dissolved organic carbon entering the Strait of Georgia from freshwater runoff has recently been estimated to be comparable in amount to that produced in the Strait by the resident photosynthetic organisms.[17]

Fibers of processed cellulose — which can only be toilet paper — have been found in the Straits of Florida and near Atlantic ports in quantities sufficient to interfere slightly with light transmission to plankton.[18] Cellulose is not a normal constituent of the marine ecosystem and so is essentially nonbiodegradable in the ocean, in the same way that agar (the structural compound of algae) is nonbiodegradable by terrestrial bacteria and so can be used as an inert culture medium in bacteriology.

The environmental effects of nutrient and carbon enrichment processes are probably becoming more and more significant each year as more and more wastes are dumped into rivers which lead to the sea. The effects of the nutrient enrichment that result directly from agricultural activity have not been well documented in the sea, although effects in smaller aquatic systems have been shown and continue to be a subject of intensive study (Chapter 10 and reference 14).

In recent years the disappearance of the giant kelp, *Macrocystis,* in the vicinity of sewer outfalls in southern California has been the cause of considerable concern. Initially it was believed that the sewage, perhaps by being toxic, was directly responsible for the disappearance of the kelp beds. Research has shown, however, that the effect of sewage upon the kelp was not direct, for the sewage itself (when diluted sufficiently by seawater) increased the growth of the kelp and was not responsible for its death and disappearance. It subsequently became apparent that the sea urchin, a common inhabitant of kelp bed areas and grazer of kelp, multiplied significantly in the presence of the sewer effluents. The resulting increase in sea urchin populations led to greater kelp grazing pressures, which led to the destruction of the kelp beds in the vicinity of sewer outfalls. Once these kelp beds were greatly reduced or absent, reestablishment of some of them could be achieved by reducing sea urchin abundance in the affected area.[19] The disappearance of the kelp beds naturally affected the kelp-harvesting industry adversely and also significantly affected the kelp bed sports fishery in these same areas of southern California.

Instead of fighting nature by spending time and tax money repeatedly dumping chemicals on sea urchins in order to preserve the kelp that shelters the beaches that protect the cliffs that support the homes of Point Loma, we might simply help the sea otter repopulate his original range (which extended well south of San Diego). He likes to eat sea urchins. In addition, his devotion, adaptability, and tool-using mark him as an interesting neighbor.

The disposal of domestic sewage in the marine environment often produces more direct effects such as noxious algal blooms, reduction in the diversity of benthic and perhaps planktonic organisms, reduced water transparency, and production of surface films or scums. Coliform bacteria introduced into the marine environment by domestic sewage are often sufficiently numerous in bays, harbors, and estuaries to constitute a health hazard which requires closure of the area to water contact sports or to the local shellfisheries.

The real drawback to disposing of sewage into the ocean is not so much its effect on the ocean, but its effect on land.[20] It is becoming increasingly clear that artificial fertilizers are not adequate to maintain soil fertility. A group at Penn State has shown how sewage recycling can be integrated into a technological urban environment to provide water reclamation, nourishing food, and green space, for about the same cost as polluting the ocean.[21] Why throw valuable material into the sea?

*Waste and Spilled Oil*

Of the nearly $2 \times 10^9$ tons of oil produced yearly, $10^9$ tons are shipped by sea. Routine shipping losses amount to 0.1 percent, or $10^6$ tons. An order of magnitude more (10 million tons) may reach the ocean in production and transportation, accidents, sewage, and atmospheric fallout from incomplete combustion.[22]

It appears that man's contribution is approaching parity with Nature's in volume, although the composition of pollution and natural hydrocarbons is significantly different. The most volatile fraction of spilled oil evaporates and ultimately takes part in atmospheric photochemical reactions. The remainder eventually passes through the biosphere.

The *Torrey Canyon, Tampico,* Santa Barbara, Florida, and recent Louisiana and Cape Cod oil spills have amply demonstrated the inadequate technology available for transporting petroleum by sea and in producing offshore oil deposits. The damage to marine life such as fish, invertebrates, seaweeds, and mammals resulting from crude oil may or may not be obvious. The high mortality of marine life experienced in England associated with beach contamination by *Torrey Canyon* oil is attributable to the toxic detergents used there to "clean up" the oil contamination. Areas treated with detergents have still not returned to "normal," while a few oil-contaminated beach and rock areas which were not treated with detergents are today in excellent condition. In France, where methods other than detergents were employed to treat the oil slick, damage to the marine biota was not as great as in England. During the Santa Barbara incident detergents were used sparingly in the vicinity of the leak area; straw was the main agent used to treat the slick. However, an immediate biological effect of this spill was a massive bird mortality, principally of diving birds. Other studies recently completed or still in progress relating to effects on the seaweeds, large zooplankton, and mesopelagic fish have shown virtually no detectable immediate effect. Since sampling problems are severe in the marine realm, probably anything but extremely striking effects would not be detected. Long-term effects remain to be evaluated. Certain red algae and eel grass were destroyed by the oil; other plants were apparently unaffected. In some instances the entire biota living on rocks was killed when the rocks remained covered with a thick film of crude oil. Recolonization of these rocky surfaces has been slow.[23]

Even the toxicity of crude oil in the marine ecosystem is not known, except that short alkanes (straight-chain and branched-chain hydrocarbons) damage marine larva, simple aromatics (ring systems) are generally toxic, and polynuclear aromatics (complex ring systems) are known carcinogens; there are suspicions that some components may mimic pheromones which marine organisms use as chemical messengers. Yet limpets ingest oil from coated rocks with no apparent ill-effects.[24] As far as can be determined, no studies on the effect of oil slicks upon the neuston, the sea surface film plant and animal community, have been made. Intuitively, one would expect this biotic community to be severely damaged by the presence of oil.

The physical behavior of oil on the sea is equally mysterious. From the time a slick drifts out of sight, little is known of its history until it reappears in a few weeks or months as irregular tarry lumps 1 to 100 mm in diameter.[25] Although laboratory experiments show considerable variation between the behavior of crude oil from different regions, there is a general pattern of hardening of the oil and breakup into small lumps. These tar balls regularly foul surface plankton nets in the Mediterranean and North Atlantic and seem to accumulate in the Sargasso Sea, but are now found in all oceans. Heyerdahl reports sailing the *Ra* through long stretches south of the Sargasso where the sea was covered with oily refuse as though they were in the wake of a tanker. He also observed many polystyrene cups and similar nonbiodegradable jetsam.

The tar balls are inhabited by an isopod (*Idotea metallica*) and a stunted goose barnacle (*Lepas pectinata*), and are covered with a gray film of unidentified bacteria which slowly consumes the tar.[25] Hydrocarbons are what is left over after anoxic biodegradation of organic material, and so can be expected to be resistant to further biological oxidation. The observed decomposition rate, under optimal circumstances of ample oxygen and complete coverage by bacteria, is so slow (2 weeks for a 10-$\mu$m drop) that dispersal of spills with detergents is not an ecologically acceptable method, because of the high probability that the droplets will be consumed by filter-feeders rather than bacteria. Even low-toxicity detergents like Esso's Corexit 7664 increase the toxicity of the oil itself. Once in the food chain, oil remains, for — dead or alive — all organisms are eaten in the sea. Furthermore, biodegradation of dispersed oil requires large quantities of oxygen which are not available except at the surface; oil on the sea floor can be expected to remain for long periods. Finally, we don't know what bacteria produce when they degrade oil: it is possible that the degradation products are more toxic than the oil itself. Thus, if recovery is not possible, the best available disposal method at the moment seems to be burning with one of the various wicking aids like Cab-O-Sil ST-2-0. The resulting air pollution is felt to be much the lesser of the two evils, and the neuston which is destroyed by fire was probably already doomed by the oil itself.

The tar balls, surprisingly, retain the volatile toxic alkanes. Epipelagic fish such as the saury (*Scomberesox saurus*) are indiscriminate feeders and consume the smaller lumps, providing a mechanism for passing large quantities of toxic material up the food chain to mammals, large predaceous fish, and man[25], although one suspects that the light "anaesthetizing" alkanes will gradually escape from even cold-blooded organisms.

Inshore refined oil spills, which amount to about half of the tonnage lost from ships, have been found to contaminate bottom sediments in 10 meters of water after mixing by a gale. The sediments have released unaltered highly toxic oil for months, killing worms, crustacea, mollusks, and fish, and forcing the closing of nearby commercial scallop and oyster beds because of the objectionable taste. The high toxicity appears to be related to the high volatility of refined fuels. The *Tampico* spill produced much more severe biological damage than occurred in Santa Barbara, which may be attributable in part to the greater volatility of the diesel oil spilled from the *Tampico*.[26] A relatively small spill of aviation gasoline west of Santa Barbara in 1968 killed thousands of lobsters, fish, and beach-dwelling invertebrates. Nelson-Smith[27] lists a large number of oil pollution incidents in harbors and estuaries and their ecological effects.

The effects of oil in calming waves are legendary, but other surface effects are less known. The familiar rainbow films that spilled oil forms on wet city streets and harbors are caused by multilayer molecular films and are characteristic of partially oxidized surface-active oil from industrial pollution. If we formed such a multi-layer film over an appreciable portion of the ocean (molecular films go a long way!) it might result in a noticeable effect on large-scale transfer of energy through the air-sea interface. Such films greatly reduce capillary ripples, and thence the rate of momentum transfer from air to sea and the rate at which carbon dioxide and oxygen are exchanged across the surface. The reflectivity of the sea to incoming radiation is increased, and the heat loss by evaporation reduced. A persistent multilayer film over an appreciable area of the North Atlantic could alter ocean currents, weather patterns, and fisheries. The "oil on troubled waters" with which mariners have traditionally calmed wild seas is just such a rainbow film — but one made of ANIMAL oil, which is naturally surface-active. However, crude oil and unused refined oil appear not to form persistent rainbow films, and the ocean is (somewhat fortuitously) safe from surface-chemical pollution by oil.

But it is not clear that immunity will last. The Japanese Ministry of International Trade and Industry is feeling the shortage of coastal land for oil refineries, and proposes processing crude oil in a seagoing refinery ship accompanying a normal oil tanker. The two ships together would carry 200,000 tons of oil, transferring it at sea, often in the monsoon areas of the Indian Ocean. One of the subsidiary advantages cited was that "the accompanying pollution experienced near refining units is removed from congested areas"[28] — out of sight, out of mind! There is no telling what such floating chemical factories might spill on the ocean in the future.

Oil pollution infests the coasts of all developed nations. From Norway to Morocco, including Great Britain and the Baltic, only the Adriatic Coast and the Aegean were not among the "most frequently polluted areas" during the last decade.[29] Of 156 fishing and bathing areas of the Italian coast, 5 percent had adequate installations for purification of sewage and industrial pollution, 24 percent were polluted by oil from ships, 35 percent by other oil, 39 percent by industry, and 68 percent by sewage.[29]

The psychological effects of such beach and water pollution have not been investigated.

Public tolerance of this sort of unnecessary insult is remarkably high, and only two reasons seem to be forthcoming. One is that the entrenched power of the oil companies is so large that the protests of injured individuals (or cities) are believed to be ineffectual; the other is that man is so adaptable that he can learn to enjoy himself on polluted beaches. Let us hope that the first is the real reason, for ways are slowly being found to cajole and coerce polluters into good behavior. If the second reason is valid — as the spectacle of begrimed surfers riding blackened waves suggests — then God help us: We'll adapt ourselves into extinction.

The effect of oil on sea birds has been well publicized, but it is worth repeating that it is almost invariably lethal (99+ percent). Chronic oil pollution in the Baltic (from deliberate dumping) has reduced the population of European long-tailed ducks to 10 percent of its 1940 value. Other North Atlantic birds in trouble from oil pollution include divers, grebes, scoters, eiders, mute swans, razorbills, guillemots, and the puffins.[29] In other parts of the world flamingos and penguins have been killed by oil.[30] Except when they are caught unawares, sea gulls (like pigeons, English sparrows, starlings, rats, and houseflies) can live comfortably in man's world.

At present it is not known if the mortality of seals and elephant seals originally reported from the San Miguel colonies during the Santa Barbara spill was due solely to oil: Autopsies on dead animals failed to provide definitive answers and more information is still required to determine the cause of the observed mortality. In an effort to be impartial, when birds, killer whales, hair seals, sea lions, and sea otters were found dead together in Alaskan waters, no one would admit that the oil which covered them all had been the cause of death. But killer whales are pretty tough beasts, and these showed no wounds.

The risk of large-scale ecological disruption by marine oil pollution seems sufficiently great that we should no longer be sidetracked by dilatory tactics such as calls for "further research," but instead should take reasonable precautions to minimize the effects of the next oil spill. Many of these precautions are not complex and many causes of oil pollution already have known technological fixes. But the laws that specify even minimal preventive technology are too frequently evaded by "waivers" obtained from complaisant officials. Legislation providing strict liability, enforceable environmental damage claims, and public hearings prior to all waivers will go far to inspire greater care and better ecological housekeeping. Industry has survived corrective legislation ere this (for example, child labor laws).

*Pollution by Metal*

The introduction of toxic heavy metals into the atmosphere, rivers, lakes, estuaries, and the sea is likewise of grave concern. In Sweden and Norway the accumulation of mercury in pike, *Esox lucius,* fish-eating birds such as the osprey (*Pandion haliaetus*), and the great crested grebe (*Podiceps aristatus*), and in invertebrates has been attributed to agricultural and industrial sources.[31] Recently in Lake Erie high mercury concentrations attributable to industrial pollution have been observed in chain pickerel (*Esox niger*).[32] In Minimata Bay, Japan, a nervous disease which caused in excess of 100 human deaths was traced to mercury accumulation in fish and shellfish eaten by Minimata Bay residents.[33] The source of the mercury was found to be contained in industrial wastes which were dumped into streams entering the Bay.

The progressive contamination of the surface layer and atmosphere of our planet by lead is well documented. The fact that polar snow is deposited in distinct annual layers has enabled Patterson, Chow, and Murozumi to examine lead concentrations in polar snow since 1750 in some detail (Figure 5).[34] A combination of radiochemical dating techniques and sophisticated geochemical analyses were used to obtain the data presented in this figure, based on over 400 separate analyses. The curve shows very low lead levels at 800 B.C. (ca. 4 micrograms of Pb per ton of snow); between 1750 and 1924 a gradual increase is noted, followed by a very rapid increase following the introduction of leaded antiknock gasoline in 1924, with concentrations exceeding 200 micrograms per ton observed in 1965. This increase corresponds with the increase

in lead smelter production following the industrial revolution and the increase in use of leaded gasoline in recent times. If one makes the assumptions that the sampling sites are uncontaminated from any immediate source of lead and that the mechanism of lead transfer to the snow is caused by the scrubbing action of rain and snow in the atmosphere, this curve should also reflect the relative concentration of lead in the atmosphere.

Although the surface area and volume of the ocean is very great it may seem surprising that we can already detect lead contamination resulting from man's activity in the open sea. Vertical distributions of lead have been obtained by the above authors in the Pacific Ocean roughly 200 miles southwest of San Diego, in the western tropical Atlantic in the vicinity of Bermuda, and in the Mediterranean Sea. These distributions are quite anomalous for trace elements in that maximum concentrations of lead are observed in the upper or surface layers and that minimum concentrations are observed below 1000 meters depth. Barium, for instance, a similar chemical

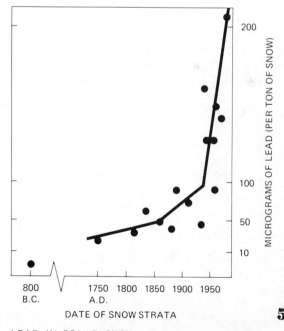

LEAD IN POLAR SNOW. The amount of industrial lead in snow taken from the Greenland Ice Sheet. The more recent the sample, the higher the concentration of lead Source: C.C. Patterson and J.D. Salvia, *Environment 10* [Formerly *Scientist and Citizen*] : 66-79.

**5**

species, becomes more concentrated with depth. Furthermore, as regards lead, the highest concentrations are observed in surface water adjacent to the highly populated and industrialized areas (the Pacific and Mediterranean stations) and the lowest in the waters of Bermuda. It is generally believed that most of this lead contamination of the sea is attributable to lead contained in antiknock gasoline. Isotopic composition data show that the composition of lead in the atmosphere of San Diego is similar to that of the lead in gasolines sold in the San Diego area.[35] The environmental effects of lead in the marine biosphere are not known. We do not know if lead is being concentrated by marine organisms adjacent to populated areas, nor what the effects of any accumulation might be, but we do know that lead is toxic in other circumstances.

## DDT

DDT exists in water in three forms: dissolved, at a concentration no more than $1.2 \times 11^{-12}$ (1.2 parts DDT per trillion parts water by weight); adsorbed onto (collected on the surface of) particles such as clay and organic detritus; and absorbed into lipid particles (fats and oils).

The ocean and its nurseries, the estuaries, are full of plankton, which specializes in scavenging particulate material, both living and dead. It is a rare particle that escapes being eaten once or twice en route to the bottom. As a class filter-feeders are optimists, ingesting every bite-sized particle that comes their way in the hope that it will be food. If DDT (or petroleum hydrocarbon) is consumed the plankton has no way of digesting it or excreting oil-soluble material. It is simply stored in fat. Thus much of the DDT (and oil) that reaches the sea surface will find its way into the biosphere and be consumed by low trophic levels and concentrated as it passes to higher trophic levels. There is beginning to appear evidence that DDT levels of the order of 0.5-10 ppm in gonads and eggs of fish may affect reproductive success.

Roughly $10^5$-$10^6$ tons of DDT have been produced the last 27 years, a portion of which (by codistillation with water vapor) finds its way into aquatic systems by aeolian (wind) transport and by river runoff. If this quantity were uniformly mixed into the surface water of the ocean the concentration would be 5.00 parts per trillion, or only one order of magnitude less than that found in a grossly polluted Long Island estuary. Table III shows the "biological magnification" of DDT up the food chain in this estuary. This magnification is such that fish-eating birds contain DDT concentrations which exceed by a factor of at least a million the concentration found in the water. Bird-eating birds, such as the peregrine falcon, would have shown even higher concentrations. Unfortunately the peregrine falcon, which feeds on mergansers, is now extinct in the United States east of the Rockies, and was not available for this study.

Menzel et al. have shown that phytoplankton, like birds, varies greatly from one species to another in its response to chlorinated hydrocarbons. Some species, such as the naked green estuarian flagellate *Dunaliella tertiolecta*, are used to man as a neighbor and are insensitive to

| Sample | DDT residues (ppm) |
|---|---|
| Water | 0.00005 |
| Plankton, mostly zooplankton | 0.040 |
| Shrimp | 0.16 |
| *Opsanus tau*, oyster toadfish (immature) | 0.17 |
| *Gasterosteus aculeatus*, threespine stickleback | 0.26 |
| *Spartina patens*, shoots | 0.33 |
| *Fundulus heteroclitus*, mummichog | 1.24 |
| *Strongylura marina*, Atlantic needlefish | 2.07 |
| *Spartina patens*, roots | 2.80 |
| *Sterna hirundo*, common tern | 3.42 |
| *Butorides virescens*, green heron | 3.57 |
| *Larus argentatus*, herring gull (immature) | 5.43 |
| *Sterna hirundo*, common tern (five abandoned eggs) | 7.13 |
| *Larus argentatus*, herring gull | 9.60 |
| *Pandion haliaetus*, osprey (one abandoned egg) | 13.8 |
| *Larus argentatus*, herring gull | 18.5 |
| *Mergus serrator*, red-breasted merganser | 22.8 |
| *Phalacrocorax auritus*, double-crested cormorant (immature) | 26.4 |
| *Larus delawarensis*, ring-billed gull (immature) | 75.5 |

DDT RESIDUES. DDT + DDE + DDD in samples from Carmans River estuary and vicinity, Long Island, N.Y., in parts per million wet weight of the whole organism, showing biological magnification along the food chain. Source: reference 36. Copyright 1967 by the American Association for the Advancement of Science.

DDT up to concentrations of 1 ppm. Others, such as the open ocean centric diatom *Cyclotella nana*, are more particular and show a sensitivity to concentrations of 0.0001 ppm.[38]

DDT has had some very serious effects on some bird populations which appear to be a complicated function of food chain length and nature and sensitivity of the species. Twelve hundred nesting attempts by California brown pelicans on Anacapa Island raised at most 5 young in 1969[40] and one in 1970.[41] DDT residues in the eggs ran as high as 2500 ppm. DDT interferes with the carbonic anhydrase enzyme system of breeding females, preventing the mobilization of calcium in the oviduct so that eggs may be laid with no shell at all. Hatching success is reduced by shell-thinning with dietary doses of 10 ppm of DDT.[42] Eggs of the double-crested cormorant suffer similar thinning: none hatched in California in 1969.[40] There are signs of eggshell thinning throughout the world and there is a distinct possibility that pelagic sea birds are destined to extinction.

Because of high levels of DDT fish from inland lakes (coho salmon) have been condemned as unfit for human consumption by the FDA. Since the well-publicized Lake Michigan incident, however, the FDA has also condemned commercial shipments of pacific mackerel from the Pacific Ocean because they contained 10 ppm DDT.[40] This does not bode well for the future of food from the sea!

Mammals are relatively tolerant of DDT, and it does not cause a fourfold statistical increase in cancer until the dose reaches 50 ppm of body weight.[42] At 3 ppm/day for a 6-month period DDT has been used therapeutically to reduce serum bilirubin levels in jaundiced humans.[43] The DDT concentration in the fat was 200 ppm at the end of the treatment, and the patient, apparently, in better health than when he started. Because of the very low degradability of DDT much of the DDT produced still resides on earth. For this reason the concentration in the ocean off Southern California already appears to be about 3 parts per trillion.[44] Although some has been degraded to nontoxic products (the half-life for bacterial degradation [Figure 6] of DDT is slow — estimated at 10 to 20 years)[44],

the degradation product is likely to be DDE, which is itself toxic and seems to persist indefinitely.

*Pollution by Other Chemicals*

It took us from 1945 to 1962 (when Rachel Carson's *Silent Spring* was published) to become aware of the biocidal nature of insecticides, from 1962 to 1969 to take token action, and an unknown time into the future will pass before meaningful action is taken (species-specific biodegradable insecticides, biological control, and acceptance of a 10 percent crop loss — which we had before DDT and which we still have — as a normal tithe to the world ecosystem to keep it running). In the meantime we have apparently exterminated another dozen species of birds. The question arises, Are we doing this same thing with other chemicals than the chlorinated hydrocarbon insecticides? One group of chemicals under suspicion are the suite of polychlorinated biphenyls, or PCBs, which were never intended to kill, but merely to make flexible such commercial items as paint, pipe, tires, plastic sheeting, and vast quantities of "disposable" plastic goods. It has been shown that PCSs are toxic to insects and also increase the toxicity of DDT and dieldrin.[45] Combustion temperatures in commercial incinerators do not destroy, but do volatilize, PCB, and it is also slowly released by weathering of exposed plastics. PCB has been detected as widely in the biosphere as has DDT and in similar concentrations in Southern Hemisphere shearwaters (*Puffinus tenuirostri* and *P. griseii*) that spend most of their time at sea and nest on remote islands.[40] If PCB or some other presently unsuspected component of commercial plastics proves to be a broad-scale biocide, corrective action will be more difficult than for DDT. Developing methods of recycling, rather than "disposing" of plastic goods suddenly becomes as important as recycling paper, glass, and metals.

This is not the end of our biocidal problems. The United States has sprayed $2 \times 10^4$ tons of 2,4,5-T [(2,4,5-trichlorophenoxy)acetic acid] alone on Vietnam[46], most of which will wash into the sea on the monsoon floods. There have been no reported studies of the effect of these

METABOLIC PATH OF DDT IN THE ENVIRON-
MENT. A first approximation. Bracketed forms are
some of the known intermediate products in biochemical degradation. The commercial biocides DDT, DDE,
and DDD are fat-soluble and accumulate in the marine
biosphere, where the products with the lowest acute
toxicity appear to have the most serious long-term effects. There is no convincing evidence for a significant
pathway toward the water-soluble (and excretable)
DDA except other than degradation by mammalian enzyme systems. Nothing is known which metabolizes
DDE.

poisons on the marine food chain — but it
seems too much to hope that ecocide on this
scale will not lead to undesirable consequences.

*Oxygen Depletion?*

Among the many horror stories circulating
about pollution is a solitary one that can be dis-
counted. This is the tale that threatens us with
loss of oxygen if we so pollute the ocean that
green plants can no longer grow in it. If this happened, 70 percent of the world's oxygen PRODUC-

TION (not the "standing crop") would cease —
but so too would 70 percent of the oxygen consumption. Every plant consumes as much oxygen
during its decay (or its assimilation and burning
by an animal) as is set free during its growth. The
only net change in the world's oxygen-carbon
dioxide system is the shift caused by burning fossil fuels (Chapter 15), for the entire free oxygen
supply of the earth is balanced by the small percentage of plants that died over geological time
and were buried before they could be oxidized.
Fortunately most of this buried carbon is not in
coal or oil but disseminated widely into black
shales and other rocks, where it is useless as fuel
and safe from technology. Oxygen is the least of
our worries.

*Energy and the Sea*

The growth rate of energy use is just twice the
population growth rate, or 4 percent per year.
Much of this additional energy goes into main-

taining the status quo, as, for instance, the increase in power required to process increasingly low grade metal ores.[47] The continual search for new power sources inevitably involves the ocean.

Hydroelectric power installations in the United States extract less than 30 percent of the potential hydropower. If we dam our remaining wild rivers (a process which would be complete by 2010 at the present rate) we can temporarily obtain $10^5$ MW(e) [megawatts, electrical; a large hydropower plant produces $10^3$ MW(e)]. The temporary feature is that reservoirs fill up with sediments in a century or two. Most of these sediments used to reach the ocean, where the resistant particles became beach sand. Beaches are not static features of the landscape, but portions of a dynamic longshore transport process in which waves meeting the beach at a small angle slowly but steadily move a stream from river mouth to undersea canyon, whence it is lost to the sea floor.

Thus, hydropower generation (and flood control, where cities are built on floodplains) causes a subtle form of oceanic pollution. Beaches are the most characteristic positive value of the ocean for many people, and diminution of a positive value is as much pollution as addition of a negative value. It is, perhaps, encouraging that the Army Corps of Engineers stands ready to haul sand back from the depths (beach replenishment) to compensate for the damming and paving of our rivers.

Another long-dreamed-of scheme is to harness tidal power, because it produces no noxious wastes and consumes no energy resources. One such installation began operating in 1966 on the la Rance estuary on the Channel coast of France (Chapter 5).

In spite of assurances that tidal power produces minimal disturbance to the ecologic and scenic environment, one wonders about the effect of turbines — even gentle axial flow turbines — upon the estuarine wildlife that must pass through them. Also, it seems unlikely that man's peak power needs will coincide with the established tidal rhythm to which estuarine organisms are adapted, and whose clock somehow governs their behavior even when they are isolated in aquaria. There may be more dis-

advantages to tidal power than we have realized.

Although rivers and tides can provide some of our estimated power needs — at a price — utility companies are betting on nuclear fission, which is growing at 31 percent per year. These plants raise two oceanic pollution problems. The obvious one is radioactivity, the other, heat.

There are two extremes in handling the RADIOACTIVE WASTES from fission. One approach seeks to extinguish all radioactivity by storing fission products for 20 half-lives before exposing them to the biosphere, and ingenious are the methods employed. The other extreme disposal method is to attempt dilution of fission wastes into the ocean (Chapter 12). Although this is totally inadequate for the future, it is the economically preferred approach for some reactors today, such as Hanford, which dumps some 350,000 curies per year into the Columbia River.

A number of British installations also dump radioactivity. In each case the dumping is controlled so that the level of activity accumulated in organisms used as human food remains below the known hazard to man. Man is not only the most concerned animal, but also one of the most sensitive to radiation damage, so this approach protects all those members of the marine ecosystem whose dietary tastes are similar to man's.

Organisms possess an ability to concentrate elements from seawater which is only occasionally related to an obvious nutritional need. These concentration factors range from 2 (for sulfate) to 2,000,000 (phosphate), with metals ranging from 100 to 5000, and the manner in which wastes are distributed into the biosphere is essentially unpredictable.[48] Thus, safety limits must be established by experiment at each location: at Windscale the legal limit is ruthenium-106 accumulated on the edible seaweed *Porphyra umbilicalis,* or "laver"; at Winfrith, Ru-106 and cesium-137 on lobsters and lobster pots; at Dounreay, zirconium-95 and niobium-95 on debris on shore; and at Bradley, Berkeley, and Hinckley, zinc-65 on oysters, silt, and fish. Windscale alone dumps some 90,000 curies into the Irish Sea, and bottom invertebrates within 40 km of Windscale show activities over 100 picocuries/gram, 25 times the normal dose. A large portion of the activity in river waters is adsorbed into microscopic suspended clay particles, which are coagulated into larger particles by contact with salt water, and are of just a size to be tempting to sessile filter-feeders like oysters. Thus, high activities have accumulated in the biosphere near the mouth of the Columbia River, leading to some problems with Zn-65 on oysters there. In situations like this, the apparent concentration factor from water to animal may be 100 times the expected value.

Thermodynamically, nuclear plants are less efficient even than steam plants, and must reject nearly 75 percent of their energy as waste heat — the source of THERMAL POLLUTION. Unlike steam plants, which send most of their heat into the atmosphere, nuclear plants are dependent upon water for cooling, and accordingly are located on rivers and coasts. But any time three times as much energy goes into a body of water as flows into a city, we can expect serious consequences to organisms in the water. As an example, Florida Power and Light's Turkey Point installation on Biscayne Bay generates 720 MW(e) at 25 percent efficiency. With the waste heat, it raises water temperature at its outfall by $8°C$, damaging or killing organisms within a 1.5-km radius. The ultimate design power is 1360 MW(e), at which time it will be rejecting nearly 4000 MW(t) (thermal megawatts) into the Biscayne National Monument. The Interior Department has brought suit to prevent this, under an 1899 refuse law: Although heat qua heat is not yet legal refuse, the dead organisms that drift away are.[49]

### The Baltic — A Case History

A symposium volume published in 1956, entitled Man's Role in Changing the Face of the Earth,[50] failed to mention Lake Erie once in 65 papers and nearly 1200 pages. Yet 10 years later we suddenly discovered that over the last century Lake Erie had gradually been converted from a healthy, productive inland sea into an urban-industrial cesspool. (Fortunately the residence time of Lake Erie is only 2.5 years, so that it can, if we wish, be restored to health in another decade or two.) (Chapter 10). Taking his cue from our proven ability to pollute inland seas,

Paul Ehrlich has written of the "Death of the Ocean, 1979."[51] Is it that imminent?

One place to look is at the Baltic Sea — a shallow estuarine arm of the ocean only 15 times the size of Lake Erie. Since it is being studied by some 14 oceanographic institutions on its shores, we should know well in advance of any serious environmental degradation. With an average depth of only 200 meters and a residence time of some 25 years (long enough to make flushing a century-long problem if it gets unbearably contaminated), it is surrounded by industrial nations and is probably the most vulnerable part of the ocean. The rash of symptoms suggests that it is indeed seriously sick.

In the order in which we discussed contaminants earlier, the situation in the Baltic seems to be the following:

Sewage is dumped in quantities large enough to consume some $1.2 \times 10^6$ tons of oxygen annually. The trouble is that the deep water in the Baltic is renewed either by sinking of surface water in particularly cold winters, or by an influx of North Sea water over the shallow sill in the Danish Belt — a phenomenon which has occurred only rarely since the 1930s. In either case this dense water fills the bottom basins and gradually loses its oxygen until vast areas are lifeless deserts (300,000 $km^2$ in 1959). The addition of biological oxygen demand from sewage accentuates this deoxygenation of the bottom waters and diminution of habitat. The Landsort Deep (500 meters) is anoxic to the extent of producing evil-smelling hydrogen sulfide (which is considerably more poisonous than cyanide). Goteborg's sludge, although dumped outside these deep unventilated basins, has reduced the species diversity noticeably among the bottom fauna. Sludge that does not contribute to oxygen consumption because it refuses to decay — like the cellulose fibers from pulp mills — simply accumulates on the bottom, entombing the fertile bottom habitat in a blanket of sodden papier-mâché.

Man's 19,000-ton annual phosphate input to the Baltic is approximately equal to Nature's. Only about half of the total input leaves the Baltic, so that about 21,000 tons/ year accumulates, and already dense algal blooms in several regions have been attributed to this dystrophication.[52]

We have already mentioned the deliberate dumping of oil in the Baltic, and the consequent reduction of some bird populations to 10 percent of their normal number.

Mercury has been much studied in the Baltic because of its use as an algicide in the pulp lumber industry. Effluent from some 100 miles on the Swedish coast has raised the methylmercury content of Baltic water sufficiently that fishing has been banned in 1 percent of Sweden's commercial fisheries (both lake and coastal). Enforcing the practical residue limit for mercury in human food proposed by the World Health Organization would mean banning fishing in all Swedish fishing areas. The Swedes, feeling that "the choice of a safety factor is arbitrary and usually chosen so that certain pesticides ... can still be used in practice," have simply adopted their own "allowable daily intake" of mercury at a level some 12 times the international recommendation. At this level they admit that they cannot exclude possible fetal or genetic effects. Already a small portion of the Swedish population consumes enough contaminated fish to put them into the danger zone.[53]

The usual problems with chlorinated hydrocarbons exist, except that for uncertain reasons the DDT concentration in Baltic seals is up to 10 times higher than in similar North Sea species. The Baltic peregrine falcon population (a sensitive indicator because peregrines accumulate DDT from the marine food chain) is in serious trouble, if not moribund.

The fate of the Baltic is in the hands of the International Council for the Exploration of the Sea — a 13-nation group which studies fisheries and attendant oceanography. Like all international groups it moves ponderously, and it remains to be seen whether political corrective action or exponentially growing synergistic polytechnic pollution will win.

We have made some specific recommendations in those cases where rather simple fixes are evident. These are largely first-aid repairs; what is needed is a fundamental reevaluation of man's relation to his environment. The idea that the natural world was put here for Western man to EXPLOIT is only an assumption, and, like earlier assumptions relating to the flatness of the Earth and the geocentricity of the universe, is really only egoism and superstition writ large. We suggest that it is time to investigate alternative hypotheses, and as oceanographers, urge that high priority be given to this one: The pelican, like the miner's canary, is an ecological warning of what lies ahead for man in the direction he is going. Survival requires that exploitation be replaced by intelligent stewardship.

## References

1. **Fremlin, J. H.** 1964. How many people can the world support? *New Scientist, No. 415:* 285-287.
2. **Grassle, S.** 1970. Ecological effects of a spill of fuel oil near Woods Hole, Massachusetts. Address given May 15, 1970, at University of California, Santa Barbara.
3. **McHarg, I. L.** 1969. *Design with Nature,* Natural History Press, Garden City, New York; **H.T. Odum,** 1967, Biological circuits and the marine systems of Texas, in *Pollution and Marine Ecology* (T. A. Olsen & F. J. Burgess, eds.), pp. 99-157, esp. p. 152 ff. Interscience, New York.
4. **Lauff, G. H.,** ed. 1967. *Estuaries,* American Association for the Advancement of Science, Publication #83, Washington, D.C. See especially chapters by G. Gunter, J. L. McHugh, and T. V. R. Pillay.
5. **Craig, R. A.** 1965. *The Upper Atmosphere,* p. 37. International Geophysics Series, Vol. 8. Academic Press, New York.
6. **Bull, G. A., and James, D. G.** 1966. Dust in the atmosphere over Western Britain on 3 and 4 April, 1956. *Met. Mag. 85:* 293-297.
7. **Junge, C. E.** 1963. *Air Chemistry and Radioactivity,* p. 364. International Geophysics Series, Vol. 4. Academic Press, New York.
8. **Bolin, C., and Stommel, H.** 1961. On the abyssal circulation of the world ocean—IV. *Deep-Sea Res. 8:* 95-110.
9. **Williams, P. M., et al.** 1969. Reported in *Institute of Marine Resources Annual Report,*

p. 18. IMR Reference 69-12. University of California.

10. **Montgomery, R. B.** 1958. Water characteristics of Atlantic Ocean and of World Ocean. *Deep-Sea Res. 5:* 134-148.

11. **Wyrtki, K.** 1961. The thermohaline circulation in relation to the general circulation on the oceans. *Deep-Sea Res. 8:* 36-64.

12. **Delaney, A. C., et al.** 1967. Airborne dust collected at Barbados. *Geochim. et Cosmochin Acta 31:* 885-909.

13. **Sverdrup, H.U., Johnson, M.W., and Fleming, R.H.** 1942. *The Oceans,* p. 220. Prentice-Hall, Englewood Cliffs, New Jersey.

14. **International Symposium on Eutrophication.** 1967. *Eutrophication: Causes, Consequences, Correctives.* Proceedings of a symposium held in Madison, Wisconsin.

15. **St. Amant, L.** 1970. Personal communication.

16. **Seki, H., Skelding, J., and Parsons, T.R.** 1968. Decomposition of sedimented material and its utilization by bacteria. *Limnol. and Ocean 13:* 440-447.

17. **Seki, H., Stevens, K.V., and Parsons, T.R.** 1969. The contribution of allochthonous bacteria and organic materials from a small river into a semi-enclosed sea. *Archiv. Hydrobiol. 66(1):*37-47.

18. **Manheim, F.T., Meade, R.H., and Bond, A.** 1970. Suspended matter in surface waters of the Atlantic continental margin from Cape Cod to the Florida Keys. *Science 167:* 371-376.

19. **North, W.H., and Hubbs, C.L.** 1968. *Utilization of kelp-bed resources in Southern California.* Fish Bulletin 139, California Department of Fish and Game, 264 pp.

20. **Albrecht, W.A.** 1956. Physical, chemical, and biochemical changes in the soil community. In *Man's Role in Changing the Face of the Earth* (W.L. Thomas, Jr., ed.), pp. 648-673. University of Chicago Press, Chicago, Illinois.

21. **Parizek, R. R., et al.** 1967. *Waste Water Renovation and Conservation.* Pennsylvania State Studies No. 23, University Park, Pennsylvania.

22. **Blumer, M.** 1969. Oil pollution of the ocean. In *Oil on the Sea* (D.P. Hoult, ed.), pp. 5-13. Plenum Press, New York.

23. **Holmes, R.W.** 1969. The Santa Barbara oil spill. In *Oil on the Sea* (D.P. Hoult, ed.), pp. 15-27. Plenum Press, New York.

24. **Smith, J.E., ed.** 1968. Torrey Canyon. In *Pollution and Marine Life.* Cambridge University Press, Cambridge, England.

25. **Horn, M.H., Teal, J.M., and Backus, R.H.** 1970. Petroleum lumps on the surface of the sea. *Science 168:* 245-246.

26. **North, W.J., Neushul, M., and Clendenning, K.A.** 1964. Successive biological changes observed in a marine cove exposed to a large spillage of mineral oil. *Proc. Symp. Poll. Mar. Microorg. Prod. Petrol. Manoco:* pp. 335-354.

27. **Nelson-Smith, A.** 1968. A classified bibliography of oil pollution. In *The Biological Effects of Oil Pollution on Littoral Communities* (J.D. Carthy and D.R. Arthur, eds.), Suppl. to *Field Studies,* Vol. 2, pp.165-196. Field Studies Council, London.

28. **Ocean Industry.** 1970. New idea: Process crude oil while tanker is at sea. *Ocean Industry 5:* 15-16.

29. **International Conference on Oil Pollution of the Sea.** Record of Proceedings. October 7-9, 1968, Rome.

30. **Bourne, W.R.P.** 1968. Oil pollution and bird populations. In *The Biological Effects of Oil Pollution on Littoral Communities* (J.D. Carthy and D.R. Arthur, eds.). Suppl. to *Field Studies,* Vol. 2. Field Studies Council, London.

31. **Johnels, A. G., and Westermark, T.** 1969. *Chemical Fallout* (M. Miller and G. Berg, eds.). Charles Thomas, Springfield, Illinois, 531 pp.

32. **Abelson, H.** 1970. Methyl mercury. *Science 169:* 3942.

33. **Irukayama, K.** 1966. The pollution of Minimata Bay and Minimata disease. *Advan. Water Pollut. Res. 3:* 153-180.

34. **Patterson, C. C., with Salvia, J.D.** 1968. Lead in natural environment. How much is natural? *Environment 10* [Formerly *Scientist and Citizen*] : 66-79.

35. Chow, T. J. 1970. Personal communication.

36. Woodwell, G. M., Wurster, C. F., Jr., and Isaacson, P. A. 1967. DDT residues in an east coast estuary: a case of biological concentration of a persistent insecticide. *Science 156:* 821-824.

37. Wurster, C. F., Jr. 1968. DDT reduces photosynthesis by marine plankton. *Science 159:* 1474-1475.

38. Menzel, D. M. 1970. Marine phytoplankton vary in their response to chlorinated hydrocarbons. *Science 167:* 1742-1746.

39. Sladen, W. J. L., Menzie, C. M., and Reichel, W. L. 1966. DDT residues in Adelie penguins and a crabeater seal from Antarctica: ecological implications. *Nature 210:* 670-673.

40. Risebrough, R. W. 1969. The Sea: should we now write it off as the future garbage pit?? *13th National Conference of the U.S. National Commission for UNESCO,* Background Book, Supplement, pp. 1-23.

41. Kirven, M. 1970. Personal communication.

42. Peakall, D.B. 1970. Pesticides and the reproduction of birds. *Sci. Amer. 222 (No. 4):* 72-78.

43. Thompson, R.P.H., et al. 1969. Treatment of unconjugated jaundice with dicophane. *Lancet 2:* 4-6.

44. Cox, J.L. 1970. Personal communication.

45. Lichtenstein, E.P., Schultz, K.P., Fuhrmann, T.W., and Liang, T.T. 1969. Biological interaction between plasticizers and insecticides. *J. Econ. Entomol. 62:* 761-765.

46. Gruchow, N. 1970. Curbs on 2,4,5-T use imposed. *Science 168:* 453.

47. Lovering, T.S. 1969. Mineral resources from the land. In *Resources and Man,* Chapt. 6. Committee on Resources and Man. National Academy of Sciences — National Research Council. W.H. Freeman, San Francisco, California.

48. Craig, H. 1957. Disposal of radioactive wastes in the ocean: The fission product spectrum in the sea as a function of time and mixing characteristics. In *The Effects of Atomic Radiation on Oceanography and Fisheries,* pp. 34-42.

49. MIT. 1970. The power versus the Glory. *Technol. Rev.,* June, p. 66. (MIT, Cambridge, Massachusetts)

50. Thomas, W.L., Jr., ed. 1956. *Man's Role in Changing the Face of the Earth.* University of Chicago Press, Chicago, Illinois.

51. Ehrlich, P.R. 1969. Eco-Catastrophe. *Ramparts,* September.

52. Fonselius, S.H. 1970. Stagnant sea. *Environment 12:* (No. 6): 2—11.

53. Berglund, F., and Berlin, M. 1969. Human risk evaluation for various populations in Sweden due to methyl mercury in fish. *Chemical Fallout* (M.W. Miller and G.G. Berg, eds.), pp. 423-432. C.C. Thomas, Springfield, Illinois.

# 12 Ionizing Radiation

## Earl Cook

Ionizing radiation is a natural environmental hazard whose potential for physiological (somatic) and genetic damage has been augmented greatly by man's discovery of atomic power.

With advances in technology, the beneficial uses of man-produced radiation, especially in the production of electric power, are being continually multiplied, but so are man's chances of exposure to harmful radiation. The long hazard life of some radioisotopes (hundreds to thousands of years), the lack of knowledge of the effects of low chronic radiation doses, and the fact that dangerous isotopes introduced into the biosphere at low and perhaps harmless levels may be selectively concentrated by biological processes in man's food chain make adequate environmental protection a matter for cautious balancing of benefits and risks.

There are many kinds of radiation, but only radioactivity, cosmic rays, and cathode-ray tubes produce radiation capable of tearing electrons away from, or IONIZING, atoms with which they interact. When the atoms disrupted by ionization form part of living molecular tissue, serious bio-

logic damage may occur, ranging from reduced life expectancy to almost immediate death; cancer and leukemia may be induced; and genetic damage to the species may arise from inherited defects that result from increased mutation rates.

Rational management of man-produced radiation, so that its benefits can be enjoyed without a long-range cost in human misery and death from environmental pollution, is a supreme test of man's decision-making capability.

Before discussing radiation as an environmental hazard, we need to review some basic facts of nuclear and health physics. The structure of atoms and the nature of isotopes of elements are described in Chapter 5.

### Radioactivity

Of the more than 320 isotopes (Chapter 5) that exist in nature, about 60 are radioactive. In addition, man has learned how to create, through nuclear fission, radioactive isotopes not found in nature; about 200 of these "artificial" radioisotopes have been identified.

Radioactivity involves a spontaneous nuclear change that results in the formation of a new element. The nuclear change takes place by emission of high-energy particles; a radioactive material is said to DECAY by disintegration. Each isotope decays at its own particular rate regardless of temperature, pressure, or chemical environment. ALLOWING ISOTOPES TO DECAY NATURALLY IS THE ONLY PRACTICAL MEANS OF ELIMINATING THEIR RADIOACTIVITY. The time required for any given radioisotope to decay to half of its original quantity is called its HALF-LIFE. Half-lives range from microseconds to billions of years.

EARL COOK is Professor of Geology and Geography at Texas A & M University. Born in 1920, he received his doctorate in geology in 1954 from the University of Washington. In a career that has combined engineering, science and administration, he has had considerable opportunity to observe the impact of technology on environment. As staff officer of one of the committees of the National Academy of Sciences, he has investigated the problems of protecting the Earth from radioactive pollution. Currently he is studying the process of decision-making about environmental problems.

Radiation exposure or dosage is measured by the rem, rad, or roentgen. The most useful of these for our purposes is the rem, which measures the extent of biological injury of a given type that would result from the absorption of nuclear radiation.

All common matter on earth is radioactive in some degree. Organisms on the earth are subjected continuously to a low level of radiation from radioactivity within their tissues, from the immediate environment, and from cosmic rays. The principal internal radiation source is potassium-40 of the bones; the main external natural sources are cosmic rays from outer space and gamma rays from the earth's crust. The range of estimated average annual gonadal radiation doses (radiation on the sex cells) to the general population from natural sources is given in Table I (a millirem, mrem, is 0.001 rem). Total dosage is 0.081 to 0.172 rem per year.

| Source | Annual dose, mrem |
|---|---|
| External sources | |
| Cosmic rays from space | 32–73 |
| Gamma rays from crust | 25–75 |
| Internal sources | |
| Potassium-40 | 19 |
| Radium-226 | 3 |
| Carbon-14 | 2 |
| Total | 81–172 |

**AVERAGE ANNUAL GONADAL RADIATION DOSE.**
Source: Federal Radiation Council Report No. 1, 1960.

Total radiation doses from environmental sources vary with altitude, because cosmic rays penetrate the thinner atmosphere of high places more readily than the heavier atmosphere of sea level; they vary with latitude because of the differences in travel paths of cosmic rays through the atmosphere; they vary with the nature of the underlying and adjacent rocks because granitic rocks contain more radioactive thorium, uranium, and potassium than other kinds of rocks; they vary with height above the land surface because of dilution of radon (a radioactive gas common to the three most important natural radioactive decay series); and they vary with the built environment because radon gas from natural building materials can become concentrated in closed spaces.

In the open ocean at the equator the average total radiation dosage is only 53 mrem per year, but at mile-high Denver near granitic rocks, the background is 170 mrem per year, and on a 20,000-foot granite peak at 55° north latitude, background rises to 560 mrem per year.

As we shall see later, radiation protection guides or standards are set in DOSE RATES, a fraction of a rem per week or month for radiation workers, or per year for the general population. It may be useful to keep in mind, as we discuss levels of radiation, that a guideline of the Federal Radiation Council sets 5 rem per generation (30 years), or about 170 mrem per year, as the maximum permissible gonadal dose for the general public, above the background level and excluding medical irradiation. This dose rate represents a little more than a doubling of the average background dose.

A little-known "natural" source of radiation to which man has exposed himself is radium in groundwater. In several areas of the United States deep wells have penetrated geologic formations containing water whose radium content exceeds the maximum permissible concentration in drinking water as set by the Public Health Service.[1] Some of these wells are used as sources of municipal and domestic water; others are used mainly for stock, irrigation, and industry. Like uranium mines, these high-radium wells show that man can greatly increase his exposure to "natural" radiation, apart from his ability to produce "artificial" radiation.

Man-produced ionizing radiation includes x rays from x-ray machines and television sets, and the radiation from the products of nuclear fission. Bombardment of a fissionable isotope by neutrons splits its nucleus and produces an enormous release of energy as well as a wide variety of fission products, almost all of which are radioactive. Many fission products are not only extremely radioactive but have half-lives as long as 33 years. If we use the commonly accepted guideline of 20 half-lives to safety, such isotopes will be dangerous for 600 years.

In terms of environmental pollution, the most important fact about nuclear fission is that the fissioning of 1000 grams of a fissile isotope produces 999 grams of waste materials (fission products and neutrons) which are either radioactive or capable of making inert material radioactive.

It is important to remember that man's additions to natural radioactivity have both intensity and time factors. All are essentially ephemeral in a geologic sense, for most artificial radioisotopes have half-lives less than 30 years and hazard lives less than 600 years. On the other hand, these are very long times in terms of man's generations, population shifts, and environmental changes. Furthermore, continued production of radioactive materials will extend the environmental hazard indefinitely.

It is also important to recognize the environmental distinction between x radiation and radiation from radioactive isotopes. X rays add to the radiation dose and to the biological hazard of the individuals exposed to them, but they cannot raise the level of environmental radiation, for they cease to be propagated when their energy source is turned off, and they attenuate or fade very rapidly in passing through air. Radioactive isotopes, on the contrary, add to the environmental or natural radiation level, because they endure and continuously emit radiation as they decay.

## Somatic Effects of Ionizing Radiation

In discussing biological damage from ionizing radiation, we must distinguish SOMATIC damage from GENETIC damage. The differences between the two kinds of damage are crucial and the distinction should be kept in mind at all times.

In terms of energy delivered to a living cell, ionizing radiation is by far the most potent of all agents, physical or chemical; for example, about 100 million times more energy has to be introduced as cyanide to produce an equally deadly effect.[2]

Ionizing radiation disrupts chemical bonds in the molecules of living cells that absorb energy from the incident rays. New chemical bonds, if established, may be in a changed configuration that may not be compatible with normal life processes. Because the living cell contains giant molecules whose structure is vital to their function, the rupture and rearrangement of bonds may have far-reaching consequences.

Depending on the nature of the exposure, radiation injury takes many forms, ranging from small and long-delayed effects to short-term lethal effects. In the individual, the biologic damage ranges from reduced life expectancy through cancer and leukemia to death.

Different parts of the body vary in their response to radiation. The gonads are especially radio sensitive and the eyes only slightly less so. Human individuals appear to get less sensitive to radiation as they grow older. The embryo in utero is highly sensitive. It has been suggested that this sensitivity reflects the percentage of body cells undergoing cell division, and that these are the cells most susceptible to cancer induction; consequently, irradiation early in life is much more serious in increasing cancer occurrence than irradiation later in life.

The biologic effects of radiation are known from the following studies:

1. Studies of the survivors of Hiroshima and Nagasaki by the Atomic Bomb Casualty Commission

2. Observation of victims of accidental high acute radiation exposure

3. Study of patients treated by radiation for nonmalignant diseases

4. Study of the occurrence of lung cancer in uranium miners

5. Study of leukemia and other cancer in children whose mothers received irradiation during the pregnancy

6. Many experimental studies on animals subjected to various doses, dose rates, and kinds of radiation

The most acute damage is radiation sickness; it ranges from short-term effects from which the individual recovers fully to death within minutes. Radiation sickness is the direct consequence of a nuclear accident or of warfare. The gross effects of very high radiation doses are given in Table II.

Cancer of the skin, marrow, bone, lung, and thyroid gland, as well as leukemia can be induced by radiation. There is a latency period of 5-20 years after exposure before the cancer appears. Leukemia is perhaps the most likely form of malignancy; its occurrence in survivors of Hiroshima has been correlated with nearness to the hypocenter of the explosion.[3] Several studies suggest that very small exposures to radiation before conception or during pregnancy may increase by 50 percent the child's risk of leukemia.

Some radioisotopes show a tendency to become concentrated in a specific biologic environment. For example, there are bone-seekers, all of which are known to be carcinogenic; plutonium is both an extremely toxic element and a bone-seeker. Other bone-seekers are radium-226 (tenaciously retained, found in bones 25-35 years after exposure), strontium-90, barium-137, thorium-232, and actinium-227.

Finally, general physiological aspects such as growth, development, and aging are affected. In Hiroshima child survivors, as radiation exposure increased, there were small but statistically significant decreases in body measurements at all age levels, and in growth rate at postpubertal age levels. Animal experimentation has shown that ionizing radiation can induce a shortening of life span attributable to no specific disease but to an accelerated occurrence of disease in general. In Hiroshima and Nagasaki survivors, a general increase in mortality, exclusive of death from leukemia, was found.

*Genetic Effects of Ionizing Radiation*

A subtle and serious consequence of some radiation injuries is genetic transmission of physiological defects following an increase in mutation rates. Thus the species may suffer genetic damage from inherited defects. A mutation is a chemical or physical accident that changes the composition of a gene. Mutations induced by radiation are no different from spontaneous ones. Indeed, geneticists believe that 5-12 percent of the "spontaneous" mutations are caused by background radiation.

The effects produced by mutations are mostly harmful. Some have an immediate effect, some lie hidden for many generations. Mutations are responsible for a substantial part of human premature death, illness, and misery.

*Dose-Response Characteristics*

Determination of the biological risk of any toxic substance requires knowledge of the relation between the dose and the corresponding response. It also requires a search for a possible threshold level of exposure.

Some toxic substances can be taken in small quantities without detectable effects. As the quantity or dose is increased, the most susceptible individuals begin to show an effect. This may or may not be a threshold dose, the dose below which there is no effect. It may simply be the dose below which actual effects are not detectable, because they are widely dispersed in a large population and cannot be related to a single cause, or because they are concealed as genetic defects that may not become visible for several generations. If greater doses increase the observed effect more than proportionately, there is probably a threshold. But if the curve relating response to dose is linear, any exposure probably has some effect (Figure 1).

It is known that for radiation sickness a given dose is more biologically effective when absorbed in a single brief exposure than when absorbed in multiple exposures or in an exposure protracted at a low dose rate. In other words, there appears to be a threshold dose below which there is no permanent damage. This phenomenon is ascribed to the ability of the physiological system to repair tissue damage from background (and a little more) radiation at about the same rate at which damage occurs. If the total dose is prolonged at a low rate rather than concentrated in time, the system has time for recovery and replacement of damaged and dying cells. If the dose is concentrated or if it falls above the threshold, repair is no longer possible and permanent injury results.

| Dose, rem | Effect |
|---|---|
| 100,000 | Death in minutes |
| 10,000 | Death in hours |
| 1,000 | Death in days |
| 700 | Death for 90% within months, but 10% survive |
| 200 | Death for 10% within many months; 90% survive |
| 100 | No deaths, but chances of cancer and other forms of reduced life expectancy greatly increased; can induce permanent sterility in females, 2-3 year sterility in males |

**II**

**EFFECTS OF HIGH RADIATION DOSES.**

Whether or not the threshold phenomenon applies to the delayed somatic effects of radiation exposure is not known, and at the present time there is great disagreement over the question of cancer induction by prolonged or chronic exposure to low levels of radiation. There may be a threshold level below which radiation has no carcinogenic effect. However, similar carcinogens such as ultraviolet light show no threshold effect[4] (there is a linear relation between dose and response down to very low dose levels) and their effects are cumulative. The most reasonable assumption is that all doses of radiation, however small, can cause cancer in some fraction of the population.

There is also argument over the way in which radiation adds to the incidence of cancer produced by other sources. Some scientists assume a fixed risk per rem that should be added to the "natural" incidence of any particular form of cancer to calculate the carcinogenic effect of radiation, whereas others point to evidence like that now available on uranium miners of the Colorado Plateau to support their contention that radiation acts with other carcinogens to MULTIPLY the number of cancers induced.

The data on respiratory cancer deaths in white uranium miners of the Colorado Plateau are as follows[5]:

|  | Smokers | Nonsmokers |
| --- | --- | --- |
| Person-years | 26,392 | 9,047 |
| Cancers expected[a] | 15.5 | 0.5 |
| Cancers observed | 60 | 2 |

[a]If uranium miners react to smoking like everyone else and if the observed group of nonsmokers has the normal incidence of cancer in the U.S. male white population.

The fact that leaps from these simple statistics is that radiation exposure multiplied the smokers' risk by four times, as it also multiplied the risk of the nonsmokers, instead of just adding a fixed risk or number of deaths to each category.

Radiation-induced mutations are known to be induced at a rate proportional to the total amount of radiation received (that is, the dose-response curve is linear), regardless of the duration or time distribution of the exposure. In other words, there is no threshold below which

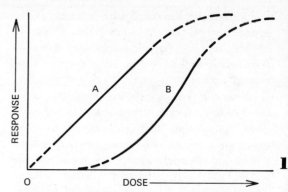

DOSE-RESPONSE CURVES. (A) Nonthreshold curve. Holds for genetic damage and probably for some cancer induction. (B) Threshold curve. Holds for radiation sickness and possibly for delayed somatic damage.

radiation is genetically harmless. The genetic effects of radiation doses are cumulative both in the individual and in his offspring; an increased mutation rate in a descendant of irradiated parents will be multiplied in proportion to the dose the descendant receives during his lifetime. PERHAPS THE MOST IMPORTANT HAZARD RELATED TO RADIATION POLLUTION IS THIS SNOWBALL GENETIC EFFECT: An increased radiation level which produces little adverse effect in the first few generations may, if maintained through those generations, produce disastrous effects, even extinction, in far-distant generations.

In summary then, we know that for acute exposures to nonlethal doses of ionizing radiation, the body has some ability to repair damage, and that there is a dose threshold below which there is no permanent injury. On the other hand, no convincing evidence exists for a threshold dose below which no cancer or leukemia will be induced by ionizing radiation; the only safe assumption is that such a threshold does not exist. Finally, there is surely no threshold for radiation-induced mutations and consequent genetic damage to the human species.

*Background Radiation: Benign or Malign?*

Although many people, including some scientists and engineers, speak of background or the "natural level" of radiation as if it were benign, or harmless to man, the steady background dose of ionizing radiation which cannot be reduced may be the cause not only of a fraction of the "spontaneous" mutations in man but also of a certain very low incidence of cancer.

The assumption of harmlessness of background radiation is based on the belief that man, over thousands of years, has adapted himself physiologically to life in a sea of radiation, and that his body can repair damage from natural dosage levels. This benign assumption is questioned more and more as linear response curves based on animal experiments and on studies of humans exposed to chronic or continued radiation doses are extended to lower and lower dose levels.

Although no one argues that a rem of man-made radiation is more dangerous than a rem of natural radiation, such an attitude seems implicit in radiation protection guides that define permissible limits of exposure ABOVE background. It is difficult to understand why 280 mrem per year, exclusive of medical irradiation, is unsafe or "unacceptable" for a man who lives in New York City, but safe or "acceptable" for a man who lives in Denver. The rationale for such standards appears to be that permissible limits expressed in total exposure would tend to restrict nuclear industry to coastal areas and to deprive the higher parts of the country of their fair share of new industrial development.

At least for genetic effects, and probably for long-term somatic effects, man-made radioactivity released to the environment is simply an increase in a hazard already present.

## Cosmic Rays and the SST

Natural radiation is a hazard to astronauts as well as to persons who will use the supersonic transport (SST). At the high cruising altitude of the SST (60,000-80,000 feet), cosmic radiation is tens of times more intense than at sea level. Although under normal cosmic conditions the great speed of the SST will keep the cumulative exposures of its crew and passengers within present "permissible" dose limits, solar flares pose a very real hazard to SST (and outer space) travel.

The solar component of cosmic rays consists of protons and heavier nuclei emitted in outbursts called solar flares. Such flares are brief, highly variable in intensity, and not accurately predictable. The giant flare of 23 February 1956 is estimated to have produced enough radiation to give a dose of 40 rem during 1 hour at SST elevations in the polar regions, a much larger dose than is permissible even for radiation workers. Such a dose would not be fatal, but the chances of cancer would be greatly increased in those exposed to it. Obviously such flares must be avoided, and ways need to be found for early detection and avoidance of solar-flare radiation by the SST. Alternatively, we can decide not to use the SST.

## Uranium Mining and Milling Hazards

The highest natural background radiation levels on the earth's surface are found over deposits of uranium ore. Man can greatly augment his dosage from this natural source by sinking mines into the uranium orebodies where he will be exposed to dose rates of 5600 mrem (5.6 rem) per year or greater, some 60 times the surface background at New York City. In addition, the miner will inhale radon gas, a decay product of uranium; the radioactive daughters of radon are solid and will probably lodge in his lungs, where their potential for damage is much greater than on his skin.

The hazard of the uranium mine environment was first revealed in the late 1930s by a study of pitchblende miners of the Erzgebirge in Germany and Czechoslovakia. Pitchblende is a mineral source of radium as well as uranium; it was then mined for its radium content. About 15 years after the start of pitchblende mining in this area of central Europe, the miners began to die of lung cancer. Ultimately, about 50 percent perished from this disease, and 80 percent of the remainder died from other lung diseases. Miners in other kinds of mines showed a much lower incidence of lung cancer. Beyond statistical doubt, the high lung-cancer mortality rate was related to the pitchblende ore.

Despite the ominous evidence from the Erzgebirge, when uranium mining started in the United States in the 1940s standards of individual exposure and mine ventilation were not set high enough to prevent a recurrence of the tragedy. In 1955, U.S. Public Health Service tests on air samples from 75 United States uranium mines showed that most far exceeded standards set by the International Commission on Radiological Protection (ICRP). A 1967 study[5] of 3414 U.S. uranium miners indicated that 46 of them had already died of lung cancer due to their mine exposure to radon and suggested that more of the studied group would yet have their lives shortened by their mining experience. Charles C. Johnson, Jr., head of the U.S. Consumer Protection and Environmental Health Service has said that "of the 6000 men who have been uranium miners, an estimated 600-1100 will die of lung cancer within the next 20 years because of radiation exposure on the job." In 1967, more than 20 years after the start of mining, exposure standards for U.S. uranium miners finally were set at levels which MAY be adequate for protection. Both the Atomic Energy Commission (AEC) and the U.S. Department of Labor now have permissible exposure limits for uranium miners; the fact that the Labor Department's standard is more than three times as stringent as that of the AEC reflects a continuing argument over the shape of the lower end of the dose-response curve.

Another hazard belatedly recognized involves the finely ground waste material, called tailings, from the uranium ore processing mills. In the upper Colorado River basin, these tailings are known to contain a total of about 10,000 grams of radium-226, as well as significant amounts of thorium-230 and lead-210, all of which are radioactive.

Radium-226 is a significant environmental hazard. It is readily leached from the tailings by rainwater and enters streams in solution. It is highly toxic, having the lowest maximum permissible concentration in drinking water of any of the 264 isotopes (natural and man-made) considered in the ICRP standards. It has a long half-life (1622 years), remaining hazardous for thousands of years. It decays to radon gas which can concentrate in buildings built on tailings used as landfill.

Radium leached from tailings has raised radium concentrations, at some places and times far above the permissible, throughout thousands of miles of the Colorado River system, and has contaminated groundwater reservoirs. In places where tailings have been used as convenient

landfill, buildings can contain hazardous concentrations of radon gas. In January 1970, two homes in Uravan, Colorado, were evacuated because of their radon gas levels and 1000 homes in Grand Junction may have to be evacuated for the same reason.

*Nuclear War and Reactor Accidents*

The greatest potential for worldwide radioactive pollution of the environment lies in nuclear war and related weapons testing. There seems little reason to discuss this disastrous potential in detail here. Man has developed the ability to render the entire surface of this planet uninhabitable. Although a nuclear war probably would stop somewhere short of annihilation of the human species, environmental conditions for the survivors would be so changed that the content of this chapter would be of no more than historical interest to them.

The greatest potential for local radioactive pollution of the environment lies in the possibility of reactor accidents (excepting catastrophic release of stored high-level wastes by flood or earthquake, or a conflagration at a plutonium plant; these sites are many times fewer in number than reactor sites, but each has more releasable radioactivity than any single reactor). No explosion like that of an atom bomb can occur in a nuclear reactor of the type in use today. However, several types of major accidents are possible. Any of these may result in melting or physical disruption of the reactor core and possible release of some of its great load of radioactivity to the local environment. This type of accident is assumed to be highly unlikely, because of the elaborate and comprehensive safety design requirements for nuclear power plants. On the other hand, the disastrous consequences of such an accident and the fact that it can occur (reactor safety design does not consider sabotage or warfare, for example) has caused commercial insurance companies to refuse to assume the risk inherent in a commercial power reactor; under the provisions of a law known as the Price-Anderson Act, this risk is jointly "assumed" by the Federal Treasury and the exposed public. How bad such an accident might be is indicated by a 1957 report of the Atomic Energy Commission on *The Theoretical Possibilities and Consequences of Major Accidents in Large Nuclear Power Plants,* which concluded that a single major accident might result in 3400 deaths at distances up to 15 miles, 43,000 injuries at distances up to 45 miles, and property damage of as much as $7 billion. Present estimates of damage, based on the assumptions of the 1957 report, might be even greater because of the larger power plants now being constructed. Although nuclear experts speak of the "exceedingly low" possibility of a serious nuclear power plant accident, the Joint Committee on Atomic Energy in 1965 admitted that there had not been "sufficient operating experience to form an adequate judgment of risk." Although reactors continue to be licensed on the assumption of "no undue risks to the public," the Price-Anderson Act in effect recognizes an undue (or at least unknown) risk to industry in the operation of the same reactors, for it indemnifies the utilities and equipment manufacturers against a risk neither they nor the commercial insurance companies are willing to assume.[6]

A kind of reactor accident that is much more likely than an accident in a commercial power reactor is the loss of a nuclear-powered vessel at sea. Indeed, such an accident has already happened. The U.S. nuclear-powered submarine Thresher, lost in the North Atlantic in 1963, released a large quantity of radioactivity to the marine environment.[7]

## Medical Irradiation

As early as 1900, a physician described the "irritating" effects of x rays. The first death from a radiation-induced tumor occurred in 1904. Then reports began to appear in the medical literature describing mentally retarded children with small heads born of mothers who had received radiotherapy during early pregnancy. Over the ensuing years it was noted that x-ray workers, including physicists and physicians, had a much higher incidence of skin cancer than could be expected from random occurrence. During the same period many dentists developed cancer of those fingers used to hold dental x-ray films in the mouths of patients. A 1944 report showed that leukemia was reported 1.7 times

more often as a cause of death among all U.S. physicians than among the general population of adult white males. An increase in leukemia incidence has been verified among patients treated by x rays for ankylosing spondulitis, an arthritic condition of the back. A 1965 study of 877 Nova Scotia women who received numerous fluoroscopic examinations while being treated for tuberculosis showed clear evidence of radiation-induced breast cancer at approximately 24 times the normal incidence. Recent studies show that children born after in utero radiation of embryos for diagnostic purposes have about 50 percent more danger of developing leukemia and other forms of cancer than do other children.

Although the use of x rays in medicine is still expanding, there is a strong movement within the profession to reduce radiation exposure from diagnostic x rays. Not only are techniques available for grossly reducing the radiation exposure, but many doctors now use x rays only when they judge the patient would be in more danger without the exposure than with it. Medical irradiation gives the average individual in the United States a yearly dose of about 60 mrem.

## X Rays from Television Sets

Any electronic tube operating at a potential above a few thousand volts may be a source of x radiation. Such sources include oscillographs, electron microscopes, and television tubes. Of these the home television tube is of greatest interest because a high percentage of the population is involved.

Television tubes in general are designed so that the maximum emission at a distance of 5 cm from the tube surface is less than 0.5 mrem per hour. On the basis of an average yearly viewing time of 1000 hours, and correction factors for viewing distances of 100 cm (children) and 200 cm (adults), it has been calculated that the average yearly gonadal skin dose for such viewers would be 40 mrem (100 cm) and 10 mrem (200 cm).[8]

In 1967, many color television sets were found to be emitting excessive radiation, generally from the sides, top, bottom, or back, and in 1969 the U.S. Bureau of Radiological Health warned viewers of color television against the hazard of sitting closer than 6 feet from the screen, and of exposing themselves for long periods to the sides or back of an operating set. Because children's cells are more sensitive to radiation, and because they have a tendency to sit closer to the TV screen, they need to be impressed with the importance of observing these rules of viewing.

## Releases from Nuclear Explosives

Fallout from atmospheric tests of atomic explosives prior to the Limited Nuclear Test Ban Treaty of 1963 raised background radiation levels throughout the northern hemisphere, most dramatically in areas downwind from the Nevada test site. Averaged over the United States, however, the fallout during the years of maximum testing has been calculated at about 30 mrem per year, well below the guide of 170 mrem per year. Because of the test ban treaty, no nuclear weapons tests since that time have been carried out in the atmosphere, and the total environmental radioactivity due to fallout has greatly decayed.

Since 1963 the danger of environmental contamination from nuclear explosives has come from underground weapons tests and from underground nuclear explosives of the Plowshare program. Plowshare is a program of the Atomic Energy Commission to promote the peaceful use of nuclear explosives in a wide range of applications, from the creation of underground storage facilities to the blasting of artificial harbors and canals. Although the potential engineering applications of nuclear energy are vast, the potential for environmental contamination is also great. Unlike the man-made radiation of nuclear reactors and their wastes, which can, with proper care in design and practice, be kept out of the biologic environment, the man-made radiation of an underground nuclear explosion is created in that environment and cannot be kept out of it. Cratering explosions release 10 percent of their radioactivity directly to the atmosphere and produce fallout characteristic of atmospheric weapons tests. Some of the 90 percent of the radioactivity that remains in the ground may be leached and transported by moving groundwater to points of potential water use. Completely contained underground nuclear detonations create a

similar danger of groundwater contamination, and in addition, may involve deliberate releases to the environment such as occurs in the flaring of radioactive natural gas after a shot designed to stimulate its production from geologic formations of low permeability.

Although environmental contamination from one properly placed underground nuclear blast might be nothing to worry about, the contamination potential of hundreds or thousands of such blasts within a relatively small area is causing concern. The Bureau of Natural Gas of the Federal Power Commission has stated: "In order to substantially increase natural gas availability . . . thousands of nuclear devices will have to be detonated . . . such large-scale application might not gain public acceptance."

Natural gas "stimulated" by Plowshare blasts will itself be too radioactive for use; therefore it is planned to add it slowly to gas distribution systems so that it will be diluted to acceptable or permissible levels by "clean" gas from other sources.

## Reactor Wastes

A fission reactor produces a great quantity of radioactivity as waste. This radioactivity is generated in the core of the reactor which houses the fissionable fuel. (Figure 2 diagrams three kinds of fission reactors.) Reactor fuel consists of uranium in metallic, oxide, or carbide form, fashioned into rods or plates put together into what are called fuel elements. The elements are encased in zirconium-alloy or stainless-steel cladding. The kinetic energy of fission is converted to heat which is picked up by water or gas (air or carbon dioxide) circulating among the fuel elements. The heat is used to generate steam, either directly (boiling water reactor) or indirectly (pressurized water or gas-cooled reactors), and the steam drives a turbine generator that produces electricity.

Only a small portion of the material in the fuel elements is actually burned up at the end of a fuel cycle. Much of it is not fissionable, and for technical reasons not all of the fissionable portion can be used or burned. Consequently, when it comes time for the fuel elements to be removed from the reactor core (about 20 percent

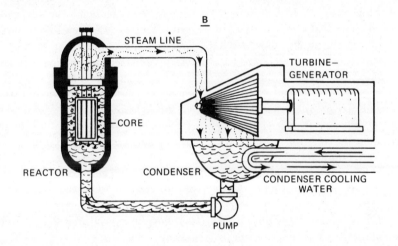

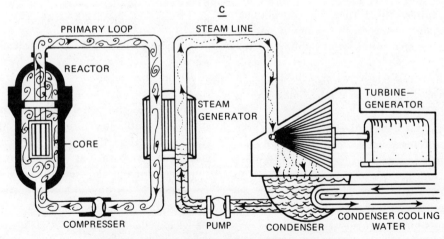

**2**

FISSION POWER REACTORS. Examples of the three types of reactors in commercial use. Pressurized water reactors: Yankee Atomic Electric Company, Rowe, Massachusetts and Consolidated Edison Company, Indian Point, New York. Boiling water reactors: Commonwealth Edison Company, Dresden Nuclear Power Station (near Chicago, Illinois). Gas-cooled reactors: Hinkley Point, Somerset, England.

are removed and replaced annually), there remains in them some highly valuable unspent fuel which it is economically important to recover. This recovery is done at fuel-reprocessing plants. However, by the time the fuel elements are removed they have become highly radioactive and extremely dangerous. The cladding and the unburned contents not only absorb most of the radioactive fission products but, although previously inert, become radioactive themselves under the neutron bombardment that takes place during fission. By far the greater part of the radioactive waste of a nuclear reactor is contained in the spent fuel elements. If the elements are properly handled, none of this radioactivity is released to the environment at the power-plant site.

During operation of the reactor, radioactivity also builds up in the primary coolant (water or gas), in two ways. Fission products escape from the fuel elements by diffusion or through defects in the metal cladding. In addition, radioactive products, especially tritium ($^3$H or T), are formed in the water by neutron activation. Water ($H_2O$) in which one of the ordinary hydrogen ions (H) is replaced by a tritium ion (T) is called tritiated water (HTO). Chemically and physically (except for its radioactivity) tritiated water is very similar to ordinary water, and it is not possible to separate the tritium by conventional waste-treatment processes. It is common practice to release tritiated water, after dilution by uncontaminated water, into the ground at reactor sites. Tritium has a relatively long half-life (12.36 years) and as tritiated water can become a serious environmental hazard.

Another hazardous radioisotope that has been difficult to manage in reactors is krypton-85. On a laboratory scale, it is possible to remove krypton from gas streams, but until recently no commercially feasible technique had been developed and krypton-85 is released to the atmosphere at present reactor sites.

Radioactive iodine (two of the iodine isotopes are radioactive), an extremely noxious waste, was released as a gas in considerable quantities into the atmosphere from the early commercial reactors, but reactors now under construction are designed to remove well over

99 percent of the produced iodine from the gaseous effluent. Iodine-131, much the more abundant of the two isotopes, has a half-life of only 8 days. If it can be trapped, concentrated, and contained for a period of 150 days or so, it will decay to an innocuous level; on the other hand, because it becomes concentrated by organisms this short half-life is not the protection it might appear to be.

Here it is important to note that a continuous advance in the technology of managing the radioactive wastes of reactors appears to have culminated in a zero-release design that is technically feasible and economically practical. Westinghouse Electric Corporation in May 1970 announced the development of a nuclear reactor system designed to eliminate radioactive-waste discharge completely. In the new system, krypton-85 will be concentrated and stored. Tritium will be fed back into the reactor system and, in effect, stored there. Two 1100-megawatt power plants being built by the Commonwealth Edison Company at a site 40 miles north of Chicago will incorporate the new zero-release system. Adoption of a zero-release reactor system would focus the entire radioactive-waste disposal problem of the nuclear power industry at the fuel-reprocessing plants.

*Wastes from Fuel Reprocessing*

A fuel-reprocessing plant is a chemical plant where the fuel elements are dissolved in nitric acid and the depleted fissionable fuel is recovered.

Until 1966, the AEC did all fuel reprocessing at its own plants in South Carolina, Idaho, and Washington. Then the first private reprocessing facility was established at West Valley, about 30 miles south of Buffalo, New York. Construction has begun (1970) on another at Morris, Illinois, and several others are planned. Each fuel-reprocessing plant is designed to serve a local or regional cluster of reactors. As more power reactors come into operation, the demand will increase for more and larger reprocessing plants.

Although private ownership of fuel-reprocessing plants will allow their siting near reactors, thus reducing the hazards of transporting highly radioactive fuel elements through populous regions, the factor of economics that dominates commercial enterprise raises a question in regard to environmental safety, for THE FUEL-REPROCESSING PLANTS REPRESENT BY FAR THE MOST SERIOUS ENVIRONMENTAL HAZARD IN THE NUCLEAR POWER INDUSTRY.

When the spent fuel elements are removed from the core of a reactor they are highly radioactive and must be handled with great care. The spent elements are stored at the reactor site for a period of about 150 days, during which time their radioactivity is greatly reduced by decay. They are then transported by truck or railroad in large lead and steel casks weighing as much as 70 tons to a fuel-reprocessing plant, where all the radioactive waste materials are extracted. After extraction, some of the radioactive wastes are in liquid form, while others are gaseous.

Most of the radioactivity is contained in high-level liquid wastes. Recently published AEC procedures for handling this very dangerous waste, which contains strontium-90 and cesium-137 with hazard lives of 600 years, call for storage at the reprocessing plant for a period not to exceed 10 years, conversion to a solid form, and shipment to a designated federal repository. If adequate safeguards are maintained during storage, conversion, and shipment of this high-level waste, and if its "ultimate disposal" is in a deep salt formation, it should constitute no significant environmental hazard. On the other hand, location of such a plant near any large city increases the hazard inherent in the possibility of the accidental rupture of a high-level waste storage tank.

The principal environmental threat of a fuel-reprocessing plant lies, not in the high-level wastes, but in its "low-level" liquid and gaseous wastes, which in current practice are discharged to the local environment. These wastes contain the radioisotopes that are difficult to trap, notably tritium, krypton-85, and radioactive iodine, as well as very small quantities of many other isotopes.

A commercial fuel-reprocessing plant of the minimum economic size will discharge 100,000 to 500,000 gallons per day of low-level liquid waste, depending on the waste-management techniques used. Most of the radioactivity in this liquid waste comes from the evaporator used to concentrate the high-level wastes. It is from the evaporator that krypton-85, xenon-133, and iodine-131 are released into the atmosphere, after being mixed with large volumes of air. Virtually all the radioisotopes except tritium CAN be removed from the liquid waste, but in practice significant quantities of isotopes like strontium-90, cerium-144, and iodine-131 (in solution) remain in the liquid when it is discharged. Also in this low-level waste is a minimum of 750 curies of tritium (the curie is a unit of quantity of radioactivity, originally defined as the radioactivity of 1 gram of radium); the larger reprocessing plants of the future may discharge ten times this amount.

*The Fusion Rainbow*

Fusion (of certain light elements into heavier elements; see Chapter 5) frequently has been described as a "clean" or nonhazardous way of producing nuclear power because the end product of fusion will be nonradioactive helium, which constitutes no environmental hazard. But the deuterium-lithium reaction discussed in Chapter 5 is clean in theory only; abundant tritium will be produced in the operating cycle, and it has been estimated that as much as 13 percent of the tritium generated may be lost from (and absorbed in) the reactor. Calculations by Dr. Frank Parker, formerly of Oak Ridge, suggest that the problem of tritium losses from a fusion reactor may be worse than the problem of tritium disposal from fusion reactors and associated fuel-reprocessing plants.[9] It appears that fusion power will not be clean power until a better method for tritium containment than is now known can be found.

*Biological Concentrating Processes*

Although maximum permissible concentrations for radioactivity in air and water have been set to protect the public from harmful biological effects of gaseous and liquid effluents from nuclear reactors, fuel-reprocessing plants, and nuclear explosions, these standards do not take into account certain biological processes which may concentrate radioactivity in the food chain of man (Chapter 1).

Just as DDT and other pesticides may be concentrated in the living tissue of fish and birds, so may radioisotopes be concentrated to levels thousands of times greater than their concentrations in the air and water surrounding the living organisms. Below the Hanford, Washington, plant of the AEC, for example, eggs of ducks and geese have been found to contain radiophosphorus in concentrations 200,000 times greater than the effluent solution.

The interception and retention of fallout by plants leads to the rapid injection of radioactive material into terrestrial food chains. In the days of bomb-test fallout it was discovered that Eskimos of the Arctic were being subjected to a unique hazard because Arctic lichens collect radioisotopes from the air and concentrate them. Caribou feed on the lichen and retain the radioisotopes in their bodies, with a further concentration. Finally, the Eskimos eat the caribou, ingesting the radioisotopes which then become selectively contentrated in various parts of their bodies.

Biological concentration is a limiting factor on the level of radioactive waste discharged into the sea at the Windscale works in England. Extensive studies have shown that the persons liable to the greatest exposure from this discharge are those who eat a special type of bread made from edible seaweed of the area. Accordingly, the discharges have been lowered to protect this bread-eating group. In the United States, on the other hand, when it was discovered that certain Tennessee mountaineers were eating fish cakes made from the meat and bones of fish taken from the Clinch River, into which low-level wastes from Oak Ridge are discharged, the AEC attempted to "educate" the mountaineers to remove the bones (in which certain radioisotopes are concentrated) before making their cakes.

Studies of iodine-131 and strontium-89 from fallout from Project Sedan (a Plowshare cratering test in Nevada) showed that desert plants collected these radioisotopes and that they were further highly concentrated in the thyroids of jackrabbits that feed on the plants.[10] After deposition on pasturage, iodine-131 can make its way swiftly into cow's milk and thence into the human body; unacceptable concentrations were found in milk in southwest Utah after Nevada

bomb tests in 1962. Although iodine-131 has a short radioactive half-life (8 days), it has a BIO-LOGICAL HALF-TIME of about 3 months, because it is quickly taken up by the thyroid gland and is eliminated slowly. Biological half-time is the time required for the amount of a particular element in the body to decrease to half its initial mass through elimination by natural biological processes. It is important to understand also that the biological effectiveness of a radioisotope is inversely related to its radioactive half-life: A given mass of a radioisotope of short half-life will decay and emit particles at a greater rate than the same mass of another isotope which has a longer half-life. Consequently, the radioisotope with the shorter half-life is more biologically "effective" or damaging. The radioisotopes representing the greatest internal hazard are those with a relatively short radioactive half-life and a comparatively long biological half-time. However, any radioisotope with a long biological half-time, including those with long radioactive half-lives, can be a serious internal hazard; two of these are radium-226 and plutonium-239.

*Radioactive Waste Storage and Disposal*

We have seen that radioactive wastes are generated in nuclear reactors and associated fuel-reprocessing plants. Although research, experimental, and production reactors (those which produce fissionable isotopes like plutonium-239) produce wastes that represent local environmental hazards, the great bulk of the radioactive wastes of the future will come from commercial power reactors.

In mid-1970 there were 17 nuclear power plants operating in the United States; 40 more were under construction and another 44 were in various stages of planning. The AEC has predicted that the installed nuclear electric capacity will rise from 7000 megawatts in 1970 to 734,000 megawatts in the year 2000. The accumulated total of all fission products will rise in the same period from 19 to 4250 metric tons.[11] The annual production of high-level liquid wastes will grow from 31,000 gallons in 1970 to 3,400,000 gallons in 2000. Accumulated strontium-90, the most hazardous fission product in the waste, will increase from 18 million curies in 1970 to 8.6 billion curies in 2000. The strontium, however, will largely be contained in stored high-level wastes. More significant is the planned release to the environment of krypton-85 and tritium, whose total activity levels by 2000 will have reached 1 billion curies ($^{85}$Kr) and 36 million curies (T); these amounts will represent unacceptable levels of environmental pollution, if all or most of the krypton and tritium have been released to the environment.

Storage of radioactive wastes implies that the material is retrievable; disposal, that it is not. Highly radioactive wastes, solidified and placed in salt mines, may be regarded as stored, even if they are to be there hundreds of years, for the radioactive slugs can be retrieved if the need arises. If the same solidified waste were to be placed in a weighted drum and dropped to the bottom of the sea, that would be disposal.

Methods of storage and disposal fundamentally depend on the biological harmfulness of the radioisotopes involved, their hazard lives, their concentrations, and the physical state of the waste material (solid, liquid, or gas). Other factors that may affect specific practices are economy, expediency, and faith in printed standards and in the capacity or willingness of the environment to cooperate.

Although most present methods for storage and disposal of radioactive wastes appear satisfactory in terms of existing quantities and present knowledge, some will certainly not be acceptable for the much higher quantities of the future and may not be acceptable even in terms of present quantities as our knowledge of the biological risks improves.

A common classification of current disposal methods for fluid (liquid and gaseous) wastes is the following: concentrate and contain; delay and decay; dilute and disperse.

CONCENTRATE AND CONTAIN applies to treatment of the high-level (tens to thousands of curies per gallon) liquid wastes produced at the fuel-processing plants. These wastes must be stored, for they are too dangerous to be placed where they could not be retrieved. So far, no method of permanent storage has been adopted, although several methods have been under research and development by the AEC for a number of years. Almost 80 million gallons of hot, high-level wastes, concentrated by evaporation,

are stored in about 200 steel-and-concrete tanks at AEC reprocessing sites (140 of these are at the Hanford, Washington site). Some of the waste has been there for over 20 years; all of it will be hazardous for at least 600 years. The tanks must be strong, corrosion-resistant, leak-protected, and provided with a constant cooling mechanism. As the tanks age, the hazard from leakage becomes serious. The most promising procedures for permanent storage would convert the wastes to solids in the form of glass or ceramic slugs, after which they could be interred in salt formations deep underground or in concrete-and-metal bins at or near the earth's surface. In either method, it is critically important to keep the radioactivity isolated from circulating groundwater and thus from the biological environment. Underground storage in salt is preferable, because salt beds are highly impervious to groundwater flow, act plastically to seal any fractures that form in them, are insulated from the effects of rain and snowfall, and underlie about 400,000 square miles of the United States.

DELAY AND DECAY applies to treatment of most of the radioactive gaseous wastes of the nuclear power industry, for they are mainly composed of short-lived isotopes. The gases may be compressed and stored in tanks until the radioisotopes, such as iodine-131, decay to innocuous levels; but iodine-131 needs to be stored for less than 6 months to be harmless, whereas krypton-85 has a hazard life closer to 50 years.

In some places intermediate-level (from a microcurie to a few curies per gallon) liquid wastes are discharged directly into the ground. Such discharge is based upon a judgment that the hydrologic factors, the ion-exchange properties of the soil, and local population distribution will allow sufficient time for the radioactivity to decay to nonhazard levels as the waste moves slowly through the soil; the fundamental assumption that these factors will remain constant throughout the hazard life of the waste material is open to serious question, and the practice itself is a temporary expedient with an inherent long-term hazard potential.

At Oak Ridge a unique delay-and-decay disposal method for intermediate-level wastes involves injecting them as a slurry into hydraulically induced fractures in shale at depths of

700-1000 feet where the slurry "sets" into a con-
cretelike solid. This method is safe only for locations below the level of circulating potable
groundwater and where vertical fractures in the
overlying rock are essentially nonexistent; such
locations are probably rare.

DILUTE AND DISPERSE applies to low-level
(less than a microcurie per gallon) wastes when
diluted by water or air and discharged into the
environment. In many cases the most EXPEDIENT
method of dealing with a radioactive gas is to
discharge it to the atmosphere from a high stack
and thus to dilute the radioactivity to a "permissible" level.

It should be emphasized that any disposal of
radioactive waste to the biosphere or to any geological environment where there is a risk of contaminating the biosphere is not a safe practice.
However, it has been and it continues to be done;
if not safe, it is at present "permissible."

The tremendous volume of the ocean might
seem to make it an ideal medium for the dilute-
and-disperse technique of radioactive waste disposal. According to recommendations of the International Atomic Energy Agency, low-level and
intermediate-level wastes may be discharged into
the ocean under controlled and specified conditions. As in all releases to the biosphere, how-

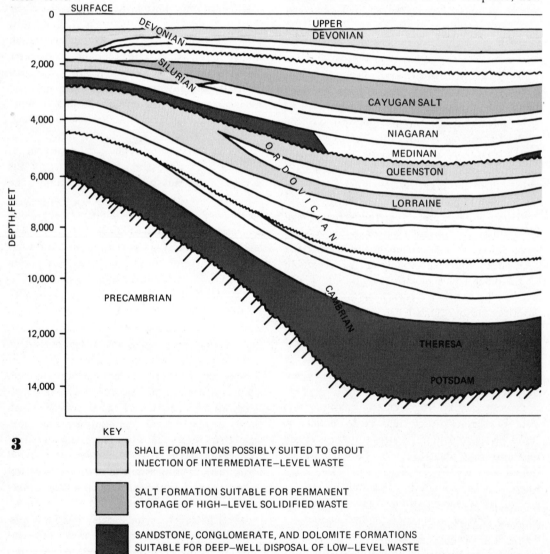

**3**

KEY

SHALE FORMATIONS POSSIBLY SUITED TO GROUT
INJECTION OF INTERMEDIATE—LEVEL WASTE

SALT FORMATION SUITABLE FOR PERMANENT
STORAGE OF HIGH—LEVEL SOLIDIFIED WASTE

SANDSTONE, CONGLOMERATE, AND DOLOMITE FORMATIONS
SUITABLE FOR DEEP—WELL DISPOSAL OF LOW—LEVEL WASTE

ever, there is widespread concern for the unknown hazard potential in the ability of certain organisms of man's food chain to concentrate radioactivity.

Solid radioactive waste (contaminated objects, not solidified liquid waste) is buried. If high-level, it is stored in vaults above the water table. If lower-level, it may be buried in relatively shallow trenches at sites where calculated groundwater movement and ion-exchange capacity of the soil make it certain that decay and dilution will reduce the radioactivity to permissible levels by the time the radioisotopes reach places where the water is available for human use.

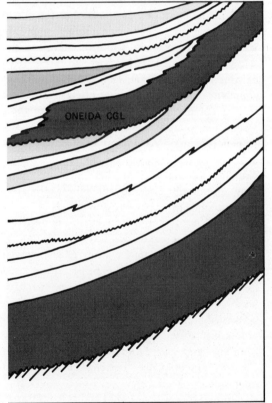

SUITABLE GEOLOGIC FORMATIONS. Geologic cross section along 42d parallel, western New York, showing formations of the Appalachian Basin suitable for three types of underground storage and disposal of radioactive waste. Source: T. P. McCann, in reference 14.

In 1966, the Committee on Geologic Aspects of Radioactive Waste Disposal of the National Academy of Sciences issued the following warning:

> The current practices of disposing of intermediate and low-level liquid wastes and all manner of solid wastes directly into the ground above

or in fresh-water zones, although momentarily safe, will lead in the long run to a serious fouling of man's environment. Such methods represent a concept of easy disposal that has had and will continue to have great appeal to operators, but we fear that continuation of the practices eventually will create hazards that will be extremely difficult to eliminate.[12]

The same committee pointed to the necessity of taking a long-range view of waste storage and disposal. Not only are some present environmental disposal sites and practices unsuited for disposal of the much greater quantities of wastes that will be produced by the growing nuclear power industry, but they may be subject to serious hydrologic changes during the 600 years or more of the hazard life of some of the long-lived isotopes. In arid regions like central Washington and southeast Idaho, irrigation projects and dams can change hydrologic conditions from safe to unsafe within a few years.

### Safe Underground Storage and Disposal

Short-lived radioisotopes can be contained or delayed until they decay to safe levels, in artificial containers or in surface ponds and soil layers sufficiently distant or isolated from points of water use. Long-lived radioisotopes, however, pose a different problem. Eventually the present practice of discharging long-lived radioisotopes to the environment, even in dilute concentrations, must be stopped, for the hazards of buildup and biological reconcentration in the environment are too great. Geologic and hydrologic research carried out over the past decade indicates that there is an alternative, that long-lived radioisotopes can be effectively isolated from the biological environment during their hazard lives. All indicated safe methods involve intelligent use of the underground, nonbiologic environment.[12,13]

High-level liquid wastes can be solidified and placed in safe permanent storage in natural salt formations. Economic studies at Oak Ridge indicate that the cost for the safer, permanent storage of solidified wastes in salt mines is about the same as that for perpetual tank storage. Intermediate and low-level liquid wastes can be injected through deep wells into deep geologic basins in tectonically stable portions of the continent where water movement is extremely slow, on the order of a few feet a year.[13] Figure 3 shows a cross section of such a basin and indicates geologic formations suitable for three types of underground storage and disposal.[14]

1. A permeable geologic formation (for example, sandstone), from which upward migration of fluids is prevented by an impervious overlying formation (for example, shale), and in which fluid motion is say only 3 feet a year, is almost ideal for disposal of liquid radioactive waste: Tritium, which takes perhaps 75 years to decay to harmlessness, would in that time move only 225 feet from the injection well; cesium-137 and strontium-90 would move not more than 600 yards away from the well before becoming innocuous.

2. Under favorable geologic conditions, intermediate-level waste may be injected into shale as a self-cementing slurry (grout).

3. Solid wastes containing long-lived radioisotopes could be placed in permanent underground storage in an environment isolated from circulating groundwater. The concept of one or two national burial grounds for long-hazard wastes has much to commend it; salt-mine interment of solidified high-level liquid wastes could be supplemented by a desert cemetery for contaminated solid wastes.

It should not be assumed, from these statements, that finding suitable underground storage and disposal sites is easy, or that just about any place will do. Suitable geologic environments for radioactive-waste disposal are relatively rare. But they exist, and in such size as to contain readily all the radioactive wastes of the foreseeable future. Before any subsurface storage or disposal operations are undertaken, the underground environment needs to be investigated thoroughly, so that the risk of contaminating the biosphere can be made vanishingly small. To be avoided are earthquake zones and places where the rocks are fractured and might leak radioactivity into formations from which water is drawn into the biosphere. Any subsurface injection of waste materials, radioactive or not, should be carried out in accordance with the Federal Water Quality Administration's 1970 *Policy on Disposal of Wastes by Subsurface Injection,* which requires the following conditions: (1) demonstration that subsurface injection is the best available disposal alternative; (2) pre-injection tests sufficient for prediction of the fate of the wastes; (3) evidence that such an injection will not constitute an environmental hazard; (4) best practicable pretreatment of the wastes; (5) best possible design and construction of the injection system; (6) provision for adequate and continuous monitoring of the operation; and (7) provision for securing the environment if the disposal operation is discontinued.

*Siting of Fuel-Reprocessing Plants*

None of the AEC plants which produce large quantities of radioactive wastes, from Savannah River in the southeast to Hanford in the northwest, appears to have been located with safe waste disposal in mind. The main factors in site selection seem to have been distance from existing centers of population and availability of abundant dependable supplies of fresh water for reactor cooling. As it turned out, none of these plants was located near a favorable area for permanent disposal. As a consequence, economic and operational expediency has led to storage and disposal practices at these sites which are only temporarily safe and which must ultimately be abandoned in favor of safer methods.

This failure to foresee the critical importance of good geologic conditions for waste disposal is now being repeated in the siting of commercial fuel-reprocessing plants. The siting criteria used for the first three of these appear to have been: (1) nearness to the cluster of reactors to be served; (2) availability of water for the reprocessing cycle; and (3) reasonable distance from any large city. Site testing for underground disposal potential has been given little consideration.

Disposal of low-level liquid and gaseous wastes is (or should be) the critical problem in siting a reprocessing plant.[15] The high-level liquid wastes represent a minor siting factor, for they are to be stored at the reprocessing plant for not more than 10 years, after which they will be solidified and transferred to one of a limited number of federal repositories which will provide "permanent isolation of the wastes from man's biological environment."

Most of the waste tritium of the nuclear power industry is released at the reprocessing plant. Tritium as tritiated water is readily incorporated into living tissue. To keep tritium from the biologic environment requires containment of tritiated water in closed-cycle recirculating systems, and disposal of that which is released in deep geologic formations in which the contained water moves so slowly that the tritium will decay before entering the biological environment. Such disposal requires that the reprocessing plant be located over geologic formations which have been proved by test wells to be suitable for safe disposal of liquid radioactive wastes. An alternative, but probably more expensive, way of handling excess tritium would be to separate it from tritiated water by a distillation process, condense it ($^3$H is a gas), and contain it until decay.

Fission-product gases like krypton-85 and xenon-133 are released in significant amounts at fuel-reprocessing plants. Recent Oak Ridge studies show that these gases will (or should) impose the most severe limitations on siting of reprocessing plants. If releases of krypton-85 to the atmosphere were to continue at the present rate per megawatt, by the year 2060 the radiation exposure of the general public from the radioisotope ALONE could equal more than half the permissible dose.[16] Isolation of these chemically inert gases from the biological environment during their hazard life requires either concentration and surface containment, or injection into geologic formations in which they will be trapped or delayed and dispersed in their rise to the surface.

If, instead of being contained or disposed of underground, low-level liquid and gaseous radioactive wastes are to be deliberately released to the environment from fuel-reprocessing plants, then the plants should be located in remote areas, suggested in a 1968 report by the energy policy staff of the Office of Science and Technology,[17] which went on to point out that there is a great deal of flexibility in siting a reprocessing plant because of the relatively low cost of transporting the small tonnage of solids involved. But of the first two commercial reprocessing plants, one is only 30 miles from Buffalo, and the other is 60 miles from Chicago.

"Low-level" liquid waste from the western New York plant (West Valley), which approaches maximum permissible concentrations some distance BELOW its point of discharge into a surface stream, eventually finds its way to Lake Erie. Because of continued great difficulty in meeting effluent standards, the plant operators in 1970 asked permission to put in a deep (7000-foot) waste-disposal well but were turned down by the AEC. The site appears well suited for deep-well disposal (although this was not a factor in its selection) and the alternative disposal into surface streams cannot − or should not − long continue without serious objection being raised; consequently, the sustained official reluctance to test the underground for disposal capabilities is difficult to understand.

The northern Illinois (Morris) site was chosen with no regard for any sort of waste disposal. Only now (1970) is there talk of testing the disposal potential of underground formations at the site.

*The Decision Matrix*

The three principal peacetime sources of potential environmental pollution from ionizing radiation are (1) nuclear reactors, (2) nuclear fuel-reprocessing plants, and (3) Plowshare blasts.

Public concern about possible radioactive pollution has been expressed recently in a number of confrontations with planners or operators of nuclear projects. Plans to excavate harbors in Alaska and Australia and to blast out an underground storage cavern in Pennsylvania with nuclear explosives have been abandoned or delayed because of public protests. Opposition to nuclear power plants in California, Minnesota, New York, and elsewhere has caused abandonment of sites, modification of designs, and delays in construction or operation. For purposes of illustration, three such confrontations, each representing one of the main potential sources of pollution, will be described briefly.

THE MONTICELLO NUCLEAR POWER PLANT. In 1967, the Atomic Energy Commission issued a construction permit to the Northern States Power Company for a 545-megawatt boiling-water reactor and power plant to be built near Monticello, Minnesota, on the Mississippi about 35 miles upstream from the point where St. Paul and Minncapolis extract their water. When the power company applied for a waste-disposal permit from the newly created Minnesota Pollution Control Agency (MPCA), it ran into trouble. Citizens led by University of Minnesota scientists criticized the projected discharge of low-level radioactive wastes to the environment, even at levels considerably below those considered by the AEC as acceptable; questioned the effluent standards set by the AEC; and accused the AEC of a conflict of interest because it is required to promote the use of nuclear power as well as protect the public.

The power company countered these charges by arguing that standards stricter than those of the AEC were unnecessary, that liquid discharges below the Monticello plant would contain less radioactivity than domestic tap water, and that a person living beside the plant would receive about half the radiation an average American receives from watching television.

In February 1969, the MPCA, acting upon the recommendations of a consultant who pointed out that the AEC standards neglect the problem of multiple sources of radioactive pollution, issued a waste-disposal permit limiting radioactive discharges from the reactor to levels much lower than those permitted by the AEC.

In August 1969, its plant almost completed, Northern States Power Company brought suit against the state pollution agency, challenging its authority to set radioactive discharge standards. A few days later Governor LeVander of Minnesota received the unanimous endorsement of the National Governors' Conference in support of the principle that state governments should have independent authority to protect their residents from environmental dangers, even in fields such as radioactivity where federal agencies such as the AEC claim exclusive jurisdiction. Later, 17 states announced intention to enter the lawsuit as friends of the court in support of Minnesota's position.

RADIOACTIVE WASTE DISPOSAL AT NRTS IN IDAHO. A wide range of activity levels is represented in liquid wastes produced, largely from fuel reprocessing, at the National Reactor Testing Station (NRTS) located on the Snake River Plain near Idaho Falls, Idaho. For years, both low-level

and intermediate-level liquid wastes have been discharged into the ground at NRTS, despite the fact that the site lies above one of the nation's great underground sources of fresh water. Reliance has been placed on the considerable depth to the water table, on the ability of the soil to capture radioisotopes by ion exchange, on the aridity of the region, and on the distance from the disposal site to places where ground water is available for use by the public. Solid waste materials, also representing a wide range of hazards, are buried in the same environment. Plutonium-contaminated wastes, highly hazardous in perpetuity (half-life: 24,360 years), are given shallow burial in steel drums on the same assumption under which the liquid wastes are discharged to the environment. Radioactive solid waste shipped from Japan is now being buried at NRTS.

Although in 1960 and again in 1966 a committee of the National Academy of Sciences had expressed concern about "overconfidence" in the protection afforded by aridity at both NRTS and the Hanford works,[12] this did not become public knowledge until 1970, when in response to questioning by Senator Frank Church of Idaho the committee report was made public. Senator Church's action reflected the expressed concern of some Idaho citizens who live "downstream" from NRTS in terms of groundwater flow. At the request of the Senator, four federal agencies investigated and recommended substantial changes in the disposal program. The Federal Water Quality Administration, for example, urged the AEC to stop burying contaminated solid waste at NRTS and to halt the discharge of tritiated water into the ground above the Snake River Plain groundwater reservoir (aquifer); FWQA recommended subsurface, deep-well injection of the tritium into a pretested, slow-flushing formation below the aquifer.

PROJECT RULISON. In 1969, a public storm blew up in Colorado over the AEC's Project Rulison. In partnership with the Austral Oil Company, the AEC announced plans for a 40-kiloton nuclear explosion deep below the scenic surface of western Colorado, in hope of stimulating natural gas production and recovery from the enclosing low-permeability Mesaverde Formation of the Rulison Gas Field.

Citizens concerned about possible detrimental effects to the environment (contamination of ground water, induced earthquakes, surface and atmospheric contamination from subsequent flaring of the radioactive gas) found they had no right even to a hearing, under a law that gives full decision authority to the AEC.

The Colorado Open Spaces Council and the American Civil Liberties Union thereupon sued the AEC in an attempt to halt Project Rulison. Two federal courts upheld the AEC's right to proceed with the test, subject only to the condition that no reentry and flaring take place until at least 6 months after the shot. The blast took place on September 10, 1969. No radioactivity was vented, no earthquake induced. Critics of the project were far from reassured that all would be well, however; their concern went beyond Project Rulison, to the potential environmental effects of the hundreds or even thousands of such shots that may be required to develop the field if Rulison proves successful from the economic and engineering points of view.

Recurrent themes in these and other public confrontations with the proponents of nuclear-energy projects are the questions, What is safe? How are protection standards set? If these standards involve acceptance of risk in return for benefits, why does the concerned and exposed public find it so difficult to participate in the acceptance or assumption of the risk?

We shall briefly consider each of these questions in turn.

*What Is Safe?*

Safety from the effects of ionizing radiation is difficult to define. Absolute safety does not exist, because some genetic damage is caused by any sustained level of radiation. Therefore we can speak only of relative safety, the determination of which depends on a knowledge of the risks inherent in various levels and durations and kinds of exposure to ionizing radiation. But we don't have the fundamental information necessary to calculate risks at low levels of chronic exposure; we haven't enough experience with reactors to be able to calculate the risk of serious accident; we don't know enough about the con-

centrating and transporting mechanisms for radioisotopes in the biosphere to be able to forecast the ecologic risks of man-made radiation; and we have very imperfect means of estimating how technologic, demographic, political, and even geologic events of the future may serve to compound (or perhaps alleviate) present risks.

At relatively high levels of both acute and chronic exposure, we are beginning to know some of the risks of ionizing radiation fairly well. But these are risks of somatic damage to individuals exposed under rather special environmental conditions, such as the children who grow from irradiated embryos or the uranium miners of the Colorado Plateau. What we need to know is how much we shall have to pay in shortened lives and human misery for each increment of radioactivity that is deliberately released to the biological environment. Although such calculations of human costs have been made, they are based on unproved assumptions and vary widely. Estimates of the number of deaths from radiation-induced cancer and leukemia to be expected in the United States from sustained radiation exposure at the guideline dose rate of 170 mrem per year range from 160 per year[18] to 32,000 a year.[19]

The United States in 1970 had an environmental level of man-made radiation that was only a small fraction of the guideline level of 170 mrem per year above background and medical dosage; of the approximately 200 mrem per year average gonadal exposure in the United States, less than 5 mrem was attributable to nuclear energy; most of the rest was from background and medical irradiation. The human cost of nuclear energy, in other words, is not yet very high. But since a human price is paid for any increase in the environmental level of ionizing radiation, there can be no truly safe level, only levels which are deemed acceptable in terms of the benefits and costs involved.

*How the Standards Have Been Set*

Protection standards have been set to represent "acceptable" tradeoffs between calculated benefits and the incalculable risks. Because the risks are not calculable, standards have been set at levels where the consequent biological damage will be difficult if not impossible to distinguish or measure. The standards have been set by technical experts who determined their public acceptability without recourse to the trial of public review and debate.

The two main standard-setting organizations whose guidelines are used in the United States are the International Commission on Radiological Protection (ICRP) and the Federal Radiation Council (FRC).

The ICRP states that "the problem in practice is to limit the radiation dose to that which involves a risk which is not unacceptable to the individual or to the population at large" and that "long-term effects should be a major preoccupation of the collective conscience."

In its first report (1960) the Federal Radiation Council, established the year before to advise the President on radiation standards, expressed a similar philosophy:

> Fundamentally, setting basic radiation protection standards involves passing judgment on the extent of the possible health hazards society is willing to accept in order to realize the unknown benefits of radiation.

> There should be no manmade radiation exposure without the expectation of benefit resulting from such exposure.

The FRC has also stated its conviction that "exposure from radiation should result from a real determination of its necessity."

The permissible dose of 5 rem per person per generation (30 years) exclusive of natural background and medical exposure appears to have been selected because it was thought that a doubling of the natural background level would involve neither serious genetic risk nor measurable somatic effects. Both groups, however, have repeatedly pointed to the lack of knowledge of the biological effects of low chronic radiation doses.

AEC regulations are based on FRC and ICRP guidelines. They are designed to protect both workers and public exposed to man-made radioactivity and are set in terms of dose rates and maximum permissible concentrations. They are not designed to limit total amounts of radioactivity released to the environment by any single plant or project or by any combination of plants or projects. They are not designed to protect against slow buildup in the environment of long-lived radioisotopes or against biological concentration in the food chain.

Early in 1970 Robert H. Finch, then chairman of the Federal Radiation Council, ordered a new review of federal radiation guidelines; the review will be conducted by the National Academy of Sciences, which will convene a committee of technical experts for the purpose.

## Who Accepts the Risk?

The risks to the exposed public are inherent in radiation protection standards. The experts who set the standards, by their own testimony, have weighed the possible health hazards "acceptable to society" against the expected benefits to be gained from the use of radiation. They have accepted the risk for the public. Many critics of the present regulatory and licensing system charge that the setting of protection standards, as well as the siting of a nuclear power plant or the decision to implement a Plowshare project, involve moral and political judgments made by persons whose limitations of competence and responsibility should restrict them to scientific and engineering judgments.

The furor over fallout in the 1950s and early 1960s and the present concern about the siting of nuclear power plants and underground nuclear explosions may stem as much from frustration over exclusion of the affected public from the decision process as from worry about the biological harm of the resultant radiation.

Atomic experts grow exasperated with citizens who fuss about a risk which the experts feel they can demonstrate is many times less than that of driving a car on a public highway. But risks imposed are much more difficult for some people to accept than risks voluntarily assumed.

A recent agreement with Sweden for the purchase of nuclear fuel rods produced in the United States requires that the rods be reprocessed in the United States. It appears that most if not all radioactive wastes developed from use of U.S. nuclear fuel will, as a matter of U.S. policy, be returned to the United States for disposal. Even solid wastes are now being shipped from Japan for burial in Idaho. The added risk to the U.S. environment from adoption of such a policy was accepted without referral to the public.

## Dual Role of the AEC

Atomic energy was developed for military purposes under wartime restrictions. Under those circumstances, it was natural that the development of applications as well as the protection of those exposed to radiation hazard should be vested in the same organization.

When, in 1947, responsibility for development of a national atomic energy program was given by Congress to the Atomic Energy Commission, it still seemed appropriate, in view of the continuing importance to the nation of the military applications of nuclear energy, and the fact that almost all of the nuclear technologists in the country worked for the AEC, that the Commission be given sole authority to review reactor designs and sites, and to license reactors.

The fallout experience of the western states in the 1950s and early 1960s, however, raised some question about the dual promotion-protection role of the AEC. Perhaps in defensive reaction to mounting criticism, the Atomic Energy Act of 1954 explicitly confirmed the intent of Congress to remove jurisdiction over radiation hazard from the states and vest it solely in the AEC. Although a 1959 amendment to the act deleted the preemption statement, the AEC continues to exercise this jurisdiction. In 1969 the state of Minnesota, as noted earlier, challenged the AEC by prescribing stricter standards for effluent from the Monticello reactor.

The conflict of interest inherent in the dual role of the Commission to promote the applications of nuclear energy and to protect the public from its hazardous effects has been repeatedly pointed out, as has the fact that every modern nation in the world that has a commercial nuclear power program, except the United States, vests the promotional and regulatory functions in separate agencies. Recent developments, both in the Congress and in the Office of the President, suggest that the United States, too, may soon vest these functions in separate agencies.

## Where Do We Go from Here?

Present standards for effluents from nuclear facilities and projects, as pointed out earlier, are designed to protect workers and the nearby public from the effects of radiation released by that plant or project. There is nothing built into such standards that will prevent a slow buildup of radioactivity in the environment as nuclear facilities and projects proliferate, and there is nothing in them that will protect the public from the ill-effects of ingesting radioisotopes which have been biologically concentrated in man's food chain.

It is not technologically necessary to release any radioactivity to the human environment from either nuclear reactors or fuel-reprocessing plants. Releases are made for reasons of cost. It is technologically difficult to capture the noble gases like krypton-85 from the gaseous waste and almost, if not actually impossible, to recover tritium from the liquid waste. But these technical difficulties do not mean that these harmful substances have to be released to the human environment. Given proper containment design and adequate siting relative to geologic and hydrologic disposal criteria, even krypton and tritium could be kept out of the biosphere. These substances will set an upper limit to the development of nuclear power only if their release to the environment is allowed to continue at, or anywhere near, the present release rate per unit of installed energy capacity (per megawatt, for example).

Any radioactive release to the biological environment, the National Academy of Sciences Committee on Resources and Man recommended in 1969,[20] should be monitored by an agency truly independent of the organization promoting the activity causing the release. Such release should be analyzed in terms of national and global environmental consequences, not just their effects on the health of the nearby human populations. Both the data and the analyses should be made available for public information and independent review.

There is usually not just one way of reaching a social goal. More often there are several, each involving a different set of costs and consequences, and each affecting in some manner the march toward other social goals.

Meeting the increasing demand for electric power at a cost which will allow wide participation in its benefits is a social goal. Restoring and maintaining a healthy and clean environment is a social goal. Assuring our nation of a continuing supply of the mineral sources of energy (coal, oil, and natural gas, uranium and perhaps thorium) is a social goal. Optimum realization of these three goals requires a thorough knowledge of available resources and of the available technological alternatives, and it demands a continuing comparison of the benefits to be derived, and of the costs and risks to the public and to the environment inherent in each technological alternative. We have good means of obtaining the needed knowledge and of making the necessary calculations. We have poor means of comparing alternatives and of making reasoned public choices among them.

We need improved means for public participation in the choices that have to be made in our use of energy. We want cheap, dependable power. We want a clean, healthy environment. We can't have the best of both (cheapest power and cleanest environment). Be it power from fossil fuels or radioactive materials, we have to decide how clean an environment, and what reduction of risk to ourselves and to our descendants we want at what price in the increased cost of power.

At the present level of environmental releases and human risk, the economic cost of environmental protection is not great. It has been estimated that the cost of radioactive waste containment, treatment, and disposal may run as low as 1.0-1.5 percent of the capital and operating costs of the large nuclear plants now being designed. Westinghouse states that its zero-release system will add only about $1 million to the cost of a 1000 megawatt plant; currently such a plant costs about $250 million. Eliminating the accident risk by placing the reactors securely underground would increase the capital cost of a large plant by only a few percent[21] and should add almost nothing to the operating costs. Placing power reactors in remote places like Hudson Bay and transmitting the power over high-voltage direct-current lines to urban areas would entail both increased capital costs and transmission losses, but not of a size that an affluent society could not absorb without difficulty. More important, siting on Hudson Bay might turn the gross impediment of thermal discharge into an advantage. Even in urban locations, the hot water from power plants can be used to heat buildings and homes; little consideration appears to have been given to this sort of alternative in site planning.

In blasting canals and harbors with nuclear explosives, as well as in underground stimulation of natural gas production by nuclear blasts, there is no zero-release alternative to consider. Some radioactivity will always be released to the human environment by a Plowshare project. Consequently, consideration of technological alternatives and comparison of costs and consequences become even more important.

*In Summary*

There is no absolutely safe level of ionizing radiation. Any man-made addition to the natural level increases the potential for biological harm. Consequently, the use of radiation and nuclear energy materials that release radioactivity to the environment involves a balancing of benefits and risks. Reducing the risk means reducing the benefits (if only by increasing the cost of the product). Choice of benefit:risk ratios involves political and moral decisions, not scientific and technical ones.

There is no technical necessity for release to the human environment of radioactivity from nuclear reactors or fuel-processing plants. Not only can reactors be made as clean as one may wish to pay for, but they can be made as safe as one is willing to pay for. Although reactor design engineers feel that modern reactors are very safe, there will always remain some risk of accident, and a reactor accident could be catastrophic. Edward Teller has said "In principle, nuclear reactors are dangerous . . . [they] belong underground."[22] An underground reactor (Sweden, Belgium, and Switzerland already have them) without radioactive effluents could be both safe and clean, in almost absolute terms.

Present radiation standards have little relation

to environmental contamination, because they do not take into account radioactivity buildup in the environment from multiple sources, and they do not protect against biological concentration of radioactivity in the food chain. They appear to represent levels of exposure below which the harmful effects of man-made ionizing radiation are at present impossible to distinguish.

The rapid growth of the nuclear power industry, the promotion of large seacoast agro-industrial complexes powered by huge reactors, and the pollution potential of Plowshare projects presage a great increase in the quantity of radioactive wastes that must be guarded against and disposed of. Present practices which depend on dilution and dispersal of radioactive wastes cannot be continued without a significant buildup of radioactivity in the environment.

Decisions made today on human exposure to radiation and on releases of radioactivity to the environment will be of great concern to posterity. High-level wastes from nuclear fuel-processing plants have a hazard life of 600 years or more. Plutonium has a half-life of 24,360 years and its hazard life may extend beyond the duration of our species. Even at fairly low levels of exposure, radiation-induced mutations may, through a score of generations, wreak more havoc than a nuclear war. Any buildup of long-lived radioisotopes in the environment will, for practical purposes, be almost irreversible. It is this long-lived lethality that makes man-made radiation not just another environmental hazard, but the ultimate environmental hazard.

The great benefits of nuclear energy in the production of electric power, in medical diagnosis and treatment, in scientific research, and perhaps even in some underground engineering applications, can be realized without contamination of the biological environment and with a very small risk to mankind. However, the frightening prospects for harm to mankind inherent in the atomic nucleus make it mandatory that decisions be based on sound scientific knowledge, be made with great moral concern (by an educated public, informed by technical experts), and be carried out with a high degree of technological care.

## References

1. **Scott, R. C.** 1963. Radium in natural waters in the United States. *Radioecology*, pp. 237-240. Reinhold, New York.

2. **Pollard, E. C.** 1969. The biological action of ionizing radiation. *Am. Scientist 57:* 206-236.

3. **Miller, R. W.** 1969. Delayed radiation effects in atomic-bomb survivors. *Science 166:* 569-574.

4. **Blum, H. F.** 1959. Environmental radiation and cancer. *Science 130:* 1545-1547.

5. **Lundin, F. E., Jr., et al.** 1969. Mortality of uranium miners in relation to radiation exposure, hard-rock mining and cigarette smoking — 1950 through September 1967. *Health Physics 16:* 571-578.

6. **Green, H. P.** 1968. "Reasonable assurance" of "no undue risk." *Scientist and Citizen 10:* 128-140.

7. **Polikarpov, G. G.** 1966. *Radioecology of Aquatic Organisms.* Reinhold, New York.

8. **Braestrup, C. B., and Mooney, R. T.** 1959. X-ray emission from television sets. *Science 130:* 1071-1074.

9. **Parker, F. L.** 1968. Radioactive wastes from fusion reactors. *Science 159:* 83-84.

10. **Martin, W. E.** 1965. Interception and retention of fallout by desert shrubs. *Health Physics 11:* 1341-1354.

11. **Blanco, R. E., Blomeke, J. O., and Roberts, J. T.** 1966. Future magnitude and proposed solutions of the waste disposal problem. In *Proceedings of the Symposium on the Solidification and Long-Term Storage of Highly Radioactive Wastes.* U.S. Atomic Energy Commission TID-4500 (CONF-660208), pp. 3-14.

12. **National Academy of Sciences.** 1966. Unpublished report to the Atomic Energy Commission by the Committee on Geologic Aspects of Radioactive Waste Disposal. 92 pp. On open file, National Research Council, Washington, D.C. Reprinted in *Underground Uses of Nuclear Energy,* hearings of the Subcommittee on Air and Water Pollution of the Committee on Public Works,

U.S. Senate, Nov. 18, 19, 20, 1969, pp. 461-512.

13. **Galley, J. E.** 1968. Economic potential of geologic basins and reservoir strata. In *Subsurface Disposal in Geologic Basins. Am. Assoc. Petrol. Geologists Memoir* 10: 1-10.

14. **McCann, T. P., et. al.** 1968. Possibilities for disposal of industrial wastes in subsurface rocks on north flank of Appalachian Basin in New York. In *Subsurface Disposal in Geologic Basins. Am. Assoc. Petrol. Geologists Memoir* 10: 43-92.

15. **De Laguna, W.** 1968. Importance of deep permeable formations in location of a large nuclear-fuel reprocessing plant. In *Subsurface Disposal in Geologic Basins. Am. Assoc. Petrol. Geologists Memoir* 10: 21-31.

16. **Coleman, L. R., and Liberace, R.** 1965. Nuclear power production and estimated krypton-85 levels. *Radiological Health Data and Reps.* 7: 615-621.

17. **Executive Office of The President.** 1968. *Considerations Affecting Steam Power Plant Site Selection.* Office of Science and Technology, 133 pp.

18. **Storer, J.** 1969. Comments on manuscript "Low Dose Radiation, Chromosomes, and Cancer" by J. W. Gofman and A. R. Tamplin in *Environmental Effects of Producing Electric Power.* Hearings of the Joint Committee on Atomic Energy, Part I, pp. 653-654. 91st Congress, October 28-November 7, 1969.

19. **Gofman, J. W., and Tamplin, A. R.** 1970. The cancer-leukemia risk from FRC guideline radiation based upon ICRP publications. Hearings of the Joint Committee on Atomic Energy. Part II. 91st Congress, February 20, 1970.

20. **Hubbert, M. K.,** 1969. Energy resources. In *Resources and Man,* Chap. 8. W. H. Freeman, San Francisco, California.

21. **Bernell, L., and Lindbo, T.** 1965. Tests of air leakage in rock for underground reactor containment. *Nuclear Safety 6:* 267-272.

22. **Teller, E.** 1965. Energy from oil and from the nucleus. *J. Petrol. Technol. 17:* 505-508.

## Further Reading

**Cember, H.** 1969. *Introduction to Health Physics.* Oxford, Pergamon Press, New York, 422 pp.

**Glasstone, S.** 1967. *Sourcebook on Atomic Energy,* 3rd ed. Van Nostrand Reinhold, New York, 883 pp.

**Novick, S.** 1969. *The Careless Atom.* Houghton Mifflin, Boston, 225 pp.

**Parker, F. L.** 1969. Status of radioactive waste disposal in USA. *J. of Sanitary Engineering Division, Am. Soc. Civil Engineers 95:* 439-464.

**Upton, A. C.** 1969. *Radiation Injury.* University of Chicago Press, Chicago, Illinois, 126 pp.

# 13 Pesticides

Robert L. Rudd

The presence of novel chemicals in natural systems is a consequence of technological man. The appearance of such synthetic chemicals and the effects that they produce have no precedent in organic evolution. Most pesticides as we know them today have no natural counterparts. Thirty years ago most did not exist. Accelerated use of organic pesticidal compounds occurred during the years after World War II. The residues of many pesticidal compounds, most notably DDT, are distributed worldwide. One DDT metabolite — DDE — may be the commonest and most widely distributed synthetic chemical on the globe. DDE can now be found in biological tissues from the open ocean to the polar ice caps, in airborne dusts over cities, and in plants, animals, and waters in remote forests and mountains.

Pesticides are biologically active chemicals. They must be highly so to achieve the intended purpose of pest control. The spectrum of activity is, however, sufficiently broad in most instances

ROBERT L. RUDD is Professor of Zoology at the University of California, Davis. Born in Los Angeles in 1921, he earned his doctorate at the University of California, Berkeley, in 1953, after an interruption of three years during World War II, in which he served as a pilot in the Army Air Corps. He has spent most of his academic career at Davis, but has lectured at many institutions and conferences in the United States and abroad. He is the author of *Pesticides and the Living Landscape* (University of Wisconsin Press). His current research interests include pesticide kinetics, the tropical rain forest as a three-dimensional ecosystem, and the activity rhythms and speciation mechanisms of shrews.

to justify the most applicable word, BIOCIDE. In sum, therefore, pesticides are widely distributed by natural means; but, in contrast to natural materials such as dusts, they retain a good part of their biocidal activity.

To the ecologist, normal pesticide use poses two major difficulties. First, pesticides are biologically active and regularly strike at nontarget organisms as well as their intended targets. Normally, both biological effects and the judgments rendered about these effects are short term. Secondly, necessarily viewed in a long-term perspective are effects attributable chiefly to the residues of pesticides, whose biological consequences cannot be easily forecast. This second category of effects is more serious. Not only are these effects unpredictable, but they act at temporal, biological, and spatial distances whose routes of transfer and action are poorly known.

This second set of problems can be enumerated as follows:

1. Many pesticides persist and we cannot dispose of them.

2. They may cause unintended effects in place; usually these are population phenomena (for example, resistance, faunal displacement).

3. They may occur at considerable distances from points of origin. Clearly, fluid transport systems (air and water flows) are chiefly responsible for dispersal.

4. Following dispersal of residues, differential magnification (concentration) in biological systems may cause unintended and unexpected results.

One may be able to categorize the problems associated with the use of pesticides broadly and simply. In so doing, however, it is equally easy to lose sight of three elementary facts:

1. There is a great body of information already accumulated dealing with pesticide technology.

2. Pesticides, that is, chemicals used in pest control, are only a part of the more general problem of pest control. Too many scientists and technologists have obscured the fact that the control of offending animal and plant populations is a BIOLOGICAL problem, not primarily a chemical one.

3. Whatever our knowledge, the further fact is that we are all largely unaware of the longer term consequences of continued pesticide use. We have in progress a global experiment whose conclusions have yet to be fully foreseen.

This chapter attempts to provide a general understanding of the two questions — why chemical control is needed and what the general environmental consequences of chemical use are. Neither question should be overlooked in assessing the importance of pesticide use. Throughout this chapter I shall stress the environmental effects. But it is important to understand first why pesticides are used.

## Competitors with Man

Most people recognize only a few dozen kinds of animals or plants that affect — either help or hinder — them directly. They may be cereal grains and fruits, game species for recreation, domestic animals, plants and animals providing fibers for clothing, and a few that are moral or political symbols. Pests are a special category of animals and plants affecting man. Although most people believe that the word "pest" is clearly definable, it is important to realize that the word has no biological meaning. A pest may very well be a hazard to us because we have made it so. For example, the Colorado potato beetle originally, like most insects, was not a pest at all. It fed on wild members of the family Solanaceae to which the potato and nightshade belong. The movements of people and, more particularly, changes in agricultural practices, allowed this normally benign beetle to increase its numbers and its range and, particularly in Europe, to cause great damage.

When the numbers of an offending animal or plant are reduced to levels causing no important hazard or inconvenience, we can no longer properly call it a pest. Reduction to such low numbers is the object of pest control, in which chemical agents figure prominently.

The competition between man and living things takes many forms. Only some competitors are pests. Competition with man may be divided into the following categories.

1. *Living things that are a direct and immediate hazard to an individual man*

Included here are vertebrate animals that attack human beings. Pest is not quite strong enough a word to describe the poisonous snake that injects a fatal dose of venom. The same is true of predatory mammals. Whether hazardous to man or his livestock, tigers, bears, lions, and other large animals are no longer a general "pest" problem. Traps, guns, and poisons render likely their reduction in numbers or extinction.

Also included in this category are diseases and parasites of man. Direct chemical therapy is standard medical practice in treating resulting irritations or illnesses.

2. *Living things that are a direct but delayed hazard to an individual man*

Many infectious microorganisms find their way to human beings in the bodies of other living animals. Such disease hosts are called VECTORS. The best known examples are the mosquitoes that carry the sporozoan parasite *Plasmodium* which causes malaria in human beings. The control of vector-caused disease is approached in two ways. The first is drug therapy when disease symptoms manifest themselves in the human individual. The second is with attempts to reduce or eliminate the vector population carrying the disease. At the present time chemical pesticides are very widely used for that purpose. The scientists who work on vector control problems bear many labels — epidemiologist, entomologist, ecologist, to name a few. The importance of their work is obvious. Still, general environmental contamination (notably by DDT) is a frequent consequence of their efforts.

3. *Living things that directly harm domesticated animals*

Almost all domesticated animals of basic importance to man are birds and mammals. Unfortunately, these warm-blooded animals are subject to the same kinds of hazards as man. Predatory animals are controlled through trapping, shooting (aided by bounty systems), or poisoning. In the United States sheep and poultry bear the brunt of attacks by predators now. Although frequently unjustifiable economically, large-scale poisoning programs still continue. Compound 1080 and strychnine are the most widely used chemicals. Fear of predatory mammals is a deeply ingrained human characteristic. We have, we might say, institutionalized an overreaction to that fear in continuing poison programs on the scale we do.

Disease and parasites also plague domestic animals. Veterinarians depend primarily on therapeutic chemicals for the treatment of a wide variety of afflictions. Systemic insecticides, for example, are commonly used against bot fly infestations in the skin of cattle.

4. *Living things that directly harm commodity production*

No agricultural or forest crop can possibly be grown in an insect- and disease-free environment. Animal and plant pests consume a significant part of commodity production. The efficient producer wants to keep pest losses to a minimum. There are many ways of attempting this, but pesticides without doubt are one of the most important. Most of the variety and the volume of pesticide chemicals are used in agriculture and the great magnitude of environmental effects and the current concern stem largely from this source. The use of pesticides is clearly encouraged by economic considerations. Some scientists say (rather generously, I think) that, generally, $1 spent on pesticides results in $3 of increased yield. In some specialty crops chemical dependence is so great that, given present production methods, they could not be grown economically without pesticides. The yield increment attributable to pesticide use in all commodities is translated into economic terms.

The general case can be illustrated as in Figure 1. Economic density or injury level simply means the level of population at which pest damage becomes too serious to overlook. Below the threshold level the grower's efforts in pest control would not return full value to him. Actual eco-

nomic injury is rarely calculated; the BELIEF that injury will occur is more frequently the stimulus to apply pesticides. The extent of pest control operations is staggering. In California, for example, major control programs are waged against some 200 pest species annually. The approximate cost of these efforts is about a quarter billion dollars per year. A good part of this cost is for pesticides.

5. *Living things that are nuisances only*

Throughout the world there are many kinds of interfering animals and plants that pose no serious economic or health hazard. These nuisance species range from fleas to elephants, from algae to trees. Human life is more comfortable without direct impingement of these nuisance species. Where we can, we try to control them. Pesticides are frequently used — particularly in urban areas — to attempt control. The control used is normally sporadic and localized. Systematic effort, such as that characterizing commodity production, rarely occurs. The result is that general nuisance abatement has not been too successful.

*The Creation of Pests*

Man's every action affects the biological world in ways often disguised and unknown. A few

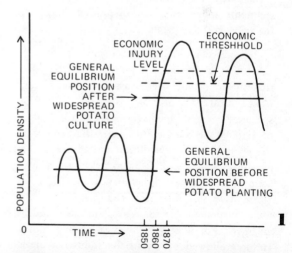

**1**

GROWTH OF THE COLORADO POTATO BEETLE AS A PEST. Economic injury levels in relation to numbers of a pest species and man's agricultural enterprise. The example here is the Colorado potato beetle, which became a pest as agriculture expanded in the nineteenth century.

examples: Kentucky blue grass originally came from Europe. The grasslands of California may look wild and natural, but most species of grasses date from early Spanish occupation. The house sparrow and the starling — now so common in the United States — came from only a few birds introduced less than a century ago. Baboons have become serious crop pests in Africa, possibly because the demand for leopard skins has reduced the number of predators.

The foregoing examples illustrate the range of species, not necessarily pests, whose ecological relationships have been altered by man. Pests are "made" in the same fashion — in an altered environment. Basically, pests important to man are created in four ways.

1. Certain species of plants and animals are selected by known evolutionary processes to become more numerous and successful.

2. Many thousands of species of plants and animals are moved from one place on earth to another. Many species, such as crop plants, are intentionally moved, but most are carried by man accidentally.

3. A reduction in biological diversity often takes place, sometimes intentionally and sometimes accidentally.

4. Living things may adapt to changed environments and, in the case of pest species, "biological weeds" are produced.

The first point can be dismissed quickly because it is obvious. Yet it is, of course, profoundly important. It concerns the entire history of agriculture (Chapter 3). Essentially, most crop species were developed very early in the history of man. Modern agriculture, classified solely by the plants it uses, is Neolithic agriculture. Mechanization and chemicalization began on a large scale in the nineteenth century. On the basis of these two technological changes, traditional monocultural (single species) plantings could be enlarged. For a century ever-expanding monocultures allowed by essentially industrial methods have produced a variety of social changes, the rural-urban shift being the most prominent. But in crop production itself yield increase became increasingly depending on mechanical and chemical tools. The result has been an increasing-ly precarious ecological pattern in most basic crops. Large-scale monoculture produces in an accelerating cycle more pest numbers that must be held down by increasing the use of pesticides (or other pest control means). A large part of the present concern for uncontrolled pesticide residues in the environment stems from the so-called successes of modern technology-based agriculture.

BIOLOGICAL TRANSLOCATIONS are the natural product of species dispersal. Yet, geologically speaking, the process was slow enough to result in a clear identity for each of the zoogeographical regions of the world. The biotic isolation characterizing much of the earth's history has recently undergone dramatic change. Much pest control — and the need to use pesticides — comes about because of man-carried animals and plants introduced into areas favorable for their multiplication.

Whether man-carried or naturally dispersed, pest species had to find in their new sites an environment that was favorably reconstructed, that is, modified by man for the pest's advantage before it could become established. A series of environmental "bridges" is often required. The cotton boll weevil — nemesis of cotton growers and beloved by folk singers — originally lived in Mexico. Not until the barriers of southwestern deserts had been bridged by irrigation schemes and agricultural plantings did the weevil gain entrance into the United States. Its presence is clearly felt. Probably no other insect species is sprayed or dusted with insecticides so often. The Colorado potato beetle (Figure 1) moved eastward in the United States on a "potato bridge," whence it moved to Europe by other means.

Most species are transported accidentally. There are now some 5000 species of insect pests worldwide. Adding all other kinds of pests — plant and animal — brings the list to 10,000 species. And these are only the economically important ones. The exchange of organisms continues daily; without too much exaggeration, one can say that, for major crop types, the one-time continental isolation no longer exists. One may speak of citrus, cotton, or wheat pests and be reasonably sure that they are the same kinds of arthropods whether from Israel, Australia, South

Africa, or the United States. The exchange of pests — worldwide — became nearly complete before stringent quarantine was enforced.

A pest in one land is usually not a pest in its native land. When it is carried to an alien shore, it usually leaves behind its predators and parasites, thus allowing its numbers to increase greatly in its new habitat. As indicated earlier, many environmental conditions created by man favor pests. Chiefly responsible is the need to reverse successional stages (Chapter 1). The economic need to plant single species in large stands further abets the problem by favoring the dispersal and food supply of the pest species. REDUCTION IN BIOLOGICAL DIVERSITY is a normal consequence of clearing and planting. Further reduction can also be planned for special reasons. Still further reduction — with inherently catastrophic instability — can be the unplanned consequence of many pest control procedures, particularly those depending on chemical pesticides.

The total biological changes that follow breaking of virgin ground could not have concerned pioneers too much. Crop production was the goal and unintended pest production the likely consequence. The two aspects have only recently been associated and documented. The best-studied example to illustrate that the simple ploughing of land for planting reduces biological diversity and produces pests comes from the recent massive agricultural plantings in the virgin Steppe of Kazakhstan in the USSR. Insect fauna from both original and modified (wheat field) environments were identified, counted, and studied. These were the general conclusions: (1) There were more than twice as many species in the virgin steppe than in the wheat fields. (2) The density of insect populations in the wheat fields was almost double that of the steppe. The number of dominant and constant species in the steppe was twice that of wheat fields, but in the steppe they comprised only half the fauna, whereas in wheat they amount to 94 percent. Therefore, there was a greater variety of species in the population of the virgin steppe and a better numerical balance between the species. In the wheat fields a few species became dominant. Finally[3], most of the dominant species in the wheat fields were important pests.

The foregoing changes took place in an amazingly short time — only 2 years. This pattern is followed wherever man clears, cultivates, and plants. This reduction in biological diversity — sometimes called artificial simplification — is therefore a normal, although not totally desirable, thing.

The process can be reversed in certain instances, thereby requiring less pesticidal control. A specific instance is the use of strip-harvesting in California alfalfa fields. Three strips of alfalfa 120 feet wide are cut at different times. The uncut strip provides a reservoir of pest enemies immediately available to the regenerating, newly cut strip. Actual counts of insect predators and parasites from alfalfa fields in which both regular and strip cutting were practiced were made by University of California scientists. Three groups of arthropod insects illustrate the important difference, as shown in Table I.

| Natural enemies | Regular farming | Strip-farming |
|---|---|---|
| Lady bird beetles | | |
| Adults | 46,000 | 205,000 |
| Larvae | 11,000 | 232,000 |
| Parasitic wasps | 70,000 | 287,000 |
| Predatory spiders | 105,000 | 1,094,000 |

ARTHROPODS IN ALFALFA FIELDS. Average number per acre.

There were almost four times as many controlling insects where diversity was maintained by strip-farming than where it was not. The expenditure for pest control was correspondingly reduced. Moreover, the yield of alfalfa hay was almost 15 percent greater under the strip-farming system.

Pesticides are used largely to combat the disturbances arising from a reduced and unstable biological community. It is unfortunate that unknowingly we make the problems of both production and pollution worse with pest control chemicals.

Figure 2 illustrates a simple case of a control problem aggravated by pesticides. The ladybird, or vedalia beetle, had been introduced into California from Australia in the nineteenth century to control a scale insect pest of oranges. The predaceous beetle quickly established itself

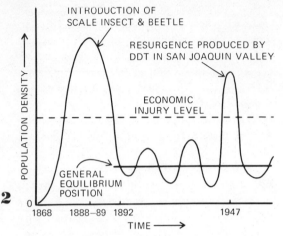

**2**

THE HISTORY OF A PEST SPECIES. A scale insect of California citrus orchards and effect of the ladybird beetle successfully introduced for its control. Note particularly the resurgence of pest numbers when DDT came into use following World War II (see text).

and for over 60 years kept the scale in check. In 1946 the newly discovered DDT found its way into use in citrus groves. Very quickly, the susceptible beetle became rarer, and, as quickly, the scale insect again became a major pest. The withdrawal of DDT restored the "natural balance" but 3 years were required in most citrus orchards before control was again satisfactory.

Continued pesticide use not only influences the numbers in single species but can affect the composition of the entire animal community. As an illustration, Cornell University scientists made a comparison between soil organisms from orchards frequently treated with pesticides and those from nearby untreated orchards. There were several times more organisms in the treated orchards but biomass (total living weight) was less. Continued treatment resulted in more of fewer kinds and these weighed less. Larger predatory forms particularly were reduced in the treated area. In fact, predatory organisms were seven times more abundant in untreated soil. The opportunity for natural control is clearly much greater in the untreated area. More disturbing was the discovery that there was a downward shift in the trophic level in the treated orchard. This shift simply means that repeated pesticide treatment resulted in vastly greater numbers of plant-feeding forms. The presence of these chemicals is another form of environmental pol-

| Chemical group or action | Examples |
|---|---|
| **Insecticides and Acaricides** | |
| Inorganic | |
| Arsenicals | Lead arsenate |
| Copper-bearing | Copper sulfate |
| Organic, naturally occurring | |
| Nicotine alkaloids | Nicotine sulfate |
| Pyrethroids | Pyrethrum |
| Rotenoids | Rotenone |
| Organic, synthetic | |
| Chlorinated hydrocarbon compounds | Aldrin, benzene hexachloride, DDD, DDT, endrin, heptachlor, methoxychlor, ovatran, toxaphene |
| Organic phosphorus compounds | DDVP, malathion, parathion, Phosdrin, schradan, TEPP, Systox |
| Carbamates | Isodan, pyrolan, Sevin |
| **Fungicides** | |
| Mercurials | Mercuric chloride, "organics" |
| Dithiocarbamates | Nabam, ziram |
| Others | Captan |
| **Herbicides** | |
| Contact toxicity | Sodium arsenite, "oils" |
| Translocated (hormones) | 2,4-D; 2,4,5-T, dalapon |
| Soil sterilants | Borates, chlorates |
| Soil fumigants | Methyl bromide, Vapam |
| **Rodenticides (Mammal Poisons)** | |
| Anticoagulants | Pival, warfarin |
| Immediate action | Endrin, phosphorus, sodium fluoroacetate ("1080"), strychnine, thallium |
| **Other Vertebrate Targets** | |
| Birds | Strychnine, TEPP |
| Fishes | Rotenone, toxaphene |

lution producing results very similar to those described for the Russian Steppe.

The simplest definition of a WEED is that it is a plant in the wrong place. The word "weed" like the word "pest" biologically has no meaning. The idea of weeds, however, can be extended very easily to any living thing that changes its natural relationships due to the activities of man. Logically, animals can be thought of as weeds as well as plants. Whether animal or plant, they occur where we don't want them, in numbers that are competitive. They are alien to the area where they are considered as pests and almost always they are aided by man's activities. They also maintain higher densities in disturbed areas than they did in their native habitats. They may have compensatory mechanisms such as increased reproductive rate to counter efforts to control their numbers. Pests are mainly biological weeds created by man-made environments. The necessity to use pesticides is most frequently a crude attempt to correct an ecologically unbalanced agricultural ecosystem.

*Chemicals in the Control of Pests*

The great variety of chemicals and their uses dictates against a full description.[1,2] About 10,000 commercial pesticidal formulations are registered in the United States. Only a few dozen basic pesticide chemicals are commonly used (Table II). Many thousands of chemical compounds have been screened for their biocidal capabilities. But the magnitude of this screening effort marks a fundamental change in the use of pesticides. The era of synthetic organic chemicals in pest control began with the discovery of the insecticidal capacity of DDT in 1941, coupled with wartime development of the nerve poisons (organic phosphorus compounds) in Germany. Synthetic compounds have dominated pest con-

trol for a quarter century. Their heavy and widespread use during this period is one of the major changes from Neolithic agriculture. A host of technologists — ranging from developmental chemists in industry to agricultural extension advisors — have arisen to accommodate this new development. Unfortunately, the emphasis has been largely on chemical development and application, a view leading both to narrowness and controversy.

The ecologist or environmentalist must take a point of view that is expanded in both time and space beyond that of the usual pesticide technologist. At once he must consider the entire living community and the physical factors on a global scale that influence the distribution of pesticides. The broadest range of pest control methodology is outlined in Figure 3. This chapter concerns itself only with chemical pesticides and more particularly with new synthetic materials widely used. The next chapter emphasizes bioenvironmental alternatives.

Two general themes underlie the ecologist's criticisms of present pesticide application practice. These are lack of selectivity and lack of controllability. All environmental problems, whether they are the immediate difficulties of the pest control practitioner or the broadest problems of the social humanist, stem from these two lacks.

Lack of selectivity along with basic P E S T I-

PEST CONTROL METHODS. A general outline of the varied ways by which pests may be controlled. Chemical pesticides are only one means.

| PURPOSE | LIMITATION OF NUMBERS | | |
|---|---|---|---|
| GENERAL METHOD | ALTERATION OF PHYSIOLOGY OR ECOLOGY | PREVENTION OF ACCESS | DIRECT KILLING |
| MEANS | BIOENVIRONMENTAL<br><br>HOST RESISTANCE<br>BIOLOGICAL CONTROL<br>CULTURAL MEANS<br>SEXUAL STERILITY<br>ATTRACTANTS | PHYSICAL MEANS:<br>BARRIERS<br><br>CHEMICAL MEANS:<br>REPELLANTS<br>BARRIERS<br>QUARANTINE | PHYSICAL MEANS<br><br>CHEMICAL PESTICIDES |

CIDE KINETICS, or transfer, are illustrated in Figure 4. Later figures illustrate the range of residue uncontrollability and subsequent ecological effects. Figure 4 describes well how so-called broad-spectrum pesticides are applied. The announced intention of many pesticide technologists is selectivity. The fact is that very little success toward that aim has been achieved in practice, whatever the character of the chemical types used.

I have indicated the general themes and viewpoints associated with chemical pest control. Technical aspects cannot be reviewed in detail in this chapter (see Further Reading). I have elected to discuss generally two important aspects of chemical use. One is mode of action, using common chemical classes and well-known pesticides involved in contention within them. The second is the concept of toxicity versus hazard as normally viewed by the toxicologist and pest control advisor. The last section of this chapter is essentially an expansion of this concept to the social arena.

## Mode of Action of Pesticides

A chemical can enter an animal's body by three main routes: ingestion — by being eaten; respiration — by being breathed; dermal assimilation — by absorption through the skin or body covering. These are referred to, respectively, by toxicologists, as oral, respiratory, and dermal routes of entry. The same terms are used when the toxicity of a chemical is being examined. Thus we have oral toxicity of a particular chemical, dermal toxicity, and so on. The description of both route of entry and comparisons of toxicity by different routes are not simply conveniences. The basic character of the chemical and its technical formulation — as well as the structure of the pest — interact to assure that one route of entry is favored over another. For example, most DDT formulations have a low dermal toxicity. They normally must be eaten

PESTICIDE KINETICS. The general case of persistent pesticide kinetics. A large fraction of spray goes to the intended area. A sizable fraction drifts onto unintended surfaces. A portion is carried into the atmosphere. Surviving residues at the surface may leach into water or enter the organic food chain, where biological concentration begins.

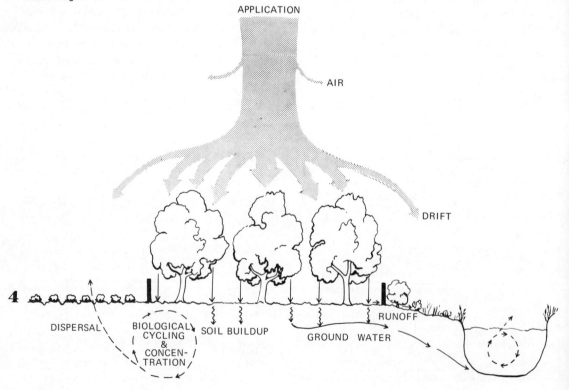

APPLICATION

AIR

DRIFT

4

DISPERSAL

BIOLOGICAL CYCLING & CONCENTRATION

SOIL BUILDUP

GROUND WATER

RUNOFF

before becoming effective. The "nerve gas" parathion on the other hand has a very high dermal and respiratory toxicity. The rodenticide strychnine is simply not hazardous unless eaten. The same is true of the sodium arsenite in ant baits.

Further decisions about the routes of entry must be made according to the group of animals and its particular structure. The chitinous exoskeleton of insects is relatively impervious to most common chemicals. This is certainly not true of mammals. A chemical may be highly toxic by one route of entry to one group of organisms and hardly toxic at all by the same route in another group. The structure and physiology of all animal groups likely to be exposed must be known so as to assess both pest control efficiency and hazard. For example, a small concentration of DDT or toxaphene in a lake will not directly harm a swimming man even if he gulps a fair amount of water. Yet that same concentration will be very toxic to the gill-breathers — fishes and invertebrates — of the lake. Examples of this sort are legion and make responsible pest control a very complicated affair.

With some pesticides, and particularly with their actions on certain groups of organisms, contact with part of the body surface is all that is needed for a toxic reaction. The surface may be skin, gills, the alveoli of the lungs, or the intestinal wall. The pesticide barely enters the body. For example, DDT affects the gills of fishes directly by immobilizing the blood supply, hence suffocating the affected fish. But with most pesticides, the chemical must not only contact and penetrate a part of the body surface, it must also be circulated to the part of the body most sensitive to its action. The circulating pesticide by itself does not differ at this stage from any of the hundreds of other compounds carried by the blood and lymphatic system. Inevitably, a sensitive area — usually a part of the nervous system — will be reached and, if the concentration is high enough, a toxic reaction can be expected.

The physiological target of a toxic chemical is usually some phase of nervous control. It may be central, that is, the brain or the spinal cord may be affected. These central nervous system poisons are exemplified by the chlorinated hydro-

carbon insecticides such as DDT. Toxicity may be manifest in the peripheral nervous system. This is the action of the organophosphates. Their pest control ability rests on "shunting out" the nerves that control body muscles. They do this by destroying the enzyme cholinesterase that is necessary for nervous transmission at the nerve ends. Or, as a third kind of attack on nerves, the nerve supply of a vital organ may be destroyed or disrupted. The rodenticide sodium fluoroacetate (1080), for example, kills by disrupting nervous control of the heart.

The vital system that the pesticide seeks may not be directly a part of the nervous system. The rodenticide warfarin, for example, acts to lower the prothrombin (a clotting factor) level in circulating blood. In time, blood loses its important ability to clot. The affected animal hemorrhages internally and dies. Another example is the chemosterilant Metepa. Its purpose is to slow or prevent the production of sperm. Although the animal carrying the chemosterilant may not be noticeably poisoned, it has no ability to reproduce. The effect, given time, is to lower population numbers in the next pest generation. Reducing numbers is the chief purpose of pesticides. The time involved, organs and systems affected, and efficiency in accomplishing this purpose differ according to chemical character.

Of the wide range of herbicidal chemicals available, by far the greatest use is made of growth accelerators. The best known of these are 2,4-D [(2,4-dichlorophenoxy)acetic acid] and 2,4,5-T. The sprayed material passes through the phloem of a plant to an area where food is being utilized. When in responsive plant tissue, 2,4-D apparently acts rather similarly to the natural growth hormone, 3-indoleacetic acid. This hormone encourages the cell wall to take up water with resulting elongation of the cell. In the normal plant cell, various mechanisms operate to control the rate of growth, including the destruction of the growth hormone when too much is present. The plant reacts to 2,4-D as it does to indoleacetic acid. Yet it is unable to oxidize or in any way inactivate the herbicide. Hence, unlimited growth continues until the plant dies. 2,4-D acts chiefly on dicotyledonous (broadleaved) plants. Although broad-spectrum in one sense, it can be used as a selective herbicide to remove weeds from fields of cereal grain, all monocotyledons. Moreover, the volatility and solubility of 2,4-D can be modified by formulation; hence, the herbicide can be used in a variety of specific ways. One illustration is its use as a defoliator, producing "partial death" by removing leaves but, at least for a short time, not killing the plant. Cotton fields may be defoliated for easier mechanical harvest. Or, as a military weapon, entire stretches of tropical jungle have recently been sprayed with 2,4,5-T to enable the discovery of men and installations (producing, among other effects, a great deal of social concern).

The second group of herbicides inhibits growth, perhaps to the point of death, and does so by interference with the cell machinery. The action may be on enzyme formation or in disturbance of an oxidative reaction. These herbicides produce biochemical lesions. The chemical nature of herbicides causing this type of effect is extremely varied, ranging from copper sulfate and the arsenical compounds to totally new organic products recently synthesized. Many are used particularly as fungicides on seed or in soil. Some, such as dinitrocresol (DNOC), can, according to formulation, be used as herbicides, fungicides, or insecticides.

I have termed the third group "species enhancers". In a real sense this is not a chemical but an ecological category. Many chemicals may do the job. Sometimes they are referred to as selective soil sterilants or pre-emergence herbicides. These chemicals are normally applied to soil and their action is on seeds or newly sprouting and rooting plants. They remove unwanted plants and make more likely survival and good growth of desirable kinds. Careful selection of chemical type ensures that result. How the favored kind is able to respond in this way is more of an unknown. It is known that many plants, particularly common, rigorous "weedy" kinds, exude chemicals from their root systems that prevent the establishment of roots of other individuals. The diffusates may reach many inches, sometimes feet, away from the parent root. Any herbicide that removes such a plant then produces an effect on the survival of another plant that is not directly a chemical effect. In the context of community ecology, we can conclude that the effect is a partial floral sterility.

Whether herbicide or insecticide, and irrespective of mode of action, almost every application made is characterized by the two criticisms of the ecologist indicated earlier — lack of selectivity and lack of controllability.

## Toxicity Versus Hazard

Toxicity is the inherent capacity of a chemical to harm. Hazard is the total risk taken when the chemical is used practically. Almost any chemical is toxic if taken in too large a dose. But relatively few are genuinely hazardous. Yet it does no practical good to say that table salt or water can be toxic. Concern should be with those chemicals that are known to be poisons. In this way all pesticides are toxic. The purpose of these chemicals is to harm something living. That this something is called a pest makes no difference. Almost any pesticide sufficiently active physiologically to kill a pest can harm some other living organism. This fact brings us to hazard. Very few application techniques can be considered thoroughly safe as far as potential hazard to people and nontarget organisms under all conditions of use is concerned. The same applies to medicinal chemicals prescribed by physicians. Therefore, a degree of hazard, or risk, is inherent in almost every pest control operation. The controversial aspect of pest control chiefly stems from the word "risk." Or, rather, it stems from the fact that different people do not agree on what that risk is. Inevitably, the question of particular interests and values enters the risk equation. A judgment on practical use, a conclusion on the degree of risk, must always be made.

Since most pests occur in large numbers, the effective toxicity of a pesticide is usually described in the percentage reduction of numbers in a pest population. We use a death measure for those chemicals that kill directly. The normal expression of toxicity is the lethal dosage, simply abbreviated, LD. Total death to a test population is expressed as the $LD_{100}$. The most reliable figure is that amount of chemical formulation that will kill one-half of a test population. This value is called the $LD_{50}$. Other indices may be used as well. The effective dosage (ED) must be defined according to desired effect. Frequently, death is not the goal of measurement. It may be, perhaps, that amount of chemical that produces a noticeable rise in heart beat in one-half of an experimental population (hence an $ED_{50}$). Special problems require special measures. In fishes, for example, the standard measurement of toxicity is the median tolerance limit following a 96-hour exposure. This is symbolized 96-hr $TL_M$ and has about the same meaning as the $LD_{50}$, except that a temporal factor is added.

Temporal effects of toxic chemicals are sometimes broadly indicated by the terms acute and chronic. Acute is usually taken to mean immediate toxic reactions from a single exposure. Chronic is even less precise. Exposure may be single or continuing, but the effects may appear either over or only after a long period of time. With the discovery that subtle effects may be long delayed following exposure to poisons, tests may now run as long as 2 years. The distinctions between the two temporal descriptions may be indistinct.

The actual amounts of toxicants are normally expressed in fractions of a million by weight or volume. Parts per million (ppm) is the way it is usually seen. Recently, however, the greater sensitivity of chemical detection procedures has often allowed us to express contamination ratios in parts per billion (ppb). This expression is particularly useful in the analysis of aquatic environments, where even the slighest traces of pesticides may have important biological effects.

Risk decisions must be made. Toxicity quantified in the ways just described has become the normal measurement by which hazard is assessed. Both success in pest control and contamination levels in environment and living tissue are judged relative to an ACCEPTABLE THRESHOLD amount. The environmental monitoring schemes of public health agencies and the food-sampling programs of the Food and Drug Administration have established safety margins based on the threshold concept. As shown later, THE CONCEPT HAS LITTLE VALIDITY IN ECOSYSTEMS. The true extent of risk in the broad sense is rapidly becoming apparent. The basic themes of this section illustrate why risk determinations in the recent past have been entirely too narrowly based.

The hard reality of risk determination regarding human health is that it is based almost entirely on toxicological and marketing considerations. Varying field conditions and differing social and traditional values play small roles in determining use in the United States. Yet the incidence of accidental death or injury is large and mounting. The U.S. Department of Agriculture reported 181 deaths due to pesticides (chiefly organophosphates) in the United States in 1969. About 1250 cases of pesticide injury were officially reported in California in 1966. Twenty-six of these, including 18 suicides, resulted in death. Occupational exposure among field workers is not only common, but full of unknowns. Why is it, for example, that peach and strawberry pickers commonly show signs of phosphate poisoning after parathion applications in which all regulations have been followed? Recent work suggests that parathion on foliage converts to paraoxon which is more stable and 10 times as toxic as parathion. Yet this fact is not yet recognized in regulatory practices. The herbicide 2, 4, 5-T is probably teratogenic (causes birth defects). But it has been used widely in Vietnam and is commonly used in the United States, even by the U.S. Department of Agriculture.

Newspaper accounts of accidental poisonings are now commonplace. Official accounts are often paradoxical. For example, the World Health Organization recently reported that in a survey of 200,000 workers occupationally exposed to DDT not a single human death was attributable to the chemical. Yet that organization regularly issues a *Circular on Toxicity* chronicling the hundreds of annual instances of death and morbidity resulting from DDT and other pesticides. As a further example of paradox, why has Japan totally banned the use of parathion and tetraethyl pyrophosphate (TEPP) when these and similar materials have increased in use threefold in the United States in the last 5 years? And the ultimate example of paradox, Why do we "allow" residual amounts of chlorinated hydrocarbons in human milk considerably in excess of those legally allowed in dairy products?

The risk of pesticide poisoning to human beings is normally judged by acute toxicity. The presence of residues in human tissues is now universal, ranging from an average low of about 3.0 ppm in Eskimo in Alaska to about 25.0 ppm in India. The average is about 12 ppm in the United States.[2,3] No one is fully confident that these insidiously acquired residue loads are without effect. A recent study in Florida suggests a relationship between the concentration of DDT (and metabolites) and liver tumors, cirrhosis, and hypertension. For example in terminal cases showing liver malignancy the mean $p,p'$-DDE (dichlorodiphenylethane) concentration in fat was three times normal and seven times as high in liver. Race and socioeconomic status are other elements in the risk equation. Southern negroes, for example – particularly children – consistently show higher residue levels than southern whites. [3,4]

## The Future of Pesticide Production

The production and use of pesticides continues to grow throughout the world. Synthetic organic pesticide production in the United States continues to increase at about 15 percent per year. Total sales anticipated by 1975 are estimated at $3 billion annually. Rates of increase in different chemical categories are not equal. Herbicide sales, for example, have risen 271 percent in the period 1963-69. This increase is more than double that for all other pesticidal classes. Herbicidal sales alone are expected to be $1.35 billion in the United States by 1974. The United States produces 50 to 75 percent of all pesticides and regularly exports about a third of its production. Both production and export of DDT have declined since 1967, but increases in other chlorinated hydrocarbon and organophosphate insecticides have more than compensated for that decline. On the world market the dominant pesticides in use are insecticides and fungicides, and this domination is expected to continue indefinitely. The conclusion that an environmentalist may clearly draw is that synthetic pesticidal use will increase world wide, with attendant ecological hazards.

## Some Chemicals Survive

The chemicals used in pest control have their value only when they intimately intrude into the pest's environment. Normally in agriculture the major portion is directed toward the leaf surfaces of plants. Pesticides as well, depending on purposes, may be placed on walls, water surfaces, or the surface of the ground. Very rarely is the method of use so precise that only the minimal area required is actually treated. More often a much larger area is treated simply because there is no choice. Moreover, these pesticides normally drift or drip or leach into other areas nearby so that the area covered by the spray or dust is increased.

The actual fraction of pesticide reaching the target surface and remaining there is small. A significant part vaporizes into the atmosphere either before it reaches the crop or shortly thereafter as the spray is drying. In one orchard where DDT was used for 20 years, measurements of DDT in soil, plants, and runoff accounted for only 50 percent of the total dosage. The remaining half probably entered the atmosphere at or shortly following spraying. In another study, a

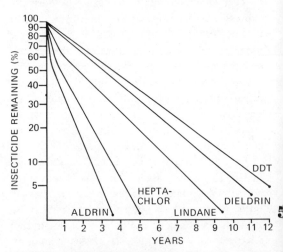

PESTICIDE DISAPPEARANCE RATES. The normal method of showing persistent pesticide disappearance rates in soil. Note that total "loss" is expected and predicted on essentially a straight-line basis. The representation, common though it is, is ecologically naive. First, in both inorganic and organic environments, soils are among the poorest media for showing insecticide survival. Second, no indication is given of the survival and enhancement of residues in living systems.

maximum of 38 percent of DDT applied to a cornfield by air actually ended up on the corn plants or in the soil.[5]

The chemical mixture, wherever it does fall, however, forms a deposit whose presence is necessary for pest control. This deposit does not normally keep its original chemical character for very long. Change comes about as the deposit is acted upon by living systems and by heat, light, and water. The remainder of this transformed deposit is called a PESTICIDE RESIDUE. This remaining portion will contain reduced amounts of the original toxic substance, physically and biologically transformed chemical derivatives of the original substance, and parts of the original solvent or diluent carriers.

All pesticides in common use produce residues that survive for noticeable periods on foliage or soils. It may be only a day or two as for TEPP or perhaps a couple of weeks for parathion. Or it may be for a very long time — many years — as with DDT. Figure 5 illustrates the average survival of several chlorinated hydrocarbon insecticides in soil taking into account the many environmental variables in different locations.[6] Probably the upper limit to residue survival is shown in Table III. This study was atypical in the sense that all factors contributing to the decomposition of residues were minimized. In this situation survival times ran several times longer than in the average case. The clear "winner" is

| Pesticide | % Remaining |
|---|---|
| | 14 Years Later |
| Aldrin | 40 |
| Chlordane | 40 |
| Endrin | 41 |
| Heptachlor | 16 |
| BHC | 10 |
| Toxaphene | 45 |
| | 15 Years Later |
| Aldrin | 28 |
| Dieldrin | 31 |
| | 17 Years Later |
| DDT | 39 |

**LONGEVITY OF CHLORINATED HYDROCARBONS.** The maximum longevity of chlorinated hydrocarbon insecticides in soils. Survival of residues in this instance is maximal because of experimental design. Source: reference 7.

DDT, 39 percent of which survived in original form for 17 years.[7]

The period of persistence is important information. There are two ways of viewing such information. One relates to the original purpose: the length of time that residual protection from pests can be expected. The other is the judgment of hazard. In this instance, the persistence period indicates how soon before harvest or before food consumption the chemical can be applied. It indicates, too, how likely is the chance of hazard from toxic residues to living things other than man and the animals or plants he has set out to control. For these reasons a great deal of research effort has gone into determining how long a pesticide chemical survives in various environmental situations.

For practical purposes those chemicals that survive for only a few days — or even weeks — can be termed nonpersistent. Those that survive for longer periods — months or years — are called persistent. Both use and hazard depend on how long and in what form pesticide chemicals survive. A nonpersistent chemical not only "disappears" in a short space of time but it has no opportunity to disperse widely. On the other hand, a sizable fraction of the original deposit of a persistent chemical remains. These residues become scattered so that they are no longer found only on the area where applied. A small amount will predictably have been carried outside the general area to some distant point. The ways in which residues are dispersed are many and varied. Natural forces, both physical and biological, are responsible. Residue dispersal is clearly important practically and a new field of study called pesticide kinetics has become established in recent years.

Most chemicals now used in pest control are synthetics, that is, they are made, not found in nature. Man must decide where and when to use these chemicals. Since these chemicals are usually toxic to many living things, including man, in sufficient amount, not only must pesticide kinetics be understood but practical steps to avoid excessive contamination of our own environment, particularly of our own foodstuffs, must be taken. The way food technologists view residues as they apply to human foods is illustrated in Figure 6.

Persistent chemicals in foods are a small fraction of the total amount applied in the agricultural environment. Moreover, the greater fraction on foodstuffs degrades in a few days' time and the processing and marketing phases allow still more to degrade or to be removed. Human concern is the "final food residue." This quantity of the original toxic material present in foods cannot be allowed to exceed certain values (tolerances) judged to be within safety limits. There have been many arguments about these final residue values. What exactly is safe? On the one hand, food production is vital and yields of foodstuffs are increased by the use of pesticide chemicals. On the other hand, there are many unknowns in the judgment. Much scientific effort goes into the determination of what the maximum permissible residue values will be. There remains constant concern about the correctness of judgments. New data often force changes. There are also some people who, on personal, religious, or philosophical grounds, argue that no traces at all of any of these chemicals should be allowed in foods.

Unfortunately, the problem of residues doesn't stop with human food. The ecologist must attend to the much greater amounts of residues that do not remain on foods. A quick inspection of Figure 6 shows that the application rate of pesticides is many times larger than the maximum possible contamination of "edible parts only." Domestic animals and wildlife also eat. It is possible to build up residues in soil to such levels that they might harm plants — become phytotoxic — or that they might once again pose residue problems for us.

## Pesticide Distribution

The greatest staying power is among the chlorinated hydrocarbon insecticides. Figure 5 shows the "survivorship curves" of five common pesticides in this group.

Both physical and biological transfer systems have been imputed to account for the spatial distribution of residues. In general, the transfer of residues in physical systems can be directly measured. There is a variety of data demonstrating that residues occur in aerial dust and smog, rainfall, in air far at sea, in ground and flowing waters, and in soils at different depths and of different types. No one has yet conducted a full study of pesticide kinetics in natural ecosystems. Our present studies at Clear Lake, California are an attempt to do this in an ecological microcosm.

Generally, fluid movements — air and water — are responsible for residue transfers over long distances. Vaporization and codistillation with water are the primary entries into air. Slowly we are acquiring the belief that larger fractions (up to 50 percent) than previously thought enter the atmosphere in this way. Pesticide residues in water tend to adsorb differentially to suspended (particularly organic matter) particles. In both air and water the smallest particles seem to carry the greatest residue burden because of their abundance.[5]

The occurrence of residues in air and water at points distant from sites of application is now established. DDT (also DDE and DDD) occurred in atmospheric dust over the Barbados Islands in the amount of 41 ppb (Figure 7).[8] DDT in dust over Pittsburgh in the latter half of 1964 averaged 0.25 parts per trillion (ppt).[9] Residues in

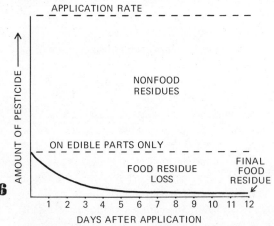

**6**

PESTICIDE RESIDUES ON FOOD. The normal manner of representation of surviving pesticide residues on human foodstuffs. Important as is this approach for human welfare, it, too, is ecologically naive. The implication that pesticide residues no longer are significant because "tolerance limits" are not exceeded on foodstuffs overlooks the ecologic fate of the much larger remainder.

British rainwater in 1966 and 1967 showed measurable amounts of BHC (lindane), dieldrin, and DDT. Even in the remote Shetland Islands, where pesticides are rarely used, total residues measured 229 ppt.[5] At this station as well as others in the United Kingdom, it is postulated that pesticides were being carried in the air over thousands of miles of ocean waters, in this case in the prevailing westerly winds from North America. On the basis of an average concentration of 170 ppt of all residues at all stations in Britain, one can calculate that 1 inch of rainfall would deposit 1 ton of residues. Or, in other terms, with an average rainfall of over 40 inches per year, Great Britain receives over four times the amount of pesticide residues that the Mississippi River dumps into the Gulf of Mexico annually. The estimated maximum amount of residues of DDT and metabolites in Antarctic snow and ice is over 2400 tons.[10] Almost 2 tons of residues a year enter San Francisco Bay from the Sacramento and San Joaquin Rivers.[11] Even so, this amount is scarcely sufficient to explain the almost total contamination of the biota from the confluence of these rivers and in the ultimate marine environment. Air transport must be the major disseminator of residues. How else, as an example, can one explain that all frogs examined

TRANSPORT OF PESTICIDE RESIDUES. Aerial transport of residues and subsequent biological magnification reaching toxic levels in an ultimate consumer. This example is extreme, but generally describes how residues enter biological tissues in areas remote from points of application. Source: reference 8.

(several hundred), including those above 5000 feet, in the Sierra Nevada are contaminated with DDT products (average 3.19 ppm)?[12] And in a totally different ecological environment, how can one explain average levels of DDT and metabolites in the blubber of gray and sperm whales amounting to 0.36 and 6.0 ppm, respectively?[13] The differential can be explained rationally because sperm whales eat larger organisms, higher up the food chain. But the presence of residues in migratory mammals from the open ocean is more difficult to account for. Atmospheric fallout must be the source.

Biological mechanisms in residue transfer are often inferred. Descriptions of amounts in tissue are, of course, easily made. But to assess transfer mechanisms a good knowledge of the life histories of implicated species and of trophodynamics in ecological communities is required. Too often, the basic ecological information needed for full assessment is not available. Schematic representation of the biological and physico-biological systems involved in these assessments is provided in Figures 8 and 9. These models have been developed from my own detailed studies at Clear Lake, but they have a general applicability to freshwater ecosystems anywhere. With appropriate substitution of ecological information the same pathways in an open ocean environment can be illustrated (Figure 10).[8,14]

Pesticide residues in animal tissues have their source in an environment normally containing traces of residues. Initial entry into the animal

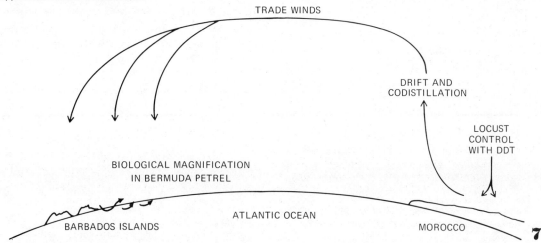

TRADE WINDS

DRIFT AND
CODISTILLATION

LOCUST
CONTROL
WITH DDT

BIOLOGICAL MAGNIFICATION
IN BERMUDA PETREL

ATLANTIC OCEAN

BARBADOS ISLANDS

MOROCCO

**7**

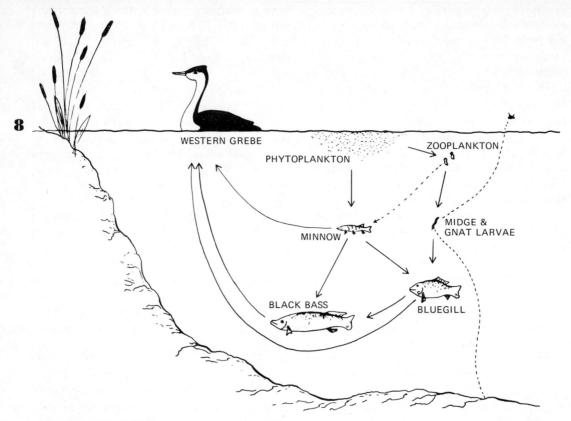

8

WESTERN GREBE

PHYTOPLANKTON

ZOOPLANKTON

MINNOW

MIDGE &
GNAT LARVAE

BLACK BASS

BLUEGILL

AQUATIC FOOD CHAINS. A simplified representation of aquatic food chains at Clear Lake, California. Slow release of persistent pesticide residues from the surrounding watershed and the lake bottom enables biological "capturing," storage, and magnification in the food chain. As a general rule, it is the last link in the food chain (the ultimate consumer) that shows toxic symptoms of concentrated residues.

food chain normally is by means of contaminated foods. This source must be essentially the only way that terrestrial animals acquire tissue residues. Contaminated foods are also major sources of tissue residues among aquatic animals, but are particularly important as secondary links in the food chain. Initial entry into aquatic food chains may derive from the tendency of pesticides to adsorb on suspended particulate matter which is consumed by filter-feeding organisms known to be environmental concentrators. There is some evidence as well that living organisms in environments in which sublethal amounts of residue are present may acquire residues directly through the gills and skin.

Two serious areas of ignorance remain. The first concerns the physicobiological interface. How precisely are residual transfers made from an inorganic environment to a biological community? The second is the amount and nature of return residues to a biological community following death of contaminated tissues. In short, what is the nature of biological recycling of pesticide residues? This question rests on the observation that residues simply do not degrade in biological environments at the rate predicted from physical evidence (Figure 5).

## Proof of Environmental Contamination

The argument persists that recent environmental contaminants cannot be responsible for some of the major biological effects that have been observed. When DDT residues were first announced in Antarctic wildlife in 1965, the standard response of chemical producers and users was that chromatographic analyses were artifacts, either due to naturally occurring chemicals or to incompetence of analysts. Either de-

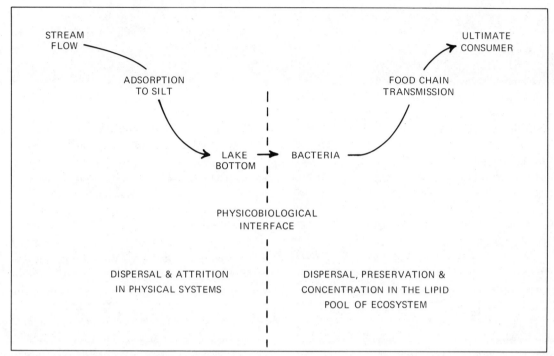

**9**

PESTICIDE KINETICS IN LAKES. Schematic representation of pesticide kinetics in lacustrine ecosystems. Residues disperse and degrade in the physical component but are entrapped, survive, and their amounts enhanced in the biological segment. The relatively inert lipid fraction amounts to an ecological preservative for these residue "fossils."

fense has been shown to be foolish. Yet it is true that the major evidence linking biological effect in the field and environmental contamination is correlative, not experimental. Ecologists regularly depend on correlation between events to reach conclusion; experimentalists seldom do.

I offer here two examples of residual occurrences linked with major biological events whose discovery was first made by field biologists and later confirmed by experimental work. The first concerns mercury in Swedish fish and wildlife. Mercury in Sweden derives primarily from point sources, that is, industrial effluents on streams, but agriculture where mercuric seed dressings are use is a major general source. Studies of fish and birds first showed high levels of mercury in tissues (over 1 ppm). A series of investigations elucidated the general problem and led to stringent industrial controls in 1966 and to the abolition of organic mercury as a seed treatment in

1967.[4] Sweden does not have naturally occurring mercury. Confirmation of the relatively recent nature of environmental contamination by mercury was provided by a study describing mercury content in feathers of 11 species of birds in museums collected over a century's time.[15] In all species mercury was relatively constant in the period 1840-1940. Beginning in the 1940s mercury content increased 10-20-fold. As expected

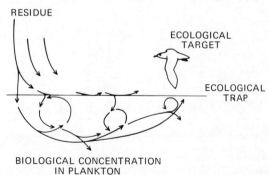

**10**

PESTICIDE KINETICS IN THE OCEAN. One means of ecological "entrapment" and confinement of pesticide residues. Airborne particles of pesticide striking a water surface do not disperse below the "skin." Rapid uptake by planktonic "environmental concentrators" ensures spatial confinement of residues to the top biological layers in which residue magnification occurs.

on biological grounds, highest levels (up to 30 ppm) were in fish-eating birds and the lowest in seed-eaters.

The second illustration links the eggshell thickness of peregrine falcons with time.[16,17] Thinning of eggshells due to DDE, dieldrin, and PCB (polychlorinated biphenyl) has now been experimentally established.[18,21] Before such confirmation, correlations between eggshell thickness and time strongly suggested a cause-effect relationship. The "coincidence," now shown in several species of raptorial and fish-eating birds, is clearly shown in Figure 11. The remarkable (and statistically significant) decline in shell thickness in the 1947-1952 period correlates well with the first general use of DDT. That the observable effect is related to environmental foci of residue concentration is shown in Figure 12. It is shown that eggshell thickness (in herring gulls) is a function of DDE concentration, which in turn is a measure of local environmental contamination. Only in Wisconsin were reproductive effects observable. The herring gull

EGGSHELL THICKNESS VS. TIME. Thickness of 614 peregrine falcon eggshells collected since 1891. The dotted horizontal line is the midpoint between the 95 percent confidence limits of the 1947-1952 group compared to all prior groups. The heavy horizontal lines are mean values; the open rectangle represents 95 percent confidence limits for each group. Source: reference 16.

colony there lived on the highly polluted shores of Lake Michigan in which all fishes have also been shown to be heavily contaminated with residues.[22]

*Biological Magnification*

The diversity of responses of living things to environmental contaminants is probably beyond knowing. Because residues of many types persist, are distributed widely, and are incorporated into biological systems, the most important response to environmental contamination is that of biological magnification.

"Capturing" existing residues occurs either by living environmental concentrators or by food-gatherers in a biological chain. Magnification or concentration of captured residues may occur by three methods. PHYSIOLOGICAL concentration occurs when residues are stored and accumulated by particular tissues within the bodies of individual organisms. A nearly straight-line relationship exists between lipid or fatty fractions of a tissue and the amount of residues contained. BIOLOGICAL concentration occurs in those instances in which residues are picked up directly through the skin or respiratory surface. This method is rather common in aquatic environments. TROPHIC concentration — or food-chain concentra-

**11**

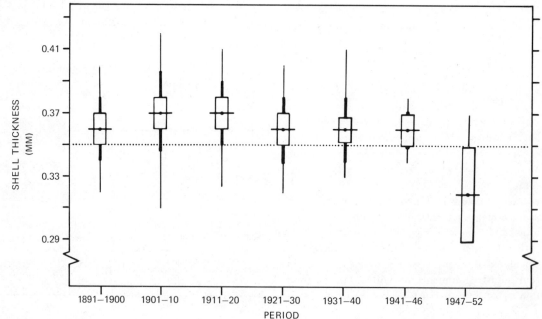

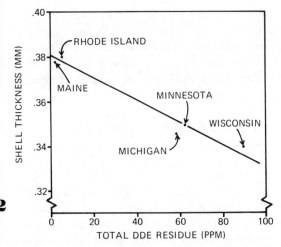

EGGSHELL THICKNESS VS. DDE CONCENTRA-TION. Variation in eggshell thickness and DDE concentrations in herring gulls collected from several locations in 1967. Only at the highest residual concentration (Wisconsin) were reproductive effects of pesticide contamination observable. Source: reference 16.

tion — occurs simply because one organism depends upon another for something to eat. Stored residues, of course, accompany ingested foods and are assimilated and stored in the predator which, in turn, if eaten, passes along a larger amount of residues. All three methods of concentration lead to magnified quantities of residues in secondary consumers in food chains. The hazard, needless to say, is greatest for the ultimate consumers.

Too frequently, environmental contamination as measured in soil and water is dismissed as negligible because residual values are usually very low. Overlooked is the incredible ability of natural mechanisms to concentrate residues. In an Ohio marsh, for example, DDT labeled with radioactive carbon concentrated 3000-fold in algae within only 3 days of application. Studies by the U.S. Fish and Wildlife Service show that many filter-feeding organisms have an unusual capacity to pick up and store residues from the environment around them. Oysters, for example, can concentrate DDT residues 70,000-fold after only 1 month's exposure.[4]

Differences in food habits reflecting positions in food chains are easily discoverable in residual levels of contamination. In Maine forests, for example, the litter fauna was sampled for pesticide residues over a period of 9 years.[23] In this

instance the major emphasis was on residues in areas sprayed only once with DDT at 1.0 lb/acre. Some areas, however, were treated at the same rate as much as three times over a period of years. Whether single or multiple application, persistent residues occurred in all fauna examined. Table IV compares mice and voles with shrews. The persistence of residues is striking. It took 9 years for mice and voles to approach residue levels occurring in nontreated areas. In areas treated three times values remained 5-6-fold above untreated areas. Carnivorous shrews, on the other hand, showed values ranging 10-40-fold above those for the herbivores. Probably about 15 years would be required, after only a single DDT treatment, before residue levels in shrew tissues could return to normal. The effects of higher residue levels are not known. Where multiple treatment occurs, those levels would remain high, having effects not only on the individual organisms, but more likely harming animals that prey upon them. Local extinction of both predator and prey are likely consequences.

Entire ecosystems can be contaminated with residues. Trophic concentration has now been documented in many instances. In my own studies at Clear Lake, California, the magnitude of concentrations of DDD in tissues over that originally occurring in water was shown to be as follows: plankton, 265-fold; small fishes, 500-fold; predaceous fishes, 85,000-fold; predaceous birds (grebes), 80,000-fold.[1]

A similar pattern of residual concentration is shown in studies by University of Wisconsin scientists working on Lake Michigan.[22] The fol-

| Years since single treatment | Mice and voles, ppm | Shrews ppm |
|---|---|---|
| 0 | 1.06 | 15.58 |
| 2–3 | 0.07 | 0.72 |
| 3–4 | 0.08 | 2.50 |
| 5–6 | 0.10 | 1.43 |
| 6–7 | 0.05 | 1.81 |
| 8–9 | 0.04 | 1.88 |
| Untreated | 0.03 | 0.30 |
| Multiple treatments (3X) | 0.17 | 4.77 |

**IV**

DDT RESIDUES IN SMALL MAMMALS. Total residues of DDT and metabolites in small mammals collected from plots in Maine forests with variable treatment history. Mean values (ppm) only are shown (Source: reference 23).

lowing listing indicates residue levels of chlorinated hydrocarbon insecticides in a trophic sequence.

| | |
|---|---|
| Bottom sediments | 0.0085 ppm |
| Small invertebrates | 0.41 ppm |
| Fishes | 3.0-8.0 ppm |
| Herring gulls | 3177 ppm |

The most complete community study yet made of residual contamination centered on a salt marsh bordering Long Island Sound.[24] Arrangement of residue levels of DDT in order of increasing value showed a clear progression related to both size of organism and trophic level. Larger organisms and higher carnivores had greater concentrations than smaller organisms at lower trophic levels. Total residues ranged through three orders of magnitude — from 0.04 ppm in plankton to 75 ppm in a ring-billed gull. Shrimp contained 0.16 ppm; eels, 0.28 ppm; marsh insects, 0.30 ppm; and predaceous fishes, 2.07 ppm. In general, concentrations of DDT were 10-100 times as high in carnivorous birds as in the fishes on which they fed. Actual values of DDT residues in water were about 0.00005 ppm. Based on this value, birds near the top of the food chain have concentrations of DDT residues a million times greater than the concentration in water. This example among others suggests that DDT residues are moving through the biological and chemical cycles of the earth at concentrations that are having far-reaching, yet little-known effects on ecological systems.

Most notably in raptorial and fish-eating birds, declines in numbers seem to be clearly related to the presence of pesticide residues. In our continuing work at Clear Lake, high residue levels are clearly correlated with inhibition of reproductive success in Western grebes. The rare Bermuda petrel clearly shows these residue effects on reproduction.[25] Yet, more dramatically, the total failure of brown pelicans to breed successfully on the coastal islands of California in 1969 and 1970 is probably attributable to biological magnification of pesticide residues "trapped" and preserved in marine ecosystems. In 1970 only one young pelican among 552 nests studied survived to fledge. Recently imputed as potential contributors to these disastrous reproductive effects are also lead, mercury, and polychlorinated biphenyls (PCB). Although the source of these materials is normally not pest control, the effects can be the same.

Species decline, that is, decline in numbers and distribution, presumably caused by ubiquitous residues, has been observed in many species of animals. The evidence is strongest in raptorial and fish-eating birds, representing in ecological terms ultimate consumers, the ends of food chains. Most concern lies with the peregrine falcon, whose decline in numbers correlates very closely with expanding use of DDT (Figure 11). Several studies focus on observations and mechanisms to explain the decline in numbers. Young birds have died; clutch size has been reduced; eggshell size and thickness has decreased; and egg-breaking by adults has increased. These changes have been linked in part to aberrant calcium metabolism. DDT and DDE (as well as PCB) have shown to be powerful inducers — at very low residual levels — of liver enzymes that degrade estradiol.[18],[19] Estrogenic hormones in female birds play an important role in calcium metabolism. Insecticide residues — uncontrolled in environment and concentrated in animal tissues — can now be shown to have altered the normal hormonal balance in wild species, leading unfortunately to species-wide effects. Some 10 families of birds now seem to be affected in this manner (Figure 13). How far these effects ultimately extend in birds or other animal groups is not known. Importantly illustrated by this action is that the threshold concept of toxic effects has to be discarded. Residues not only act by accumulation ecologically or physiologically to yield toxic effects, but they can also act in TRACE amounts to result in species disaster. Only recently has this subtlety of contaminant effects been appreciated.

*A Concluding Commentary*

Pesticide chemicals will continue to be used in pest control, and they will continue to cause effects in place. The broad-spectrum activity of these chemicals ensures that nontarget organisms will be affected as well as intended targets. Some effects and alternative methods that might lessen or eliminate these effects are considered in the succeeding chapter.

But the second category of major effects described at the beginning of this chapter is of more serious concern to the environmentalist. Surviving pesticide residues are at once insidious, uncontrollable, and unpredictable in their actions. The only conclusion to draw is that all pesticides whose toxic effects cannot be confined to the site of application must be banned. Sufficient risks remain even with such a restriction in use. These risks are properly the responsibility of the pest control practitioner and range from hazard to the farm worker to pesticide resistance in pest species. Even with total banning of persistent pesticides, sufficient amounts of residues will remain in the earth's ecosystems to ensure ecological disruptions for decades. Estimates of

these amounts range upward into the millions of pounds. These estimates are, at best, guesses. The actual amounts make no real difference, however. Examples of biological disruption are now sufficiently documented to establish that existing uncontrolled residues, whatever their amounts, are seriously damaging.

Further evidence of the subtlety with which pesticide contaminants can act is provided by an example which, if established as generally occurring, could have staggering ecological consequences. It rests on the question, "How do insecticide-resistant vertebrates affect the organisms that feed upon them?" Recent work at Mississippi State University provides a first answer.[26] In experimental studies, 95 percent of the vertebrate predators (11 species) died after consuming one endrin-resistant mosquito fish (*Gambusia*). In other terms, resistant mosquito fish tolerate endrin residues sufficient to kill potential predators several hundred times their own weight. These were laboratory studies. No one can yet say that the effects occur in nature, but, even if locally applicable, resulting ecological disruptions could be catastrophic.

CYCLE CAUSING THIN EGGSHELLS. A simplified diagram illustrating the physiological mechanisms by which species declines in raptorial and fish-eating birds might be induced. Numbers decline in these "ultimate consumers" as pesticide residues increase. The breakdown of estrogens affects the circulating calcium level in the blood, in turn affecting both adult and unhatched egg (see references 16 and 19).

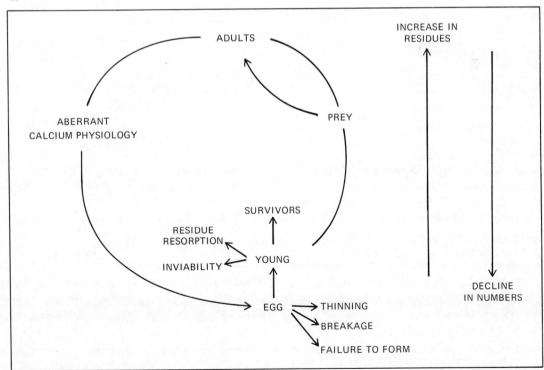

13

In effect, with pesticidal chemicals we have introduced an evolutionarily new, density-independent factor into the environment. We have argued the need for these chemicals in pest control. It is now necessary to argue for stringent pesticide control, to depart from the major emphasis on pests alone. Pesticides are now uncontrolled. We need to recognize that pest control is basically an ecological, not a chemical, problem. The dizzying changes induced into the earth's ecosystem in the last two or three decades constitute an experiment out of hand, whose consequences now seem ecologically catastrophic. Restoring control requires perspective and judgment. Sufficient facts are available. No one need dodge behind the welter of data points — of $LD_{50}$s, $TL_M$s, and chemical formulas. Neither pest control nor the uncontrolled effects of pesticides is toxicology simply extrapolated. The scientist must not only seek facts; he must judge facts in entire systems, including those within the human community. Ecologists are obligated to serve this human expectation. Through them the primary goal — the reestablishment of a WORKING CONTROL SYSTEM — can be achieved. Persistent pesticides, along with many more waste products of technological man, cannot be allowed to continue to work against such a controlling system.

## References

1. Rudd, R.L. 1964. *Pesticides and the Living Landscape.* Univ. of Wisconsin Press, Madison, Wisconsin, 320 pp.

2. U.S. Dept. of Health, Education and Welfare. 1969. Rept. of the Secretary's Commission on Pesticides and their relationship to environmental health, 677 pp.

3. Davies, J.E., Edmundson, W.F., Schneider, N.J., and Cassady, J.C. 1968. Problems of prevalence of pesticide residues in humans. *Pesticide Monitoring J. 2:*80-85.

4. Miller, M.W., and Berg, G.G., eds. 1969. *Chemical Fallout — Current Research on Persistent Pesticides.* C.C. Thomas, Springfield, Illinois, 531 pp.

5. Frost, J. 1969. Earth, air, water. *Environment 11:*14-28, 31-33.

6. Crosby, D.G. 1964. Intentional removal of pesticide residues. In *Research in Pesticides* (C.O. Chichester, ed.) Academic Press, New York, pp. 213-222.

7. Nash, R.G., and Woolson, C.A. 1967. Persistence of chlorinated hydrocarbon insecticides in soils. *Science 157:*924-927.

8. Risebrough, R.W., Huggett, R.J., Griffin, J.J., and Goldberg, E.D. 1968. Pesticides: Transatlantic movements in the northeast trades. *Science 159:* 1233-1236.

9. Cohen, J., and Pinkerton, C. 1966. Widespread translocation of pesticides by air transport and rain-out. In "Organic Pesticides in the Environment." *Amer. Chem. Soc., Advan. Chem., Ser. 60:*163-176.

10. Peterle, T.J. 1969. DDT in Antarctic snow. *Nature 224:*620.

11. Bailey, T.E., and Hannum, J.R. 1967. Distribution of pesticides in California. *J. Sanitary Eng. Div., Amer. Soc. Civil Engr., Proc. 5510:*27-43.

12. Cory, L., Fjeld, P., and Serat, W. 1970. Distribution patterns of DDT residues in the Sierra Nevada Mountains. *Pesticides Monitoring J. 3:*204-210.

13. Wolman, A.A., and Wilson, A.J. 1970. Occurrence of pesticides in whales. *Pesticides Monitoring J. 4:*8-10.

14. Risebrough, R.W., Reiche, P., Peakall, D., Herman, S., and Kirven, M. 1968. Polychlorinated biphenyls in the global system. *Nature 220:*1098-1102.

15. Berg, W., Johnels, A., Plantin, L.O., Sjöstrand, B. and Westermark, T. 1966. Mercury content in feathers of Swedish birds for the last 100 years. *Oikos 17:*71.

16. Hickey, J.J., and Anderson, D.W. 1968. Chlorinated hydrocarbons and eggshell changes in raptorial and fish-eating birds. *Science 162:*271-273.

17. Hickey, J.J., ed. 1969. *Peregrine Falcon Populations — Their Biology and Decline.* Univ. of Wisconsin Press, Madison, Wisconsin, 596 pp.

18. Peakall, D.B. 1967. Pesticide-induced enzyme breakdown of steroids in birds. *Nature 216:*205.

19. **Peakall, D.B.** 1970. Pesticides and the reproduction of birds. *Sci. Amer. 222:*72-78.
20. **Porter, R.D., and Wiemeyer, S.N.** 1969. Dieldrin and DDT: Effects on sparrow hawk eggshells and reproduction. *Science 165:*199-200.
21. **Bitman, J., Cecil, H.C., Harris, J.J., and Fries, G.F.** 1969. DDT induces a decrease in eggshell calcium. *Nature 224:*44-46.
22. **Hickey, J.J., Keith, J.A., and Coon, F.B.** 1966. An exploration of pesticides in a Lake Michigan ecosystem. *J. Appl. Ecol. 3 (suppl.):*141-145.
23. **Dimond, J. B., and Sherburne, J.A.** 1969. Persistence of DDT in wild populations of small mammals. *Nature 221:*481-487.
24. **Woodwell, G.M., Wurster, C.F., and Isaacson, P.A.** 1967. DDT residues in an east coast estuary: A case of biological concentration of a persistent insecticide. *Science 156:*821-824.
25. **Wurster, C.F., and Wingate, D.** 1968. DDT residues and declining population in the Bermuda petrel. *Science 159:*979-981.
26. **Rosato, P., and Ferguson, D.E.** 1968. Toxicity of endrin-resistant mosquito fish to eleven species of vertebrates. *Bioscience 18:*783-784.

Further Reading

**American Chemical Society.** 1969. Cleaning our environment — the chemical basis for action. Report of the Subcommittee on Environmental Improvement, Committee on Chemistry and Public Affairs. Washington, D.C., 249 pp.

**Anderson, D.W., Hickey, J.J., Risebrough, R. W., Hughes, D.F., and Christensen, R.E.** 1969. Significance of chlorinated hydrocarbon residues to breeding pelicans and cormorants. *Can. Field-Nature. 83:*91-112.

**Carson, R.** 1962. *Silent Spring.* Houghton Mifflin, New York, 368 pp.

**Kennedy, J.F.** 1965. Restoring the quality of our environment. Report of the Environmental Pollution Panel, President's Science Advisory Committee, The White House, Washington, D.C., 317 pp.

**Moore, N.W.,** ed. 1966. Pesticides in the environment and their effects on wildlife. *J. Appl. Ecol. 3 (suppl.):* 311 pp.

**Moore, N.W.** 1967. A synopsis of the pesticide problem. *Advan. Ecol. Res. 4:*75-129.

**Nicholson, H.P.** 1967. Pesticide pollution control. *Science 158:*871-876.

**Rudd, R.L., and Genelly, R.E.** 1956. Pesticides: Their use and toxicity in relation to wildlife. *Calif. Dept. Fish and Game, Game Bull., No. 7,* 209 pp.

**Tatton, J.O'G., and Ruzieka, J.H.A.** 1967. Organochlorine pesticides in Antarctica. *Nature 215:*346-348.

**Wurster, C.F.** 1968. DDT reduces photosynthesis by marine phytoplankton. *Science 159:*1474-1475.

# 14   Better Methods of Pest Control

Gordon R. Conway

The preceding chapter was concerned with the pollutant effects of modern organic pesticides. As we saw, these compounds pose serious hazards to wild animal and plant life and to man. By itself this is quite sufficient justification for seeking alternatives to pesticides or, at least, trying to minimize their use. But pesticides are not only pollutants; they now also commonly fail to control pests.

Furthermore, these two aspects of the pesticide problem are related to each other. The particular characteristics of many modern pesticides which produce the failures in pest control are also partly responsible for the wider environ-

GORDON R. CONWAY is a Research Fellow in the Environmental Resource Management Research Unit at the Imperial College of Science and Technology in London. He received his B.S. in zoology from the University College of North Wales and then studied agriculture at Cambridge and at the University of the West Indies in Trinidad. From 1961 to 1966 he was entomologist at the Agricultural Research Centre in the State of Sabah (North Borneo), Malaysia, responsible for controlling "everything from elephants to red spider mites." He then went to the University of California at Davis where he earned a doctorate in biomathematics. Conway writes: "I was very dissatisfied with the empirical approach to pest control I had been following in Borneo. I wanted to see to what extent mathematics and the techniques of systems analysis could provide a better way of tackling pest problems." In recent years he has acted as a consultant on environmental problems in the developing countries, in Asia for the Ford Foundation and in Africa for WHO.

mental problems. In this chapter we will look first at the pattern of pesticide failure and analyze some of the underlying causes to show this connection. As a next step it should then be possible to define the features of an approach to pest control which is better both in terms of being more efficient and of producing fewer hazards in the environment. The rest of the chapter will be devoted to reviewing, on this basis, alternatives which have been or are being developed. The emphasis will be on the problems of insect pest control because, as we have seen, insecticides tend to be the worst environmental polluters and because most of the failures of pest control have been associated with their use. However, many of the arguments that will be developed also apply to a lesser extent to other pests such as fungi, nematodes, and weeds.

## The Early Successes

In the early years of modern pesticide use, during and immediately after the Second World War, the successes were impressive and frequently spectacular. Many pests of crops and of man and his domestic animals were controlled to a degree which had been quite impossible before. The first large-scale use of DDT was a classic of this kind. Applied to over 3 million people in the area of Naples in 1944 it rapidly brought about the end of an outbreak of louse-carried typhus. Then, after the Second World War, DDT and a related organochlorine insecticide, dieldrin, were widely and successfully used to control the mosquito vectors of malaria. Death rates from this disease in Madagascar and Ceylon, for example, were almost halved in the first 2 years of DDT spraying campaigns.

302

In agriculture the story was the same. For instance, in the 4 years prior to 1944 over 15 percent of American apple crops were lost annually to the ravages of the codling moth, but in the 4 subsequent years use of DDT brought this loss down to 4 percent. As they became available other organic insecticides worked with even greater success. And along with the new insecticides came new acaricides for mite control, nematocides for nematode control, fungicides for controlling fungus diseases, and herbicides for controlling weeds. Table I shows examples of the kind of gains which were achieved on a variety of crops in the United States from this "pesticide revolution."

There were failures, though, from the beginning, and by the middle 1950s poor control and worsening pest problems began to show up in an increasing number of situations. Insecticides and acaricides were by far the worst offenders but, as we shall see, some of the other forms of pesticides were also involved.

*The Pattern of Failure – Cotton*

To illustrate the pattern of pesticide failure which developed, we will take the cotton crop and its pests as an example. Cotton is an important crop both in the United States and in many other countries, and it has been affected by the problems associated with pesticide use to perhaps a much greater degree than any other. Not only does it provide examples of the variety of ways in which pesticide use is deficient; it also serves as a warning of the kind of situation that may well arise in other crops.

Over a hundred species of insect and spider mite attack cotton in the United States. But only a few of these in any area are key pests in the sense that if not controlled they would, year after year, cause serious damage to the crop. Over most of the cotton-growing acreage in the United States the boll weevil (*Anthonomus grandis*) is the key pest, and before the use of organic pesticides it caused considerable losses of cotton. There are, in addition, a number of other pests of lesser importance, such as the American bollworm (*Heliothis zea*), the cotton fleahopper, the cotton leafworm, and the cotton aphid. In 1943 when DDT became available it was found to control the bollworm and the fleahopper, although not the boll weevil or the other pests. But then 2 years later benzene hexachloride (BHC), another organochlorine insecticide, was found to be effective against all the pests that DDT did not control. In the years that followed, cotton pest control came to rely very heavily on these two compounds and on a number of other organochlorine compounds. Although resistance by cotton aphid to BHC and by leafworm to toxaphene began to show up quite soon, in the early 1950s growers and entomologists felt confident that cotton pests were well under control.

In 1955 this confidence was shattered by the development of high resistance to a range of organochlorine insecticides by the boll weevil in the lower Mississippi Valley. This proved to be the beginning of the development of widespread resistance in nearly all the other major cotton pests. The change was made to organophosphorus insecticides and then to carbamates, but in each case it was not long before resistance occurred. As a report of a panel of the President's Science Advisory Committee has stated[2]: "By the end of the 1963 season, almost every major cotton pest species contained local populations that had developed resistance to one or more of the chlorinated hydrocarbons, organic phosphorus or carbamate insecticides, or mixtures of chlorinated hydrocarbons. Moreover,

| Crop | Pest | Yields/acre | | Cost of treatment/acre | Net gain/acre |
|------|------|-------------|---------|------------------------|---------------|
| | | Untreated | Treated | | |
| Seed cotton | Bollworm | 7203 lb | 7860 lb | $16 | $126.50 |
| Pea seed | Fungi | 456 lb | 610 lb | $ 0.70 | $ 21.25 |
| Tomatoes | Diseases | 5.4 tons | 11.8 tons | $40 | $100 |
| Sugar beets | Root maggot | 11.8 tons | 14.5 tons | $ 2.25 | $ 32.20 |

**PESTICIDE BENEFITS.** Some examples of gains in terms of yield and net dollar returns from pesticide use on crops in the United States. Source: reference 1.

strains have developed in the laboratory that are resistant to all of these." In addition to this resistance effect, the heavy insecticide spraying had severely depleted the numbers of beneficial parasites and predators, and upsurges occurred of many pests which had hitherto been considered of secondary or minor importance. The American bollworm and other related bollworms, spider mites, and aphids were among the species which became considerably more important than before.

### The Canete Valley Story

A similar pattern of events occurred on cotton in other countries and to emphasize this shared, global nature of the problem, it is worth recounting the recent history of cotton growing in a small valley in Peru. The valley is called the Canete Valley and its story is, by now, virtually a classic in the history of pest control.[3] It is a coastal valley, one of many in Peru each separated from the other by stretches of arid land lacking in vegetation. The valleys receive little rainfall and the crops depend on irrigation water brought from the valley rivers. Each valley is an isolated agro-ecosystem in miniature. The Canete Valley originally grew sugar cane but in the 1920s shifted to cotton, and now some 15,000 hectares, or about two-thirds, of the valley are under the crop. The cotton growers are very technologically advanced: They have their own association and support their own experiment station. Cultivation of the crop is mechanized and many advanced agronomic techniques have been adopted. But when the growers turned to modern organic pesticides to solve their pest problems a situation developed which produced near-disaster.

In the years before the new pesticides were introduced there were three important pests of cotton in the Canete Valley: *Anthonomus vestitus*, which is related to the American boll weevil, a cotton leafworm, and a caterpillar, *Mescinia*. Before and during the war control of these pests was based on inorganic pesticides such as nicotine sulfate or various kinds of arsenicals. In the late 1940s some use began to be made of the organic insecticides and at the same time the

practice of ratooning (letting the cotton remain in the ground for 2 or 3 years) was adopted. Two more pests, the cotton aphid and a bollworm, *Heliothis virescens*, then became important. During the period when mostly inorganic pesticides had been used average yields ranged from 415 to 526 pounds per acre. In 1949, however, with the heavy outbreak of bollworm and aphids the yield dropped to 326 pounds per acre.

In the face of this drop of yield the growers decided to use more organic insecticides, principally DDT, BHC, and toxaphene. Some new strains of cotton were also introduced, the irrigation was improved, and there were changes in cultural practices. What followed is described by Professor Ray Smith of the University of California at Berkeley (personal communication):

> At first these procedures were very successful. Cotton yields nearly doubled. The average yield in the Canete went from 440 pounds per acre in 1950 to 648 pounds per acre in 1954. The cotton farmers were enthusiastic and developed the idea that there was a direct relationship between the amount of pesticides used and the cotton crop, i.e., the more the better. The insecticides were applied like a blanket over the entire valley. Trees were cut down to make it easier for the airplanes to treat the fields. The birds that nested in these trees disappeared. Other beneficial forms such as insect parasites and predators disappeared. As the years went by, the number of treatments was increased; also, each year the treatments were started earlier because of the earlier attacks of the pests. In late 1952, BHC was no longer effective against aphids. In the summer of 1954, toxaphene failed to control the leafworm, *Anomis*. In the 1955-6 season, *Anthonomus* reached high levels early in the growing season; then *Argyrotaenia sphaleropa* appeared as a new pest. Next *Heliothis virescens* developed a very heavy infestation and showed a high degree of resistance to DDT. Substitution of organophosphorus compounds for the chlorinated hydrocarbons became necessary. The interval between treatments was progressively shortened from a range of 8-15 days down to 3 days. Meanwhile, a whole complex of previously innocuous insects rose to serious pest status.

In the 1955-56 season the situation came to a head. Yields plummeted to 296 pounds per acre and, with the high cost of pesticides, the growers experienced heavy losses. In nearby valleys which had either not used organic pesticides or used them only to a limited extent the problems did not arise and the yields remained high.

The situation was retrieved by the adoption of integrated control techniques; we shall discuss this later in the chapter.

Drawing on these experiences in the United States and Peru and on close observation of cotton growing elsewhere in the world, Professor Smith shows that there is a quite discernible pattern in the history of cotton pest control which applies almost ubiquitously. He identifies five phases, progressing from subsistence farming through exploitative agriculture, to crisis and disaster, which may then be overcome by resorting to integrated control (see Table II).

The story of cotton as an illustration of the failings of modern pesticides is by no means unique. Similar case histories, although perhaps not quite so dramatic, could be described for a number of crops, such as apples and citrus in North America or cocoa in the tropics. There is also evidence that throughout the world many cereal crops are following the same pattern. The problem, then, is not a minor one nor is it restricted to special situations. It is a general and growing problem equal to, if not more important than, the direct consequences of pesticide use on wildlife and man.

In analyzing the cotton problems and experience with other crops it becomes clear that there are three major reasons why pesticide control is breaking down. First, pesticides are nonregulatory; second, they are countered by pest resistance; and finally, they interfere with natural regulatory mechanisms. We will examine each of these in turn.

### Pesticides as Nonregulators

In the first chapter we saw that many or most organisms are kept relatively stable in number by natural regulating mechanisms. Processes within populations or agents acting from outside govern population size by producing changes in numbers which are density-dependent. The proportionate mortality increases with rising density and vice versa. Moreover, the stability is more or less permanent. The agents which bring it about are continuously present in the ecosystem and come

into play whenever there is a shift in population size.

However, pesticides do not act in a density-dependent manner. When a pesticide is applied it produces a certain percentage kill of the pest population, a percentage which is unrelated to the numbers of the organism present. If the pesticide persists the kill may continue, the percentage decreasing with time, but other than this there is no further effect. The population is reduced, but only for a relatively brief period since no mechanism responsive to population change has been introduced. The only way in which a low, stable pest population can be achieved is by

I.   Subsistence Phase

   1. Cotton is not irrigated, part of subsistence agriculture
   2. Yields below 200 pounds lint per acre
   3. Crop protection dependent on natural control, inherent resistance, hand picking, cultural practices, rare insecticide treatments, and luck

II.   Exploitation Phase

   1. Cotton grown on newly irrigated land
   2. Crop protection schemes based on chemical pesticides
   3. Intensive pesticide use often on fixed schedules
   4. Initially high yields

III.   Crisis Phase

   1. More frequent pesticide applications needed
   2. Treatments start earlier in growing season and extend later into harvest period
   3. Pest populations resurge rapidly to new higher levels after treatment
   4. New pests arise

IV.   Disaster Phase

   1. Pesticide usage increases costs
   2. Marginal land removed from production
   3. Eventually cotton can no longer be grown profitably in area

V.   Integrated Control Phase

   1. Crop protection system devised which relies on a variety of control methods
   2. Environmental factors are modified and fullest use is made of natural mortality and biological control

**II**

COTTON PEST CONTROL PHASES. The five phases which have occurred worldwide in cotton pest control. Source: R. F. Smith, University of California at Berkeley, personal communication.

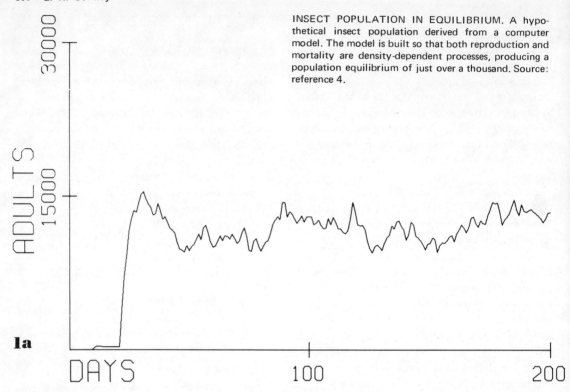

INSECT POPULATION IN EQUILIBRIUM. A hypothetical insect population derived from a computer model. The model is built so that both reproduction and mortality are density-dependent processes, producing a population equilibrium of just over a thousand. Source: reference 4.

repeated applications of pesticide timed to hit the population whenever it begins to recover or by using a compound which persists for a very long period.

We can illustrate this by means of a model of a simple insect population which has been programmed for a computer. Figure 1a shows the changes in the population over time when no control is attempted. The model has been so arranged that the population is highly regulated by natural factors: both natality and mortality are programmed as density-dependent processes. The population starts out as a few eggs and, as can be seen, grows exponentially and then levels off at a stable level. In Figure 1b spraying with a pesticide is simulated. The application is made on day 100 and is programmed to give a 90 percent kill on the first day with subsequently a 5 percent reduction in kill on each following day. As can be seen, as the effect of the pesticide wears off the population rebounds to the previous level. Only when further pesticide applications are made is the population prevented from rebounding (Figure 1c).

One consequence of this characteristic of pesticide use is that environmental contamination is persistent. Wildlife and man in affected ecosystems are being constantly exposed to pesticides. If the exposure was less prolonged there would be fewer environmental problems. For pest control the direct consequence is that pesticide use is costly in materials, time, and manpower. Often the need for repeated pesticide applications results in farmers adopting so-called spray schedules whereby the pesticides are applied on a regular basis determined solely by the calendar. In crops such as cotton the costs of such spray schedules are threatening to make the crop uneconomic. However, perhaps more important than this effect, the need for persistent or repeated pesticide applications contributes to the other two components of pesticide failure.

## Resistance to Pesticides

This is not a new problem; pest populations developed resistance to the older inorganic compounds. As early as 1908, for example, the San

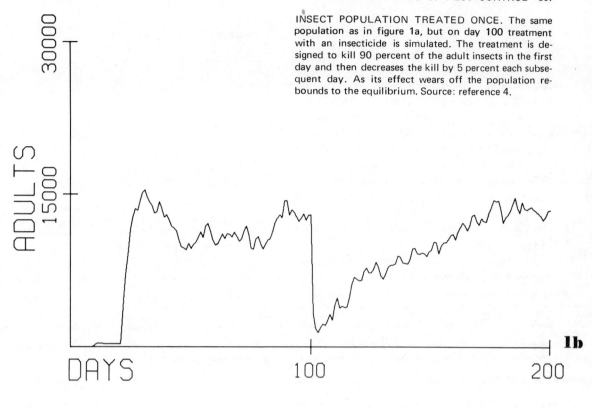

INSECT POPULATION TREATED ONCE. The same population as in figure 1a, but on day 100 treatment with an insecticide is simulated. The treatment is designed to kill 90 percent of the adult insects in the first day and then decreases the kill by 5 percent each subsequent day. As its effect wears off the population rebounds to the equilibrium. Source: reference 4.

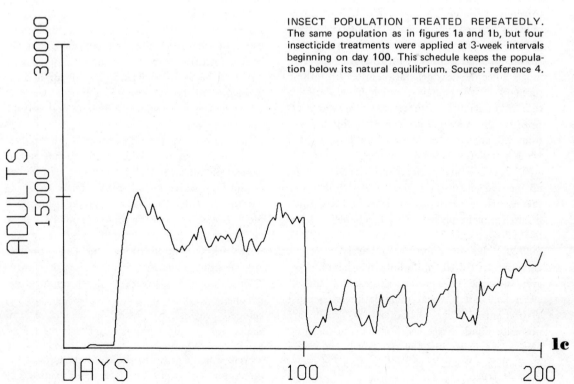

INSECT POPULATION TREATED REPEATEDLY. The same population as in figures 1a and 1b, but four insecticide treatments were applied at 3-week intervals beginning on day 100. This schedule keeps the population below its natural equilibrium. Source: reference 4.

Jose scale, which is a pest of apples, showed resistance to lime sulfur. By the 1940s there were some ten pest species exhibiting resistance, principally to hydrogen cyanide and arsenic compounds. But with the introduction of organic pesticides the number of resistant species began to increase rapidly. By 1958 there were 60 such species and by 1967 over 200[5],[6] (see Figure 2). the present rate of increase continues all of the estimated 5000 species of insect and spider pests in the world will be showing resistance to one or more pesticides by the year 1990. The increase will probably not continue at the same rate, but this calculation gives some idea of the magnitude of the problem.

The term "resistance", in this context, does not refer to a process of habituation to a pesticide. Individual insects do not develop immunity through progressive exposure. In fact, usually the reverse occurs: Adult houseflies exposed to daily sublethal doses of DDT or dieldrin became increasingly susceptible to them. Pesticide resistance is a genetic phenomenon. It occurs because a few individuals in a population possess a genetic structure which confers on them the ability to survive exposure to a pesticide. When the pesticide is applied all, or nearly all, of the susceptible individuals are destroyed and the survivors are predominantly those with the genes for resistance. Since the next generation arises from these survivors it will contain a much higher proportion of individuals with resistance. As applications of the pesticide are repeated this proportion will continue to increase until finally the whole population is resistant.

The genes actually confer resistance by setting up mechanisms in the individual which detoxify the pesticide. Resistance to DDT, for example, results from the presence of a mechanism whereby hydrogen chloride is removed from the DDT molecule, leaving only the relatively nontoxic compound DDE (dichlorodiphenylethane). However, since the genes producing these mechanisms are usually rare in natural populations they must also confer other characteristics which are normally disadvantageous. It is only in the presence of pesticides that the resistant genes have a clear advantage and so spread, in time and space, through the population. This process of acquiring

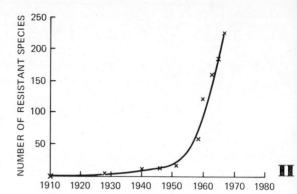

RESISTANCE TO INSECTICIDES. The growth of resistance to insecticides. The number of resistant species refers to the number of different insects and mites with resistance to one or more pesticides.

pesticide resistance is thus one of simple natural selection in the Darwinian sense. It is, in fact, a classic example of microevolution.

Since acquiring resistance depends on selection in this way, it also follows that the stronger the selection pressure the more rapidly does the population become resistant. With very complete pesticide coverage of the population, very few of the survivors will be susceptible, and hence a very high proportion will be resistant in the ensuing generations. Here we can clearly see the significance of the point, already established, that because pesticides are nonregulatory they have either to be very persistent or to be applied repeatedly. This failing, important in itself, leads to a much worse resistance problem than would otherwise occur.

In addition to selection pressure, the rapidity with which resistance is acquired depends on the generation time of the pest. Species with short generations which breed continuously throughout the year develop resistant populations that much faster. The two factors combined set up a vicious circle. Rapidly breeding pests elicit frequent pesticide applications which, in turn, create a strong selection pressure for resistance. Then as populations recover earlier, applications become even more frequent and resistance is developed progressively faster. Some idea of the speed and spread of population resistance can be gained from Figure 3.

It is not surprising, then, that the first species to show resistance were those which breed

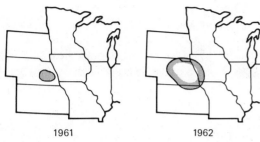

1961                    1962

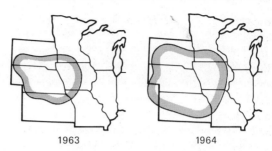

1963                    1964

SPREAD OF INSECTICIDE—RESISTANT POPULA-
TION. Annual spread of resistance to dieldrin-related
compounds in the western corn rootworm in South
Dakota, Nebraska, Kansas, Minnesota, Iowa, and
Missouri. Source: reference 6.

rapidly and live in continuously favorable environments, such as occur in tropical regions or
in human dwelling places. Nor is it surprising that
the species involved have tended to be of medical
and veterinary importance, since these have been
subject to the most intensive pesticide pressures.
The most widespread resistance has been shown
by houseflies, biting flies, flies of cattle, mosquitoes and midges, bedbugs, and cockroaches. For
example, 21 species of the mosquito genus
*Anopheles* alone have developed resistance to
organochlorine insecticides.

However, resistance is by no means confined
to pests of this kind. Resistance in cotton pests
has already been described and pests of many
other crops are now included in the resistant list.
Also, resistance has developed in several mammal
pests. The most serious case is the resistance
evolved in the brown rat, *Rattus norvegicus*, to
anticoagulant rodenticides such as warfarin.[7]
This was first observed in 1958 in wild brown
rats near Glasgow in Scotland and 2 years later
was found on the borders of England and Wales
and also in Jutland in Denmark. Attempts have
been made to contain the resistant rats in the
areas where they were first observed. But this has
not been very successful and by 1970 resistant
brown rats were occupying an area of 1200
square miles in the English-Welsh borders.

Resistance, in fact, will develop in most organisms subjected to the pressure of chemical toxicants. Bacteria causing human, animal, or plant
disease readily evolve resistance to various antibiotics. Fungi can also develop resistance to fungicides; for example, *Helminthosporium avenae*,

a fungus which attacks oats, has developed resistance to organomercury compounds.

A further aspect of the problem is the occurrence of cross-resistance. When a pest population
shows resistance to DDT, for example, it may
also show resistance to several related compounds, such as methoxychlor and DDD (di-
chlorodiphenyldichloroethane). There are, in
fact, four groups of insecticides within each of
which resistance to any one member may also
confer resistance against any other. Two of the
groups are organochlorine insecticides — the
DDT group and the cyclodiene derivative group,
to which dieldrin belongs. The other two groups
comprise the organophosphorus compounds and
the carbamates. Table III shows clearly the extent
to which this kind of cross-resistance can occur.
It may also be present between groups but only
in certain directions. Resistance to organophosphorus and carbamate insecticides may confer resistance to organochlorines but the reverse has
not been reported.

| Compound | Times increase in resistance over a normal population |
|---|---|
| Trithion | 15,000 |
| Iso-Systox | 8,570 |
| Methyl Systox | 8,000 |
| Schradan | 2,000 |
| EPN | 1,400 |
| Parathion | 883 |
| Phosdrin | 350 |
| Pyrazoxon | 300 |
| Systox | 266 |
| Tetram | 111 |
| Delnav | 100 |
| Disyston | 25 |
| Diazinon | 12 |
| Malathion | 8 |
| Ethion | 8 |

CROSS-RESISTANCE. The resistance to various other
organophosphorus sprays shown by a population of
citrus red mites which had first acquired resistance in the
field to Systox. Source: reference 8.

Taken together these factors add up to a very serious situation. But the point that needs stressing most is that the resistance genes and the detoxifying mechanisms occur naturally in pest populations. They are present in the populations long before any exposure to pesticides. Pests have been, in this sense, preadapted to resist the pesticides which have been devised so far. It is possible, of course, that new and radically different compounds will be developed which are not vulnerable in this way. But the probability is that genes are already in existence which will confer resistance against the pesticides of the future.

*Interference with Natural Enemies*

As we saw in the first chapter, one way in which animal numbers can be regulated is through the mortality caused by natural enemies, such as parasites or predators. The third failing common to the majority of modern organic pesticides is their ability to interfere with this natural regulation.[9]

Provided that natural enemies are able to respond rapidly in their attack rate to changes in the numbers of their hosts or prey, they can bring about very tight control. In many cases, though, this is at a level which allows the pest to cause economic damage, and additional pest control measures have to be taken. If pesticides are applied and they kill off relatively more of the natural enemies than the pest or interfere with the regulation in some other way, then the pest is liable to rebound following the application and may well reach a level much higher and more damaging than before. This phenomenon is termed "resurgence."

In recent years resurgences have become increasingly common in a wide variety of pests. To quote one example, populations of cyclamen mite on strawberries can increase from 15 to 35 times following parathion spraying, because this insecticide is less lethal to the cyclamen mite than to another mite which preys upon it. In another instance, resurgences of bagworms on oilpalms in Malaya occurred apparently because pesticide applications broke the synchrony between the life cycles of the pest and its natural enemy. Before the pesticides were applied the pest had continuous overlapping generations. At any one time all stages of the pest were present on the crop and the natural enemy, which had a shorter life cycle, was able to keep up. But the pesticide killed all but one stage of the pest. Subsequent generations became distinct and the enemy species died out because its attack stage did not coincide with the susceptible stage of the pest.

Natural enemies also keep many potential pests more or less permanently at harmless levels. A pesticide may have little or no effect on the natural enemies of the pest against which it is applied but instead it may kill off the enemies of hitherto harmless species which will then build up to pest status. New pests caused in this way are usually referred to as "upset" pests.

One of the classic upset pests is the fruit-tree red spider mite, which has become an important pest in apple and other fruit orchards following intensive pesticide use.[10] In England it arose in the 1920s following the first use of tar oils as winter washes. These oils did not affect the winter eggs of the mite but they did kill many of its hibernating enemies, such as ladybug beetles and predacious mites, both directly and by destroying the mosses and lichens which gave them protection. The outbreaks of red spider mite which followed were, nevertheless, small compared with those triggered off by the use of DDT and BHC after the war. At that time over 40 species of beneficial insect were known to occur in apple and DDT and BHC proved to be lethal to nearly all of them. In 1950 organophosphorus acaricides were added to the spray program, but this resulted in even greater red spider mite outbreaks.

Sometimes the response to one upset pest only serves to create another. In this way a whole chain of pests is created, as has occurred on tea in Ceylon.[11] Dieldrin was used there against a shot hole borer, *Xyleborus fornicatus,* which attacks the twigs and branches of the tree. It controlled the borer but, in so doing, killed off a parasite which was regulating a leaf-feeding caterpillar. DDT was then used against the caterpillar, but it in turn produced outbreaks of various mites. In time, a chain of events such as this may lead to a pest situation in a crop totally different from, although just as serious as, that at the beginning.

There are several reasons why many pesticides appear to be so lethal to natural enemies. The way in which predators concentrate pesticides has been described in the preceding chapter; this is undoubtedly one reason for their greater susceptibility. A predator can be killed by feeding on a number of pest individuals, each of which has received only sublethal doses of a pesticide. Parasites, on the other hand, are probably more vulnerable because they are usually smaller and more delicate in structure than pest species. Both predators and parasites are also at greater risk because they tend to be more mobile. They have to search out their respective prey or hosts and in so doing are more liable to encounter insecticide deposits. Some insecticides only act after they have been ingested, but the majority can be picked up by insects through the "skin" or cuticle and so are particularly lethal to natural enemy species.

In this third component of pesticide failure we can once again see the link with the wider environmental problems that have occurred. A great many of the wild animals whose populations have been diminished in recent years are predators or other animals which range widely through diverse habitats and so pick up and concentrate pesticide deposits. The common cause of both pest control failure and environmental damage is that most pesticides are insufficiently specific in their toxicity.

## The Alternatives

Our analysis of pesticide failure provides us with three characteristics to look for in alternative methods. First, they should be capable of more or less permanently regulating pests at harmless densities; second, they should not be vulnerable to the development of resistance; and third, they should work with and not against the natural controlling mechanisms provided by parasites and predators. If we can combine these features we will, moreover, have gone a considerable way toward minimizing the environmental problems which hitherto pest control has left in its wake.

First we will discuss how far it is possible to satisfy these objectives simply by using pesticides in better ways. Then we will turn to the several categories of nonpesticidal techniques which bring about control through regulatory mechanisms. Finally, we will look at a number of new nonpesticidal techniques which hold out the promise of pest eradication.

## Better Use of Pesticides

Pesticides can sometimes be a useful tool, producing little environmental hazard, providing the right compounds are chosen and are used sparingly and well.

The basic prerequisite for better pesticide use is accurate pest monitoring. By keeping a regular account of the numbers and composition of pest populations, pesticide applications can be planned more rationally. More efficient control can be obtained but with fewer, well-timed applications. Often a crop is only vulnerable to attack for a relatively short period of the growing cycle; for example, during flowering or when the fruit is setting. By monitoring the pest population early in the season and obtaining estimates of its growth potential it may then be possible to ensure that the vulnerable period of the crop is protected by just one or two critically timed applications.

In many cases the numbers of a pest may be largely determined by the climate, so that the pest assumes an importance only in some years. Where pesticides are being applied according to a fixed schedule this will then result in many unnecessary applications being made. But with a well-designed forecasting system sufficient warning of pest buildup can be given and applications made only as required. Forecasting systems are already in operation for many pests in the United States and elsewhere. In the states of the Corn Belt there are schemes which warn of buildup of the European corn borer, for example. Also, individual farmers can often contract on a private basis with independent agencies to obtain forecasts and assessments for their own farms.

The extent to which pesticide applications can be reduced through pest monitoring is very considerable. A recent report on cotton growing in Colombia states that, whereas a few years ago the crop there was sprayed 18 to 20 times in a season, now through careful observation of pest incidence only some 9 to 10 applications are needed. And in the United States it is estimated that pesticide application could be reduced by up to 50 percent if this approach were fully adopted. Such a reduction would be the surest way of postponing the development of resistance and it would also be a major step in minimizing environmental pollution.

By careful timing and placing of pesticide applications or by using suitably selective compounds it is also possible to get pest control without upsetting natural enemy regulation. Some parasites and predators live in very close association with their hosts or prey; they have synchronized life cycles and occupy the same microhabitats. But, in many cases, pest species and their natural enemies only meet at certain times or in well-defined localities. It is then possible to apply pesticides so that the pests are affected and the enemy species largely spared. This has been done successfully in Malaya as part of the control program for cockchafer beetles on rubber. The cockchafer grubs which feed on the roots of the rubber trees are parasitized by scoliid wasps and tachinid flies, but Dr. Rao of the Rubber Research Institute found that the parasites complete their life cycle and emerge from the soil before the cockchafer grubs pupate. A soil insecticide can thus be safely applied in the period between the emergence of the parasites and the emergence of the cockchafer beetles. In Europe another cockchafer pest, the May beetle, tends to congregate in the early spring on certain areas of high ground. By identifying and mapping these areas Swiss entomologists are able to localize the pesticide applications and so avoid both affecting the cockchafer's natural enemies and contaminating the environment over a wide scale. One method which ensures that only the pest species is affected is to combine the pesticide with a specific bait or sex-attractant chemical. Fruit flies have been very successfully controlled in this way and baits are particularly suited to control of mammal or bird pests. Providing the bait is attractive only to the pest species or the bait container allows only the pest to gain access, then the number of other animals affected can be greatly minimized.

A selective pesticide is one which kills the target pest but is harmless to natural enemies or other animals which may become exposed to it. By their nature contact-acting pesticides rarely have this ability; they kill most organisms they contact. But varying degrees of selectivity are to be found among the stomach-poison and systemic pesticides. The stomach poisons, as their name suggests, act only after ingestion. When applied to crop plants they only affect those insects which actually eat the plant material. The systemics act in a similar way. They are taken up by plants and translocated through the sap and in consequence tend to affect only sap-sucking insects. In some cases systemics may also show contact toxicity, but this can be overcome by applying them to the seed. When the seed sprouts the systemic is translocated through the sap of the growing seedling, giving control of the sucking pests with little effect on the enemies. In general, the stomach poisons and systemics can be relied on to spare parasites, but predators can still be affected through the prey they feed on.

When the many problems associated with broad-spectrum contact-acting pesticides were first realized much hope was placed on their being replaced by selective compounds. However, the number developed so far is very small and few are really truly selective. Part of the problem is due to the continued lack of detailed knowledge of the mode of action of pesticides. It is still not possible to produce a "blueprint" for a selective pesticide. Also, the sheer cost of discovering, testing, and developing pesticides (between 1/2 and 4 million dollars per compound) discourages production of highly selective forms. Broad-spectrum compounds with a variety of applications can be sold over a wide market and bring a better economic return on the high development cost.

*Physical and Mechanical Agents*

The oldest method of pest control is simple physical destruction. The classic example is the use of the fly swatter. In the past pests have been burned, drowned, beaten, or trapped using a variety of tools, some of which were extremely ingenious. Today most physical or mechanical methods are less efficient than pesticides and too expensive in time and labor, although, under certain conditions, they can provide a viable alterna-

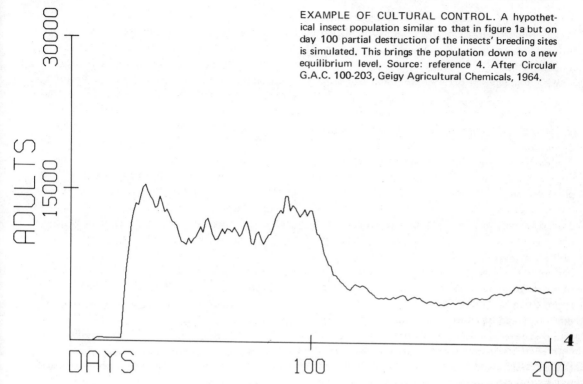

EXAMPLE OF CULTURAL CONTROL. A hypothetical insect population similar to that in figure 1a but on day 100 partial destruction of the insects' breeding sites is simulated. This brings the population down to a new equilibrium level. Source: reference 4. After Circular G.A.C. 100-203, Geigy Agricultural Chemicals, 1964.

tive to pesticide use. They have one advantage in that there is little chance of pests becoming resistant to them. They can also be selective; for example, light traps if operated properly need only catch the pest species. Their principal drawback, though, is that, like pesticides, they can only produce a simple density-independent mortality.

*Regulatory Techniques*

In Figure 1 we saw that when a pesticide was applied to a hypothetical insect population, the numbers dropped and then recovered to their previous level as the effect of the pesticide wore off. If we now look at Figure 4 we see that something has been done to the model population that permanently changes the equilibrium to a new and lower level. In this case the change has been brought about by simulating the partial destruction of the breeding sites of the population. The "carrying capacity" of the pests' environment is reduced so that the population size becomes permanently limited. Environmental manipulation which brings about population regulation in this

way is referred to as "cultural control." Also under this heading come those measures which allow existing regulatory agents such as natural enemies to act in a more efficient manner. A second approach, biological control, brings about the same effect by introducing new species of natural enemies into an environment. Finally, populations of pests can be regulated, at least with respect to the crops themselves, by developing pest-resistant plants or by creating physical or chemical barriers which limit the number of attacking organisms.

*Cultural Control*

Mosquito control furnishes perhaps the best known example of the value of destruction of breeding sites. Many fly species including mosquitoes, biting midges, houseflies, and deerflies have larval stages which live in or near to water. The drainage and filling of ponds and marshes and the removal of shoreline vegetation in lakes and rivers can greatly reduce the populations of pests such as these. Over much of Europe and North America malaria had already disappeared long before the appearance of modern pesticides, because industrialization and urban growth had brought about the destruction of mosquito breeding sites.

With some pests, plants other than the crop may serve as breeding sites or as hosts for alternate generations, and removing these can bring about control. For example, the sorghum midge overwinters on johnson grass which grows along the borders of the fields and the midge is able to build up for two or three generations on this plant before moving onto the sorghum blooms.

Pests can also be limited environmentally by crop rotation. The principle involved is a simple one: By alternating susceptible with nonsusceptible crops the growth of pest populations is periodically checked. It is a method particularly suited to plant diseases and in the United States approximately 24 diseases on 17 different important crops can be controlled in this way. But it is also effective against a number of insect pests and against nematodes. In the southeastern United States rotation has virtually eliminated the wheat gall nematode as a pest. Much the same kind of effect can be produced by destroying the residue of a crop after harvesting.

Rotation and destruction of residues aim to limit population size by providing a break in continuity. However, when cultural control measures are used to try and enhance natural enemy regulation they are designed to work in exactly the opposite way. The principle is again a simple one. By producing continuity both for the pests and for the parasites and predators the efficiency and permanence of regulation can be increased. When crops are grown in rotation each crop in turn goes through a similar sequence of plant growth, invasion, and buildup of pests which is in turn followed by an increase in natural enemies. Each phase lags behind the other and frequently it is only after much of the damage by the pest species has been done that the natural enemies build up sufficiently to exercise control. However, in perennial crops and when the same annual crops are grown in succession, the buildup phase tends only to occur once, when the crop is first planted, and thereafter regulation may remain more or less uninterrupted. For example, in South Africa a number of brassica pests can be kept under control by growing various varieties of brassica in close succession. This approach tends to be most useful in countries with equable climates, since the continuity is unlikely to be upset by changes in temperature or rainfall.

In some cases, though, continuous cropping may not be sufficient to provide all the continuity that is required. Some natural enemies require plants other than the crop to complete their life cycle. For example, it was recently found that a leafhopper on vines in California could be controlled effectively by providing blackberry plants around the vine fields. This was because the parasite of the leafhopper could only survive the winter months by parasitizing another insect species which lives on blackberry.

Hedgerows and uncultivated land in general, have an important influence on the presence of natural enemies in crops. As a rule, the diversity of animal species increases in the vicinity of hedgerows (Figure 5) and this implies that there are many more natural enemy species present. It has been found in work on cabbage aphids that there are usually fewer aphids near hedgerows because of the higher incidence of predation by ladybugs and hoverfly larvae. In the latter case this is because the adult hoverflies feed on the pollen in the wild hedgerow flowers.

Natural enemies may also be favored by changes in shade or in cover crops or by different spacing and pruning practice. The possibilities of environmental manipulation are endless. The advantages of the method lie in the permanence of control which can often be attained and the low cost that is usually involved. However, there may be serious disadvantages. Changes in cropping practice may bring about good pest control but may reduce yield or farming efficiency in other ways. Hedges may be costly to keep up and may interfere with the efficient use of farm machinery. Furthermore, environmental changes which are favorable for pest control may be deleterious to wild animals and plants. For example, draining ponds and marshes as part of mosquito control has severely reduced the populations of many fish and birds.

## Biological Control

Introducing natural enemies to control pests is a practice of great antiquity. The cat was domesticated by man to control rats and mice in his granaries and home, and still in many parts of the world its primary role is as a predator rather than a pet. The modern interest in biological control, however, stems from two highly successful introductions against, respectively, an insect pest at the end of the last century and a weed in the 1920s. Both these stories are by now classics of biological control. The full details make colorful reading but the bare outlines are as follows:

In 1887 the citrus industry in California had become very seriously threatened by infestations of the cottony-cushion scale *Icerya purchasi,* which had been introduced accidentally a few years earlier. A prominent government entomologist, C. V. Riley, thought that the scale had probably been introduced from Australia or New Zealand and suggested that a search should be made there for the natural enemies of the scale which could then be imported to California. The next year, after some opposition, a search was made and a number of parasites and also some predators were found, including a ladybug *Rhodalia cardinalis.* It was first thought that the parasites were likely to be the most valuable but when the various species were tried out in California in the field, it was the ladybug which showed the greatest potential. It was a voracious feeder on the scale and farmers who heard of its powers were soon eager to obtain colonies for their own orchards. Within a year Los Angeles county had tripled the citrus fruit harvest. Soon the scale was

reduced to insignificant numbers throughout the State and it has remained so for the last 80 years, except for a brief period in the 1950s when in several counties DDT and malathion sprays killed off the ladybugs.[13]

The second story also involves the Americas and Australasia but the roles are reversed. At the end of the last century several species of a cactus plant, the prickly pear, *Opuntia,* were introduced as garden plants into Australia from their home in Mexico. But they spread from the gardens and became very serious weeds of pasture land. By the 1920s 60 million acres had become infested and over half of this had so dense a cover of the cactus that it was impenetrable to man or large animals. A search was then mounted for suitable plant-eating insects in the Americas. Some 50 species were found and several of these showed a good potential. But in 1925 the ideal insect was found in Argentina. It was *Cactoblastis cactorum,* the larvae of which tunnel in the cactus pads and bring about complete destruction of the plants. A single importation of nearly 3000 eggs was made. From these a breeding stock was established and in the next 3 years eggs were released in the field. Massive destruction of the prickly pear occurred and by the early 1930s large areas were under control. Today it only occurs as individual plants or in small patches, regulated at this very low level by *Cactoblastis.*[14]

In the last 40 years there have been many other successful examples of biological control. A recent estimate puts the number at over 100, spread over 60 countries. And in addition to using natural enemies some success has been obtained with viruses, bacteria, and other microorganisms as control agents. The control of cottony-cushion scale and prickly pear, though, illustrate the principal features of most of the subsequent successes.

First, biological control has been most readily achieved when the pest species itself is exotic, that is, has been introduced from another region of the world. Endemic pests usually have a full complement of natural enemies and if these are not already producing a sufficient degree of control it is not easy to find and introduce further enemy species that will improve on it. On the other hand, introduced pests will have brought few of their parasites or predators with them.

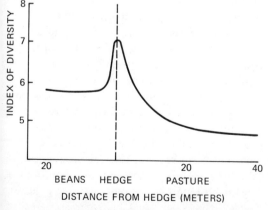

FAUNA NEAR A HEDGEROW. The changes in diversity of the fauna in the air above a bean field and a pasture and the intervening hedge. The hedge is approximately 2 meters high. Source: reference 12. Used by permission of the British Ecological Society.

The natural enemy "niche" is wide open and there is a good chance that it can be filled by the original enemy species of the pest, providing they can be located.

Second, if the introduced parasites and predators do "take" they can frequently bring about a very high degree of regulation which persists almost indefinitely, providing there are no major environmental changes or there is no interference from pesticides. One danger is, of course, that the parasites or predators may be so effective in destroying the pest species that they will run out of food and so become extinct. However, this probably happens only rarely. Even in the case of the prickly pear control where the *Cactoblastis* moth has no alternate host plant, a delicate balance is set up, apparently through a remarkable process of self-regulation in the moth. In some instances, though, absence of alternate hosts can result in insufficient reservoirs of the enemy species to cope with sudden increases in the pest. This has happened in the case of the pine shoot moth in Ontario and a very ingenious solution to the problem has been proposed. The parasite of the moth, in its native home in Europe, also attacks a tortricid moth which feeds solely on the noxious klamath weed. By introducing the tortricid, it may be possible both to improve the control of the pine shoot moth and reduce the klamath weed.

Third, biological control can be achieved very inexpensively. The cost of introducing the coccinellid against cottony-cushion scale in California was only $2000, which was a small price to pay even in 1889.

*Plant and Animal Resistance*

In considering the drawbacks to pesticide use we saw how pests can evolve resistance to pesticides. In a similar way plants and animals can evolve resistance to the attack of pests and this can be utilized in pest control.

In nature the resistance of an organism is essentially its ability to avoid being wiped out by other organisms which feed upon it. This resistance evolves through the process of natural selection and tends to result in a fairly stable balance between plant and herbivore and between herbivore and parasite or predator. But in a crop plant (or domestic animal) the resistance may be insufficient or may be absent. The crop plant may be able to survive the attacks of pests but nevertheless at the cost of a loss in yield. Alternatively, the resistant factors of the natural plant may have been lost during the process of breeding a cultivable variety. Finally, it is possible for the plant to be resistant to the organisms which attack it in its natural environment, but in the crop environment to be exposed to quite different organisms, for which it has no resistance.

There are three principal mechanisms of resistance. First, resistance may be due to a form of deterrence. There may be a physical or chemical characteristic of the plant or animal which prevents pest attack. Biting flies, for example, are deterred by the thickness of animal skins. The structure of plant surfaces may prevent the entry of fungal spores. Second, there may be a positive antibiosis. The host may be able to kill the pest or, at least, affect its reproductive capacity. Cotton, for example, produces the compound gossypol which retards growth in the bollworm, *Heliothis zea*. Third, the resistance may be simply that the host is able to contain the activities of the pest so that no vital damage is caused. In Borneo it was found that a single boring larva of the moth, *Endoclita*, was liable to kill a cocoa tree. Yet a secondary forest tree which the borer also attacked could accommodate large numbers of boring larvae and be little affected. The forest tree was resistant but the cocoa was not.

One of the earliest ways of improving the resistance of a crop was by grafting the susceptible plant onto a related resistant variety or species. This works well providing the pest only attacks a certain part of the plant. Species of grape *Vitis* occur both in Europe and America. Over a hundred years ago an aphid, *Phylloxera*, was imported to Europe on American vines. The aphid feeds only on the leaves of American vines and does little harm to them, but, on the European vines it also attacks the roots, causing galls. Attacked vines usually died and soon large areas of the French wine-growing regions were affected. In 13 years, over 1.5 million hectares of vines were destroyed and wine production was cut

two-thirds. Much effort was wasted on insecticidal and other forms of control, but then the
simple suggestion of grafting the French vines
onto American roots was made. This immediately solved the problem. The practice was
widely adopted and continues to be used to the
present day.[15]

However, improved resistance has been mostly
brought about by crossing and selection. In general, the degree of resistance in a crop will vary
from plant to plant. By careful screening it is
possible to identify those individuals in which
the resistance is exceptionally high. These can
then be selected and used as parents to produce
more resistant lines. Alternatively, the resistance
may have to come from outside and it then becomes necessary to screen related varieties and
species. In some cases the process involves widespread searching throughout the countries where
the crop and its relatives occur. The resistant species and the crop plant are then crossed to produce a hybrid, which will combine the characters
of both parents. The hybrid is then repeatedly
back-crossed with the crop plant parent until
finally a plant is obtained which is identical with
this parent except that it retains the resistant
factors of the other.

Breeding for resistance has been perhaps the
most successful of the nonpesticidal approaches
to pest control. Today most crop varieties have a
built-in resistance to one or more insect pests or
diseases. Resistance makes a particularly high
contribution to disease control. For example,
over 95 percent of the acreage of small grains and
a similar proportion of the alfalfa acreage in the
United States is now planted to disease-resistant
varieties.

The advantage of the resistance approach is
that it can bring about more or less permanent
control with little recurring expense. Most of the
cost is incurred during the breeding program.
This can be fairly short: For example, new varieties of alfalfa resistant to spotted aphid were
developed in 3 to 5 years. Nevertheless, it can
take up to 15 or 20 years to perfect a new resistant variety and, where disease is involved, the
control may not be very long-lived. Fungi and
bacterial pathogens all have short generation
times and there is thus a great likelihood of their

evolving characteristics which will overcome the
resistance. For instance, new races of rust disease
are thrown up every 3 or 4 years in the United
States and each time this happens there has to be
a new countereffort in wheat breeding. In such
situations pest control involves a neck-and-neck
race between the pathogen and the crop breeder.

*Physical Barriers and Repellents*

The use of physical barriers or repellents in
pest control is in principle the same as utilizing
resistance. By creating barriers between the crop
plant or domestic animal and the pest population
the level of attack is reduced. But unlike resistance the barriers are not incorporated in the
plant or animal.

Physical barriers can be very effective in protecting crops or stored food from pests, although
they tend to be expensive in time and labor. For
example, well-built fences can keep deer or wild
pigs from crops, and well-designed barns can
keep rats from stored grain.

The oldest form of repellent is the scarecrow.
It was, however, rarely very effective and today
is supplanted by a variety of sophisticated scaring
devices based on a detailed understanding of animal behavior. For instance, it is possible to scare
off birds such as starlings by playing recordings
of their characteristic distress cries. Chemical repellents are best known for their use against mosquitoes and other biting flies on man. Similar
kinds of repellents have been used to protect
crops, but only in a few situations. Unfortunately, a common drawback of repellents is that
they rarely have more than a temporary effect,
so that their use is limited.

*Techniques of Eradication*

The alternatives considered so far have been
aimed at regulating pest numbers. Often in the
past pesticides have been applied in the hope that
pest populations would be totally wiped out, but
this rarely has occurred. However, in recent
years, a number of techniques have been developed which hold out the promise of eradica-
ting pests on a much wider scale.

These techniques come under the general
heading of genetic control, since in one way or

another they involve manipulating or changing the hereditary characteristics of the pests themselves. There are two kinds of technique. The first involves the use of sterile matings: The pest population is eradicated by increasing the proportion of matings which are sterile. The second brings about eradication by introducing a lethal hereditary factor into the population.

*The Sterile Mating Technique*

The most successful form of this technique involves breeding large numbers of the pest species in the laboratory. These are then sterilized by irradiation and released in the field in sufficient numbers to swamp the natural population. Providing the sterilized and normal individuals mate readily with one .another, a high proportion of the ensuing matings will produce no offspring and this will result in much smaller populations in the next generation. If the releases are continued in each subsequent generation a higher and higher proportion of matings will be sterile until finally the population becomes extinct. The principle can be clearly shown in terms of simple arithmetic, as in Table IV.

**IV**

| Generation | No. of fertile insects | No. of sterile insects | Ratio of sterile to fertile insects | No. of insects reproducing |
|---|---|---|---|---|
| Parent | 1,000,000 | 9,000,000 | 9:1 | 100,000 |
| $F_1$ | 500,000 | 9,000,000 | 18:1 | 26,316 |
| $F_2$ | 131,560 | 9,000,000 | 68:1 | 1,907 |
| $F_3$ | 9.535 | 9,000,000 | 944:1 | 10 |
| $F_4$ | 50 | 9,000,000 | 180,000:1 | 0 |

EFFECT OF STERILE MATING. A simple arithmetic model showing how a population is eradicated by repeated releases of sterile male insects. It is assumed that there is a fivefold rate of increase in the normal population. Source: reference 16.

This method first received world-wide attention 10 years ago when it was used to wipe out the screwworm in the southeast of the United States.[17] The screwworm, *Cochliomya hominivorae*, is a serious pest of cattle. The adult fly lays its eggs in the skin of the animals and the larvae which hatch out feed on the flesh, causing large wounds. Before 1958 the screwworm produced considerable losses to the livestock indus-

try in Florida, Georgia, and Alabama and in the states along the Mexican border. It was known, however, that the adult female fly mated only once and this gave Dr. E. F. Knipling the idea that the pest could be eradicated by releasing large numbers of sterile male flies. A massive operation to rear screwworms was begun in 1957, and from January 1958 over 50 million sterile flies were produced for release each week in the affected southeastern states. The operation was spectacularly successful and within a year the screwworm was eradicated.

Since the screwworm program there have been one or two other successes. In 1962 on the island of Rota in the Pacific the melon fly was eradicated by releases of sterile flies of both sexes. The melon fly, unlike the screwworm, can mate several times and this success demonstrated that monogamy was not an essential prerequisite for the technique. However, as in the case of the screwworm, the pest population was small and isolated. Prior to the releases the melon flies were, in fact, deliberately reduced by insecticide applications.

It seems unlikely that the release of sterile insects will succeed against large populations which are continuous over wide areas. The problem lies in the logistics of rearing and releasing the immense numbers of insects that would be required. An alternative approach that has been suggested is to sterilize directly populations in the field by means of chemosterilants mixed with bait. A great deal of attention is being paid to finding suitable compounds, but so far the method has not been tried out successfully on a large scale. One problem, of course, lies in devising very specific baits or in finding sterilizing compounds which will be harmless to other animals.

Finally, sterile matings can be produced by releasing incompatible strains of the pest species. The mosquito, *Culex fatigans*, for example, can be separated into different strains which show varying degrees of incompatibility with each other because of an hereditary cytoplasmic factor. When the sperm nucleus from one strain enters the egg of another it is prevented from fusing with the egg nucleus, so producing a deformed embryo which subsequently dies. A strain of the species from Germany which was incompatible with the local strain in a village in Burma was released there in 1967. The natural population varied between 4000 and 20,000 and at first insufficient males of the introduced strain were released. However, after the release of about 5000 males per day the percentage of hatching eggs dropped sharply. Within 12 weeks no eggs were hatching and the population was eradicated.[18]

In the tsetse fly it has been discovered that crosses between two related species, *Glossina swynnertoni* and *G. morsitans,* produce offspring which are sterile but otherwise normal. This also occurs in another mosquito complex, *Anopheles gambiae,* only here the males which are produced as a result of crosses between species in the complex are not only sterile but show hybrid vigor: They have an increased mating ability compared with the normal males. Situations such as these which can be exploited for genetic control probably occur in a number of important pests.

### The Lethal-Factor Technique

This technique is even more experimental. Quite a number of lethal mutant genes have been identified in pest species. In mosquitoes of the *Aedes* genus, for example, there are two mutants which appear to have considerable potential. The first is called *bronze*. Females with this mutant lay eggs with poor shells which die within a few hours of oviposition. The second mutant, *proboscipedia,* produces female mosquitoes with torsi or leg joints in the place of a proboscis. The females cannot feed and hence do not produce eggs. By introducing sufficient numbers of individuals with these mutants into natural populations it is theoretically possible to bring about eradication.[19]

A particularly intriguing possibility for genetic control was suggested by the discovery that mutants can occur on the sex chromosomes of insects which result in a biased sex ratio.[20] Sex is usually determined by the X and Y chromosomes, the sex chromosomes. Commonly if a Y chromosome is present the insect is male and if it is absent, a female. It has been found though that a mutant can occur on the Y chromosome which

enables the Y-bearing sperm to fertilize more readily than the X-bearing sperm. Males carrying the Y mutant thus produce nothing but male offspring. It is therefore theoretically possible that if a few individuals with the mutant are introduced into a natural population, the mutant will spread, the sex ratio will become more and more biased, and eventually the population will become extinct.

The great potential power of all these techniques of genetic control lies in the fact that they are autocidal; that is, they cause the insect pests to turn on themselves. The high genetic variability shown by most pests enables them to evolve resistance to most pest control techniques. But in genetic control it is this variability itself that is used. Coupled with the speed with which eradications can occur it ensures that there will be little chance of resistance occurring. Also it follows that the techniques are highly specific and as a consequence there is less likelihood of environmental hazards.

Nevertheless these are still largely experimental techniques. They have so far been successful only in limited or specialized circumstances. It remains to be seen how extensively they can be applied.

### The Systems Approach to Pest Control

So far in this chapter, we have discussed eight major alternatives to using broad-spectrum, contact-acting pesticides in pest control. Many of these methods have been shown in the field to be really viable alternatives, producing effective control, often at less cost, and with less environmental contamination and upset. But the position is not a simple one of contrast between good and bad methods. Some of the alternatives can bring about serious and deleterious environmental effects. For example, the older but more selective compounds such as the arsenicals can be as equally toxic to wildlife as the modern organic compounds. And we have seen that the destruction of habitats which occurs when breeding sites or the alternate hosts of pests are removed, can produce even more far reaching effects than pesticide use. Under certain conditions biological control, too, can get out of hand. For example, herbivores brought in to control weeds may turn to crop plants, and the mongoose, which has been introduced in a number of countries to control snakes, has often become a predator of domestic fowl.

Furthermore, these alternatives vary in their effectiveness from pest to pest and from one situation to another. Often a method which works against a species on one crop will not work against the same species on a different crop. Similarly, one method of control, for example crop rotation, which is effective against one member of the pest complex of a crop, may well reduce control of another. Economic factors are also important. Control techniques which are intensive and costly can be borne by a high-yield, high-return crop such as tomatoes or chrysanthemums, but much cheaper methods are necessary for a crop such as rice or cotton. In some situations all of the alternatives will be ineffective or too expensive and then broad-spectrum, contact-acting insecticides will have to be used, despite the inherent danger. DDT, which for good reason is being withdrawn from use in many of the industrialized countries, will continue to be used in the developing countries for mosquito control, for some time to come. It is effective and cheap, and no better alternative as yet exists.

*Integrated Control*

What has clearly been needed for some time is an approach which looks at each pest situation as a whole and then comes up with a program which integrates the different control methods in the light of all the factors present. Unfortunately, the development of such an approach has been hampered by intense rivalries between protagonists of the different techniques of pest control. Before the Second World War there was good reason to believe that pest control would emerge as a sound ecologically based branch of applied science. However, the discovery of the organic pesticides was seen as the solution to all the pest problems and it heralded an era of widespread chemical control in which ecological considerations took second place. Then, as the reaction to pesticide use grew, biological control was pushed forward as the new panacea, but only

to be replaced, in turn, by each of the other alternatives. In recent years it has been the sterile-mating techniques that have been most vigorously pressed. Nevertheless, amid all this there has been slowly growing a school of pest control workers who have been writing about an integrated approach and have been successfully putting it to work in practice.

The origins of integrated control lie in early attempts to apply chemicals selectively so that they would not interfere with the effectiveness of natural or imported enemies. As early as the late 1940s, Dr. Pickett and his colleagues in Nova Scotia devised a program of this kind for control of apple and pear pests. It was very successful and at one time it was in use in over 80 percent of the orchards in Nova Scotia. The term "integrated control" was, however, invented by a group of Californian entomologists to describe the program they had developed to deal with the spotted alfalfa aphid, *Therioaphis trifolii.* This had been introduced accidentally to California in 1954, where it had soon increased to the extent that it threatened the whole crop. Initially, broad-spectrum organophosphorus insecticides were used, but these interfered with the buildup of a number of native predators and of parasites which were specially imported. The problem was solved very successfully (costs and losses attributable to the aphid dropped to a sixth) by replacing the pesticides then being used by different and more selective compounds which allowed the natural control to be retained.

At about the same time, in Peru, an integrated approach much broader in concept was being developed in an attempt to solve the problems of the Canete Valley. The cotton crop, it will be remembered, had yielded less than 300 pounds per acre in the 1955-56 season. The new plan which was quickly thought up consisted of the following key measures:

1. Cotton was no longer to be grown on the marginal land in the valley.

2. There was to be no more ratooning, that is, allowing the crop to persist for 2 or 3 years.

3. The soil was to be "dry-cultivated" in order to kill the bollworm pupae.

4. Beneficial insects were to be reintroduced from other valleys.

5. Dates were to be fixed for planting and irrigation and for destroying crop residues.

6. Synthetic organic pesticides were to be prohibited except by dispensation of a special commission. Reliance instead would be placed on arsenical and botanical insecticides. If organic compounds were used they should be of the selective kind.

The plan was approved by the Peruvian Ministry of Agriculture and put into action. The result was dramatic. The upset pests returned to their former unimportant role and the key pests diminished. In the years 1957 through 1963 average yields were 798 pounds per acre.

In the last 10 years there have been quite a large number of similarly successful examples of the integrated approach, in situations ranging from glasshouse crops in England, to cocoa, oil palms, and rubber in Malaysia. In the United States the alfalfa program now covers all the pests in the crop and it is being further expanded into a much wider integrated control program aimed at the combined pest problems of alfalfa and cotton in situations where they are grown together.

But it has been largely true that these integrated programs have developed as a response to crisis or near-crisis pest situations brought on by bad pesticidal control. And, in large measure, they have been developed empirically. In this respect they differ little from the more traditional and narrow pesticidal approach. Ideally, integrated programs need to be devised early in the development of a new crop and on the basis of a thorough understanding of the crop ecosystem and the wider environment. The problem, though, is the sheer complexity of ecosystems, even the more simplified agro-ecosystems. The pest control worker has a formidable task in gathering and analyzing the information upon which he needs to build an integrated program. For example, we have seen that hedgerows may favor some pests because they contain alternative food plants, yet may help to control others because they support natural enemies. Furthermore, because of their physical characteristics they may induce aerially borne pests to settle and so form foci of infestations. They may also impede the use of agricultural machinery and

they are usually costly to maintain. Again, at a different level, they are part of the aesthetic landscape and thus have a very real social value. A good integrated control program needs to take all the factors into consideration.

Fortunately, two recent developments offer hope of overcoming this problem. First, a number of relatively simple techniques have been devised by ecologists which enable field information to be gathered and analyzed in a more meaningful manner. Second, attempts are being made to use the methods of systems analysis and modern electronic computers to carry the data analysis further and to plan the actual control programs.

### Life Tables and Key Factors

The new ecological techniques center around the construction of population life tables.[21] Such tables have long been used by actuaries in computing human life expectancies and have formed the basis for issuing life insurance policies. However, their value as a means of studying the populations of animals other than man has only just been recognized.

Most of the effort involved in building life tables goes into planning the necessary sampling techniques and acquiring the data. We do not have space to go into this, but the table itself is relatively straightforward. Table V shows an example for a hypothetical pest population. In the first column the various distinct stages in the life cycle of the pest are listed. The next column

| Life stage | No. alive at beginning of each stage | Factor | Mortality | | k value[a] |
|---|---|---|---|---|---|
| | | | No. | Percentage | |
| Eggs | 100 | Parasites | 20 | 20 | 0.1 ($k_1$) |
| Small Larvae | 80 | Frost | 30 | 37 | 0.2 ($k_2$) |
| Large Larvae | 50 | Predators | 10 | 20 | 0.1 ($k_3$) |
| Pupal | 40 | Parasites | 38 | 95 | 1.3 ($k_4$) |
| Adults | 2 | | | | |
| | | | | | $K = 1.7$ |

**V**

LIFE TABLE. A life table for a hypothetical insect population. See text for explanation.

[a]For example, $k_2$ = log small larvae − log large larvae
= log 80 − log 50
= 1.9031 − 1.6990
≈ 0.2

322   G. R. Conway

gives the number alive per sample or per unit area at the beginning of each stage. This is followed by a naming of the factor or factors responsible for the mortality within each stage. Next comes the actual number dying and then the percentage dying in each stage. The final column gives the *k* value, which is computed by taking the difference between the logarithms of the numbers alive at the beginning and the end of each stage. The *k* value is a measure of the strength of the mortality factor at each stage. *K*, the sum of all the *k* values, is a measure of the total mortality.

One life table gives the breakdown of the population over one generation. If data are acquired over several generations or seasons, a series of life tables can be completed. It is then possible to determine which mortality factor is consistently the most important. This can be done simply by plotting all of the *k* values and *K* over time (Figure 6). The mortality factor associated with the *k* value which most closely follows *K* will be the key factor, that is, the factor largely responsible for changes in population.

In Figure 6 the key factor is clearly pupal parasitism. Somewhat surprisingly, in nearly all of the pest populations for which life tables have been built, a single key factor usually stands out in this way. A recent review found that of ten such populations, in seven the key factor was a parasite, predator, or disease; in two it was weather, and in the final one it was the food supply.

The value of life tables and key-factor analysis for the integrated approach is enormous. For example, in populations of the eye-spotted bud moth, a pest of apples in Quebec, the key factor was found to be frost below −21°C. Populations experiencing this degree of frost do not build up to economic proportions the following season. It is this kind of information which makes it possible to obtain efficient pest control with fewer insecticide applications. The extent to which parasitism or predation is a key factor can also significantly help in the planning of biological control or of cultural control methods which encourage natural enemies. Further, if life tables are constructed during or following application of control measures they will provide information on the success or failure of the control.

*Systems Analysis*

A pest control worker, like the manager of a factory, is concerned with making decisions about how a complex organized system can be manipulated to produce an "optimal result." The factory manager desires to maximize production and the pest control worker to minimize pests or pest damage, but in both cases subject to obtaining the highest return for the least cost. This problem of finding maxima or minima is one which can be concisely expressed in mathematical terms.

If we take a simple equation such as

$$y = 45 - 20x + 4x^2$$

which is graphically represented in Figure 7, then the minimum value of *y* is the value at the

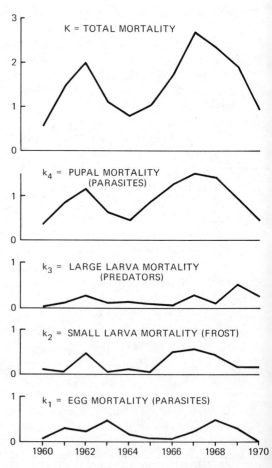

KEY—FACTOR ANALYSIS OF A HYPOTHETICAL INSECT POPULATION.

bottom of the curve. It can be determined accurately by simple differentiation

$$dy/dx = -20 + 8x$$

so when $dy/dx = 0$, $x = 2.5$, that is, $y$ is at a minimum when $x$ equals 2.5. If $y$ is the number of pests and $x$ is a factor, such as rate of insecticide application, which determines their numbers, then from this equation, the number of pests will be minimized when the insecticide is applied at 2.5 pounds per acre.

In practice the equation will, of course, be much more complicated, for example,

$$y = aX_1 + bX_2 - cX_3 + dX_4X_5 \ldots$$

where the $X$'s are different factors affecting the number of pests. Some of the $X$'s will be natural factors such as parasites or the weather, others will be control factors such as rate of insecticide applications. Each will in turn be defined by other equations. For example, in order to prevent environmental pollution there may be an upper limit to the amount of insecticide ($X_3$) that can be applied:

$$X_3 \leqslant 10$$

(The value of $X_3$ must be less than or equal to 10 lbs/acre)

Systems analysis was developed some 30 years ago to enable very complex systems to be analyzed in this way. Briefly, a program of systems analysis consists of taking the following steps. First, the objective is clearly defined in terms of precisely what is to be minimized or maximized and the constraints that are imposed; second, the system which bears on this objective is broken down into its component parts. Then data are obtained for each of the components and these used to produce a series of equations. Finally, by one of a number of mathematical techniques the optimal solution is found. Because of the large amounts of information that have to be processed and the complexity of the mathematical techniques involved, much of the analysis will of necessity have to be carried out on a computer.

Although obviously applicable, a full analysis of this kind has not yet been carried out on a pest problem. Unfortunately there are very few problems for which sufficient information is available; there are large gaps in our knowledge

of even the most important pests. However, considerable progress has been made in building mathematical models of isolated components of pest systems. It has been found that the programming languages of computers can be used to create models which very closely mimic biological events and processes. By manipulating or playing with these models on the computer it is possible to gain a better understanding of how pest populations are affected by natural factors and how they can be controlled. Figures 1 and 4, which were referred to earlier in the chapter, show the results of very simple exercises in this kind of computer modelling.

*Future Prospect*

In the early years of pesticide use it was widely thought that before long the great majority of pest problems would cease to exist. But today there is little sign of this. Many problems have resulted from bad pest control and many more are being created by the pressure for greater agricultural production. Some of the biggest problems are yet to come. In the developing countries vast areas are being planted to monocultures of the new cereal varieties. The pest problems on these are only just appearing, but they promise to be serious and if the wrong approach to pest control is adopted they may well turn out to be disastrous.

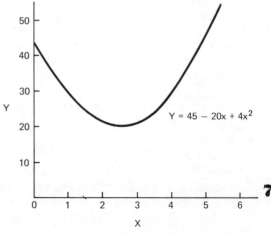

SAMPLE SYSTEMS ANALYSIS EQUATION. Graph of the equation $y = 45 - 20x + 4x^2$. The minimum value of $y$, which is 20, occurs when $x$ equals 2.5.

The growing problems in the United States and abroad pose a tremendous challenge to present and future generations of pest control workers. Pest control still has a long way to go before it is an applied science as sophisticated as, say, civil engineering. As we have seen, it is still predominantly empirical and narrowly reliant on the use of unselective pesticides. Nevertheless, developments of recent years suggest that it is quite firmly moving away from this. The mainstream is in integrated control and as the new techniques of field ecology and systems analysis become developed its position will become more and more assured. In all of this, concern with wider environmental effects must play an increasingly important role. As we have seen, the environmental problems are commonly linked with the inability to get good pest control. As one improves so, we hope, will the other.

## References

1. Rudd, R. L. 1966. *Pesticides and the Living Landscape.* University of Wisconsin Press, Madison, Wisconsin, 320 pp.
2. Watson, J., et al, 1965. *Cotton Insects.* A report of a panel of the President's Science Advisory Committee. The White House, Washington, D.C., 19 pp.
3. Smith, R. F., and van den Bosch, R. 1967. Integrated control. In *Pest Control – Biological, Physical, and Selected Chemical Methods* (W. W. Kilgore and R. C. Doutt, eds.), pp. 295-340. Academic Press, New York.
4. Conway, G. R. 1970. Computer simulation as an aid to developing strategies for Anopheline control. *Misc. Publ. Entomol. Soc. Amer. 7:* 181-193.
5. Brown, A. W. A. 1958. The spread of insecticide resistance in pest species. *Advances in Pest Control Research* (R. L. Metcalf, ed.), Vol. 2, pp. 351-418. Interscience, New York.
6. Brown, A. W. A. 1967. Insecticide resistance – genetic implications and applications. *World Rev. Pest Control 6:* 104-114.
7. Lund, M. 1967. Resistance of rodents to rodenticides. *World Rev. Pest Control 6:* 131-138.
8. O'Brien, R. D. 1960. *Toxic Phosphorus Esters. Chemistry, Metabolism and Biological Effects.* Academic Press, London, 434 pp.
9. Ripper, W. E. 1956. Effect of pesticides on balance of arthropod populations. *Ann. Rev. Entomol. 1:* 403-438.
10. Massee, A. M. 1958. The effect on the balance of arthropod populations in orchards arising from the unrestricted use of chemicals. *Proc. 10th Intern. Congr. Entomol. 3:* 163-168.
11. Cranham, J. E. 1961. The natural balance of pests and parasites on Ceylon tea, especially tea tortrix and *Macrocentrus. Tea Quart. 32:* 26-36.
12. Lewis, T. 1969. The diversity of the insect fauna in a hedgerow and neighboring fields. *J. Appl. Ecol. 6:* 453-458.
13. Doutt, R. L. 1958. Vice, virtue and the vedalia. *Bull. Entomol. Soc. Amer. 4:* 119-123.
14. Holloway, J. K. 1964. Projects in biological control of weeds. *Biological Control of Insect Pests and Weeds* (P. de Bach, ed.), pp. 650-670. Reinhold, New York, 844 pp.
15. Ordish, G. 1967. *Biological Methods in Crop Pest Control.* Constable, London, 242 pp.
16. Knipling, E. F. 1964. *The Potential Role of the Sterility Method for Insect Population Control with Special Reference to Combining This Method with Conventional Methods.* ARS 33-98, Agricultural Research Service, U.S.D.A., Washington, D.C.
17. Knipling, E. F. 1960. The eradication of the screw-worm fly. *Sci. Amer. 203:* 54-61.
18. Laven, H. 1967. Eradication of *Culex pipiens fatigans* through cytoplasmic incompatibility. *Nature 216:* 383.
19. Craig, G. C. 1967. Genetic control of *Aedes aegypti* L. *Bull. World Health Organ. 36:* 628-632.
20. Hamilton, W. D. 1967. Extraordinary sex ratios. *Science 156:* 477-488.

21. **Southwood, T. R. E.** 1966. *Ecological Methods.* Methuen, London, 391 pp.


Further Reading

**Bosch, R. van den, and Stern, V. M.** 1962. The integration of chemical and biological control of arthropod pests. *Ann. Rev. Entomol. 7:* 367-386.

**Chant, D. A.** 1964. Strategy and tactics of insect control. *Can. Entomol. 96:* 782-201.

**Clark, L. R., Geier, P. W, and Hughes, R. D.** 1967. *The Ecology of Insect Populations in Theory and Practice.* Methuen, London, 232 pp.

**Conway, G. R.** 1971. Ecological aspects of pest control in Malaysia. In *The Careless Technology: The Ecology of International Development* (T. G. Farvar and J. Milton, eds.) Doubleday Natural History Press, in press.

**De Bach, P.** 1964. *Biological Control of Insect Pests and Weeds.* Reinhold, New York, 844 pp.

**Food and Agricultural Organization (U.N.).** 1966. Proceedings of the F.A.O. Symposium on Integrated Pest Control October 1965 — Rome. Parts 1, 2, and 3.

**Kennedy, J. S.** 1968. The motivation of integrated control. *J. Appl. Ecol. 5:* 492-499.

**Kilgore, W. W., and Doutt, R. L.** 1967. *Pest Control: Biological, Physical and Selected Chemical Methods,* pp. 293-342. Academic Press, New York.

**McGovran, E. R.,** et al. 1969. *Insect-Pest Management and Control. Principles of Plant and Animal Pest Control 3.* National Academy of Sciences Publication No. 1695, Washington, D.C., 508 pp.

**Southwood, T. R. E., and Way, M. J.** 1970. Ecological background to pest management. In *Concepts of Pest Management* (R. L. Rebb and F. E. Guthrie, eds.). North Carolina State University Press, Raleigh, North Carolina.

**Watt, K. E. F.** 1968. *Ecology and Resource Management.* McGraw-Hill, New York, 430 pp.

# 15  Pollution, Weather and Climate

Gordon J. F. MacDonald

The evidence continues to mount showing that human activities are changing the state of the atmosphere. It is important to examine this subject at this time, for at least three reasons. First, the growing population and the more complex activities of man may be altering climate in a way that will, in the long term, be undesirable. While, as I will emphasize, we do not know in detail what man is doing to his climate, the delicate balances within the atmosphere and the history of climate in the past suggest that man, through his inadvertent actions, may cause a disastrous ice age or an equally disastrous melting of the ice caps. Second, the study of inadvertent modification — both on the planetary and local scale — may identify means by which weather and climate can be altered to produce desirable effects. The science and engineering of weather modification are still in their infancies. They may grow more rapidly if we understand what is

GORDON J.F. MACDONALD is Vice Chancellor for Research and Graduate affairs at the University of California, Santa Barbara. Now on leave, he is serving as a member of the President's Council on Environmental Quality. He did both his undergraduate and graduate work at Harvard, and was a junior fellow there from 1952 to 1954. After teaching at MIT, he went to UCLA, where he became chairman of a new department of Planetary and Space Science. Professor Mac-Donald has served on the President's Science Advisory Committee and has been a consultant to NASA and the U.S. Department of State. He has made important contributions to the study of the interior of the Earth, the upper atmosphere, the modification of weather, and the origin of the moon and the planets.

happening in the atmosphere as a result of what man is doing. Finally, it has long been known that the climate of cities differs from that of the surrounding countryside. Only recently it has been recognized that these climatic differences may affect the behavioral and social attitudes of the urban population. The feelings of alienation and discouragement which we find so prevalent today in the core of the cities are not independent of the problems of suffocating smog, agitating noise, and the heat of the cities. Because of these barely perceived but important connections, the problems of inadvertent weather modification are more than important. They are fundamental.

## Urban and Rural Climates

It has long been recognized that the climate of cities, which represent the most concentrated form of environmental modification by man, differs appreciably from the climate of adjacent rural areas. In addition, there is a growing body of literature showing that industrial activities are modifying atmospheric properties and in some cases may be profoundly changing the weather.

Cities on the average have a temperature $0.5^\circ$ to $1^\circ$C higher than the surrounding countryside. The effect is even more marked in the winter, when the minimum temperature reached may be $1^\circ$ to $2^\circ$C higher than that of the surrounding areas. In addition to the difference in temperature, cities are more frequently covered with clouds and the frequency of fog in wintertime can be twice that of the suburbs. Accompanying the increased frequency of cloud cover is a higher total precipitation. Table I summarizes the relative climates of cities as compared with the adjacent countryside. These are general averages; in very large metropolitan areas the differences can be greater.

| Parameter | City as compared with rural surroundings |
|---|---|
| **Temperature** | |
| Annual mean | 0.5 to 1.0°C higher |
| Winter minima | 1.0 to 2.0°C higher |
| **Cloudiness** | |
| Clouds | 5 to 10% more |
| Fog, winter | 100% more |
| Fog, summer | 30% more |
| **Dust particles** | 10 times more |
| **Winter speed** | |
| Annual mean | 20 to 30% lower |
| Extreme gusts | 10 to 20% lower |
| **Precipitation** | 5 to 10% more |

**CLIMATIC CHANGES PRODUCED BY CITIES.** Sources: references 1 and 2.

Several factors contribute to the higher temperatures in urban centers. The direct energy input from home heating units, industry, and air conditioning all lead to the higher annual mean temperature and to raising the minimum temperature. In addition, buildings naturally shelter the city so that wind speeds are less and the turbulent transfer of energy from the city to moving weather systems may be decreased. The increased cloudiness over cities, together with the effect of buildings and pavements on the amount of solar heat retained, can further accentuate the direct input of heat into the atmosphere.

The increased precipitation in cities is probably due also to a number of factors. The heat of the city in effect causes a "thermal mountain" in the air flow. The heat of the sun together with the heat produced by furnaces, automobiles, factories, and homes warms the air in the city. The warmer, less dense air rises in comparison with the cooler air of the suburbs and surrounding regions. As the air rises, it expands and therefore cools. When the air contains water vapor, the cooling can cause the water vapor to change to liquid drops or even ice crystals. When this happens a cloud forms. If the droplets or ice crystals coagulate to a large enough size, they drop from the clouds as rain or snow. The actual formation of precipitation is much more complex than indicated in this simplified account, but over cities the basic mechanisms involve the heating, rising, and expanding of the air.

Laboratory experiments have shown that if one cleans the air of all solid particles, the air can hold much more water at a given temperature before condensing or crystallizing than it can when small particles are present. In nature, the small particles act as nuclei to which the water molecules can become attached. The particles can be dust or salt particles from the ocean, and over cities, the bits of matter produced by the burning of oil, coal, and wood, and to a large extent the exhaust particles of internal combustion engines. These artificial nuclei can aid the formation of precipitation when there is a deficiency of natural nuclei. In cases where the artificial nuclei are abundant then many droplets form and a fine drizzle or fog is produced.

Support for the theory that particle pollution plays a role in precipitation has recently been offered by R. H. Frederick of the Environmental Science Services Administration.[3] He shows the existence of a rather systematic tendency for cold season precipitation at 22 urban Weather Bureau stations in the eastern United States to average several percent greater on weekdays than on weekends, when there is less dust around. This is an important finding which, if substantiated in further studies on other urban areas, would go far in explaining the difference in precipitation between cities and the country.

The most dramatic cases of the relation of industrial pollution and weather are found in regions where the pollutants are concentrated in valleys. Hosler[4] has illustrated how the emission of water vapor and condensation nuclei from the stack of a single wood pulp mill in Pennsylvania can cause fog formation. Fog sometimes fills a valley several miles wide and 20 miles long and spills into adjacent valleys. Hobbs and coworkers[5,6] have shown that Washington State pulp and paper mills are prolific sources of cloud condensation nuclei and that clouds often form downwind of these activities. Hobbs argues that regions of abundant artificial condensation nuclei show an annual precipitation in the last 20 years which is 30 percent greater than in the previous 30 years. Furthermore, these studies have established a higher ice nuclei abundance by as much as an order of magnitude over urban Seattle, compared with stations removed from industrial activity. These observations, taken along with those of Frederick, clearly show the potential importance of man-introduced particulate matter in influencing the weather in regions of high industrial activity. The effects of individual urban centers produce local and regional changes in weather. The sum of the contributions of many metropolitan areas can bring about changes in climate over large regions.

### Changing Climate

The study of geologic and historical records clearly shows that major climatic fluctuations have taken place in the past. Since the last advance of the ice sheet in Eurasia — about 10,000 years ago — the permanent ice cover in the Northern Hemisphere has been limited largely to the Arctic Ocean and to some islands in the higher latitudes. Even during the last 10,000 years periods of marked warming and cooling with time scales of centuries have been noted. Over the last two centuries — for which instrumental data are available — climatic fluctuations have continued.

Climate is much too complicated to be described by a single parameter. A useful guide is the temperature of the atmosphere measured at the earth's surface and averaged over 1 year over the entire earth. Climatological data show that from 1880 to 1940 this average temperature increased by about 0.6°C, while in the last 25 years the average temperature has decreased by about 0.3°C.[7, 8] Thus, during the last three decades, one-half of the warming that had occurred during the preceding six decades has been erased.

Associated with increasing temperature were northward movements of the frost and ice boundaries, pronounced aridity in the south-central parts of Eurasia and North America leading to dust bowl conditions, strong mean motion (wind) parallel to the lines of latitude in the Northern Hemisphere, and a northward displacement of the polar fronts. In more recent times, the lowering of temperatures has been associated with the shifting of the frost and ice boundaries to the south, a weakening mean motion along lines of latitude, and marked increases in rainfall in parts of the previously arid continental areas. For example, sea-ice coverage in the north Atlantic in 1968 was the most extensive in over 60 years. As a result, Icelandic fishermen suffered losses and the accompanying colder weather shortened the growing season. In contrast, the rains in the central continental regions, particularly in India and in East Africa, contributed to very high wheat yields. These experiences emphasize two further points about climate. The complex pattern of human activity is sensitive to relatively small changes in climate, and our ability to predict such changes is very limited.

The fluctuations observed, with a time scale of decades, are still small compared with the climatic variations obtained during the "Little Ice Age" of 1650-1840, the warmer period between 800-1000 A.D., and the still larger variation that is associated with the ice age and its retreat. However, it is important to note that, while fluctuations of only a few tenths of a degree are involved, fluctuations of about 4 to 6°C either way can lead to melting of the ice caps or to a new ice age.

### Causes of Climatic Fluctuation

Are the climatic fluctuations of the past 90 years due to the natural and as yet poorly understood changes in atmospheric processes or have the activities of man intervened in some subtle way? We can identify at least six ways in which man could perturb the atmospheric heat balance and thus affect the climate in a significant way. These are as follows:

1. Increasing the carbon dioxide content of the atmosphere by burning fossil fuels (carbon dioxide pollution).

2. Decreasing atmospheric transparency by small particles (aerosols) resulting from industry, automobiles, jet planes, and home heating units (particle pollution).

3. Decreasing atmospheric transparency by dust put into the atmosphere as a result of improper agricultural practices (dust pollution).

4. Direct heating of the atmosphere by burning fossil and nuclear fuels (thermal pollution).

5. Changing the albedo (fraction of the incoming solar radiation which is diffusely reflected out into space by land, sea, and cloud cover) of the earth's land surface through urbanization, agriculture, deforestation, and construction of reservoirs (surface pollution).

6. Altering the rate of transfer of thermal energy and momentum between the oceans and atmosphere by an oil film resulting from the incomplete combustion and the oil spill from ocean-going vessels (ocean oil pollution).

These activities directly affect the radiation budget of the atmosphere. Others may have an indirect effect. For example, certain kinds of industrial processes emit cloud condensation nuclei and thus affect the frequency of fog and low stratus which, in turn, affect the radiation balance. Also, forest fires produce cloud condensation nuclei and ice nuclei as well as large quantities of heat and water vapor. In this connection, the large-scale burning of trash forest products and of accidentally set forest fires which are particularly prevalent in the Western states, might result in serious modification of climate as well as of local weather.

Carbon dioxide pollution has long been recognized as potentially able to affect worldwide climate. The possible effects of urban, industrial, and agricultural activities on climate, as opposed to local weather, however, have only recently been noted.[9,10]

*Atmospheric Carbon Dioxide*

Carbon dioxide makes up only one three-thousandth of the atmosphere yet it influences how much of the sun's heat is retained in the atmosphere and in so doing can change climate. Further, carbon dioxide in both the atmosphere and oceans (one ten-thousandth of the ocean is dissolved carbon dioxide) is of vital importance to all biologic activity. Carbon is the key element of all living matter and carbon is derived either directly or indirectly from atmospheric carbon dioxide.

Most of the energy used by man to drive modern technology is derived from fossil fuels.

The carbon contained in these fuels was once present as carbon dioxide in the atmosphere and the process of oxidation returns carbon dioxide to the atmosphere. This interchange is a speeded up version of part of a cyclic process in which carbon participates over geologic time.

During the 4½ billion years of earth history volcanic and related activity have poured carbon dioxide into the atmosphere. The total amount introduced is uncertain but it is at least 40,000 times the amount now present in the atmosphere. Part of the carbon dioxide released from the earth's interior has dissolved in the oceans. There it can combine with calcium and magnesium, supplied by the weathering of rocks, to form limestone and dolomite. A portion of the dissolved carbon dioxide and of the atmospheric carbon dioxide enters the biosphere and it is taken up by plants. About one-fourth of the total quantity of carbon dioxide has been reduced by plants to organic carbon compounds and become buried in sediments. A fraction of this material has been transformed by a variety of geologic processes into gas, coal, lignite, oil shale, tar, sand, and petroleum.

The burning of fossil fuels (primarily lignite, coal, petroleum, and natural gas) now releases annually about $1.5 \times 10^{16}$ grams of carbon dioxide. This figure should be compared with the amount of carbon dioxide annually consumed in photosynthesis, about $1.1 \times 10^{17}$ grams. Thus, today the combustion of fossil fuels produces an amount of carbon dioxide which is an appreciable fraction (approximately one-seventh) of the carbon dioxide entering the photosynthesis cycle each year. It is, furthermore, about four orders of magnitude (10,000 times) greater than the return of carbon to the fossil reservoir; the rate of release of carbon dioxide into the atmosphere by natural oxidation during respiration of recently grown organic materials replaces all but one ten-thousandth of the amount consumed in photosynthesis.

Until recently, it was not clear how much of the carbon dioxide being released by combustion accumulated in the atmosphere and how much entered the oceans and the terrestial biomass. Callendar[11] calculated that the carbon dioxide had increased at approximately a constant rate from the nineteenth century level of about 290 ppm to about 330 ppm in 1960 (0.03 percent of the atmosphere). In order to sustain such an increase, about three-fourths of the carbon dioxide released through combustion would have to remain in the atmosphere. More recently, Keeling has undertaken a detailed monitoring program at Mauna Loa Observatory in Hawaii and at the Pole station in Antarctica. He has found that the annual average $CO_2$ levels measured at Mauna Loa and at the Pole station agree to within 1 ppm (part per million). Furthermore, both stations show a consistent increase over the past few years. Keeling[8] finds a concentration of $CO_2$ of about 314 ppm and that the rate of increase averages about 0.2 ppm/yr. This implies that each year the mass of carbon dioxide in the atmosphere increased by $5 \times 10^{15}$ grams. Thus, of all the $CO_2$ produced by combustion, one-third remains in the atmosphere and two-thirds are taken up by the oceans and by the biomass. At the current rate of deposition in the atmosphere of carbon dioxide, the amount of manmade $CO_2$ doubles every 23 years. Assuming a mass of atmospheric $CO_2$ of $2.2 \times 10^{18}$ grams, this is an increase in atmospheric $CO_2$ of over 0.2 percent per year or 2 percent per decade.

*Sources of Increasing Carbon Dioxide*

At present, the world's use of energy is increasing annually at about 4 percent, which corresponds to a doubling time of 17 years. Of all the energy produced, about 98 percent comes from oil, coal, and natural gas, while water power contributes only 2 percent and on a global scale nuclear energy is still negligible. At present, the total thermal energy produced from crude oil, coal, and lignite corresponds to $3.8 \times 10^{12}$ kwh/yr, which corresponds to $8.5 \times 10^{-3}$ watts per square meter (watts/m$^2$) averaged over the surface of the earth. This can be compared with the energy production in 1940 of $3.1 \times 10^{-3}$ watts/m$^2$ averaged over the earth's surface.

Not only has the total amount of energy used by modern industrial society increased very greatly but, also, the sources of the energy have changed. Since 1800, the principal sources of the world's industrial energy have been the fossil fuels and water power. Before 1900 the energy derived from oil, as compared with that obtained from coal, was almost negligible. Since 1900 the contribution of oil to the total energy supply has steadily increased and is now approximately equal to that of coal, and is increasing more rapidly (Chapter 5). If natural gas and natural gas liquids are added to crude oil, the petroleum group of fuels represents about 60 percent of all the energy derived from coal, petroleum, and water power. Since World War II the production of coal has grown at a constant rate of about 3.0 percent, with a doubling period of 20 years. World production of crude oil, except for a slight retardation during the depression of the 1930s and during World War II, has increased from 1890 to the present at a nearly constant exponential rate of 6.9 percent per year, with a doubling period of 10 years.

The rates of growth of a highly industrialized nation differ substantially from the world average. The U.S. production of total energy from coal, oil, natural gas, and water power divides into two distinct growth periods. From 1850 to 1907 energy in the United States was produced at a growth rate of 7 percent per year, with a doubling period of 10 years. From 1907 to the present, the growth rate dropped to 1.8 percent per year, with a doubling period of 39 years.

Keeling's observations on the current increase of $CO_2$ in the atmosphere, together with the fact that about one-third of the $CO_2$ released through combustion enters the atmosphere, implies that man's activities have added about $1.7 \times 10^{17}$ grams of carbon dioxide to the atmosphere. This is 8 percent of the $2.2 \times 10^{18}$ grams now present. In consideration of climate, it is not only the total amount of $CO_2$ introduced into the atmosphere that is important, but also the rate at which it is introduced. Although coal has been mined for about 800 years, one-half of the coal produced during that period has been mined during the last 31 years. Half of the world's cumulative production of petroleum has occurred during the 13-year period since 1956. Thus, $9 \times 10^{16}$ grams of $CO_2$ have been introduced into the atmosphere since 1950, and $1.3 \times 10^{17}$ grams have been introduced since the mid-1930s.

An estimate of the maximum amount of $CO_2$ that man might introduce into the atmosphere can be made from estimates of the total fossil fuels that are available. Averitt[12] estimates that $7.6 \times 10^{12}$ metric tons of coal represents the maximum available. This is about twice the coal resources established by actual geologic mapping. Estimates of petroleum resources vary considerably. Weeks[13] and Ryman[14] estimate that approximately $2 \times 10^{12}$ barrels of oil are ultimately recoverable. Hubbert (Chapter 5) appears to favor the somewhat lower figure of $1.35 \times 10^{12}$ barrels. If these fossil fuels were burned, they would add to the atmosphere $3.3 \times 10^{18}$ grams of $CO_2$. This figure should be compared with the $2.2 \times 10^{18}$ grams now in the atmosphere. Thus, man is capable of increasing the current $CO_2$ content by about 150 percent.

Hubbert (Chapter 5) estimates that 80 percent of the ultimate resources of the petroleum family — crude oil, natural gas, tar, sand oil, and shale oil — will be exhausted in less than a century. The time required to exhaust 80 percent of the world's coal resources would be 300 to 400 years, but only 100 to 200 years if coal rather than nuclear power is used as the main energy source. These rates of consumption imply that, in the next century, the content of the $CO_2$ in the atmosphere could be doubled. We can also estimate that over the next 30 years it could be increased by about one-third.

Projected possible increases of carbon dioxide in the atmosphere must be viewed with caution. The oceans, for example, contain 60 times more carbon dioxide than does the atmosphere. If the atmosphere's average temperature increased, either as a result of the increasing carbon dioxide content or through some other means, the heating would tend to drive some of the carbon dioxide now dissolved in the oceans back into the atmosphere. Alternatively, the increasing flow of nutrients into the ocean, resulting from improper agricultural practices, would stimulate the growth of phytoplankton and increase, through photosynthesis, removal of carbon dioxide from the atmosphere. Looking to the future, we cannot say with any precision what the carbon dioxide content of the atmosphere actually will be.

What we can say is that man has changed the total amount of carbon dioxide by several percent and, further, that he is capable of more than doubling the carbon dioxide content over the next hundred years.

## Thermal Effects of Carbon Dioxide

Weather and climate are determined by how much of the solar energy is converted by the atmosphere-ocean-land system into the motion of the atmosphere. The heat energy input into the atmosphere depends on the albedo of the earth including clouds, the interchange of heat by the atmosphere with the land and water and by the absorption of radiation by gaseous constituents in the atmosphere. Carbon dioxide is nearly transparent to visible light so that it has only minor effect on the incoming solar radiation. However, it is a strong absorber of infrared radiation given off by the land, sea, and clouds. Carbon dioxide then radiates back to the surface a portion of the absorbed thermal energy so that a fraction of the heat that would be lost in space remains to warm the atmosphere. This effect is sometimes misleadingly termed a greenhouse effect. A greenhouse, however, operates not only by trapping of radiation but also by dampening turbulent heat exchange with the wind.

The most complete calculations of the net effect of altering the carbon dioxide content of the atmosphere are those of Manabe and Wetherald.[15] These numerical calculations show that increasing $CO_2$ content results in warming of the entire lower atmosphere, the amount of warming being dependent in part on the water vapor concentration of the atmosphere. With the assumption of fixed concentration of water vapor, together with conditions of albedo, cloudiness, radiation, and other parameters chosen as typical of the midlatitudes, an increase of 10 percent in the $CO_2$ concentration leads to a warming of $0.2°C$. For the assumption of a fixed relative humidity (actual water vapor pressure as a percentage of vapor pressure required for condensation) with all other conditions remaining the same, a 10 percent increase in content of $CO_2$ raises the temperature by $0.3°C$. Manabe and Wetherald consider the latter assumption of fixed relative humidity conditions as being more realistic. If the amount of carbon dioxide in the atmosphere is doubled at constant relative humidity, the temperature is increased by 2.4°C.

In addition to carbon dioxide, water vapor also absorbs infrared radiation. In a humid atmosphere the net effect of carbon dioxide is less than in a dry atmosphere. The third component of importance in the atmosphere is ozone. In the upper region of the atmosphere, above 40,000 to 50,000 feet, ozone absorbs some infrared but its principal effect on air temperature is due to its absorption of ultraviolet and visible sunlight. Of the three components that affect the radiation balance, so far man has only changed in a measurable way the concentration of carbon dioxide. However, the possible introduction of a fleet of commercial supersonic transports presents a potential problem for the future. Aircraft add water as a result of combustion of jet fuel. In the lower atmosphere this water mixes rapidly and does not change the radiative properties of the atmosphere. However, the higher atmosphere is relatively dry, with a water content of only about 2 parts per million. The water introduced in the stratosphere (about 10 to 30 km altitude) remains there for a least 18 months. This water can lead to an increase in temperature; a fivefold increase in concentration would raise the surface temperature by about 2°C. A fleet of 400 SSTs flying in this region would change the concentration by about 25 percent if the water were distributed uniformly through the stratosphere.

Another potential effect of the water introduced into the stratosphere by SSTs is on the concentration of ozone. Water can react with ozone, converting it to molecular oxygen in photochemical reactions. These reactions could lower the ozone concentration with consequent effects on the radiation balance. However, uncertainties in the nature of the reactions, their rates, and the natural concentration of ozone and water vapor make any estimate of the overall change in temperature most uncertain.

*Particles and Turbidity of the Atmosphere*

Is the observed decrease in the temperature of the last 2½ decades due to man or is it the result of whimsical nature that is now overwhelming the effects of carbon dioxide? The answer is by no means clear, but Bryson has argued that there is increasing evidence that urban and industrial pollution, perhaps aided by agricultural pollution, may be in part responsible for decreasing the surface temperature at a rate which is large compared with the effects of carbon dioxide in increasing the temperature. What is not clear is whether agricultural and industrial pollution have effects that are comparable to those due to natural volcanic dust.

Particle pollution, whether urban and industrial aerosols or whether agricultural dust, can affect the thermal balance in at least two ways, one direct and one indirect. The presence of small particles in the atmosphere decreases the transparency of the atmosphere to the incoming solar radiation. This partial shielding of the surface is usually described in terms of the turbidity of the atmosphere. The decreased solar radiation reaching the surface will lead to lower temperature, but the small particles also affect the outgoing long-wave radiation. The net effect on the total radiation balance depends on the abundance and size distribution, and the altitude range of the small particles. Calculation of this net effect is still primitive; however, Bryson[9] estimates that a decrease of atmospheric transparency of only 3 or 4 percent could lead to a reduction of surface temperature of 0.4°C. What is important is the net amount of radiation reaching the surface, and this is composed both of the direct solar radiation and the infrared radiation which is both reflected and reradiated back by clouds, carbon dioxide, and water vapor.

Secondly, the indirect effect of particles introduced by man on the thermal budget of the atmosphere arises because air, particularly the air that has been over the ocean for some time, is often deficient in cloud condensation nuclei and ice nuclei. The introduction of manmade condensation nuclei into the atmosphere aids the formation of fog and low cloud layer from water-vapor-laden air. These artificially stimulated clouds will reflect some fraction of solar radiation back out into space and block the infrared radiation from reaching the surface.

The effect of particles in encouraging the formation of low clouds and fog further enhances the modification of the thermal balance. Low clouds have a large effect on the net energy reaching the surface; Manabe and Wetherald[15] show that a 1 percent change in the average low cloud cover the world over will bring about a decrease in temperature of 0.8°C − four times the observed drop over the past two decades. At present, on the average, about 31 percent of the earth's surface is covered by low cloud; increasing this percentage to only 36 percent would drop the temperature about 4°C − a decrease very close to that required for the return of an ice age!

There are few reliable observations of the transparency or turbidity of the atmosphere extending over long periods of time. McCormick and Ludwig[10] discuss data from Washington, D.C. and Davos, Switzerland that indicate increases of turbidity of approximately 10 and 20 percent per decade, respectively, for the period 1910 to 1960. Somewhat larger changes have been reported from the results obtained at the observatory in Mauna Loa, but these observations have been questioned on instrumental grounds.

Davitaya[16] presented data on dustfall on snow in the high Caucasus Mountains. The quantities increased by an order of magnitude between 1930 and 1960, with most of the changes occurring since 1950; however, there are uncertainties as to how much of the dust is locally derived and how much is representative of the overall atmospheric content.

While the local increases of fog and low cloud cover over urban areas are well documented, the overall increase of cloud cover, if indeed there has been one, is not known. Only with the availability of satellites have data been obtained on a fairly routine basis over ocean areas, but these data are often incomplete since high clouds may hide clouds at lower levels, and the perturbation in the thermal balance depends critically on cloud-height distribution.

Mitchell[8] has critically examined the hypothesis that man-made aerosols play a significant role in controlling the radiation balance. He concludes that a major part of the turbidity variation is due to volcanic activity introducing fine-grained particles into the stratosphere. Mitchell's calculations are based on estimates of the total debris associated with volcanic explosion, an assignment of 1 percent of this total to stratospheric dust, and an assumption of a 14-month lifetime for the stratospheric dust. All these numbers can be questioned but, if they are accepted, it would appear clear that volcanic dust dominates urban and agricultural pollution.

The above remarks are not intended to imply that there is a proven case that urban, industrial, and agricultural pollution or volcanic dust is the principal cause of the recent cooling trend. What is significant is that the apparent changes in atmospheric transparency may be sufficient to bring about the observed cooling of the earth's surface. Further, the direct effects of transparency can be amplified by increased formation of low clouds and fogs which greatly affect the thermal balance of the earth's surface.

If the pollution interpretation is correct, then we face an urgent problem of global climate modification, since atmospheric pollution is increasing at an exponential rate and there are, as yet, no acceptable means of impeding this growth.

*Thermal Pollution*

The mean annual difference between absorbed solar radiation and long-wave radiation into space (that fraction of the solar radiation available to drive the atmosphere) is about 68 watts/m$^2$. Most of this radiation balance is used in the evaporation of water, heating of the atmosphere, and driving various meteorological processes (Chapter 5). A tiny part, less than 1 percent, is used in the photosynthesis of green plants and is turned into a relatively stable form of chemical energy. Man's industrial activities directly affect this thermal budget since industrial heat represents a new source of heat additional to that from solar radiation. Averaged over the surface, man at present is producing about $8.4 \times 10^{-3}$ watts/m$^2$, or somewhat more than 1/10,000 of the radiation balance of the atmosphere. While this fraction is at present much too small to affect climate on a large scale, it certainly alters local microclimate. What is important is that in the future the direct input of energy into the atmosphere may be of major importance.

In a primitive society, the utilization of energy is pretty well limited to the food used by the individual. This corresponds to about 100 thermal watts per capita. The present world average is somewhat in excess of 1000 thermal watts per person, while a highly industrialized society such as the United States uses about 10,000 thermal watts per capita. Projecting into the future, we see that if the world population goes to 5 billion and if the worldwide average of energy use is 10 kilowatts per person, then the direct energy input into the atmosphere would be 0.14 watts/m$^2$, or about 1/500 that of the natural radiation balance. Indeed, if the present rate of energy increase of 4 percent per year is maintained (a doubling time of 17 years), then in 200 years artificial energy input into the atmosphere would equal one-half of the radiation balance. This level would be reached in only 100 years with a 10 percent yearly increase of energy. As Budyko[17] has argued, an increase of only a few tenths of one percent in the radiation balance (0.2 to 0.6 watts/m$^2$) would be sufficient to cause the melting of polar ice. With a doubling time of 17 years, we would increase energy production 25-fold in about 80 years to reach an artificial energy input of 0.2 watts/m$^2$.

The combined effect of carbon dioxide pollution and direct heat pollution is strongly in the direction of warming the earth's atmosphere. On the other hand, urban and agricultural pollution tend to lower the earth's temperature. Which pollution will win in the end? Will we drown or freeze? Can we, as we obscure the sky, neatly balance the lost solar radiation through fission and fusion? These will become critical questions in the not too distant future.

*Albedo*

The albedo of the earth averages about 34 units. Of the 100 units of solar radiation entering the atmosphere 34 units are reflected directly back into space. Increasing the albedo will result in a lower average surface temperature since less heat is available to the atmosphere. Manabe and Wetherald[15] calculate that a unit increase in albedo of the earth's surface will produce a decrease in average surface temperature of 1°C. Thus man-made alteration of the albedo at the earth's surface, if large enough, can bring about substantial changes in climatic conditions. Densely built up regions have a higher albedo than do forests and cultivated soils. Deserts, some of which may have resulted from man's activities, have a much higher albedo than do grass-covered fields. While local changes of albedo have been measured, the long-term global variation is unknown even as to sign. The vast proliferation of urban areas and highway systems suggests that man may, at present, be increasing the surface albedo.

Man's construction, lumbering, and farming change not only the radiative properties, but other surface features that can influence the thermal state of the atmosphere. The ground exchanges heat with the air primarily through the irregular motion in the atmosphere known as turbulence. The degree to which the flow of air is turbulent depends on the roughness of the surface. For example, on a small scale, the air temperature at a height of a few feet over a hot airfield runway can be 1 to 2°C cooler than over the cooler grassy surroundings. The flow of the air over the smooth surface is less turbulent than over grass and less heat is transferred from the hot surface upwards into the air. Further, the roughness also affects the actual flow of the air, particularly in the vertical direction.

The calculation of the net effect of changing surface characteristics is uncertain because of incomplete information on the overall thermal effects of changing albedo and surface roughness. However, both the magnitude of man-made surface changes — direct, as in construction, and indirect, as in the formation of deserts — and the sensitivity of the atmosphere to such alteration suggest these should be carefully studied.

*Ocean Pollution*

The possible effects of spreading oil in a very

thin film on the ocean surface are poorly understood. It is generally assumed that the oceans,
with their vast store of thermal energy, act as a
balance wheel to climate. The atmosphere exchanges energy with the ocean not only through
the radiative processes but through the mechanical processes associated with air moving over a
wave-roughened surface. The strength of the
mechanical interaction depends on the roughness
of the surface at various length scales, and the
roughness is determined by the surface properties
of the water as well as by the velocity and the
irregularity of the wind blowing over the surface.
Very thin oil films can perturb the interchange
by reducing the turbulent flux of the heat and of
the momentum, reducing the evaporation, and
lowering the amount of energy radiated by the
surface.

We do not know whether oil pollution is a
significant factor in climatic change. Data on the
extent of oil pollution, the lifetime of an oil film
on the sea's surface, and the detailed thermal effects of such a film are not available, so that even
the sign of the effect of ocean oil pollution on
the surface temperature is not known.

## Conclusions

I have briefly reviewed six major ways in
which man could be altering the planet's climate;
there may be others of comparable importance
such as contrails from jets and supersonic aircraft. Of these six ways, we know most about the
effect of carbon dioxide but, even here, the uncertainties are large.

Examination of the possible ways in which
man affects climate on a large scale leads to certain important generalizations:

1. Large-scale man-made changes may be taking place in the environment. These are, for the
most part, inadvertent, and some have been only
recently recognized.

2. The magnitude of the changes produced by
man is of the same order as that caused by
nature. For example, the carbon dioxide added
to the atmosphere can bring about a change of
several tenths of a degree in the average tempera-

ture; and a change of this magnitude has been
observed to occur naturally.

3. The alterations produced by man can no
longer be regarded as local. Direct heat input by
a city changes the microclimate of that city. The
combined effect of many cities can change the
climate of the planet.

4. Our understanding of the physical environment is sufficient to identify inadvertent modification but it is far too primitive to predict confidently all the consequences of man's unwise use
of his resources.

5. Despite the very long term importance of
understanding changes in our environment if we
are to maintain a habitable planet, inadvertent
modification is a neglected area of research —
neither fashionable to the scientists and engineers
nor, until recently, of high priority to the
money-distributing government agencies. For example, there are at most a handful of small research groups throughout the country studying,
in a professional way, the influence of man's
activity on climate. Of the monies provided by
the U.S. Federal Government for research in
weather modification, only about 1 percent is for
the support of programs studying inadvertent
modification.

## References

1. **Landsberg. H.** 1956. The climate of towns In
   *Man's Role in Changing the Face of the
   Earth.* University of Chicago Press, Chicago,
   Illinois.
2. **Geiger, R.** 1965. *The Climate Near the
   Ground.* Harvard University Press, Cambridge, Massachusetts.
3. **Frederick, R. H.** Personal communication.
4. **Hosler, C. L.** 1968. *Weatherwise 21:* 110.
5. **Hobbs, P. V., and Locatelli, J. D.** 1969. *J.
   Atmos. Sci 26:*
6. **Hobbs, P. V., and Radke, L. F., and Shum-
   way, S. E.** 1969. *J. Atmos Sci 26:*
7. **Mitchell, J.** 1963. *Changes of Climate.*
   UNESCO Symposium,

8. **Mitchell, J.** 1969. *Global Effects of Environmental Pollution.* (S. F. Singer, ed.). AAAS Symposium

9. **Bryson, R.** 1968. *Weatherwise 21:* 56-61.

10. **McCormick, R., and Ludwig, J.** 1967. *Science 156:* 1358-1359.

11. **Callendar, G.** 1958. *Tellus 10:* 243-248.

12. **Averitt, P.** 1969. *Coal Resources of the United States, Jan. 1, 1967.* U.S. Geological Survey Bulletin. 1275.

13. **Weeks, L. H.** 1958. *Amer. Assoc. Petrol. Geol. Bull. 42:* 431-438; see also Hubbert, Chapter 5.

14. **Ryman, W. P.** 1969. quoted by Hubbert.

15. **Manabe, S., and Wetherald, R. T.** 1967. *J. Atmos. Sci 24:* 241-259.

16. **Davitaya, F.** 1965. *Trans Soviet Acad. Sci. Geogr. Sov.*, No. 2.

17. **Budyko, M.** 1967. *Meteorologiya i gidrologiya*, No. 11.

# ENVIRONMENT & SOCIETY

# 16 Man and the Urban Environment

Robert B. Smock

ROBERT B. SMOCK is Professor of Sociology at the University of Michigan's Dearborn campus, where he teaches human ecology and demography and directs the Center for Urban Studies. He has worked extensively on urban planning, particularly transportation systems. He earned his doctorate in 1962 from Wayne State University. His strong interest in social organization has led to two current projects, one on family planning in the lower classes and one on social functions of the upper class.

## Cities and the Ecological Crisis

Many reasonable observers are alarmed by the fact that the world's human population is increasing at the rate of about 2 percent per year. This rate means a doubling of population in about 35 years, and no one seems to know how the food and housing supplies, the capacities of transport and water and sewage systems, and all the rest of the needed goods and services can be doubled that quickly. Furthermore, the rising expectations of underdeveloped countries and of poor people everywhere make a more-than-doubling of resources important for the purposes of peace and political cohesion.

It is especially alarming that the world's population in cities of 1 million or more is increasing at the rate of 4 percent per year, or twice as fast as population in general.[1] ("Cities" here and elsewhere in this chapter are defined as whole urbanized areas, regardless of the number of units of local government within them.) The doubling of population in these giant concentrations in only 18 more years deserves the most serious thought, because their ability to more than double their facilities seems especially doubtful.

There are now about 200 cities around the world with million-plus populations, and they contain 375 million people, or about 10 percent of the total world population. This is remarkable in view of the fact that, as recently as 1950, only 4 percent, or about 161 million, of the world's people, were in cities that large. It is unlikely that any cities grew that large before modern times.

The long-range implications of such rapid world urbanization are challenging because there is no known upper limit to the process. In the United States today no more than 7 percent of the population is involved in rural farming, and computerized farms might be operated from cities someday. So the urban environment seems destined to be the home of our entire species by the end of the lifetimes of many babies who are already born, if present trends continue.

The rapid urbanization of population has two special meanings for everyone concerned about the viability of ecosystems. First, it seems unlikely that agricultural societies could ever grow large enough, or could ever develop the necessary technology, to reduce the entire earth to a dead hulk. But urban societies could do just that. Every city in the world has polluted air above it, polluted water flowing from it, and polluted land under piles of solid waste surrounding it. In the tragic drama of environmental degradation, there is no doubt that the city is a major villain.

The second ecological meaning of urbanization may be less obvious, but it is equally important. It has to do with the reasons for the emergence of urban organization as the dominant form of human organization. All species of monkeys and apes live in social groups, and the reason emerging from recent studies is that these groups enhance the opportunities for learning.[2] This seems to be exactly what cities can do for human beings. The first cities most likely emerged in areas that contained differing subenvironments and communities which, through social interaction, learned from one another and cooperated, rather than holding aloof from, or going to war against one another.[3]

In other words, cities are settings in which people have been more flexible and adaptable than they have been in other settings. To whatever extent this is true, it raises doubt about the idea (expressed by a few) of solving ecological problems by withdrawing to smaller, rural-type communities. If cities have been successful adaptive organizational mechanisms in the past, then they may now be our best hope for adapting to environments becoming exhausted and degraded by our ignorance and rapid growth.

Until now cities have been the villains of the ecological drama; perhaps in the near future they will become the heroes, too. This chapter is devoted to exploring how cities have changed the pattern of human activities to become the kinds of environments they are today, for the purpose of discovering how they might be directed to change in ways conducive to ecological well-being tomorrow.

The first obstacle to such change is lack of awareness of the need for it. Most of rural environment grows; most of urban environment is constructed. This difference can create a false sense in cities of an independence from nature. In reality, of course, not a single law of nature is suspended for urban men, and they are very much dependent on nature's resources and regularities. Urban communities begin to be comprehensible when viewed as ecosystems just as do salt water marshes or tropical rain forests.

Like all ecosystems, those that contain human communities consist of interdependent components of population, organization, environment, and technology.[4] Earlier chapters have touched on their POPULATION and TECHNOLOGY components, and they will be discussed less extensively here. The ENVIRONMENTAL component is distinctive in urban ecosystems because of its largely "constructed" character, and it will be described here in a little more detail. The organi-

zation part of urban ecosystems, as it applies to the human population, contains the important reasons why cities are doing so badly in their environmental-technology relations. It is the character of urban social organization which is preventing cities from applying know-how they already possess to the goals of ending pollution and recycling wastes. So this discussion is focused upon ORGANIZATION.

### Why Organization Is Important

The relevance of social organization is revealed by the reasons given by planners, businessmen, politicians, and other urban decisionmakers for why so little is being done. One reason is the problem of GROWTH. It is very difficult, for example, to have a sewer system ready to accommodate the wastes of a larger future city population when the size of the future population is not reliably known. Another reason is the problem of COST. New York, for example, needs to decide whether to pay about 8 million dollars more a year for exhaust-control systems on its new cars, or about 15 million dollars a year to remove sulfur dioxide from Consolidated Edison Company smoke, or both, or any number "of many similar options, all of them expensive."[5]

The connection between social organization and the cost problem is the system of social stratification, which allocates varying proportions of wealth to the various social classes. It seems reasonable that ecologists expect the United States to be the first society to recycle everything and to abolish pollution, because it has the most technological resources. It also seems to be expected that the wealthiest businesses within the United States will absorb the costs of necessary changes. It seems reasonable, but it is not. Probably in any stratification system, and certainly in the existing one, the costs of ecological reform will be paid only with large increases in general prices and taxes. Beginning to pay the costs of production-plus-disposal, instead of just production, will hit the economy like a surge of inflation. Consumers must begin to receive fewer goods and services per dollar because every dollar must come to cover its share of the cost of circulating a large proportion of the materials.

The poorer people are, the more they may be expected to resist paying these new costs. If there were not poor people in the United States there would still be a cost problem. But given some 20 percent in poverty and an even larger percentage already feeling economically insecure,[6] this aspect of social organization seems likely to account for a long and dangerous delay in the resolution of the ecological crisis.

The connection between organization and the growth problem is similar. The poorer people are, the more they contribute to the natural increase of population (births in excess of deaths).[7] It is certain that high-income and middle-income populations will have to slow their rates of growth, too; but growth rates are still highest among low-income populations, particularly in underdeveloped countries. Perhaps this subject is familiar enough to need no further emphasis here, but there is one more way in which the stratification aspect of organization is relevant.

The poorer people are, the more conformist and the less adaptable they are to most kinds of social change.[8] Since ecological reform seems likely to call for important changes in economic processes, in political policies, in community patterns, and right down into domestic practices in individual families, this resistance to change is highly significant. It is certainly as significant as the more widely recognized conservatism of the elite, or the "Establishment."

Ecologists experience an understandable temptation to blame wealth for environmental degradation. The wealthier people are, the more they consume and the more waste they produce. But this observation can lead to ecologically wrong conclusions if human population is imagined to be a homogeneous entity. In fact it is an organization of widely differing parts. Increasing the gross wealth of a total society does increase the ecological problem. But the solution of the ecological problem, the reversal of the presently declining life expectancy of the living environment, depends upon increasing the per capita wealth of poor people within the population, in the United States and everywhere else on earth.

For some time to come, that kind of increased wealth will concomitantly reduce the rate of population growth, increase the ability to pay the costs of ecological reform without starvation or rebellion, and improve the chances for a human organization adapted to nature in a life-supporting way. No existing form of organization, in the United States or anywhere else, is increasing the per capita wealth of poor people very rapidly. Perhaps stratification systems need to change so that relatively poor people receive a larger share of economic growth; perhaps they need to change so that the relatively poor receive all the growth while the amount received by the relatively wealthy is stabilized; perhaps already in some places the limits of productivity have been reached, and the relatively poor can be upgraded only in proportion to the downgrading of the relatively wealthy. However it is achieved, the UP-GRADING OF POOR PEOPLE in terms of income, education, and occupational skills is a prerequisite of ecological reform.

This is where cities come in. Over the past century cities in the United States have absorbed millions of relatively poor people, mostly peasants (in the general sense of non-land-owning farmers) from Europe and from the South, and over a generation or two turned them into relatively wealthy urban workers. But during the most recent two decades the process has encountered snags, and urban unrest — springing from frustrated expectations of opportunities for upgrading — has emerged as a major social problem.

Cities have always been hard on their natural environments. London's fog (smog from burning soft coal in fireplaces) was a problem before industrialization. It appears to be no more than a coincidence that the problems within urban organization and the environment problem have hit at the same time. History may record that it was a fatal coincidence from which the human population never recovered. But man has worked on his technology for so long, and invested so little money and time in coming to understand the organization component of ecosystems with cities in them, that it is far too early to give up.

Throughout the following sections of this chapter two questions are considered: (1) In urban ecosystems, what are the patterns of organization which have upgraded population in terms of income, education, and occupation? (2) What accounts for the ecosystem problems in the relations between population, organization, environment, and technology right now?

## Detroit as a Typical City

The urbanized area of Detroit has experienced all the changes contributing to the contemporary urban crisis. Its population has grown rapidly, its urbanized land area has grown even more rapidly, its central city has declined in many ways, its black minority has grown and challenged the discrimination against it, its suburbs have experienced growing pains, and it has become aware of its degrading impact on its physical environment. It is a good example for our consideration.

Much of the available information about Detroit comes from the national census taken every 10 years. In addition, in 1953 and again in 1965 surveys were made in a 700-square-mile area including the city of Detroit as part of the process of regional transportation and land use planning.[9] In 1953 this area included an outer ring a mile or more wide which was still in agricultural use; in 1965 nearly all of the area was urbanized (see Table I).

| Year and place of residence | Population | Land area, sq. miles | Black workers |
|---|---|---|---|
| 1953 — Total | 2,969,000 | 709 | 135,000 |
| Detroit | 1,849,000 | 140 | 123,000 |
| Suburbs | 1,120,000 | 569 | 12,000 |
| 1965 — Total | 3,533,000 | 709 | 159,000 |
| Detroit | 1,571,000 | 140 | 146,000 |
| Suburbs | 1,962,000 | 569 | 13,000 |

DETROIT POPULATION, LAND AREA, AND BLACK WORKERS. "Workers" are persons going to work on an average weekday. Source: 1953 Detroit Metropolitan Area Traffic Study, and 1965 Detroit Regional Transportation and Land Use Study; see reference 9.

## Detroit's Population.

In the 12 years between 1953 and 1965, the population of the Detroit AREA increased by 564,000 (19 percent) to a total of over 3½ million. This large amount of growth was not unprecedented, but it was not readily predictable either. The central CITY of Detroit itself grew by half a million between 1910 and 1920, and by

half a million more between 1920 and 1930. Between 1930 and 1940, however, the increase was about a tenth that much, at 54,000. The central city of Detroit increased in size between every 10-year census from 1820 to 1950, then it experienced an abrupt decline which WAS unprecedented.

The Detroit urban AREA population has grown larger in EVERY 10-year period without exception since its first census, although at widely varying rates. The increase was 112 percent in 1910-1920, only 9 percent in 1930-1940, and somewhere between 19 percent and 65 percent in every other decade since 1850-1860. Much of this increase has been due to migration. There were more than half a million foreign-born white Detroiters in 1930, compared with fewer than 100,000 before the turn of the century. There are now more than half a million black Detroiters, compared with fewer than 100,000 in 1920.

The major change in population in 1953-1965 was not a matter of growth, however, but of distribution. The combination of a 75 percent increase in the suburbs and a 15 percent decrease in the central city had never occurred before. It represents a changing relationship between population and environment, in the form of declining density.

## Detroit's Environment.

The base of Detroit's environment is an area of land subdivided by access streets and built upon or otherwise developed for urban as opposed to agricultural use. This urbanized area has, of course, increased with the growth of population. For 226 years (until 1927) a process of periodic annexation kept the urbanized area, plus a ring of undeveloped land reserved for further urban growth, inside Detroit city limits. That is, political Detroit was as large or larger than the urbanized area, or physical Detroit.

After a century as a French, English, or American fort or town, Detroit became an incorporated city in the contemporary legal sense in 1806. In 1861, a second city (Pontiac) was incorporated within the three-county area surrounding Detroit; in 1867, there was a third (Wyandotte);

1879, a fourth (Mt. Clemens). Then there were
o more until 1915. When the automobile began
o make interurban travel easier, suburbs began
o proliferate around the central city.

With a final annexation in 1927, governmental
Detroit encountered an iron ring of suburbs and
as not been able to annex again. There con-
nued to be vacant land inside the city limits
ntil the early 1950s. Then, from 1953 to 1965
nd to the present), all the growth of the popu-
tion of the area occured in the suburbs.

The variety of environments within the De-
roit area takes on some pattern against this his-
orical background. For example, the inner part
f the central city consists of about 15 square
iles which were inside the city limits of 1890.
lost of the housing there is old, some of it on
edarpost foundations and originally built with-
ut plumbing, electricity, or central heating. The
vorst of the city's slums are there. Also there is
he central business district, with some new,
arge, and beautiful buildings.

On many acres of the inner city, the original
tructures have been demolished, to be replaced
ometimes by large, publicly owned row houses
nd apartments for low-income people, and
ometimes by large, privately owned row houses
nd apartments for high-income people. There
re belts of industrial land along the railroads and
he Detroit River which bound the area. A very
ifferent kind of environment is provided by a
arge medical center and still another kind by a
enter consisting of a university, a library, and
useums.

Rising incomes, a network of freeways, and
he redevelopment of land have combined to re-
uce the residential population in these inner-
ity environments from half a million in the
920s to about 200,000 now. The highly desir-
ble decline in density from 32,000 per square
ile to 14,000 per square mile is somewhat il-
usory, because it has been produced partly by
vithdrawing land from residential use and by dis-
ossessing thousands of families from their hous-
ng. There is still a great deal of crowding among
hose who remain. It seems doubtful that the
rea can provide an acceptable residential en-
ironment for more than about 150,000 people.
robably a majority of people living in the inner

city occupy a physical environment which has
not seemed desirable by any American standard
since the First World War.

Around this inner city is a middle city of 45
square miles of land in a ring annexed between
1890 and 1920. Here the residential neighborhoods were often developed under the Building
Code of 1911, the first building code, and are
still structurally sound and often attractive. But
residential lots are rarely wider than 30 feet and,
given the marked propensity of Detroiters for
single-family or at most two-family houses, this is
insufficient for the desired garages and yards.

At its peak in 1930, the population of this
middle city was over 800,000, at about 17,000
per square mile. It is now a little over 600,000 at
14,000 per square mile, and if average incomes
continue to rise the density may not stabilize
above 10,000 per square mile.

There are about 10,000 people per square
mile today living in the 80 square miles in an
outer ring of land annexed by Detroit between
1920 and 1927. These nearly 800,000 persons
occupy houses developed under a subdivision regulation of 1918, which was a kind of city plan, as
well as a zoning ordinance of 1940. Lots and
streets are relatively wide, and residential neighborhoods tend to be protected from commercial
and industrial land uses. There is no decline of
population in this outer city.

The kinds of environments in the suburbs are
at least as various as in the central city. Older
suburbs may have rings of progressively older
houses from their city limits to their own central
business districts, with smaller-scale versions of
the central city's slums in their oldest, dilapi-
dated, most densely settled parts. Newer suburbs
sometimes have no central business district at all,
but consist of mile after mile of mass-produced
houses which are all wooden boxes for lower-
income families or all brick boxes for middle-
income families.

There are in the suburbs many square miles of
urban housing in settings with rural and small-
town charm. They represent life's goal for many
families and would represent a desperate deprivation to others whose joy is in the bustle of city
street life and heterogeneous social interaction.
There are spots of rural slums — very rarely

even shacks with dirt floors — inhabited by people who are too poor or too private for the city slums, which are crowded and at the same time protected by building codes which raise costs.

In all this urban area, there are no slums where hundreds crowd together to sleep in the streets as in some cities of the East. There are no vast estates with palaces, with servant families in separate buildings, as in or near some cities of the East and West. But there is just about everything between.

This pattern of metropolitan urban environment is often labeled urban sprawl, or perhaps suburban sprawl. It is often roundly condemned as economically and politically inefficient, which it certainly is. The metropolis constitutes a single economic system, and it would be far more efficient if it were a single political system. In metropolitan Detroit, the 130 units of local government (cities, villages, and townships) could save many tax dollars simply by jointly purchasing their office supplies, not to mention what savings could be accomplished by their merger.

To be understood, the problem of urban sprawl needs to be analyzed as two separate problems: the problem of the "wasteful" use of land and the problem of "inefficient" multiple local governments. The first problem is probably not going to be solved because its solution would require a smaller, or a less-urban, or a less-affluent population, and none of these changes seems probable.

Most families with children want more space and more privacy and will pay whatever they have to pay, and can pay, to get it. When they settle in small suburbs their local taxes do not cover their fair share of the costs of governing the metropolis. So state or national governments will have to collect higher taxes and subsidize needy units of local government, including both poor and aging central cities and poor and aging suburbs.

The problem of multiple local governments is probably not going to be solved either, because (for one reason) a metropolitan mayor would, in many instances, represent more political muscle than the governor of the surrounding "sovereign" state or states. The doctrine of States' Rights is

too important a defender of regional differences between North, South, and West to be abandoned in the foreseeable future. Significantly, it is STATE laws governing local incorporation and annexation which would have to change in order to end suburbanization. Now that suburban residents outnumber central city residents, the opportunity for such change is probably past.

In summary, the environment of "urban sprawl" is probably here to stay for a long time. It may be preferable to any feasible alternative IF population growth stops short of destroying essential nonurban ecosystems, AND its full costs are paid somehow, AND special-purpose metropolitan authorities provide such essential metropolitan systems as water, sewer, parks, and transportation.

*Detroit's Technology.*

Considering technology in relation to urban social organization calls for two points to be made. First, it is the continued mechanization of agriculture which accounts for much of the rapid growth of cities like Detroit. Before 1920 it was the export of farm labor by Europe which was relevant. In the United States while the total labor force grew from 42 million to 64 million, the farm labor force declined from 11 million in 1920 to 4 million in 1960, and a fair share of rural-to-urban migrants settled in Detroit.

Second, the continued mechanization of industrial processes is having a profound effect on Detroit's organization. This is apparent in the information for 1953 and 1965 which indicates a DECLINE of 69,000 in the number of blue-collar workers going to work on an average weekday and an INCREASE of 79,000 in the number of white-collar workers (see Table II).

There is a clear implication here that the present trend of change in technology is bringing about the upgrading of population which is so desirable for the purpose of ecological reform. White-collar workers with their higher incomes, lower fertility, and greater education and adaptability are replacing blue-collar workers. Urban discontent, blue-collar unemployment, and a shortage of professional and technical workers suggest, however, that social organization is not responding to changes in technology as rapidly as it might.

*Social Organization*

The complexity of the organization of a population is proportional to the amount of differentiation within it. Every human population is organized at least to the extent that there is a pattern to the ways that different age and sex groupings are expected to relate to one another. Commonly there are at least two additional kinds of differentiation in urban populations: Those producing subcommunities and those producing strata.

Human communities are divided into SUBCOM-MUNITIES by the presence of in-marrying groups within them. That is, if a member of any particular subgroup in a population normally selects a mate from within that subgroup, and their offspring normally become a part of that subgroup, then whatever difference it is that distinguishes the subgroup continues over the generations and marks off a subcommunity. Black Detroiters comprise one such subcommunity, as do Japanese Christians in Japanese cities or Irish Protestants in Irish cities.

The second kind of differentiation is between the STRATA of the population having differing shares of resources such as income, education, and power. The number of people on differing occupational levels is an indicator of strata because families headed by blue-collar workers (such as craftsmen, operatives, or laborers) have on the average less income and less education than families headed by white-collar workers

| Year and place of residence | all workers | blue collar | white collar |
|---|---|---|---|
| 1953 — Total | 1,004,000 | 585,000 | 419,000 |
| Detroit | 664,000 | 394,000 | 270,000 |
| Suburbs | 340,000 | 191,000 | 149,000 |
| 1965 — Total | 1,014,000 | 516,000 | 498,000 |
| Detroit | 460,000 | 263,000 | 197,000 |
| Suburbs | 554,000 | 253,000 | 301,000 |

**DETROIT WORKERS RESIDENCE AND OCCUPATIONAL LEVEL.** "Workers" are persons going to work on an average weekday. Sources: 1953 Detroit Metropolitan Area Traffic Study, and 1965 Detroit Regional Transportation and Land Use Study; see reference 9.

(such as clerks, sales people, businessmen, or professionals).

The organizing of heterogeneous urban populations in subcommunities and strata is a trial-and-error process, and what is effective and becomes lasting is that particular organization which favors activities beneficial to a particular population with a particular technology in a particular environment. There appear to be four general kinds of activities which are universal in cities (as well as other social systems) because their consequences — or "functions" — are prerequisites for social survival. These are domestic, communal, economic, and political activities.

DOMESTIC ACTIVITIES are those having to do with maintaining the pattern of the community by producing children and raising them properly. They are also concerned with the care and feeding of the human organism, giving it a place to sleep, and emotional support, whether it is young or old. Domestic activities have to vary in systematic ways, so that people are "turned out" who find it appropriate to be janitors and barbers and riveters and electricians and scholars and clerks and salespeople and housewives and grocers and mayors and ministers and engineers and all of whatever kinds of people a community needs.

COMMUNAL ACTIVITIES are those having to do with integrating into workable groups all the various kinds of individuals turned out by families. Any kind or degree of specialization is a waste of time and a threat to cohesion without appropriate and sufficient integration. Some communal activities are informally organized — friendship cliques, for example. Some communal activities are formally organized — education and religion, for example. The family is the traditional setting for domestic activities; the neighborhood is the traditional setting for communal activities.

ECONOMIC ACTIVITIES are those having to do with providing the resources necessary for maintaining all the other kinds of activities. Economic resources include food, clothing, shelter, medicine, automobiles, or whatever is necessary for the survival of ways of life, and money is a representation of all such resources. Nonmaterial resources such as power or education may be valued for themselves or for their contribution to control over material resources.

POLITICAL ACTIVITIES are those having to do with decisions about who gets what. Generally such decisions are made according to the rules of the game within the family, the community, or the business. But whenever there is uncertainty or conflict, the "rules of the game" may be invented or clarified by political activities. This leadership function becomes of critical importance when an organization is under attack from within or from without.

A system of social organization is essentially an arrangement for integrating strata and subcommunities so that the necessary domestic, communal, economic, and political activities are carried out without undue social conflict.

*Detroit's Organization.*

Like many other cities, Detroit has had serious organizational problems.

Subcommunities as inmarrying groups maintain distinctive patterns of domestic and communal activities. Nearly all Detroiters are members of one or another of four subcommunities: white Protestant (41 percent), black Protestant (15 percent), white Catholic (35 percent), or Jewish (4 percent). Nearly all parents wish to have their children marry within their group, and their children comply anywhere from 4 out of 5 times (among white Protestants) to 99 to 100 times (among black Protestants).[10] In Detroit it is the racially different subcommunities which now SEEM to pose the major organizational problem.

Until the 1960s many white and black Detroiters thought that the Detroit black Protestant subcommunity was maintained separately only by discriminatory practices of white Detroiters. As racial integration began to emerge as an important community goal, however, it began to seem that there were distinctive patterns of domestic and communal activities in which black Detroiters took pride — distinctive practices of language, child rearing, religion, friendship, and leisure, for example.

It came to be observed that some white Protestants, some white Catholics, and some Jews wanted to "integrate" with other subcommu-

nities, but most of each group did not. Most wanted their children to marry within their subcommunity and live in neighborhoods which offered friends, churches, stores, and other facilities distinctive to their subcommunities. Many black Detroiters began to decide they wanted the same option of integration or VOLUNTARY seg-regation open to them. But this desire applied only to domestic and communal activities. To understand how Detroit came to be wracked by racial violence in 1967 requires consideration of the various strata and of "classes."

Generally speaking, the more valued the economic activities of an individual are, the higher is his money INCOME The more valued his political activities are, the greater is the POWER he has to exercise. The more valued his communal activities are, the greater is the PRESTIGE he is accorded. A larger amount of any one of these resources tends to create some kind of claim or expectation or at a least a wish for a larger amount of the other two. The more valued the domestic activities of an individual are, the greater is the ESTEEM (or love) he is accorded, but this distribution is perhaps independent of the other three. The Detroit population is stratified in levels ranging from negligible income to income in excess of a million dollars a year, in levels ranging from no power at all to very great power indeed, and from no prestige to the highest prestige.

Social classes come into existence as significantly different ways of life to the extent that domestic and communal activities are adapted to distinctive economic and political experiences. In other words, classes are kinds of subcommunities which are created when families adapt to strata positions. Classes persist to the extent that they are inmarrying groups and to the extent that economic and political experiences continue to reward the adaptations they reflect.

It is probable that there is a very loose system of five social classes in Detroit as in other American cities.[11] There are as many versions of a LOWER-CLASS way of life among about 10 percent of Detroiters as there are nationality, regional, racial, and religious groupings among them. One common element is some kind of handicap that prevents regular employment, such as the absence of education, or chronic physical or mental ill health, or a personality reflecting nonurbanized culture, especially when such culture is disorganized upon importation into the city.

Lower-class life is adapted to an absence of regular earnings so that there is relatively little valuing of "ambition" in the higher-class sense; but money is valued. Lower-class life is adapted to an absence of power so that there is relatively little valuing of the ability to exercise "authority" in the higher-class sense; but strength is valued. The absence of prestige seems to weaken the valuing of "virtue."

About 40 percent of Detroiters more or less reflect a WORKING-CLASS way of life adapted to the regular receipt of hourly wage income from blue-collar jobs. Sometimes participation in labor unions gives working-class people more experience with political power and the exercise of authority than can be had in the next higher class. Their relatively low prestige allows working-class people to drink beer from cans while sitting on their porches in their undershirts, as would never be done in good higher-class families, but they value "virtue" enough to strive to "keep out of trouble" with external authority.

Another 40 percent of Detroiters are LOWER MIDDLE CLASS, and more or less reflect a way of life adapted to the relatively greater prestige accorded to holders of salaried white-collar jobs than to wage earners. They defend their prestige by valuing "virtue" more than any other class. But lower middle class ambition is limited to 35-or-40-hour-a-week positions and to the education which promises better positions. Their exercise of power tends to be limited to voting.

The (perhaps) 9.9 percent of Detroiters in the UPPER MIDDLE CLASS are more likely to be involved with power in the nominating and campaigning activities of the political parties. But their most distinctive trait is their ambition, which is greater than that in any other class. Upper middle class families can come to revolve around the 70 or 80 hour work weeks associated with their heads' careers. Their salary, profit, or professional fee incomes are likely to be supplemented by dividends or interest or rent because they are the apprentice wealthy as well as the

apprentice powerful. Their secure prestige may allow them a little less virtue and a little more pleasure, at least in the form of the cocktail hour, or less sexual inhibition, or the enjoyment of some kinds of culture.

The 0.1 percent of Detroiters in the UPPER CLASS (an estimated 3500 people) may pursue the enjoyment of life even more freely because they need not be quite so laboriously ambitious. This is not to say that it is easy to manage family wealth so as to derive a good family income while continuing to augment capital. But help can be hired for that task while more time is given to the specialty of this class, which has been described as "gracious living." When it is called for, they generally exercise power so as to conserve the social system which has rewarded them so well.

These greatly oversimplified sketches hide more of the complexity of social stratification processes than they reveal. They are intended only to give some substance to the generalization that the experiences of life in different strata are so different that having adapted to one stratum makes it difficult, later, to adjust to another. Generally speaking, this is why more jobs at higher occupational levels can be produced by a changing technology more rapidly than people can change so as to be ready to take them: It is because of social class. To repeat, social classes come into existence as significantly different ways of life to the extent that domestic and communal activities (in families, cliques, schools, and churches) are adapted to distinctive economic and political experiences.

Of all the components of social organization, social classes are the most important to the ecological problem. It is the lower classes which have the highest rates of growth. One study suggested reproduction rates of 1.52 for farm laborers, of 1.35 for urban laborers, 1.22 for blue-collar workers, 0.98 for clerks and salespeople, and 0.87 for professional people.[11] (Large families are reprehensible in upper and middle strata, too, of course.)

It is the lower classes which have the least ability to bear the costs of ecological reform. (Of course, there will also be resistance to increased costs from upper and middle strata.) And it is the lower classes which are least likely to direct themselves to rational changes from the practices approved by traditional authority: "Men of lower class position, who do not have the opportunity for self-direction in work, come to regard it as a matter of necessity to conform to authority, both on and off the job," and raise their children accordingly.[8]

This self-perpetuating adaptation of a domestic activity (in child rearing) to an economic activity (on-the-job experience), in conjunction with the observation that Detroit has always had a lower class, could lead to a great deal of pessimism about the likelihood of population upgrading. But another fact to consider is that Detroit as an urban ecosystem is known to have successfully upgraded one lower class after another during the past century of industrialization. Classes, like cities themselves, represent adaptations, and they change along with changes in the ecosystem characteristics to which they are adapted.

At the turn of the century it was Irish hooligans whose names crowded the police blotters. Today Detroit's police commissioner is named Murphy. In the 1920s, it was Italians and Poles who predominated in the crowded slums. Now there are jokes about the great frequency with which Italian and Polish names appear on the roster of Detroit policemen, and the mayor of Detroit is of Polish descent. This upgrading has been accompanied by sharp declines in the birth rates of these groups.[12]

It was not until World War II that black Detroiters were allowed to enter white-collar jobs in any number. Since that time, the beginning of the end of racial discrimination has revealed a tremendous reservoir of black ambition and talent. The number of black Detroiters in white-collar positions increased by 73 percent between 1953 and 1965. The sons of factory workers (and sometimes the grandsons of slaves) are salesmen and teachers, photographers and chemists, professors and judges.

But that is where the happy story must end, for the present. The fact is that (as of 1965) 76 percent of black Detroiters are still blue-collar workers at a time when the number of blue-collar jobs is shrinking. The percentage of black households headed by someone unemployed and looking for work is three times the percentage of white households. The resulting discontent is a major Detroit problem. Of course, Detroit is not alone with this problem. Blacks face whites in competition and conflict in cities all over the United States and in a few other Western nations as well. In fact, it is highly interesting and important that a major problem in the social organization of urban ecosystems in many parts of the world is this problem of subcommunity conflict.

The battles between the strata foreseen by Marx and Lenin have not developed exactly as predicted. But some of their concerns about class conflict are involved in subcommunity conflicts as blacks face whites in Detroit, Moslems face Hindus in New Delhi, as Buddhists face Catholics in Saigon, as Biafrans face other Nigerians in Lagos, as Catholics face Protestants in Dublin, and so on and on. Everywhere the subcommunities are in conflict over social organization and its stratification system for the distribution of wealth, power, and prestige. People do not want to be all alike, but increasingly they demand equal opportunities for upgrading, for getting ahead.

This is an old story in Detroit, as in many cities. An original organization of northern white Protestants has competed and conflicted with a long series of migrating waves of white Catholics (subdivided among many nationalities) and of Jews (subdivided at least into western and eastern Europeans). The numerically smaller but equally sharp contemporary problem posed by some white Protestant migrants from the American South (so-called hillbillies) establishes the fact that this is not a matter of any specific religious or racial differences; it is a more general problem of subcommunities within urban social organization. How, then did this urban ecosystem work so as to upgrade subcommunities which came earlier into its organization? This is the theme in the following consideration of interaction between the ecosystem components.

## Population and Environment

A first principle of urban development reflects the interaction between population and environment: Physical cities expand outward from their centers as their populations grow. Given density limits of any kind this is obvious enough, but it has some important implications. For one thing, it implies that in the absence of continued annexation a "flight to the suburbs" (in the sense of a continually increasing suburban percentage of urban-area population) is inevitable if the population is growing, even if the population is all one race. This has been overlooked in some discussions.

Another implication is that housing will tend to be newer in rings at increasing distances from the city center.[13] To the extent that newer housing is better housing (and it always is if everything else is equal), higher strata within the population will tend to live farther from the city center. Exceptions to this principle are numerous in Detroit, ranging from expensive apartments at the center to dirt-floor shacks on the outer edge of the suburbs. But if incomes of families in broad rings out from the old inner city are averaged, the averages are progressively higher with increasing distance from the center. Median employment earnings in 1965 were $6400 in inner Detroit, $8500 in outer Detroit, and $9600 in the suburbs.[9] This measure understates the differences, because lower nonemployment incomes (from retirement and welfare sources) are more frequent in the older rings, and higher nonemployment incomes (from investments) are more frequent in the newer rings. A consequence of this pattern is that the upgrading of subcommunities has been accompanied by their mobility outward through the rings of the physical city, which might be called the upward and outward principle.

There are many neighborhoods in Detroit which have been successively "invaded" by families of a series of nationalities and religions, in the order in which they migrated to the city. A particular working-class neighborhood might have been successively occupied by Irish, then Italian, then Jewish, then black working-class families. Another consequence of these principles is that the growth of the size of each stratum leads to another kind of "invasion" of neighborhoods so that some, as they age, have been successively occupied by middle-class, then working-class, then lower-class families.

This means, of course, that high rates of crime, of dependency, and of other traits associated with the lower strata have always tended to be concentrated in the central inner city of Detroit, regardless of what subcommunities happened to be the newest and the most centralized at any given time. Subcommunities tend to develop a taste for law and order after they have achieved some of the fruits of upgrading which they then wish to conserve. It is likely that the most violent and nonconformist of the newcomer groups were the earliest, from western Europe, rather than the latest, from the South.[14] Regardless of such possible variations, upward and outward has persisted as a first principle relating the organized population to its environment.

*Technology and Environment*

One relationship between technology and environment is reflected in the spatial distribution of places of work. Both industrial and commercial work places, like residences, have tended to occupy land on a less and less concentrated basis. In the eighteenth and nineteenth centuries, businesses were concentrated where overland routes met at the Detroit River. In the late nineteenth and the twentieth centuries five major railroad routes converged on Detroit, and they were linked to form a band of rails roughly following around the city limits of 1890. (All the railroad rights-of-way presently serving Detroit were in existence in 1890.)

During the growth period accompanying the rise of the automobile (Detroit grew from less than half a million to over a million and a half between 1910 and 1930), industry spread away from the river along the rail lines which had encircled the city, while the city expanded all around this industrial belt. Then, particularly after World War II, the car and the truck allowed industry and commerce to move to less expensive land on the edge of the urbanized area while remaining accessible to raw materials, to workers, and to customers.

Both the deconcentration of the residential population and the deconcentration of places of work reached a turning point in Detroit in the 1953-1965 period. In 1953, Detroit was a place of RESIDENCE for 66 percent of the area's workers; in 1965, for only 45 percent. In 1953, Detroit was the place of WORK for 66 percent of the area's workers; in 1965, only 48 percent. The City's loss of its majorities was not due simply to a slower rate of growth. It experienced a net loss of 204,000 resident workers and of 174,000 places of work (see Table III).

| Year and place of Residence | All workers | Place of work | |
|---|---|---|---|
| | | Detroit | Suburbs |
| 1953 – Total | 1,004,000 | 660,000 | 344,000 |
| Detroit | 664,000 | 510,000 | 154,000 |
| Suburbs | 340,000 | 150,000 | 190,000 |
| 1965 – Total | 1,014,000 | 486,000 | 528,000 |
| Detroit | 460,000 | 302,000 | 158,000 |
| Suburbs | 554,000 | 184,000 | 370,000 |

**III**

DETROIT WORKERS RESIDENCE AND PLACE OF WORKING. "Workers" are persons going to work on an average weekday. Sources: 1953 Detroit Metropolitan Area Traffic Study, and 1965 Detroit Regional Transportation and Land Use Study, see reference 9.

If all that was involved here was a less intensive use of the central city's land, with reduced densities of homes and businesses, the city's problems would be quite different than they are. But the character of the ecosystem — particularly the upward and outward population process and the process of technological change — has meant a much more difficult situation. Consider this: Between 1953 and 1965 Detroit lost 131,000 BLUE–COLLAR workers, while the suburbs gained only 62,000. The one thing Detroit kept a majority of was blue-collar workers (51 percent of all in the area in 1965). Detroit lost only 73,000 WHITE–COLLAR workers, but the number living in the suburbs increased by 152,000. The benefits of population upgrading due to technological change have accrued much more to the suburbs than to the central city.

To say it another way, the central city plays a specialized role in the urban ecosystem. The character of that role is revealed by the nature of the work trips made by the area's workers. There are about a half million jobs and about a half million resident workers in Detroit; another half million jobs and half million workers in the suburbs. Yet 342,000 work trips cross the Detroit city limits on an average week day. In relation to worker income, there are twice as many low-

income Detroiters going to work in the suburbs as there are low-income suburbanites going to work in Detroit. And the number of high-income suburbanites who go to work in Detroit is about twice as high as the number of high-income Detroiters who go to work in the suburbs (90,000 compared to 47,000).

This means that Detroit provides a pool of low-income workers for suburban jobs and a pool of high-income jobs for suburban workers. Detroit gets the problems; the suburbs get the resources. Perhaps the most revealing single work-trip statistic is the increase by 4000 in the number of work trips from Detroit homes to suburban jobs (from 154,000 to 158,000) in 1953-1965. Since the number of jobs in Detroit is greater than the number of workers living there, this particular increase might be unexpected. On closer inspection, it proves to be the net result of 14,000 fewer white Detroiters going to suburban jobs and 18,000 more black Detroiters going to suburban jobs. In one stroke the net increase is an index of (1) the segregation of black Detroiters within the city, (2) the concentration of black Detroiters in blue-collar jobs, (3) the shift of blue-collar jobs to new factories in the suburbs, and (4) the decline in number of blue-collar jobs, so that blue-collar workers must go where new jobs are, or not work (13,000 inner-city workers were unemployed in 1965, which was 8.5 percent of the inner-city labor force, while the rate in outer Detroit was 2.9 percent, and in the suburbs 1.6 percent).

At this point some of the obstacles to the upgrading of poor people in Detroit begin to become clearer. Not only are blue-collar jobs fewer in number; they are also increasingly inaccessible to inner-city workers. Work trips taking an hour or longer increased from 11 percent to 14 percent of all work trips by inner-city workers between 1953 and 1965; hour-long trips DECREASED from 9 percent to 6 percent of all work trips in the area as a whole.

Part of the reason is that fewer inner-city workers have cars. There are six cars for every ten workers in the inner city; six cars for every six workers in the outer city; six cars for every five workers in the suburbs. There are no buses to many of the suburban sites of new factories, while, on the average, the percentage of jobs held by workers who live in the inner city is twice as high in census tracts reached by bus as in census tracts not reached by bus.[15] A newly formed regional transit authority has been trying for a few years to create an area-wide bus service, and it may someday succeed. Still, one imagines more and more inner-city workers on more and more buses chasing fewer and fewer blue-collar jobs farther and farther into the suburbs, into an impossible future.

The contrast between the work-trip situation just described and the work-trip situation in the early decades of this century, when the upgrading of European migrants was underway, could hardly be greater. The streetcar and bus were able to link all places of residence with all places of work from the time the urbanized area covered 15 square miles (in 1890) until it covered 150 square miles (in 1940). But now that over 500 square miles are urbanized, the most recent migrants from the southern United States face a situation in which over a third of a million jobs are in census tracts unreached by public transportation.

*Technology and Organization*

Another important change is in the interaction between technology and the economic activities of urban organization. It was the rapid increase in jobs for factory workers (the semiskilled, or operatives) which made cities like Detroit a goal for European immigrants. The number of such jobs in the cities of the United States grew from 3 million in 1900, to 6 million in 1920, to 9 million in 1940, to 12 million in 1960. An increase of 3 million jobs every 20 years is rapid growth indeed. But notice the falling rate of increase. It was 100 percent in 1900-1920, only 50 percent in 1920-1940, and only 33 percent in 1940-1960. There has been no comparable decline in the rates at which migrants come looking for such jobs.

Now the situation is even worse, as the continued mechanization of urban technology has reversed the trend completely, and the number of manual jobs is actually declining. The European migrant to United States cities was sucked up the urban occupational ladder by the vacuum created by industrialization. The mi-grant now moving into cities from American farms and small towns is being blown off the bottom rung of the urban ladder by the negative winds of "automation."

The European immigrant was also pushed up the urban ladder by the floods of newcomers who followed him. There was an increase of tens of thousands of foreign-born whites in the Detroit area in every decade between 1880 and 1930, when the number peaked at more than half a million. Countless immigrants and their children, after a little time, found work outside the factories, supervising and selling and clerking and teaching and administering, because what little experience or skill they may have accumulated looked valuable in comparison to the lack of experience and skill of those thousands who were even newer to urban life and work.

The big push "upwards and outwards" no longer characterizes the urban ecosystem. The most recent increment of nonurban migrants to the city population may indeed be the last, since less than 7 percent of the national labor force remains in agriculture. Increasingly, the average migrant to the city is in the same stratum as the average person already in the city, as rural-urban migration is replaced by interurban migration. No more big upward push by migrant masses entering the bottom stratum is to be expected. This change not only accounts for some of the difficulty in upgrading contemporary urban poor people. It also suggests that one last victory in changing "peasants" to urbanites can remove the urban lower class from all future pages of American history. Just one more time . . . .

*Interaction Within Organization*

Perhaps this is a good point at which to note that one terrible problem elsewhere in the world does seem to have disappeared from the pages of the history of Detroit (and other American cities). This is the problem of interreligious conflict, such as sees Catholic and Protestant at war in Dublin, and Jew and Moslem at war in Jerusalem, for example.

Such violence is not unknown in Detroit. Within living memory groups including Italian–Catholic and Jewish gangsters terrorized Detroit homes and businesses. But that was merely a minor regression (occasioned by the social tragedies of Prohibition in the 1920s and Depression in the 1930s), and by no means as serious as the waves of crimes, vice, violent strikes, and riots which characterized most American and European cities in the nineteenth century.[16]

The way that such groups became sufficiently integrated to compete instead of to do battle has not been documented in Detroit as it has for Italians in New Haven,[17] for example, or for other groupings elsewhere, but there is no reason to suppose that the process has varied greatly. First of all there was the step of one common communal activity for everyone — education in a single integrated school system. Public schools were first established in Detroit in 1838, when the city was divided into seven school districts each to levy its own assessment. The results were unsatisfactory because the wealthier districts promptly had good schools going while the poorer districts did not. In 1842, a citywide school tax was authorized, and a single Board of Education was selected.

For the next hundred years the Detroit school system operated as a keystone of ecosystem organization. It took most of its taxes from the wealthier districts and operated schools everywhere which set definite limits on the extent to which domestic practices could convince the young English or Irish or Polish Detroiter that his or any other group was always inferior or superior to others. To the extent that it offered a roughly equal education to all, the city's school system played a crucial role in population upgrading and religious accommodation. After 1950, the multitude of suburban (and parochial) school systems put the physical city's organization back where it had been in 1838-1842, with regard to education. Wealthy suburban school systems are not helping with upgrading OR with racial accommodation.

The second step in the effective integration of the religious subcommunities seems to have been the replacement of family firms and elitist local governments by large corporate and political bureaucracies. For all their problem of rigidity, these entities did reduce (without eliminating) the obstacles to upgrading represented by nepotism and favoritism. What suburbanization and the deconcentration of business have done is to make a third of the jobs physically inaccessible to inner-city workers, and to replace one local government with 130 city, village, and township governments. What the single city government did for local politics was the same thing the single school system did for education. It allowed ward politics which soaked the rich (as much as they were willing to permit) and gave legal, medical, financial, and all kinds of social services to poor people from the hands of ward bosses in return for votes.

Bureaucratized social work is probably capable of doing even more effectively everything that machine politics ever did for upgrading the poor. But the rich — as represented by new homes and new work places — are no longer in the city to finance it, and state and federal government has been slow to provide the essential substitutes. The present crisis will not rekindle religious animosity only because no religious group is concentrated in the inner city.

This is not to say that the physical city is without religious segregation. Catholic, Jewish, and WASP (white Anglo-Saxon Protestant) neighborhoods are common.[10] WASP neighborhoods make clear why it is that religious segregation does not lead to violence in contemporary Detroit. They tend to be both the wealthier or, when occupied by Appalachian whites or hillbillies, among the poorest, and therefore do not suggest unequal opportunity FOR THE SUBCOMMUNITY. Religious segregation in Detroit is largely (1) voluntary, (2) based on pride, and (3) relatively independent of class, in the sense that each religion has richer and poorer neighborhoods.

This seems to have been the third and final step toward peaceful religious integration in Detroit. For those minorities who wanted it, the voluntary segregation of domestic and communal activities has remained possible. Involuntary segregation remains fraught with friction.

But what has been absolutely essential is the substantial integration of all subcommunities in their economic and political activities.

The way to religious integration in the earlier urban ecosystem is probably the way to racial integration in the future urban ecosystem. There would seem to be no necessity to return to the violent and disorganized cities of the pre-industrial period, because history shows what it took to bring them to "law and order." The noted social historian Oscar Handlin wrote in 1961 that racial differences were a problem: "Apart from this exception, however, the city has achieved a greater degree of internal order, with less social tension, than ever before in its modern history."[16] It is ironic that he wrote at the beginning of a decade of widespread racial conflict.

It is conventional to suppose that racial differences are much harder to integrate than religious and nationality differences, but that may not be the whole truth. After all, the United States only began a concerted effort to spread the American Dream across racial lines AFTER urban ecosystems were in serious trouble for other reasons. Religious and nationality violence in cities elsewhere, and relative racial peace in cities of South America, Hawaii, and Canada where racial mixtures were established before the present period, might raise doubts about race as an inevitable cause of conflict. Perhaps the more important cause is severe disappointment about upgrading, relative to expectations.

When rapidly industrializing cities were rapidly upgrading their newcomers, those newcomers were generally integrated in the three steps of (1) common public schooling, (2) advancement by merit in corporate and governmental bureaucracies, and (3) voluntary domestic and communal segregation. The present analysis of the interaction of urban ecosystem components has pointed to new and serious problems which have interrupted rapid upgrading — problems of "automation" and of suburbanization in particular. Solving the problem of white racism — as essential as it is — will not solve the other elemental problems of urban ecosystems. It seems possible that racial

conflict has obscured ecosystem problems which would be much (although obviously not entirely) the same were the total population of a single race. Would racial homogeneity increase the number of blue-collar jobs, or get buses from the inner city to new suburban factories, or give the central city anything other than an aging tax base depreciating in value?

Racial homogeneity would probably yield a more nearly equitable allocation of prestige than is now the case. But Jewish Detroiters are an interesting case in this regard. They have usually experienced prejudice, or a denial of prestige, wholly inappropriate to their moral conformity. But their urban experience before they immigrated (often occasioned by laws forbidding them to own land in European nations) gave them a valuable head start in competition with immigrant peasants in American cities. For that reason, if for no other, they have probably experienced a more rapid upgrading than any other group in the United States. And they have been a notably nonviolent subcommunity. It seems, then, that the mere fact of the denial of prestige is insufficient to elicit violence from a subcommunity if there is also sufficient opportunity for upgrading.

This suggests that getting the urban ecosystem functioning again so as to resume the rapid upgrading of newcomers might solve the urban problem, as well as helping to solve the environmental problem. Before considering how urban ecosystems change and what it might require to change them in the desired direction, the question of variations from the Detroit model deserves consideration.

## How Cities Differ

Detroit and most other American cities serve interchangeably as examples of major trends in the urbanization of America,[18] and the general study of urbanization finds similar patterns and problems in cities all over the world.[3] For example, the presence of strata and subcommunities in large cities seems near-universal. Also, no societies WITH CITIES seem inclined to resist opportunities to industrialize, in spite of all the problems associated with such change. Preurban hunting and fishing societies, in contrast, can hold out against both trends of urbanization and industrialization for centuries (American Indians present a strange, tragic, and in some ways admirable example of such a preurban society).[19] The tendency of rapidly growing industrial cities to form rings of development is another common trait.

Other patterns of settlement and land use, in addition to rings, are also common, however, and provide a major source of variation. When the uses of land are examined in any detail in Detroit and other cities, it becomes clear very quickly that consistent differences between rings are the result of averaging a large amount of variation within rings. This variation reflects the operation of several other principles of urban development.

One is the extension of industrial and commercial land out along major transportation routes (water, rail, and highway) from city centers. Such strips or belts tend to devalue adjacent land for residential use, and create sectors of distinctive land utilization which cut through the rings. Rivers, mountains, and even minor topographical variations usually distort the ring pattern at least a little. Also, subcenters can form at transportation intersections and produce on a smaller scale rings of their own, interrupting the pattern of larger rings spreading from the original center. Older suburbs can constitute large and important subcenters of development. Finally, neighborhoods sometimes hold on to their symbolic character (as high-status sections, or ethnic quarters, or vice districts, or cultural areas) by the force of tradition when the force of ring development would dictate otherwise.

The rings apparent in the description of Detroit are not only the product of a great deal of generalizing; they are also the product of rapid industrial growth. In the early nineteenth century before industrialization, the settlement pattern of Detroit had a kind of "ring" distribution, but its quality was reversed from what is now the pattern. The homes of the wealthy were located on tree-lined streets just off the central city square, and the poorest housing tended to be on much less expensive land far removed from the center. Nonindustrialized towns and cities in and outside the United States still often reflect this pattern.[3]

In brief, the physical city is shaped by variation and interaction of population (for example, growing or not), environment (for example, rivers and heights), organization (for example, strata and subcommunities), and technology (for example, industrial and other). There are some clear principles of development, but they all act at once and the results are rarely predictable except at a very general level. The behavior involved is purposive, but the consequences which comprise the city are commonly unanticipated. Therefore, physical cities differ widely in the details of their structure. The urban ecosystem is the product of a process of trial and error; many people build some part of it, but nobody can be said to have built the city.

A major difference between older industrial cities like Detroit and cities in the economically underdeveloped countries is different kinds of growth. Detroit industrialized while American birth rates were falling and the city's population was probably not replacing itself. Since birth rates were lowest in the higher strata, this gave opportunities for migrant upgrading.

> The overwhelming contribution to the present growth of the urban population in the underdeveloped areas is by natural increase in the cities — the excess of births over deaths ... rural to urban migrants, coming to the city in India, are competing with newborn people or the youth already in the city, for whatever jobs the city can provide ... it is a fundamentally new situation.[1]

The added difficulty for population upgrading created by such rapid natural growth is apparent, and it seems it will be a long time before the industrializing nations will be able to help save the earth. Presumably it is true for these new urban migrants, as it has been for so many others, that, "as soon as it looks as though fewer children will make an economic difference, they have fewer."[19] But today's industrializing nations do not have the immense wealth that the colonizing European nations had, nor the immense natural resources of the United States. Having fewer children does not make much economic difference on the bottom stratum in nations industrializing more slowly. Everywhere the problem is how to speed population upgrading.

A difference between cities in communist and capitalist countries is as follows: Cities like Detroit have an ecosystem organization in which dominance or leadership functions are divided on a competitive basis between business and government. [20] This is an essential meaning of the "capitalist" system, and it has the incalculable value of limiting the concentration of power. It also has the shortcoming that there is no single institution with the responsibility and authority to plan to cope with such broad urban problems as environmental pollution and population upgrading. Even if physical Detroit had one government instead of 130, that government could not direct industrial processes (such as those which are increasing pollutants and decreasing blue-collar jobs) without risking attacks as "socialist."

Communist countries, where political activities clearly dominate economic activities, are at an opposite extreme, and most other countries fall in between. European urban planners (from both sides of the Iron Curtain) who visit the United States commonly marvel at the relative professional impotence of their American counterparts. European planners can make much more meaningful and ambitious plans for coping with the urban ecosystem than American planners can.

In the writer's experience, however, European planners when pressed for solutions to the big problems confess to the same difficulties with growth and cost and the intractable forces of urban expansion which trouble Detroit and other American cities. The amount of centralized control must make some differences between the cities of the world, but everywhere the organization of urban ecosystems needs to change if population is to be upgraded and the life expectancy of environment is to be extended.

## How Cities Change

Human ecosystems, like all living systems, consist of matter activated by energy inputs. The energy activating men in cities does not move them in a random way, but according to definite instructions, or "information." There are three different kinds of "information" which interlock with one another, and together act as a kind of blueprint maintaining the general structure of urban ecosystems over the generations. [21] One or more of these kinds of information will have to change if cities are to survive.

The first kind of information is PHYSICAL. It consists of "things" distributed in time and space. One of the reasons that inner-city people act differently in the new Metropolis than they did in the old City is that the physical information they receive is different. The factories are now many miles away in the suburbs, for example. Physical information has been called "ecological" information, but the other two kinds are just as important for explaining urban ecosystems.

The second kind of information is GENETIC. The "instructions" forming each successive generation through their genes set limits on what people can do which are just as definite as the physical information in the world they come to occupy. But there is no reason to suppose that the genetic information we contain, even in combination with existing physical information, is such as to prevent solutions to our problems. The American continent presented the same basic physical information (in the form of topography and natural resources) to the Indians and to the Europeans who came here. Furthermore, it seems highly unlikely that the genetic differences between Indians and Europeans account for the difference in what they did with the continent. That difference is due to the different CULTURAL information possessed by the two groups.

This third kind of information — the cultural — includes the ecosystem component of technology. It includes a major part of the factors determining the size and mobility of population. It determines the character of the constructed part of the urban environment. [22] And it determines the variations in the forms of social organization. Cultural information always acts within the limits set by physical and genetic information. But modern culture has shown itself to be highly adaptable, so that we ought to be able to change it in problem-solving ways.

To be realistic, however, we have to observe that all through human history prophets and reformers, teachers and preachers have attempted to change patterns of culture without much success, beginning long before ecologists arrived on the scene. Individuals can change — they can "learn," they can "grow up," they can be "converted," they can exercise "free will." But in the meantime, basic cultural differences have distinguished one nationality from another for centuries. Even within American culture the Southerner, the Northerner, and the Westerner have maintained competing subcultures for more than a hundred years (not to mention the subcultures maintained by subcommunities and classes within the same city).

It is as if cultural information developed by a kind of "evolution" no more under the control of men than the evolution of the species.[2] NO ONE DESIGNED OUR CITIES. They just grew. No one "decided" that preindustrial cities would be arranged in residential rings from the higher strata outward to the lower strata, or that industrial cities would be arranged with the rings tending to run in the opposite way. They just grew that way. I have no doubt at all that if they continue to just grow, then famine and pestilence and war will set the upper limit on the size of urban populations.

Nature's way tends to preserve species (although many have become extinct), but not necessarily to preserve particular individuals. If men as particular individuals wish to avoid famine, pestilence, and war, then they will have to take conscious control — for the first time — of the evolution of their cultures and direct them toward social and ecological adaptation and reform.

We know only enough about the dynamics of the flow of cultural information to realize how very difficult this will be.[23] We know that some human individuals in every culture "do" just about everything it is possible to do. They worship other individuals and they eat other individuals, for example. Only some of the things people do become "symbolized" so that they can be shared between the members of an organized population. Symbolization is the first step in the creation of culture. The practice of running

sewer pipes into rivers came to be symbolized as "pollution" only recently. That was an essential first step, but cultural information ending water pollution requires more than that.

Some symbolized activities become "institutionalized" in the sense of becoming expected, and institutionalization is the second step in the creation of culture. Marriage, religion, working, and voting are institutionalized; so are the activities which maintain human poverty and environmental degradation. Human groups apply tremendous pressure on their members to secure conformity to their institutions, even when they are unaware of doing so. But usually not much pressure is needed.

The reason is that some symbolized, institutionalized activities become built into the personalities in a human group in the process of child rearing. This "internalization" of cultural information is the third and final step in the creation of an effective flow of cultural information. Internalization explains why we act like Americans (or whatever we are) even when we are alone, or even when we might not want to.

Cultural symbols, social institutions, and personal habits run together to make the flow of cultural information like a mighty river. Ecologists who want to change basic economic and political activities are throwing rocks up Niagara Falls.

This is a realistic assessment. But it is equally realistic to recognize that culture is constantly changing. Two facts make sense of this paradox. One is that nobody lives forever; every generation has another chance. The other is that living systems are usually cybernetic in character; they operate on a trial-and-error basis.

In cybernetic systems actions produce feedback informing an actor of the consequences of each act. Changes in feedback MAY produce new actions. Cities are giving us feedback REQUIRING new actions. We will fail to adapt only to the extent that the old culture is considered "sacred."

That is precisely why cities are likely to be the heroes of the new culture. All through human history cities have proven to be the graveyards of one sacred culture after another and the cradles of new stages in cultural evolution. In the midst of dynamic urban heterogeneity, establishments and masses of all kinds have found it impossible in the long run to sustain the myth that any one way of life is divine.

Such a myth CAN be sustained in any rural village (or hippie commune) with an organization segregated from "strangers." In that situation cultural evolution can stop, and only "outside" pressure from changing technology or environment can begin the process of social change again. It is not necessary, today, to begin to change cities. They are changing now in the disorderly, trial-and-error way they have always changed.

The greatest threat to adaptive change probably is NOT the repressive force of conservatism. It is not as strong today as it was in 1776. The greatest threat is ignorance, and particularly ignorance about the consequences of old culture and of new culture for ecosystems. It is, for example, a cause for shame that real data on the costs of suburbanization are only now becoming available.[24]

After decades of work the nation finally produced economic indicators which keep us informed of shifts in economic quantities. What we need now are social indicators informing us about shifts in the quality of life.[25] This is partly a matter of learning about the distribution as well as the gross amount of economic resources. Not nearly enough people know that the poorest 20 percent of the population has been receiving the same 5 percent of the national income every year since the 1940s, without any progress at all toward the reduction of relative poverty.

There is no national goal more important than a redistribution of income, to reduce the tremendous difference between the bottom and the top strata. This does not mean a "middle-class society." We probably need a working class, a lower and an upper middle class, an upper class, and maybe some new classes no one ever heard of before. But we do not need a lower class.

There is no national goal more important than a redistribution of income, but there are a number of goals equally important.[26] The essence of the ecological view is the recognition of the interdependence of all ecosystem components. We have to become as sensitive to changes in the Pollution Index as we are to changes in the Consumer Price Index, for example. The only reasonable goal for the 1970s is an extension of a goal popular in the 1920s — "a sound mind in a sound body" in a sound organized population with a sound technology in a sound environment.

With ecologically realistic goals and realistic indicators to tell us when we approach them, the other thing we need is urban variety. It not only "takes all kinds" to make an urban world; it takes all kinds of each kind to assure the emergence of the necessary adaptive changes. We need more than both hippies and hard hats; we need some patriotic hippies, some pacifist hard hats, and some socially radical ecologists. Nothing is sacred except life itself. Today's two-or-three-child family is no more sacred than yesterday's fertility goddess; the growth of population must soon stop because the alternative is rising death rates. Today's profits are no more sacred than yesterday's prophets; the costs of change must be paid.

## References

1. **Davis, K.** 1969. In *Growth of Population* (M. C. Shelesnyak, ed.). Gordon and Breach, New York.
2. **Lenski, G. E.** 1970. *Human Societies.* McGraw-Hill, New York.
3. **Hauser, P.M., and Schnore, L. F.,** eds. 1965. *The Study of Urbanization.* Wiley, New York.
4. **Duncan, O. D.** 1964. Social organization and the ecosystem. In *Handbook of Modern Sociology* (R. E. L. Faris, ed.). Rand McNally, Chicago, Illinois.
5. **Wolman, A.** 1961. The metabolism of cities. In *The Future Metropolis* (L. Rodwin, ed.). Braziller, New York.
6. **Myrdal, G.** 1963. *Challenge to Affluence.* Pantheon, New York.
7. **Svalastoga, K.** 1964. Social differentiation. In *Handbook of Modern Sociology* (R. E. L. Faris, ed.). Rand McNally, Chicago, Illinois.
8. **Kohn, M. L.** 1969. *Class and Conformity.* Dorsey, Homewood, Illinois.

9. **Smock, R. B.** 1967. *The Inner-City Worker.* Center for Urban Studies, The University of Michigan Dearborn Campus.

10. **Lenski, G. E.** 1961. *The Religious Factor.* Doubleday, Garden City, New York.

11. **Kahl, J. A.** 1957. *The American Class Structure.* Holt, Rinehart and Winston, New York.

12. **Mayer, A. J., and Marx, S. A.** 1957. Social change, religion, and birth rates. *Amer. J. Sociol. 62:* 383-390.

13. **Duncan B., Sabagh, R., and VanArsdol, M. D., Jr.** 1962. Patterns of city growth. *Amer. J. Sociol. 67:* 418-429.

14. **Graham, H. D., and Gurr, T. R.** 1969. *Violence in America.* National Commission on the Causes and Prevention of Violence, Washington, D.C.

15. **Smock, R. B.** 1968. *The Accessibility of Workplaces by Bus and the Employment of Inner-City Workers.* Center for Urban Studies, The University of Michigan Dearborn Campus.

16. **Handlin, O.** 1961. The social system. In *The Future Metropolis* (L. Rodwin, ed.). Braziller, New York.

17. **Myers, J. K.** 1950. Assimilation to the ecological and social systems of a community. *Amer. Sociol. Rev. 15:* 367-372.

18. **McKelvey, B. F.** 1963. *The Urbanization of America.* Rutgers University Press, New Brunswick, New Jersey.

19. **Tax, S.** 1969. In *Growth of Population* (M. C. Shelesnyak, ed.). Gordon and Breach, New York.

20. **Hawley, A. H.** 1950. *Human Ecology.* Ronald Press, New York.

21. **Margalef, R.** 1968. *Perspectives in Ecological Theory.* University of Chicago Press, Chicago, Illinois.

22. **Michelson, W. H.** 1970. *Man and His Urban Environment.* Addison-Wesley, Reading, Massachusetts.

23. **Smock, R. B.** 1969. *The Social Necessity for the Concept of Ecological Dependency.* Center for Urban Studies, The University of Michigan Dearborn Campus.

24. **Hawley, A. H., and Zimmer, B. G.** 1970. *The Metropolitan Community.* Sage, Beverly Hills, California.

25. **Bauer, R. A., ed.** 1966. *Social Indicators.* M.I.T. Press, Cambridge, Massachusetts.

26. **U. S. Department of Health, Education, and Welfare.** 1969. *Toward a Social Report.* U.S. Government Printing Office, Washington, D.C.

## Further Reading

**Duncan, O. D., and Duncan, B.** 1955. Residential distribution and occupational stratification. *Amer. J. Sociol. 60:* 493-503.

**Hawley, A. H.** 1944. Ecology and human ecology. *Social Forces 22:* 398-405.

**Lenski, G.** 1966. *Power and Privilege: A Theory of Social Stratification.* McGraw-Hill, New York.

**Schnore, L. F.** 1965. *The Urban Scene: Human Ecology and Demography.* Free Press, New York.

**Vayda, A. P., ed.** 1969. *Environment and Cultural Behavior.* Natural History Press, Garden City, New York.

**Wrigley, E. A.** 1969. *Population and History.* McGraw-Hill, New York.

# 17  Environment and Economics

Kenneth E. Boulding

## Spaceship Earth and Economic Growth

We are now in a long transitional period in which our image of man's relationship to his environment is changing. We are ridding ourselves of the notion that we live on a physical frontier. But we still have a long way to go in making the moral, political, and psychological adjustments implied in this transition. In particular, economists have not come to grips with the consequences of the transition from an open to a closed system. But the closed earth requires a closed economy — a "spaceman economy" — as opposed to what I have called the open, "cowboy economy."

In an economic system materials flow from mines and so on (leaving a noneconomic reservoir), pass into what one might call the econosphere, and then leave it as effluents into a second noneconomic reservoir. At any one moment the econosphere can be thought of as the total capital stock — all the people, objects, and organizations involved in the system of economic exchange. The cowboy economy typifies the frontier attitudes of recklessness and exploitation. Consumption and production are considered

---

KENNETH E. BOULDING is Professor of Economics at the University of Colorado. Born in Liverpool, England in 1910, he did both his undergraduate and graduate work at Oxford. He taught at Iowa State College, McGill University, and the University of Michigan, among others, before joining the Colorado faculty in 1967. He is one of the Program Directors at Colorado's Institute of Behavioral Science and has published a number of books and articles. His current interest centers on the economics of disarmament.

---

good things and the success of the economy is measured by the amount of THROUGHPUT deriving in part from reservoirs of raw materials, processed by "factors of production," and passed on in part as output to the sink of pollution reservoirs. The Gross National Product (GNP) roughly measures this throughput.

In the spaceman economy, by contrast, reservoirs of materials are finite — the reservoirs for pollution are finite and cannot accept input too quickly and still remain in equilibrium. Man is seen to be in a circular rather than a linear ecological system. Then throughput is considered something to be minimized rather than maximized; it is the COST of maintaining the capital stock, rather than a measure of economic success. It is with this in mind that I have suggested calling the GNP the GROSS NATIONAL COST.[1] It should be obvious, but does not appear to be generally accepted, that income is not the real measure of economic welfare at all. Economic welfare is measured by the conditions of the person or the society, the extent, quality and complexity of the bodies, minds, and things in the system; income is simply the unfortunate cost of keeping up with decay. Gadgets and clothes wear out, one has to consume food and gasoline, which consumption is simply decay. It also follows that the bigger the economic system — the capital stock — the more it decays and the more we have to produce simply to maintain it.

When we have developed the economy of the spaceship earth, in which man will persist in equilibrium with his environment, the notion of the GNP will simply disintegrate. We will be less concerned with income-flow concepts and more with capital-stock concepts. Then technological changes that result in the maintenance of the total stock with LESS throughput (less production and consumption) will be a clear gain.

The spaceman economy is some way off in the future. How imminent it is is not clear, though the accumulating evidence of the physical consequences of the closed earth suggest that we should evolve to it soon. There is, indeed, evidence from an analysis of the GNPs of different countries that the very rich countries may approach an equilibrium state naturally, though I would not put too much faith in this natural process! If one plots the logarithm of the RATE OF INCREASE of per capita GNP against the actual per capita GNP itself, for all the countries where information is available, for the period 1900-1960, we find two interesting facts. The first is that most countries in the temperate zone are represented by points lying on a straight line sloping downwards, with Japan at the top left (10 percent annual increase in per capita GNP) and the United States at the bottom right (less than 2 percent annual increase).[2] That is, the richer a country is, the slower it grows economically. If the trend continued into the future, all these countries would stop economic growth when they are two or three times richer per capita than the United States is now. Before then, though, we will surely have been forcibly stopped by our limited environment.

The second fact is that the other group of nations, almost all in the tropics, occupy a roughly circular area in the bottom lefthand corner of the graph. They are poor and they are almost not growing in per capita wealth as fast as the rich countries. They seem to have a sort of Brownian movement. This suggests that there is a "development line" — if you're rich you get richer, but more and more slowly — but if you are in the underdeveloped group you're not going anywhere.

*Economics and Environmental Degradation*

If the transition to a spaceman economy is some way off in the future, the problems of environmental degradation are of the here and now. The environment of a person consists of all those objects which are relevant to him — the chair he sits in, the clothes he wears, the room he oc-

cupies, the meal he is eating, the air he breathes, the sounds he is hearing, and even, we might add, the vast internal environment of his memories and images. The environment of mankind is the sum of the environments of all individuals.

The environment, whether personal or total, can be divided roughly into two subsets — the ECONOMIC ENVIRONMENT and the NONECONOMIC ENVIRONMENT. The economic environment consists of those items which participate in exchange, actually or potentially, or which are valued in some sense in terms of exchangeables and hence appear in somebody's balance sheet. The distinction is not wholly clear because many noneconomic items in the environment affect the value of economic ones and vice versa. Thus, the starry sky is pretty clearly part of the noneconomic environment. Nevertheless, we may be prevented from enjoying it by smog or we may have to pay to go someplace where it can be seen. The economic environment can be divided roughly into private goods and public goods. Private goods are appropriated by individuals; the enjoyment of such a good on the part of one individual precludes its enjoyment by another. Public goods, like roads at low traffic densities, can be enjoyed by one person without excluding anybody else. Goods may be either positive, that is, productive of utilities or welfare, or negative, that is, productive of disutilities or illfare, in which case it is perhaps simpler to call them "bads."

Concern about environmental quality is related closely to the production of bads, both public and private. Bads, in general, are more difficult to deal with than goods and it is not difficult to see why. An individual who owns a private good has strong incentives to administer it wisely and carefully, for any benefits which come from such wise administration accrue directly to him. This is indeed the origin of the "magic of property" which is observable in all societies, even in socialist societies. The peasants' private plots in the Soviet Union are much better cared for and much more productive than the collective farms, simply because of the marginal incentives involved. Bads, however, unless they can be turned into goods, are nobody's business. The private incentive is to get rid of private bads as cheaply and unobtrusively as we can. We make bargains, of course, about both goods and bads. Thus, we pay garbage men to dispose of our garbage, which thus has a negative price. In the exchange of goods, each party is concerned to present his goods in an attractive and well-organized form. There is very little incentive to present garbage in an attractive and well-organized form. If we produce bads, we simply want to get rid of them as quickly and as cheaply as possible.

The difficulty of organizing bads is brought out very clearly when we look at the legal system, a considerable part of which is devoted to establishing property, or at least responsibility, in the production of bads. Thus, the law of torts, which enables us to sue for damages, is in effect a device for making A pay for the bad which he has forced B to accept. If your car runs into my house and so deteriorates the quality of my domestic environment, I can sue you for this and in a great many cases obtain compensation. The identification of the producer of the bad, the setting of its price, and forcing the producer to pay for it is, therefore, a main function of this branch of the law. Nobody, however, is very satisfied with the operation of the system as it stands. Many bads are produced for which the producer is not penalized and the "consumer" is not compensated. The system is extremely expensive, so that the costs of obtaining compensation often eat up a good part of the compensation itself; as a result the system operates better on the side of penalties than it does on the side of compensations. The greatest difficulty of the system, however, arises because of the frequent difficulty in identifying the producer of the bads. In a great many cases we have a system which produces bads fairly randomly, so that it is extremely hard to apportion the blame for their production, as it is a result of the system as a whole rather than of the action of any particular individual within it. Under the simple law of torts, anybody who receives a bad for which nobody else is to blame is not compensated unless he is insured. Insurance, while it helps to spread the risks and is the obvious device for seeing that the person who suffers a bad does in fact get compensated for it, is also costly and where it is not universal may act quite inequitably.

The legal system continues to struggle with these problems. We see, for instance, in the establishment of special laws for workman's compensation a failure of the traditional law of torts in the industrial relationships. An injury to a workman may be part of the inherent risks of the system and may not be the "fault" of his employer. Hence, the system as a whole is assessed for responsibility of the production of these bads, so that suffering can be compensated. Automobile insurance is another area where the allocation of blame is often so difficult that some states, such as New York, are experimenting with a "no fault" insurance plan in which the emphasis is on the compensation of the sufferer rather than the penalization of the guilty. In the criminal law, on the other hand, the shoe seems to be on the other foot. All the emphasis is on the penalization of the guilty, and as a result there are often grave injustices done to the victim. These considerations may seem at first sight a little remote from problems of the environment, but it is important to recognize that a deterioration of the environment, which is the production of a special kind of bads, is part of a much larger problem of the production of bads in general and cannot really be separated from the larger problem.

It is difficult enough to organize society for the proper handling of private bads, but the public bads are still more difficult to deal with, simply because of the high level of political and social organization required. Similarly, public goods are more difficult to deal with than private goods, because they too require a level of political and social organization and even social self-consciousness far beyond what is required for the adequate production of private goods. In the case of public bads, the law of torts is no remedy at all. If a factory pollutes the air which I breathe and induces disease or dirties my clothes so that they have to be cleaned, it is usually not worthwhile for me as a single individual to try to sue the factory owners for so small a part of the total damage. The suppression of public bads, like the provision of public goods, requires political organization. It cannot be done through the market mechanism alone, although the market mechanism can be used as a supplementary device. There must ultimately be an invocation of the police power and the legitimated threat system of the law. There is a further question of constitutionality as to how we protect ourselves against bad government, in this case, the failure of government to eliminate public bads or to provide public goods. This is largely a matter of developing a feedback process from those people who are affected by government decisions and by legal enactments, into the process which produces these decisions and enactments. This indeed is the major justification of democratic institutions. The problem is complicated, however, by the fact that government, political, and legal institutions have a certain tendency to produce public bads, as well as to suppress them, and there are very few legal and constitutional remedies for this. If, for instance, my government threatens my life and property through an irresponsible and foolish foreign policy, there is very little I can do about this in the way of legal remedies. Constitutional remedies are supposed to be the answers to problems of this kind, but very often are not.

Before we can be very successful in constructing political and social institutions which will suppress the production of bads, both public and private, we must ask ourselves the more fundamental question as to what subsystems within the general framework of society are in fact productive of bads. The problem is particularly acute in the case of what might be called cumulative bads, in which we have a process that accumulates negative capital goods and which continually increases the total stock of bads in the society. The concern about the environment, for instance, which is so strong at the moment, arises mainly because there is a perception that certain elements of the environment, such as the atmosphere and the oceans, are deteriorating in quality, that is, are becoming structures with more bads and fewer goods in them from the point of view of the welfare of mankind. The environmental question, therefore, resolves itself very largely into the question of the identification of deteriorating dynamic systems, that is, systems within society which go from bad to worse rather than from bad to better. We cannot, of course, judge these systems in terms of simple

market values alone, although market values are a legitimate part of the total valuation process. We are dealing here, however, with the total environment, of which the economic environment is only a part. One of the major difficulties in assessing whether a system is in fact deteriorating is the difficulty of finding some index of value which measures, or at least assesses in some way, the direction in which the system is moving. For most of these cases, we do not really have to have very exact quantitative information. We do, however, need to know "which way is up" and even a question as simple as this is often quite difficult to answer. It is possible, however, to identify a number of subsystems within society which are likely to produce a deteriorating dynamic. Each of these may have different properties and may have to be treated differently. Any system which produces bads is suspect, although, of course, the production of bads in itself does not necessarily mean that the system is a deteriorating one, as the production of bads may be more than counterbalanced by the production of a larger quantity of goods. The following seven systems within society are suggested as good candidates at least for classification as deteriorating systems.

1. MALEVOLENCE. If A is malevolent towards B, the diminution in B's welfare increases A's utility. Hence, A may produce bads for B, that is, A may diminish B's welfare and diminish the quality of B's environment. If B retaliates and produces bads in turn for A, we may get a mutually deteriorating system. Unfortunately, malevolence frequently tends to produce malevolence, so that it does tend to escalate. Benevolence, by contrast, in which A's perception of an increase in B's welfare increases his utility, also tends to escalate and tends to increase the production of goods.

2. TRIBUTE. A may threaten to produce bads for B unless B gives A goods. B's goods are then given to A as tribute. If B fails to come through, A may carry out the threat, and so may increase the production of bads. Tribute does not necessarily imply malevolence, that is, A may not feel malevolent towards B. He simply wants his goods. On the other hand the use of the threat

system to extract tribute frequently creates malevolence in the victim, and malevolence in the victim may easily produce malevolence in the threatener. The deteriorating quality of the slave system and its low horizon of development is probably mainly due to this factor.

3. DETERRENCE. Tribute, which is essentially the threat-submission system, often tends to pass into defiance, or into deterrence if the victim refuses to submit. Deterrence is a system of threat-counterthreat in which each party threatens to produce bads for the other unless the other refrains from producing bads for the first party. Deterrence may be stable in the short-run, though even then it produces implicit bads by withdrawing resources in the production of threat capability. Deterrence furthermore cannot be stable; otherwise it could cease to deter. Hence it is always tending to break down into the production of bads. Submission and tribute may sometimes be less costly to the victim than deterrence, but the situation is complicated by the fact that threat may not merely be to the goods of the persons involved but also to their identities. Deterrence then tends to yield more satisfactory identities than submission. It is a more equalitarian system in the sense that the threat-counterthreat relationship is one of approximate equals, whereas the threat-submission system is a relationship of unequals. Consequently, there is a tendency for deterrence to be preferred even when it is much more costly than tribute. The international system with its constant tendency to break down into war is, of course, the most striking example of a deterrence relationship and is probably the greatest single threat to the environment.

4. EXTERNALITIES. This is the more traditionally "economic" source of production of bads. It occurs when bads are produced in a process of joint production along with goods that do not have to be paid for in accordance with their negative value, that is, the bads do not form part of the COST of the operation. Under circumstances in which the producer has to bear the cost of the bads, too many resources would be devoted to those processes of production which produce these bads. Air and water pollution from business enterprises are a good case in point. If business had to pay an assessed value for all the bads which they produced, they would very soon tend to move towards processes of production which produced fewer bads and more goods, and processes of production which produced such expensive bads that they were no longer profitable would tend to disappear.

5. INVISIBILITIES. I just made up this term, as it is badly needed. Invisibilities are the production of bads which are so small, in the case of the individual producer, that they are not noticed, but which cumulatively may be very large. Automobile exhaust and DDT are examples. These are very close to being "public bads"; just as a public good is something which I can use without diminishing your enjoyment of it, so a public bad is something from which my withdrawal will not noticeably affect your discomfort. If a single person stops driving a car, this doesn't do much for the smog problem.

6. SELF–GENERATING OR ARTIFICALLY GENERATED DEMANDS. In any realistic appraisal of the social system we must go beyond the conventional assumption of economics that the preferences, especially of private persons, are givens of the system which are not subject to further discussion. In fact, of course, preferences are learned and because of this it is legitimate to examine the learning process with a view to detecting possible perversities in it. Consumption that is addictive, such as tobacco or heroin consumption, and which has adverse physiological effects, obviously comes under this category of perverse degenerative demands, and almost everyone will agree that it should be controlled in some way. A more difficult and touchy case is that of fashion and the perversion of taste through fashion. The demand to be fashionable in itself would seem quite legitimate, as it is an expression of the identity of an individual with a community. A fashion for virtue, however, may satisfy the desire to be fashionable and is obviously to be preferred to a fashion for vice. There are tastes also which have external diseconomies, like the taste for being an alcoholic, which produces a good deal of misery for other people. A very different question is the taste for sensation and nonsense. The sort of taste which produced Hitler with his enormous external disecon-

omies, or even the taste which perverts science into sensationalism, can legitimately be recognized as candidates for inclusion in deteriorating systems.

7. POPULATION. This is the classical Malthusian problem of the pressure of population on the environmental base. The larger the number of people in any given environment, at least beyond a certain point, the more likely is the environment to deteriorate. A crowded one-room shack is more likely to deteriorate than a suburban dwelling. A crowded country produces pollution of all sorts which is hard to control. Population pressure should perhaps be classified more as an underlying condition which makes deteriorating systems of other kinds more likely rather than a deteriorating system itself. Insofar as unrestricted increase in population is a direct producer of deteriorating quality of human life, however, we can perhaps justify classifying this with the others.

Each of these systems requires quite different means for its control. Malevolence control is very little understood. The church and the family try to do something about it, not always very successfully. One grave difficulty here is that a common malevolence towards a particular object is very often a source of a feeling of community, especially in the national state. Consequently, the national state often actively encourages malevolence towards those other states which it regards as its enemies. Any organization indeed which is bound together by a common enmity, whether this is a sect, a political party, a class, or a nation, or even a philosophical school, is apt to develop malevolence towards its enemy and this malevolence is frequently reciprocated. Furthermore, organizations and communities which are built on a common malevolence towards an external enemy frequently find that the malevolence generated creates a frame of mind in which malevolence is easily turned inward in factionalism and personal hatred within a community itself. The problem of control of malevolence, therefore, is doubly difficult because many of the agencies which ought to control it in fact propagate it in the interests of their own community. A critical question here is what elements in the social system encourage the development

of personal identities which do not require malevolence towards others in order to establish the personal integrity and community identities which are based on mutual benevolence rather than on mutual malevolence towards an external enemy.

Private tribute, for instance, by bandits, is brought under control by the development of law and the institutions of government. On the other hand, government then begins to extract tribute in the form of taxation on a scale which even the Mafia cannot emulate, so again we must identify tribute control as one of the major unsolved problems of society. Taxation has a peculiar status. At its best it is a kind of "willing tribute." People are prepared to coerce themselves, as it were, as long as everybody is coerced. The provision of public goods on a purely voluntary basis is never successful, mainly because of the "freeloading problem," that is, the individual who enjoys the goods, but who doesn't want to pay for them. A democratic tax system by which people, as it were, vote to tax and hence to coerce themselves is a possible solution to this problem. On the other hand, the tax system, once it is set up, is always subject to abuse, and it is possible to pass by gradual stages from a voluntary tax system into a tyranny in which the only reason why people pay taxes is that they will be shot if they don't.

Deterrence probably holds the greatest threat to mankind today and is also very difficult to control. The only two known methods are the development of a superior hierarchy of threat systems, for instance, in the present case, in world government, or through the development of other systems, such as exchange or integrative systems which gradually weaken and replace the threat system. Here again we know very little about the dynamics of systems of this kind. We do, in fact, get out of deterrence systems as we pass, for instance, from societies of personal violence into civil societies in which deterrence is rarely exercised between individuals except in relatively mild forms. How we make the transition into a world civil society is perhaps the most fundamental problem which faces the human race at the moment, and the solution of all other problems depends upon it. The greatest threat of all to the environment is war.

Of all forms of environmental deterioration, externalities are probably the easiest to control, although in many cases there are severe problems of identification. The ideal method of control consists of a system of legal penalties for producing bads, such as effluent taxes, so that anybody who produces a bad has to pay for it, either to the government or to the injured party. This, of course, has to be imposed politically through political sanctions. This means also that the problem of estimating how large the effluent tax ought to be is not solved by the ecological process of the market, but has to be the result of a political decision, and hence it is quite easy to get it wrong. However, even bad effluent taxes are probably better than no effluent taxes. The penalties for producing bads may also take the form of prohibitions, fines, or criminal sanctions, but these are usually less satisfactory as ways of changing behavior. Bads are often the product of the activities of relatively powerful people against whom prohibitions and legal penalties are almost universally inadequate as deterrents, as witness the antitrust laws. It is probably a wise strategy in this case to lay off the moral invective, avoid malevolence as far as possible, and treat the matter on rather coldly cost-benefit terms (but see also Chapter 18). A real problem here is the backwardness of the physical and biological sciences in measuring pollutants and in providing monitoring equipment which can detect their production. This is one of those rather unusual cases where the economics of the problem is very easy, but the physics and biology is quite difficult. We do not know the physical costs, for instance, in many cases of air and water pollution in terms of health deterioration, medical expenses, cleaning bills, and so on. In the absence of this information, it is very hard to impose effluent taxes which are just. Nevertheless, these items of information are frequently not in the information system precisely because penalties are not imposed and an apparatus for producing effluent taxes would very soon produce strong pressure to produce the requisite information.

Invisible externalities are much more difficult to deal with than visible ones. Effluent taxes are virtually impossible because the effluence cannot be detected. It may be that the only answer is the development of "counter-institutions," such as government-subsidized consumer research, with some sort of tax powers on manufacturers who are producing products which in turn produce invisible bads. The legal problems here are quite tricky and need much further exploration. The possibility of a constitutional amendment which would give individuals the right to sue on behalf of the environment, as we have a certain parallel in the antitrust laws, might have rather salutory effects, but might also be very disorganizing. There is a real danger that the environmental concern will lead into a prohibition-like activity which would be an oversimple solution to a particularly complex problem.

The control of the production of perverse tastes is an extremely difficult and intractable problem. Even such relatively simple aspects of the problem as control of harmful drugs, in which one should presumably include tobacco, has been notoriously unsuccessful, especially in the United States. Here the prohibitionist state of mind forces drug users into a criminal subculture almost immediately, a subculture which has strong incentives to perpetuate and expand itself. This seems to be a clear case where one should penalize the seller but not the buyer, mainly on the grounds that the demand is induced by the seller. The problem of how to transform the identity of the drug taker and the community of the drug taker is one which has so far baffled society completely. Our experience with alcohol, which quantitatively is probably a much worse pollutant than drugs, and causes much more human misery, has also been a resounding failure, and it is hardly too much to say that all attempts to deal with it have been unsuccessful. The problem here goes very deep into family and religious subcultures, which are usually not particularly accessible to the control mechanisms of the larger society.

Population control has turned out to be a very intractable problem, perhaps because we really understand very little about the totality of the forces, both social and biological, which govern fertility. The problem is one of reducing fertility to correspond with reduced mortality, so that we can achieve a stationary population with a long average length of life. Thus, in an equilibrium population in which the average age of death is

70, the birth and death rate would have to be about 14 per thousand, whereas the biological maximum birth rate for the human population seems to be somewhere between 40 and 50 per thousand. No government policy in regard to the population has been at all successful, and we may need further social inventions even as extreme as my own "green stamp plan" of marketable licenses for children beyond the second child[3] (see also Chapter 2).

One of the most difficult problems in environmental control is its impact on the distribution of income and wealth. Much of the pressure on the environment today arises because the poor, as a result of economic development, are now enjoying things which used to be the privilege of the rich, such as travel, increased protein diets, and high consumption of power. Solutions to environmental problems frequently involve repressing or confining the activities of the poor, while leaving the rich much as they were. There have been at least two previous periods of strong concern about the environment in the United States, one around 1900 involving the first conservation movement, associated especially with the names of Governor Pinchot and Teddy Roosevelt. This produced the Bureau of Reclamation and an extension of the national parks and forests system. These were in many respects highly creditable achievements. Nevertheless, the overall effect may easily have been adverse to the poor. The Bureau of Reclamation, in spite of its somewhat socialist ideology and its emphasis on the family farm, did very little for the very poor farmer, especially for the Indian and the Spanish-American in the West. National parks and national forests, by raising private land values in their environment, have quite effectively kept poor people out of the mountains, so that the mountain West on the whole has not become an Appalachia. The second period of strong interest in the environment was in the 1930s, following the dust bowl phenomenon. This produced the Soil Conservation Service, which again has done an excellent technical job and has certainly transformed the look of the American landscape. It was the richer farmers, however, who were most able to benefit from it, and it is part of a general

agricultural policy which has driven poor farmers off the land into the urban ghettos and has materially subsidized the rich farmers. One is a little afraid that the present excitement will lead to the solution of high taxes on automobiles to subsidize public transportation, which will leave the rich with their automobiles and will force the poor onto subways. Even effluent taxes might easily turn out to be regressive if they force a rise in the price of low-cost housing, domestic power, and processed food, as they well might. Unfortunately, the distributional impact of almost any economic policy is virtually unknown. This is the great desert of economic science.

It may be hard to solve these problems under a market-type society, but there is very little evidence that centrally planned economics do any better. The pressure to fulfill a plan indeed may be more destructive of the environment than pressure from a profit system, and the fact that prices in socialist societies correspond very poorly to social costs means that even the possibility of control through effluent taxes and manipulation of the price system is likely to be quite ineffective. Furthermore, the bias of most socialist societies towards heavy industry, their bias against agriculture, and the tendency of most socialist societies to exploit their working classes in the interest of national power certainly gives very little comfort to those who seek the solutions to the environmental problems simply in slogans of the left.

Another very tricky problem in this connection, which is perhaps even more acute in socialist societies than it is in capitalist societies, is the problem of justice in distribution among the generations. This is the problem of how far the present generation should be sacrificed for the benefit of its posterity. One can hardly help having a sneaky sympathy with a man who says "What has posterity ever done for me?" and only a very strong ethic of intertemporal community can justify the present generation's making large sacrifices for its posterity, especially when these sacrifices are imposed by the state.

Implicit in any environmental program indeed is a rate of time discounting, and also a rate of uncertainty discounting which is even more difficult. Time and uncertainty discounting apply not only to the problem of distribution between the present generation and its posterity. It is of great relevance also in the problem of the rate at which the present generation should use up its exhaustible resources, as this also, of course, will effect the welfare of posterity. The further we look into the future, of course, the more uncertain it becomes. As we use exhaustible resources to produce knowledge, this knowledge in turn produces more resources. It may be indeed that this process cannot go on forever and that we have to regard the present as a peculiar time in human history when we have to transform the exhaustible resources involved in fossil fuels and ores into enough knowledge to enable us to do without them. If we could do that our own interests and the interests of posterity would be served.

It may be indeed that the key word in environmental control is a very unpopular one, that is, "patience." It is impatience that leads to the destruction of the present environment for immediate ends and a neglect of the interests of the future. Impatient young people, therefore, who think that environmental control is something revolutionary and radical, something for which we wave a magic political wand and all our pumpkins turn into effluent-free coaches (and, incidentally, nobody has yet produced an effluent-free horse) are likely to be grieviously disappointed. Environmental control is conservative rather than radical, evolutionary rather than revolutionary. It is more likely to be achieved through capitalistic instruments, like the price system suitably modified, than it is through socialistic planning. Nevertheless, it does require something like a socialist ethic with strong emphasis on the realization of the ability of the individual to identify himself with the world society which stretches forward into the future.

Perhaps one could describe this as a planetary ethic rather than a socialist ethic, but it is an ethic which is based ultimately on man's sense of stewardship for his beautiful blue and white planet with its incalculably precious freight of genetic material. The ethic of the environment indeed is an ethic of the stewardship of the evolutionary process which is falling more and more into man's hands and which he has the power to destroy as well as to foster. When man finds his identity as the steward of his planet, the problems of environmental control will move towards solution, though the institutions by which they are solved may be highly diverse.

## References

1. **Boulding, K. E.** 1970. Fun and games with the gross national product: The role of misleading indicators in social policy. In *The Environmental Crisis* (H. W. Helfrich, ed.). Yale University Press, New Haven, Connecticut.
2. **Boulding, K. E.** 1970. Gaps between developed and developing nations. In *Toward Century 21: Technology, Society, and Human Values* (C. S. Walling, ed.). Basic Books, New York and London.
3. **Boulding, K. E.** 1964. *The Meaning of the Twentieth Century*, Chap. VI, The population trap. Harper and Row, New York.

## Further Reading

**Boulding, K. E.** 1966. Environmental quality in a growing economy. In *Essays from the Sixth RFF Forum*. John Hopkins Press, Baltimore, Maryland.

# 18   Environment and the Law[1]

Victor J. Yanacone, jr.[2]

Many of our environmental problems arise from activities based on inadequate ecological knowledge. Pesticide abuse is a classic example. The indiscriminate use of broad-spectrum, persistent pesticides such as DDT, dieldrin, endrin, aldrin, toxaphene, and heptachlor have so altered the ecology of agricultural ecosystems that more resistant pest species have evolved and new species have become pests. Modern agrichemical methods ignore the potential value of integrated control techniques in which specific chemical bullets are used to augment the armory of natural and biological insect controls.

Utilizing our water resources for waste disposal is still another example. Oceans and rivers, lakes and streams are just like any other sink — they have a finite capacity for waste, after which they back up. Moreover, they fight back as algae blooms quickly decay into sulfurous miasmas.

VICTOR JOHN YANNACONE, JR. is an attorney who has pioneered in the field of environmental law. A working trial attorney since 1959, he began the first sustained legal assault on DDT, culminating in the pending civil antitrust action seeking $30 billion in reparations from the manufacturers of DDT for false and misleading advertising. Yannacone is responsible for establishing the Trust Doctrine, the Ninth Amendment of the Constitution, and the general principles of equity jurisprudence as the cornerstones of successful environmental litigation. He is the senior author of a comprehensive treatise on environmental law, *Environmental Rights & Remedies*. He lectures widely on litigation as an alternative to revolution. Currently he is working with several groups in the United States to apply the techniques of systems ecology to environmental problems.

Our atmosphere is not a limitless sink into which we can pour countless tons of noxious gases and poisonous particulates. The atmosphere too has a finite capacity for waste, and we are reaching that limit today.

Our high-speed air transportation system has begun to alter our weather patterns and climatological cycles. High-altitude clouds from commercial jet contrails have begun to reduce the amount of incident solar radiation received by green plants on the ground.

Man's apparent dominion over the environment is but a license from nature with the fee yet to be paid. We should have learned from the disastrous effects of radionuclide fallout that what we sow we must also reap, yet the fallout of lead and other heavy metals, chlorinated hydrocarbons and other toxicants continues at an increasing rate. Mankind has ears, yet has not heard the warnings shouted from the environment all around him. More and more noise is tolerated, increasing the toxic environmental stresses already imposed on urban and ghetto dwellers throughout the nation. We are proceeding to develop a commercial supersonic jet transport, even though it seems that continued random awakenings can produce transient psychoses in stressed populations.

Man has been warned. He has been given the unique opportunity to choose whether his species will drown in its own sewage, be buried under its own garbage, choke to death on air it cannot breathe, or be driven to homicide or suicide by the noise around.

During the spring of 1968, the alumni of a prestigious law school, who claim among their numbers many Justices of the U.S. Supreme Court, held a reunion. The intellectual theme for that reunion weekend was *Law and the Urban*

*Crisis.* Five prominent legal educators were invited to address the alumni on this urgent question, but just as the proceedings were to begin, a group of black law students, together with members of the city's Black Coalition, entered the auditorium and began to address themselves to the all-white speakers on the platform and the all-white alumni audience.

"You just don't understand the problem at all," they said, "The problem is not Law AND the Urban Crisis; law IS the urban crisis!"

And now when we look to the law for answers to many of our social and environmental problems, we find that the law itself is the cause of many of those problems.

It is "the law" that zones the housing patterns which lead to building too many highways for too many autos.

It is "the law" that expropriates public property for private profit.

It is "the law" that permits environmental degradation.

It is "the law" that guarantees equal protection of that law for the corporation — that fictional bastard child of the law endowed by the U.S. Supreme Court with all the God-given rights of a human being but without any soul to save or tail to kick — while the Court effectively denies such equal protection of the law to the poor, the Indian, the Black, women, the inarticulate, and the politically weak or ineffective.

It is "the law" that forbids the public distribution of birth control information in many states.

It is "the law" that denies women in many states the freedom to determine the use to which their wombs will be put.

It is "the law" that created and now maintains a tax system that encourages overpopulation by penalizing those who would remain single or with few children.

Always it is "the law!"

## Law and Environmental Protection

There are three avenues of appeal to the law for protection of the environment.

Legislative

   Utilizing existing statutory law: federal, state, and local

Developing new legislation that is ecologically sophisticated, environmentally relevant, socially responsible, and politically feasible

Administrative

   Reliance upon federal, state, and local regulatory (administrative) agencies to effect their statutory missions in such a way as to protect the environment

Judicial

   Appeal to the Courts, federal, state, and local, for protection of the environment in:

   Litigation based on statutory interpretation, and the common law of nuisance, negligence, and trespass

   Litigation seeking both declaration of the rights of the people (class actions for declaratory judgment), and equitable relief (injunction, reparations) based on ancient common law equity principles (the Trust Doctrine; *sic utere tuo alienam non laedas* — use your own property so as not to injure the property of others) and on the Constitution of the United States, particularly on the "unenumerated rights" guaranteed by the Ninth Amendment, and protected against Federal action by the "due process" and "equal protection" clauses of the Fifth Amendment and against state interference by the "rights, privileges and immunities," "equal protection," and "due process" clauses of the Fourteenth Amendment.

## Legislation

The first and, deceptively, the simplest approach is through the legislatures. If this approach is successful, there will be, of course, no need for other than occasional interpretive litigation. The ways of legislatures, however, are slow and ponderous, and many national natural resource treasures are in immediate danger of serious, permanent, and irreparable damage.

The FLORISSANT FOSSIL BEDS represent a classic example of legislative ineffectiveness in a crisis situation. At stake were the unique and irreplaceable Florissant fossil beds, a 6000 acre area 35 miles west of Colorado Springs, where seeds, leaves, insects, and plants from the Oligocene period 34 million years ago are remarkably preserved in paper-thin layers of shale. These fossils, studied by scientists from all over the world, are the richest of their kind anywhere on earth. One hundred and forty-four different plant species and more than 60,000 insect fossil specimens have already been found.

Following a subcommittee hearing at Colorado Springs on May 29, 1969, the U.S. Senate unanimously passed a bill establishing the Florissant Fossil Beds National Monument. But while the Congress was deliberating, four land speculators purchased over half the land to be included within the National Monument and announced that they intended to begin bulldozer excavation of roads to open the area for development immediately, unless the land was purchased by government or private groups.

The Defenders of Florissant, an *ad hoc* organization of scientists and citizens dedicated to protection of the fossil beds, finally turned to the courts, filing suit "on behalf of all the people of this generation and those generations yet unborn who might be entitled to the full benefit, use and enjoyment of that unique, national, natural resource treasure, the Florissant fossil beds."[3] They demanded a temporary restraining order prohibiting disturbance of the fossil shales by the speculators until such time as Congress had completed its deliberations.

On July 9, 1969, the U.S. District Court for Colorado held that no federal court could interfere with the absolute right of private property ownership and the only way to save the fossil beds would be to buy them, at whatever price the speculators demanded. The Defenders of Florissant appealed to the U.S. Court of Appeals for the Tenth Circuit that same afternoon, but the court questioned its own power to grant a temporary restraining order and demanded to know what law the speculators had violated. The defenders had to concede that Congress, in its infinite wisdom, had never seen fit to pass a law protecting fossils, so the Court of Appeals then demanded to know what right it had to interfere with an individual's use of his own land so long as use didn't violate any statute law.

All that was left to do was to point to a fossil palm leaf that had been discovered at Florissant

and plead: "The Florissant fossil beds are to geology, paleontology, paleobotany, palynology and evolution what the Rosetta stone was to Egyptology. To sacrifice this 34 million old geologic record, a record you might say written by the mighty hand of God, for 30 year mortgages and basements for the A-frame ghettoes of the '70s is like wrapping fish with the Dead Sea Scrolls."[4]

In a precedent-setting ruling, the Court of Appeals restrained the speculators from disturbing the fossil beds. That temporary restraining order terminated on July 29, 1969, and on that day the District Court heard testimony and argument for a preliminary injunction. Meanwhile, Congress had cleared the bill through a subcommittee of the Committee of Interior and Insular Affairs and the bill was pending before the entire Committee prior to release on the House floor for action. Nevertheless the District Court again held that there is nothing in the Constitution to prevent a landowner from making whatever use of his property he chooses, and if the fossils were to be saved they had to be purchased at the speculators' price.

Again it was necessary to appeal to the Tenth Circuit Court of Appeals, and at the hearing the speculators explained that they only intended to scrape off the top layer of the fossil shales and that would still leave more than sixteen feet of fossils remaining. We told the court, "You could just as well say scraping the paint off the Mona Lisa would cause no real damage because the canvas was left." And again the 34 million year old fossils were rescued by a last-minute Court order. A preliminary injunction was granted by the Court of Appeals just as the bulldozers were poised at the boundary of the National Monument.

Although Congress finally passed the bill, the difficulty with the legislative approach to environmental protection is best summed up in the words of the Clerk of Court of Appeals, "Will you please get that bill through Congress soon and give us some rest."

*Administrative Agency Action*

Recognizing the delay inherent in the legislative process, legislatures attempted to meet the needs of modern technological society by creating administrative agencies to which they ceded some of the powers of the legislative, executive, and judicial branches of government in order to give speedy effect to the will of the people as manifest by act of Congress. Unfortunately, the administrative approach carried within itself the seeds of its own abuse. Any administrative agency, no matter how well intentioned, is not a court, it is a Star Chamber — its own judge, jury, and executioner. All in the public interest, of course! The narrow jurisdiction and mission-oriented viewpoint of administrative agencies, particularly those charged with industry regulation, make them inherently incapable of considering environmental matters with the requisite degree of ecological sophistication.

The Scenic Hudson Preservation case marked the fork in the road for those concerned with the legal defense of the biosphere. In that case the U.S. Court of Appeals for the Second Circuit decided that, if the conservationists were willing to submit the controversy to the Federal Power Commission (FPC) (the federal regulatory agency charged with the mission of regulating the generation and distribution of electric power in the United States), then that agency could hear and consider evidence on natural values in addition to the usual evidence on the economics of electric power generation and distribution. The alternative was for the conservationists to stay in court and challenge the suitability of the FPC as a forum for the resolution of ecological conflict.

The tragedy of the Scenic Hudson Preservation case occurred when the Scenic Hudson Preservation Committee, a special interest, local conservation organization concerned primarily with protecting the view of Storm King Mountain from the exclusive residential neighborhoods on the east side of the Hudson River north of New York City, yielded to the FPC jurisdiction to hear and determine the environmental impact of the Consolidated Edison Electric Utility company application to build a pumped storage generating facility on Storm King Mountain. This coalition of preservationists and aesthetically concerned conservationists, to avoid challenge to established bureaucracy, thus yielded to the FPC the ultimate authority to make ecological judg-

ments binding on generations yet unborn, cloaking the FPC with a mantle of ecological competence it does not possess and cannot attain within the narrow limits of its statutory mission.

The Federal Power Commission did, in fact, perform as might be expected. After lengthy and expensive hearings (costing the conservationists more than $1,000,000 to date) the FPC effectively ignored the testimony on the ecological impact of the project and approved the permit application. Since the conservationists were given their "day in court" and chose to take that day before an administrative agency rather than in a court of equity, the findings of fact made by the FPC are now binding on the conservationists.

The administrative agencies are legislative creations. In theory, they exist to effect policy established by the elected legislative representatives of the people. To accomplish this the legislature ceded rule-making power from its legislative mandate under the Constitution, the executive ceded a certain amount of administrative power, and the judiciary ceded certain judicial functions, in particular fact-finding and preliminary hearing. As a result of this tripartite grant of power, administrative agencies represent not a fourth branch of government as some seem to think, but the foundation of all practical government operations: Administrative agencies provide the substantial bulk of bureaucracy.

It is now clear that the worst offenders in the process of environmental degradation are not the ruthless entrepreneurs dedicated to wanton exploitation of our natural resources — the profiteers and abusers of the public's air and water — but those short-sighted, mission-oriented, allegedly public interest agencies such as the Department of Transportation, its Federal Highway Administration and Federal Aviation Administration, the Department of Agriculture and its Division of Pesticide Registration, the Army Corps of Engineers, and the Atomic Energy Commission and their many regional counterparts. The mission-oriented, statutorily enshrined determinations of these agencies preclude any consideration of the long-term ecological consequences of their decisions.

If we must find a common denominator for the serious, environmental crises facing all technologically developed countries regardless of their nominal form of government, it would have to be entrenched bureaucracies which are essentially immune from criticism or public action. These self-perpetuating, self-sufficient, self-serving bureaus are power sources unto themselves, effectively insulated from the people and responsible to no one but themselves. One of the strange inconsistencies of bureaucracy is the reluctance of administrative agencies to expose themselves to public scrutiny. A review of the published reports of Nader's Raiders and similar citizen vigilante investigative groups chronicle tales of evasion, suppression of information, and a general policy of restricting public information. Assuming the best of motives on the part of bureaucrats and politicians, this course of conduct can only be explained by a kind of totalitarian paternalism totally inconsistent with Constitutional concepts of American government.

*Pesticide Litigation*

The bankruptcy of administrative bureaucracy and administrative agency protection of the environment is disclosed by examining the record on litigation seeking to substitute the citizen as representative of other citizens, that is, the class action. The citizen here is substituting himself for the regulatory agency. Recent pesticide litigation provides some good examples.

We need look no further than the Division of Pesticide Registration of the U.S. Department of Agriculture and its handling of the DDT controversy to understand the failure of the existing regulatory agency system and at the same time sense the power of the courtroom and the effect of equity litigation in the struggle to protect the environment. In 1966, a citizen sought equitable relief from a toxic insult to the community ecosystem and sued not just a local mosquito control commission using DDT, but 1,1,1-trichloro-2,2-bis(*para*-chlorophenyl)ethane, the chemical DDT itself. Finally in a New York court of equity the full weight of scientific evidence against DDT was presented to the social conscience of the community in a forum protected from the political, economic, and bureaucratic pressures that for a decade or more had successfully suppressed the evidence of DDT's world-

wide damage to the environment. At long last the agrichemical-political complex was forced to put its propaganda to the test in the crucible of cross-examination.

The New York State Supreme Court issued a temporary injunction restraining the County of Suffolk from using DDT in mosquito control on August 15, 1966 and continued this "temporary" injunction until December 6, 1967 holding that:

> DDT has, by its inherent chemical stability, become a continuing factor in some ecological life cycles so as to profoundly alter them and the environmental equilibrium. Thus, it is reasonably apparent that DDT is capable of and actually has to some extent caused extraordinary damage to the resources of this county. If in no other way, the chemical by its very stability has introduced an element of instability in the general ecosystem. For instance, by reducing a food source of some of the larger wildlife and so reducing the over-all larger wildlife population, lesser elements multiply more quickly. These lower forms are presumably more of a nuisance, assuming they in turn survive. Furthermore, DDT affects wildlife directly. Its ingestion, from whatever source, has the capability, it seems, to disrupt reproductive processes or even more simply act as a poison. It is fairly apparent then that the application of DDT in Suffolk County has and is continuing to have a demonstrable effect on local wildlife, reducing it slowly but surely, either directly across the board or indirectly from the top down, but reducing it nevertheless.
>
> We have a situation where plaintiff has at least minimally sustained a massive effort to validate the allegation that DDT does in fact do biological harm.[5]

Although the Court dismissed the complaint on procedural grounds it continued the temporary injunction pending legislative review of the entire matter. That review culminated in a determination by the Suffolk County Legislature to discontinue the use of DDT for mosquito control throughout the county in July 1968. From the date of the first temporary injunction in 1966, DDT was finished for mosquito control in the state of New York.

In the Court of Appeals for the state of Michigan in 1967, an action was brought to stop the aerial application of over 5600 pounds of dieldrin along the shores of Lake Michigan. The Michigan Department of Agriculture and the U.S.

Department of Agriculture, with the assistance of entomologists from Michigan State University, declared an infestation of Japanese beetles present in Berrien County, Michigan, and in order to prevent quarantine of the agricultural produce of Berrien County set about to eradicate that infestation.

There on a witness stand under cross-examination, representatives of the U.S. Department of Agriculture, the Michigan Department of Agriculture, and Michigan State University admitted that the Japanese beetle infestation supposedly justifying the application of more than 5600 pounds of the broad-spectrum, persistent chemical biocide, dieldrin, had been declared after extensive beetle trapping had shown a total population of Japanese beetles of less than 1000. As one of the judges of the Court of Appeals asked an agriculture department witness during an aside, "5600 pounds of dieldrin to eradicate less than a thousand Japanese beetles? Doctor, do you intend to poison the beetles or bury them?"

The Court of Appeals issued a temporary injunction restraining the aerial application of dieldrin, and although the Michigan Supreme Court later lifted the injunction, the aerial application was never again attempted. A year later, the Michigan Department of Agriculture supported a hand application of dieldrin to selected sites of Japanese beetle infestation amounting to less than 500 pounds of active material and at the same time the Michigan Department of Natural Resources came out strongly against "hard" or persistent pesticides, ultimately succeeding in having them banned for all practical purposes throughout the entire state of Michigan.

In 1969 at Madison, Wisconsin, in another courtroom challenge of DDT, Dr. Harry W. Hays, Director of the Pesticide Registration Division of the U.S. Department of Agriculture testified: "If the data appear to us . . . to be adequate . . . the product is registered. We look at the data furnished by the manufacturer, but we don't look at it analytically . . . We don't check it by the laboratory method."[6] At long last the people were told that the Department of Agriculture relies entirely upon data furnished by the pesticide manufacturers and does not do any independent tests of its own.

The incredible lack of concern for the safety of the American people became apparent on further cross-examination when Dr. Hays admitted that if a pesticide was checked at all, it was checked by an entomologist only for its effectiveness against the target insect and not for its effect on beneficial insects or fish and wildlife. "We don't assume that the intended use will cause any damage," he explained. Moreover, Dr. Hays further admitted that although he had personal knowledge of published scientific studies showing damage to fish and wildlife from DDT, the Division of Pesticide Registration was not doing anything about possible environmental hazards from the pesticide.

Dr. Hays had testified previously, on behalf of the Industry Task Force for DDT of the National Agricultural Chemicals Association, that the U.S. Department of Agriculture is solely responsible for the registration of pesticides and for determining whether they may be shipped in interstate commerce. He also testified that these determinations are not subject to revision except on appeal by the pesticide manufacturer. Then Dr. Hays reluctantly admitted that the public had no access to USDA records of pesticide registration.

Thus, only in an adversary judicial proceeding was it finally demonstrated that the U.S. Department of Agriculture is really serving the agrichemical industry and not the American people, while remaining at the same time essentially immune from responsibility to the American people.

Perhaps the new Environmental Protection Agency will be an improvement. Only time will tell.

*Damage Litigation*

Conventional tort litigation suits for money damages on behalf of private citizens represent another avenue of appeal to the law on behalf of the environment, yet this avenue also leads inevitably to questions without answers. What do you do about a toxicant like DDE, the metabolite of DDT which is ubiquitous, distributed throughout the lipid tissues of every living element of the biosphere? What do you do about a toxicant whose toxic effects cannot be demonstrated as the proximate cause of any particular personal injury or disease?

In the struggle to protect natural resources against the predations of short-sighted, limited vision government agencies such as the Army Corps of Engineers, the Department of Agriculture, the Federal Aviation Administration, or the Atomic Energy Commission, any attack on their agency decisions must NOT be based on damage to any particular private economic interest. The Everglades will never be saved from the Army Engineers and the Central & South Florida Flood Control District by showing potential loss of income to the hot-dog vendors at the Everglades National Park, as the National Audubon Society attempted to do in the Canal 111 case. The futility of any attempt to protect the environment by alleging private damage in a court of law is best illustrated in the history of the rape of Pennsylvania by the coal industry during the nineteenth and early twentieth centuries.

Now, in spite of the lessons of more than fifty years of nuisance law development, timid lawyers and timid conservationists are still hoping that "through conventional damage suits, such as those downstream property owners might bring against upstream polluters, what amounts to a citizen's right to a clean environment may be established."[7]

That kind of wistful, wishful, thinking has been put to rest by a recent New York case involving a notorious cement plant and quarry near Albany, the state capital.

> Involved in this appeal are eight separate actions commenced by residents of the Town of Coeymans whose homes and businesses are in the immediate vicinity of defendant's main cement plant and quarry located in the Town of Coeymans, Albany County, adjacent to U.S. Route 9W. The relief sought in these actions was an injunction restraining defendant from emittion dust and other raw materials and conducting excessive blasting operations in such a manner as to create a nuisance and the recovery of damages sustained as a result of the nuisance so created.
>
> Despite its conclusion that the defendant in the operation of its plant had, in fact, created a nuisance with respect to plaintiffs' properties, the trial court refused to issue an injunction. In reaching its decision on the propriety of granting the injunctive relief sought, the court carefully considered, weighed and evaluated the respective equities, relative hardship and interests of the parties to this dispute and the public at large. Re-examining the record, we note the zoning of the area, the large number of persons employed by the defendant, its extensive business operations and substantial investment in plant and equipment, its use of the most modern and efficient devices to prevent offensive emissions and discharges, and its payment of substantial sums of real property and school taxes. After giving due consideration to all of these relevant factors, the trial court struck the balance in defendant's favor and we find no reason to disturb that determination.
>
> The trial court did award damages based upon the loss of usable value sustained. Plaintiffs' contention to the contrary notwithstanding, we find no ground for interfering with either.[8]

The damages awarded now amount to a license fee enabling the cement company to continue its pollution. This is the same effect that the proposed $10,000 dollar per day fine to be levied on polluters of Lake Michigan would have. Upon payment of a mere $3.65 million dollars per year, industries with gross sales of many billions of dollars each year would have a license to continue polluting Lake Michigan, which already hangs like a festering appendix on the great bowel of midwest civilization.

*Environmental Legislation*

Before abandoning the attempt to make the legislative process relevant to environmental protection, let us consider the problem of pesticide contamination of the biosphere. Look at this particular environmental problem through the eyes of the legislature for a change. There are cries now throughout the country to "Ban DDT!" and a public hue and cry has been raised against the compound that was once hailed as the saviour of mankind. But if we have to wait until we have accumulated the kind of evidence we now have against DDT before we can restrict the use of other broad-spectrum, persistent chemical toxicants, we will always be reacting with too little action, too long after the damage has been done. The problem is to draft a law that is ecologically sophisticated, environmentally relevant, and politically feasible.

The Supreme Court's ruling on "one man — one vote" and even the subsequent reapportionment of many state legislatures have not eliminated voting blocs from the political structure of the states. There are still Italians, Irish, Poles, Germans, Slavs, Blacks, Jews, Spaniards, Puerto Ricans, Mexicans, teachers, steel workers, miners, farmers, ranchers, cattlemen, sheepmen, oilmen, gasmen, city dwellers, suburbanites, commuters, industrialists and industries of all kinds, public power interests, private utility companies, the highway men, the senior citizens, the teenagers, the young people, students, the middle-aged, the hawks and the doves, the hippies, the yippies, the YAFs, the conservatives, the liberals and, yes, even Democrats and Republicans. Each individual voting group must be at least partially satisfied with the overall legislative program of the administration in office or that administration just won't be reelected and returned to office. Even scientists and conservationists are beginning to understand that a governor, a senator, a congressman, or a state representative is only effective while in office. The best-intentioned governor, senator, congressman, or state representative in the country can do little good if he is unable to steer effective legislation through the legislature or if he cannot be reelected.

Historically, conservation as a social movement has been an upper-class and upper-middle-class phenomenon. Under the early leadership of such American aristocrats as Theodore Roosevelt and Gifford Pinchot, it appeared that all the "conservationists" wanted were ducks in the marsh, deer in the forest, trout in the streams, salmon in the rivers, robins on the lawn, a few parks here and there, some scenic highways to get there, and a Conservation Commissioner, just so that they had the ear of government. Today, the conservationists demand wilderness in sight of the city and clean air and clean water — now! — while conveniently forgetting that government action programs cost public monies which in large measure are derived from the very activities being challenged.

Consider the DDT problem. Any law simplistically banning the use or sale, or manufacture or distribution of DDT in your state, county, city, or even the United States, without at the same time establishing an ecologically sophisticated pesticide regulation program, is a bad law. It won't satisfy anyone very long and will permanently polarize agriculture and conservation to such an extent that common problems can no longer be considered in rational discourse.

While it has long been obvious that existing pesticide regulation laws at the federal, state, and local level are inadequate, the initial reaction from conservationists throughout the country is merely to demand conservation representation on existing pesticide control boards, or to insist that any new pesticide control agency have conservationist representation. In 1968, we began to search for a way to write a pesticide control law that would be essentially immune to the makeup of the body administering the law. A law that would protect the environment whether the board administering it was made up entirely of farmers or entirely of bird-watchers or entirely of agricultural chemical company executives. A law that would encourage efforts to maximize agricultural production over a long period of time while minimizing disturbance to the environment and cost to the farmer over similarly long periods of time. A law that would encourage application of systems concepts in entomology, ecology, political science, and agronomy.

The key to such a law is in the criteria for administration action. The criteria for administrative judgment must be written into the law so that the determination of the administrative bodies can later be tested in a court of law, if necessary, against some kind of objective standard.

The conservationists would have us prohibit the use of any material that killed anything other than target insect organisms. This, of course, would reduce insect control methods to the fly-swatter, the hammer and the block — and certain biological control processes — totally inadequate for the feeding of all who are hungry. Again the DDT lawsuits furnished the answer.

Economic entomologists supplied by the Industry Task Force for DDT of the National Agricultural Chemicals Association told us about the damage from insects, and entomologists from the University of California told us about biological control and indicated that the ultimate control would be an integrated combination of biological controls and selected chemicals. It became obvious that the key definitions for any pesticide control law were three: "control," "economic threshhold," and "pest."

"Control" means maintaining pest population density at or below the economic threshhold.

"Economic threshhold" means the pest population density above which there is significant damage to man or his interests.

"Pest" means any organism that is present at a population density above the economic threshhold.

Our definitions were definitions that each vested interest — agriculture, chemical company, and environmentalists — could tolerate, grumble as they might. The definitions are acceptable. And acceptability is the hallmark of politically successful legislation.

The next important element of pesticide legislation is the information requirement. Again we must satisfy both the farmer and the bird-watcher.

In order to encourage national standards, the applicant for registration — and we can assume that this will be the chemical company manufacturing the product rather than any individual user — must demonstrate compliance with the registration procedures of the U.S. Department of Agriculture and then, in order to protect the environment, the applicant must furnish

> Reliable scientific data showing:
> (a) The amount of pesticide, determinable in units of treatment concentration for specific methods of application, required to reduce pest populations to or below the economic threshold.
> (b) The ecological characteristics of the pesticide in the environment, particularly its:
> (1) chemical stability (persistence)
> (2) mobility
> (3) solubility characteristics
> (4) effect on non-target organisms.[9]

Immediately there will be a hue and cry as to the difficulty of furnishing this information, but again, the model law places the burden on those most able to pay — the agricultural chemical industry itself, and imposes a duty of continued disclosure.

Now even if these companies do contribute, directly or indirectly, to elections, they still cannot produce the number of actual votes that a

good pesticide law, satisfying a majority of agricultural and conservation interests, will produce. As a wise old political mentor in my home town told me a long time ago, "People still vote, even when they vote for machines."

Finally, no law is complete without a safety valve, that provision in the law that makes it acceptable to all parties — the provision for judicial review on citizen demand or industry demand, meaning that in a matter of great controversy the issues will be settled in court. And since our courts are allegedly nonpolitical, and all elected politicians have an established policy of noninterference in judicial matters, whatever the courts decide, the politicians will have done their best, and they will have done it in the highest and best political spirit of nonpartisan government. In other words, whatever the courts decide, it won't be the politicians fault.

The model pesticide regulation law provides for a speedy, summary industry appeal through familiar administrative review channels, while the citizen is afforded a declaratory judgment procedure through the courts. Provision is also made to protect industry from harassment of frivolous litigation.

*Equity*

The truly unique element of our legal system is the concept of equity. Some scholars would have you believe that equity is unique to the Anglo-American system of jurisprudence, but that statement is more supported by chauvinism than history. Equity jurisprudence as a system of remedial law evolved from a number of common sources. It can be found in the Talmud and the earliest writings of the Roman law. It can be found today, though it is somewhat less than obvious, in the current system of civil jurisprudence derived from the Code Napoleon and used throughout most of Europe.

In its most elementary form, the fundamental principle of equity jurisprudence is the command: SO USE YOUR OWN PROPERTY AS NOT TO INJURE THAT OF ANOTHER. And the law, in order to give effect to this right provides for appeal to the ultimate power of society, be it king, parliament, state, or people, with a corollary maxim: EQUITY PERMITS NO WRONG TO BE WITHOUT A REMEDY! The effective assertion of equitable rights by an individual or group of individuals is limited only by the rule that a party seeking equitable relief must come forward with "clean hands" — the party must be morally right as well as legally justified. There is an additional rule of restraint self-imposed by courts of equity: the relief granted must be commensurate with the injury suffered by the party seeking relief and tempered by the needs of society.

We have seen an example of equity litigation in the DDT controversy discussed earlier in the chapter. To provide a deeper understanding of equity, the next few sections provide an historical account of its origins and development.

### The Origin of Jurisdiction in Equity

Aristotle asserted that all law is universal and thereby cannot admit of exceptions, yet Aristotle was wise enough in the ways of the world to recognize that what happens in society is that laws promulgated to cover a broad range of human action frequently cause injustice to some innocent individual because his particular case does not appear to be covered by the application of the universal law. He then reasoned, perhaps with tongue in cheek at the period of history, that when the lawmakers make a law, they make it for the good of the community, therefore some legal remedy must be available to the individual treated unjustly by the application of a particular law. In order to determine whether the individual was indeed being treated unfairly by the law, one must look to the intent of the lawmaker and the operation of the law. The remedy for the individual unjustly treated in a particular case by application of a general law was termed by Aristotle *Epicheia,* which translates loosely as "There should be an exception." It was left up to the judge deciding each particular case to determine whether a general or universal law was applicable, and if not, to make the appropriate exception in order to preserve the intention of the lawmaker, which was to ensure the good of the community.

The early Roman lawgivers accepted this concept, named it equity, and used it as a corner-stone for the development of what we now call the Roman Law. The intention of the Roman lawgivers was that one person should not benefit by a law while another person was injured by that law unintentionally and unnecessarily.

During the Middle Ages the heir apparent to the Roman legal system, the Christian church, developed the concept of equity even further, establishing the principle that "for every injury there must be some legal remedy," on the philosophical grounds that if the lawmaker did not provide some remedy for injury to an innocent individual, the law would allow certain injustices to go unpunished while others were punished, and this would be unjust. Since it was then an accepted principle that lawmakers were just, they could not have intended an injustice to follow from their laws, therefore, they intended to provide the legal remedy and the court would simply serve as the means to provide that which they intended to provide all along. Although such circumlocution might have found favor with medieval philosophers, there was, nevertheless, a singularly practical reason for development of the principle. For if there was no procedure for individual relief from the unintended application of a general law, and sufficient individuals were oppressed by the unintended application of that law, then the individuals would tend to look with disfavor on the lawmakers and, in spite of the repression inherent in the feudal system, there might be civil unrest, a condition not conducive to the maintenance of the tenuous existence of the feudal estates which represented civilization in western Europe during the Middle Ages.

Equity jurisprudence developed throughout the ecclesiastical courts following the decline and fall of the Roman Empire, but it was to see its most dramatic development in England following the Norman conquest.

The common law, as distinguished from the customary law of the popular courts, originated in the establishment by Henry II of a national court administering a law for the entire nation, and by the end of the reign of Henry II, we find established a *Curia Regis,* a court of the King, which was a true court of law in the modern sense, administering a national law, common to the entire country, and which had largely displaced the customary laws of the different parts of the country. This continued during the thirteenth century, so that by its close, the common law was definitely established as the law of the nation, displacing the customary law and the local courts which were limited to local petty matters. The law of the *Curia Regis,* which had been the law of the very great, extended and adapted to the needs of the people so as to become the common law of a nation.

So long as the common law remained a flexible system with its field undefined, its power of inclusion unlimited, and its organs undifferentiated, there was no reason for distinguishing between the common law and equity. But soon the law became so fixed and inflexible and its practitioners so absorbed in nice questions of form and pleading, there was no longer room for equity. By the early fourteenth century, the common law, which had supplanted the ancient customary law, had now, in its turn, become the regular system of remedial justice, but with gaps and defects where sufficient remedies were not provided, and resort was necessary to the ancient power of the King as the fountain of all justice.

Equity did not directly contest the existence of settled legal rights. Rather, after recognizing those rights, equity went on to insist that the holder of such legal rights if they were acquired or retained unconsionably, or if they were being used in an unconscionable attempt to interfere with the fundamental rights of others, should be subject to the jurisdiction of the "Chancellor" or the "Keeper of the Conscience of the King" as the source of all legal rights.

## Equitable Relief

It is a fundamental principle essential to the very existence of organized society, and civilization as we know it, that every man, in exercising his personal rights and in the use of his property shall respect the rights and properties of others. Every man must so conduct himself in the enjoyment of the rights and privileges which he may enjoy as a member of society in such a way that he shall prejudice no one in the possession and enjoyment of their personal rights or the rights they hold in common as members of society. When there is an invasion of the rights or privileges of the public or the rights and privileges of any individual held in common by reason of the existence of civilized society, the absence of exact precedent and the fact that commentators on the law do not discuss the subject is of no material importance in awarding equitable relief.

That the exercise of the preventive powers of a court of equity is demanded in a novel case is not a fatal objection. In social evolution, with the march of the arts and sciences, and in the resultant effects upon organized society, it is quite intelligible that new conditions must arise in personal relations, which the rules of the common law, cast in the rigid mold of an earlier status, were not designed to meet. It would be a reproach to equitable jurisprudence, if equity were powerless to extend the application of the principles of common law, or of natural justice, in remedying a wrong, which, in the progress of civilization, has been made possible as the result of new social or commercial conditions.

Equity is the agency by which law is brought into harmony with society. It is one of the factors which operate in judicial evolution. It succeeds legal fictions — those judicial assumptions through which a rule of law is modified in its operation — and it precedes legislation.

Equity has neither fixed boundaries, nor logical subdivisions, and its origin, both in Rome and in England, was that there was a wrong for which there was no remedy at law. As Lord Chancellor Cottenham observed:

> It is the duty of this court, [equity], to adopt its practice and course of proceeding to the existing state of society and not, by a strict adherence to forms and rules, under different circumstances, to decline to administer justice and enforce rights for which there is no other remedy . . . If it were necessary to go much further than it is, in order to open the doors of this court to those who could not obtain [justice] elsewhere, I should not shirk from the responsibility of doing so.[10]

A distinguishing feature of equity jurisdiction is that it will apply settled rules to unusual conditions, and mold its decrees so as to do justice between the parties. Peculiar and extraordinary cases will arise in the complex and diversified affairs of men, which perhaps, cannot be classed under any of the distinct heads of equity jurisdiction, but which must be acknowledged, nevertheless, to come within the legitimate powers of a court of equity because complete justice cannot otherwise be done between the parties. Therefore, when no remedy exists at law, courts of equity, to prevent injustice and in many cases on principles of general policy, will go far in granting relief.

Such was the law of equity at the start of the eighteenth century. If that rule of law had been developed with vigor much of the human and environmental degradation of the Industrial Revolution might have been avoided.

Since that time, two anomalous rules have evolved, interfering with the principle that for every wrong there is a remedy. The first of these anomalies concerns the artificial distinction between public and private nuisance and the second is the doctrine of "sovereign immunity." Both of these doctrines can be attributed to the meddling of Sir William Blackstone (1723-1780).

## Public and Private Nuisance

Until Blackstone there was no distinction made between public and private nuisance. The rule had been well established that any individual could apply to a court of equity to abate a nuisance. But during the later part of the eighteenth century, Blackstone created a new rule of law that was to represent a classic manifestation of the obfuscation of simple legal principles by "self-proclaimed" legal scholars. This new rule of law proclaimed by Blackstone was to contribute substantially to the environmental and social crisis of today and represents the kind of antisocial perversion of the law that made the common law of England during the seventeenth, eighteenth, and nineteenth centuries such an inviting target for the diverse talents of William Shakespeare, Charles Dickens, and W. S. Gilbert.

Blackstone created a difference between public and private nuisance, and the significance of that difference is to be found in the attributes of the public nuisance: (1) only a public nuisance may be made the basis for a criminal prosecution, and (2) only the public, through the proper officer, may sue to enjoin or abate a public nuisance, In the absence of special damage to a particular private individual — damage which is substantially greater than that suffered by other individuals in society — a public nuisance is subject to correction only at the hands of public authority. The mischief done and the disastrous consequences of Blackstone's whim are still evident.

In 1965, an action was brought on behalf of the people of the Town of Brookhaven, in the County of Suffolk, New York, by a group of citizens, to restrain the Long Island duck industry from discharging the raw, untreated sewage equivalent to that of a city of one million people into the waters of Great South Bay, which was once one of the finest shellfishing and marine recreation areas on the east coast of the United States. The duck industry defended the action by admitting that the eight million ducklings grown along the estuaries of the Great South Bay did in fact deliver the raw sewage effluent equivalent of a city of one million people into the Bay, but they demanded that the Court dismiss the action on the grounds that such an affront to the public waters was so great that it was a "public nuisance" not a "private nuisance" and as a "public nuisance" it could only be attacked by the Attorney General of the state of New York, not by any private citizens, unless of course those private citizens could establish "special damages" different from the damages sustained by the public at large.

A New York State Supreme Court, the same court that less than a year later in a dramatic reversal of precedent would issue the first injunction against the use of DDT ever granted by a Court, dismissed the case against the duck industry, accepting without question the argument that a public nuisance could not be abated by a private citizen or group of citizens.

How could this strange concept have crept into the law of equity? What is the justification for this strange anomaly in that body of law that holds no wrong may exist without a remedy? In 1858, the Court of Appeals of the State of New York identified the source and expounded the justification for this onerous rule,

> A contrary rule would be productive of very great inconveniences. . . . No private person or

number of persons can assume to be the champions of the community and in its behalf, challenge the public officers to meet them in the courts of justice to defend their official acts.[11]

The court continued and discussed the theory of the decision,

> The general rule is that for wrongs against the public, whether actually committed or only apprehended, the remedy, whether civil or criminal, is by a prosecution instituted by the state in its political character, or by some officer authorized by law to act in its behalf. . . .
>
> The principle is further exemplified in questions respecting nuisances. Common or public nuisances, which are such as are inconvenient or injurious to the whole community in general, are, as all are aware, indictable [the People of the State can take action in a criminal proceeding] only, and not actionable [any citizen can sue]; for as **Blackstone** [*Blackstone's Commentaries*, Book 4, p. 167] says, "it would be unreasonable to multiply suits by giving every man a separate right of action for what damnifies him in common only with the rest of his fellow-citizens.[11]

Just who was Sir William Blackstone that he should exert such a restraint on the general application of equitable principles? Referring to the eleventh edition of the *Encyclopaedia Britannica*, published in 1911 and drawing on continual revisions from the first English edition in 1771, the following information may be elicited under the entry, "Blackstone, Sir William (1723-1780)":

> . . . In 1746 he was called to the bar. Though but little known or distinguished as a pleader, he was actively employed during his occasional residences at the university (Oxford), in taking part in the internal management of his college. In May 1749, as a small reward for his services, and to give him further opportunity of advancing the interests of the college, Blackstone was appointed steward of its manors. In the same year, on the resignation of his uncle, he was elected recorder of the Borough of Wallingford. . . . He accepted a seat on the bench, and on the death of Sir Joseph (Yates) succeeded him (in the court of common pleas). He died on the 14th of February, 1780 . . . .
>
> Blackstone was by no means what would now be called a scientific jurist. He had only the vaguest possible grasp of the elementary conceptions of law. Austin, who accused him of following slavishly the method of Hale's Analysis of the Law, declares that he "blindly adopts the mistakes of his rude and compendious model; missing invariably, with a nice and surprising infelicity, the pregnant but obscure suggestions which it proffered to his attention, and which would have guided a discerning and inventive writer to an arrangement comparatively just.
>
> From the small place which equity jurisprudence occupies in his arrangement, he would scarcely seem to have realized its true position in the law of England.
>
> Bentham accuses him of being the enemy of all reform, and the unscrupulous champion of every form of professional chicanery. Austin says that he truckled to the sinister influences and mischievous prejudices of power, and that he flattered the overweening conceit of the English in their own institutions. "He displays much ingenuity in giving a plausible form to common prejudices and fallacies. . . ."

For more than a century the opinion of that one man has stood in the way of a proper disciplined application of a fundamental principle of equity jurisprudence, "equity will not suffer a wrong without a remedy."

Just what happened at the time of Blackstone? It was obvious that Blackstone set himself to the task of codifying the laws of England, but in the process of attempting to build a logical and consistent body of legal principles he lost the basic insight of the Anglo-American system of jurisprudence, the common law.

The common law grew with civilization and the practices and customs of society. As the oppressed peasants obtained certain remedies during the Middle Ages, these remedies became a part of the common law. That is why the English legal system to which we are heirs, depends on case law or precedent rather than elaborate codes promulgated by a legislature or king. A system of administering justice based on precedent rather than statute is inherently more flexible and capable of meeting the needs of society because the court is free to interpret the law with reference to, and by analogy with, past cases of similar import, though not precisely identical.

There is no doubt that Blackstone did a reasonable job of tidying-up the law, but in his attempt to make of law an axiomatic science little different from geometry, he lost the essential elements of equity jurisprudence, particularly the rule that for every injury there must be a legal remedy.

## Sovereign Immunity

Blackstone's justification for striking the principle that for every injury there must be a legal remedy from the law of England arose from his belief that the King could do no wrong. Reasoning that failure to provide an adequate legal remedy for an injury was wrong, and that the King could do no wrong, it was obvious that there was no need for a rule of law providing a remedy for every wrong, because the King had obviously provided the remedy, since the King could do no wrong and failure to provide a remedy for an injury would be wrong. This perfectly circular argument has been exposed by many legal scholars, yet it still appears in decisions of courts that should know better.

Consider for a moment the ideological basis for establishing American independence. The founding fathers of this country were asserting the fundamental equitable principle that no wrong should exist without an adequate legal remedy. They did not deny the right of George III to tax his American colonies, they asserted that certain taxes were the wrong taxes, at the wrong time and for the wrong purposes. Taxation without representation was wrong. In other words, the King could, in fact, under certain circumstances, do wrong, and the equitable rule of law that no wrong should exist without a legal remedy was a fundamental human right.

Unfortunately, the founding fathers had short memories and quickly established Blackstone's principle that the King could do no wrong in a slightly modified form, applying the doctrine of sovereign immunity to the action of the newly established federal government. This principle was quickly asserted by the states and until very recently courts regularly asserted the principle that the federal government and each state government were immune from suit by any citizen unless the government itself specifically authorized the suit. Again the stumbling block in the way of free access to the courtroom for protection of the environment requires historical analysis before it can be overcome.

The general doctrine of the immunity of the United States from suit without consent of Congress is a rule conceived by the federal judiciary. There is no basis for this rule either in the Constitution itself or in any specific statute of Congress, but rather sovereign immunity is a rule adopted by the U.S. Supreme Court.

Apparently the first assertion of the sovereign immunity of the federal government was the dictum by Chief Justice John Marshall in *Cohens v. Virginia.* "The universally received opinion is, that no suit can be commenced or prosecuted against the United States; that the Judiciary Act does not authorize such suits."[12]

But, Justice Wilson had previously specifically stated that the term "sovereign" was "unknown" to the Constitution of the United States:

> [T]he term sovereign has for its correlative, subject. In this sense, the term can receive no application; for it has no object in the Constitution of the United States. Under that Constitution there are citizens, but no subjects. . . . [T]he people . . . of the United States . . . have reserved the Supreme Power in their own hands; and on that Supreme Power, have made the [government] dependent, instead of being sovereign . . . .[13a]

He had traced the establishment of despotic governments to the doctrine of sovereignty:

> [In] almost every nation which has been denominated *free,* the *state* has assumed a supercilious pre-eminence above the *people,* who have *formed* it: Hence the haughty notions of *state independence, state sovereignty* and *state supremacy.* In *despotic* Governments, the *Government* has usurped, in a similar manner, both upon the *state* and the *people:* Hence all arbitrary doctrines and pretensions concerning the Supreme, absolute, and incontrolable, power of *Government.* In *each, man* is degraded from the *prime* rank, which he ought to hold in human affairs . . . .[13b]

Justice Wilson also indicated that in England the sovereignty had been described as being in Parliament, with the people ignored; to Wilson this was a description of a despotic government:

> From the crown of *Great Britain,* the sovereignty of their country passed to the people of it . . . [T]he people, in their collective and national capacity, established the present Constitution. It is remarkable that in establishing it, the people exercised their own rights, and their own proper sovereignty, and conscious of the plentitude of it, they declared with becoming dignity, "We the *people* of the *United States,* do ordain and estab-

lish this Constitution." Here, we see the people acting as sovereigns of the whole country. . . .[13c]

By contrast, in England the doctrine of sovereignty was based on feudal principles that considered the prince as sovereign and the people as his subjects. Such feudal principles contemplated the sovereign

> . . .as being the fountain of honor and authority; and from his grace and grant derives all franchises, immunities and privileges; it is easy to perceive that such a sovereign could not be amenable to a Court of Justice, or subjected to judicial control and actual constraint. It was of necessity, therefore, that suability became incompatible with such sovereignty. Besides, the *Prince* having all the Executive powers, the judgment of the Courts would, in fact, be only monitory, not mandatory to him, and a capacity to be advised, is a distinct thing from a capacity to be sued. The same feudal ideas run through all their jurisprudence, and constantly remind us of the distinction between the *Prince* and the subject. No such ideas obtain here; at the Revolution, the sovereignty devolved on the people; and they are truly the sovereigns of the country, but they are *sovereigns without subjects* . . . and have none to govern but *themselves;* the citizens of *America* are equal as fellow citizens, and as joint tenants in the sovereignty.
>
> . . . Sovereignty is the right to govern; a nation or State-sovereign is the person or persons in whom that resides. In *Europe* the sovereignty is generally ascribed to the *Prince;* here it resides with the people . . . Their *Princes* have *personal* powers, dignities and pre-eminences, our rulers have none but *official;* nor do they partake in the sovereignty otherwise, or in any other capacity, than as private citizens.[13d]

In fact, it is clear that the majority of the Supreme Court, just five years after the adoption of the Constitution of the United States, rejected the idea of the United States as sovereign — and necessarily the rule of sovereign immunity from suit — because "suability became incompatible with such sovereignty."[13e] The people were the sovereign, not the United States government.

However, a century later, the doctrine of sovereign immunity had crept back into the courts, and in 1882 the Supreme Court of the United States reviewed the reasons underlying this judicially created doctrine of sovereign immunity.

> In this, as in most other cases of like character, it will be found that the doctrine is derived from the laws and practices of our English ancestors:

> What were the reasons which forbid that the King should be sued in his own court, and how do they apply to the political body corporate which we call the United States of America?[14]

The doctrine of sovereign immunity first scorned by the Supreme Court, then hesitantly justified by the Supreme Court as an inherited concept from the English Common law, is now justified solely on grounds of policy.

> The reasons for this immunity are imbedded in our legal philosophy. They partake somewhat of dignity and decorum, somewhat of practical administration, somewhat of the political desirability of an impregnable legal citadel where government as distinct from its functionaries may operate undisturbed by the demands of litigants.[15]

> [W]hile the political theory that the King could do no wrong was repudiated in America, a legal doctrine derived from it that the Crown is immune from any suit to which it has not consented was invoked on behalf of the Republic and applied by our courts as vigorously as it had been on behalf of the Crown.[16]

The doctrine of sovereign immunity from suit, a fiction created by the federal judiciary, is today based upon the desirability of leaving the government — the sovereign — unfettered from accomplishing its business. But the people are the sovereign under the Constitution of the United States; the officers of the government "are the agents of the people,"[17] and if indeed "The government of the Union . . . is emphatically and truly, a government of the people. In form and in substance it emanates from them. Its powers are granted by them, and are to be exercised directly on them, and for their benefit,"[18] then the doctrine of sovereign immunity is an unconstitutional infringement on the standing of individual citizens, under the Ninth and Tenth Amendments of the United States Constitution to contest the validity of governmental activities.

## Popular Sovereignty

There is one vestige of the concept of sovereignty that does inure to the benefit of the people. From time immemorial, land — all land — was the absolute personal property of the sovereign and could be used, abused, given, or taken at the whim of the sovereign. In some societies the king was the sovereign, in others the state was the sovereign, and in the United States, the people, collectively, in common, are the sovereign. Throughout the history of civilization, wars and revolutions have been fought over land, its control, or its utilization. In the United States, all powers with respect to land once held by the Kings of England, France, or Spain, are now held by the people of the United States collectively and exercised, by permission of the people, by the executive, legislative, and judicial branches of the federal government, and the governments of the several states, with these governmental systems acting as the agents, trustees, or keepers of the power of the people.

The constitution of the United States provides that the rights not explicitly given by the people of the United States to the federal government are retained by the people of the Unites States as collectively assembled in the several states, and the second repository of sovereign powers is in the people of the several states.

> The enumeration in the Constitution, of certain rights, shall not be construed to deny or disparage others retained by the people. (*United States Constitution*, Ninth Amendment)

> The powers not delegated to the United States by the Constitution, nor prohibited by it to the States, are reserved to the States respectively, or to the people. (*United States Constitution*, Tenth Amendment)

As the individual state constitutions were formulated, the rights of individual owners of private property were strengthened, but at no time did the sovereign, the people of the United States, give up the ultimate right to determine the highest and best use of land on behalf of the American people. Neither did the people of the individual states give up their rights collectively as the sovereign state, to provide for the common good and insist on behalf of all the people that land use be according to the highest and best use of the land as determined by the physical and environmental parameters of the land and the region of which it is a part. The justification for any restriction on the individual use of land is found in the concept of sovereignty.

If we are to live in harmony with that which has been given to us from preceding generations and from the earth before man, we must make certain assumptions with respect to every available piece of open land in the United States:

> The area is vulnerable.

> Development of some kind is inevitable.

> Development of the land to its highest and best use as an element of human ecology must be accommodated.

> Development must be determined by the environment of the region and its inherent ecological characteristics.

> The area should contain all prospective growth without limiting its highest and best use as an element of human ecology.

> Planned growth towards the highest and best use of the land and its associated environment is more profitable to the region and its population than unplanned growth.

> The police power of the state, the ultimate sovereignty of the people, and the maintenance of traditional American concepts of private property ownership are all compatible and can join together in the harmonious, mutually beneficial development of the area.[19]

### Zoning: Master Planning Manifest in Law

Recognizing the limited availability of land itself and the place of land as the basic capital asset and fundamental natural resource of civilized man, land use historically has been limited by executive, legislative, and judicial process.

The judiciary in the United States has upheld the attempts of the several states, and at the local level, municipalities, to restrict the use of land in accordance with some rational plan, usually designated euphemistically as the Community or Regional Master Plan.

> Zoning is not just an expansion of the common law of nuisance. It seeks to achieve much more than the removal of obnoxious gases and unsightly uses. Underlying the entire concept of zoning is the assumption that zoning can be a vital tool for maintaining a civilized form of existence only if we employ the insights and the learning of the philosopher, the city planner, the economist, the sociologist, the public health expert and also the other professions concerned with urban problems. . . .

> This fundamental conception of zoning has been present from its inception. The almost universal, statutory requirement that zoning conform to a "well-considered plan" or "comprehensive plan" is a reflection of that view [See Standard State Zoning Enabling Act, U.S. Dept. of Commerce (1926).] The thought behind the requirement is that consideration must be given

to needs of the community as a whole. In exercising their zoning powers, the local authorities must act for the benefit of the community as a whole following a common deliberate consideration of the alternatives, and not because of the whims of either an articulate minority or even majority in the community. . . . Rather, the comprehensive plan is the essence of zoning. Without it, there can be no rational allocation of land use. It is the insurance that the public welfare is being served and that zoning does not become nothing more than just a Gallup poll.[20]

### Ecologically Sophisticated Zoning Legislation

Zoning laws have been upheld by the courts on the grounds that they represent an attempt by an individual community, government agency, or state to determine the highest and best use of its limited land resources for the greatest good of the greatest number of people without any undue infringement on the individual rights of property owners. The key to successful zoning legislation is the determination of the highest and best use of land resources. Of necessity this must be done by a team of individuals trained in the various disciplines necessary to define the environmental parameters of a regional ecosystem. The community itself, particularly its people, constitute elements of that regional ecosystem just as surely as do the basic land area, its topography, hydrology, meteorology, and climatology.

The determination of the highest and best use of the land in a regional ecosystem will never be made by traffic engineers who call themselves master planners, or by architects who call themselves city planners. The adequate determination of the highest and best use of the limited land resources of a regional ecosystem mandates a systems analysis approach coupled with modern computer capabilities in order to determine the boundary value solutions and elemental optimizations of the complex nonlinear higher order relationships that describe the region as it actually exists, in real time, rather than as a stylized formalization which is little more than a figment of the imagination of some self-proclaimed expert. Nevertheless, even when the analysis of interrelationships has been made and the matrix of functional relationships described, it will still be necessary to proceed with the process of synthesis and a thorough study of information transfer within the regional system.

Now just what does all this esoteric talk of sovereignty really mean to the local municipality, the homeowner, or the state official?

It means that any zoning law which does not fully reflect the ecological verities of the region in which it intends to operate is fatally defective in the legal sense. It can not be sustained in the courts in the face of an ecologically sophisticated attack.

It means that any zoning law which does in fact reflect the ecological elements of the region in which it intends to operate can be sustained in the public interest, even if it appears to infringe upon the sacrosanct right of private property ownership.

It means that any master plan which fails to consider the ecological integrity of the region and does not fully determine the interrelationships among each element of the land and the landscape and each natural resource is scientifically incomplete and legally defective.

It means that any master plan which does in fact consider the ecological integrity of the region and does fully determine the interrelationships for each element of the land and landscape and each natural resource is complete and can be sustained as the basis for legal restraints on land use even when they appear to violate the sacrosanct right of private property.

Any so-called master plan, be it for village, town, city, county, state, or region, which fails to evaluate fully the effects of any proposed land use on the overall ecological integrity of the system is an inadequate plan at best and is ultimately doomed to become a costly and deadly hoax on the community. Any zoning law — local, state or federal — based upon such inadequate evaluation must fail. It should fail as legislation, and it will fail in the courts; just as every attempt to ignore the natural limitations imposed on man's use of his natural resources must fail.

Attorneys sometimes shudder at the temerity of challenging the sacrosanct right of private property, the concept upon which great fortunes have been built, governments established, legislatures suborned, and courts misled, but before you dismiss the foregoing material as the figment of the imagination of some dewy-eyed revolutionary, remember the success of the arguments which saved the Florissant fossil beds.

## Airport Sites and Air Travel

As a practical example of the application of the principles of equity jurisprudence and the sovereignty of the people, consider the problems of site selection for major airports. Although the problem of airport siting is quite complicated today, particularly because of urban encroachment[21] and inadequate (nonexistent?) regional planning, it should be possible to assert two fundamental statements of fact which can become principles of law at equity:

> The air traveler is entitled — as a matter of absolute right — to the safest possible flight which the state-of-the-art in modern aviation technology is capable of providing.
>
> The homeowner and the man on the street are entitled to protection from the hazards of aircraft operations.[22]

An ecologically sophisticated, socially relevant, politically feasible, legally supportable airport zoning law can be written with remarkable ease and be readily comprehensible — as zoning laws go in this country — by simply depending upon those two simple principles.

There are certain areas about airports and in the vicinity of aircraft operations which are inherently dangerous. The area of most probable hazard to ground operations in the vicinity of a military airfield, for instance, is the area 7½ miles along the longitudinal axis of an active runway, and 1-3/4 miles on each side of that active runway.[21] Once this zone of maximum hazard has been established for the operations of a given airport, no residential housing or high-density human activities should be permitted in the area.

It makes little difference whether this is accomplished by legislation or litigation, so long as it is accomplished. There is no right to build a residential dwelling or worse yet a residential development in this zone of maximum hazard from aircraft operations. There is also no right to build any structure or conduct any activity which will increase the risk to aircraft operations in that zone.

"But," the landowner says, "if you limit my use of my own land, you are taking my property without due process of law and must pay just compensation." Nonsense! This is not taking, this is protection. If the land is vacant, and its development is restricted to those uses which do not involve human habitation or high-density human occupation, its ultimate increase in value is assured. If there is residential activity in the area already, and it moved in after the airport facility was in operation, the homeowner is not entitled to compensation since any diminution in the value of his property is not the result of new public action, but his own actions. The homeowner in effect knew, or with the exercise of reasonable prudence or due care should have known, that the area of maximum ground hazard from aircraft operations nearby is not the place to build or purchase a home. If the airport moves into an area where homes are already present, then the burden of relocating the homeowner out of the zone of maximum hazard must be borne by the airport authority.

Ultimately, the permitted uses in this zone of maximum hazard — agriculture, horticulture, forestry, certain industrial operations requiring minimum human density, transportation facilities, and airport-associated industries — will build up the area and buffer the outlying residential areas throughout the useful life of the airport. It should be obvious to all, and it is certainly an urban fact of life, that the location of an airport irrevocably determines the environmental characteristics of the area in which it is located, altering the intrinsic suitability or unsuitability of that area for certain types of development.

As the zone of maximum hazard is buffered by limited permitted uses, and these permitted uses fill the space, their existence at that location will determine the further development pattern of the area, and residential development will tend to concentrate further away from the airport rather than move towards the airport — the apparently suicidal tendency encouraged today by conventional zoning laws.

## Recovery of Public Property

There is a second example of the potential application of equity jurisprudence and the concept of popular sovereignty. Consider the California redwoods. There is considerable national sentiment favoring some protection of these magnificent trees for the enjoyment of future generations. There is already on the record Congressional action seeking to establish Redwood National Park such that these trees can be protected. Unfortunately the redwood forests are now owned in large measure by commercial forest product development corporations which consider them a source of income through harvesting and reforestation with faster-growing, shorter lived, more commercially valuable species. The timber companies apparently have no objection to losing their redwood forests, provided they are compensated at the reasonable market value of the trees as commercial lumber. This so raises the cost of the land acquisition to the public agencies, Congress, the state legislatures, or nonprofit public benefit organizations such as the Nature Conservancy, that only inadequate areas can be acquired and protected. What can be done?

There is no doubt that under our existing concepts of justice the owner of the land taken for a public use is entitled to just compensation. The issue is, What is "just compensation?" Is it the fair market value of the forest as commercial timber? No. It is an amount equal to the original cost of the land to the present owner, plus the taxes the present owner has paid on the land since it was acquired, plus the reasonable rate of interest on such an investment, together with the cost of removal of the owners operations. But isn't the landowner entitled to the reasonable lawful use of his property and shouldn't the condemnation award reflect the most profitable use of the land to the owner — in the case of a redwood forest, timber?

Yes, but only if the property was the owner's personal property originally, and this is where the concept of popular sovereignty is needed. The timber company is not the real owner of property that has been vested with the public interest. The timber company acquired the property — if we trace the chain of title far enough back — from the sovereign, either the king or the government, and now the sovereign wants its property back. Before the Constitution furnished the citizen with some protection of his property

from seizure by the sovereign, the sovereign would simply take the property and usually the head of the subject at the same time in order to limit protest. Today we require that the sovereign pay just compensation. How much is "just compensation"? It is certainly not an unconscionable profit at the expense of the sovereign. In this country the sovereign is the people of the United States and the people are obligated only to make the property owner whole, the people have no obligation to furnish the property owner with a windfall profit at the expense of the people.

The principles of equity jurisprudence can be asserted by the people under the concept of popular sovereignty. They can take direct legal action to protect national natural resource treasures and the environment of man while at the same time assuring wise use of such resources in a salubrious environment by the people of this generation and safeguarding those generations yet unborn.

Legal defense of the environment today depends in large measure on a sense of history. If the environmental defender accepts that historical position which asserts the king can do no wrong and the titular sovereign is immune from suit, then we must sit back and wait for the Congress or the state legislatures or the President of the United States or the governors of the several states to act. Reliance upon such ill-founded legal principles has led to the ridiculous proposition that we must amend the Constitution to assure each citizen certain basic environmental rights such as the right to clean air and potable water, and the maintenance of diverse viable populations of plants and animals. Nonsense! Just think of the affront to our founding fathers that such a proposed constitutional amendment represents. Think of the true meaning of such a constitutional amendment. What the proposers of such an amendment are really saying is that the men who were far-sighted enough to have guaranteed freedom of religion; freedom of speech; freedom of the press; the right to peacefully assemble to petition for redress of grievances; the right to be secure against unreasonable search and seizures; the privilege against self-incrimination; protection against double jeopardy; trial by jury, due process, and equal protection, reasonable bail and protection from cruel and unusual punishments — the men who were visionary enough to secure all those rights for the generations yet unborn and then wise enough to state that "The enumeration in the Constitution of certain rights, shall not be construed to deny or disparage others retained by the people" just in case there might be future assaults on the citadel of liberty — these men were not concerned enough to guarantee the American citizens of the twentieth century the right to breathe. All right, all of you who sincerely believe that we need a constitutional amendment in order to secure our right to breathe, stop breathing!

What can you do when a government agency decides to drown the Grand Canyon or most of Central Alaska, or when a combination of government agencies acts in concert to destroy the delicate ecological balance of the entire state of Florida?

What can you do when a municipality decides that the highest and best use of a mighty interstate river system is a local, open sewer?

What can you do when the U.S. Department of Agriculture refuses to consider the effects of chlorinated hydrocarbon pesticides on nontarget organisms, and the manufacturers of DDT and the other persistent, broad-spectrum chlorinated hydrocarbon pesticides refuse to furnish the American people with the information from their own research on the long-term toxic effects of their products?

What can you do when an entire industry, such as the nonferrous metals industry, continues to avoid installation of state-of-the-art pollution control systems at their smelters, refineries, and foundries?

What can you do when timber and paper companies cut down entire forests of redwood and other magnificent species in order to "reforest" the area with fast-growing pulp wood trees?

What can you do when builders and developers insist on dredging estuaries to fill salt marshes or strip the topsoil from prime agricultural land in order to plant houses?

What can you do about an automobile industry that insists on major style changes every three years while continuing to reproduce the same

inefficient, air-polluting internal combustion engine?

Just what can you do?

Today, while there is still time,

## SUE THEM!

You must knock on the doors of courthouses throughout this nation and seek equitable protection for the environment. You must not wait for Congress or state legislatures, or local government to pass laws, you must assert the fundamental doctrine of equitable jurisprudence — a doctrine as old as civilization, as old as the Talmud or the New Testament, or the Roman Law, or the Middle Ages — a doctrine as new as today and as advanced as tomorrow: SO USE YOUR OWN PROPERTY AS NOT TO INJURE THE PROPERTY OF ANOTHER.

At this time in history, the environment must be defended by direct legal attack on environmental degradation asserting the fundamental human right to life by demanding air clean enough to breathe and water clean enough to drink safely, as well as diverse populations of plants and animals dynamically stable enough to provide a supporting ecological system for mankind.

As far as industry is concerned, this means demanding the cleanest air and the cleanest water that the existing state of the art in pollution control technology can provide. As far as government is concerned, this means insisting that government is the trustee for the sovereign people and that all of our natural resources are held in trust for the full benefit, use, and enjoyment of all the people, not only of this generation, but of those generations still to come, subject only to wise use for the advancement of civilization in each generation.

Conventional conservation education will not save the Everglades, the Oklawaha, the Grand Canyon, the Yukon, or any other national natural resource treasure which has become the object of private greed or public blundering. Only imaginative legal action on behalf of all the people entitled to the full benefit, use, and enjoyment of such national natural resource treasures, of this and future generations, in class actions for equitable relief, particularly declaratory judgments to declare the rights of the people and injunctions to prohibit actions which can infringe such rights, will present the facts and raise the issues in a forum where the conscience of the community in the person of a court of equity can resolve the conflict, essentially free of the political, economic, and bureaucratic influences which have controlled our national environmental policy to date.

In matters of heated environmental controversy there is considerable difficulty in presenting information, especially scientific data, in a forum where it can be received in an unemotional and objective atmosphere. Some consider mass demonstrations the most effective way to carry the environmental message to the people and move the public to demand action from elected officials and government bureaus. The same experts also consider public demonstrations the best way to secure media coverage of the information presented. Perhaps such methods once had value — there is no doubt that informational picketing during the early days of labor organization was effective — but today one must contrast the effects of a student demonstrator lying in a pool of blood in the gutter holding a picket sign for 30 seconds of coverage on late night TV news with the same student sitting in a witness chair giving evidence in a courtroom. Industry and government can ignore protests and informational picketing, government can certainly repress demonstrations, but no one in industry or government ignores that scrap of legal foolscap that begins:

YOU ARE HEREBY SUMMONED TO ANSWER THE ALLEGATIONS OF THE COMPLAINT ANNEXED HERETO WITHIN 20 DAYS OR JUDGMENT WILL BE TAKEN AGAINST YOU FOR THE RELIEF DEMANDED!

No one from government bureaucrat to corporate officer ignores a summons from a court.

Rest assured that the corporation president reads it; the chairman of the board reads it; their house counsel reads it; their Wall Street counsel reads it; and most important to the citizen, the defendants named must answer it. And it must be answered in court, not in the media where public relations budgets can influence coverage;

not in the market place where concentrated economic power is effective control; but in the courtroom where, as far as facts and evidence are concerned, the individual citizen is the equal of any corporation or government agency.

All of the major social changes which have made America a hospitable place to live have had their basis in fundamental constitutional litigation. Somebody had to sue somebody before the legislature, in enlightened self-interest (for the public benefit, of course) acted. Our adversary system of trial litigation has been the means of presenting facts and evidence to the conscience of the community since Magna Charta. The courtroom is the last arena where the individual citizen can meet big business or government bureaucracy and hope to survive. Litigation is civilization's only alternative to revolution. If you do not forsake your courts they will not forsake you — the citizen — in your hour of need. Thomas à Becket and Thomas More are only two of the many who gave their lives that you, the citizen, can have your day in court.

## References

1. Copyright 1971, Victor John Yannacone, jr., all rights reserved. The material in this chapter is taken from the substance of certain speeches and articles dealing with environmental law presented during 1969 and 1970 by the author, together with new material prepared for this book.
2. Yannacone, V. J., jr., and Cohen, B. S. 1971. *Environmental Rights & Remedies,* Lawyers Cooperative Publishing Co., Bancroft, Whitney & Co., Rochester, N.Y. Any of the topics presented in this chapter can be pursued in depth in *Environmental Rights & Remedies* by consulting the index or the table of cases. Hereafter, specific points are not referenced.
3. Defenders of Florissant, Inc. v. Park Land Company et al. 1969. Verified Complaint filed in U.S. District Court for the District of Colorado, Denver, Colo.
4. Defenders of Florissant, Inc. v. Park Land Company et al. 1969. Argument before the

U.S. Court of Appeals for the Tenth Circuit by Victor John Yannacone, Jr., Attorney for Defenders of Florissant, July 9.

5. **Carol A. Yannacone v. Dennison et al.** 1967. Supreme Court, Suffolk County, 55 Misc2d 468, 471, 472; 285 NYS2d 476.

6. In re **Petition of the Citizens Natural Resources Association of Wisconsin** for a ruling declaring DDT a pollutant. 1969. Docket 3 D R, Wisconsin Department of Natural Resources.

7. *Science 158: 1552-1556 (1967).*

8. **Boomer v. Atlantic Cement Co.** 1969. 55 Misc2d 1023, 287 NYS2d 112, affirmed 30 AD2d 480, 294 NYS2d 452 reversed 26 NY2d 219 1970.

9. **Model Pesticide Law.** 1969. Prepared by Victor John Yannacone, Jr., and presented to the 1969 Mid-Winter Republican Governors Conference, Dec. 10-12.

10. **Wallworth v. Holt.** 4 Myl & C 619 (England).

11. **Doolittle v. Supervisors of Broome County.** 1958. 18 NY 155, 159, 160, 163.

12. **Cohens v. Virginia.** 1821. 19 US (6 Wheat.) 264, 411-12.

13. (a) **Chisholm v. Georgia.** 1793. 2 US (2 Dall) 419, at 456, 457. (b) *ibid.,* at 461 (emphasis in original); (c) *ibid.,* at 470-471 (emphasis in original); (d) *ibid.,* at 471, 472 (emphasis in original); (e) *ibid.,* at 471;cited in V. J. Yannacone, Jr., Plaintiff's brief against Project Rulison, *Cornell Law Review LV:* 761.

14. **United States v. Lee.** 1882. 106 US 196, 205-209.

15. **United States v. Shaw.** 1940. 309 US 495, 501.

16. **Feres v. United States.** 1950. 340 US 125, 139.

17. **Chisholm v. Georgia.** 1793. 2 US (2 Dall.) 419, 472.

18. **McCulloch v. Maryland.** 1819. 17 US (4 Wheat.) 316, 404, 405.

19. **McHarg, I.** 1969. *Design With Nature.* Natural History Press, New York.

20. **Udell v. Haas.** 21 NY2d 463; 235 NE2d 897 288 NYS2d 888.

21. **Sims, Maj. William R.** and **Cerchione, Capt. Angelo J.,** 1969. *In Search of an Aviation Master Plan,* Air University Review, Vol. XX, No. 6, pp. 64-72, Sept-Oct, 1969.

22. **Yannacone, V. J., jr.** 1970. Aviation and the law. In *Master Planning the Aviation Environment.* Univ. of Arizona Press, Tucson, Arizona.

# 19 Environment and Administration: The Politics of Ecology

Lynton K. Caldwell

Administration is to policy as means are to ends. But means and ends are often interrelated in diverse ways and the distinction between them is not always clear. The difference often is relative because what may be ends for one purpose may be means to another; or the means toward an objective may in certain respects become ends in themselves. For example, protection of the environment is a goal of responsible government, but not all means to this end are equally acceptable in all societies. In the United States, public opinion and political tradition favor open, democratic, and predictable procedures in the execution of public law and policy. Procedures perceived to be arbitrary or autocratic are widely rejected in principle and are usually avoided (but are sometimes camouflaged) in practice.

Administrative procedures characteristically are shaped by a variety of influences of which an official statement of goal or purpose, for example a law, is only one. This is because understandings of what is intended are never exactly the same for all of the individuals involved, and the goals or purposes of policy and administra-

---

LYNTON K. CALDWELL is Professor of Political Science at Indiana University. After earning graduate degrees at Harvard and the University of Chicago, he served on the faculties of Chicago, Syracuse University, and the University of California at Berkeley. He has been a consultant to the Argonne National Laboratory, the National Institutes of Health, and NASA, and has served on special assignments in Colombia, Pakistan, India, Thailand, Turkey and Indonesia. His major professional interest focuses on the interaction of science and public policy in modern society, with emphasis on the role of government in the relationship between man and environment.

tion are neither formulated nor pursued with anything approaching absolute freedom. All human action occurs in a context set by history and the existing state of the physical world. The world is dynamic — history evolves from past to future. And so all human ends and means, all public policies and administrative procedures, must, to the extent necessary, conform to the conditions that prevail. Unfortunately for the convenience of those concerned, the extent of this necessity is usually indeterminate. In each circumstance it must be discovered by trial and error.

This is not to say that human actions are completely predetermined by events. But it is clear that a large part of human activity, particularly in relation to the environment, is a response to conditions or events. The evolution of technology — invention in clothing, housing, agriculture, energy, and medicine, for example — illustrates man's response to circumstances in his environment. Many of the new public efforts toward ecological protection and control are reactions to disastrous consequences of previous interactions of human society with its environment. The unfolding and interactions of these circumstances and events have brought human society to a point in time at which comprehensive management of man's environmental relationships has become a practical necessity. Although there may be strong dissent to this proposition, an examination of man's situation in relation to his environment readily reveals why this is so.

## The Man-Environment Predicament

During the twentieth century human society has moved from an open-space to a closed-space world. In a strictly physical sense the earth belongs to an open-space cosmic system, receiving and reflecting solar energy. In a practical sense the world was always a closed system. Until the advent of space flight, man was absolutely confined to the biophysical conditions on earth. He remains dependent for survival on the planetary life-support system of air, water, soil, and living things. Space technology has not altered this circumstance, it has only modified it to the extent that man may now leave the earth for relatively brief intervals provided that he carries a life-support system with him. The earth is still his indispensable base, but the growth of his numbers, his technologies, and his exploitive patterns of behavior have radically altered his relationship to this planetary base. The ecological crisis, present or impending, is a consequence of man's slowness to adapt his behavior to these changed circumstances.

In brief, as other essays in this volume have pointed out, modern man has sought infinite expansion in a finite world and is now being faced with the inevitable consequences of this ultimately self-defeating course of action. Among these consequences are overpopulation, environmental pollution, resource depletion including soil exhaustion, the extinction of plant and animal species, degenerative disease, new forms of psychological stress, social instability, and individual despair. The environmental quality movement emerged during the second half of the twentieth century as a response to a slowly growing popular awareness that modern man was rapidly impairing his life-support base and endangering his own survival and that of all living things. By 1970, the accumulating evidence of man's ecological predicament had become so clear that no thoughtful· and informed person could honestly deny it. But honest opinions differ as to how modern man can get out of this predicament into which his own short-sighted ingenuity has placed him.

Four courses of policy have been distinguishable among the welter of opinions on how to deal with man's environmental crisis. Oversimplified for clarity they may be summarized as follows:

1. No special action is necessary beyond prevention of immediate or incontrovertible lethal effects. This laissez-faire attitude assumes that man is a tough animal in a tough world, and that having survived vicissitudes in the past he will do so in the future. Holders of this opinion deny that there is an ecological crisis and decry "alarmist" prophecies of gloom and doom.

2. There is, or soon may be, an ecological crisis, but technology can overcome it. This is the optimism of the "technological fix." Its advocates argue that the world can support indefinitely expanding populations and resource demands because technology will find a way of meeting human needs. This opinion has been widely held among engineers, Marxists, free-enterprise industrialists, and some scientists, and has been popular among Westernized intelligensia in "underdeveloped countries."

3. Technoscientific industrialism is the cause of our ecological crisis and must be abandoned or rigidly repressed. This attitude is sometimes ridiculed by its critics as a "back-to-nature" obsession. It holds suspect most efforts to restore the quality of the environment through governmental action or technological innovation. Its adherents see governmental and industrial bureaucracies as the principal architects of our ecological predicament and question the logic of relying upon those institutions that led us into it to get us out of it. Extreme antitechnologists would abandon cities, restore subsistence agriculture, and make "harmony with nature" the criterion of wise and moral public policy.

4. Technoscientific industrialism has indeed resulted in an ecological crisis, but modern man has built himself into the technoscientific culture so completely that he cannot voluntarily abandon it even though he might wish that he could. The way out of his predicament is neither through rejecting science-based technology nor uncritically relying upon it. The only practicable policy would be to control the uses of science and technology toward ecologically wise ends. But "wise ends" implies an "edited culture" in which the future shape of society would be socially planned and guided in accordance with ecological criteria.

Of these four lines of policy only the fourth seems feasible. Neither the laissez-faire nor the technological fix policies afford any practical assurance of reversing the worsening crisis of ecology. They offer simplistic approaches to a complex situation. Sometimes there is a case to be made for less government control and for the use of technology in solving environmental problems. But to rely primarily upon either of these approaches precludes our drawing upon the full range of possibilities in coping with our environmental problems. Both approaches impose unnecessary constraints upon public policy and leave a large number of man-environment problems without any practicable method of solution.

The antitechnology, antibureaucracy approach is utopian and naïve in its implication that modern man in the aggregate can be persuaded voluntarily to return to a preindustrial way of life. Modern society has become dependent upon artificial systems to a degree that precludes their summary abandonment without massive loss of life. Supplies of food, water, clothing, and medicine depend upon the continued functioning of technological systems even though their maladministration has created many of our environmental problems. To phase down this dependence in any time period less than several decades would require a massive shift in public attitudes, the exercise of totalitarian political power, and immense bureaucratic efficiency. The type of regime capable of dismantling the technoscientific industrial apparatus would be rejected by large numbers of antitechnologists, and no adequate power base for such a regime is apparent in modern society.

Arguments over which course of policy is most likely to bring modern society out of its ecological predicament are thus largely theoretical. There is truly only one course open to modern industrial man that offers a real prospect of solving his ecological problems. No course offers assurance, but an "edited" culture and a guided economy based on ecologically valid principles offers the only realistic, operational possibility. Unless the intelligence, aggressiveness, and ingenuity that got man into his ecological mess can transcend past performance and get him out of it, the "descent of man" will take on a new grim meaning.

If man is to work his way out of his ecological crisis, a clear articulation of ends and means is required. Society blundered into its present predicament largely because goals and outcomes were inadequately considered, seldom specified, and rarely appraised in the light of verifiable knowledge. Until very recently the knowledge necessary to formulate positive environmental policy was grossly inadequate. But even this inadequate knowledge was inadequately used. Efforts to enlarge and perfect ecological understanding were (and still are) minimal because the need for the requisite kind of knowledge has been insufficiently understood. Today, however, there is sufficient knowledge to begin to formulate public policies for man-environment relationships on ecologically sound principles. The excuse that "we don't know enough" is no longer good enough. We know enough to desist from ecologically dubious undertakings and to cease practices that have been demonstrated to be ecologically damaging. Human health, personal freedom, safety, and happiness are increasingly threatened by competing acts of man in a finite environment. If dealing with these difficulties are not the proper functions of government, then an effective substitute for government will have to be discovered. What this might be belongs for the present to the realms of conjecture and science fiction.

## Foundations for Political Ecology

If the salvation of society lies in the thoughtful application of science and technology to an edited culture, a fundamental task of society is to determine what that culture is to be. But "societies" are abstract entities and as such make no determinations — only living people do that. And, although scientific knowledge and technology would be indispensable to shaping the course of cultural development, ALL  f o r m s  of knowledge would be contributory to this end. Social, ethical, and esthetic values, subject to scientific analyses of their implications, would afford more significant criteria for cultural "editing" than relying primarily either upon science or the humanities for guidance.

In the absence of agreement as to the general character of the society, there is no adequate basis for social determination of the ends toward which science and technology should be directed.

Nor is it possible to ascertain what areas of science and technology ought, in the public interest, to be further developed. Certainly any serious effort to cope with the ecological problems of modern society implies a commitment to specified social goals and planning. But not all people accept these implications as feasible or desirable. Opponents of the planned application of science tend to cluster in the following three groupings: (1) convinced democrats, (2) laissez-faire conservatives, and (3) science individualists.

CONVINCED DEMOCRATS include persons whose interpretation of democracy and the "rights" of individuals and minorities appear to be incompatible with the idea of cultural editing. Who, they ask, is to decide how the culture is shaped? The question is obviously legitimate, reflecting a fear of an imposition of social goals by a self-selected elite. But the question often is asked in a rhetorical spirit that suggest that any answer will be impractical or otherwise unsatisfactory. Objections from this viewpoint might partially be overcome by a system that facilitated widespread popular participation in goal-setting and decision-making. But some critics would remain skeptical of the capacity of people for cooperation and consensus on any basis other than perceived self-interest. These skeptics tend to agree with laissez-faire conservatives that impersonal market mechanisms are the safest means to feasible social decisions.

LAISSEZ-FAIRE CONSERVATIVES tend to be distrustful of elites AND of popular participation in the making of social choices. Their objectives are directed primarily to future choices, adherence to past social choices being the essence of conservatism. The concept of cultural editing would be especially disturbing to advocates of free enterprise. Editing implies restriction and suggests guidance and the elimination of those aspects of the economy that are "not in conformity with the general plan." If the general plan is to preserve, protect, and restore the life-support capabilities of the biosphere, activities that are ecologically harmful would logically be marked for elimination. This could mean that certain hitherto legitimate businesses and ways of doing business could become illegal.

SCIENCE INDIVIDUALISTS believe that only the individual scientist can determine goals of scientific research. In fact, however, many scientists accept the feasibility of social goals for science, provided that the determination is made by scientists collectively or is made upon the basis of scientific judgment. The view that scientists cannot be made to pursue lines of inquiry that do not interest them is only a half-truth. Individual scientists in large numbers have been attracted into lines of research for which ample funding was provided and which were "fashionable" within the relevant communities of science. Nuclear physics, space science, and molecular biology are cases in point. Scientists as a group have evidenced concern with the goals of science and the interrelations between science and social development. The proposition that social goals should be ecologically valid is consistent with values widely held among scientists, and especially with the belief that it is more rational to be guided by confirmed knowledge than by tradition or conjecture. Determination of the goals of science can never be more than, in part, an individual judgment.

Regardless of these and other misgivings regarding social planning, the predicament of modern man forces him into it. The attempt to cope with problems of human demands upon a finite world cannot succeed without a mutually consistent set of operational methods. Our present methods of dealing with the environment often work against one another and indeed are often employed for purposes that are conflicting. For example, our efforts to conserve fisheries through regulations of the catch are contradicted by the filling of tidal and estuarial breeding grounds. Mutually consistent methods cannot be developed without the assistance of a coherent and popular explanatory theory of man in context (for example, man in relation to his evolved and contrived environment). What is needed is a scientifically confirmable theory of man in nature that points to verifiable principles of conduct and rational modes of action. This is the philosophical basis for the ECOLOGICAL ATTITUDE.

Having committed himself to the necessity for management of his environment, it remains for modern man to undertake the task of developing goals and guidelines for this action. In doing this, it will be necessary to construct a conceptual foundation for the policies and activities that are undertaken.

Throughout most of history to date, human societies have proceeded generally upon assumptions that have become less and less tenable. Old assumptions misled and continue to mislead modern society. The spaceship is the paradigm or symbolic expression of the ecological state of contemporary humanity. Some coherent and believable model of man in context is necessary to obtain popular acceptance of the necessities of the new age. The growth of the human economy in a finite world cannot be infinite. At some point, presently undetermined, man must either achieve a homeostatic (or steady-state) social condition, or must periodically experience sharp declines of population and a permanent impairment of the quality of life. The harsh alternatives to rational limitation of population growth were described by Robert Malthus and, as ultimate consequences, have never been disproved.

A homeostatic condition in society would, therefore, seem to be an ultimate necessity for human welfare. It should be understood, however, as a tendency rather than as a static condition. Many, and perhaps all living systems are subject to oscillations in levels of population. The difference between a homeostatic condition and a cycle of exponential growth and catastrophic decline may be one of degree. But the degree of difference can amount to a fundamental difference of condition, especially when a population "crash" results in the extinction of whole species or even genera of living things. Nevertheless, the achievement of a self-containing and self-renewing society on a worldwide basis would probably be the most difficult task that civilized man has attempted. We cannot even be sure that the human animal is capable of achieving or maintaining the self-control necessary to a homeostatic state.

Efforts to achieve a steady-state society — and opposition to these efforts — afford a new area for political conflict. Evidence of this conflict is already appearing in issues concerning population control, environmental pollution, land use, and resource depletion. The conflict would be less confused and might even be constructive if it proceeded on the basis of agreed-upon assumptions regarding the state of man in nature. Such assumptions would be practical expressions of a confirmable theory of man in context which, of course, embraces a theory of man in relation to man. In the absence of such a theory, expressed in operational terms, there appears to be no practicable way to bridge the gap between ecological analyses of threats to man's life-support base, on the one hand, and technical proposals for meeting these threats, on the other. To bridge this gap requires decisions as to priorities, laws, institutional arrangements, physical and esthetic outcomes, and the quality of society itself.

To be realistic is to recognize that no theory of man in context can be valid that is not formulated with reference to the flow of time. In a world of inevitable and apparently irreversible change, no homeostatic state can be validly interpreted as unchanging. And, because of the complexities of the processes of change and the limitations of human knowledge, no theory of man in context can be scientifically confirmable in absolute terms. The politics of ecology must, therefore, be a politics of probabilities, supported by a theory of nature that draws realistic distinctions between those things about which certainty is possible and those that are indeterminate.

A politics of ecology is, therefore, the practical expression of a theory of man in nature that is confirmable by scientific method, is amenable to correction, is probabilistic, and takes account of the phenomena of time, change, and indeterminacy. Such a theory implies an ethic, or in the words of René Dubos, a "theology of the earth."[1] In the effort to understand the place of man in nature, science and religion converge. If this convergence leads to a synthesis and the synthesis is made operational through a plan of action, a powerful political ideology could result. An explanation of the power of Marxism has been that it is a universal theory of history with an implicit ethic which leads directly to action. The politics of ecology could be more persuasive than Marxism, for example, has been, to the extent that its propositions are based upon science rather than upon an unverifiable philosophy of history. And unlike most ideologies and theologies, a valid politics of ecology must possess a capacity for self-correction as required by new knowledge.

Unlike politics and theologies based on revelation and final truth, a politics of ecology is evolutionary. It is, therefore, less susceptible to dogmatism, obsolescence, and irrelevance. Problems of heresy and deviation are less likely to arise to the extent that there are objective methods for ascertaining the truth of a proposition. It is consistent with the character of ecological theory to abstain from final judgment because of insufficiency of evidence. A politics of ecology is, therefore, less arbitrary than many modern ideologies, although it is also less amenable to bargaining. Its great advantages are factual verification as a test of truth and, as ecological science develops, a capacity for reliable prediction.

The ability to predict would enable a politics of ecology to delineate the probable consequences of alternative solutions to environmental problems. And so, although in one sense politics of ecology would be less democratic than advocates of decision-making through bargaining might prefer, it could in fact provide more meaningful popular participation and influence than bargaining situations usually permit. This wider involvement of people is possible to the extent that politics sets forth alternative courses of action with reliable estimates of their costs and consequences.

Insofar as this approach to popular decision can be followed and is followed, the decisions of government are more likely to become popular decisions than they are when decisions are negotiated between competing interests, with the secondary consequences for society neither ascertained nor considered. In the long run, the politics of ecology would be more consistent with popular participation and choice than the kinds of democracy that are now in effect. One need not argue that the science of ecology has all or most of the answers needed for rationalizing all ecologically related social decisions. The science of ecology is far from adequate for our needs, but it affords a more reliable basis for political decisions than those that have underlain most of our major public laws and policies to date. Moreover, commitment to an ecological politics would

force an intensification and broadening of ecological research, especially in the areas referred to as "human ecology."

In the following discussions of administrative policies and procedures, the concomitant of an ecologically based politics is assumed. Without this kind of politics in our public life no lasting inroad upon our environmental problems can be expected. In the absence of a comprehensive and comprehensible philosophy of man and nature that is operational, techniques of policy analysis and decision-making are merely veneers covering traditional methods of negotiation and bargaining based upon physical, bureaucratic, or economic power. The ecological approach implies a problem-solving approach to policy questions. We have observed that the mental and moral capabilities of man in the aggregate may not be adequate for this task. But the advantages to human welfare and happiness in the ecological approach are so great that an effort to create this kind of politics is justified regardless of the probability of its success.

### Existing Modes of Public Action

Nowhere do present political institutions in the aggregate reflect an ecological view of man and society. Efforts to meet the mounting problems of Spaceship Earth have most often proceeded by modifying existing structures and procedures. And, because perception and understanding of our growing ecological problems tends to be restricted to a relatively highly educated minority, the prospects for arousing sufficient public concern to obtain fundamental reforms in priorities and administrative agencies affecting the environment are uncertain. To alter the orientation of an entire governmental system is a task of truly Napoleonic proportions. Such changes are seldom made peaceably or democratically, nor can their actual character be assured on the basis of previous experience. Institutional changes, structural or procedural, that have thus far been developed to cope with environmental problems have been relatively minor and incremental.

This caution has doubtless been prudent, as neither experience nor analysis has shown us clearly the best way to reorganize our institutions for environmental administration. Nevertheless, present efforts and past failures are enabling us to identify the principal obstacles to success and to formulate criteria for effective performance. We will examine these obstacles and emerging criteria; but in order to establish an informational base from which to make this examination, it is first necessary to review the methods presently being used to govern man's use of his environment.

Most of the modes and methods by which public policies for the environment are put into effect are not new. The specific forms that this action takes are the familiar ones of persuasion, regulation, adjudication, and management. But precedent to these methods of applying public policies are two other modes of public action: legislation and planning.

The conventional method of declaring public policies is through LEGISLATION. There are, of course, many ways in which law is formulated and expressed. Principal among these are written constitutions, treaties, statutes, executive orders or decrees, legislative resolutions, municipal ordinances, and administrative rules or regulations. Law is used to establish goals, to specify means, and to provide the incentives, procedures, penalties, and resources needed to achieve policy objectives.

The most common vehicle for the expression of public environmental policy is statutory law, which is the kind of legislation that most people have in mind when they say that "there ought to be a law." Statutes are enacted pursuant to or consistent with more fundamental expressions of law called "constitutions," and they are the basis for more detailed legislative acts or for administrative rules, regulations, or managerial action undertaken to carry out or enforce the legislative intent. A list of the more important national legislative acts establishing environmental policy in the United States is given in Table I.

An example of an important legislative statute (or law) establishing public policy for the environment in the United States is the National Environmental Policy Act of 1969 (Public Law 91-190). This legislation, which took effect with its signing by President Richard M. Nixon on

January 1, 1970, declares that protection and improvement of the environment is a policy of the Congress of the United States. The act specifies the content of the policy and provides specific procedures for its enforcement. We will examine the substance of this act later in this chapter. It is cited here as an example of the use of legislative action in laying a foundation for the other modes of public action, administrative and judicial, through which public policies directly affect the lives of people.

Insofar as people voluntarily conform to ecologically sensible patterns of behavior, the function of the law is primarily goal-setting and declaratory. People cannot cooperate except upon the basis of some common purpose or objective. For large complex societies, the goals and objectives of social conduct must be stated where they will have visibility and legitimacy. In order to obtain coordinated public effort, especially on a voluntary basis, there must be at least a minimal degree of common order. For this order to be generally accepted, it must be based upon some agreed-upon procedure for obtaining social consensus. In self-governing commonwealths, this procedure has been the enactment of law in some appropriate form (for example, statute, constitutional amendment, or resolution) by elected representative assemblies. Upon the basis of this legislation, executory and implementing procedures may be developed. But increasingly the

---

Water Pollution Control Act of 1948: 80-845
Air Pollution Control Act of 1955: 84-159
Clean Air Act of 1963: 88-206 (Amended in 1965: 89-272, and in 1966: 89-675)
National Wilderness Preservation Act of 1964: 88-577
Land and Water Conservation Act of 1964: 88-578
Water Resources Planning Act of 1965: 89-80
Water Quality Act of 1965: 89-234
Motor Vehicle Air Pollution Control Act of 1965: Title II of 89-272
Solid Waste Disposal Act of 1965: Title III of 89-272
Highway Beautification Act of 1965: 89-285
Clean Water Restoration Act of 1966: 89-753
Air Quality Act of 1967: 90-148
National Water Commission Act of 1968: 90-515
National Trails System Act of 1968: 90-543
Wild and Scenic Rivers Act of 1968: 90-542
Radiation Control for Health and Safety Act of 1968: 90-602
National Environmental Policy Act of 1969: 91-190
Water Quality Improvement Act of 1970: 91-224

**ENVIRONMENTAL LEGISLATION.**

attainment of social goals necessitates complex and extensive procedures that cannot wisely be specified in advance in detail. This circumstance partly results from the size, complexity, and dynamism of modern societies and is partly a consequence of the application of scientific experiment and technological innovation to the solution of perceived problems. Rapid changes in the state of knowledge and technique make impractical detailed and mandatory prescriptions in the law. Legislative specification of social goals and objectives has, therefore, led to increasing use of planning as a mode of public action.

As with legislation, the term PLANNING covers a wide range of activities. Our concern with it here is as a formal process for determining how to accomplish specified goals of public action (see, for example, reference 2, especially the two chapters cited). The planning that is intended to affect man-environment relationships is largely "physical" planning. It includes such familiar activities as the design of bridges, location of highways, layout of towns, and determination of land use. But the environment is also affected by other forms of planning and these affects are not always foreseen or desired. For example, financial planning may ignore environmental consequences of taxation in relation to the use of land, improvements to property, and the exploitation of natural resources. Urban sprawl and the destruction of the rural environs of American cities may, in part, be attributed to the household finance policies of the federal government that were not accompanied by adequate planning for individual home-ownership.

Two major weaknesses in formal planning for public action are first, that it tends to be incomplete and, second, that it has too seldom been properly implemented.

The extent to which planning should be comprehensive — should try to take everything relevant into account — is controversial among professional planners. Obviously how far comprehensiveness should be taken is at issue because the extremes of focus on one single thing or on everything are impossible to achieve. As Garret Hardin has observed, it is not possible to do just one thing. Every action has multiple consequences and every plan, however narrowly conceived, has implications that will affect its outcome or the outcomes of other efforts. Therefore, planning must to some extent be comprehensive if it is to be relied upon for its intended purposes. Planning that is concerned with ecological factors, including ecosystems, is inadequate and even dangerous if it is substantially less comprehensive than the interrelated phenomena that are involved. Many of the worst consequences of planned efforts in agriculture, public works, transportation, and housing may be attributed to narrowly conceived planning that ignored the full range of ecological factors in the thing that was attempted.

The second weakness in public planning has been in making it operational. In countries in which formal planning bodies have been established, separate and apart from executory agencies, plans have frequently been ignored or half-heartedly executed. American city and regional planning offers a seemingly endless array of abandoned, rejected, or distorted plans. Perhaps some of these plans should not have been implemented, but many well-conceived and badly needed plans have been shelved because of inadequate provision for their implementation. There are some persuasive arguments for separating the actual planning process from its implementation. An implementing agency that generates the plans that it carries out may assume a self-perpetuating character, and planning may be done more for the advantage of the agency than for any real public need. In the United States, for example, the Army Corps of Engineers has been criticized for promoting the plans that it subsequently is called upon to execute.[3,4] A major problem of environmental administration is, therefore, how to obtain an effective implementation of planning without making the planning process into a vehicle that serves the interest of the implementing agency first and the public interest second. In brief, how can the public interest in planning be protected?

This problem may become more acute in the future than it has been heretofore. The politics of ecology would require an articulated sequence of investigation, planning, execution, evaluation, review, and further planning. The separation of planning from other phases of the political process would only be methodological or sequential. The entire process of environmental planning and administration must be integral to be effective. But to keep this process responsible and responsive, some means of independent review of planning and plan execution must be provided. The politics of democracy obviously requires this check upon planners, but the problem of accountability is hardly less in totalitarian governments. Plan implementation has been a continuing problem in the Soviet Union and in Communist China. The magnitude, complexity, and specialization of modern government and society make comprehensive large-scale planning extremely difficult to control. No guaranteed prescription for effective and responsible large-scale planning can honestly be offered today.

Successful planning most frequently is found where public goals are clearest, where public consensus is high, and where the personalities and technical capabilities of the planners and their political associates are conducive to cooperation. Examination of what actually happens leads to the pessimistic conclusion that cooperative, comprehensive planning is a mode of public action essential to the maintenance of civilized society in a crowded industrialized world, and that human beings, for the most part, are indifferently equipped by culture, and perhaps by genetics, for high levels of cooperative, coordinative action. Competitiveness, egoism, aggressiveness, and short-sightedness are among the common human traits that defeat the effectiveness of public planning. Whether "human nature" can transcend these common limitations is conjectural. But the question is of highest importance, as people and nations can plan themselves into destruction as well as out of their ecological difficulties. And as matters stand in the world today, public planning is to some extent unavoidable.

*Modes of Policy Implementation*

The goals or objectives of public action are set by law and planning. They are commonly implemented through a variety of means, often used in combination. There is no generally accepted way to categorize or describe these modes of policy implementation, and readers who wish to examine them from a variety of perspectives will need to consult the literature of public policy or public administration (as a beginning the works in references 5 and 6 might be consulted). For convenience in discussing the implementation of public policy for the environment, principal modes of action were categorized earlier in this chapter as persuasion, regulation, adjudication, and management. PERSUASION, when effective, is an efficient means to goal attainment if its overhead or operational costs are low. The ideal result of persuasion is a pattern of behavior internalized in the individual. Voluntary cooperation may then take place on behalf of declared public goals with minimal psychic or material cost. To obtain this internalized behavior and resultant cooperation may, however, require a major effort of education or indoctrination. Campaigns to reduce littering of roadsides and to include voluntary restrictions of family size illustrate this method of policy implementation. Ideas may be powerful persuaders, and efforts such as that of the Scientists Institute for Public Information (at Rockefeller University, 30 East Sixty-Eighth Street, New York, N. Y. 10021)[7] and the program to establish community ecology centers[8] are examples of the use of information to change the attitudes and behavior of people. To the extent that people are persuaded that a given policy is desirable or necessary, other modes of public action are facilitated or are less needed. Without some minimal degree of persuasion no other mode of action can be fully effective.

REGULATION is a more formal and usually a more costly method of action. It involves the adoption, in pursuance of law, of rules under which certain activities in society may be carried on. Regulations may be sought to control behavior in which general compliance with public policy cannot realistically be expected. Regulated activities are frequently those in which individual self-interest easily conflicts with the general interest. Land speculation, destructive resource exploitation, and the projection of industrial wastes onto the public environment are activities in which it might pay the individual or the organization to be a bad citizen. In these instances, public regulation is invoked to protect the public interest. There are a large number of government agencies whose regulatory activities incidentally or collaterally affect the environment. Examples are the rules of the Federal Aviation Agency regarding operations of aircraft, and the regulations of the Food and Drug Administration and the Department of Agriculture on the use of pesticides.

Regulatory agencies may thus have certain similarities to courts of law. They do not directly manage or administer the affairs of the interests, individuals, or corporations that they regulate. Characteristically, public regulators are boards or commissions, although individual public administrators, judges, or courts of law, may be given regulatory responsibilities. Fish and game commissions, air or water pollution control boards, land-use zoning appeal boards, and public utility commissions are examples of regulatory agencies that control activities without being responsible for either the success or failure of those activities.

Regulatory action includes the right to issue (or deny) licenses and permits, to adopt rules governing specified activities such as hunting, fishing, burning leaves, or subdividing land, and to investigate alleged violations of those rules. Because the perceived self-interest of the regulated is served by favorable action by the regulator, the regulatory process has a "built-in" tendency toward abuse. Corruption is an ever-present danger when the regulated attempt to persuade the regulators toward a favorable line of action. Bribes have been offered to planning or zoning commissions exercising regulatory power over the subdivision or utilization of land. But short of outright monetary bribery, which appears to be very exceptional in the more technologically advanced countries, the regulatory process is vulnerable to "symbiotic" relationships between the regulatory agency and the regulated interests.

For example, members of a natural resources commission in a western American state might develop a point of view toward the exploitation of minerals that is almost identical with that of the officials of the mining companies whose activities they regulate. Under these circumstances, the full range of public interests in the natural environment might be subordinated to the particular interests of mining. These symbiotic relationships in public regulation occur most often when there are frequent movements of personnel between the regulatory agency and the regulated interests, or when the economic and political stakes in the regulated activity are high enough to make worthwhile the taking of risks in bringing influence to bear upon the regulatory officials. (Some examples of the impact of interest groups on regulatory agencies are given by Gable.[9])

ADJUDICATION may be administered either by executive agencies or courts of law. Regulation may ultimately be enforced by adjudicative procedures. A common objective of the procedure is to determine whether a given regulation has, or has not, been violated. Adjudicative action may be sought by private individuals through law suits or by public law enforcement agencies. By traditional practice in the United States (and to a similar extent in all judicial systems based on Anglo-Saxon law), alleged rights of the individual in the environment have been enforceable chiefly by self-help through suits for damages in the courts. This after-the-fact remedy is NO REMEDY for many types of environmental abuse. Moreover, traditional judicial procedures are poorly adapted to a science-based, probabilistic politics. It appears, therefore, that findings of fact on environmental issues will increasingly be left to administrative determination. The courts may continue, however, to perform indispensable services in determining constitutional questions and holding administrative agencies to constitutional procedures.

In recent years greater use has been made of judicial procedures to prevent damage to the environment by governmental agencies and business corporations. To overcome the limitations on self-help as a means of obtaining adjudicative action, organizations have been formed to reduce the risk and cost to individual citizens in seeking remedies through the courts. Among these organizations are the Environmental Defense Fund and the Conservation Law Society of America (Chapter 18). Moreover, conservation organizations such as the Sierra Club and the National Audubon Society have effectively used legal remedies on behalf of environmental quality and ecological values.

The availability and scope of judicial remedies in the United States have been greatly enlarged in recent years by federal and state legislation and by judicial interpretations of older legal provisions. The action of the Second U. S. Court of Appeals in 1966, setting aside of license granted to the Consolidated Edison Company by the Federal Power Commission to build a hydroelectric facility on Storm King Mountain in New York, was described by the *Wall Street Journal* as a precedent-setting decision.[10] In this case, the regulatory agency, the Federal Power Commission, was directed by the court to reconsider the companies' application, giving due consideration to "preservation of natural beauty and of national historical shrines." The National Environmental Policy Act of 1969 has been invoked in cases involving the Florida Everglades jet airport and the trans-Alaska oil pipeline. Thus, with a clearer legislative commitment to environmental quality and ecological values and with organized and depersonalized means for distributing the costs and risks of litigation, the self-help means of law enforcement through adjudication may acquire a new effectiveness and increased use.

MANAGEMENT is the most direct form of public action and may be the most common form of public action in the future. In free-enterprise countries, there exists a general popular bias against direct management of natural resources and the environment by government. Yet even in the United States there are a large number of environment-shaping activities directly administered by government. Government agencies may, nevertheless, contract with private business organizations for actual performance of the operational tasks. In the federal government of the United States, the Corps of Engineers, the Bureau of Reclamation, the Atomic Energy Commission, the Forest Service, the National Park Service, and the Bureau of Public Lands directly manage various aspects of the environment in various ways.[11] Most of the agencies also perform regulatory functions. The Corps of Engineers issues permits for construction on or adjacent to navigable waters; the Atomic Energy

Commission has certain licensing controls over radioactive substances and nuclear power facilities; and the Bureau of Public Lands regulates grazing on the public domain. But these agencies also directly act upon the environment through their own employees and in pursuance of policies and programs that they have formulated.

Because much of the discussion that follows pertains to the managerial mode of public action, no further discussion will be developed here. Instead we will examine the obstacles to the formulation and administration of ecologically sound public policies. This overview of difficulties is necessary to provide background for considering what future changes in public policy and institutions may be required if a politics of ecology is to be implemented effectively.

The OBSTACLES to effective policy formulation and execution are numerous and, as with modes of public action, there is no single orthodox way to describe them. Similarly, the various obstacles are interrelated, each contributing to the obstructive character of the others. The discussion that follows will consider obstacles to policy effectiveness under three headings: (1) Ecological Relationships Misinterpreted, (2) Problems Wrongly Diagnosed, and (3) Institutions Poorly Adapted. These sections will be followed by a discussion of criteria for a more effective administration.

*Ecological Relationships Misinterpreted*

Ecological relationships that are misunderstood or not understood at all include interrelationships between men and societies of men as well as man's relationships with the natural environment. The subject of man-environment relationships has been characterized by serious problems of semantics or of meaning. These have been treated at length by Harold and Margaret Sprout.[12]

If the political theories that have dominated modern thinking have inadequately or incorrectly interpreted the true state of man in nature, their continued dominance can only frustrate and retard man's ability to cope with his self-made ecological crisis. It is for this reason that a valid politics of ecology must precede or accompany public action to protect and improve the environment. That there is already an emergent politics of ecology is evident by public action, especially since 1968, on international as well as national and local political levels. There is also a literature on the politics of ecology, but it does not appear that the concept has as yet received a definitive statement.[13]

The argument that a philosophy of man's relation to nature is also a philosophy of man in relation to other men is illustrated by one of the major conceptual difficulties of creating institutions for environmental administration. This is the dichotomy between the public and private aspects of life. An extension of this dichotomy is the distinction between governmental and nongovernmental activities. These distinctions are, of course, more cultural and legal than ecological. But human ecology does have cultural as well as physiological dimensions. Moreover, interpretations of interpersonal and social relationships influence the way in which men think about their environments and affect their readiness to cooperate in measures to protect or to improve environmental conditions. Political theory and ecological thought are not separate and unrelated, and much of our failure to protect environmental values through public action may be fairly attributable to failure to recognize this.

The formal boundaries between public and private or between governmental and nongovernmental areas are set by culture and made explicit by law. These boundaries and distinctions differ among cultures. And within a culturally heterogeneous society such as that of the United States widespread differences of interpretation may exist. Perceptions and realities also differ, complicating public agreement concerning what is necessary and "realistic." For example, the term "private" is often applied to organizations and activities that functionally are public; large-scale corporate enterprise is an example. In addition, technological and ecological change may extend public concern to activities and relationships that could once be viewed as private. The "right" to unlimited child-bearing is a case in point. As the fit between a society and its physical environment becomes tighter, the scope of strictly private activities may be sharply restricted. In the

congested environments of modern industrial societies, activities as diverse as the burning of leaves, the consumption of beef, and the keeping of household pets may become matters of public concern and public policy.

Invasions of traditional privacy are more often the consequences of population pressure and unguided technology than of willful impairment of "private rights" by government. The principal obstacles to the personal freedom of modern man and to the impairment of his environment are the competing and incompatible activities of other men. A major motivation toward a politics of ecology has been the mutual frustration of competing interests. Conflicts over land use and the allocation of water resources have stimulated coordinative efforts by government, even when no ecological viewpoint or environmental policy was present. The public is now concerned with the location of privately owned airports, with the application of agricultural pesticides, and with the composition of household detergents. But public concern over these issues has been fragmented and based as much upon invasions of private rights or public rights as on the ecological wisdom or folly of the actions involved. This is, of course, a logical consequence of the precedence of historically defined personal and public rights over more recent ecological concepts. Ecological or environmental rights, individual or public, have with few exceptions (for example, public nuisances) only recently been defined by law. Indeed, the question of human rights to a healthful or pleasing environment is still very much unsettled in the United States and has been the subject of at least two proposed amendments to the Constitution [91st Congress, 1st Session, House Joint Resolution 54 (January 3, 1969, Ottinger) and 91st Congress, 2nd Session, Senate Joint Resolution 196 (January 19, 1970, Nelson)].

In order to build institutions for the more effective management of man's ecological relationships, a more sophisticated and realistic interpretation of personal freedom and social responsibility in relation to man's environmental situation must become current in society. Ecological relationships are flagrantly misinterpreted in treating the artificial boundaries between nations and other political jurisdictions as if they were intrinsically more "real" and more significant than ecological boundaries. The biosphere affords no basis for doctrines of national sovereignty, and few worldwide ecological problems (for example, those affecting the atmosphere and the oceans) can be resolved on an exclusively national basis. The Spaceship Earth concept is the true paradigm of man's environmental situation, but it is not yet the model for the prevailing interpretations of man's relationship to his environment.

Were it not for rivalries and ideological conflicts among nations, it might be easier to construct effective environmental agencies on an international basis, where there is little past experience, than in nations where historical constraints are strong. On the basis of clearly evident need and objective criteria, nations might cooperate to build new international policies and structures that might not be supportable under their domestic political ideologies and systems. The readiness of nations to participate in international environmental control depends, however, upon the recognition of the need to do so on the part of their leaders, and upon their peoples possessing the collective will and the means to honor international commitments on behalf of the environment.

*Problems Wrongly Diagnosed*

Because of the comprehensiveness and complexity of most environmental problems, various but mutually consistent methods are required for their solution. It is axiomatic that the nature of the problem determines the suitability of methods for its solution, and this is why the importance of the conceptual foundation for policy and administration has been stressed in the foregoing pages. To the extent that the general problem of man-environment relationships has been improperly formulated, attempts to deal with it through technology, law, and administration have been unsuccessful. Some examples of this mismatching of problem and methods may be instructive.

In the United States, billions of dollars and uncalculated effort have been spent on flood control in river valleys. The problem has been posed in terms that tend to brush aside or belittle hydrological and climatological realities. Periodically the floodplains of rivers are flooded. But through the engineering of dikes, levees, reservoirs, channel straightening, and drainage ditches, efforts have been made to permit human activities on the floodplains to proceed just as they would on flood-free uplands. The costs of attempting to impose human will upon natural systems of continental drainage have been enormous. They have also been unnecessary, as two other solutions are available, either of which is more consistent with ecological realities.

The first would be to follow the common-sense solution long used in Southeast Asia. In monsoon climates, floods are a regular seasonal event, and homes, factories, and villages are constructed for year-round safety. In the dry season, buildings along a river appear to stand on stilts, well above the water level. During floods the water rises to the lower level of the buildings, but without inconvenience to the occupants other than the removal of domestic animals and equipment from the land that is normally flooded.

A second alternative would be to prohibit permanent or perishable installations on the floodplain. Agriculture could be carried on with occasional crop losses covered by insurance. Activities not vulnerable to flooding (forestry, for example) could be undertaken with minimal engineering protection. Commercial structures could be permitted provided that they were built according to a flood protection zoning code that would insure against their becoming public burdens or nuisances as a result of damage through flooding. In countries such as the United States, in which the pressures on the land are not unduly great in the principal river valleys, there is little practical need to build on flood plains. The incentive to do so is often related to ecologically unwise policies affecting construction on waterfront land and encouraging speculation in land prices.

Obviously either method interferes with the right alleged by some people to assume their own risks and to live and build where and as they please.[14,15] Stubborn insistence on rebuilding in flood-hazard areas would not be given public acquiescence or financial support in an ecologically rational society. This is not to argue that some management of river systems would not be desirable even in a political economy that was strongly nature-oriented. But the elaborate system of waterway management that Americans have undertaken commits them indefinitely to high costs of maintenance and to the permanent flooding of upstream acres, to some extent offsetting those for which protection is provided downstream. If artificial control measures are taken near the seacoast, they often destroy interesting and biologically productive deltas and estuaries, and often cause the attrition of beaches. A politics of ecology would attempt to correct this misapplication of engineering technology through methods appropriate to natural conditions. It would seek to minimize the costs of working against nature and would refuse to concede to any individual, business, or governmental agency the right to commandeer from society the money and effort required to maintain irrational patterns of activity in the flood plain.[16,17]

Another set of examples of wrong solutions to misstated problems applies to the irrigation of arid lands. There are circumstances in which the support of human populations through irrigated agriculture is fully justifiable. But many irrigation projects today are not efforts toward enriching human diet or regularizing the productivity of good agricultural land with erratic rainfall. Large-scale irrigation projects today often are responses to economic opportunities related to affluence and to population pressure. In the Central Arizona project, for example, the real reason for building dams in the Colorado River (Chapter 7) was to raise real estate values in the desert and to permit agricultural speculators to grow price support crops, such as cotton, that the great majority of the American people neither needed nor wanted. In underdeveloped countries, dam-building is often undertaken for reasons of political propaganda. The ribbon-cutting ceremony is often the most persuasive reason for the project as it is perceived by public officials. In an ecologically rational world, most land that was naturally arid would remain desert. Its highest value would be found in its esthetic, recreational, and buffering potentialities.

Although the use of arid lands by nomadic herdsmen has been disliked by government officials, social reformers, and numerous economists, there are ecologists and some economists who view ecologically intelligent pastoralism as the most efficient and productive use of most arid lands.[18] For example, wildlife harvesting and game ranching may be more productive for man in parts of Central Africa than conventional methods of agriculture or animal husbandry.[19] In the polar regions, in tropical rain forests, in highly mountainous areas, and on high dry plains, a roving or rotational pattern of residence may also be ecologically preferential to permanent settlement. (Note arguments of Kraenzel[20] for consistency of institutional arrangements with regional ecology.) But for reasons quite irrelevant to human happiness and welfare, bureaucrats, economists, welfare workers, educators, and the police tend to force people into permanent settlements where they can more easily be helped, watched, taxed, and conscripted. The almost universal efforts of governments to suppress "nomadism" may be a minor aspect of modern political activity, but it is symptomatic of the nonecological character of most modern governmental policy.

### Institutions Poorly Adapted

It is at least a reasonable working hypothesis that institutions of government — legislative, juridical, or administrative — must have been sufficiently well adapted to the conditions under which they were developed to have, in fact, been successfully established and to have survived. But it does not follow that institutions, once established, continue to be appropriate to existing conditions if those conditions change and the institutions change only partially or not at all. Administrative institutions tend, in the long run, to reflect political realities. But in the short run, institutional inertia slows the pace of change. New or reorganized institutions tend to be pulled back into the established order of bureaucratic procedure unless their leadership or the intensity of the forces that support them can maintain their innovative character.

Traditional structures of government have become increasingly out of phase with the changing ecological conditions of man and with space-age technologies. The abilities of modern men to manipulate their environments have expanded more rapidly than have the abilities of men, individually or through institutional arrangements, to cope with the consequences of the use of these new powers. A visible consequence of this incongruity has been the relative declining ability of governments to cope with the more important environmental problems of their peoples. In certain of its technical processes, the effectiveness of the government has demonstrably improved. But these improvements tend to be in such traditional functions as tax collection, fiscal planning, and personnel management. The structures and programs of most governmental agencies have not been designed to cope with the ecological crisis that modern man has created. They have, in fact, contributed to it.

A major obstacle to a reform of government for environmental administration is that, in many countries, the changes required contradict deep-rooted tradition. In the United States, for example, the increasing inability of political institutions to perform in practice as they were intended to perform in theory, has not induced a popular move to replace them. Over large areas of the United States, local government is responsive chiefly to an interlocking system of local economic interests united primarily in promoting land development and in the manipulation of real estate values. In effect, local governments frequently act to advance the interests of business regardless of other considerations. The structure and procedures of most American cities and counties tend to negate the influence of the individual citizen. Unless he is an individual of exceptional political influence, he will receive little consideration from local bodies, such as planning commissions, which tend to respond to the pressures of those who can punish them politically or economically. These pressures may come from overwhelming numbers of voters, but they rarely do. More often it is the banks, law firms, business corporations, and economic development promoters who are influential.

Even if traditional American local government operated as it was intended to operate, it would still be incompetent to cope with a broad range of environmental problems. Problems of air and water pollution and of solid waste management are beyond the capacity of most localities to solve without the cooperation of other jurisdictions. The politically dominant interests in many localities are not served by a vigorous administration of environmental quality programs. Rigorous enforcement of zoning codes, subdivision regulations, outdoor advertising ordinances, and pollution controls "hurt business." Tax returns from business enterprise and real estate assessment are hardly sufficient criteria for making substantive policy decisions, but they are nevertheless the primary concern of many local officials. The decay and disorder that characterize large sections of urban (and rural) America have developed under the domination of these self--serving and narrowly focused interests. Their voluntary modification by statewide or nationwide environmental quality programs can be expected, at best, to be no more than slow-moving and half-hearted.

Intergovernmental arrangements have been initiated to overcome the limitations inherent in American local government. Among them are special districts (for example, for water supply, sanitation, recreation, or fire protection), metropolitan councils of government, interstate compacts, federally established administrative regions, and federal-state grants-in-aid. Some of these devices have been moderately successful, especially when compared with conditions existing prior to their creation. Nevertheless, they tend to be cumbersome, inflexible, and uneconomical of either time or money. Where these infirmities have been overcome, as in the interstate Port of New York Authority, objections have been raised regarding their accountability. Efforts to patch up the old system have produced some improvements in the public administration of environmental services, but the remedies fall far short of meeting the needs. Evidence for this assertion may be found in the failure of increasing public efforts on behalf of environmental quality to match the pace of increasing environmental deterioration.

The root of the institutional problem lies in the relation of institutions to the political culture that creates and sustains them. Institutions are structured expressions of the way the world is viewed. When, as with man-environment relationships, man's cultural evolution renders his traditional viewpoint obsolete, his institutions are also threatened by obsolescence. Until man's perception of his relation to the world is corrected, the prospect for reforming his institutions is poor. And, as perception of the need for change differs very widely among people in the world today; the environmental issue inevitably becomes a focus for political conflict.

Having surveyed some of the obstacles to effective environmental administration, it is now feasible to examine CRITERIA for reorganizing institutions and revising procedures so that these and other obstacles can be surmounted. Two categories of criteria are required for establishing a rational and systematic environmental administration. The first of these are the components of a policy for the environment. They are specifications of the substance of a public policy to guide or control administrative action in relation to the environment. The second set are criteria for the establishment of effective structures for environmental administration. Thus, the first category deals with objectives, and the second deals with organizations and procedures.

At the national level the immediate need in most countries is the establishment of an ecologically based public policy for the environment. Until this is done, there is not adequate basis for the coordination of existing environment-shaping activities and for the curtailing or elimination of ecologically harmful practices. But it is not sufficient merely to assert public responsibility for the quality of the environment. The criteria of quality must be specified with sufficient clarity to afford a basis for action. An example of how this may be done has now been provided by the United States in Public Law 91-190, The National Environmental Policy Act of 1969.

## The National Environmental Policy Act

Although to some extent modeled after the Employment Act of 1946, the Environmental Policy Act encompasses a broader and more complex set of issues. It created one new institution, the three-member Council on Environmental Quality in the Executive Office of the President, to keep the Congress, the President, and the public informed regarding the changing state of the environment and to review the impact upon the environment of the actions of other governmental agencies. The act also provides procedures to help control the environmental actions of the federal agencies. In future program planning, the agencies are now required to consider the environmental consequences of their proposals and to review their own legislative authorizations and administrative policies for consistency with the act. Failure to observe these procedures in good faith opens the agency to legislative, executive, or judicial challenge.

But perhaps the most important feature of the act is its declaration of policy, because the specific provisions of this declaration afford criteria for determining, in a legal sense, what environmental quality in America means. For the United States, the National Environmental Policy Act may help to overcome the unecological biases of popular attitudes toward the environment that have obstructed environmental policy-making and execution. Criteria for policy effectiveness would include specification of (1) the goals of policy and (2) the means to their realization. The Environmental Policy Act does both. Section 101 of the Act sets forth the following six objectives or elements of an environmental policy for the nation:

(1) fulfill the responsibilities of each generation as trustee of the environment for succeeding generations;
(2) assure for all Americans safe, healthful, productive, and esthetically and culturally pleasing surroundings;
(3) attain the widest range of beneficial uses of the environment without degradation, risk to health or safety, or other undesirable and unintended consequences;
(4) preserve important historic, cultural, and natural aspects of our national heritage, and maintain, wherever possible, an environment which supports diversity and variety of individual choice;
(5) achieve a balance between population and resource use which will permit high standards of living and a wide sharing of life's amenities; and
(6) enhance the quality of renewable resources and approach the maximum attainable recycling of depletable resources.

It is an axiom of coherent policy that a statement of purpose should embody the proposed means to its realization. Section 102 of the act does this in relation to the agencies of the federal government. This section establishes principles to guide federal agencies in relation to action affecting the environment and specifies procedures to which they must adhere. These principles and procedures provide a means for testing the conformity of agency action to the intent of the Congress as expressed in the act. As an example of a coherent, action-forcing policy declaration, Section 102 deserves careful study and is, therefore, cited in full:

> Section 102. The Congress authorizes and directs that, to the fullest extent possible: (1) the policies, regulations, and public laws of the United States shall be interpreted and administered in accordance with the policies set forth in this Act, and (2) all agencies of the Federal Government shall —
>
> (A) utilize a systematic, interdisciplinary approach which will insure the integrated use of the natural and social sciences and the environmental design arts in planning and in decision-making which may have an impact on man's environment.;
>
> (B) identify and develop methods and procedures, in consultation with the Council on Environmental Quality established by title II of this Act, which will insure that presently unquantified environmental amenities and values may be given appropriate consideration in decision-making along with economic and technical considerations;
>
> (C) include in every recommendation or report on proposals for legislation and other major Federal actions significantly affecting the quality of the human environment, a detailed statement by the responsible official on —
>
> (i) the environmental impact of the proposed action,
>
> (ii) any adverse environmental effects which cannot be avoided should the proposal be implemented,
>
> (iii) alternatives to the proposed action,
>
> (iv) the relationship between local short-term uses of man's environment and the maintenance and enhancement of long-term productivity, and
>
> (v) any irreversible and irretrievable commitments of resources which would be involved in the proposed action should it be implemented.
>
> Prior to making any detailed statement, the responsible Federal official shall consult with and obtain the comments of any Federal agency which has jurisdiction by law or special expertise with respect to any environmental impact involved. Copies of such statement and the comments and views of the appropriate Federal, State, and local agencies, which are authorized to develop and enforce environmental standards, shall be made available to the President, the Council on Environmental Quality and to the public as provided by section 552 of title 5, United States Code, and shall accompany the proposal through the existing agency review processes;
>
> (D) study, develop, and describe appropriate alternatives to recommended courses of action in any proposal which involves unresolved conflicts concerning alternative uses of available resources;
>
> (E) recognize the worldwide and long-range character of environmental problems and, where consistent with the foreign policy of the United States, lend appropriate support to initiatives, resolutions, and programs designed to maximize international cooperation in anticipating and preventing a decline in the quality of mankind's world environment;
>
> (F) make available to States, counties, municipalities, institutions, and individuals, advice and information useful in restoring, maintaining, and enhancing the quality of the environment;
>
> (G) initiate and utilize ecological information in the planning and development of resource-oriented projects; and
>
> (H) assist the Council on Environmental Quality established by title II of this Act.

## International Policy Statements

Criteria for guiding the actions of governments in relation to the environment have been proposed or published by various international conferences or agencies (for example, reference 21.) Among the more comprehensive of these were the resolutions of the Biosphere Conference convened by UNESCO in Paris in 1968.[22] A more general declaration of human rights in the environment will probably be made by the United Nations Conference on the Human Environment in 1972. These statements cannot easily be made operational as the conferences that make the declarations have no power to force the compliance of governments. Nevertheless, they help to overcome a major obstacle to environmental administration by giving high and universal visibility to the environment as a focus for policy, and their texts usually set forth the principal ecological arguments for protection of the biosphere, thus having an educational as well as a political effect.

## Criteria for Administrative Structures

Policy statements such as the National Environmental Policy Act may specify certain administrative procedures to carry out the policy intent, but they seldom deal with the organization of administrative agencies in more than very general terms. These terms ordinarily apply only to the agency primarily charged with execution of the act. But a large number of agencies in every national government have functions that impinge upon the environment. And, because there is usually a direct relationship between the organization structure of an agency and the activities that it carries on, attention to the effect of structure on policy is necessary wherever there is concern that the policy be faithfully administered (for further discussion on this point see reference 23).

Institutional inertia has been identified as a leading obstacle to effective policy implementation. Because few public agencies have been established on the basis of regard for ecological facts or for the full range of human values in the environment, administrative reorganization is today an almost inevitable concomitant of effective environmental policy implementation. The range of environmental problems is broad and the existing structures for environmental policy implementation differ greatly, so that any discussion of the reorganization of government for environmental policy purposes could easily become very extended. The development of institutions well adapted to the effective implementation of environmental policies is a task largely yet to be accomplished.

In considering criteria for administrative effectiveness, the term "criteria" must be loosely interpreted. A number of official studies of environmental policy needs in the United States have indicated changes in administrative organization or procedure believed to be necessary to achieve policy objectives.[24-26] As these reports differ in format, scope, and emphasis, a comparative analysis of their recommendations does not yield general conclusions as to how to organize the government for purposes of environmental administration. Nevertheless, these and other descriptive and analytic studies of governmental organization for the management of natural resource and environmental policy have provided enough information regarding the difficulties and failures of policy implementation to give us some indication of the characteristics required of agencies that may be expected to perform effectively in this field.

The following criteria are not necessarily exclusively relevant to environmental policies. They may be equally relevant to other aspects of public administration. But they are essential to the effective management of environmental affairs. In summary, operational effectiveness for environmental management agencies depends upon their being:

(1) structured for problem-solving on a basis coextensive with their responsibilities;
(2) cybernetic or self-correcting in operation in order to (a) test their effectiveness (through "feedback") and (b) to revise their programs or redirect their course as experience indicates;
(3) adaptable in internal organization and personnel;
(4) capable of cooperative interaction with other agencies toward the attainment of environmental policy goals.

Marked deficiencies in one or more of these criteria account for inadequacies in many of the presently operating environmental management agencies. It is to provide capabilities corresponding to these criteria that new forms of administrative action are being sought as environmental policy objectives are developed.

Criteria of another category are located conceptually between policy objectives and administration. These are the criteria for estimating the state of the environment. They are often described as "indicators" of environmental quality. Because their data are primarily scientific (physical or biological), these criteria are not discussed in this chapter, but their important function in the administration of environmental policy should be emphasized. They are discussed at length in the reports cited in references 24-26.

Given the present ad hoc and incremental approach to environmental administration, it may be more useful to examine what needs to be done and what is now being initiated to develop new institutions than to dwell primarily upon

408   L. K. Caldwell

established efforts. Many of the processes that environmental administration requires are already being employed. What is now needed is for them to be used on a greatly extended scale and in systematic and coordinated relationship to one another.

*Setting Behavior Patterns*

Persuasion, as we have noted, is the most economical and ultimately the most effective mode of obtaining a desired course of public action. Environmental management is, of course, the management of human behavior in relation to the environment. It is, therefore, firstly the management of people and only secondarily, the rearrangement of things. But environmental management, being purposeful or goal-directed, implies cooperative or coordinated public action consistent with a goal or purpose. Therefore, a major part of the action in environmental management is to cause or to prevent certain types of public behavior. And because the ways in which human behavior affects the environment are seemingly without end, environmental policy, as a practical matter, must deal with behavior in the aggregate more than directly with individual acts. To the extent that attitudes or modes of behavior can be inculcated in a population, the managerial aspects of the environmental policy task are correspondingly eased. Social or mass persuasion is, therefore, a fundamental element in all policy implementation; and this explains the presence of philosophical, hortatory, or moralizing provisions in many public laws, especially those pertaining to man-environment relationships. These measures may, therefore, be described accurately as institutions for mass persuasion.

The National Environmental Policy Act, for example, declares "that each person should enjoy a healthful environment and that each person has a responsibility to contribute to the preservation and enhancement of the environment." To implant or strengthen this sense of responsibility requires a multiplicity of subsidiary educational and institutional measures that as yet have nowhere been brought together in a coherent public effort. One new type of institution that has been

established to develop this sense of public responsibility is the environmental awareness center. To some extent these centers have grown out of conservation or nature education centers established primarily in the United States and several European countries by conservation organizations. Illustrative of these organizations are the Environment Awareness Center at the University of Wisconsin, the Nature Camps of the National Audubon Society, and the nature interpretation services of the U.S. National Park Service and the Forest Service. (The magazine *Environmental Education*[27] is a continuing source of information on these efforts.)

More formal means of setting behavior patterns, regulations for example, have been invoked to control air and water pollution, the use of pesticides, disposal of solid wastes, and other environment-affecting acts. Penalties for littering public highways, regulations governing burning of trash, and ordinances against excessive noise, are examples of the use of law to influence behavior. Standard-setting legislation generally has this behavior-influencing objective. To the extent that people, business firms, or government agencies observe and conform to the rules or standards, the laws do not require major enforcement efforts. Administrators and courts are required only to deal with noncompliance and exceptions.

The influence of education has already been noted in the establishment of environmental awareness centers. Much of this education, however, is informal and self-sought. Formal education in schools and colleges is of greatest importance in the establishment of public attitudes and behavior, including the development in people of the capacity to receive the message of the environmental awareness centers. Moreover, formal education is the one medium through which, over time, everyone in the nation learns common norms and concepts at the most impressionable ages. The development of environmental studies programs and of ecology courses throughout the educational institutions of the United States may significantly change the behavior of Americans toward their environments in coming years. This is not to suggest that everyone's behavior will be changed, but that public priorities with respect to the environment and public willingness to bring governmental efforts to bear upon environmental problems may be significantly affected.[28],[29]

*Structural Patterns and Innovations*

Since the late 1960s, the rate of institutional change in relation to environmental problems has accelerated, and the trend continues. The rapidity of the change and its often incremental character make it difficult to describe. This is because there has been a widespread tendency, not only in the United States, but in many other nations, to begin to cope with environmental problems on an improvised, minimal, and partial basis, and then progressively to enlarge and reorganize the effort.

Control of air and water pollution in the United States is a case in point. First efforts were intended to encourage state action, constitutional scruples among political conservatives discouraging direct federal intervention. The next stage saw air and water pollution treated under the then acceptable rubric of public health with control agencies established in the U.S. Department of Health, Education and Welfare. When public concern with the broader range of values in water use became stronger, water pollution control was moved to the Department of the Interior. By 1970, all of the environmental pollution control functions of the federal government could be brought together in the Environmental Protection Agency, which may or may not be the long-term structure for public action in environmental pollution control.

A similar process of ad hoc creating, regrouping, consolidating, and restructuring has occurred in federal activities for research and monitoring with respect to geophysical environmental change. In 1965, the U.S. Weather Bureau, the Coast and Geodetic Survey, and several other agencies that had had independent histories were brought together in the Environmental Science Services Administration (ESSA). In 1970, following an extended prior study by the Commission on Marine Science, Engineering, and Resources, ESSA and several other agencies concerned with marine activities (for example, the Bureau of Commercial Fisheries), became components of

the National Oceanographic and Atmospheric Administration located in the U.S. Department of Commerce.[30]

This process of adaptation, growth, and restructuring is, in principle, the only feasible way to proceed in developing new structures for more effective environmental management. It is hardly possible to create comprehensive and coherent public agencies in advance of public policy decisions regarding goals and functions. The criteria that we have identified as indicators of effective organization provide little guidance in determining the substance of policies to be administered, and they do not point to goals or specific outcomes of public action. They do, however, suggest that some types of structures are preferable to others when effective management of environmental affairs is the objective.

For example, the flexibility that may be gained through the corporation form of organization may be advantageous in dealing with environmental services in localized areas where the services are largely technical in character. Water supply and sewage disposal are cases in point and can be provided by public corporations with certain fiscal and procedural autonomy not normally available to government departments. But the extension of these services and the levels of quality provided are not routine or technical questions, and decisions regarding them should not be left to essentially commercial or technological considerations.

The following section gives some examples of present types of environmental management and some possibilities for the future.

*Water, Air, and Waste Management*

Of possible importance for corporate enterprise in the future, especially in water-deficient areas, is the closed water-sewage system installation. Modeled on the principles of spacecraft, this system would continually purify and reuse water within a given area, such as a city, replacing only that water lost through transpiration, evaporation, or leakage. There are obvious economic advantages in water usage under this arrangement, but there are also problems. Possibly the psychological difficulty is greatest.

People seem more disposed to use treated water that has carried other peoples' sewage than to reprocess water used in their own community. More serious is the possible accumulation of pathogenic organisms in a closed system. Not all microorganisms, viruses for example, are amenable to treatment by methods now in use. Technical solutions to the difficulty may be found, and indeed must be found, before prolonged space flight becomes practicable. The science of "cabin ecology" assisted by biochemistry and bioengineering may ultimately make closed water-sewage systems practicable outside of spacecraft.

But before this occurs, it may be necessary to charge for the taking of water from natural sources. As long as water is treated as a free good, the economics of the closed system may be unfavorable to its construction and operation. The aerospace industry, which has developed technical competence in this type of work, has an understandable interest in its development, particularly in view of the probability of diminished activities in outer space in the years immediately ahead. It would seem feasible for a public corporation, or even a privately owned corporation under contract, to construct and operate such a system. Privately managed municipal water systems have not been uncommon in the United States.

Not all forms of corporate or collective enterprise for environmental management are new, although some may be new to certain countries or localities. For example, the Ruhrverband, an association for the control of pollution of the Ruhr River, has functioned for more than 50 years to provide treatment of effluents. This organization combines private, industrial, and public organizations in an association under governmental supervision. It has provided relatively effective control of water pollution within a localized area, but it does not appear to be the answer to control of pollution in the multination drainage basin of the Rhine River.

For river system management, governmental agencies are the common form of organization; the size and political involvement of river-basin authorities usually renders them unsuitable for private undertaking. In Great Britain and the United States, the historical method of water pollution control was through public boards or commissions with jurisdiction over a particular drainage basin. Earlier efforts often included flood control. In the United States, the Miami Conservancy District was created under local initiative and at local expense to control the water of the Miami River in the state of Ohio. Since that time, however, the idea of locally developed and controlled river management systems has been displaced by a preference for federal planning and control. The Tennessee Valley Authority is the principal American innovation for large-scale multistate river systems. Although cooperative relations have been established between the Tennessee Valley Authority and state and local jurisdictions, it is a corporate agency of the U.S. government.[31] The Ohio River Valley Water Sanitation Commission[32] and the Delaware River Basin Commission[33] are interstate bodies established under the compact clause of the U.S. Constitution. The federal government is a partner in these compact authorities and, in any case, has jurisdiction over interstate navigable waters administered chiefly by the U.S. Army Corps of Engineers.

Even in the specific area of the management of water resources, the variety of structures and arrangements is so great as to make any concise or general description impracticable.[34, 35] The multiple uses of water complicate its management. Moreover, priorities among uses differ among localities and over time in the same locality. For example, recreational use of rivers and lakes has greatly increased in recent decades, and the traditional uses of water for waste disposal and industrial processes now face competing priorities that were formerly of minor consequence. In the arid regions of the American Southwest, industrial uses of water are gaining in economic importance over traditional agricultural usage. Thus, the design of comprehensive and coherent systems for water management is a complex task with many variables that are not easily measured or controlled.[36] Out of present experimentation, some selectivity among the more successful structures may be possible. But it would be rash to predict what structures for water management may prevail by the year 2000.

Air quality control and the management of solid wastes appear to present somewhat simpler organizational problems. In both cases, techno-economic factors may influence the structuring of organizations in the future. The air-shed concept is an equivalent to the drainage basin or watershed for organizing air quality control on a regional basis.[37, 38] If it becomes technically and economically feasible to stop air pollution at its source, the air-shed concept and any regional structure to control emissions would become redundant.

Solid waste management offers possibilities for structural innovation, especially in recycling metals, cellulose, and other reusable materials. Existing economic systems and practices have made ecologically harmful forms of solid waste disposal economically attractive. In the future, shortages of strategic minerals and lack of available space for dumping wastes on land or at sea may force recycling and increase its economic attractiveness. This aspect of environmental control would seem to be especially susceptible to private management under some form of corporate structure. But public assistance would be required to prevent or to discourage traditional practices of waste disposal that line the banks of American rivers with cast-off automobile tires and fill the ravines of the American countryside with discarded automobile carcasses. Taxes on various consumer products, especially upon automobiles, have been proposed to provide for their ultimate disposal. But no general system of solid waste management on a national scale has yet emerged.

### Administrative Disjunction

There are evident gaps between environmental policy and environmental administration in the United States and in most industrialized nations. These inconsistencies are not peculiar to environmental issues, but are markedly characteristic of them, and are explained by the same factors that have caused administrative restructuring for environmental management to be ad hoc, incremental, and progressive. The changing relationship of man to his environment, detailed at the beginning of this chapter, has only been gradually perceived. The institutions of government previously established to deal with specified aspects of the environment were premised on attitudes and beliefs that science and experience have in many instances shown to be erroneous. But is is difficult to redirect long-standing habits and practices. Thus public declarations of new policies for the environment may coexist with governmental practices in direct contradiction to proffessed policy.

For example, public programs for the conservation of wetlands (marshes, lakes, and estuaries) have been launched without significantly affecting the draining and filling of wetlands under public auspices. These conflicts are not necessarily consequences of uncoordinated competition among separate branches of government. They may occur within a single agency in which the agency head, for example, the Secretary of the Interior in the United States, may advocate one policy, and certain subordinate personnel or bureaus may rely upon other authority, for example statutory authorization, to pursue opposing policies or to ignore the announced policy of the agency as a whole.

No government has as yet elevated the custody and care of the environment to a status equal to foreign affairs, defense, or social welfare. For this reason, our examination of administrative structures has dealt more with organization for specific environmental purposes than with the comprehensive administration of environmental policy. There is now a tendency among the American states to create high level boards or committees to develop environmental policy and to review trends in the environment. We are in the midst of a period of institutional development, but it would be premature to predict how far and how fast it will go and what its ultimate configuration may be. The foregoing pages, in effect, selectively sample these developments, which as matters now stand, is about all that can be attempted.

In summation, the process of structural innovation thus far has been largely ad hoc and experimental. No pervasive controlling philosophy or concept has pointed the way to one set of structural solutions as opposed to others. Improvisation has been the usual approach to innovation, and instances of generally effective organizational arrangements (for example, the Ruhrverband or the Tennessee Valley Authority) have seldom been emulated. If one expects to find dramatic new forms of environmental management being organized, he will be disappointed. Novel organizations may, probably must, come into existence if modern society copes effectively with its environmental problems. But these new structures will probably be based on past experience, and their novelty will be relative. The most probable area for institutional innovation in the near future is international. There are environmental problems that ultimately can only be attacked upon a global basis. Because almost no international institutional structure for environmental control presently exists, what is done will necessarily be innovative. The concluding section of this chapter will briefly survey the rapidly developing field of international action for protection of the environment.

*International Policy and Administration*

One of the most powerful incentives to deter people from damaging the environment is their desire to live in an undamaged world. Yet because the mass of people do not appear to be gifted with creative imagination, it may happen that fear will prove a more potent incentive than hope in promoting environmental good citizenship. As evidence of ecological damage accumulated during the 1960s, prophecies of ecological catastrophe became more numerous.[39-41] Prospects for severe ecological disasters before the end of the century were widely accepted as probable among well-informed scientific observers. And unfortunately for human society, the nature of biological chain reactions could conceal a fatal sequence of ecological change until the final phase of disaster. The introduction of a particularly potent and persistent biocide into the global ecosystem might trigger off a sequence of destruction that would proceed at first quietly and covertly until, perhaps a quarter of a century after the damage had begun, the full enormity of its effects became evident. The death warrant for the human species could already have been signed by man himself in the release of toxic agents into the sea.

Environmental good-housekeeping by a few wisely governed nations will no longer suffice to protect their citizens or to safeguard the ecological welfare of the world. Unless nations can somehow surmount their political differences to provide for an effective worldwide system of ecological monitoring and control, the prospects for man and the natural environment are discouraging. Fortunately an awareness of this circumstance is becoming widespread among scientists and government officials around the world. This awareness has been reflected in the 1968 UNESCO conference on "Rational Use and Conservation of the Resources of the Biosphere" and the UNESCO-sponsored follow-up program "Man and Biosphere," the creation by the International Council of Scientific Unions of a Scientific Committee on Problems of the Environment (SCOPE), the International Biological Program, the 1971 Economic Commission of Europe Meeting of Governmental Experts on Problems Relating to Environment, and the 1972 United Nations Conference on Human Environment. The outcomees of these efforts will almost certainly point toward some degree of international environmental control.

Proposals for international environmental controls have already been under consideration in relation to outer space, Antarctica, and the deep sea bed.[42,43] For outer space and Antarctica, international treaties have been negotiated to prevent some of the more obvious abuses of these environments, especially in relation to military activities. The future governance of the oceans and the bed of the deep sea have been on the agenda of the General Assembly of the United Nations and under consideration by numerous conferences and study groups. It seems probable that an international policy for the oceans and an organization to implement it will come into existence before the end of the 1970s.

International cooperation is most readily achieved where application of technical procedures are primarily involved and where interference with the behavior of people and of nations is minimal. This may explain why the World Weather Watch sponsored by the World Meteorological Organization (WMO) is the first continuing organized environmental monitoring effort to be established. But perhaps the alloca-

ENVIRONMENT AND ADMINISTRATION: THE POLITICS OF ECOLOGY

tion of broadcast frequencies by the International Telecommunications Union should also be considered as a form of environmental management. The electromagnetic environment of the earth is an integral part of man's total environment even though it is invisible to him. The increasing use of electronic radiation, especially in the form of microwaves, has created environmental health and safety problems in addition to the technical, economic, and political aspects of telecommunications transmission. This is an area of physical science and engineering in which public policy concern may be expected to increase.

Environmental relationships are of concern in various ways to the United Nations Educational, Scientific, and Cultural Organization (UNESCO), to the World Health Organization (WHO), and to the Food and Agriculture Organization (FAO). Cooperation has developed among the United Nations-affiliated organizations in a number of environment-related efforts. For example WHO and FAO have worked together on agroclimatological studies and both UNESCO and FAO have assisted the nongovernmental International Union for the Conservation of Nature and Natural Resources (IUCN). This Union has been primarily concerned with the protection of natural ecosystems, wildlife, and distinctive landscapes. It operates through a series of commissions on ecology, education, national parks, landscape planning, and policy, law, and administration, and it sponsors a Survival Service for the protection of threatened wildlife.

The International Council of Scientific Unions, which has traditionally focused its efforts on international cooperative research in science, has now extended its concern to policies and institutions for the protection of the biosphere. Through its Scientific Committee on Problems of the Environment (SCOPE), it has under consideration the development of worldwide systems of monitoring environmental contamination and organizing data sources needed for environmental policy-making and administration.

A detailed account of international organizations and their concurrent action on behalf of environmental matters, and of international agreements, could easily become a book in itself. (A list of relevant books and articles is given in reference 44.) Some of these efforts are effective, others only moderately or not at all. But there have been successes, and precedents are being established and experience acquired that may in time be applied on a larger scale.

*A Concluding Observation*

Whatever uniformities may hold true for physiological man, cultural behavior does not appear to be regularized, repetitive, or easily predictable. For this reason there is a tentativeness about any description of an ongoing social development such as the politics of ecology. The incompleteness and uncertainty that characterize this state of affairs may be intellectually unsatisfying. But this indeterminancy is inherent in the processes of human society, and it would be dishonest to present the circumstances as more logical and complete than they really are. The human mind and human motivations are still largely mysteries, and their response to the environmental issues of our time can be estimated, but only with great caution.

The area of public policy and administration lies between the scientific study of the environment and the application of techniques for environmental protection and control. It is the area of linkage between knowledge and action, and it is the most poorly understood and developed of the three. The crisis of the environment is, therefore, more a crisis of will and rationality than it is of knowledge or of technical or engineering capabilities.[45, 46] Informed men know what must be done if the world is to survive man's demands upon it. They also know how to accomplish substantial parts of the task of environmental renewal. What remains to be discovered is how to bring human will and effort to bear upon the task in sufficient strength and in sufficient time to safeguard the continuing existence of the living world.

References

1. **Dubos, R.** 1969. *A Theology of the Earth.* A lecture delivered on October 2, 1969 at the Smithsonian Institution in Washington, D.C. under the sponsorship of the Smithsonian Office of Environmental Sciences.

2. **Gross, B. M.**, ed. 1967. *Action under Planning: The Guidance of Economic Development.* Shafer, R. J., What is national planning? pp. 257-263; Caldwell, L. K., The biophysical environment, pp. 84-108. McGraw-Hill Book Co., New York.

3. **Drew, E. B.** 1970. Dam outrage: the story of the Army engineers. *The Atlantic 225* (April 1970): 51-62.

4. **Maas, A.** 1951. *Muddy Waters.* Harvard University Press, Cambridge, Massachusetts.

5. **Lerner, D., and Laswell, H. D.**, eds. 1951. *The Policy Sciences: Recent Developments in Scope and Method.* Stanford University Press, Stanford, California.

6. **Bauer, R. A., and Gergen, K. J.** 1968. *Study of Policy Formation.* Free Press, New York.

7. **Science.** 1964. Volume 44: 616.

8. **Ecology Center Foundation.** Various publications. 710 Montgomery Street, San Francisco, California 94111.

9. **Gable, R. W.** 1958. Interest groups as policy shapers. *Ann. Amer. Acad. Political and Social Sci. 319:* 84-93.

10. **Wall Street Journal.** 1966. Struggle over scenery. Editorial page, June 16.

11. **Dreyfus, D. A.** 1970. *A Definition of the Scope of Environmental Management.* U.S. Senate, Committee on Interior and Insular Affairs, 91st Congress, 2nd Session. Committee Print.

12. **Sprout, H. and Sprout, M.** 1965. *The Ecological Perspective on Human Affairs with Special Reference to International Politics.* Princeton University Press, Princeton, New Jersey.

13. **Huxley, A.** 1963. *The Politics of Ecology – The Question of Survival.* Center for the Study of Democratic Institutions, Santa Barbara, California.

14. **Kates, R. W.** 1962. Hazard and choice perception in flood plain management. In *Research Paper No. 78,* Department of Geography, University of Chicago, Chicago, Illinois.

15. **White, G. F.** 1964. Choice of adjustment to floods. In *Research Paper No. 93,* Department of Geography, University of Chicago, Chicago, Illinois.

16. **Sutton, W. F.** 1964. The use of flood plains. *The Military Engineer 374:* 4140416.

17. **Cypra, K., and Peterson, G. L.** 1969. Technical service for the urban flood plain property management: Organization of the design problem. *Natural Hazard Research Working Paper No. 12,* University of Toronto, Toronto, Canada.

18. **Darling, F. F., and Farvar, M. T.** 1971. Ecological consequences of sedentarization of nomads, and Heady, H. F., Ecological consequences of Bedouin settlement in Saudi Arabia. In *The Careless Technology* (J. C. Milton and M. T. Farvar, eds.), Natural History Press, New York, in press.

19. **Talbot, L. M.** 1971. Ecological consequences of rangeland development in Masailand. And **West, O.**, The ecological impact of the introduction of domestic cattle into wildlife and tsetse areas of Rhodesia. In *The Careless Technology* (J. C. Milton and M. T. Farvar, eds.). Natural History Press, New York, in press.

20. **Kraenzel, C. F.** 1955. *The Great Plains in Transition,* pp. 324-346, 361-389. University of Oklahoma Press, Norman, Oklahoma.

21. **Davies Memorial Institute.** 1968. *Principles Governing Certain Changes in the Environment of Man.* The David Davies Memorial Institute of International Studies, London. And by the same publisher, undated, *Draft Rules Concerning Changes in the Environment of the Earth.*

22. **UNESCO.** 1969. *Intergovernmental Conference of Experts on the Scientific Basis for Rational Use and Conservation of the Biosphere, UNESCO House, Paris, 4-13 September, 1968, Final Report.* UNESCO, Paris: SC/MD/9-6 January 1969.

23. **Fox, I. K., and Craine, L. E.** 1962. Organizational arrangements for water development. *Natural Res. J. 2:* 1-44. And Ostrom, V. The water economy and its organization. *Ibid.:* 55-73.

24. **U.S. House of Representatives.** 1968. *Managing the Environment.* A report of the Subcommittee on Science, Research and Development of the Committee on Science and Astronautics.

25. **National Academy of Sciences.** 1970. *Institutions for Effective Management of the Environment.* A report of the Environmental Study Group.

26. **U.S. House of Representatives.** 1970. *The Environmental Decade (Action Proposals for the 70's)*, p. 38. Twenty-fourth report by the Committee on Government Operations.

27. **Environmental Education** (1969) University of Wisconsin, Madison, Wisconsin.

28. **Caldwell, L. K.** 1966. The human environment: a growing challenge to higher education. *J. Higher Educ. 37:* 425-438.

29. **Steinhart, J. S., and Cherniak, J. S.** 1969. *The Universities and Environmental Quality, Committment to Problem Focused Education.* A report to the President's Environmental Quality Council, September 1969.

30. **Popkin, R.** 1967. *The Environmental Science Services Administration.* Praeger, New York. Also *The Washington Post,* June 6, 1970; *Science 168:* 1433-1435.

31. **Selznick, P.** 1949. (2nd ed., 1966). *T.V.A. and the Grass Roots: A Study in the Sociology of Formal Organization.* University of California Press, Berkeley, California.

32. **Cleary, E. J.** 1967. *The Orsanco Story: Water Quality Management in the Ohio Valley under an Interstate Compact.* Johns Hopkins Press, Baltimore, Maryland.

33. **Martin, R. C.** 1964. *River Basin Administration and the Delaware.* Syracuse University Press, Syracuse, New York.

34. **Hart, H. C.** 1961. *Administrative Aspects of River Valley development.* Asia Publishing House, New York.

35. **Chapman, J. D.,** ed. 1963. *The International River Basin.* University of British Columbia Press, Vancouver, Canada.

36. **Maas, A.,** et al. 1962. *Design of Water Resources Systems.* Harvard University Press, Cambridge, Massachusetts.

37. **Kneese, A.** 1968. The problem shed as a unit of environmental control. *Arch. Environmental Health 16:* 124.

38. **Lieber, H.** 1968. Controlling metropolitan pollution through regional airsheds: administrative requirements and political problems. *J. Air Pollution Control Assoc. 18:* 86-93.

39. **Ehrlich, P. R.** 1970. Eco-catastrophe! In *The Environmental Handbook* (G. De Bell, ed.). Ballantine Books, New York.

40. **Holling, C. S.** 1969. Stability in ecological and social systems. In *Diversity and Stability in Ecological Systems.* Brookhaven Symposia in Biology, Vol. 22, pp. 128-141.

41. **Cole, L. C.** 1968. Can the world be saved? *BioScience 18:* 679-684.

42. **UNESCO.** 1969. *UNESCO Courier 22* (January 1969), whole issue.

43. **United Nations.** 1969. *Problems of the Human Environment.* Report of the Secretary General (E/4667, May 26, 1969).

44. **Caldwell, L. K., and DeVille, W. B.** 1968. International technoscientific organizations. In *Science, Technology and Public Policy: A Syllabus for Advanced Study,* Vol. 1, pp. 135-138. Department of Government, Indiana University, Bloomington, Indiana.

45. **Caldwell, L. K.** 1970. A crisis of will and rationality. *Environmental Education.* pp. 18-19. Scientists' Institute for Public Information, New York. Not to be confused with the journal *Environmental Education,* published at the University of Wisconsin.

46. **Woodwell, G. M.** 1970. Science and the gross national pollution. *Ramparts 8:* 51-52.

# 20 Environment and the Equilibrium Population

William W. Murdoch

One question continually recurs in discussions of environment: What is the upper limit to world population set by resources and/or by pollution? For several reasons there is no definitive answer to this question.

## Uncertainties in Resources

In the first place we do not know enough now and conditions in the future will change unpredictably. For example, to some extent we not only discover but we also invent resources, and predicting invention is difficult. Thus 20 years ago we could not have predicted the present green revolution (Chapter 3). Now, because of that revolution, if everything goes well we should be able to feed the population over the next 30 years at least as badly as we do now and possibly a little better.

A similar uncertainty faces us in other resources such as minerals. We will run out of presently known commercial reserves of certain important minerals around the turn of the century (Chapter 4), but for some of them we will probably find substitutes or mine lower grades. Will we find substitutes for them all? Such an assumption is certainly implicit in our use of resources and is made explicitly by many economists.[1] Finding substitute resources is a particular example of one type of general solution which has been proposed, namely the "technological fix." Whether or not we can rely upon the technological fix to solve our problems in the foreseeable future is a fundamental and arguable proposition which is not resolvable in an absolute way. (It can be ruled out as a LONG-TERM solution to indefinite expansion in a finite world.) The dilemma with respect to resources is exemplified by the following colloquy between two scientists, both of whom welcome "good" tech-

nology where it is appropriate. The discussion was part of evidence given before a Congressional committee.[2] Dr. Revelle has just commented that technology virtually assures our long-term survival and progress.

> *Dr. Cloud:* First, I would like to comment that that is an act of faith, an act of faith which some of us don't share . . .
> *Dr. Revelle:* Which?
> *Dr. Cloud:* The assumption that technology is going to find a way out.
> *Dr. Revelle:* If it does not, we are sunk.
> *Dr. Cloud:* We sure are.
> *Dr. Revelle:* You must have this faith.
> *Dr. Cloud:* No, you must not. Suppose you make a mistake; isn't it better to have made a mistake on the side of being sure that you were living within the limits of your resources.
> *Dr. Revelle:* Expressed in terms of petroleum, you cannot live within the limits of your resources.
> *Dr. Cloud:* Of course, we are already on the downgrade. By a miracle, a technological miracle, atomic energy comes along just in time to save our necks.
> *Dr. Revelle:* I doubt it is a miracle. It is an inevitable consequence of man's evolution.
> *Dr. Cloud:* I think that is an act of faith which I don't share.

Faith is not generally a good basis for prediction. But equally no one can categorically state that substitutes or alternative sources will not be found for a given resource at a given time in the future.

In the second place, a given resource is unlikely to become unavailable globally all at one time. For example, mineral resources are distributed very unevenly throughout the world and nations are more or less dependent on their free flow across the face of the earth. All industrial nations, except possibly the Soviet Union, are net importers of most of the minerals and ores that they use, and the United States is expected to rely more and more heavily on foreign sources.[3] At the same time world demand for industrial metals has been growing at 6 percent per annum for a decade, that is, 3 times faster than the population, and the underdeveloped countries in particular have enormous room for increased demand. Since many important minerals occur largely in underdeveloped nations it is not at all obvious that any nation can comfortably expect the free flow of minerals to continue unchecked in the future.

A third reason why the question of limits is difficult to answer is that each resource cannot be examined independently of other resources. Resources interact. Thus, to produce enough food on land we need a highly developed technology to produce machinery, fertilizers, and (for the present) pesticides. Each of these in turn is dependent upon a finite resource. Fertilizers have to be mined and manufactured. To produce all this material huge industrial development, pressing on limited resources and economies, will be needed in the developing nations. We shall see also below that exploitation of different resources often involves interference, and eventually we shall have to choose among such resources.

## Pollution and Catastrophes

Similar uncertainties arise in discussing environmental degradation as a limiting factor. If we suffer from pollution and environmental dislocation in a world of 3½ billion people, of which only 1 billion are industrialized, the imagination boggles at the specter of a population of 10 billion in which a higher proportion have evolved into the technological state — yet 10 billion is only 50 years away at current growth rates. But how can we tell what will become technically or economically feasible or politically acceptable in dealing with pollution?

One can reasonably argue that we ALREADY have too much pollution and too imminent a major ecological dislocation, and that in itself should constitute a limit. But we also benefit from the pollution-producing activity and we might argue that the overall benefits outweigh the social costs.

This matter of costs and benefits raises the question of evaluating future environmental catastrophe. If our continued growth implies a high probability of catastrophe, growth should stop. The crux of the matter is: How probable is the catastrophe and, less important, how large are the potential benefits of growth? The larger the potential castastrophe, the less probable it need be before we give up the activity. We must not be misled here by the fact that people do things which are irrational as judged by this kind of analysis; they climb mountains, for example. We cannot use as a yardstick for measuring SOCIAL costs and benefits the actions taken by INDIVIDUALS at individual costs and for individual benefits.

Where we can expect essentially infinite social costs and there is also a relatively high probability of the occurrence of disaster, rational analysis is easy. This is especially true if the potential benefit is low. For example, a major accident in a biological warfare facility could destroy our present society. The probability of such a disaster is rather high, since mistakes have already occurred — let us say it is 1 in 10,000 or 100,000. If such a facility is maintained under these circumstances, it is hardly based on rational analysis.

Other situations tend to be much less clear. However, we can probably place the detonation of large numbers of nuclear devices for digging canals and other purposes in the "clearly irrational" category. Similarly, nuclear reactor accidents seem to have very low probabilities of occurrence, but since the potential human cost is high, the additional economic cost of placing reactors underground is clearly worthwhile. Leaving them above ground is irrational. The economic costs of making fission power safe (Chapter 12) are also in this category of rational economic costs. Much more difficult is the question of pesticide use in the underdeveloped countries. And pesticides illustrate the further problem that frequently we cannot measure the environmental costs. The social and economic benefits of pesticides, in the form of increased food for undernourished people are tangible and measurable. But the environmental costs in the form of destabilized ecosystems are largely hidden and may not be measurable until some future date when the lag effects occur. The necessity to feed people is so great, that here we probably have to continue to use pesticides and take a chance on catastrophe, but we must increase efforts to find alternatives. It may turn out, as pesticides become less efficient at controlling pests (Chapter 14), that we will cease to use them because the benefits have declined, rather than because the environmental costs have risen.

It appears that at the present we have no very good estimates of the probability or imminence of global environmental catastrophe (see, for example, Chapter 15). That is, there is no clear basis for rational action. The cautious procedure would be to arrest growth until such a basis is available.

*Interaction of Resources and Pollution*

This analysis brings us to the important point that exploitation of resources, and pollution, are simply different sides of the same coin. They are not separate and cannot be treated separately. Gilbert White has written:

> Notwithstanding public cries of impending water shortage, there is little reason to fear serious economic dislocations through failures in water quantity. The likelihood that the quality of human life will be impaired by misuse and degradation of the *quality* of available water is much greater. There is no realistic prospect that the community pulse of Los Angeles will ebb slowly to a halt or that New Yorkers will fall gasping of thirst on their grimy pavements through lack of water in the United States. Quantity seems manageable in the foreseeable future, although not without difficulties. Quality is less predictable.[4]

I would like to illustrate the interactions between different resources and between resources and pollution with a brief analysis of the ocean harvest. The world's oceans present a large but limited set of resources. About 20 percent of our protein comes from the oceans and about 5 percent of our minerals. Of the latter, 98 percent come from the continental shelf. Estimates vary, but about 80 percent of the oceans' fishery yield comes from the continental shelf or within about 30 miles of land. Productivity is particularly high inshore, and estuaries are an important source of fishery products. In the future some minerals, but particularly some fish, will be taken from further offshore. But the inshore zone will continue to dominate as the production zone.

For the next 30 years, the oceans can play a very important role in providing man with some protein. Diligence can probably ensure that the oceans can continue to provide about as much protein per head as they do now, and this contribution might even increase. However, the production is dependent on long food chains and is rather sensitive to a variety of sources of disturbance which can effect either the harvest itself or the complex food web (Chapter 11).

Many of the adverse effects on the ocean harvest come from the land. Estuaries are destroyed or polluted; rivers are channelled and dammed; microbial pollution from domestic sewage closes shellfisheries; excessive nutrients from domestic, industrial, and agricultural sources cause eutrophication and even toxic algal growths; heavy metals such as lead, mercury, and arsenic either kill off fish or other organisms or accumulate in the food chain and poison people. There are even cases of very high radioactive concentrations in seafood. The most ironic sequence is that biocides such as DDT and persistent inorganic pesticides (containing heavy metals), used to increase the yield of carbohydrates on land, pose a threat to the yield of proteins from the oceans.

Thus, resource exploitation in one place becomes environmental degradation either in the same or in some other place. We may be approaching the time when we will have to choose between different resources in some areas. We may want to drill the ocean floor for oil, dredge the bottom for minerals, and grow oysters, but we simply may not be able to do all three together. We may get higher yields of rice and wheat, but to get them we may have to put up with declining offshore fisheries in some areas.

At present, this interaction between land and sea does not appear to be very serious on a global scale. Probably not many people have died or suffered from ocean pollution. It is true that some losses occur — shellfish areas on the east coast of North America have been closed, some fish production in the Mediterranean has declined, a large number of single instances of fish kills have been recorded, many beaches in the Mediterranean are too dangerous to visit. But on a global scale the problem is still relatively minor. It seems likely, though, that interference with the ocean harvest will become a major problem within the next 30 years if current trends persist. Although prediction is risky, the following account gives some idea of likely trends.

The world population of 3.6 billion will approximately double, but the problems of effluent from industry are likely to be much more than doubled. Real GNP in the United States tends to increase at about 3-4 percent per year and we can expect a massive trend to industrialization in nations currently less developed. An increase in industrial activity by at least a factor of 4 does not seem an unreasonable guess for the next 30 years. However, this problem is likely to be compounded by two other processes. The first is that, as in the case of population, there is a trend in the United States and Europe at least, for industry to move to the coast, especially for industries that produce waste effluents and that will come under increasing pressure not to pollute inland rivers and lakes. The second factor is the changing nature of the industrial effluent towards more exotic compounds. For example, the chemical industry in Europe doubled in 8 years between 1953 and 1960.[5] During the same period the output of petrochemicals increased 8-fold and plastics 4-fold (United States 4-fold also). Doubling times of 8 years give about a 16-fold increase in these products over the next 30 years.

The special problem of growth in the coastal zone is even worse in estuaries. One-third of the U.S. population now lives and works close to estuaries. The United States has lost to "progress" some 40 percent of its estuarine area.[6] As building land becomes scarcer and rivers and coastal areas are managed to prevent flooding and so on, estuaries must continue to dwindle unless some provision is made for them and the rivers which serve them. Since they act as a sink for pollution they will inevitably feel the brunt of populational and industrial changes.

While the population will only double, some agriculturalists at least, hope to feed the population much better. This will require massive increases in two serious polluters: fertilizers and, unless radical changes occur, pesticides. It is significant that the new strains of cereals being planted in the tropics require pesticides and fertilizers where they were never used before, or if they were used, at least twice as much insecticide and 4 times as much fertilizer are needed. The great increase in use of these two types of products will take place in the tropics, especially in the southern hemisphere, exactly where our hopes lie for increased ocean production.

The increases are likely to be on a mammoth scale. Excluding mainland China, about 56 million metric tons of fertilizer is used globally, almost all in the advanced countries, where about 80 percent of it is produced. Application rates are extremely low in the poor nations. For example, in 1967-68 in India it was 8 kg per arable hectare, in Asia as a whole 15 kg, in Africa only 5 kg. By contrast the rate was 219 kg in Britain and 70 kg in the United States. The rate of consumption has increased by about 10 percent over the past 5 years, and if this trend continues we can expect consumption in 30 years to be about 10 times higher than it is now. In fact it is likely to be higher than this — possibly 700 million tons.[7] Thus inshore waters off the poorer countries of Asia and Africa are likely to have massive increases in "excess nutrients" and a consequent imbalance of nutrients.

Pesticides in ocean food chains already present a health hazard (at least one fish harvest in California has been declared too contaminated for consumption). They also have killed off or are killing off several dozen species of marine birds. It seems quite likely that if production and use go on increasing at current rates, or as much as they will "need" to for the green revolution, the concentration in the ocean in 30 years will be such as to reduce significantly productivity at the lower trophic levels. In the United States pesticide production increased three-fold in the 8-year period 1953-60.[5] Were such a fantastic rate to continue, pesticide production would increase about 80 times by the turn of the century. Presumably the rate will be much lower. The recent rate of increase over 5 years seems to have been about 8 percent, giving a doubling time of about 9 years.[8] This would lead to an eight-fold increase in 30 years. However, an added problem with pesticides is their long persistence periods (Chapter 13). So, as pesticides accumulate, an increase in production rate of only five-fold would probably push up the concentrations in the ocean to dangerous levels (Chapter 11).

It is important that those responsible for developments on land should take account of consequences for the oceans and of the "openness" of ecosystems in general. Consider for a moment, for example, the viewpoint of a proponent of a massive dam across the Amazon, Robert B. Panero of Herman Kahn's Hudson Institute in New York.[9] He points out that there are various ecological risks inherent in the plan. This huge dam would stop most of the sediment flowing out of the Amazon into the ocean. These mineral nutrients are now carried northwards in the Atlantic currents to the waters of the Caribbean and off the southeast United States. He notes that this might have an effect on, for example, the fishing off Florida — we don't know. In addition, the inland lake that would be created (about one-third the size of France) might well affect local climate. "We would expect none of these risks, though, to prevent construction of the dam. Such risks are present in all dams and reservoirs and have never really prevented any from being built!"

*Sustainable Population Limit*

A final reason why it is difficult to estimate the earth's carrying capacity is that the number of people the earth can support over an extended period of centuries is certainly less than the number it might support at any one time. It is this SUSTAINABLE limit that concerns us, even though it is a more complex problem. There is guarded optimism among agriculturalists that we can feed the 6 or 7 billion people who will be on earth at the turn of the century (Chapter 3). Others believe that we can feed 20 billion or even a wildly optimistic 100 billion. But there exists real doubt that the earth can sustain even 6 billion OVER LONG PERIODS. Indeed, Hulett has estimated that, if we take account of all resources and of our effects on the environment, and if the total population came to have current U.S. standards of living, then the total sustainable world population would be only 1 billion — less than a third of the current number.[10] It has been argued that considering simply the food supply, the sustainable capacity is only 1.5 billion.[11]

The argument about the food supply, here, is based on the fact that to feed 6 or 7 billion people we will have to do things to our food-producing ecosystems which are liable to impair their capacity to produce food in the future. I made this point above for the oceans, surely the ecosystem we consider LEAST vulnerable. Brown and Finsterbusch made the same point for the land in Chapter 3. Consider for example that our hopes for feeding more people rest mainly on the new cereal grains. This means raising fertilizer applications in the developing countries by 10-fold and even up to 27-fold.[11] But many of the soils in the developing countries already have a very poor structure and there is recent evidence that continued heavy application of fertilizers in even good soil may decrease its future productivity and its response to added fertilizers. So we might wind up with worse soils than we started with. Again, as increasing use is made of pesticides in poor countries we may see the kind of burgeoning of pest problems described in Chapter 14. The resultant ecosystem may become so denuded of alternative control systems that yields may begin to decrease. Similar arguments can be developed for other aspects of the world's rapidly increasing food production.

These unhappy possibilities may or may not transpire. But the dangers are there and their likelihood is uncertain. The cautious procedure is to assume that they are highly probable. This means that we should place more emphasis on long-term solutions rather than on short-term "fixes" that may interfere with our chances of achieving a stable environment.

Probably no one knows what the long-term sustainable population is. However, the doubling population and its greatly increased activities will place terrific and increasing strains on the environment over the next, say, 30 years. In trying to gauge the severity of the problem, a moderately conservative guess is that some global environmental problems are likely to become severe and possibly even catastrophic within 30 years. (Some local problems are already severe.) A sober evaluation of these points and of others made throughout this book indicates that in some respects we may be reducing the carrying capacity of the environment and suggests that we may be at, approaching, or exceeding the sustainable limit.

Discussion of maximum limits is illuminating and even necessary. However, the question of limits is to a great extent the wrong question insofar as it aims us towards the wrong goals. There is a more rational goal than living to the limits of our ecosystem, particularly when we don't know where the limits are and when we are likely to overshoot them in finding out.

*The Case for Optima*

A more sensible course is to substitute optima for maxima in our goals. Although ecologists' concern over growth is frequently construed as a "negative" approach, it actually provides us with the stimulus to develop a positive approach in determining our relationship with our environment.

A basic assumption I make is that, over some specified period of time and for defined conditions, there is an OPTIMUM population size — for the earth or any part of it — and that the optimum is smaller than the maximum size set by the physical and biological constraints of the environment. We can further define the optimum as one which allows long-term persistence of the population IN EQUILIBRIUM with its environment. By equilibrium I mean that resources and wastes are circulated so that long-term survival is achieved and that the environment is kept as a diverse provider of our needs, including aesthetic needs. A final refinement is that the optimum population can be said to have been reached when the addition of more members results in a lowering of the quality of life of those already present.

Estimating the optimum population size for some point in time, or even defining suitable techniques and criteria for doing so, is an extraordinarily difficult job. It is a job, too, which is not yet being tackled to any extent. Yet it is one of the most important tasks facing us in the next few decades.

Similarly, "quality of life" is hard to define. It is affected by our physical and mental health and comfort, by our material standard of living, by social interactions, and by other factors. But it surely also must be higher when we have clean air and water, diverse surroundings, space for recreation and solitude, a rich culture willing to preserve manifestations of its history, and interesting and fine cities where social stress, congestion, and crime are at a minimum.

The goal of an optimum population seems eminently reasonable. Yet it is a puzzling, but I believe valid observation that a nongrowing equilibrium population is not widely accepted as a worthwhile aim, as is illustrated by several recent essays by social scientists.[1,2]

In the nonhuman world ruled by the direct forces of natural selection, of course, there is generally strong pressure for population growth, and perhaps our desire to continue this is a dark atavism. However, it is hard to develop a compelling argument for population growth in a rich country with a large population such as the United States and even harder for poor, highly populated countries. Even if economic growth were our goal, most economists assure us that population growth per se is not necessary for economic growth. In the nuclear age U.S. population growth is not necessary for national defense. On the other hand, there is a great deal to be said in favor of a stable optimum population — in a nutshell, that it will be optimum with respect to the quality of the individual's life.

*Optima and the Economy*

A population in equilibrium with its environment will have an economy rather different from our present affluent and rapidly expanding economies. Such an equilibrium system would have over long periods: (1) a stationary population, (2) continual recycling of a large proportion of mineral and other resources, to prevent both their irretrievable loss to the population, and their accumulation as waste. Thus, for many technologically crucial materials we would expect a fixed resource pool, possibly even a gradually diminishing one over the long term. Also, in the equilibrium system, (3) great care would be taken to maintain a high-quality environment and this would impose limits on energy and other resource use at levels below the maximum possible. These circumstances presumably would lead to low and declining rates of economic growth, especially in the manufacturing sector.

This subject of a "spaceman" economy has been discussed by a number of economists, for example, Boulding (Chapter 17 and reference 13). There is disagreement on whether or not a zero growth economy would be approached. A contrary viewpoint to the one presented here is that continued growth is consistent with a sound environment. Of the three features listed above, an increasing population is not generally considered important to economic growth, and it can be argued that the economy would keep expanding with a stationary population. However, Japan's economists have recently proposed increasing Japan's birth rate to provide more labor for sustained economic growth, suggesting that this assumption may not always hold, and at least one economist considers population growth crucial.[14] With respect to a fixed resource pool, it is clear that economic growth in the past HAS meant an increase in resource utilization: to replace existing capital goods, to produce new capital goods (investment), and to produce more consumer goods. For example, between 1905 and 1938 more metal was produced than had been produced in man's entire history before 1905, and metal consumption since 1939 is equal to the entire metal consumption before that period.[3] The world's industrial metal production has been growing at over 6 percent for 10 years. Earlier in this chapter I mentioned other large increases in industrial output (that is, resource utilization). However, one component of economic growth which would remain is technological innovation, and the prospects for growth in manufacturing in an equilibrium society would depend upon such innovation — a more parsimonious use of rarer resources, new combinations of materials, and so on. It is claimed that such technological innovation (together with capital accumulation) has been largely responsible for U.S. economic (per capita) growth in this century[15], but the fact remains that it was accompanied by expanding markets and resources. Whatever the exact outcome, a change to equilibrium with respect to population, resources and environment would seem to imply major changes in the pattern and magnitude of economic growth. Since we have all been born in an era of growth, it may be difficult to conceive

of any other sort of system, but potentially more worthwhile goals include a more equitable distribution of affluence or even the achievement of an "optimum standard of living."

In using the phrase "optimum standard of living" I am suggesting that there is an optimum per capita income which can be less than the maximum possible per capita income. From an environmental viewpoint the GNP is more relevant, but putting it in terms of per capita income underlines the point that we can be too affluent, and that establishing an equilibrium system will entail less affluence for the average individual than is potentially possible. Defining an optimum standard of living, like the optimum population, is a complex problem, for it must be a function of population size, population distribution, technology, environmental quality, and so on.

The ecological case for an optimum standard of living below the maximum rests on the argument that a high level of affluence, and in particular a high rate of economic growth in an affluent society, produces dangerous pressure on long-term resource use and a high degree of environmental degradation.

The proposed solution to problems of growth, namely not to grow, is apparently simple. However, since growth is a major goal of our society, a change to an equilibrium, "environmentally conscious" society would be revolutionary. "Revolutionary" is used in a quite strict sense. Previous technological revolutions have all enabled man to expand: the prehistoric agricultural revolution, the agrarian and industrial revolutions of a few centuries ago, the technological revolution of the middle period of this century. A change to nongrowth would call a halt to the growth aspects of the past 8000 years of history. It is important, therefore, to examine briefly the pressures in society towards growth.

*Pressures for Growth*

One of Western man's most pervasive and firmly held beliefs is that economic and technological "progress" is not only an unmitigated good but is a major purpose of our existence. Progress has several components, such as increased control over the environment or faster communications, but its most obvious manifestation is growth. Growth of all sorts, but certainly, in particular, economic growth and the growth of institutions. What university president would proudly point to a declining student body? What corporation would acclaim a reduction in its output? Indeed Galbraith has argued that the aim of corporations is growth rather than the maximizing of profits.[16]

Though the desire for growth is well-nigh universal in contemporary Western society, it is possible to single out important groups which have growth very much at heart and whose influence is powerful. The business man, owners of public utilities, labor unions, and most politicians are excellent examples. Many influential economists consider growth to be the major goal of the nation's economy, though there are exceptions. The following quotation illustrates the point[17]: "The Real Growth Imperatives arise from the fact that a strong economy is a growing economy. An economy with a high per capita income such as ours generates a large volume of private saving which must flow into capital accumulation if the economy is to sustain itself. In other words, the continued vitality of the system requires growth." This is especially true in a Capitalist system where the major source of capital is private savings.

Frequently the desire for economic growth is for political reasons, and it is here in particular that the cold war anticommunism comes to the fore. Thus in the opening pages of the standard undergraduate text on economics is a diagram of United States and USSR economic growth and the following remarks:

> Two decades from now, will the Soviet Union have overtaken the United States as the most affluent society in the world? . . . Not only are Americans and Russians concerned with the outcome of this economic sweepstakes, but so are Asians and Africans interested in choosing that form of economic organization which will move them most rapidly along the road of development.[15]

Again

> There are a number of important considerations that merit close examination.
> *The Soviet Threat* is one of these. The Soviet threat is real and has many points of thrust. It would be perilous to underestimate the danger.

But how is it related to our own economic growth? Some people fear that the Russians will "catch up" to us someday and so fulfill the Khrushchev boast about burying us. Others fear that rapid Soviet growth will increase Russian military potential so greatly as to jeopardize the free world's defenses. Still others fear possible adverse "demonstration effects" of rapid Soviet development – that underdeveloped and uncommitted nations will turn to communism as a way of achieving national strength, politically and economically. All these fears merit sober consideration.[17]

Placing economic growth above other goals may have been appropriate in the past, given the prevailing conditions and assumptions about the relationship between wealth and social welfare (or quality of life). It still is a major goal for poor countries. But our affluent population is still imbued with economy-based values, and narrow economic considerations override social, environmental, and other issues. Economic growth ought to be a means to social ends, but has become an end in itself.

A second important group which fulfills its Parkinsonian destiny of growth can be loosely termed "technocrats": those scientists and engineers concerned with the application, development, and growth of technology. I distinguish here between pressure for GROWTH and technological INNOVATION. One is certainly in favor of safer and more efficient nuclear power facilities but not necessarily in favor of more nuclear reactors.

This pressure for expansion is illustrated by an editorial in the magazine *Science* by a member of the National Academies of Science and of Engineering and a former President of American Electric Power Company.[18] He contends that environmental considerations are interfering with the "needed growth" in our energy supply and that such opposition to growth will bring about a catastrophic situation.

> The scientific and technological community has a vital role to play. It, above all others, is in a position to appreciate the importance to the future of our society of placing no obstacles in the way of providing adequate energy. And it must rise to the social challenge of achieving, through knowledge enhanced by research, compatibility between expanding use of energy and environmental health.

The managers of the energy-producing industries must assume their share of the heavy burden of responsibility for maintaining a clean environment, but they must do so without sacrificing efficiency, prudent investment, and responsibility for continuity of production.[18]

It is not clear that in fact environmental health — or environmental quality — IS compatible with expanding energy use, maximum efficiency, and so on, and in the long run it certainly is not. Furthermore, we do not NEED expanding energy sources — we WANT them, and the distinction is important. In fact, it is often a moot point whether such developments are responses to industrial growth — to "need" — or are precursors of the growth and the need. Thus localities sometimes vie for power stations because they attract new industries and STIMULATE growth.

In selecting particular groups as examples I am not suggesting that the "blame" for growthmania can be laid at their door. The entire society is caught up in the growth spiral. The economist can certainly argue that the values and priorities that he incorporates into his model are GIVEN to him by society; his job is merely to translate these priorities into economic procedures. However, this seems altogether too modest an appraisal of the role the economist plays.

### Growth and Faith in Technology

An integral part of the growth syndrome is faith in technology; the faith that problems produced by technology have technological solutions. A common lament of socially conscious citizens is that we have enough science and technology to put a man on the moon (sometimes), but we cannot maintain a decent environment in the United States. The implicit premise is clear: it is that the solution to our environmental crisis is a technological one, and probably what we need is some "ecological engineering."

It is true that we need to develop and apply improved technologies to deal with these problems, as has been discussed in this book; that a sensible ordering of priorities would divert money and effort from space and military technologies to the technology of improving the general and urban environment. But that technological answers provide a final solution and allow us to have a continuously expanding system is untrue. This has been discussed for mineral resources in Chapter 4. Hardin has pointed out that there is no purely technological solution to the problem of stopping population expansion, which is a social, political, cultural, and moral problem.[19] Indeed he suggests there exists a whole class of "no technological solution" problems. Thus, there is no evidence that we can increase production, resource use, food production, and so on, without putting ever greater stress on the environment and causing more environmental degradation, even though it is true that some local pollution problems in the past have been worse than some local problems now. For example, if we solve the power problem by using cheap and fairly "clean" nuclear energy we will probably aggravate current resource and pollution problems. This arises from the essentially positive feedback nature of technology. When unlimited power becomes available, we will stretch ourselves to the limit to use it. That means more resource exploitation, more "side products" of manipulating these resources into consumer goods, more consumption, and more garbage. Waste is not a side effect, it is a principal component of economic processes of all kinds.

The application of technological "solutions" contains a more subtle danger.[20] The technological complex — the society, its structures, and machinery — is already a system composed of mainly positive feedbacks. The inherent danger of technological solutions to environmental problems is that they give the impression that the problem is being tackled and, in a society geared to growth, this allows the system to continue its headlong rush. In tinkering with the juggernaut of technology (which produced the problems) we are oiling its wheels. The spiraling effect of pesticide use is a good illustration, and a more familiar one is the current "antismog" devices on automobile exhausts. These devices will not solve the air pollution problem, indeed there are reports that they make some aspects worse; but they give the impression that something is being done and that we can go on using more and more automobiles. By contrast, technological solutions need to be applied within an overall framework of seeking remedies for the basic cause (namely growth) as well as for symptoms. The basic problem of changing our relationship with the environment to an equilibrium one is not technological, and the opiate of purely technological solutions dulls our perception of this fundamental fact.

## Growth and the "Quality of Life"

I have said that in an affluent society we can conceive of an optimum standard of living which is below the maximum we could achieve, and that we should therefore consider putting an end to economic growth as we know it. This implies that increasing affluence is not necessarily correlated with an increasing quality of life, and that in the United States we may already be experiencing a decline in the average quality of life as our COLLECTIVE wealth increases. Since we measure quality of life subjectively, for example, including aesthetics, the case necessarily rests to some degree on personal judgment, leaving much room for disagreement.

The weight of evidence as exemplified in this book favors the hypothesis that as we grow richer in the United States the quality of our shared environment declines. One can even try to measure this by indexes such as the clarity of the air, the dirtiness of the water we drink and swim in, the ratio of wilderness or National Park area to people and the fact that soon visits to National Parks may have to be rationed, the number of wildlife species lost or being lost, the number of feet of clean beachfront per person, the time spent in nonvacation trips in one's car, the average noise level in the city, the increased probability of environmental disaster, and so on. A few horror stories do not measure the decline, but they illuminate it. For example, the frequent warning to children in Los Angeles not to run, skip, or jump on very smoggy days; smog in Yosemite valley; the fact that mothers' milk has so much DDT it would be banned from interstate commerce.

The case is surely easy to make for the city dweller. Smog, noise, traffic, mental stress, all the apparently necessary trappings of a healthy economy. Mishan[21] sees: "The spreading suburban wilderness, the near traffic paralysis, the mixture of pandemonium and desolation in the cities, a sense of spiritual despair scarcely concealed by the frantic pace of life", and notes that "such phenomena, not being readily quantifiable, and having no discernible impact on the gold reserves, are obviously not regarded as [economic] agenda."

It might be said in reply that people choose to live in such conditions, they want this kind of life, therefore by definition wealth has brought them increased social welfare. Los Angeles, for example, is a rather unpleasant city, saved largely by what is left of its pleasant climate, yet it is one of the fastest growing in the United States. Clearly people "choose" to come to Los Angeles. But in fact, people need jobs and they go where jobs are, or where they think there is opportunity for economic success. Secondly, they have been led to believe that more money necessarily means a better life, and they go where there are highly paid jobs. That is, they make a choice based on misinformation. Madison Avenue has been assuring us for years that our sexual potency is directly related to the various consumer goods we own, and we do not choose impotency. Finally, it is inaccurate to say that people have chosen to live in a city such as Los Angeles rather than some very different kind of city, since in fact there exists essentially no choice. Almost all of our cities have the same problems as does Los Angeles. But surely there must be other models than that collection of villages being slowly suffocated by a miasma of freeways and highways and the resultant smog: a city fit for (air-conditioned) cars to crawl through but not for people to live in.

The matter of where people choose to live illustrates that, contrary to myth, increasing collective wealth does not necessarily increase individual choice. As Mishan[21] has said: "As the carpet of increased choice is being unrolled before us by the foot, it is simultaneously being rolled up behind us by the yard." Consider, for example, the restriction in one's freedom to choose a pattern of living. Because of the impact of the car (that bastion of economic growth) it is essentially impossible for most people to live close to work, to walk there or cycle there, or to go by efficient public transport.

It would be foolish to blame all of the problems of urban life on population and economic growth. Clearly, major reasons for these problems include the fact that successive national administrations (and the voters) have placed higher priorities on military excursions and the space race than on the welfare of the poor, and in particular the poor black urban citizens, on educating people, or on the quality of life generally. Other reasons include our stress on private consumption rather than public spending and quite simply poor planning and administration. Nevertheless, the spread of disamenities which has put a blight on urban life in general is directly attributable to the headlong rush of production and growth, and part of the physical and administrative problems of cities is attributable to their high growth rate.

One of the clearest illustrations of the possible inverse relation between national wealth and individual welfare is the supersonic transport (SST). By building SSTs, and flying them, we will increase the GNP, assuming that we don't concomitantly reduce production of other goods. It is difficult to see just who will benefit. A few businessmen will now be able to get from a traffic jam in New York to a traffic jam in London in possibly 2½ hours less. But they will still take 2 or 3 days to adjust physiologically to the change in time zones. During the flight they will subject themselves to the potentially serious hazards of increased radiation (Chapter 12). They will subject some of the rest of the world to sonic booms (even if they fly only over the oceans, which would be uneconomical for the airlines) and they will probably interfere with our weather (Chapter 15). SSTs will also aggravate the problem of scarce oil resources.[22] They would use about 2½ times as much fuel per passenger mile as existing jet transports. Six hundred SSTs are projected to be in service by 1985, at which time they would consume about 11 percent of the projected world oil demand. As early as 1980 they would be using 3 times as much oil as Africa! It is even doubtful that the SST is a sound proposition economically; no corporation has been willing to finance the project, which will be 90 percent financed by the government (that is, by the public).[23] For most of us, on balance, the SST cannot possibly raise our quality of life and will quite probably reduce it.[24]

Now, it is clear that, in fact, we could go on increasing GNP for some time AND improve the quality of our lives, by redirecting resources. Thus it has been estimated that we need $100 billion over the next 5 years just to get clean water. Governor Rockefeller of New York has guessed that the cities will need $30 billion per year, and a decent public transport system which would move people efficiently and use much less power, would certainly run into several hundred billion dollars.

However, if we eventually convert to an ecologically sound system in which the population and the systems of production are in equilibrium with our environment, continual increase in cleaning up operations will not be necessary. As Heilbroner has pointed out, economic growth as western capitalists have come to know it, would not continue long in an equilibrium society.[25]

## Economic and Other Values

Basic to the argument about standard of living versus quality of life is the assumption that values other than economic values exist and must be reckoned with. If we provide more food, so saving a man from the pain and despair of starvation and illness, I assume we have added to his welfare in ways which cannot be measured economically. No doubt we can ALSO place an economic evaluation on his improved contribution to society, but I would deny that such an evaluation is exhaustive.

The assumption has wide import. The current conventional wisdom is that we can solve environmental problems by economic means such as internalizing externalities, and so on (Chapter 17). The basic premise of this wisdom is that the economic model embraces or can embrace all our priorities and values and the constraints on our future action. Acceptance of the universality of the economic model implies that economic parameters (especially prices) measure the significant features of our world and that economic values provide the basis for action. The competing contention (which a number of economists would agree to) is that the economic model is strictly limited, that the larger physical or, very loosely, ecological model of reality is more general and subsumes the economic model, forcing it to conform to ecological constraints.

If we accept the ecological model, we can simply say that certain phenomena lie outside economics. Thus we would deny that the economist can necessarily commensurate the incommensurables, which he needs to do to internalize all externalities. For example, the California pelican, being irreplaceable, can be said to have some absolute noneconomic value. The same might be said for the unique pastoral Norman church in Buckinghamshire, England, which will be destroyed if London's third airport is built near it. People may, and undoubtedly will, try to put a dollar value on such things, based on numbers of visits per year, or the amount of earnings we might willingly forego to see them. But economics works by discounting the future. How does one put a dollar value on future generations' right to these things? Furthermore, one can simply claim that they have a value not measurable in economic terms. We may still decide to raze the church and kill the pelican, but we cannot pretend to be able to measure the loss.

The danger of extending economic values to cover the incommensurables is that it makes it more difficult to change our goals, which are already based on such values. If we do try to evaluate everything in economic terms, we must emphasize that frequently this will be only a PARTIAL evaluation. Indeed, one of the more valuable contributions made by recent discussions of the environment is a deepening of our appreciation of this one concept — that economic considerations provide inadequate criteria for judging the quality of our lives and for deciding the future direction of society. We need, therefore, nothing less than a change of values. The need for such a change and an eloquent indictment of our current values have been made by others such as McHarg[26] and White.[27]

### The Problem of Altruism

Although I have singled out some groups as special forces for growth, the fact is that it is the sum of all our individual decisions which produces growth and other aspects of our society

which degrade our environment. The problem is quite simple: Whatever the collective good may require, it is almost always to the individual's benefit to increase his personal wealth, thereby driving on the economy. This problem is exacerbated by the advertiser's creation of personal dissatisfaction, but it seems that this only accelerates a process already in motion.

The dilemma is familiar to biologists. The strict analogy in biology has been termed the problem of "genetic altruism." Thus, natural selection, by definition, ensures that those genotypes survive and increase that produce more reproductive offspring than do competing genotypes — EVEN THOUGH THIS GENERALLY IS A FORCE TOWARDS INCREASING POPULATION DENSITY. If the population increases too much, the POPULATION AS A WHOLE may perish by destroying its environment. Thus it is in the population's interest not to overexploit its environment, yet at the same time each genotype is selected for its capacity to increase. Hence, the welfare of the individual genotype is at variance, eventually, with the general welfare. (Under conditions where other factors such as enemies keep the population sparse this problem does not arise.)

One possible answer, to save the population from increasing too much, is for some genotypes to be ALTRUISTIC. That is, they give up their reproductive potential for the common good. It should be immediately clear that there is usually no way for such genetic altruism to be selected. Individual organisms whose genotypes program them for such worthy action leave no offspring (or few — the effect is the same), and that genotype soon is selected against. This, then, is the dilemma.

The genetic altruism analogy can be applied to the common exploitation of finite resources. Hardin has discussed essentially this subject in his "Tragedy of the Commons."[19] Thus, the individual shepherd stands to gain more by adding one sheep to the common grazing land than he stands to lose by the marginal overgrazing caused by that one sheep. However, when ALL shepherds act this way in their own interests, the grazing land is destroyed and they ALL lose, other things being equal.

The analogy can also be pursued with respect to environmental degradation. Thus, in the United States, by buying a car one gains more in convenience and comfort than one loses in health and comfort by adding marginally to traffic congestion and smog. However, since we are all of us making this individual decision, our collective decisions result in a general decrease in comfort and health. At the same time, there is little to be gained by foregoing the purchase of a car — "consumer altruism" — since the loss in convenience more than offsets the tiny marginal reduction in smog. Furthermore, loss in convenience is greatly magnified because the existence of efficient public transport is made impossible by well-nigh universal car ownership. In general, then, in a society where the general trend is to greater economic wealth, there is generally no INDIVIDUAL gain to be derived from economic altruism. Indeed, great personal satisfaction is gained from increases in relative rather than in absolute wealth and, since everyone strives for this, the inevitable consequence is an increase in collective economic wealth.

It should be realized that individual altruism as I have used the term here is not always a desirable population trait. When cars are sparse, buying a car can lead to both personal and general gain. When all incomes are low, increasing individual wealth can produce individual and general gain. This simply says that populations and societies can exist below optima. However, when environmental limits are reached, or populations have exceeded optima, then the case for altruism is well founded. The dilemma then is to select for altruism through social evolution.

Biological systems "solve" the selection dilemma in two ways. The first is to ensure that individual selection and population selection (that is, control below disastrous levels) are both achieved by the same means. This is done, not by altruism, but by selecting for individuals in such a way that population can be controlled. For example, in some bird species, there is selection for those genotypes that are the most aggressive, can defend territories and rear productive young, and can prevent other genotypes (other birds) from reproducing. Each successful bird then defends a territory which is large enough to allow it to rear its young and large enough that the food supply is not depleted. The elements of such a system are certainly fundamental to our private enterprise arrangements, but its success as a model for our economic system would require probably rather more social inequity than we are willing to bear and rather more foresight in husbanding resources than our corporate leaders seem to possess.

In the second and rarer type of biological system, selection occurs largely at the POPULATION level and some individuals "willingly" are altruistic. Examples of individual altruism are common among social insects. For example, in some termite species when the colony is attacked, some individuals in the colony sacrifice their lives when they plug up holes in the colony walls by sticking their heads into the holes. In other systems, such as ants and bees, the altruism is "predetermined" since some individuals are reared under conditions that make them sterile — they simply work to make sure that the queen passes on her genes. This can be selected because they are the queen's offspring and she therefore passes on their genes for them.

The crux of the matter is that successful altruistic systems are probably all family systems. Thus, all the individuals in a colony or population are very closely related genetically. It then becomes possible for an individual to forego reproduction because other family members are passing on his genes for him. In most other "normal" populations, of course, the various individuals are genetically very different and therefore compete with each other.

Analogies have limited utility, and I do not wish to pursue this one too fully. However, there are two aspects relevant to the human condition. First, this social type of system is successful, and altruism persists, because the individuals have shared, rather than competing, genetic interests. Secondly, this mechanism helps selection to work at the population rather than the individual level and, most important, it allows the members of the population to react to environmental conditions AS A POPULATION and with the long-term survival of the population as a goal. An example of this again comes from social insects. When environmental conditions are favorable and the population is low, some ant species can increase the proportion of sexual individuals in the colony, thereby increasing the population quickly. When the population becomes too large for prevailing conditions the proportion of sexual individuals is reduced and the population declines. This complex population mechanism requires that the colony receive information about the quality of its environment — for example, via the amount of food available. The response to such signals is then made by varying the diet given to developing ants.

There are several implications. First, since the functional population in human systems is not the family unit, we must somehow substitute social mechanisms for such genetic mechanisms of cooperation. Our economic system involves individual or group competition, and therefore makes it hard to develop a population approach to the environment. This is an even more fundamental reason for changing our value system than the fact, discussed above, that the dollar fails as a yardstick for measuring social welfare. Second, somehow we have to develop techniques for assessing the relationship between our population size and activities and the environment. We must develop ways of measuring present and future demand on environmental resources and current and future environmental effects. We have developed economic indexes, Smock (Chapter 16) suggests we should develop social indexes, and there is no doubt we need environmental/population indexes. We are quite capable, of course, of ignoring such indexes, and a third requirement is that we develop the capacity to make decisions at the population level, based on such information. Unlike the social insects, we will need to use intelligence in solving our problems.

We continually return to the stumbling block that any change such as those described will involve collective decisions which will run contrary to the majority of individual's desires — desires based on individual self-interest or more important, the desires of those in power. This change should not be impossible, but it will be tremendously difficult. It is surely likely to work better

if two conditions are fulfilled: (1) that all individuals are aware of the relationship between population and environment, they are ecologically aware or have an "ecological attitude"; (2) that individuals participate in such population decisions. Success will almost certainly require social coercion, which in a democracy is more likely to be effective where these two conditions hold.

We have ample evidence that coercion can be widely accepted in the population and that such coercion can work. For example, very few people give away money to the poor, but they still go along with a moderately progressive income tax system. Similarly, it is in each person's self-interest not to pay money to the school system but to let other people do the paying. Yet school bonds are frequently voted more or less voluntarily, even by people who do not have school-age children. Such coercion, to some extent, is formalized altruism. Whether we are sufficiently farsighted to formalize the altruism needed to produce the equilibrium society remains to be seen, but the prognosis is not wholly negative. Coercing the average couple by economic or other means into having the replacement 2.1 children should provide a good test case (Chapter 2).

The equilibrium population is not altogether a utopian dream. Human societies have existed and do persist that are in equilibrium with their environment and that limit their populations to preserve a way of life. Such societies comprise a negligible minority of mankind but they do exist. Freeman has argued that "primitive" hunting-and-gathering societies regulated and do regulate their populations, by various social mechanisms, to a level WELL BELOW the food supply.[12] For example, the Kalahari Bushmen spend relatively little time getting food, and much of that is spent collecting preferred food species in the presence of abundant other species. Fertility is limited so that the tribe can be mobile, that is, the population is regulated "to maximize certain culturally-defined goals with respect to the kind of life they wish to enjoy." Only 20-30 percent use of the food supply has been suggested for such societies. Although we may not approve of their actual methods of population control, our "advanced" society appears to have a good deal to learn about optimum population from such primitive people.

*Implications of Equilibrium: Social Inequity*

The "environmental crisis" in the United States has been rightly recognized by some urban sociologists as the new fashionable concern of the affluent white middle class. They have pointed out that the poor, and especially the black urban poor, have other priorities than clean air, clean beaches, or some other irrelevancy such as a "balanced ecosystem." This is in spite of the fact that it is frequently the poor who suffer most from pollution. They cannot afford to move from airport flight patterns or from the smog- and lead-polluted freeway that runs past their house; it is poor farm laborers who suffer from acute pesticide poisoning in California and their children who are ill and dead from drinking water high in nitrates. However, the poor undoubtedly have their priorities right. One hardly will worry about the side effects of DDT if food itself is scarce; strontium-90 concentrates in milk, not corn; and why concern oneself about filthy beaches and overcrowded national parks if you never leave the ghetto to visit them?

Some sociologists and political scientists see the environment issue as a red herring, distracting us from the more important problems of war and racial and economic injustice. In particular they are worried about the "defection" of the youth from these causes, since whatever small gains have been made in the past decade in ameliorating the Vietnam War and racial inequality are owing largely to the efforts of the college generation of the '60s. Schaar and Wolin see the students' new concern for the environment as a retreat from politics by the very generation which became the most deeply political one in recent history. Nor is this retreat due simply to chance.[28] "It is not accidental that at the same time as the Nixon Administration is using environment to forge a new unity, it has been shelving, retarding, or neglecting most of the previous policies dealing with blacks, the poor, education, and the cities . . . The Nixon consensus, by placating the silent majority, is also capitalizing

upon the despair of the confused minority of activists who had struggled for racial justice and economic improvement and who now, by the commitment to nature, were tacitly conceding that racial and economic injustice were ineradicable facts of American Society." By emphasizing in his State of the Union message (January 22, 1970) that the environment was the special concern of youth, "Nixon captured the issue which might allow for peace between the political system and the younger generation." This peace, these commentators fear, will draw off the steam which powers the movement for social improvement.

I will suggest below that at least the problem of economic injustice cannot be separated from environmental problems, and racial injustice derives in large part from economic inequality. For the rest, one has to hope that we can deal with more than one problem at a time. At least one point which these authors and others have made, that the environmental issue brings together the radicals and the establishment, the young and the old, "the hippies and the Hickels," promises success in attacking that issue, though it may also have its sinister aspects as they claim.

There need be no conflict between the aims of environmental equilibrium in our rich society and of increased social justice and affluence for the poor. Indeed, I contend that it is crucial that we achieve greater equality if we are to reach environmental equilibrium. The traditional way of making the poor richer, in theory, is to increase collective wealth, so that even the poor are dragged upwards. Of course, enormous inequality remains, generating economic competition among individuals and groups and producing more pressure for economic growth. Since it is important to reduce such sources of economic competition in order to slow down the pressure for growth, the obvious solution is to have a more equitable distribution of wealth than we now have. It is difficult to see how one could achieve economic equilibrium in a free society without economic equality.

Furthermore, Smock (Chapter 16) has proposed a wide range of reasons why we need increased economic equality to solve our urban problems. He notes also that, overall, birth rates decline with rising income (though they don't decline enough). This is also true among nations. The fact that environmental concern is a middle-class virtue suggests that the existence of poor people who do not share this concern is an obstacle in the way towards environmental equilibrium. Apparently one needs to feel relatively secure economically and to have a certain minimum of absolute affluence to develop this concern. Obviously I am not suggesting that the environment will be saved once everyone joins the middle class. Indeed it is the collective activities of the average American that cause the problem. However, it does seem that a more even distribution of wealth would increase the chances of developing a consensus on the environment. This point is supported by Davies's discussion of the relationship between concern over pollution and a person's income and position on the socioeconomic scale.[29]

A basic problem which environmentalists must face is that many of the changes required to maintain a decent environment will INCREASE the inequality between rich and poor, unless this inequality is alleviated at the same time as steps are taken to improve the environment. Boulding (Chapter 17) has perceived this potentiality in current plans to "internalize industries' externalities." He points out that "solutions to environmental problems frequently involve repressing or confining the activities of the poor, while leaving the rich much as they were," and that "one is a little afraid that the present excitement will lead to the solution of high taxes on automobiles to subsidize public transportation, which will leave the rich with their automobiles and will force the poor onto subways. Even effluent taxes might easily turn out to be regressive if they force a rise in the price of low-cost housing, domestic power, and processed food, as well they might. Unfortunately, the distributional impact of almost any economic policy is virtually unknown. This is the great desert of economic science".

The reverse side of the coin of effluent taxes and other internalizing activities is public, or government, spending. Because of the common-property nature of many environmental problems a good case can be made that public spending, as opposed to private spending, is necessary to improve environmental conditions. Essentially this argument was made by several economists during a discussion of the "crisis of affluence."[30] But some of these same economists, including Galbraith, Harrington, and Thurow, point out that public spending in the presence of marked economic inequality in the population, frequently leads to an INCREASE in inequality since it benefits the rich much more than the poor. Boulding[13] and Lauter and Howe[31] made the same point in observing that state universities subsidize the rich, not the poor.

## Implications of Equilibrium: Power Structure

The current idea that the way to clear up pollution is to force industry to internalize its externalities through the price or market system is attractive (Chapter 17). For example, the price of every article could include the cost of its "disposal," or better, it should include the cost of readying the article for recycling. However, whether or not the present private enterprise, corporate capitalist system is suited to this mechanism is open to discussion.

First, a major function of the corporation is to grow.[16] If a sound environment implies a reduction and possible cessation of growth, it is questionable that the corporation can make the necessary metamorphosis. Corporations and those in favor of growth are likely to argue that we can have growth AND a sound environment if only we develop a clean technology and resource substitutes. That is, they have tried and will continue to try to mold environmental issues so that they fit into the existing corporate model. Thus arguments about whether or not the "technological fix" is a feasible long-term solution will remain central.

Second, the private corporation might well serve as a useful means of maintaining environmental quality if there were effective means of regulating its activities. In such an ideal situation, the people and therefore government might decide that a certain industrial activity was causing too much pollution. Government would therefore pass legislation defining the limits of acceptable pollution. This would be so low that the activity would stop or a clean one would be substituted. In other cases, where an effluent tax existed, this would lead to the installation of costly plant to reduce pollution and would increase the cost of the product. The regulation would be enforced by a regulating agency with adequate powers and nothing to lose by enforcing such regulations.

The reality, of course, is far from this ideal. The crux of the matter is that large corporations not only have the power to pollute, they have the economic and political power to prevent, delay, and water-down regulatory legislation. They also have the power and connections to ensure that the regulatory agencies don't regulate as they ought to. In theory this can all be sorted out, but in practice the system is most likely to be self-perpetuating.[32,33] The history of regulatory legislation against private industry with a view to increasing social welfare illustrates the problem. In the face of powerful evidence that poor automobile design kills people, Detroit has successfully delayed and emasculated car safety legislation for a decade. Another example is the coal industry, which has successfully combated legislation against pollution from sulfur oxide.[29]

Third, conceivably the leaders of private industry might be convinced of the worthiness of the cause of social welfare, including the value of a clean and stable environment. In this case they might be willing to internalize the externalities because they have well-developed social consciences. This system has the same appeal as benevolent dictatorship, being benevolent oligarchy. The problem here is that all the evidence points to the conclusion that the safety and welfare of the public are not a prime concern of the leaders of private industry, recent advertisements to the contrary notwithstanding. I have already pointed to the lack of concern over car safety shown by Detroit — this in spite of the fact that the automobile industry has long had access to accident statistics from Cornell.[34] The same industry did so much foot-dragging on air pollution control that the Justice Department in January 1969 filed suit against four major auto manufacturers and their trade association on the grounds that they had conspired to delay the development and use of devices to control air pollution from automobiles. (The power of the companies is shown by the fact that the Federal government later agreed to settle the suit by a consent decree which did not penalize the companies and sealed the grand jury records.)[29] Pesticide sales pitches and the high-pressure pesticide salesmen provide another example. An even more serious disregard of public safety occurs in the nuclear power industry (Chapter 12).

There are, of course, other reasons why the large corporations are undesirable features of our system. Corporate decisions frequently determine the shape of our lives. The corporations are only mildly responsive to public concerns via the market, since they themselves tailor much of the demand. Since corporate leaders are not voted into their position nor are removable from it by the people at large (or even by the vast majority of their stockholders), and since they are relatively uncontrollable by the elected government, they are in fact not responsible to the public over what they do with the public's environment. Yet they are able to shape that environment.

This problem of lack of public control has become even greater with the growth of great multi-national corporations. These have great wealth and therefore great power; some of them have an annual turnover in excess of most Gross National Products. This means that they can determine the pattern of resource exploitation on a global scale. For example, huge oil companies are rich enough to come to financial agreements with the ruling elite of poor countries to remove their natural petroleum resources, without necessarily taking into account the welfare of the people or of the environment.

This is not to say that corporate leaders are necessarily less moral than the rest of us, or that they are forcing an unwilling populace to ever greater feats of environmental degradation. Indeed, a case can be made that, with their power and organization, the corporations could help solve environmental problems. However, we need to change values, and it may be easier to change individuals than great institutions whose very purpose is growth. Further, given that values do change, such institutions are sufficiently powerful to impede the implementation of such change. Doubt falls upon the corporations AS A SYSTEM.

## Alternative Systems

It is by now passe to observe that the system in the USSR is more similar to that in the United States than different from it. Decisions are taken there by a remote elite of ruling bureaucrats obtaining power nor from property, but from their position in the political party. Certainly we would not expect such a totalitarian system to be responsive to the public or sensitive to environmental concerns. And from the environmental point of view the results are essentially the same as in the United States. Both countries are hell-bent on economic growth. Since the USSR is poorer, environmental problems are less severe there. But they are bad enough and will get worse as Russia becomes more industrialized. The Soviet Union's problems with pollution in Lake Baikal and the Caspian Sea are notorious by now. Even the caviar-producing sturgeon faces extinction.

The elaboration of alternative systems to corporate and state capitalism and totalitarian collectivism is the job of the political scientist, not the ecologist, and I would not dream of attempting it here. (Chapters 17-19 deal with some aspects of the problem.) However, probably such a system requires a population educated to environmental realities and a decision-making apparatus sensitive both to the desires of this population and to these environmental realities. Along these lines, it may be possible to learn something from a recent Swedish experiment.[35]

Sweden has already shown that it is sensitive to environmental problems. It has banned the sale of some species of fish from some lakes because of the fishes' high mercury content. It is looking hard at DDT levels in Baltic fish and may soon ban the sale of some fish from there. Sweden was the first nation to impose a ban on DDT, aldrin, dieldrin, and other chlorinated hydrocarbons. Moreover, the Swedish government has recognized that even strict legislation against pollution is difficult to enforce unless the public is informed and involved. As a start towards this goal, the Ministry of Education arranged a few evening classes on the technical and legal aspects of pollution for 250,000 people. Ten thousand of these people took an extra 2 weeks' instruction. The most interesting aspect is that, from this group, about 1000 people throughout Sweden were picked to "conduct public enquiries and, in general, agitate on behalf of pollution control." Whether or not this project will work remains to be seen — but it appears to be a sound idea. Indeed, why restrict such education and agitation to the problem of pollution?

The need to obtain a widespread and fairly sophisticated understanding of environmental problems is illustrated by a recent advertisement run by Chevron Oil Co. to market a gasoline additive (F-310, a polybutine amine) which is claimed to reduce exhaust pollution.[36] This new panacea for cleaner and purer air, in fact, works by cleaning up deposits on the carburetor and intake valve. The ad is quite misleading since only a small percentage of cars have dirty enough engines to make this a problem — such engines are a very minor facet of air pollution. A much worse aspect of the campaign, however, is the picture in the advertisement. A balloon is attached to the exhaust of the automobile; in the "before additive" picture it is full of black fumes (bad) in the "after additive" picture it is clear (good). But the poisonous and smog-producing exhaust emissions, carbon monoxide, nitrogen oxide, and unburnt hydrocarbons are COLORLESS. Thus the additive will do almost nothing to lower the levels of these pollutants and the advertisement misleads and confuses the public.

Clearly, we need a large education program on the subject of the environment. One might judge the success of such a program in 10 years' time by asking a layman what he thinks of a project, let us say, to dam a large African river. If he answers that he would need to know, before answering, the dam's potential effects on the spread of schistosomiasis, on the local climate, on downstream agriculture and on health, the number of people to be moved, the nature of their destination, on the possibilities of flooding and the possible dislocations of community life, one might feel rather encouraged. Of course, if he wanted to see good evidence that the benefits would far outweigh any conceivable costs and to be assured that the people there understood the implications of the dam and wanted it, then one would certainly be optimistic.

I assume that a proper understanding of environmental issues and all their ramifications, is not only a prerequisite but a PRECURSOR of wise action. Wise action entails nothing less than a change of values, a sorting out of "standard of living" and "quality of life," and an evaluation of individual actions in a population setting. It then entails acting on the basis of such values. There are many reasons for being pessimistic about such a possibility. But there is surprising basis for optimism. A *Fortune* survey of opinion among the 8 million people between 18 and 24 who are or were in college showed that 40 percent no longer look on making money as a decent purpose for one's life.[30] Of course, inevitably our ideals deteriorate with age, but that 40 percent is a good beginning.

## References

1. **Barnett, H. J., and Morse, C.** 1963. *Scarcity and Growth. Resources for the Future.* Johns Hopkins Press, Baltimore, Maryland. See also reference 3.

2. **Government Operations Committee.** 1969. Effects of population growth on natural resources and the environment, p. 50. Hearings before a subcommittee of the Committee on Government Operations, House of Representatives.

3. **Lovering, T. S.** 1969. Mineral resources from the land. In *Resources and Man* (Preston Cloud, ed.). W. H. Freeman, San Francisco, California.

4. **White, G. F.** 1969. *Strategies of American Water Management.* University of Michigan Press, Ann Arbor, Michigan.

5. **World Health Organization.** 1968. *Research into Environmental Pollution.* Technical Report Series 406.

6. **Niering, W. A.** 1970. The dilemma of the coastal wetlands: Conflict of local, national and world priorities. In *The Environmental Crisis* (H. W. Helfrich, ed.). Yale University Press, New Haven, Connecticut.

7. **Borgstrom, G.** 1969. *Too Many.* Macmillan, London.

8. **Environment Staff Report.** 1969. Diminishing returns. *Environment 11:* 6-40.

9. **Panero, R. G.** 1969. A dam across the Amazon. *Science J. 5A* (3): 56-60.

10. **Ehrlich, P. R., and Ehrlich, A. E.** 1970. *Population, Resources, Environment.* W. H. Freeman, San Francisco, California.

11. **Allaby, M.** 1970. One jump ahead of Malthus. *The Ecologist 1:* 24-28.

12. **Taylor, L. R.,** ed. 1970. *The Optimum Population for Britain.* Academic Press, London.

13. **Boulding, K. E.** 1970. Fun and games with the gross national product — the role of misleading indicators in social policy. In *The Environmental Crisis.* (H. W. Helfrich, ed.). Yale University Press, New Haven, Connecticut.

14. **Clark, C.** 1970. The economic and social implications of population control. In *Population Control* (A. Allison, ed.). Penguin, Harmondsworth, England.

15. **Samuelson, P. A.** 1967. *Economics: An Introductory Analysis.* McGraw-Hill, New York.

16. **Galbraith, K.** 1967. *The New Industrial State.* Houghton-Mifflin, Boston, Massachusetts.

17. **Wallis, W. A.** 1969. United States growth: what, why, how. In *The Goal of Economic Growth* (E. S. Phelps, ed.). W. W. Norton, New York.

18. **Sporn, P.** 1969. *Science 166:* 556. Copyright 1969 by the American Association for the Advancement of Science.

19. **Hardin, G.** 1968. The tragedy of the commons. *Science 162:* 1243-48.

20. **Murdoch, W. W., and Connell, J. H.** 1970. All about ecology. *Center Mag. 3* (1): 56-63.

21. **Mishan, E. J.** 1969. *The Costs of Economic Growth.* Penguin, Harmondsworth, England.

22. **The Observer.** 1970. August 30, pages 1 and 2. London.

23. **Hohenemser, K.** 1970. Onward and upward. *Environment 12* (4): 23-27.

24. Hardin, G. 1970. To trouble a star. *Bull. Atomic Scientists 26* (1): 17-20.

25. Heilbroner, R. 1970. Ecological Armageddon. *New York Review of Books 14* (8): 3-9.

26. McHarg, I. L. 1970. The plight. In *The Environmental Crisis* (H. W. Helfrich, ed.). Yale University Press, New Haven, Connecticut.

27. White, L. 1967. The historical roots of our ecological crises. *Science 155:* 1203-07.

28. Schaar, J. H. and Wolin, S. S. 1970. Where are we now. *New York Review of Books 14* (9): 2-10. Reprinted with permission from *The New York Review of Books.* Copyright 1970.

29. Davies, J. C. 1970. *The Politics of Pollution.* Pegasus, New York.

30. A Center Report. 1970. Crisis of affluence. *Center Mag. 3* (1): 72-83.

31. Lauter, P., and Howe, F. 1970. How the school system is rigged for failure. *New York Review of Books 14* (12): 14-21.

32. The Nader Report. 1970. A series of separate reports on a number of administrative agencies, for example, J. S. Turner, *The Chemical Feast,* study group report on the Food and Drug Administration. Grossman, New York.

33. Carter, L. J. 1968. Water pollution: officials goaded in raising quality standards. *Science 160:* 49-51.

34. Nader, R. 1965. *Unsafe at Any Speed.* Grossman, New York.

35. Greenberg, D. S. 1969. Pollution control: Sweden sets up an ambitious new program. *Science 166:* 200-201.

36. New Scientist. 1970. Selling against pollution. Vol. *47:* 323-324.

# Index

436